CORRECTION SYMBOLS IN ALPHABETICA...

Boldface numbers refer to chapters or sections of t...

ab	Faulty abbreviation, **28**	*no ¶*	
ad	Misuse of adjective or adverb, **9**	*num*	Error in use of numbers, **29**
		p	Error in punctuation, **20–25**
agr	Error in agreement, **8**	. ? !	Period, question mark, exclamation point, **20**
appr	Inappropriate diction, **31a**		
awk	Awkward construction	ʌ,	Comma, **21**
bib	Error in bibliographical form, **35c**	;	Semicolon, **22**
		∨	Apostrophe, **23**
ca	Error in case form, **6**	" "	Quotation marks, **24**
cap	Use capital letter, **26**	: — ( ) [ ] . . . /	Colon, dash, parentheses, brackets, ellipsis mark, slash, **25**
con	Be concise, **31c**		
coord	Faulty coordination, **16a**		
cs	Comma splice, **11a–b**		
d	Error in diction, **31**	*par, ¶*	Start new paragraph, **3**
dev	Inadequate essay development, **1**	*¶ coh*	Paragraph not coherent, **3b**
		¶ dev	Paragraph not developed, **3c**
div	Incorrect word division, **30**	*¶ un*	Paragraph not unified, **3a**
dm	Dangling modifier, **14g**	*pass*	Ineffective passive voice, **18d**
emph	Emphasis lacking or faulty, **18**	*ref*	Error in pronoun reference, **12**
exact word	Inexact word, **31b**	*rep*	Unnecessary repetition, **31c–2**
fn	Error in footnote form, **35h**	*rev*	Proofread or revise, **2**
frag	Sentence fragment, **10**	*run-on*	Run-on sentence, **11c**
fs	Fused (run-on) sentence, **11c**	*shift*	Inconsistency, **13**
gl/gr	See glossary of grammatical terms	*sp*	Misspelled word, **34**
		spec	Be more specific, **3c, 4c**
gl/us	See glossary of usage	*sub*	Faulty subordination, **16b–c**
gr	Error in grammar, **5–9**	*t*	Error in verb tense, **7,** *pp. 176–80*
hyph	Error in use of hyphen, **34d**		
inc	Incomplete construction, **15c–e**	*trans*	Better transition needed, **3,** *pp. 60, 76–77, 98–99*
ital	Italicize (underline), **27**		
k	Awkward construction	*var*	Vary sentence structure, **19**
lc	Use lowercase letter, **26f**	*vb*	Error in verb form, **7,** *pp. 169–75*
log	Faulty logic, **4**		
mixed	Mixed construction, **15a–b**	*w*	Wordy, **31c**
mm	Misplaced modifier, **14a–f**	*ww*	Wrong word, **31b**
mng	Meaning unclear	*//*	Faulty parallelism, **17**
ms	Incorrect manuscript form, **App. B**	*#*	Separate with a space
		⌢	Close up the space
no cap	Unnecessary capital letter, **26f**	*x*	Obvious error
no ʌ,	Comma not needed, **21j**	∧	Something missing, **15e**

THE
LITTLE, BROWN
HANDBOOK

THE
LITTLE, BROWN
HANDBOOK

SECOND EDITION

H. Ramsey Fowler

MEMPHIS STATE UNIVERSITY

With the Editors of Little, Brown

Little, Brown and Company

BOSTON   TORONTO

Contributing Editor   Jane E. Aaron
Sponsoring Editor   Carolyn A. Potts
Developmental Editor   Janet M. Beatty
Book Editor   Susan W. Warne
Cover and Text Designer   Anna Post
Manuscript Editor   Carol Beal

Library of Congress Cataloging in Publication Data

Fowler, H. Ramsey (Henry Ramsey)
    The Little, Brown handbook.

    Includes index.
    1. English language — Grammar — 1950–
2. English language — Rhetoric.   I. Little, Brown and
Company.   II. Title.
PE1112.F64 1983   808'.042   82–17234
ISBN 0–316–28981–7

Library of Congress Catalog Card No. 82–17234

ISBN 0-316-28981-7

9 8 7 6 5 4 3

MU

Published simultaneously in Canada
by Little, Brown & Company (Canada) Limited

Printed in the United States of America

We would like to thank the following authors and publishers for permission to quote from their works.

The American Heritage Dictionary of the English Language, definitions of *conjecture* and *real.* © 1969, 1970, 1971, 1973, 1975, 1976, 1978, Houghton Mifflin Company. Reprinted by permission.
Roger Angell, from *Five Seasons.* Copyright © 1977 by Roger Angell. First published in *The New Yorker.* Reprinted by permission of Simon & Schuster, a Division of Gulf & Western Corporation, and International Creative Management.
Bonnie Angelo, from "Those Good Ole Boys," *Time,* 27 September 1976. Copyright 1976 Time Inc. Reprinted by permission from TIME.
Pete Axthelm, from "The City Game." Reprinted by permission of The Sterling Lord Agency, Inc. Copyright © 1970 by Pete Axthelm.
Peter Bogdanovich, excerpted from "Bogie in Excelsis," *Pieces of Time.* © 1973 by Peter Bogdanovich. Used by permission of Arbor House Publishing Company.
Jacob Bronowski, from *Imagination and the University.* Copyright © 1964 by Jacob Bronowski. Reprinted by permission of Mrs. Rita Bronowski.
Lynn Buller, from "The Encyclopedia Game" in Saul D. Feldman and Gerald W. Thielbar, eds., *Life Style: Diversity in American Society.* Copyright © 1972 by Little, Brown and Company (Inc.). Reprinted by permission.

(continued on page 579)

Preface

This new edition of *The Little, Brown Handbook* will look familiar to users of the first edition. The book still combines a reference guide for writers with a textbook for composition classes. Its organization — whole paper and paragraphs first, sentence chapters together, usage glossary at the back — and its correction code remain unchanged. Its reference system still provides easy and varied access both for instructors marking papers and for students seeking information on their own (see "Using This Book," p. viii). Its explanations, examples, and exercises continue to be appropriate for students who are unfamiliar or uncomfortable with the process and conventions of writing. And its recommended standard of usage remains generally conservative.

But the second edition does something that the first edition could not do: It reflects instructors' experiences with the handbook in thousands of writing courses. Along with gratifying support, we received countless well-founded suggestions for making the book more useful, and these suggestions prompted many small improvements and several large ones. Few sentences escaped some change for the better as we reexamined every line of text, every example, and every exercise for unneeded complexity and unwanted ambiguity. In response to many requests, we increased the number of exercises by over 15 percent. Eighteen new exercise sets give students extra practice on persistent problems such as case, verbs, agreement, fragments, splices and run-ons, commas, semicolons, and apostrophes. And fifty new and revised exercise sets encourage students to produce mature sentences and paragraphs of their own by expansion, imitation, and especially sentence combining.

The additions to the second edition go beyond exercises, for most of the chapters have seen some expansion. The chapters on the writing process (1 and 2) now take greater account of the writer's purpose, include more on invention and revision, and cover the formal as well as the informal outline. As before, the chapters trace the development and revision of a student essay, but the essay now compares and contrasts the relative strengths of computerized video games and Monopoly (Monopoly wins). These chapters on the whole paper and the one on paragraphs (Chapter 3) are more closely linked by approach and terminology, by additional cross-referencing, and by a new section 3e on combining paragraphs in the essay.

We also expanded many of the chapters on sentences, punctuation, and mechanics. For example, Chapter 10 on sentence fragments now begins with three tests for determining whether a group of words forms a complete sentence. Chapter 15 now includes a new section 15e on careless omission of words. The discussion of restrictive and nonrestrictive elements (Chapter 21 on commas) now illustrates the importance of context, and the examples are simpler, clearer, and more plentiful.

The material on diction (Chapter 31) and spelling (Chapter 34) is also more complete. We added euphemisms to the discussion of inappropriate words and enlarged the section on concrete and specific words. The list of commonly misspelled words is more than quadrupled to almost 500 entries.

The chapter on the research paper (35) continues to follow the development of a student paper ("How Advertisers Make Us Buy"), but almost every section of the chapter contains new material. For example, we expanded the bibliography and footnote models in *MLA Handbook* style; added the MLA's internal parenthetical style of source citation; added both the APA and science styles of documentation; included a new section (35g-2) on how and when to introduce quotations, paraphrases, and summaries into the paper; and included sample note cards in the annotations opposite the sample paper. Chapter 36 on practical writing now includes a discussion and example of the business memorandum.

The educational supplements that accompanied the first edition have also been revised and expanded for the greater benefit of both students and instructors. The enlarged handbook instructor's manual, by Robert A. Schwegler, contains detailed material on how to use the handbook in composition courses and on evaluating student writing; a bibliography of composition resources; well-tested teaching suggestions for each chapter of the handbook; and answers to the exercises. The second edition of *The Little, Brown Workbook*, by Quentin L. Gehle, continues to parallel exactly the handbook's organization, but it includes new self-tests, more sentence exercises, and new review exercises. The workbook is accompanied by a new instructor's manual containing suggestions for teaching with the workbook as well as answers to the exercises. The answers to the exercises in both the handbook and the workbook are also bound in separate booklets that may be distributed to students at an instructor's option. A poster-sized correction chart, showing the handbook's code and symbols, and two completely new diagnostic tests are also available to instructors.

Acknowledgments

We have hinted already at the large numbers of instructors who helped with this edition. We wish we had space to thank individually the hundreds of first-edition users who shared their experiences with us either through Little, Brown's field representatives or in diligent responses to our extensive and doubtless exhausting survey. Most of these instructors will see something in this new edition for which they can claim credit. We must acknowledge the fifteen instructors whose contributions in special discussion groups prompted many significant revisions: Jay Balderson, Western Illinois University; Harry Brown and Karen Reed, both of Midwestern State University; Mary Copeland and Lorene Strickland, both of Brookhaven College; Richard Cox, David Merrell, and William Walton, all of Abilene Christian University; Lyman Hagan, George Peek, and Norman Stafford, all of Arkansas State University; Natalie Maynor and Jack White, both of Mississippi State University; and Ida Short and Daniel Thomas, both of Shelby State Community College.

For consistently careful and helpful readings of parts or all of the first edition pages and the second-edition manuscript, we are especially grateful to Larry G. Brunner, Hardin-Simmons University; Barbara R. Carson, University of Georgia; C. Michael Curtis, Senior Editor, *The Atlantic Monthly;* Michael C. Flanigan, University of Oklahoma at Norman; Michael Grimwood, North Carolina State University; John T. Harwood, Pennsylvania State University; Leo J. Hines, Fitchburg State College; Margrit Loomis, Northeast Louisiana University; Michael Meyer, University of Connecticut; John R. Reuter, Florida Southern College; Cynthia L. Ricketson, Central Piedmont Community College; Robert A. Schwegler, University of Rhode Island; Cynthia L. Selfe, Michigan Technological University; and Karen W. Willingham, Pensacola Junior College. As before, we owe a large debt to Richard S. Beal, Boston University, for wise counsel and comradeship.

Using This Book

A handbook is a comprehensive reference guide to the essential information in a field or discipline, whether it be stamp collecting, home maintenance, or chemistry. *The Little, Brown Handbook* is no exception. A basic resource for English grammar, usage, and composition, it can serve you as a basic text and reference for writing not only in a composition course but also in other courses and outside college. This introduction describes the book's organization and store of information, the ways to locate that information, and the standard of usage recommended.

The handbook's organization and coverage

An overview of the handbook's contents appears inside the back cover. The first four chapters discuss the elements of the composition process such as discovering a purpose, generating and organizing ideas, composing paragraphs, being convincing, and revising. You may want to read and digest these chapters even if they are not assigned by your instructor.

You may also want to read Chapter 5, which presents the system of English grammar. Though much of the material will be familiar to you, the chapter will repay your attention because it shows that the grammar of English is more than just a hodgepodge of rules, and it provides the background needed for understanding the fourteen chapters that follow. Each of the following chapters treats a single convention or principle of either grammatical correctness (Chapters 6 to 9), clarity (Chapters 10 to 15), or effectiveness (Chapters 16 to 19). Your instructor may discuss some or all of these chapters in class or may only suggest that you consult specific chapters when you encounter problems.

Chapters 20 to 30 of the handbook describe the current conventions of punctuation and the closely related conventions of mechanics — capitalization, abbreviation, and the like. Whether or not you are assigned these chapters, you should think of them as resources to consult continually for advice on specific questions.

Chapters 31 to 34 deal with words. Chapter 31, which discusses the principles guiding effective word choice, is intended to help you express your meaning exactly and concisely. Chapter 32 introduces the features and uses of any desk dictionary. Chapters 33 and 34 suggest ways you can develop your vocabulary and master the complexities of English spelling.

The last chapters of the handbook treat specific writing tasks. Chapter 35 traces the process of writing and documenting a research or library paper for which you consult books and periodicals on some issue or question. Chapter 36 provides specific advice on writing essay examinations for college courses, letters to make complaints or requests or to apply for a job, and business memorandums.

The handbook includes three appendixes, each one addressing a specific practical problem. Appendix A explains your responsibility for acknowledging the ideas and information that you draw from other writers. Appendix B describes a widely accepted standard, which your instructor may supplement, for preparing a manuscript. And Appendix C offers specific advice on studying effectively for any course.

Two glossaries and an index conclude the handbook. The glossary of usage provides brief notes on troublesome or confusing words and expressions that plague writers at all levels of experience. The glossary of grammatical terms defines all the specialized words that appear in the handbook as well as a few others. The index contains every term used in the book and every form the term can take as well as many specific words and phrases that you may need to look up.

Finding information in the handbook

The Little, Brown Handbook provides a wealth of specific information — what form of a verb to use, how to express an idea concisely, whether to punctuate with a comma or a semicolon, whether to capitalize a word, how to arrange the title page of a paper, and so on. The handbook also provides many ways of locating such information quickly. When you seek information on your own, you can check the guide to useful lists inside the front cover; you can refer to the table of contents inside the back cover or immediately after this introduction; or you can refer to the index. The table of contents shows all the book's parts, chapters, and main sections within chapters. The sections are labeled with letters (*a*, *b*, and so on). These letters and the corresponding chapter numbers (for instance, 9d or 12a) also appear before the appropriate convention or guideline in the text itself, and they are printed in colored boxes on the sides of the pages. Thus you can find a section heading in the contents and thumb the book until you arrive at its number and letter on the side of the page. If you are uncertain of what to look for and need a more detailed guide to the book's contents, consult the index.

Your instructor may mark your papers using heading numbers and letters, symbols, or written comments. Pages 49 to 52 show samples of student work marked each way. If your instructor marks your paper with, say, 21a, you can refer to the contents to learn that you have made an error involving a comma. If you need further information to correct the error, you can then refer to the text by finding the appropriate page number or by locating 21a in a colored box on the side of the page, as described above. If your instructor uses symbols to mark your paper, you can find out how to correct the error by referring to the contents at the back of the book, where the symbols are listed by chapter, or to the alphabetical list of symbols inside the front cover. Using the latter guide, you would be directed by the symbol *frag* to Chapter 10, which discusses sentence fragments. The symbols also appear in the colored boxes on the sides of the pages. The best way to find specific handbook sections from your instructor's written comments is to consult the index. Look up the term used by your instructor and scan the subentries under it until you find one that seems to describe the error you have made. Then turn to the page number given.

The handbook's recommended usage

The Little, Brown Handbook describes and recommends the conventions of standard, written English — the written language common to business and the professions. Written English is more conservative than spoken English in matters of grammar and usage, and a great many words, phrases, and constructions that are widely spoken remain unaccepted in careful writing.

When clear distinctions exist between the language of conversation and that of careful writing, the handbook provides examples of each and labels them *spoken* and *written*. When usage in writing itself varies with the level of formality intended, the handbook labels examples *formal* and *informal*. When usage is mixed or currently changing, the handbook recommends that you choose the more conservative usage because it will be acceptable to all readers.

If you follow the guidelines discussed in this handbook, your writing will be clearer and more demanding of serious attention than it might otherwise have been. However, adhering to established conventions is but a means to the real achievement and reward of writing: communicating your message effectively.

Contents

12
Pronoun Reference

224

13
Shifts

232

14
Misplaced and Dangling Modifiers

238

15
Mixed and Incomplete Sentences

247

I

The Whole Paper and Paragraphs

1
Developing an Essay

Most of the papers you write in college are essays. Whether you argue against pesticides, describe a physics experiment, analyze a business case, interpret a novel, examine the causes of a historical event, or tell of a personal experience, you are exploring your relation to the world and presenting ideas for someone to consider. You are writing an **essay,** a nonfiction composition that analyzes and interprets a topic, offering your view of it.

All your essay writing serves a basic **purpose:** you aim to communicate something about a topic to a particular audience of readers. These three components of the essay — you the writer, the topic, the audience — interact continuously during the writing process. You choose a subject that you care about and believe readers will care about. As you develop and arrange information about the topic, you balance your view, the demands of the subject, and the needs, interests, and expectations of the audience. If you have done your part, readers will be drawn into your world and will experience the subject as you do.

The general purpose of essay writing is thus communication by a writer through a subject to an audience. But shaping materials for the benefit of an audience requires as well a more specific conception of purpose, a goal for a particular essay to achieve. Sometimes you will want to entertain readers or share with them your beliefs or feelings. More often you will want to inform readers about a subject or persuade them to agree with your opinion. These goals or intentions often overlap in a single essay. You may combine, say, persuasion and self-expression in writing about a saxophonist's unusual talent. Or you may combine information and entertainment in an essay on an especially raucous rock concert. But an essay will have a primary intention that demands emphasis on one of the three elements of the writing process. When you write mainly to express yourself, for instance, you predominate because you are the subject. In contrast, when you write mainly to persuade or entertain readers, they are your focus. And when you write mainly to inform readers about a subject, the subject itself is the focus. But always the other two elements also help determine what and how you write.

Your subject, audience, and specific purpose will lead you to write one of four kinds of essays: narrative, descriptive, argumentative, or expository. The **narrative essay** relates a sequence of events, whether factual or not. You might choose the narrative form if you wanted to entertain readers by recounting your mishaps on public transportation. If your subject were work and you wanted to persuade readers of the need for on-the-job training, you might narrate your difficulties mastering a new job without training. Your opinion of the topic would be embodied in the tone of your writing (for instance, amused or angry) and in your selection of events (the situations that job training would have helped you avoid).

The **descriptive essay** evokes a scene, person, object, emotion, or event by concentrating on distinguishing details. You might inform readers about an architectural style by describing a particular building in that style. You might try to express the sensations of smell, touch, and taste by describing the experience of eating an apple. A descriptive essay on the general subject of work might convey the fearsome (or kindly) attributes of a supervisor. Like narration, description usually implies rather than states the writer's opinion through details (for instance, the boss's towering size, stern face, dignified walk, and cold manner) and through concrete words (like *towering* and *cold*) that appeal to readers' senses.

In an **argumentative essay** you try to persuade readers to appreciate and respect — if not also accept — your position on a debatable subject. You generally state your opinion outright and then defend it logically with supporting ideas and evidence. An essay urging tighter (or looser) controls on drug use is argumentative. So is one maintaining that health care is an obligation of the government (or none of the government's business), or one calling for the abolition of college examinations. In an essay on work, you might try to persuade your readers that students who qualify for financial aid should be given first priority for jobs on campus. (Argumentation is discussed more fully in Chapter 4.)

The fourth kind of essay, **expository,** is the one used most often in college and business writing, and it is the one this book concentrates on. The primary purpose of most exposition is to inform readers about something or explain something to them. You might discuss how a baseball team ended a losing streak, how a chemical process works, or why the 1960s were a time of social upheaval. Combining the purposes of informing and persuading, you might explain why you chose to major in engineering rather than business.

An expository essay on work might outline the various jobs on campus or, perhaps with the additional intention of entertaining, give the steps in preparing a Big Mac. In developing your topic, you state your view of it directly as well as convey it in your tone and in your selection and organization of information (for instance, adopting an impersonal tone to present the making of a Big Mac as a mechanical process).

Though narration, description, argumentation, and exposition are kinds of essays, they may also provide needed information in single paragraphs within an essay. For instance, to persuade readers that needy students should receive first priority for campus jobs, you might include a paragraph narrating the unhappy job-hunting experiences of one needy student. Or an expository essay on a chemical process might include a paragraph describing the smells or colors of the chemicals. But these paragraphs would be worth including only if they advanced your larger and primary purpose of persuading or informing readers.

Focusing on purpose, audience, and kind of essay will help you throughout the writing process as you discover, clarify, develop, and shape ideas and feelings. As you write, you choose words and information to express your viewpoint coherently. Writing draws on intuition as well as reasoning, on sensation and emotion as well as fact and memory. Thus it is not always, or even most often, an orderly procedure. You and every other writer may find that the process of writing is smooth and sequential one day, disjointed or disorderly the next. No two writers approach writing the same way, and no individual approaches it the same way from one experience to the next. Because writing is as personal as thinking and communicating, it is also as varied.

As complex and varied as the writing process is, however, it can be divided into several steps that we will trace in this chapter and the next. In writing, your thoughts move over and over again from the general to the specific and from the specific to the general. You start with a broad subject and limit it to a single topic (see 1a). You generate ideas about your topic by directing your thoughts from the abstract to the concrete and from the vague to the definite (1b). You group your ideas and select from among them (1c) to discover your particular point of view (1d). Throughout the writing process you consider your readers, making your writing understandable by selecting the ideas, details, and tone that will work best (1e). You organize all the ideas and details so that relations among them will be clear (1f). And as you write and revise, you rethink your ideas and flesh out your general plan with specific words (Chapter 2).

Practicing these steps in the writing process, much as you would practice the moves of a dance or the notes of a musical piece, will help you become a more relaxed and proficient writer. But always keep in mind that the process is usually cyclical and unpredictable. If you have to alter your point of view after you organize your material, or if you must change your plan when you are halfway through writing the first draft, then you are experiencing what thousands of writers before you have also experienced.

1a
Discovering and limiting a subject

Many writers (including experienced ones) encounter their first stumbling block in trying to find a subject to write about. Your instructor may suggest a subject; but if not, you will have to invent one suitable to you.

A good way to discover an essay subject is to review your own experiences, interests, and curiosities. Look for a subject you already know something about or have been wondering about, such as some issue at your college or in your town, or a job you had or would like to have. Recall what you have discussed with others recently: perhaps an event in your family's history or a change in relations between men and women. Consider something you have read or seen in a movie or on television: for instance, a shocking book, a violent or funny movie, a television commercial. Think about things that make you especially happy or angry, such as a hobby or the behavior of your neighbors. The goal here is to think of a subject that interests you. Then you can interest your readers in it by providing details and examples that develop your viewpoint.

Your subject, whether assigned or arrived at on your own, may be "the ill effects of pollution," "popular games," "college preparation for a business career," "sports fanatics," "how politics works," or "automobiles." But these subjects are too broad to be covered interestingly or even intelligently in an essay of, say, 500 to 750 words (two or three double-spaced typewritten pages). In so little space you probably could not provide much specific information. And specific information — sensory details, facts, and so on — is essential for readers. In most writing, treating a narrow subject thoroughly works better than treating a broad subject skimpily. The broad subjects above need to be scaled down to manageable topics, subdivisions of the larger categories.

If you chose or were assigned the subject "the ill effects of pollution," for instance, you would soon find that you could not cover all effects of all forms of pollution in a brief essay. If you tried to consider the effects of water pollution, air pollution, noise pollution, visual pollution, and all the rest, you would spend 750 words just distinguishing among the kinds of pollution. Your essay would consist of general statements unsupported by details — the details readers must have if they are to understand and believe your general statements. Your treatment would probably be shallow even if you chose a subcategory such as the effects of noise pollution, for you would have to consider the noise from many different sources, including street traffic, airports, and factories. But if you pursued your interest in the subject, you would eventually arrive at a reasonable topic — perhaps a specific example such as the ill effects of living one block from an airport runway — to which you could devote an entire, convincing essay filled with specific information.

One student, Linda Balik, faces the problem of narrowing the subject for an essay whose development we will follow in this chapter and the next. From several choices Balik selects the subject "popular games." She likes to play games of all kinds — including cards, board games, and computerized video games — and she is confident she can find something specific to say about all of them. But she also sees that 750 words can barely touch on the dozen or so games that come easily to mind. Thus she seeks the kind of game or the specific game that interests her most, and she eventually decides on computerized video games. But still the subject seems too general. Among other possibilities she can try to entertain readers by describing the sights and sounds of a game; she can inform readers by narrating the evolution of the games; or she can explain to readers how to play one or two of the games, what the games have in common, or why the games are so popular. These, Balik recognizes, are likely topics for her essay, narrow enough to be treated specifically in only a few pages. In the end she decides to try to explain, in an expository essay, the attractions of the battle games. Because she is not sure herself why she and others enjoy these games so much, she also sees an opportunity to learn something while completing the assignment.

Here are some other examples of narrowing a subject to a manageable topic.

BROAD SUBJECT	MORE SPECIFIC TOPIC
The differences between high school and college. [Too many dimensions to discuss adequately. Choose a single dimension.]	Learning to live without a guidance counselor. The differences between high school and college chemistry.
Politics is a dirty business. [A judgment that needs extensive support. Perhaps choose a single example of dirty politics and explore it carefully.]	How one student government president was corrupted by power. Why it took a month to repair the sewer in front of my house.

Relations between parents and children. [Too many possible dimensions. Perhaps choose a specific kind of relation.]

The dynamics of single-parent families.

The differences in the ways parents treat the oldest and the youngest of their six children.

When choosing and then limiting your subject, try not to lose the personal perspective you started with. Select a comfortable topic and then define it carefully. Your essay will be easier for you to write and more informative and interesting for your readers.

(For information on narrowing the subject for a paper requiring library research, see 35a and 35b.)

EXERCISE 1

Review your recent experiences and interests and think of three or four general subjects for an essay. What have you read or seen that made you curious to know more? What activity have you been involved in lately? What interesting discussions have you participated in? What makes you angry?

EXERCISE 2

Narrow each of the broad subjects from Exercise 1 to a specific topic suitable for a brief essay (500 to 750 words). What aspect of the subject interests you most? What aspect can you discuss most effectively, using enough specific information to convey your perspective to your readers? How can specifying a purpose — expressing yourself, entertaining, informing, or persuading — help you narrow each subject? Can that purpose be best served by narration, description, argumentation, or exposition?

EXERCISE 3

By applying your own perspective and purpose and by focusing on the kind of essay specified, narrow each of the following general subjects to a topic suitable for a brief essay.

Description
1. restaurants
2. movie stars
3. weather
4. furniture

Exposition
5. magazines
6. music
7. automobiles
8. art

Narration
9. Saturday nights
10. sporting events
11. work
12. movies

Argumentation
13. required college courses
14. television programming
15. laws affecting minors
16. government

1b
Developing the topic

Once you have a topic, you need to develop it with specific ideas and details that will convey your intention to readers. You may find that the ideas tumble forth, especially if your topic is a very personal one. Or you may use a strategy like one of the following to generate and remember ideas.

1
Generating ideas by writing

Making a list

Ideas rarely occur in fully developed form. Instead, they straggle to the surface, often half complete, sometimes silly, usually in random order. A thought begun at dinner may not be completed until the next day, and dozens of other thoughts will intervene. To remember all your ideas, write them down as they occur to you. You may wish to consider your topic for a day or two. Or you may prefer to brainstorm, allowing only thirty minutes, say, in which to write down every thought that occurs to you. Don't edit your ideas because they seem irrelevant or dumb or repetitious. Doing so will probably slow down the flow of ideas and may cause you to delete something that could help you later.

Linda Balik makes a list to generate and collect her thoughts on the attraction of computerized video games. Here is part of it.

kinds of games: battles, sports, driving, puzzles, question-answer, backgammon, chess
battle games most popular
games have evolved a long way from original Pong
features: fast action, bright colors, sound effects
computer games more interesting than other arcade games like pinball
played indoors — arcades, pizza shops, bars, home TV
games offer space-age adventure: control of spaceship, defending from invaders
the computer — clever, all-knowing, all-capable
computer takes place of real opponents
clever marketing on TV and in magazines
escape from real problems
problem of addiction to games
expensive
some games just expensive ways to play inexpensive games like cards, chess, backgammon
player can be "violent" — control environment through violence
uses good reflexes and dexterity — little luck involved

This list is quite informal. Though Balik seems to be zeroing in on battle games, several of the ideas concern other games as well. Some items are sketchy, whereas others are fuller. Some, like "games have evolved a long way" and "clever marketing," seem unrelated to the rest. Balik has not made connections between thoughts that are clearly related: for example, between the games' space-age adventures and the escapism they provide. And some of the ideas concern shortcomings of the games (expense, problem of addiction, violence), not just their attractions. The list suggests to Balik a slightly different topic from the one she began with: Instead of explaining simply why the games are popular, she will explain their advantages and disadvantages.

Filling one page

Another way to develop a topic is to begin with a blank page, focus on your topic, and write without stopping until you have filled at least one sheet. As in making a list, you should not stop to edit but instead should force yourself to keep writing. Don't be concerned if the thoughts are not organized. Don't worry yet about the grammar of your sentences or the correct use of words. The goal now is to record as many ideas on your topic as you can, as fast as you can. The result will not be an essay, but it will very likely lead you to specific ideas that you had not considered.

2
Generating ideas by asking questions

If making a list of ideas or filling a page with them does not prove productive, you may want to try asking yourself questions. Asking a set of specific questions about a topic helps you look at the topic objectively while also providing some structure to the development of ideas.

Asking the journalist's questions

A journalist with a story to report asks a series of questions designed to uncover as much information as possible about the event.

1. *Who was involved?*
2. *What happened and what were the results?*
3. *When did it happen?*
4. *Where did it happen?*
5. *Why did it happen?*
6. *How did it happen?*

These questions can be useful in probing an essay topic as well, especially if your purpose is to entertain or to inform in narration or exposition. If you decided to relate how a summer job was a learning experience, for instance, the journalist's questions would help you isolate the important people you encountered, the main events and their order, and the possible causes of the events. Similarly, if you decided to explain the dynamics of a single-parent, single-child family, the questions would lead you to consider the characteristics of the people involved, the ways the two people interact, and the possible causes and effects of their style of interaction.

Asking exploratory questions

Also useful for probing a topic are questions that correspond to the ways we naturally think about subjects.

1. *How can it be illustrated or supported?* Focus on providing an extended example or several examples of the topic: four television soap operas, the experiences of a single woman with children. Or focus on providing reasons for your view of the topic: three reasons for majoring in English, four reasons for driving defensively.
2. *What is it? What does it encompass, and what does it exclude?* Focus on defining the topic: a word like *liberal*, an idea like good dance music.
3. *What are its parts or its characteristics?* Focus on dividing the topic: a single thing like a short story (characters, setting, plot) or a roller skate (wheels, stops, laces). *Or what groups or categories can it be sorted into?* Focus on classifying the topic: kinds of automobiles or classes of human rights.
4. *How is it like, or different from, other things?* Focus on comparing and contrasting the topic with something else: public and private transportation, two styles of architecture.
5. *Is it comparable to something in a different class but more familiar to us?* Focus on forming an analogy, an extended comparison of the topic with something else: getting through freshman year and pushing a car uphill, football strategy and battle strategy.
6. *What are its causes or its effects?* Focus on explaining why the topic happened or what its results were: the causes of cerebral palsy, the effects of a cold climate on life-style.
7. *How does it work or how do you do it?* Focus on analyzing a process: making a Big Mac, running a marathon.

As most of the examples indicate, these questions are appropriate for sharing information in exposition. But you can also use them for other purposes and other kinds of essays. To narrate a single event like a flash flood, for instance, you might recount various people's experiences of the flood. To describe a chimpanzee, you might compare and contrast it with a human. And to argue for restructuring a dangerous highway intersection, you might examine both the accidents caused by the present structure and the likely effects of the change.

After listing ideas to help refine her topic from the attractions of computerized video games to their advantages and disadvantages, Linda Balik uses the exploratory questions to develop the new topic more fully. Some approaches, such as definition and cause and effect, do not seem to apply to the topic. Others, however, open up new possibilities for development. She can explain how the battle games work, evaluating each step (inserting money into the machine, manipulating the controls, scoring points with "kills," and so on) as a positive or negative feature of the games. She can sort computer games into classes (battle games, driving games, sports games, and the like) and then evaluate each class. But the question that takes her furthest is "How is it like, or different from, other things?" She considers how the advantages and disadvantages of computerized battle games compare with those of other forms of recreation like watching television, reading, playing outdoor sports, playing other indoor games. She recognizes that the qualities she likes about computer games (escapism, reliance on skill instead of luck) are less important in other indoor games like Monopoly and Clue. At the same time the traditional board games are strong where computer games are weak, particularly in cost and in the opportunity to play real people as opponents. This, Balik decides, is the way she will develop her topic: comparing and contrasting the advantages and disadvantages of computerized battle games and board games. Since the battle games seem to her to resemble each other more than the board games do, she will treat the battle games as a group and focus on a single board game — Monopoly, the most popular. This decision prompts additional ideas as well as the beginnings of a structure for her essay.

COMPUTER GAMES	MONOPOLY
new — reflect the times	old
played on TV screen	played on traditional board
escapism	mundane economic concerns
depend on skill	luck a big factor — dice
play is very fast	play is slow, waiting for opponents
easy for children	harder for children
played indoors	played indoors
violence	greed
skills — dexterity, reflexes	skills — planning, budgeting

expensive	inexpensive
fantasy science fiction — space-age adventure	predictability of board and opponents' moves
opponent — computer	opponents — real people
addicting	nonaddicting
can be mastered, get boring	can never be mastered — luck — each game new

The ideas still overlap somewhat; for instance, the items on skills can be combined. And some of the ideas are uninformative: "Played on TV screen" versus "played on traditional board," although it is the fundamental difference between the two that prompts the comparison, tells nothing else about the games. And the fact that both games are played indoors adds nothing to the comparison. But the lists do prepare Balik for the next stage: grouping ideas.

The exploratory questions can prove very useful for developing whole essays, as we have just seen. However, they are often even more helpful for developing the details, examples, and reasons needed in paragraphs within the essay. One essay might employ different kinds of paragraphs. For instance, a paper on television soap operas that was developed by illustration might contain a paragraph analyzing the causes of their popularity. Or an essay analyzing the causes of cerebral palsy might include a paragraph-length analogy between a person confined to a wheelchair and a prisoner or a dependent child. Balik's comparison-and-contrast paper might contain a paragraph that explains how the two games are played. Because these methods of development are so useful at the paragraph level, they are discussed and illustrated more fully in the chapter on paragraphs (see 3c).

EXERCISE 4

To practice generating ideas for an essay, apply at least one of the four development methods — making a list, filling a page, asking the journalist's questions, or asking the exploratory questions — to one of the narrowed topics from Exercise 2 or 3 (p. 7).

EXERCISE 5

Fill a page on one of the following topics. This exercise will give you practice both in generating ideas and in writing.

1. who I am
2. the appearance (or taste) of an apple
3. borrowing (or lending) money
4. prejudice in my hometown
5. television news versus newspaper news
6. pigeons
7. a country music singer
8. a television show
9. a brother or a sister
10. an awkward or embarrassing moment

EXERCISE 6

Narrow two of the following subjects to more limited topics, and then generate a list of ideas about each topic by asking one or more of the exploratory questions on page 10.

1. the college grading system
2. jogging
3. reading
4. shyness
5. parties
6. patriotism
7. parents
8. radio personalities
9. basketball
10. zoo animals

1c
Grouping ideas

After thinking about a subject, narrowing it, and developing some ideas, you still may not see what you really have to say to readers or how you can best say it. The next step is to group the ideas into broad patterns. Organizing ideas brings them into order, eliminates what is irrelevant, shows which ideas need more thought, and gives you more control. Grouping your ideas will help you discover your central theme and how specific ideas relate to it.

In writing down ideas and asking the exploratory questions about her topic, Linda Balik has modified the topic from the attractions of computerized battle games to the games' advantages and disadvantages to a comparison of the advantages and disadvantages of computer games and Monopoly. The side-by-side ideas on the two games (pp. 11–12) provide a head start for grouping ideas, but the two lists are still a jumble of advantages and disadvantages. Sorting through the ideas, rearranging them, and changing some, Balik produces these groups of related ideas.

Advantages of computer games
    each game quick; instant response
    escapist — imaginary world of space-age adventure
    luck only in computer's randomness — otherwise depends on skill (dexterity, reflexes)
    player can control the game world — piloting spaceship, defending earth
Disadvantages of computer games
    expensive
    computer is only opponent
    games can be addicting
    games can be mastered and then become boring
Advantages of Monopoly
    traditional game enjoyed by young and old
    because of luck, each game a new start
    game can never be mastered
    inexpensive
    play real people as opponents

Disadvantages of Monopoly
> dealing with making and losing money — not particularly escapist
>
> takes a long time and moves slowly — waiting for opponents to play
>
> uses game board, so play is predictable
>
> depends more on luck (dice) than skills (planning, budgeting)

Sorting out the advantages and disadvantages of the two games helps Balik eliminate some ideas and combine and expand others. She still must develop the ideas more fully and tighten the relationships within and among groups. But she is ready to move on to a crucial stage, formulating a central thesis for her essay.

EXERCISE 7

Choose one of the sets of ideas you generated in Exercise 4, 5, or 6 (pp. 12–13), and group the ideas into general categories. Delete, add, or modify ideas as necessary to reflect your thinking at this new stage. These grouped ideas will provide the basis for an essay you produce by completing exercises in the rest of Chapter 1 and in Chapter 2.

1d
Developing the thesis

The activities described so far — discovering and limiting a subject, generating ideas, and grouping those ideas — are steps on the way to determining the main idea you want to communicate to your readers. An essay must be focused on, controlled by, and related to that one main idea. If it isn't, its parts will seem disjointed, and the writing almost certainly will fail to interest or convince readers. The central idea is called the **thesis.** It contains your view of your topic, your reason for writing, your goal. Your thesis does more than merely name the topic; it *asserts* something about it.

If your topic were noise pollution as experienced by someone living near an airport, your thesis might be an assertion like this one: "To discover how damaging noise pollution can be, one only needs to live a block from an airport runway." For the topic of why television soap operas are so popular, your thesis might be "Soap operas do help some people escape from their problems, but many people watch them because their own lives look simple and happy by comparison." These sentences both name the essay topic specifically and assert an opinion about it.

1
Conceiving the thesis sentence

As the two examples above illustrate, an essay's thesis is often expressed in a single sentence, called the **thesis sentence.** It generally comes near the beginning of the essay, thus alerting readers early to what they can expect and focusing their attention. As an expression of the thesis, the thesis sentence serves three crucial functions.

1. It narrows your topic to a single idea that you want readers to gain from your essay.
2. In asserting something about the topic, it conveys your purpose and your opinion, your special perspective.
3. It may provide a specific, concise preview of your ideas and of how you will arrange them in the essay.

Here are several examples of topics and corresponding thesis sentences that fulfill these three functions.

TOPIC	THESIS SENTENCE
Tapping of telephone lines by police	Though abuses have occurred and probably always will, the police should be permitted to tap a telephone line in any situation where they can demonstrate potential danger to public safety.
The effects of strip-mining	Strip-mining should be tightly controlled in this region to reduce its pollution of water resources, its permanent destruction of the land, and its devastating effects on people's lives.
Why it took a month to repair the sewer in front of my house	If you want to wait a month for your sewer line to be repaired, have an argument with a neighbor on the Public Works Commission before asking the commission to do the repair.
My city neighborhood	The main street of my neighborhood contains enough variety to make almost any city dweller feel at home.

The dynamics of single-parent families	In families consisting of a single parent and a single child, the boundaries between parent and child often disappear so that the two interact as siblings or as a married couple.
How one student government president was corrupted by power	As student government president I worked harder to gain personal favors from teachers and administrators than I did to represent the students who elected me.
What public relations is	Most of us are unaware of the public relations campaigns directed at us, but they can significantly affect the way we think and live.
The effects of climate on lifestyle	Living in a cold climate like New England's influences how you spend your money, what you do with your time, and how you feel about yourself and others.

Each of these thesis sentences reflects not only the writer's particular slant on the topic but also his or her primary intention to entertain, inform, or persuade with narration, description, exposition, or argumentation. The first two sentences clearly convey a persuasive purpose: The writers maintain that the police *should* be allowed to tap some telephone lines and that strip-mining *should* be tightly controlled. In the third sentence the writer conveys an intention to entertain and perhaps inform readers by narrating the main events in getting a sewer line repaired. The emphasis in the fourth sentence on the variety of a city street reflects a desire to inform by describing a scene. And the remaining four sentences convey their writers' intention to inform with exposition: One writer will explain the dynamics of a single-parent, single-child family; another will explain how being student government president corrupted her; another will explain the influences of public relations campaigns; and the last will explain three effects of living in a cold climate.

2
Writing and revising the thesis sentence

When you move from groups of ideas to a thesis sentence, the most important step is to discover precisely what you want to say.

How are the ideas related? What is your attitude toward them? How can you convey relationships and attitude to your readers in one specific, assertive sentence?

Working with questions like these, Linda Balik begins formulating a thesis sentence for her essay on computer games and Monopoly. She first turns her topic into an assertion.

> Computerized battle games and Monopoly both have advantages and disadvantages.

The sentence reflects Balik's intention to explain the differences in an expository essay. However, it says nothing specific about the differences, and it does not convey Balik's attitude toward the games. The sentence implies instead an objective essay like a newspaper story: balanced reporting with no personal viewpoint. Yet while formulating and arranging her ideas, Balik has been developing an attitude — namely, that computer games, with all their advantages, are not as much fun as Monopoly, even with its disadvantages. Her purpose in writing will be to persuade, then, as well as to inform, and so she reworks her thesis sentence.

> Computerized battle games have their attractions, but Monopoly is still a better game.

Balik asserts her own view here, but the sentence is no more specific than the first one. She needs to say what is good about computer games and what is better about Monopoly. For specifics she returns to her notes.

> Computerized battle games are exciting and challenging, but they are expensive and short-lived, and they do not rival Monopoly for fun.

This sentence is much more specific, but still it bothers Balik. It is unbalanced, emphasizing computer games too much by including both their advantages and their disadvantages. And the word *fun*, the one advantage given for Monopoly, is vague and therefore troubling. Balik is not sure what she means by it, and she doubts that her readers will understand either. Another look at her notes helps her define the word, and she rewrites the sentence once more.

> Computerized battle games are exciting and challenging, but Monopoly's inexpensiveness, staying power, and opportunity for interaction among people make it a better game.

In this final revision Balik grasps what she means by *fun* (the interaction among people) and balances the advantages of the two games. Her thesis sentence is *limited* to one idea and is *specific* about that idea. It is also *unified* because the parts relate to and complement each other. It expresses a clear intention — to show by comparison that Monopoly is a superior game — and thus it tells Balik's readers what to expect and promises to guide her later work. Although she may wish to revise the thesis sentence further as she writes and revises (see 2b), she can be satisfied with it now.

Here are other examples of thesis sentences revised to be limited, specific, and unified.

ORIGINAL	REVISED
Fad diets are dangerous. [A vague statement that needs limiting with specific information: Which diets? How and why dangerous?]	Fad diets can be dangerous when they deprive the body of essential nutrients or rely on excessive quantities of potentially harmful foods.
Inexpensive travel can be educational. [Too general. Why is it educational?]	Traveling on a small budget teaches one more about a country and its people than traveling expensively does.
We all feel aggression, but since it usually means violence, perhaps injury and death, we should figure out how to use it constructively. [Not unified: emphasis on violence detracts from assertion at the end.]	By deliberately channeling our natural feelings of aggression, we can express them constructively rather than destructively.

EXERCISE 8

Evaluate the following thesis sentences, considering whether each one is sufficiently limited, specific, and unified. Rewrite the sentences as necessary to meet these goals. What overall purpose and kind of essay does each sentence indicate?

1. Gun control is essential.
2. One evening of a radio talk show amply illustrates both the appeal of such shows and their silliness.
3. Good manners make our society work.
4. City people are different from country people.
5. Television is a useful baby sitter and an escape for people who do not want to think about their own problems.
6. The best rock concerts are those in which the performers transform a passive crowd into a stamping, screaming mob.
7. I liked American history in high school, but I do not like it in college.
8. We are encouraged to choose a career in college, but people change jobs frequently.
9. Drunken drivers, whose perception, coordination, and reaction time are impaired, should receive mandatory suspensions of their licenses.
10. The beach in winter is not a lonely place.

EXERCISE 9

Write a thesis sentence for your set of grouped ideas from Exercise 7 (p. 14).

EXERCISE 10

Write thesis sentences for three of the following topics. Each of your sentences should convey the purpose given in parentheses.

1. wearing blue jeans (*informing*)
2. a frustrating experience (*expressing yourself*)
3. what one can learn from travel (*informing or entertaining*)
4. why old houses or apartments are better than new ones (or vice versa) (*persuading*)
5. the sounds of the country or city (*expressing yourself or informing*)
6. why divorce laws should be tougher (or looser) (*persuading*)
7. how to care for a plant (*informing*)
8. why students attend college (*informing*)
9. deciding whom to vote for in an election (*informing*)
10. why women should (or should not) be subject to the military draft (*persuading*)
11. how a rumor spreads (*informing or entertaining*)
12. the ideal car (*informing or persuading*)
13. why public transportation should (or should not) be expanded (*persuading*)
14. a disliked person (*expressing yourself or entertaining*)
15. an exciting sports event (*entertaining or informing*)

1e
Considering an audience

As we have seen all along, the purpose of all essay writing is to *communicate ideas and information to readers.* Readers are your audience. If they do not understand what they read or do not react the way you want, then you may be at fault. The chances are good that you have not considered carefully enough what the audience must be told in order to understand and to react appropriately.

Considering your audience begins when you select your subject — when, for an obvious example, you decide not to write on macroeconomic theory for your music history teacher. You continue to consider your audience as you collect ideas and devise a thesis sentence; for an article on jobs for students, say, you focus on training positions with flexible hours, not on full-time management positions. But considering your audience becomes crucial when you think about what to *say* about your thesis and how to say it. Both your statements and the facts, details, and examples you use to support them depend on the interests and understanding of your readers. The attitude that you convey toward your material — the tone of your writing — depends on your readers' expectations and the impression you want them to gain.

1
Using specific information

When you describe, narrate, argue, or explain, you use specific information to gain and keep the attention of your readers and to guide them to accept your point of view. In description you rely primarily on sensory details to convey appearance, sound, smell, taste, and touch. In narration you focus on the important details of significant events to convey your sense of an experience or occurrence. Argumentation depends on appropriate assertions supported by reasons, facts, and other evidence. And exposition depends on specific information — details, facts, examples — to clarify an explanation. Whatever the kind of writing, however, your selection of information must suit the background of your audience: its familiarity with your topic, its biases, and its special interests.

Consider the student who needs money. He writes two letters, one to his parents and another to his school's Office of Student Aid. First he writes to his parents:

> Well, I did it again. Only two weeks into a new semester, and I'm broke already. But you know I needed a sweater, and besides, book prices have just skyrocketed and I've got this Constitutional History course that almost broke the bank all by itself ($60.00 for books!). Oh, and I've met this really great girl (more later). So anyway, I'm pretty low on cash right now and am going to need another $50.00 to make it through the rest of the month. This should be the last time I have to ask you for money, though. Starting next week I'm going to work part-time at a restaurant — doing some short-order cooking and general kinds of work — so if you want your money back . . .

Then he writes to the Office of Student Aid:

> I am writing to request a short-term loan of $50.00 for bill consolidation and for other personal reasons. Starting in ten days, I will be employed for ten hours per week, as a cook, at Better-Burgers, 315 North Main Street. Thus I will be able to repay the loan easily within the required three-month limit. I understand that if I fail to make any payment . . .

The two letters make the same request, but they contain very different information. In the first letter the student chooses details to present himself as a still scatterbrained but always lovable and almost responsible son: He's "broke already" and not, apparently, for the first time; he needed new clothes; he's serious enough about his studies to pay large sums for his books; he has a new girl friend; he's vague about his job. In the second letter he presents himself as a mature citizen who is aware of his responsibility to his creditors: He omits any mention of his purchases, his girl friend, or other personal details; he explains where he will be working and for precisely how many hours each week; he stresses the certainty of repayment; he proves he knows the regulations — the "three-month limit" and the penalties for nonpayment. If, by accident, the student mailed the second letter to his parents, they might be mystified by its impersonality. And if he mailed the first letter to the Office of Student Aid, the recipients might deny his request.

When you are preparing to write, ask yourself how much your readers already know about what you are saying. You do not want to provide so little information that they are confused; nor do you want to provide so much information that they are either bored or unable to assimilate it all. Before beginning to write her essay on computer games and Monopoly, Linda Balik asks herself who her readers are and how familiar they will be with both games. Can she assume her readers have played or at least seen a battle game and Monopoly? If not, she will have to spend a paragraph or two explaining the games' methods of play, rules, and strategies so that her comparisons will make sense. If her readers are familiar with the games, however, such explanations will be unnecessary, even boring, and she can safely omit them. For knowledgeable readers, though, she will also have to be sure to include the elements of the games that they might consider important. For instance, she cannot try to strengthen her case for Monopoly by ignoring its comparative weaknesses or the comparative strengths of computer games.

2
Adopting a suitable tone

The **tone** of your writing reflects your attitude toward both your subject and your audience. In speaking you convey varied feelings and elicit varied reactions from listeners by changing your gestures and facial expressions, your selection and pronunciation of words, and the pitch and volume of your voice. In writing you accomplish the same ends by changing words and by restructuring sentences and paragraphs.

Conceived most broadly, tone may be informal or formal, as illustrated by the two requests for money on the preceding page. In the first the student's tone is personal. His sentences are typical of conversation: loose and full of the second-person pronoun *you*, contractions (*I've, I'm*), and casual expressions like *really, pretty, so anyway*. His paragraph is loosely structured, introducing subjects like the new girl friend as they occur to him and burying the most important point, the request for money, in the middle. In the second paragraph the tone is much more formal. The student's words (*bill consolidation, employed, per week, thus*) suit his goal of seeming to be serious and responsible. He avoids *you* and contractions. His carefully constructed sentences (*Thus I will be able to repay the loan easily within the required three-month limit*) would sound stiff in most conversation. The paragraph proceeds tightly from request to assurance of repayment to acknowledgment of responsibility for nonpayment.

As these examples suggest, different tones are appropriate for different purposes, subjects, and audiences. A very informal tone, whether flippant, affectionate, or distressed, is generally suitable for personal letters and journals addressed to a sympathetic audience or to yourself. A very formal tone, impersonal and distant, usually suits informative, expository writing, such as a science report, that the audience expects to be objective. But most of your writing in college will fall between these extremes in a wide middle range of tones: perhaps somber for a self-expressive descriptive essay, humorous or eager for an entertaining expository or narrative essay, irritated or dignified for an argumentative essay, or merely calm and straightforward.

Here, for example, is the opening paragraph of a student's essay.

> All over the country people are swimming, jogging, dancing, playing tennis — doing anything to keep fit. Newspapers and national magazines claim we are in the midst of a health revolution. Yet this college has consistently refused to provide money or land for athletic facilities and programs that would benefit all students, not just varsity athletes. So far this year the administrators have denied a petition for a running track around the football field, rejected a donor's offer to build a swimming pool on unused college land, and even refused to begin a noncredit course in dance. Students thus have no place to exercise except in their own rooms and on dangerous highways. The college's administrators must begin to deal positively with the problem.

This student's tone is forceful. The similar structures of the sentences almost set up a marching rhythm. The paragraph proceeds directly from an assertion about the nationwide movement to a demonstration of how out of step the college is to a recommendation for action. The actions of the administrators are described in the negative (*denied, rejected, refused*) to stress how uncompromising they are. Other words, too, are strong: *revolution, consistently, even, dangerous, must.* Yet the student, though clearly angry, has not allowed his anger to muddle his thesis, nor has he failed to support it. If the rest of the essay is equally effective, the writer will very likely convince his readers — including nonathletic students and even, perhaps, college administrators — that his opinion is valid. He will have adopted an effective tone.

If Linda Balik directs her essay on computer games and Monopoly to readers who do not know the games, she may assume a personal, perhaps light tone to match her subject and to try to interest readers in playing the games. Such a tone may also be appropriate for fellow students who also play the games. However, if Balik anticipates that some of these knowledgeable readers will object to her favoring Monopoly, she may better reach them with a somewhat serious tone conveying reasonableness and objectivity.

(For a discussion of tone in argumentation, see 4a.)

3
Writing to a general audience

What do you do when you don't know much about your audience, when you are not writing exclusively for your parents or the Office of Student Aid or people who play games? Unless you are taking courses in advertising or the communications media, most of the writing you do in college will be directed to a general college-level audience. This group of teachers and students is diverse, to be sure, but its members have many characteristics in common. Like most people, college-level readers are skeptical and easily distracted, but they are also curious and thoughtful. They may not share all your interests, but they can understand and appreciate anything you write, so long as it is specific, clear, honest, and fresh. They will expect you to support the assertions you make and the conclusions you draw.

Of course, much of your college writing may have only one reader besides you: the instructor of the course you are writing for. Suppose you are taking an American history course and have been asked to write an essay on the economic background of the War of 1812. You certainly may assume that your instructor is familiar with your subject and expects an essay that shows careful reading of available information and your own interpretation of the facts. Your instructor will judge your essay on the clarity of your prose, the adequacy of your research, and the ability of your examples to support your conclusions.

EXERCISE 11

To practice using different kinds of information for different audiences, choose one of the following topics and list four points you would make to each audience specified.

1. the effects of smoking: for elementary school students and for adult smokers

2. your opinion of welfare: for someone who is on welfare and for someone who is not and who opposes it
3. the advantages of a summer camp: for a prospective camper and for his or her parents
4. why your neighbors should remove the wrecked truck from their yard: for your neighbors and for your town zoning board
5. the beauty of a snowfall: for someone who has never experienced snow and for someone who hates it

EXERCISE 12

Analyze the content and tone of the following paragraphs. What do the writers' selection of information and choice of words and sentence structures convey about their attitudes toward their subjects and toward their readers?

1.   It is Friday night at any of ten thousand watering holes of the small towns and crossroads hamlets of the South. The room is a cacophony of the ping-pong-dingdingding of the pinball machine, the pop-fizz of another round of Pabst, the refrain of *Red Necks, White Socks and Blue Ribbon Beer* on the juke box, the insolent roar of a souped-up engine outside and, above it all, the sound of easy laughter. The good ole boys have gathered for their fraternal ritual — the aimless diversion that they have elevated into a lifestyle.   — BONNIE ANGELO, "Those Good Ole Boys"

2.   For tens of thousands of the city's teen-agers, going to school has become a sometime thing. Some are so poor they have no time for anything but the struggle to stay alive; some are frustrated by their inability to do high school work; some are rebelling against parental and teacher authority; some are sapped of energy by asthma and other chronic ailments; some are living the half-lives of drug addicts; some are turned off by studies in which they see no sense. And there are some who stay home to avoid the gauntlet of muggers, rapists, and drug-starved predators they must pass on the way to school; some have been truants so long they think they cannot return; some play hookey simply because they know they will not be caught.   — MICHAEL STERN, "Truancy Overwhelms the Truant Officers"

3.   The tarpaulin is down, and a midafternoon rain is falling steadily. Play has been halted. The lights are on, and the wet, pale-green tarp throws off wiggly, reptilian gleams. The players are back in their locker rooms, and both dugouts are empty. A few fans have stayed in their seats, huddling under big, brightly colored golf umbrellas, but almost everybody else has moved back under the shelter of the upper decks, standing there quietly, watching the rain. The huge park, the countless rows of shiny-blue wet seats, the long emerald outfield lawns — all stand silent and waiting. By the look of it, this shower may hold things up for a good half-hour or more. Time for a few baseball stories.
                                    — ROGER ANGELL, *Five Seasons*

EXERCISE 13

Choose one topic from Exercise 11. Write a paragraph for each audience, presenting different information and adopting different tones as appropriate.

1f
Organizing an essay

If your essay is disorganized — if its ideas do not follow in a clear order or if they do not relate clearly to each other and to the thesis sentence — then much of your effort to produce an effective thesis sentence and to select appropriate details and tone will be wasted. Readers will search for your ideas, their relative importance, and their connections. But if the search is too difficult, they may mistrust what you say or give up entirely.

Writers can sometimes organize their ideas effectively *while* they write, once they have their thesis firmly in mind and know roughly what they want to say. But often they find that organizing *before* writing helps clarify the relations between ideas and speeds the actual writing later on.

▌Arranging and outlining the parts of an essay

Organizing

A carefully written thesis sentence will help you organize the parts of your essay, for it is likely to contain your main supporting ideas and point the way toward their eventual arrangement. Each of the thesis sentences on pages 15–16 suggests an arrangement for the parts of a whole essay. And in each case the suggested pattern corresponds to one of several conventional ways of organizing ideas: spatial, chronological, general to specific and specific to general (plus variations on these), and comparative. Because these patterns are customary, readers expect them and look for them. If you do not meet these expectations, readers will have trouble following you, and you will lose their attention.

A **spatial organization** is especially appropriate for description of a geographical area, an object, or a person. Following the way people normally survey something, you move through space from a chosen starting point to other features of the scene, object, or person. Describing a friend, for instance, you might begin with his shoes and move upward or begin with his face and move downward. If, instead, you moved from hands to face to shoes to arms, your arrangement would probably be less effective because your readers would have to work harder to stay with you. The thesis sentence below suggests that the writer might move in space from one end of the street to the other.

> The main street of my neighborhood contains enough variety to make any city dweller feel at home.

To illustrate variety, the writer can be expected to provide details of the shops, apartment buildings, and people encountered along the street.

A **chronological organization** reports events as they occurred in time, usually from first to last. This pattern, like spatial organization, corresponds to readers' own experiences and expectations. It suits expository essays in which you describe a process from beginning to end (for instance, the steps in making a Big Mac). And it is usually the most effective pattern for narration. In a narrative essay developed from the following thesis sentence, the author's most effective approach would probably be to proceed chronologically, from the breaking of the sewer line, to the argument, to the appeal to the commission, to the results.

> If you want to wait a month for your sewer line to be repaired, have an argument with a neighbor on the Public Works Commission before asking the commission to do the repair.

Two other common patterns of organization are from the general to the specific and from the specific to the general. You will choose a **general-to-specific pattern** if you want to present your main ideas first and then support them with specifics. This pattern often suits argumentation, where the writer may first state the entire argument generally and then provide the specific evidence for each assertion. The next thesis sentence forecasts such an organization.

> Though abuses have occurred and probably always will, the police should be permitted to tap a telephone line in any situation where they can demonstrate potential danger to public safety.

After the introduction the writer might elaborate on the thesis sentence, summarizing both the main objections to wiretapping and its effectiveness in preserving public safety. In the rest of the essay the writer might analyze each specific situation in which wiretapping should be permitted. General-to-specific organization is also useful in exposition. For instance, the following thesis sentence suggests that the body of the paper might first discuss generally the dynamics of single-parent, single-child families and then provide specific examples of the two forms of interaction.

> In families consisting of a single parent and a single child, the boundaries between parent and child often disappear so that the two interact as siblings or as a married couple.

If in exposition you wish to relate the specifics first and let them build to more general ideas, then you will want to follow the **specific-to-general pattern.** Take, for instance, this thesis sentence.

> Most of us are unaware of the public relations campaigns directed at us, but they can significantly affect the way we think and live.

The writer might develop the essay with a single, specific example of a public relations campaign, showing how it influenced people without their knowledge. Then he could explain more generally how the example typifies public relations campaigns.

Several other patterns of organization resemble the general-to-specific or specific-to-general pattern. In the **climactic pattern** you arrange ideas in order of increasing drama or importance. For example, the following thesis sentence lists three effects of strip-mining in order of their increasing severity, and the essay would cover them in the same order.

> Strip-mining should be tightly controlled in this region to reduce its pollution of water resources, its permanent destruction of the land, and its devastation of people's lives.

The climactic pattern aids argumentation, as this example shows, but it also works in other kinds of essays. In narration the most dramatic event often comes last, and in description the most dramatic feature may be saved for the end. Exposition is often enhanced by the climactic pattern. The thesis sentence below sets up an essay in which a cause precedes three effects arranged in order of increasing importance.

> Living in a cold climate like New England's influences how you spend your money, what you do with your time, and how you feel about yourself and others.

Expository essays can also be arranged in variations of this pattern. An essay on learning to play the guitar might proceed from **most familiar to least familiar,** that is, from simply plucking strings and sliding the hand up and down the instrument's neck, which most people have seen, to the less familiar styles of picking and chording. Similarly, an essay on the benefits of practicing modern dance might proceed from **simplest to most complex,** from the advantages of exercise to the increased understanding of the art of dance.

The last organizational pattern applies mostly to one of the methods of developing ideas that we discussed earlier: **comparison and contrast.** Essentially you can arrange this pattern in two ways: (1) First discuss the features of one item being compared and then discuss the features of the second item. For instance, Linda Balik can discuss all the advantages and disadvantages of computer games before turning to the advantages and disadvantages of Monopoly. (2) Discuss the two elements side by side throughout the essay, treating both under the various categories of comparison. Using this alternating pattern, Balik may discuss first the cost of both computer games and Monopoly, then the amounts of luck and skill involved in both games, and so on.

Though individual paragraphs within an essay may be organized in any of the ways discussed here (see 3b-1), the entire essay will have its own pattern. If you do not adhere to that pattern, you risk confusing or frustrating your readers. In the essay about athletic facilities, whose opening paragraph we saw on page 22, the author would weaken his case if he were to arrange his ideas like this: (1) the college will lose students (secondary reason); (2) the college's responsibility is fitness of mind *and* body (main reason); (3) faculty members as well as students would benefit (another secondary reason). Instead he should save the second reason for the end, where it is most likely to impress readers.

Outlining

Most essays consist of an introduction, a body, and a conclusion. The introduction draws your readers into the world of your essay, stating your topic and sometimes your thesis sentence. The conclusion may state what you hope readers will remember from your essay or may summarize your essay's main ideas. (Both introductory and concluding paragraphs are discussed with other special paragraphs in 3d.) The body of your essay is its center, the part in which you offer specific details, examples, or reasons to support your thesis. In an essay of 500 to 750 words the body may contain three to five substantial paragraphs, each one presenting a part of your thesis and the evidence to support it. If you decide before you write what you will cover in each paragraph, the actual writing will be easier, better organized, and less in need of major revision.

Perhaps the best method for planning an essay is to devise an outline that shows major ideas as well as supporting information. An outline differs from the preliminary groups of ideas (1c) because it occurs further along in the writing process. Now you are no longer discovering your thesis. Instead, you have your thesis sentence and a sense of what you want to say, what information and tone will suit your audience, and what overall organization might be most appropriate. But before you start to write, you need to arrange the parts of your essay in some sensible order that will guide your writing.

For many essays, especially those with a fairly straightforward structure, an **informal outline** may provide adequate direction for your writing. As we saw on page 26, the thesis of the descriptive essay about a neighborhood street suggests a spatial organization. In

the informal outline the writer sets up topic headings that will correspond to separate paragraphs of her essay, and she adds the features of the street that she will mention.

THESIS SENTENCE

The main street of my neighborhood contains enough variety to
make almost any city dweller feel at home.

INFORMAL OUTLINE

1. The beginning of the street
   high-rise condominium occupied by well-to-do people
   ground floor of building: an art gallery
   across the street: a delicatessen
   above the delicatessen: a tailor's shop, a camera-repair shop, a
      lawyer's office

2. The middle of the street
   four-story brick apartment buildings on both sides
   at ground level: an Italian bakery and a Spanish bodega
   people sitting on steps
   children playing ball on sidewalks

3. The end of the street
   a halfway house for drug addicts
   a boarding house for retired men
   a discount drug store
   an expensive department store
   a wine shop
   another high-rise condominium

This informal outline is appropriate for both the topic and the
organization. The writer should have little difficulty adhering to the
organization or supplying the missing ingredient — concrete descriptive details — as she writes. For a more complex topic requiring a
more complex arrangement of ideas and support, however, you may
want or be required to construct a **formal outline.** More rigidly arranged and more detailed than an informal outline, a formal outline
not only lays out main ideas and their support but also shows the
relative importance of all the essay's elements and how they connect
with each other. Here, for example, is Linda Balik's formal outline
for her essay on computer games and Monopoly. (This example
shows a topic outline: All headings are expressed in phrases, and
parallel headings have parallel wording. For long and complicated
projects like a research paper, an outline with full sentences may be
required. See 35f.)

THESIS SENTENCE

Computerized battle games are exciting and challenging, but Monopoly's inexpensiveness, staying power, and opportunity for interaction among people make it a better game.

FORMAL OUTLINE

I. Advantages of computer games
   A. Speed of play
      1. Fast-moving, continuous action
      2. Instant response
   B. The game "world"
      1. Escapism of space-age adventure
      2. Unpredictability of play
   C. Role of luck and skill
      1. Luck only in programmed randomness of computer
      2. Skills important
         a. Quick reflexes
         b. Dexterity

II. Disadvantages of computer games
   A. Expense
      1. Games costly
         a. Arcade games
         b. Home TV attachments
      2. Frequent breakdown and repair
   B. Staying power
      1. Mastery
      2. Boredom
   C. Opponents
      1. No interaction with other people
      2. Risk of addiction

III. Disadvantages of Monopoly
   A. Speed of play
      1. Slow-moving, interrupted action
      2. Delayed response
   B. The game "world"
      1. Real-world problems
         a. Making and losing money
         b. Buying and selling property
      2. Play somewhat predictable
         a. Forty-square board
         b. Other players' moves
   C. Role of luck and skill
      1. Luck (dice roll) crucial element of game
      2. Skills helpful
         a. Budgeting and planning
         b. Decision making

IV. Advantages of Monopoly
   A. Expense
      1. Whole game inexpensive
      2. Game set durable
      3. Parts easily replaceable

B. Staying power
   1. Single game usually satisfactory
   2. Mastery or boredom unlikely because of luck
C. Opponents
   1. Interaction with real people
   2. No risk of addiction

Balik's outline displays a logical organization and plentiful supporting details. It also adheres to several principles of outlining that can help ensure completeness, balance, and clear relationships.

1. So that the outline both clarifies the order of ideas and details and indicates their relative importance, all its parts are systematically indented and numbered or lettered: Roman numerals (I, II, III, IV) for primary divisions of the essay; indented capital letters (A, B, C) for secondary divisions; further indented Arabic numerals (1, 2, 3) for principal supporting examples; and further indented small letters (a, b, c) for supporting details. Each succeeding level contains more specific information than the one before it.

2. The outline divides the material into several groups. An uninterrupted listing of ideas like the one below would indicate a need for tighter, more logical relationships among ideas. (Compare this example with Balik's actual outline, opposite.)

   III. Monopoly
   A. Slow-moving, interrupted action
   B. Delayed response
   C. Luck a crucial element
   D. Skills helpful
   E. Whole game inexpensive
   F. Game lasts for years
   G. Parts easily replaceable
   H. Opponents real people
   I. Opportunities for interaction
   J. Mastery or boredom unlikely

3. Within each part of the outline, distinct topics of equal generality appear in parallel headings (with the same indention and numbering or lettering). In the following example points 2 and 3 are more specific than point 1, not equally general, so they should be subheadings *a* and *b* under it.

   B. The game "world"
   1. Escapism of space-age adventure
   2. Defense of earth
   3. Battle against unreal forces
   4. Unpredictability of play

4. All subdivided headings in the outline break into at least two parts because a topic cannot logically be divided into only one part. The following example violates this principle.

   C. Role of luck and skill
      1. Luck a crucial element of game
         a. Dice roll
      2. Skills helpful

Any single subdivision should be either combined with the heading above it (as the one above is in Balik's outline, p. 30), matched with another subdivision that has been omitted, or rechecked for its relevance to the heading above.

Balik's outline illustrates the kinds of choices that must be made at the outline stage. She selects categories of comparison (speed of play, expense, and so on) that apply to both games. She structures her comparison to discuss all features of computer games first and then all features of Monopoly, rather than treat them side by side, because the former method seems easier to control. The arrangement of the main subheadings — advantages before disadvantages for computer games, the reverse for Monopoly — comes from Balik's desire to begin with the advantages of computer games but end with the advantages of Monopoly, the game she prefers. The result is somewhat cumbersome, as Balik will learn when she drafts and revises her essay (see 2b), but it is a workable blueprint.

2
Maintaining unity and coherence

In devising and checking your outline, and in writing your essay, you should be aware of two qualities of effective writing that relate to organization: unity and coherence. An essay has **unity** if all its parts support the thesis sentence and relate to each other. It has **coherence** if readers can see the relations and move easily from one thought to the next. Unity and coherence underlie successful paragraphs, and so we treat them in detail in Chapter 3 (see 3a and 3b). But they are also important when you are planning the elements in the whole essay.

When your outline is nearly completed, examine it for unity. Is each primary division relevant to the thesis sentence? Within major sections of the outline, does each example and detail support the main idea of that section? You may become sidetracked by ideas that do not really fit, so you are wise to delete them at the outline stage. If you later find a way to include some of them, you can always retrieve them.

In the informal outline for an essay on the main street of a neighborhood (p. 29), the writer might have been tempted to include a section on other streets in the neighborhood or to compare her neighborhood with others in the city. Although such topics might be squeezed into the essay, they do not relate directly to the thesis sentence and would detract from the writer's purpose of demonstrating the variety of a single street. In the brief informal outline below, the writer loses control of unity at point 4.

dev

1f

THESIS SENTENCE

Caring and communicating, not simply hard work, distinguish successful teachers from unsuccessful ones.

INFORMAL OUTLINE

1. Caring and communicating

    caring is knowing students' names, showing interest in their work and problems, treating them like adults and individuals, ensuring that all students are learning

    communicating is changing approach to match students' needs, making effective contact with each student, highlighting the interesting aspects of the subject without sacrificing depth

2. Successful teachers

    know when students are in trouble

    give ample time to each student

    don't talk down to students

    vary class environment to keep interest alive

    make students eager to learn the subject

3. Unsuccessful teachers

    don't offer help — need to be asked

    treat each student the same way

    either talk over students' heads or talk down to them

    have an unchanging approach to class activities

    seem bored or hostile and make students feel that way about the subject

4. Effects on students

    unsuccessful teachers make learning a chore

    students treated like children will act like children

    need to bring attention to unsuccessful teachers — force them to change

In an essay, point 4 would distract the reader, who expects a focus on teachers, and would thus weaken the main argument. Although bad teachers' effects on students' performance and behavior and what should be done about them are both valid topics, they do not relate directly to the writer's chosen topic of the difference between teachers.

Coherence is achieved by an easy movement from one idea to another, a movement that corresponds to readers' general expectations of logical order and to their particular expectations created by your thesis sentence. In looking over your outline, be sure that the whole adheres to the organizational pattern you selected. Review the main divisions, the subdivisions, and the supporting examples and details to ensure that each relates to your thesis sentence. Ask yourself how you will move from each item in the outline to the one following. If you have difficulty perceiving a connection, then recheck to be certain that the items fit the thesis and the organizational pattern. In writing you will use transitional expressions like *although, then, for example,* and *in addition* to move from one sentence or paragraph to another. (Transitional expressions are discussed fully in 3b-6.) However, they will not by themselves make your connections clear. You must be sure that the progression of your ideas leads readers to see the relations you intend.

EXERCISE 14

List four to six main ideas to support each of five of the topics below. Arrange the ideas in the pattern specified in parentheses.

1. an unusual person (*spatial*)
2. how students release frustration or tension (*specific to general*)
3. how to do one of the following: make a great dessert, take a good photograph, make a triple play in baseball, train a dog, study for an examination (*chronological*)
4. why eighteen-year-olds should or should not be permitted to drink alcoholic beverages (*general to specific*)
5. my view of what happens after death (*climax*)
6. the elements of one of the following: training for a sport, baby-sitting, building a tree house, a religious service (*most familiar to least familiar or simplest to most complex*)
7. the similarities and differences between two friends (*comparison and contrast*)
8. why I am attending college (*climax*)
9. how self-help books can help (*specific to general*)
10. the benefits of regular exercise (*general to specific*)

EXERCISE 15

Revise the following outline so that it adheres to the principles of the formal outline given on pages 31–32. Use the thesis sentence as a guide to appropriate divisions in the outline.

THESIS SENTENCE

Strip-mining should be tightly controlled in this region to reduce its pollution of water resources, its permanent destruction of the land, and its devastating effects on people's lives.

FORMAL OUTLINE

I. Reasons for strip-mining
   A. Need for coal
      1. Energy shortage
   B. Advantages over underground mining
      1. Quicker
      2. Less expensive
   C. Safer than underground mining

II. Effects of strip-mining in this region
   A. Causes of water pollution
      1. Leaching of soil acids by rainwater
      2. Run-off of acids into streams
   B. Disappearance of fish
   C. Poisoning of water supply
   D. Appearance of hills caused by mining
      1. Scarring
      2. Destruction of vegetation
   E. Erosion of the land
      1. Topsoil removed
      2. Mud slides are very common
   F. Elimination of people's forms of recreation
   G. Health problems
      1. Illness caused by polluted water
   H. Destruction of people's farmland and homes
      1. Acid soil
      2. Mud slides
   I. Inadequate compensation for destruction of farmland and homes

III. Possible controls on strip-mining
   A. Regulation of mining techniques
      1. To limit erosion
      2. Limitations on pollution
   B. Mandatory land reclamation to replace topsoil
      1. Restore vegetation to prevent erosion
   C. Required compensation for destruction of farmland and homes
      1. Cash payments
      2. Rebuilding

EXERCISE 16

Evaluate the following outline for unity. What ideas or specific details do not support the thesis sentence?

THESIS SENTENCE

If I had a million dollars, I would treat myself to luxuries I've never had: gourmet food in fine restaurants, a classic car, and worldwide travel.

INFORMAL OUTLINE

1. Gourmet food in fine restaurants
   no McDonald's or Burger King
   good French restaurants with black-coated waiters
   whom to tip: maître d', waiters, bus boys?
   elegant desserts (puff pastry, chocolate mousse)
   no dishes to wash, no pots to scrub

2. A classic car
   no buses or subways
   a five-speed Mercedes, silver or black
   equipment: air conditioning, stereo, television, telephone
   unlimited gas, no problems with availability or cost
   danger of theft
   expensive upkeep

3. Worldwide travel
   need for a travel adviser
   first Paris, then Egypt, then China
   a trip a year, all over the world
   learn to see the benefits of the U.S.; eventually stay home
   health hazards of travel

4. Problems
   getting used to luxuries
   what to do when the money runs out?
   readjusting to the "before" life-style

EXERCISE 17

Make a list of the ideas in the following paragraph. You will see
that it is incoherent: The relations among its ideas are unclear.
Rearrange the ideas to clarify their connections and to ensure that
they fall in an expected pattern.

Being left-handed has no benefits. At dinner parties you have
to eat with your elbow tucked into your ribs, or you have to make
a fuss about the seating arrangements. As a child you are constantly told to use your right hand. It's a condition with no pluses,
unless you like being disadvantaged. In school there are few left-
handed desk chairs. You can't even make scissors work properly.
And when you write, you look to others as if you're writing upside
down. It's as if you have leprosy or a social disease.

EXERCISE 18

Using your set of grouped ideas from Exercise 7 (p. 14) and the
corresponding thesis sentence from Exercise 9 (p. 19), devise a formal outline that reflects an appropriate pattern of organization;
contains the main idea of the thesis sentence plus supporting
ideas; and, under each idea heading, includes specific details and
examples that are themselves sensibly arranged.

2

Writing and Revising the Essay

This chapter will complete the writing process, begun in Chapter 1, with the actual writing and revising of the essay. Throughout we will continue to follow Linda Balik's essay on games.

2a

Writing the first draft

In writing the first draft of an essay, you concentrate not on correctness but on recording your ideas, the connections between them, and the details to support them. Your outline should provide a map to guide you. But following the map — actually writing — also demands a certain degree of spontaneity, an openness to relationships not seen before, a willingness to admit that an idea does not fit or belongs somewhere else.

Linda Balik begins the first draft of her essay by reviewing her outline (pp. 29–31). She then writes in longhand, trying to proceed steadily without halting too often to reread. Even so, she does stop, rethink, and correct as she goes along, taking one step backward for every two or three steps forward. Occasionally, her ideas and details seem almost to rearrange themselves within paragraphs, whereas others must be wedged in and still others dropped. For instance, Balik decides to omit the cost of both games, which has been a basis for comparison almost since she conceived her topic, because cost has little to do with playing the games. Balik's method of writing is as individual as her way of thinking, but she shares with almost all writers this stop-and-go progress.

Balik completes her first draft in two hours, a reasonable time given her preparation. She then types it so she can work on it further. The draft, including its errors and larger problems, appears below.

Title?

Computerized video battle games are exciting and   1
challenging, but Monopolys staying power and opportunity for
interaction among people make it a better game.

Computer games do have their attractions. They provide   2
fast-moving, continuous action, every move of the player
gains instant response. The games draw the player into a
space-age adventure of defending yourself or beloved planet
from evil alian forces. Since the game world is far out and
unpredictable, the games are a perfect means of escape. The
problems faced by the player are also less mundane and predictable than those faced in the real world.

Some chance is programmed into the computer of the   3
battle games so the player knows the enemy will attack. But
not how or when. That is where skill comes in. Responding
quickly enough to stay alive requires very fast reflexes,
and the manipulation of the controls takes dexterity.

A disadvantage of computer games is that they do not   4
have much staying power. Anyone who plays the games for a
while eventually master them or simply tire of them. One
friend with a television game has six game cartridges
(worth well over a hundred dollars) that hes bored with and
no longer plays.

The serious weakness of computer games are that   5
playing against a computer prevents the player from interacting with other people. Even when you and another player
are taking turns to see who gets a higher score the game
is to intense for the two of you to talk to each other

2

while you are playing. Many people become addicted to the
escapism and solitude of computer games. And the places
where you play computer games don't help. Your only opportunities are in bowling alleys, arcades, bars, and pizza
shops and in front of your own television. All sorts of
undesirable characters hang around the public spots, and we
all know too much television is bad for you.

Monopoly is quite different from computer games, as
anyone knows. In many ways it is exactly opposite the
advantages of computer games match the disadvantages of
Monopoly, and the disadvantages of computer games match the
advantages of Monopoly. However the advantages of Monopoly
outweigh computer games.

6

A single game of Monopoly takes a long time to play.
The action is slow, with each persons play being interrupted
by the play of opponents. And it commonly takes many rounds
of play before a player's actions have any results. The
game world, instead of being escapist, is very down-to-
earth: players make and lose money, buy and sell property.
Both the forty squares of the game board and the actions of
opponents are predictable.

7

Monopoly also relies on luck. Dice, tools of chance,
determine all moves. Still, winning at Monopoly does depend
on certain skills--planning, budgeting, and decision making--
that players can use within the boundaries of luck to
improve their chances of winning Monopoly.

8

Besides the skills it requires Monopoly has other
advantages they correspond closely to the disadvangates of
computer games. For one thing, Monopoly has super staying

9

3

power. The urge to play lasts a long time. As long as the game set itself.

The real advantage of Monopoly is the nature of a   10
player's opponents, which is the greatest disadvantage of computer games. A single game of Monopoly usualy satisfies even the most avid player for some time so addiction is not a risk. Even if it were, at least the opponents are always real living, breathing, talking people. By interacting with them, you keep in touch with people and your communications skills are maintained. No matter how much you play it, the game does not remove you or shield you from society.

Games are meant to be played between people, so   11
Monopoly will be around for a long time to come.

EXERCISE 1

Like almost all first drafts, Balik's is rough. Read it carefully and critically. How effective is the opening paragraph in engaging your interest? Where would more details or examples make Balik's ideas clearer or more convincing? Can you find at least one place in the draft where Balik moves away from her thesis sentence? Where in the draft does she fail to make her direction apparent or fail to link ideas clearly? Which paragraphs are unified and coherent, and which are not? Where has she made errors in grammar, usage, punctuation, word choice, and spelling, and how can you correct them?

2b
Revising the first draft

Before you begin to revise your first draft, take a break for at least a few hours to clear your mind and gain some distance from your work. Then you will be more relaxed and objective as you tackle one of the most crucial stages in any writing.

Revision involves much more than proofreading for simple errors. It is a true rethinking. Your first draft tests your thesis sentence, your ideas, and your arrangement of ideas. It is the stage at which you make ideas work for your thesis or see that the thesis needs changing to encompass your ideas. In the first draft you discover how your thoughts work when spelled out in complete sentences and how those sentences interact in paragraphs. You find out what you really have to say and how to say it.

More than a few writers, including many experienced ones, have reached the end of the first draft only to reject the whole thing because they were not comfortable with their thesis or even with their topic. If you work through the planning stages outlined in Chapter 1 and adhere to your outline, your first draft will probably be workable, as Balik's is. But it will *always* need revision.

You should set aside at least as much time for revising your first draft as you took to write it. In writing you were pushing to record your ideas in sentences and paragraphs; in revising you will be looking at your materials as your readers will, critically, hunting for lapses in sense. Plan on reviewing the essay several times to examine and improve its structure; the structure of its paragraphs; the volume, relevance, and persuasiveness of supporting evidence; the effectiveness of sentences; and the precision and appropriateness of words. When you are confident that the essay achieves your purpose and presents your ideas in the best manner for your audience, then proofread it several more times to catch and correct errors in grammar, usage, punctuation, spelling, and the like.

Use the following checklist, which is divided into structural revision and proofreading, as a guide to revising your essays. (The chapter and heading numbers in parentheses refer to the appropriate sections of this handbook.)

Revision checklist

STRUCTURAL REVISION

1. What is your purpose, and what kind of essay are you writing? How are these evident in your thesis sentence and throughout the essay? (Chapter 1)
2. How does each paragraph and sentence in your essay develop or support your thesis sentence? Have you made the relationships clear? (1d and 1f)
3. What details, examples, or reasons have you provided to support each of your ideas? Which ideas need more support? (1b and 1e)
4. How is your tone appropriate for your audience? (1e)
5. What pattern of organization have you used? Have you followed it consistently? Where have you drawn relations among elements of the essay? Which connections are *un*clear? (1f)
6. How does each sentence in a paragraph help develop the paragraph? Are the paragraphs unified, coherent, and well developed? (3a, 3b, 3c)
7. How effective are your introductory and concluding paragraphs? How can they be improved? (3d)
8. How believable are your assertions? How have you supported each one? Where have you slipped into faulty reasoning? (4a, 4b, 4c)
9. Are your sentences effective? Have you used subordination and coordination (Chapter 16) and parallelism (Chapter 17) appropriately? Are your sentences emphatic (Chapter 18) and varied (Chapter 19)?
10. Have you relied on standard diction? (31a) Do your words denote and connote what you intend? Have you avoided triteness? (31b) Is your writing concise? (31c)

PROOFREADING

11. Are your sentences grammatical? Have you avoided errors in case (Chapter 6), verb form (Chapter 7), agreement (Chapter 8), and adjectives and adverbs (Chapter 9)?
12. Are your sentences clear? Have you avoided sentence fragments (Chapter 10), comma splices and run-on sentences (Chapter 11), errors in pronoun reference (Chapter 12), shifts

(Chapter 13), misplaced or dangling modifiers (Chapter 14), and mixed or incomplete constructions (Chapter 15)?

13. Is your use of commas, semicolons, colons, periods, and other punctuation correct? (Chapters 20–25)
14. Are your sentences mechanically correct in the use of capitals, italics, abbreviations, numbers, and hyphens? (Chapters 26–30)
15. Are your words spelled correctly? (Chapter 34)

When Balik returns to her first draft after half a day, she tries to read it objectively, as if for the first time. Though she immediately catches a few errors in grammar and spelling, she concentrates first on the structure: the relationship of the essay's parts to its thesis sentence, the connections between ideas, and the support for each idea. Solving problems in these areas takes the bulk of her revision time. Only when she is satisfied with the structure does she search out and correct errors in grammar, punctuation, mechanics, and spelling. Her revision begins on the next page.

The Battle of the Games
Does the enormous popularity of computerized video battle games
spell the death of traditional board games? Will Space Invaders, Asteroids, and
~~Title?~~

Battlezone soon do away with Monopoly? I don't think so. The

                                                    may be quicker, more
∧Computerized ~~video~~ battle games are∧ exciting, and

even more   than Monopoly,
∧challenging∧ but Monopoly's staying power and opportunity for

interaction among people make it a better game.

Computer games do have their attractions. They provide

                                  ⊙ E
fast-moving, continuous action∧ every move of the player

                          either instant death or instant points.
gains instant response.∧, The games draw the player into a

                                              your
space-age adventure of defending yourself or∧ beloved planet

                                            totally unlike the real world
from evil alian forces. Since the game world is ~~far out~~∧ and

unpredictable, the games are a perfect means of escape. The

problems faced by the player are also less mundane ~~and pre-~~

        real-world problems.
~~dictable~~ than ~~those faced in the real world.~~

Another attraction of computer games is that play depends on skill.
∧Some chance is programmed into the computer of the

                                                              b
battle games, so the player knows the enemy will attack.∕ ~~B~~ut

not how or when. That is where skill comes in. Responding

quickly enough to stay alive requires very fast reflexes,

                                  (dials, levers, or buttons)
and the manipulation of the controls∧ takes dexterity.

For all their advantages, though, computer games also have disadvantages.
                                  One   the games
∧~~A disadvantage of computer games~~ is that ~~they~~ do not

have much staying power. Anyone who plays the games for a

                        S   S
while eventually master∧ them or simply tire∧ of them. One

friend with a television game has six game cartridges

(worth well over a hundred dollars) that he's bored with and

no longer plays.

                                              is
The serious weakness of computer games ~~are~~∧ that

playing against a computer prevents the player from inter-

acting with other people. Even when you and another player

are taking turns to see who gets a higher score, the game

              O
is to∧ intense for the two of you to talk to each other

1

2

3

4

5

2

while you are playing. Many people become addicted to the
~~they lose touch with family and friends, pour all their money into~~
~~the games, and neglect their studies.~~
escapism and solitude of computer games.∧ ~~And the places~~

~~where you play computer games don't help. Your only oppor-~~

~~tunities are in bowling alleys, arcades, bars, and pizza~~

~~shops and in front of your own television. All sorts of~~

~~undesirable characters hang around the public spots, and we~~

~~all know too much television is bad for you.~~

    Monopoly is quite different from computer games, as

6

anyone knows. In many ways it is exactly opposite: the *wordy, awkward*
transition ?

advantages of computer games match the disadvantages of

Monopoly, and the disadvantages of computer games match the

advantages of Monopoly. However, the advantages of Monopoly
the advantages of
outweigh∧ computer games.
Among Monopoly's disadvantages are its slowness and its nonescapist qualities.
∧ A single game of Monopoly ~~takes a long time to play,~~

7

~~∧The action is slow, with each person's play being interrupted~~

by the play of opponents. And it commonly takes many rounds
(building houses on a property to increase rents, for instance) *(an opponent*
of play before a player's actions∧ have any results∧
landing on the property).
∧The game world, instead of being escapist, is very down-to-

earth: players make and lose money, buy and sell property.

Both the forty squares of the game board and the actions of

opponents are predictable.
Perhaps Monopoly's greatest weakness in comparison with computer games is its
reliance on luck.
~~Monopoly also relies on luck.~~∧ Dice, tools of chance,

8

A single dice roll can make or break a player by determining whether you collect a
huge rent from an opponent or pay one that bankrupts you.
determine all moves.∧ Still, winning at Monopoly does depend

on certain skills--planning, budgeting, and decision making--

that players can use within the boundaries of luck to

improve their chances of winning Monopoly.

    Besides the skills it requires Monopoly has other

9

which
advantages ~~they~~ correspond closely to the disadvan~~g~~a~~t~~es of
t g
great
computer games. For one thing, Monopoly has ~~super~~ staying

Because of the element of luck in Monopoly, every game is a new start. A player 3
can never master the game and thus rarely tires of it.
power.∧ The urge to play lasts ~~a long time.~~ *A*s long as the

game set itself.

   The real advantage of Monopoly is the nature of a   10

player's opponents, which is the greatest disadvantage of

computer games. A single game of Monopoly usual*l*y satisfies

even the most avid player for some time, so addiction is not

a risk. Even if it were, at least the opponents are always

~~real~~ living, breathing, talking people. By interacting with
--bargaining, trading jokes and threats, urging each other --
them∧ you keep in touch with people and∧ your communications
                                       maintain
skills. ~~are maintained.~~ No matter how much you play it, the

game does not remove you or shield you from society.

   ~~Games are meant to be played between people, so~~   11

~~Monopoly will be around for a long time to come.~~

   The dictionary suggests that the word game came from a prefix ga,
meaning "together," and the word man. No doubt computerized battle
games will become increasingly exciting, elaborate, and popular,
but they are not games in the oldest sense of the word.
For togetherness, play Monopoly.

In revising her essay, Balik supplies a title and echoes it in her substantially enlarged opening paragraph. She adds to her thesis sentence a category of comparison (speed of play) that is important in the essay but that she missed before; and she rewords the sentence to make the comparison more explicit. She eliminates some repetition. And she eliminates (from paragraph 5) any mention of where computer games are played; the topic is neither reflected in her thesis sentence nor raised again with Monopoly. She expands her concluding paragraph, partly to support her contention that games are meant to be played between people. But her most significant revisions are of two kinds. First, she adds additional details and examples to well over half the paragraphs (see paragraphs 2, 3, 5, 7, 8, 9, and 10). The original, she sees, was often not specific enough to explain her assertions and give a sense of how the games are played. Second, she works to strengthen her paragraphs — a serious weakness of her first draft — so that they will do more to lead the reader from one idea to another. To paragraphs 3, 4, 7, and 8 she adds topic sentences that remind readers of where they are in the essay and what they can expect next. After Balik finishes this work, she proofreads her essay to catch and correct errors in grammar, usage, punctuation, and spelling.

But Balik is not finished. Throughout the revision we see here, she has been disturbed by paragraph 6, an effort to make a transition from one kind of game to the other. The transition seems clumsy but she doesn't see how else to bind the two halves of the essay. It bothers her that the essay breaks so awkwardly in half, computer games on one side, Monopoly on the other. Unsure of what to do, she asks a friend to read and react to the revision. He comments only that he loses track of computer games by the time he gets to Monopoly, but that criticism crystallizes the problem for her. She has chosen the wrong form of comparative organization. Instead of covering computer games entirely before moving on to Monopoly, she will mix the two, covering both under each category of comparison. Then the essay will not divide in half, she will not need a transitional paragraph, and she will not be trying her readers' memories and patience.

Because her earlier revision has forced her to supply details and clarify connections between ideas, Balik prepares the final revision with little difficulty. She restructures the paper so that each paragraph treats both games under a single category of comparison, and she supplies new topic sentences. To link sentences within the new paragraphs and to keep the comparisons straight, she adds transitional expressions like *in contrast* and *however* and phrases like *in Monopoly* and *of computer games*. Otherwise, she finds that most sentences from her earlier revision fit in the new structure without change.

2c
Preparing the final draft

After completing her final, structural revision, Balik checks the essay several times before deciding that she has done her best. Following the guidelines in Appendix B, she types the final revision in correct manuscript form, proofreads it and corrects her typing errors, and hands in the paper.

Balik's final essay, along with her instructor's comments, begins on the next page. Her successive revisions have substantially improved her essay. Not only is it more coherent, unified, and detailed, but it is also more effectively structured. The comparisons are sharper, easier to grasp and remember; and the movement between paragraphs is less awkward. But the essay still has flaws. Balik's revision retains errors in grammar, punctuation, and spelling. Wordiness, repetition, lack of parallelism, and frequent shifts in person weaken some sentences. More seriously, the difficulties of making a side-by-side comparison show up in occasionally disjointed paragraphs.

These are the criticisms that Balik's instructor makes on the final essay. He directs her to consult appropriate sections of the handbook by using the correction code inside the back cover. And, in a final comment, he specifies the strengths and general weaknesses of the essay.

When you submit a paper, your instructor, like Balik's, will act as counselor and editor to help you see both virtues and flaws in your essay. He or she will suggest ways you can improve the essay and your future writing as well. Repeated practice in working from ideas to essay and in responding to a critical reader's comments will help you become a more efficient and capable writer.

The Battle of the Games

Does the enormous popularity of computerized video
battle games spell the death of traditional board games?
Will Space Invaders, Asteroids, and Battlezone soon do away
with Monopoly? I don't think so. The computerized battle
games may be quicker, more exciting, and even more
challenging than Monopoly, but Monopoly's staying power
and opportunity for interaction among people make it a
better game.

1

No one could sensibly deny that computer games have
distinct advantages over Monopoly. Their fast-moving,
continuous action contrasts with the slow play of Monopoly.
Instead of having to wait for other players to take their
turns, as you do in Monopoly, the computer game player is
constantly "on." And instead of having to wait through
several rounds of play to see if your actions have any
effect (for instance, waiting for someone to land on the
property you built houses on) in computer games the response
is instant death or instant points.

2

(19a)

(21b)

Computerized battle games are a perfect means of
escape. The space-age adventure of defending yourself or
your beloved planet from evil alian forces is totally
unlike any real-world activity. Monopoly, in contrast, is
very down-to-earth. Even if you are playing for higher
stakes than you would in real life, making and losing
money are all-too-familiar activities. Monopoly is also
predictable: you know the forty squares of the game board,
and you can pretty well guess what your opponents actions

3

(34)

(23a)

2

will be under different conditions. But computer games are no more predictable than a real space war would be. The play engages you completely. ⟩ 13a

4

Computer games have one other distinct advantage over Monopoly: playing them depends on skill, whereas playing Monopoly depends on luck. Some chance is programmed into computer games, so the player knows the enemy will attack but not how or when. That is where skill comes in. ⟩ 17a
Responding quickly enough to stay alive takes very fast reflexes, and manipulation of the controls (dials, levers, or buttons) takes dexterity. In Monopoly, however, dice, tools of chance, determine all moves. A single dice roll can make or break a player by determining whether you ⟩ 13a
collect a huge rent from an opponent or pay one that bank-rupts you. Still, winning at Monopoly does depend on
3a ⟨ certain skills--planning, budgeting, decision making--that players can use within the boundaries of luck to improve their chances of winning Monopoly. ⟩ 3lc

So far Monopoly may seem quite inferior to computer games, but it does have its own important advantages. One of these is staying power. Anyone who plays a computer game for a while eventually masters it or simply tires of it. Because of the element of luck in Monopoly, however, every game is a new start. A player can never master the game and thus rarely tires of it. The urge to play lasts as long as the game set itself. Whereas one of my friends ⟩ 3b
10a ⟨ with a computer-game television attachment has six game cartridges (worth over a hundred dollars) that he's bored with and no longer plays.

5

rev
2c

3

6

An even greater advantage of Monopoly over computer
games is the nature of the opponent or opponents. Playing
against a computer prevents the <u>player</u> from interacting with
other people. Even when <u>you</u> and another player are taking
turns to see who gets a higher score, the game is too intense
for the two of you to talk to each other while you are
playing. The opponents in Monopoly, however, are always
living, breathing, talking people. By interacting with
them--bargaining, trading jokes and threats, urging them
on--the <u>player</u> keeps in touch with people and maintains
communications skills. No matter how much <u>you</u> play it, the
game does not remove you or shield you from society. Many
people become addicted to the escapism and solitude of
computer games. They lose touch with friends and family,
pour all their money into the games, and neglect their

13a

31c

13a

3b

18a-2

7

The dictionary suggests that the word <u>game</u> came from
a prefix <u>ga</u>, meaning "together," and the word <u>man</u>. No
doubt computerized battle games will become increasingly
exciting, elaborate, and popular, but they are not games
in the oldest sense of the word. For togetherness, play
Monopoly.

*Your essay is thoughtful and, for the most part, well constructed.
Your thesis provides a clear, specific assertion about your topic.
You obviously assume that your audience is familiar with
both games, and in that context you have provided good
support for your ideas. Most of your sentences are effectively
varied and effective.*

*A problem in your essay is the constant shift in person
between "you" and "player." Consult 13a in the handbook. A more
serious weakness occurs in the structure of some of your paragraphs.
Though your topic sentences move the essay along, your comparisons
are sometimes too jumbled for your connections to be clear. Consult
sections 3a and 3b in the handbook on paragraph unity and coherence.*

Instead of using the numerical correction code, Balik's instructor might have used a combination of correction symbols and verbal comments to indicate weaknesses. The sample below shows the fourth paragraph of Balik's essay marked in this manner. (The symbols appear inside the front cover of the handbook.)

Computer games have one other distinct advantage over
Monopoly: playing them depends on skill, whereas playing
Monopoly depends on luck. Some chance is programmed into
computer games, so the player knows the enemy will attack
but not how or when. That is where skill comes in.

// Responding quickly enough to stay alive takes very fast
reflexes, and manipulation of the controls (dials, levers,
or buttons) takes dexterity. In Monopoly, however, dice,
tools of chance, determine all moves. A single dice roll
can make or break a player by determining whether you   *shift*
collect a huge rent from an opponent or pay one that bank-

*A un-
stated
topic
of ¶ is
dependence
on
luck*   rupts you. Still, winning at Monopoly does depend on   *rep*
certain skills--planning, budgeting, decision making--that
players can use within the boundaries of luck to improve
their chances of winning Monopoly.

The instructor's comments should be encouraging to Balik. She knows that her revision efforts have produced greater specificity and coherence in a more effective organization. If she were to revise her essay and resubmit it, she would start by restructuring the weak paragraphs, rearranging the details to clarify the relations among them. She would also, of course, correct the other problems — if necessary, by referring to the appropriate sections of the handbook. The additional work would surely produce a very competent essay.

EXERCISE 2

To become familiar with the handbook's code, revise Linda Balik's paper to improve paragraph coherence and to correct errors, as suggested by her instructor.

EXERCISE 3

Write an essay of 500 to 750 words from the outline you developed in Chapter 1, Exercise 18 (p. 36). Revise your essay carefully, following the revision checklist on pages 42–43.

EXERCISE 4

Carefully read the student essays below, and answer the following questions about each one. (1) What is the writer's purpose, and what kind of essay is that purpose expressed in? (2) How well does the thesis sentence convey both purpose and kind of essay? What assertion does the thesis sentence make? How specific is the sentence? How well does it preview the writer's ideas and organization? (3) What pattern of organization does the writer use? Is it adhered to consistently throughout the essay? (4) What details, examples, and reasons does the writer employ to support his or her ideas? Where is supporting evidence skimpy? (5) Who do you think constitutes the writer's intended audience? What is the tone of the essay? What attitude toward subject and audience does it convey?

The Gentle Manatee

Part of the controversy over saving endangered species of animals and plants seems to center on the uselessness of these species to humans. Why save them if they do not serve us? But there is a virtue in saving living things just because they add variety to the world. One interesting endangered species is the manatee.

The manatee is a huge water-dwelling mammal. It is a vegetarian that eats only water plants. It lives mostly in rivers and shallow coastal waters in North and South America and western Africa. It cannot survive in cold waters, and the largest number in our part of the world live in southern Florida. Though they are supposedly protected by law, manatees are few in number because people break the laws and run their motorboats over the animals in shallow waters when they come up to breathe.

Manatees are slow breeding animals. Each female manatee only gives birth to one calf, and the gestation period lasts over a year. A calf after it is born nurses for up to a year and a half. A full-grown manatee may be up to twelve feet long and weigh 2000 pounds.

Besides its size, the most remarkable thing about a manatee is the way it looks. It is shaped and colored like a torpedo with a thicker middle than ends. Its body is rough, like an elephant's, but not as wrinkled. It has a small flat tail, like a whale's, that it uses to move. And it has small flippers on each side of its body, near the front. Most striking is its face. Tiny, clouded eyes peer out of a wrinkled, bristly face that can only be called ugly. Huge, fleshy lips are strong and movable enough to grasp plants and push them back into the mouth.

Manatees are harmless, and this is their most interesting characteristic. They don't have any natural predators, nor do they prey on anything but plants. They swim away from danger because they have no way to defend themselves. They are somewhat social animals that communicate by making noises and rubbing each other. They will even rub againt humans who are swimming under water and may seem to hug with their flippers.

Manatees live an ideal existence. Most of their time is spent browsing along the bottom for food or in rest. When resting, they push themselves up for air every so often and then sink to the bottom. When not eating or resting, they seem to play games like tag or follow-the-leader or they ride currents in a kind of body surfing.

Manatees are charming creatures, in many ways more charming than humans. Their friendliness and gentleness and their relaxed and harmless way could teach us humans something about living our lives.

Working in the Barnyard

Until two months ago I thought summer jobs occupied time and helped pay the next year's tuition but otherwise provided no useful training. Then I took a temporary job in a large government agency. Two months there taught me a very valuable lesson about how people work together.

Last May I was hired by the personnel department of the agency to fill in for vacationing workers in the mail room. I had seven coworkers and a boss, Mrs. King. Our job was to sort the huge morning and afternoon mail shipments into four hundred slots, one for every employee in the agency. Then we delivered the sorted mail out of grocery carts that we wheeled from office to office along assigned corridors, picking up outgoing mail as we went along. Each mail delivery took an entire half day to sort and deliver.

My troubles began almost as soon as I arrived. Hundreds of pieces of mail were dumped on a shallow table against a wall of mail slots. I was horrified to see that the slots were labeled not with people's names but with their initials — whereas the incoming letters, of course, contained full names. Without thinking, I asked why this was a good idea, only to receive a sharp glance from Mrs. King. So I repeated the question. This time Mrs. King told me flatly not to question what I didn't understand. It was the first of many sharp exchanges, and I hadn't been on the job a half hour.

I mastered the initials and the sorting and delivery procedures after about a week. But the longer I worked at the job the more I saw how inefficient all the procedures were, from delivery routes to times for coffee breaks. When I asked Mrs. King about the procedures, however, she always reacted the same way: it was none of my business.

I pestered Mrs. King more and more over the next seven weeks, but my efforts were fruitless, even counterproductive. Mrs. King began calling me snide names. Then she began picking on my work and singling me out for reprimands, even though I did my best and worked faster than most of the others.

Two months after I had started work, the personnel manager called me in and fired me. I objected, of course, calling up all the deficiencies I had seen in Mrs. King and her systems. The manager interrupted to ask if I had ever heard of the barnyard pecking order: the top chicken picks on the one below it, the second picks on the third, and so on all the way down the line to the lowliest chicken, whose life is a constant misery. Mrs. King, the manager said, was that lowliest chicken at the bottom of the pecking order in the agency's management. With little education, she had spent her entire adult life building up her small domain, and she had to protect it from everyone, especially the people who worked for her. The arbitrariness of her systems was an assertion of her power, for no one should doubt for a moment that she ruled her little roost.

I had a month before school began again to think about my adventure. At first it irritated me that I should be humiliated while Mrs. King continued on as before. But eventually I saw how arrogant, and how unsympathetic, my behavior had been. In my next job, I'll learn the pecking order before I become a crusader, *if* I do.

3
Composing Good Paragraphs

Whatever our purpose in writing and whatever our subject, we normally write in **paragraphs,** groups of related sentences set off by a beginning indention. For readers the indention signals that the following sentences work as a unit; it leads them to expect that a single topic will be developed in some depth. For the writer paragraphing provides a way to break down complex ideas into manageable parts, discuss each part separately and completely, and then relate each part to the central theme of the essay.

A paragraph resembles a mini-essay in three important ways: It is unified, it is coherent, and it is developed. (See 1e and 1f.) Because it can stand free of its context and still generally be understandable and because it has a beginning, a middle, and an end, a paragraph can also be seen as enclosed in a frame.

> Some people really like chili, apparently, but nobody can agree how the stuff should be made. C. V. Wood, twice winner at Terlingua, uses flank steak, pork chops, chicken, and green chilis. My friend Hughes Rudd of CBS News, who imported five hundred pounds of chili powder into Russia as a condition of accepting employment as Moscow correspondent, favors coarse-ground beef. Isadore Bleckman, the cameraman I must live with on the road, insists upon one-inch cubes of stew beef and puts garlic in his chili, an Illinois affectation. An Indian of my acquaintance, Mr. Fulton Batisse, who eats chili for breakfast when he can, uses buffalo meat and plays an Indian drum while it's cooking. I ask you.

> — CHARLES KURALT, *Dateline America*

In this paragraph the writer captures and focuses our attention by stating his central idea (sentence 1) and by supporting or illustrating the idea (sentences 2 through 5). By beginning each illustrative sentence with the sentence subject, the writer makes it easy for us to see how the sentences relate to each other. And we have no doubt about the writer's attitude toward his subject (he has no particular fondness for chili) and toward us, his readers (he assumes we are his allies). The paragraph presents one thought: It is unified. All its parts relate clearly to each other: It is coherent. And its assertion is well supported by detailed examples: It is well developed. These qualities are the goals of paragraph writing and the topics of this chapter.

¶ *un*
3a

3a
Maintaining paragraph unity

Since readers expect a paragraph to explore one topic, they will be alert for that topic and will patiently follow its development. In other words, they will seek and appreciate paragraph **unity,** clear identification and clear elaboration of one idea and of that idea only. If readers' attention is not rewarded and they must shift their focus from one topic to another and perhaps back again, their confusion or frustration will impede their understanding and acceptance of the writer's meaning.

In an essay the thesis sentence announces the main idea (see 1d). In a paragraph a **topic sentence** often alerts readers to the essence of the paragraph by stating the general idea and expressing the writer's attitude toward it. In the framed paragraph opposite the topic sentence is sentence 1. The author states generally that people disagree about how to make chili. The next four sentences provide specific examples of chili concoctions, and the last sentence (*I ask you*) invites us to consider the examples with amusement, as the writer does.

In an essay of 500 to 750 words, each paragraph is likely to treat one part of the essay's thesis sentence; the topic sentences simply restate parts of the thesis. A topic sentence will not, of course, guarantee a unified paragraph, any more than a thesis sentence guarantees a unified essay. The next several sections explain how to write unified paragraphs controlled by strong topic sentences.

1
Focusing on the central idea

The framed paragraph on chili works because it rewards our attention to its topic sentence. The sentences that follow the first do not stray off to other subjects, such as the other food preferences of the people mentioned or of the writer himself. Instead, each one helps us better understand the writer's topic.

The following paragraph, in contrast, begins to lose its way in sentence 5.

¶ un

3a

> One of the best-run races was the relay. The four teams' [1,2]
> runners were evenly matched for the first two laps. They were [3]
> never more than a foot or two apart. Then, just after the third [4]
> runner on each team took the baton, the runner in lane 2 took a
> ten-foot lead. The people in the stadium became hushed for a [5]
> moment and then began cheering wildly. Some spectators al- [6]
> most hurt others in their efforts to get a clear view of the track.
> All afternoon the people in the crowd alternated between quiet [7]
> watching and noisy, active cheering. Their behavior matched [8]
> the varied pace of the track meet itself.

By the end of this paragraph the author seems to have forgotten that her purpose (implied in sentence 1) was to describe a well-run race. In sentence 5 she becomes distracted herself by the excitement in the stands, and she never returns to the runners. Meanwhile we readers become confused because the topic sentence leads us to expect one thing whereas half the paragraph gives us something else.

To achieve unity in this paragraph, the author must first decide what she wants to focus on — the race, not the spectators. Then she must complete her description of the race and eliminate the sentences about the spectators (who might become the subject of another paragraph in the essay). The revision:

> One of the best-run races was the relay. The four teams' [1,2]
> runners were evenly matched for the first two laps. They were [3]
> never more than a foot or two apart. Then just after the third [4]
> runner on each team took the baton, the runner in lane 2 took a
> ten-foot lead and held it until he passed the baton to his team-
> mate. The race seemed to be decided when, suddenly, the [5]
> fourth runner in lane 3, receiving the baton, exploded in an
> amazing burst of speed that brought him alongside the runner
> in lane 2. The two ran together almost to the finish, where the [6]
> lane-3 runner lunged inches ahead of his opponent to break the
> tape and win the race.

The writer of this paragraph might have avoided disunity in the first place if she had thought out beforehand what she wanted the paragraph to accomplish and had written a **sentence of clarification** after her topic sentence, explaining exactly what she meant by *best-run*. For instance: *One of the best-run races was the relay. It showed teams of athletes working together and one great individual performance.* The second sentence defines the topic and thus helps restrict it. Consequently, when her thoughts come to the excitement in the stands, the writer is less likely to let that excitement distract her from her main purpose. In the paragraph below, the writer's second sentence clarifies what he means in his topic sentence (sentence 1) by *inaccuracy of aim rather than insufficiency of endeavor.*

Regarded from the receiving end, it seems that the princi- 1
pal failing of latter-day scientists is inaccuracy of aim rather
than insufficiency of endeavor. Researchers still insist on apply- 2
ing all their best efforts — and most of our money — to providing us with new things that we don't want. They give us the 3
Concorde when we'd much prefer a cure for the common cold.
They provide us with intimate pictures of Mars, although we'd 4
sooner have an everlasting shoelace. They present us with tran- 5
sistor radios when all we really want is a little public peace and
quiet.   — PATRICK RYAN, "It Ticks and It Talks"

Writers also sometimes pair topic sentences with **sentences of
limitation,** so their topic will not be too unwieldy nor the opportunities for wandering too many. A sentence of limitation draws tight
borders around a topic, making it more specific. In the following
paragraph the author has used his second sentence to limit the
broad topic stated in the first.

Children also attend closely to what surprises them, to a 1
novel image or event that violates their expectations about the
order of their world. Since adults often spend considerable 2
time in the effort to convince children of adult infallibility, one
of the most remarkable and pleasing novelties for children is to
observe adults making errors that children easily identify as
such. One series of *Sesame Street* segments *Street* was designed to 3
exploit the interest for children of adults making obvious mistakes while trying to solve a simple problem. "Buddy and Jim" 4
are two adults who confront a series of such simple problems,
but can never seem to get the obvious solutions quite right.
They attempt to place a picture on a wall by hammering the 5
blunt end of the nail into the wall, fail to observe that the nail
should be turned around, and then conclude that they must
walk to the wall on the opposite side of the room in order to
point the nailhead into the wall.
— GERALD S. LESSER, "Growing Up on Sesame Street"

2
Choosing a paragraph shape

Within its imaginary frame a paragraph's central idea and
supporting details may be arranged variously to correspond to various ways of developing the central idea. Thinking of the topic sentence as the point of a paragraph and the supporting sentences as its
body, we can imagine several paragraph "shapes" that are appropriate for different kinds of writing.

Central idea at the beginning

In the most common format — illustrated by the paragraphs examined so far — a general topic sentence comes first, then sometimes a clarifying or limiting sentence that amplifies or restricts the meaning of the topic sentence, then specific illustrations and details that support the topic sentence.

This model is the most helpful for inexperienced writers because it forces them to focus on a paragraph topic before writing and then to select only those details appropriate to the topic's development. The following two-sentence paragraph shows again how the model works.

> We have come to expect incompetence as a necessary fea- 1
> ture of civilization. We may be irked, but we are no longer 2
> amazed, when our bosses make idiotic decisions, when au-
> tomobile makers take back thousands of new cars for repairs,
> when store clerks are insolent, when law reforms fail to check
> crime, when moon rockets can't get off the ground, when
> widely used medicines are found to be poisons, when univer-
> sities must teach freshmen to read, or when a hundred-ton air-
> liner is brought down by a duck.
> — RAYMOND HULL, "The Peter Principle," *Esquire*

As this paragraph shows, the topic-first model is particularly appropriate in exposition, for it allows you to tell your readers at the outset what you will explain in the rest of the paragraph. For a similar reason this model is also useful in argumentation: You assert your opinion and then in the following sentences provide the evidence to support it.

In a common variation of the topic-first model, the first sentence is a transition from the preceding paragraph and the second sentence is the topic sentence. The following paragraph was preceded by a description of older brothers.

> The tactics of the younger brother are governed by differ- 1
> ent considerations. Not having had disciplinary authority dele- 2
> gated to him, he doesn't develop the authoritarian approach.
> His smaller physical size leaves him free to harass his older 3
> brother, since the parents caution the older brother not to hurt
> him, and also because the younger son may not feel obliged to
> observe adult standards. His smaller size, which puts him at a 4
> disadvantage in physical combat with the older brother, leads
> him to adopt indirect methods of aggression. He waits for a 5
> weakness in the older brother, and then, with deception and
> surprise, he ambushes him. Because his parents' expectations 6

have left him less ambitious than his older brother to win the hard way, he may feel it is enough merely to win — and forget the rules. For all these reasons, the indirect, devious style of aggression is more common among later sons than among first.
    — IRVING HARNS, "Who Would Kill a President?"

Central idea at the end

In some paragraphs the central idea (and the topic sentence) may come at the end, after supporting sentences have made a case for the general statement. The paragraph ends with a point.

Since this shape leads the reader to a conclusion by presenting all the evidence first, it can prove effective in argumentation. And because the paragraph's point is withheld until the end, this shape can be dramatic in exposition as well. For example:

He inspired scores of imitators, sold millions of records. He got drafted in the Army, got his infamous D.A. and 'burns clipped, served a tour of duty in Germany, sold millions of records. He went to Hollywood, appeared in 33 movies, sold millions of records. He played Vegas, got married, filled amphitheaters, got divorced, lived a gaudy life so high and wide that it seemed like a parody of an American success story. And he kept selling records, well over 500 million in all. The music got slicker and often sillier, turned from rock toward rhinestone country and spangled gospel. Only the pace remained the same. Elvis Aron Presley always lived fast, and last week at the age of 42, that was the way he died.
    — *Time*

Central idea in the middle

In another kind of paragraph, details and examples come first and are summed up in a topic sentence, which is then supported further with more details and examples. The point of the paragraph comes in the middle.

This paragraph form is useful in both exposition and argumentation when the central idea benefits from support both before it is stated (to awaken interest in it or to make it more acceptable) and after (to drive the point home). In the following paragraph the writer opens with an example (sentences 1–3), states its significance in her topic sentence (sentence 4), and then continues the example (sentences 5–8).

> They begin by bombarding a lonely young person with at- 1
> tention. When their subject responds, they convince him to 2
> move in with them, share their meals, participate in their activi-
> ties. By manipulating him — depriving him of sleep, alternately 3
> offering and withdrawing support — they bind him more closely
> to themselves and separate him from the outside world. In 4
> these ways and others the Moonies of the Unification Church
> employ coercive persuasion to gain and hold new members.
> The recruit, increasingly confused and dependent, loses touch 5
> with any reality besides the one created for him by the group.
> He drops out of school and refuses to see or communicate with 6
> his family or former friends. His freedom continues to decline 7
> as he is instilled with guilt for any deviation from the group's
> behavior code. Before long he, too, is preying on lonely teen- 8
> agers and young adults.   — A STUDENT

Central idea at the beginning and the end

You may want to state the topic sentence at the beginning and then restate it at the end to provide a new twist supported by the intervening sentences. This shape has a point at top and bottom.

This model works in both exposition and argumentation. In the following expository paragraph Jerzy Kosinski provides a topic sentence (sentence 1) and then restates it on the basis of new information (sentence 6).

> In the little world of television, all is solved within its 1
> magic 30 minutes. In spite of the commercials, the wounded 2
> hero either rises or quickly dies, lovers marry or divorce, vil-
> lains kill or are killed, addicts are cured, justice usually wins,
> and war ends. All problems are solved again this week, as they 3
> were last, and will be next week. Life on TV must be visual. This 4, 5
> means single-faceted, revealed in a simple speech and through
> the obvious gesture. No matter how deep the mystery or am- 6
> biguity, the TV camera claims it has penetrated it.
> — JERZY KOSINSKI, "TV as Baby Sitter"

Writers sometimes restate their topic sentence in a last-ditch effort to rescue a paragraph whose middle part has gone astray. But trying to achieve unity by forcing it will not work. To be effective, a restated topic sentence must gain something from all the sentences preceding it.

Central idea at the beginning and in the middle

In another paragraph shape, the central idea is divided into two parts, and each part is developed separately. The point appears in the beginning and the middle.

This form gives a writer flexibility because the topic can be examined a bit at a time. Thus it is especially useful in complicated explanations and arguments. In the following paragraph from *The Gettysburg Address,* his speech at a Civil War battlefield, Abraham Lincoln first states half his idea in sentence 1 and then completes the idea in sentence 4.

> But, in a larger sense, we cannot dedicate — we cannot con- 1
> secrate — we cannot hallow — this ground. The brave men, liv- 2
> ing and dead, who struggled here have consecrated it, far above
> our poor power to add or detract. The world will little note, nor 3
> long remember, what we say here, but it can never forget what
> they did here. It is for us the living, rather, to be dedicated here 4
> to the unfinished work which they who fought here have thus
> far so nobly advanced. It is rather for us to be here dedicated to 5
> the great task remaining before us — that from these honored
> dead we take increased devotion to that cause for which they
> gave the last full measure of devotion; that we here highly re-
> solve that these dead shall not have died in vain; that this na-
> tion, under God, shall have a new birth of freedom; and that
> government of the people, by the people, for the people, shall
> not perish from the earth.
> — ABRAHAM LINCOLN, *The Gettysburg Address*

This paragraph model has several hazards because its effective use requires making and following a plan. As in the diamond-shaped model, the two parts of the topic must be closely related, or the paragraph will go awry. And the second statement should not attempt merely to cover up a lack of unity.

Central idea not stated

Sometimes a paragraph's topic sentence will appear in the previous paragraph or will be so obvious that it need not be stated explicitly. The following paragraph, from an essay on the actor Humphrey Bogart, has no explicit topic sentence.

> Usually he wore the trench coat unbuttoned, just tied with 1
> the belt, and a slouch hat, rarely tilted. Sometimes it was a cap- 2
> tain's cap and a yachting jacket. Almost always his trousers 3

were held up by a cowboy belt. You know the kind: one an   4
Easterner waiting for a plane out of Phoenix buys just as a joke
and then takes a liking to. Occasionally, he'd hitch up his slacks   5
with it, and he often jabbed his thumbs behind it, his hands
ready for a fight or a dame.

— PETER BOGDANOVICH, "Bogie in Excelsis"

The effectiveness of this paragraph rests on the power of details to
describe Bogart. Thus a stated topic sentence — such as "Bogart's
character could be seen in the details of his clothing" — not only
would weaken the paragraph but would contradict its intention.
Nonetheless, the topic sentence is clearly implied.

Paragraphs in descriptive writing (like the one above) and in
narrative writing (relating a sequence of events) often lack stated
topic sentences. But producing a paragraph without a topic sentence does not release you from the need to unify. You must have a
topic for the paragraph, and the details you choose must develop
the topic.

EXERCISE 1

Identify the central idea in each paragraph below. In what sentence, if any, is it expressed? Is it clarified or limited by any other
sentence? Describe the paragraph's shape.

1.   Though they do not know why the humpback whale sings,   1
scientists do know something about the song itself. They have   2
measured the length of a whale's song: from a few minutes to
over half an hour. They have recorded and studied the variety   3
and complex arrangements of low moans, high squeaks, and
sliding squeals that make up the song. And they have learned   4
that each whale sings in its own unique pattern.   — A STUDENT

2.   Coca-Cola is the most popular beverage in the world. It is   1, 2
available in almost all countries of the world. Moreover, the   3
equivalent of nearly half the world's people drink a Coke every
day. Yet neither the federal government nor Pepsi-Cola nor any   4
of Coke's other competitors have been able to discover the key
to its flavor. The ingredients and the recipe were closely   5
guarded from the start by the Atlanta pharmacist who invented
Coca-Cola in 1886. And though most of the ingredients have   6
since become known through chemical analysis, one crucial ingredient and the formula itself remain mysteries understood by
only a handful of people.   — A STUDENT

3.   At each step, with every graduation from one level of edu-   1
cation to the next, the refrain from bystanders was strangely
the same: "Your parents must be so proud of you." I suppose   2
that my parents were proud, although I suspect, too, that they
felt more than pride alone as they watched me advance

through my education. They seemed to know that my educa- 3
tion was separating us from one another, making it difficult to
resume familiar intimacies. Mixed with the instincts of parental 4
pride, a certain hurt also communicated itself — too private
ever to be adequately expressed in words, but real nonetheless.

— RICHARD RODRIGUEZ, "Going Home Again"

4.   The two most expressive things about him were his mouth 1
and the pockets of his jacket. By looking at his mouth, one 2
could tell whether he was plotting evil or had recently accom-
plished it. If he was bent upon malevolence, his lips were all 3
puckered up, like those of a billiard player about to make a difficult shot. After the deed was done, the pucker was replaced 4
by a delicate, unearthly smile. How a teacher who knew any- 5
thing about boys could miss the fact that both expressions were
masks of Satan I'm sure I don't know. Wallace's pockets were 6
less interesting than his mouth, perhaps, but more spectacular
in a way. The side pockets of his jacket bulged out over his 7
pudgy haunches like burro hampers. They were filled with 8
tools — screwdrivers, pliers, files, wrenches, wire cutters, nail
sets, and I don't know what else. In addition to all this, one 9
pocket always contained a rolled-up copy of *Popular Mechanics,* while from the top of the other protruded *Scientific American* or some other such magazine. His breast pocket contained, 10
besides a large collection of fountain pens and mechanical pencils, a picket fence of drill bits, gimlets, kitchen knives, and
other pointed instruments. When he walked, he clinked and 11
jangled and pealed.   — RICHARD ROVERE, "Wallace"

EXERCISE 2

The paragraphs below contain ideas or details that do not support
their central ideas. Identify the topic sentence in each paragraph
and delete the unrelated material.

1.   In the southern part of the state, some people still live 1
much as they did a century ago. They use coal- or wood-burn- 2
ing stoves for heating and cooking. Their homes do not have 3
electricity or indoor bathrooms or running water. The towns 4
can't afford to put in sewers or power lines, because they don't
receive adequate funding from the state and federal governments. Beside most homes there is a garden where fresh vege- 5
tables are gathered for canning. Small pastures nearby support 6
livestock, including cattle, pigs, horses, and chickens. Most of 7
the people have cars or trucks, but the vehicles are old and
beat-up from traveling on unpaved roads.

2.   Most people don't realize how difficult it is to work and go 1
to school at the same time. If you want to make good grades 2
but need to pay your own way, the burdens are tremendous. I 3
work in an office sixteen hours a week. Each term I have to 4
work out a tight schedule that will let me take the courses I

want and still be at work when I'm needed. I like the job. The ₅,₆
people there are pleasant, and they are eager to help me learn.
In the end my job will be good training for the kind of mana- ₇
gerial position I hope to have some day, because I'm gaining
useful experience in office procedures and working with
people. It's hard for me to have a job and go to school, but ₈
when I graduate both will make me more employable.

EXERCISE 3

Develop the topic sentence following into a unified paragraph by
using the relevant information in the statements below it. Delete
each statement that does not relate directly to the topic, and then
rewrite and combine sentences as appropriate.

TOPIC SENTENCE

Mozart's accomplishments in music seem remarkable even today.

Wolfgang Amadeus Mozart was born in 1756 in Salzburg, Austria.
He began composing music at the age of five.
He lived most of his life in Salzburg and Vienna.
His first concert tour of Europe was at the age of six.
On his first tour he played harpsichord, organ, and violin.
He published numerous compositions before reaching adoles-
    cence.
He married in 1782.
Mozart and his wife were both poor managers of money.
They were plagued by debts.
Mozart composed over six hundred musical compositions.
His most notable works are his operas, symphonies, quartets, and
    piano concertos.
He died at the age of thirty-five.

EXERCISE 4

Develop three of the topic sentences below into detailed and unified paragraphs by following the instructions given in parentheses
after each one.

1. Country music (or rock music or classical music) fans come in
   (number) varieties. (*Expository paragraph with topic sentence
   at the beginning followed by a sentence of clarification.*)
2. Regulations should be tightened, not loosened, to reduce the
   impact of this pollution. (*Argumentative paragraph with topic
   sentence at the end.*)
3. Many students attend college to prepare for a specific career;
   but I need to spend this time discovering my interests and
   abilities. (*Expository paragraph with topic sentence divided between the beginning and the middle, each half developed by examples.*)

4. People should not impose their beliefs on others. (*Argumentative paragraph with topic sentence at the beginning followed by a sentence that limits the idea.*)
5. My high school was an ugly (or attractive or homely or whatever) building. (*Descriptive paragraph with topic sentence implied rather than stated.*)

3b
Achieving paragraph coherence

A paragraph is unified if it holds together — if all its details and examples support the central idea. A paragraph is **coherent** if readers can see *how* the paragraph holds together without having to puzzle out the writer's reasons for adding each new sentence. Each time readers must pause and reread to see how sentences relate to each other, they lose both comprehension and patience.

Coherent paragraphs convey the relations among sentences in many ways, and we will look at each one in detail. First, however, we will examine what makes a paragraph, like the one below, incoherent.

> The ancient Egyptians were masters of preserving dead people's bodies by making mummies of them. Mummies several thousand years old have been discovered nearly intact. The skin, hair, teeth, finger and toenails, and facial features of the mummies were evident. It is possible to diagnose the diseases suffered in life, such as smallpox, arthritis, and nutritional deficiencies. The process was remarkably effective. Sometimes apparent were the causes of death; a middle-aged king died from a blow on the head, and polio killed a child king. Mummification consisted of removing the internal organs, applying natural preservatives inside and out, and then wrapping the body in layers of bandages.

This paragraph seems to be unified: The writer sticks to the topic of mummification throughout the paragraph. But the paragraph is hard to read. It jumps back and forth between specific details about features, diseases, and causes of death (sentences 3, 4, 6) and general statements about mummies' intactness (sentence 2), the effectiveness of the process (sentence 5), and the process itself (sentence 7). Sentence 5, about the effectiveness of the process, seems to relate to sentences 3 and 4 before it and to sentence 6 after it, yet because of its placement we can't be sure. The last sentence, though related to the topic sentence, seems stuck on as an afterthought. All the sentences seem disconnected; no words signal how each one relates to the one before it. And though sentences 3, 4, and 6 seem to have parallel meaning, they are not expressed in parallel form (*The . . . were evident*; *It is possible to diagnose* . . .; *Sometimes apparent were* . . .), and their verbs shift from past to present to past (*were, is, were*).

When the paragraph is revised to solve these problems, it becomes much clearer.

> The ancient Egyptians were masters of preserving dead people's bodies by making mummies of them. Basically, mummification consisted of removing the internal organs, applying natural preservatives inside and out, and then wrapping the body in layers of bandages. And the process was remarkably effective. Indeed, mummies several thousand years old have been discovered nearly intact. Their skin, hair, teeth, finger- and toenails, and facial features are still evident. The diseases suffered in life, such as smallpox, arthritis, and nutritional deficiencies, are still diagnosable. Even the causes of death are still apparent: A middle-aged king died from a blow on the head; a child king died from polio.

This paragraph contains the same information and the same number of sentences as the previous one, but now we have no difficulty moving from one sentence to the next, seeing the writer's intentions, understanding the writer's meaning. Now, after the initial broad assertion (the topic sentence), the writer makes two related and somewhat more specific statements: First (in sentence 2) he defines the process of mummification, which the opening sentence has led us to wonder about; then (in sentence 3) he states that the process was effective. Sentence 3 automatically leads us to expect an explanation of how the process was effective, and in sentence 4 the writer proceeds to tell us: Ancient mummies have been discovered nearly intact. "How intact?" we want to know. And again the writer responds to our expectation: We can make out features (sentence 5), diseases (sentence 6), and even causes of death (sentence 7). Besides arranging his sentences so that they proceed from the general to the specific in a way we anticipate, the writer has also clarified relations in other ways. Added words now connect the sentences: *Basically* (sentence 2), *And* (3), *Indeed* (4), *still* (5, 6, 7), *Even* (7). The three examples of intactness (sentences 5, 6, and 7) are now given parallel form and consistent verb tense (*are still evident, are still diagnosable, are still apparent*). Thus we can readily see that the examples are related.

In addition to these techniques for achieving paragraph coherence — organization, transitional words, parallelism, consistency — this paragraph also employs the others discussed below: repetition or restatement (for instance, *mummies . . . mummies . . . mummification . . . the process*) and pronouns (*mummies . . . their*). As you have seen, all these techniques respond to readers' tendency to expect certain patterns and their need to understand relationships without struggle.

1
Organizing the paragraph

The above paragraphs on mummies illustrate an essential element of coherence: Information must be arranged in an order that corresponds to readers' expectations. If the paragraph begins with a general statement (as most paragraphs do), readers will immediately expect and easily follow either restriction or illustration of the generalization. Restriction may consist of one or more sentences (such as sentences 2, 3, and 4 of the second paragraph on mummies), each sentence either more specific than the last or at the same level of generality. Illustration following the opening statement or the restriction may consist of a single extended example or several shorter ones (such as sentences 5, 6, and 7 of the second mummies paragraph). As we saw in examining the first paragraph on mummies, the writer's violation of one of these patterns — placing restricting sentence 5 among its illustrations — forces readers to concentrate on piecing together meaning. It forces them to do work that the writer should have done.

Within these patterns of general and specific statements, paragraph elements at the same level of generality can also be arranged to conform to readers' expectations. The basic organizational patterns — spatial, chronological, general to specific, specific to general, and variations of the last two — correspond to the patterns of essay organization discussed in Chapter 1 (see 1f).

Spatial pattern

A paragraph organized **spatially** focuses the reader's attention on one point and scans a person, object, or scene from there. The movement may be from top to bottom, from side to side, from a farther point to a closer one, or from a closer point to a farther one. Donald Hall follows the last pattern in the paragraph below.

> Across the yard, between the cow barn and the road, was a [1] bigger garden which was bright with phlox and zinnias and petunias. Beyond was a pasture where the color changed as the [2] wild flowers moved through the seasons: yellow and orange paint brushes at first, then wild blue lupines and white Queen Anne's lace, and finally the goldenrod of August. Mount Kear- [3] sarge loomed over the pasture in the blue distance, shaped like a cone with a flattened point on top. We sat on the porch and [4] looked at garden, field, and mountain.
> — DONALD HALL, *String Too Short to Be Saved*

Notice the words that specify the spatial relationships: *Across* and *between* (sentence 1); *beyond* (sentence 2); *over* (sentence 3).

A spatial organization parallels the way we actually look at a place for the first time and thus conforms to our expectations. The writer may want the details to speak for themselves and so may not provide a topic sentence or (like Hall) may pull the scene together at the end of the paragraph. Spatial paragraphs are especially suitable for descriptive or expository essays or for fiction.

Chronological pattern

Another familiar way of organizing the elements of a paragraph is **chronologically** — that is, in order of their occurrence in time. In a chronological paragraph, as in experience, the earliest events come first, followed by more recent ones.

> There is no warning at all — only a steady rising intensity of 1
> the sun's light. Within minutes the change is noticeable; within 2
> an hour, the nearer worlds are burning. The star is expanding 3
> like a balloon, blasting off shells of gas at a million miles an
> hour as it blows its outer layers into space. Within a day, it is 4
> shining with such supernal brilliance that it gives off more light
> than all the other suns in the Universe combined. If it had plan- 5
> ets, they are now no more than flecks of flame in the still-
> expanding shells of fire. The conflagration will burn for weeks 6
> before the dying star collapses back into quiescence.
> — ARTHUR C. CLARKE, "The Star of the Magi"

The author relates the events in a clear sequence. He also provides signals to the order of events and the time that separates them: *Within minutes* and *within an hour* (sentence 2), *Within a day* (sentence 4), *now* and *still* (sentence 5), *before* (sentence 6).

Like spatial paragraphs, chronological paragraphs can be almost automatically coherent because readers normally expect the progression of events. Chronological paragraphs may also lack topic sentences, as Clarke's does. Such paragraphs appear most often in narrative essays and in expository essays that explain historical events, a process, or some other sequence.

General-to-specific and specific-to-general patterns

When a paragraph's subject dictates that neither a spatial nor a chronological pattern is appropriate, your arrangement of details must be based solely on common patterns of thinking: from the general to the specific, from the specific to the general, and variations on these. (See also 4d.) The following paragraph orders details from the **general to the specific.**

> Perhaps the simplest fact about sleep is that individual 1
> needs for it vary widely. Most adults sleep between seven and 2
> nine hours, but occasionally people turn up who need twelve

hours or so, while some rare types can get by on three or four. Rarest of all are those legendary types who require almost no sleep at all; respected researchers have recently studied three such people. One of them — a healthy, happy woman in her seventies — sleeps about an hour every two or three days. The other two are men in early middle age, who get by on a few minutes a night. One of them complains about the daily fifteen minutes or so he's forced to "waste" in sleeping.
— LAWRENCE A. MAYER, *"The Confounding Enemy of Sleep"*

After the general statement of his topic sentence, the author moves from common and less common sleep patterns (sentence 2) to the rarest pattern (sentence 3) and (in the remaining sentences) to particular people. General-to-specific paragraphs like this one, which usually take the triangular, topic-sentence-first shape discussed on page 60, are most useful in exposition and argumentation.

In the **specific-to-general** paragraph pattern the elements of the paragraph build to a general conclusion. Such is the pattern of the next paragraph.

It's disconcerting that so many college women, when asked how their children will be cared for if they themselves work, refer with vague confidence to "the day care center" as though there were some great amorphous kiddie watcher out there that the state provides. But such places, adequately funded, well run, and available to all, are still scarce in this country, particularly for middle-class women. And figures show that when she takes time off for family-connected reasons (births, child care), a woman's chances for career advancement plummet. In a job market that's steadily tightening and getting more competitive, these obstacles bode the kind of danger ahead that can shatter not only professions, but egos. A hard reality is that there's not much more support for our daughters who have family-plus-career goals than there was for us; there's simply a great deal more self- and societal pressure.
— JUDITH WAX, *Starting in the Middle*

The author first states a common belief (sentence 1) and two reasons why it is a misconception (sentences 2 and 3). Then she explains the implications, first specifically (sentence 4) and then generally (sentence 5). Usually conforming to the inverted-triangle paragraph shape with the topic sentence last, specific-to-general paragraphs are useful in exposition and argumentation when you want to present the evidence for an idea before explicitly presenting the idea itself.

In a variation of the specific-to-general organization, details may be arranged in a **climactic** pattern, from less dramatic or important to more so. Increasing drama is the basis for organizing the following paragraph, whose punch comes at the end.

> B. F. Skinner has never responded fully to any of his crit- 1
> ics, despite their number and stature. Often he has failed to un- 2
> derstand them. Sometimes he has even branded them as neu- 3
> rotic or even psychotic. Occasionally he has seemed to imply 4
> that he himself is beyond criticism. "When I met him, he was 5
> convinced he was a genius," Yvonne Skinner remembers.
>
> — *Time*

This pattern can work well in exposition, as we have just seen; in description, where the most telling detail comes last; and in narration, where the last event is often the most dramatic. The climactic arrangement is especially effective in argumentation, for each successive detail directs readers' attention to the most crucial evidence at the end.

Other variations on the specific-to-general and general-to-specific patterns are those that arrange details according to readers' likely understanding of them. In discussing the virtues of public television, for instance, you might proceed from **most familiar to least familiar,** from a well-known program your readers have probably seen to less well known programs they may not have seen. Or in defending the right of government employees to strike, you might arrange your reasons from **simplest to most complex,** from the employees' need to be able to redress grievances to more subtle consequences for employer-employee relations.

2
Using parallel structures

Another way to achieve coherence, although not necessarily in every paragraph, is through **parallelism** — similar structures for similar elements of meaning within a sentence or among sentences. Parallel structure helps make coherent the second version of the paragraph on mummies (p. 68). Because the examples of the mummies' intactness occur in sentences with similar structures, we understand almost without thinking that the examples relate equally to the general statement preceding them. In the paragraph below, Joan Didion creates parallel structure with equal effectiveness.

> Joan Baez was a personality before she was entirely a per- 1
> son, and, like anyone to whom that happens, she is in a sense
> the hapless victim of what others have seen in her, written
> about her, wanted her to be and not to be. The roles assigned to 2
> her are various, but variations on a single theme. She is the Ma- 3
> donna of the disaffected. She is the pawn of the protest move- 4
> ment. She is the unhappy analysand. She is the singer who 5,6
> would not train her voice, the rebel who drives the Jaguar too
> fast, the Rima who hides with the birds and the deer. Above all, 7

she is the girl who "feels" things, who has hung on to the fresh-
ness and pain of adolescence, the girl ever wounded, ever
young.   — JOAN DIDION, "Where the Kissing Never Stops"

In this paragraph the parallelism starting in sentence 3 signals a
shift in the paragraph from the earlier general statements to the related examples. Sentences 3 through 7 have the same basic structure: *She is the Madonna. . . . She is the pawn. . . . She is the unhappy
analysand. She is the singer. . . . Above all, she is the girl. . . .* Within
sentence 6 parallel structures echo each other (*the singer who . . . the
rebel who . . . the Rima who*) and are echoed in sentence 7 (*the girl
who*). The similarity in structures ties the paragraph neatly together.
(See Chapter 17 for more discussion of using parallel structures
within sentences.)

3
Repeating or restating words and word groups

Since every unified paragraph has only one topic, that topic is
bound to recur in most, if not all, the sentences. In fact, repeating
or restating key words or word groups is an important means of
achieving paragraph coherence and of reminding your readers what
the topic is. In the following paragraph, for example, the repetition
of *I, my mother, photograph,* and *face* both focuses our attention on
the important elements of the paragraph and holds the paragraph
together.

> I look at photographs of my mother when she was a young   1
> and a very beautiful bride. It is odd to think that when they   2
> were taken, my mother was 20 years younger than I am now.
> The stranger in the photograph — fragile, shy, with a look of   3
> dewy vulnerability — bears no resemblance to the self-con-
> tained, armored, aloof woman I call Mother now. I search the   4
> face in the photographs compulsively; my feelings are opaque
> and obscure, but I sense that if I can "read" that lovely face, I
> will understand not only my own fate but that of my daughter.
> — BARBARA G. HARRISON, "Finding the Way to Be Friends"

In the next paragraph the writer not only repeats key words
but also rephrases them, each time providing a slightly different
slant on her topic. Thus she avoids monotony while binding her sentences together.

> Since the industrial revolution work has been rearranged   1
> and much of the satisfaction has been rationalized out. Very   2
> few workers have a chance to set their own task. Jobs have   3
> been divided and subdivided so that each person performs a
> single operation upon a continuous flow of parts or papers. In-   4
> creasingly the worker is denied not only the chance to set his

own task but even the chance to finish the task someone else
sets for him. The jobs are so fragmented that few workers can   5
feel they are helping to make a car or to issue an insurance policy. They are merely repeating the same few motions, the same   6
simple calculations over and over throughout a lifetime of
labor.   — BARBARA GARSON, *All the Livelong Day*

The writer's repetitions and restatements ensure that we perceive
her central idea, the segmenting of workers' jobs. *Work* (sentence 1)
becomes a *task* (sentences 2, 4), *jobs* (sentences 3, 5), and *labor* (sentence 6). *Workers* and *the worker* (sentences 2, 4, 5) become *each
person* (sentence 3), *him* (sentence 4), *they* (sentences 5, 6). The work
has been *rearranged* (sentence 1), *divided and subdivided* (sentence
3), *fragmented* (sentence 5). It consists of *a single operation* (sentence
3), *the same few motions, the same simple calculations* (sentence 6).

Though planned repetition can be effective, careless or excessive repetition weakens prose (see 31c).

4
Using pronouns

The previous examples illustrate yet another device for achieving paragraph coherence, the use of pronouns like *my, she, him, his,*
and *they.* **Pronouns** refer to and function as nouns (see 5a-2) and
thus can help relate sentences to each other. In the paragraph below, the pronouns *he, him,* and *his* indicate that the patient is still
the subject while enabling the writer to avoid repeating *the patient*
or *the patient's.*

The experience is a familiar one to many emergency-room   1
medics. A patient who has been pronounced dead and unex-   2
pectedly recovers later describes what happened to him during
those moments — sometimes hours — when his body exhibited
no signs of life. According to one repeated account, the patient   3
feels himself rushing through a long, dark tunnel while noise
rings in his ears. Suddenly, he finds himself outside his own   4
body looking down with curious detachment at a medical
team's efforts to resuscitate him. He hears what is said, notes   5
what is happening but cannot communicate with anyone.
Soon, his attention is drawn to other presences in the room —   6
spirits of dead relatives or friends — who communicate with
him nonverbally. Gradually he is drawn to a vague "being of   7
light." This being invites him to evaluate his life and shows him   8
highlights of his past in panoramic vision. The patient longs to   9
stay with the being of light but is reluctantly drawn back into
his physical body and recovers.
                     — KENNETH L. WOODWARD, "Life After Death?"

The pronouns in this paragraph give it coherence, in part because they refer clearly to a noun. The opposite effect will occur if the reader cannot tell exactly what noun a pronoun is meant to refer to. (For a discussion of the problems associated with pronoun reference, see Chapter 12.)

¶ *coh*

3b

5
Being consistent

Being consistent is the most subtle way to achieve paragraph coherence because readers are aware of consistency only when it is absent. Consistency (or the lack of it) occurs primarily in the person and number of nouns and pronouns and in the tense of verbs (see Chapter 13). Although some shifts will be necessary because of meaning, inappropriate shifts will interfere with a reader's ability to follow the development of ideas. The writers of the following paragraphs destroy coherence by shifting person, number, and tense, respectively.

SHIFTS IN PERSON

An enjoyable form of exercise is modern dance. If *one* [1,2] wants to stay in shape, *you* will find that dance tones and strengthens most muscles. The leaping and stretching *you* do [3] also improves *a person's* balance and poise. And *I* found that [4] *my* posture improved after only a few months of dancing.

SHIFTS IN NUMBER

Politics is not the activity for everyone. It requires quick- [1,2] ness and patience at the same time. *A politician* must like [3] speaking to large groups of people and fielding questions without having time to think of the answers. *Politicians* must also be [4] willing to compromise with the people *they* represent. And no [5] matter how good *a politician* is, *they* must give up on becoming popular with all constituents. It isn't possible. [6]

SHIFTS IN TENSE

I *am developing* an interest in filmmaking. I *tried* to take [1,2] courses that relate to camera work or theater, and I *have read* books about the technical and artistic sides of movies. Though [3] I *would have liked* to get a job on a movie set right away, I *will* probably *continue* my formal education and training in filmmaking after college. There simply *aren't* enough jobs available [4] for all those who *wanted* to be in films but *have* no direct experience.

6
Using transitional expressions

In addition to the methods for achieving coherence discussed above, writers also rely on specific words and word groups to connect sentences whose relationships will not be instantly clear to readers. Sometimes the omission of these words or word groups will make an otherwise coherent paragraph choppy and hard to follow, as the next paragraph shows.

> Medical science has succeeded in identifying the hundreds   1
> of viruses that can cause the common cold. It has discovered   2
> the most effective means of prevention. One person transmits   3
> the cold viruses to another most often by hand. An infected   4
> person covers his mouth to cough. He picks up the telephone.   5
> His daughter picks up the telephone. She rubs her eyes. She   6, 7, 8
> has a cold. It spreads. To avoid colds, people should wash their   9, 10
> hands often and keep their hands away from their faces.

This paragraph is unified and fundamentally coherent because the sentences do seem related to each other. However, we can only guess at the precise relationships, which are indicated by the italicized words in the paragraph as it was actually written:

> Medical science has *thus* succeeded in identifying the hun-   1
> dreds of viruses that can cause the common cold. It has *also*   2
> discovered the most effective means of prevention. One person   3
> transmits the cold viruses to another most often by hand. *For*   4
> *instance*, an infected person covers his mouth to cough. *Then*   5
> he picks up the telephone. *Half an hour later*, his daughter   6
> picks up the *same* telephone. *Immediately afterward*, she rubs   7
> her eyes. *Within a few days*, she, *too*, has a cold. *And thus* it   8, 9
> spreads. To avoid colds, *therefore*, people should wash their   10
> hands often and keep their hands away from their faces.
>
> — A STUDENT

Now we see that sentence 1, with *thus*, is a transition from the previous paragraph. The *also* in sentence 2 indicates clearly that this discovery is a second insight of medical science, not perhaps a clarification of the first. *For instance* in sentence 4 signals that an example is coming. The time indicators in sentences 5 through 8 link the parts of the example. *And thus* in sentence 9 helps pull us out of the example and prepares us for the conclusion, signaled by *therefore*, in sentence 10.

The linking words and word groups are called **transitional expressions.** They state relationships clearly and thus enhance paragraph coherence. The following is a partial list of transitional expressions, arranged by the functions they perform.

¶ *coh*
3b

TO ADD OR SHOW SEQUENCE

again, also, and, and then, besides, equally important, finally, first, further, furthermore, in addition, in the first place, last, moreover, next, second, still, too

TO COMPARE

also, in the same way, likewise, similarly

TO CONTRAST

although, and yet, but, but at the same time, despite, even so, even though, for all that, however, in contrast, in spite of, nevertheless, notwithstanding, on the contrary, on the other hand, regardless, still, though, yet

TO GIVE EXAMPLES OR INTENSIFY

after all, an illustration of, even, for example, for instance, indeed, in fact, it is true, of course, specifically, that is, to illustrate, truly

TO INDICATE PLACE

above, adjacent to, below, elsewhere, farther on, here, near, nearby, on the other side, opposite to, there, to the east, to the left

TO INDICATE TIME

after a while, afterward, as long as, as soon as, at last, at length, at that time, before, earlier, formerly, immediately, in the meantime, in the past, lately, later, meanwhile, now, presently, shortly, simultaneously, since, so far, soon, subsequently, then, thereafter, until, until now, when

TO REPEAT, SUMMARIZE, OR CONCLUDE

all in all, altogether, as has been said, in brief, in conclusion, in other words, in particular, in short, in simpler terms, in summary, on the whole, that is, therefore, to put it differently, to summarize

TO SHOW CAUSE OR EFFECT

accordingly, as a result, because, consequently, for this purpose, hence, otherwise, since, then, therefore, thereupon, thus, to this end, with this object

(For a discussion of transitional paragraphs, see 3d-3.)

7
Combining devices to achieve coherence

The devices we have examined for achieving coherence rarely appear in isolation in effective paragraphs. As any example in this chapter shows, writers must often combine sensible organization, parallelism, repetition, pronouns, consistency, and transitional ex-

¶ *coh*
3b

pressions to help readers follow the development of ideas. And the devices also figure, naturally, in the whole essay (see 3e).

EXERCISE 5

Analyze the structure of each paragraph below. Locate the general statement of the paragraph topic and any restriction of the topic. How does the writer arrange illustrations or the details of a single illustration: spatially, chronologically, from general to specific, from specific to general, or in a variation of the last two?

1.   The losing animal in a struggle saves itself from destruc- 1
tion by an act of submission, an act usually recognized and ac- 2
cepted by the winner. In some cases, for instance, the loser presents to its rival a vulnerable part of its body such as the top of
the head or the fleshy part of the neck. The central nervous sys- 3
tem of the winner recognizes the "meaning" of the presentation, and the instinct to kill is inhibited. Typical of this natural 4
pattern is the behavior of two wolves in combat. As soon as one 5
of the animals realizes it cannot win, it offers its vulnerable
throat to the stronger wolf; instead of taking advantage of the
opportunity, the victor relents, even though an instant earlier it
had appeared frantic to reach the now proffered jugular vein.
                                    — RENÉ DUBOS, "Territoriality and Dominance"

2.   On August 18, 1951, the St. Louis Browns baseball team 1
cracked a joke and forever changed the rules of professional
baseball. On that day the Browns were playing the Detroit Ti- 2
gers. In the first inning the St. Louis manager sent to the plate 3
Eddie Gaedel, a man less than four feet tall. Detroit's pitcher at 4
first did not throw to Gaedel, but the small man held his stance,
his child's bat cocked. When the pitcher finally let one fly, the 5
ball sailed over Gaedel's head. The pitcher tried again, and 6
again the ball flew over Gaedel's head. The third pitch, too, was 7
high, and so was the fourth. The pitcher simply could not lower 8
his throws to Gaedel's strike zone. Gaedel walked to first base, 9
where he was replaced by a pinch runner who later scored.
Within twenty-four hours baseball had a new rule: no midgets 10
would ever again play professional ball.   — A STUDENT

3.   One must descend to the basement and move along a con- 1
fusing mazelike hall to reach it. Twice the passage seems to 2
lead against a blank wall; then at last one enters the brightly
lighted auditorium. And here, finally, are the social workers at 3
the reception desks; and there, waiting upon the benches rowed
beneath the pipes carrying warmth and water to the
floors above, are the patients. One sees white-jacketed psy- 4
chiatrists carrying charts appear and vanish behind screens
that form the improvised interviewing cubicles. All is an atmos- 5
phere of hurried efficiency; and the concerned faces of the

patients are brightened by the friendly smiles and low-pitched
voices of the expert workers. One has entered the Lafargue Psy- 6
chiatric Clinic.   — RALPH ELLISON, *Shadow and Act*

4.   Aside from basic money management, what did I actually 1
learn from all my summer and after-school jobs? Each one may 2
have given me some small skills, but the cumulative effect was
to deepen my belief that work was the essential aspect of
grown-up life. Even now, I am sometimes filled with anxieties 3
at the prospect of stretches of free time. When I do not imme- 4
diately rush to fill that time with work, I have to fight off guilt,
struggling mentally against a picture of a Real Grown-up shak-
ing a finger at me, someone with the droning voice of our high-
school career counselor, but with firm overtones of former employers, teachers, even my mother. "This," the voice beats 5
relentlessly into my ear, "is your preparation for life."
                              — SUSAN ALLEN TOTH, *Blooming*

EXERCISE 6

The sentences in the following student paragraphs have been deliberately scrambled to make the paragraphs incoherent. However,
the sentences contain ample clues to a coherent arrangement.
Identify the central idea in each paragraph. Then rearrange the
sentences to form a well-organized, coherent unit.

1   We hear the negative side too often, probably because so 1
much of it is true. The total volume of mail delivered by the 2
Postal Service each year makes up more than half the total
delivered in all the world. But we should not forget what 3
the Postal Service does *right*. Its 70,000 employees handle 4
90,000,000,000 pieces of mail each year. And when was the last 5
time they failed to deliver yours? In fact, on any given day the 6
Postal Service delivers almost as much mail as the rest of the
world combined. That means over 1,250,000 pieces per em- 7
ployee and over 400 pieces per man, woman, and child in the
country.

2.   Whether you arrive by car, bus, train, plane, or boat, the 1
skyline will take your breath away. A single visit to New York 2
City will tell you why the city is both loved and hated by so
many people. And the streets seem so dirty: cans and bags and 3
newspapers lie in the gutters and on the sidewalks or sometimes fly across your path. Even the people who do speak Eng- 4
lish won't smile or say "Excuse me" or give you good directions. The thrill will only be heightened when you walk down 5
the canyons formed by skyscrapers, look in the shop windows,
go to the theater or a museum, stroll in the neighborhoods
where no one speaks English. You start to notice the noise of 6
traffic and get annoyed at the crowds. But all is not perfect — 7
far from it. After a few days, when your reactions balance out, 8
you have the same love-hate feelings as everyone else.

EXERCISE 7

Study the paragraphs in Exercise 1 (pp. 64–65) for the authors' reliance on various devices to achieve paragraph coherence. Look especially for parallel structures and ideas, repetition and restatement, pronouns, and transitional expressions.

EXERCISE 8

The paragraph below is incoherent because of inconsistencies in person, number, or tense. Identify the inconsistencies and revise the paragraph to give it coherence.

I rebel against the idea of males always being the sole family provider. For me to be happy, I needed to feel useful, and so I work to support myself and my daughter. I did not feel that it is wrong for one to be a housewife while a man supports your household, but that way is not for me. I enjoy the business world, and I have been pleased with my job. Working, I make enough now to support the two of us, and I know that when I graduate, I will be able to earn even more. I can do very well as my own provider.

EXERCISE 9

Write a coherent paragraph from the information below, combining and rewriting the sentences as necessary. The topic sentence should be followed by two restrictions, each followed in turn by its relevant illustrations. When combining or rewriting the sentences, introduce parallelism, repetition and restatement, pronouns, consistency, and transitional expressions so that a reader can see connections.

TOPIC SENTENCE

The advantages of hypnosis over drugs have not been fully recognized or exploited.

RESTRICTIONS AND ILLUSTRATIONS

Hypnosis has none of the dangerous side effects of tension-relieving drugs.
Unlike drugs, hypnosis can help people permanently overcome self-destructive habits.
Self-destructive habits include smoking and overeating.
Hypnosis is far superior to drugs for relieving tension.
Hypnosis can help people sleep soundly, awake refreshed, and stay alert and productive.
Drugs cannot do all these things.
Hypnosis can do things drugs cannot do.
Hypnosis is nonaddicting.
Most of the drugs that relieve tension do foster addiction.

Drugs cannot boost self-confidence and morale for any length of
time, but hypnosis can.
Tension-relieving drugs are expensive.
Hypnosis is inexpensive even for people who have not mastered
self-hypnosis.

¶ *dev*
3c

EXERCISE 10

Develop three of the topic sentences below into coherent paragraphs, following the instructions given in parentheses after each
one. Employ parallelism, repetition and restatement, pronouns,
consistency, and transitional expressions as appropriate.

 1. Of all my courses, _____ is the one that I think will serve me
    best throughout life. (*Expository paragraph with at least three
    illustrations of the statement arranged from specific to general.*)
 2. The movie (or book) had an exciting plot. (*Expository para-
    graph with illustrations — the elements of the plot summary —
    arranged chronologically.*)
 3. We Americans face many problems, but the one we should
    concentrate on solving first is _____. (*Argumentative para-
    graph with a restriction and then illustrations — the reasons for
    the statement — arranged from the general to the specific.*)
 4. The most dramatic building in town is the _____. (*Descrip-
    tive paragraph with illustrations — the details of the building —
    arranged spatially.*)
 5. Children should not have to worry about the future. (*Exposi-
    tory paragraph with a restriction — perhaps stating why children
    should not have to worry or what they should do instead — and
    at least three specific illustrations arranged in climactic order.*)

3c
Developing the paragraph

A paragraph may be both unified and coherent but still be
skimpy, unconvincing, or otherwise inadequate. The paragraph below is unified: It adheres to the topic of bad television commercials,
and its attitude toward them is consistent. It is also coherent in the
sense that the relations among sentences are apparent. But it is not
an effective paragraph.

> Despite complaints from viewers, television commercials 1
> aren't getting any more realistic. Their makers still present 2
> idealized people in unreal situations. And the advertisers also 3
> persist in showing a version of male-female relationships that
> can't exist in more than two households. What do the advertis- 4
> ers know about us, or about how we see ourselves, that makes
> them continue to plunge millions of dollars into these kinds of
> commercials?

This paragraph gives us the writer's main ideas, but we know nothing about the specific commercials that prompted the ideas. The paragraph lacks **development,** completeness. It does not provide enough information for us to evaluate the writer's assertion in sentence 1.

Paragraph development — the adequate support of main ideas so that readers stay interested and come away convinced — always involves being specific by supplying details, examples, or reasons for your assertions. Often it also involves a specific method of development that is determined by your topic and what you want to say about it.

1
Using details, examples, and reasons

If they are sound, the general statements you make in any writing, whether argumentative, expository, narrative, or descriptive, will be based on what you have experienced, observed, read, and thought. To understand and appreciate your general statements, your readers need details of the examples or reasons on which you base them. Details, examples, and reasons form the heart of paragraph development.

Here is the actual version, written by a student, of the paragraph we discussed above. Notice how the added descriptions of commercials (in italics) make a sketchy paragraph into an interesting and convincing piece of writing.

> Despite complaints from viewers, television commercials 1 aren't getting any more realistic. Their makers still present 2 idealized people in unreal situations. *Friendly shopkeepers stock* 3 *only their favorite brand of toothpaste or coffee or soup. A* 4 *mother cleans and buffs her kitchen floor to a mirror finish so her baby can play on it. A rosy-cheeked pregnant woman uses* 5 *two babies, two packaged diapers neatly dissected, and two ink blotters to demonstrate the diaper's superior absorbency to her equally rosy-cheeked and pregnant friend.* The advertisers also 6 persist in showing a version of male-female relationships that can't exist in more than two households. *The wife panics be-* 7 *cause a meddlesome neighbor points out that her husband's shirt is dirty. Or she fears for her marriage because her finicky hus-* 8 *band doesn't like her coffee.* What do the advertisers know 9 about us, or about how we see ourselves, that makes them continue to plunge millions of dollars into these kinds of commercials?

This paragraph supplies specific, concrete examples to illustrate the more general, abstract topic sentence (sentence 1) and restrictions (sentences 2 and 6). The examples are detailed — with concrete words like *rosy-cheeked, meddlesome,* and *finicky* — and thus they not only set the scene for us but also tell us exactly what the author's attitude is.

2
Choosing a method of development

Sometimes you may have difficulty developing an idea, or you may not see the most effective way to shape the information you have. Then you can draw on various methods of paragraph development that correspond to methods of essay development (see 1b-2). Experienced writers follow these methods all the time, though usually not consciously. Inexperienced writers can ask themselves a series of questions about an idea that will suggest not only a method of development but also the supporting details.

How can it be illustrated or supported?

Some ideas need only detailed examples or reasons to become well developed. The writer of the second paragraph on television commercials developed her idea with several specific examples of each general statement. You can also supply a single extended example, as the author of the following paragraph does to illustrate his assertion (sentence 1) about cultural differences in the ways people communicate.

> One of my earliest discoveries in the field of intercultural 1
> communication was that the position of the bodies of people in
> conversation varies with the culture. Even so, it used to puzzle 2
> me that a special Arab friend seemed unable to walk and talk at
> the same time. After years in the United States, he could not 3
> bring himself to stroll along, facing forward while talking. Our 4
> progress would be arrested while he edged ahead, cutting
> slightly in front of me and turning sideways so we could see
> each other. Once in this position, he would stop. His behavior 5, 6
> was explained when I learned that for the Arabs to view the
> other person peripherally is regarded as impolite, and to sit or
> stand back-to-back is considered very rude. You must be in- 7
> volved when interacting with Arabs who are friends.
> — EDWARD T. HALL, *The Hidden Dimension*

Sometimes you can develop a paragraph by providing your reasons for stating a general idea. Such is the method used in the paragraph below.

> History textbooks for elementary and secondary schools 1
> are not like other kinds of histories. They serve a different func- 2
> tion, and they have their own traditions, which continue inde-
> pendent of academic history writing. In the first place, they are 3
> essentially nationalistic histories. The first American-history 4

text was written after the American Revolution, and because of it; and most texts are still accounts of the nation-state. In the ₅ second place, they are written not to explore but to instruct — to tell children what their elders want them to know about their country. This information is not necessarily what anyone con- ₆ siders the truth of things. Like time capsules, the texts contain ₇ the truths selected for posterity.

— FRANCES FITZGERALD, *America Revised*

In sentence 1 the writer makes a general assertion, and in sentence 2 she clarifies it. Then she provides two reasons for her assertion (sentences 3 and 5) and elaborates on each one (sentences 4, 6, and 7). The assertion is not yet proved, for the detailed illustrations will come in other paragraphs; but we understand its basis.

What is it? (*Definition*)

Definition involves naming the class of things to which something belongs and the characteristics that distinguish it from the other members of the class. You can easily define concrete, non-controversial terms in a single sentence: *A knife is a cutting instrument* (its class) *with a sharp blade set in a handle* (the characteristics that set it off from, say, scissors or a razor blade). But defining a complicated, abstract, or controversial topic often requires extended explanation (see 4b-2), and you may need to devote a whole paragraph to it. Such a definition provides details and perhaps one or more examples to identify the subject's characteristics. It may also involve other methods of paragraph development discussed below, such as division (separating things into their parts), classification (combining things into groups), or comparison and contrast.

The following paragraphs are both developed by definition, though their subjects are quite different.

A soap opera deals with the plights and problems brought ₁ about in the lives of its permanent principal characters by the advent and interference of one group of individuals after another. Thus, a soap opera is an endless sequence of narratives ₂ whose only cohesive element is the eternal presence of its bedevilled and beleaguered principal characters. A narrative, or ₃ story sequence, may run from eight weeks to several months. The ending of one plot is always hooked up with the beginning ₄ of the next, but the connection is unimportant and soon forgotten. Almost all the villains in the small-town daytime serials are ₅ émigrés from the cities — gangsters, white-collar criminals, designing women, unnatural mothers, cold wives, and selfish, ruthless, and just plain cussed rich men. They always come up ₆ against a shrewdness that outwits them or destroys them, or a kindness that wins them over to the good way of life.

— JAMES THURBER, "Ivorytown, Rinsoville, Anacinburg, and Crisco Corner"

> The neurotic, in contrast to the psychotic, cannot help reg- 1
> istering with painful accuracy all the thousand little incidents
> of real life which do not fit in with his conscious illusion. Con- 2
> sequently he wavers in his self-valuation between feeling great
> and feeling worthless. At any minute he may shift from one ex- 3
> treme to the other. At the same time that he feels most con- 4
> vinced of his exceptional value he may be astonished that any-
> one takes him seriously. Or at the same time that he feels 5
> miserable and down-trodden he may feel furious that anyone
> should think him in need of help. His sensitivity can be com- 6
> pared with that of a person who is sore all over his body and
> flinches at the slightest touch. He easily feels hurt, despised, ne- 7
> glected, slighted, and reacts with proportionate vindictive re-
> sentment.
> — KAREN HORNEY, *The Neurotic Personality of Our Time*

What are its parts? (*Division*) Or what groups can it be sorted into? (*Classification*)

Division or **analysis** involves scrutinizing a single thing by separating it into its parts or components, as we might examine a family by dividing it into its individual members — mother, father, daughter, son. **Classification** involves grouping things according to their similarities. Using classification to describe families, we might examine family structures in various cultures — matriarchal, patriarchal, nuclear, extended, and so on. Division and classification are so closely related that we often combine them in developing an idea, a paragraph, or an essay. Thus in describing the family we might first classify the types and then divide each type into the separate roles of the individual family members.

In the paragraph below, the writer divides a small portion of a daily newspaper into its parts, giving the technical name for each part.

> A typical daily newspaper compresses considerable infor- 1
> mation into the top of the first page, above the headlines. The 2
> most prominent feature of this space, the newspaper's name, is
> called the *logo* or *nameplate*. Under the logo and set off by rules 3
> is a line of small type called the *folio line*, which contains the
> date of the issue, the volume and issue numbers, copyright in-
> formation, and the price. To the right of the logo is a block of 4
> small type called a *weather ear*, a summary of the day's fore-
> cast. And above the logo is a *skyline*, a kind of advertisement in 5
> which the paper's editors highlight a special feature of the
> issue.   — A STUDENT

Division always begins with a single object or concept; in the paragraph above it is a segment of a newspaper's front page. The task is then to identify the distinct elements that constitute the object or concept. The student omits untypical elements, such as the stock market reports that appear on only some front pages, because these would clutter and confuse the analysis.

In the following paragraph the writer classifies high school hoods.

> Generally speaking, there are two kinds of hoods at Bing- 1
> ham High School: those who are considerably smaller than the
> rest of their classmates, like Jim Devaney, and those who are
> considerably larger, like Jim's friend, whose name I never
> learned. The large hoods tolerate the small ones with the same 2
> self-serving indifference that sharks extend to sucker fish. They 3
> have a symbiotic relationship founded on the unequal distribu-
> tion of hormones. Looking at the two groups together, or at any 4
> group of adolescents, it is hard to believe that a student's place
> in the society of his peers is determined by anything more com-
> plicated than physical appearance. Ductless glands are every- 5
> thing.   — DAVID OWEN, *High School*

This paragraph illustrates several principles of classification. First, the subject being classified is plural (hoods), in contrast to the single subject of division. Second, the classes or groups are alike in at least one basic way: both are in high school, both are hoods. And third, the classes do not overlap, as would tall hoods, short hoods, and, say, skinny hoods, who might be either short or tall.

How is it like, or different from, other things? (*Comparison and contrast*)

Comparison and **contrast** may be used separately or together to develop an idea or to relate two or more things. In the following paragraph Jacob Bronowski uses comparison to develop his view that scientific reasoning is the same as poetic imagining.

> Many people believe that reasoning, and therefore science, 1
> is a different activity from imagining. But this is a fallacy, and 2
> you must root it out of your mind. The child that discovers, 3
> sometimes before the age of ten, that he can make images and
> move them around in his head has entered the same gateway to
> imagination and to reason. Reasoning is constructed with mov- 4
> able images just as certainly as poetry is. You may have been 5
> told, you may still have the feeling, the $E = mc^2$ is not an imagi-
> native statement. If so, you are mistaken. The symbols in that 6, 7
> master-equation of the twentieth century — the E for energy
> and m for mass, and c for the speed of light — are images for
> absent things or concepts, of exactly the same kind as the
> words "tree" or "love" in a poem. The poet John Keats was not 8
> writing anything which (for him at least) was fundamentally
> different from an equation when he wrote,
>
> > "Beauty is truth, truth beauty," — that is all
> > Ye know on earth, and all ye need to know.

There is no difference in the use of such words as "beauty" and 9
"truth" in the poem, and such symbols as "energy" and "mass"
in the equation.
— JACOB BRONOWSKI, *Imagination and the University*

¶ *dev*
·3c

In the next paragraph E. B. White uses contrast to make us see
the unusual beauty of most Florida days. Whereas Bronowski treats
the compared subjects side by side, White discusses all of one element before turning to the other.

On many days, the dampness of the air pervades all life, all 1
living. Matches refuse to strike. The towel, hung to dry, grows 2, 3
wetter by the hour. The newspaper, with its headlines about in- 4
tegration, wilts in your hand and falls limply into the coffee and
the egg. Envelopes seal themselves. Postage stamps mate with 5, 6
one another as shamelessly as grasshoppers. But most of the 7
time the days are models of beauty and wonder and comfort,
with the kind sea stroking the back of the warm sand. At eve- 8
ning there are great flights of birds over the sea, where the light
lingers; the gulls, the pelicans, the terns, the herons stay aloft
for half an hour after land birds have gone to roost. They hold 9
their ancient formations, wheel and fish over the Pass, enjoying
the last of day like children playing outdoors after suppertime.
— E. B. WHITE, "The Ring of Time"

The most effective contrasts occur between ideas or things
that are usually perceived as similar. White's days are like that. So
are, say, two modern science fiction writers with opposite views of
the future, or two photographic techniques using the Polaroid camera. Comparisons, however, are most effective when they show similarities between ideas or things usually perceived as different, such
as reason and imagination in Bronowski's paragraph. And because
we would expect differences in the writings of two authors a century
apart, comparison could be effective in showing how they are alike.

*Is it comparable to something in a different class but more fa-
miliar to us? (Analogy)*

Whereas we draw comparisons and contrasts between elements in the same general class (appearance and behavior, Florida
days, kinds of thinking), we link elements in different classes with a
special kind of comparison called **analogy.** Most often in analogy we
illuminate or explain an unfamiliar, complex, abstract class of
things with a familiar and concrete class of things. In the paragraph
below, the author develops an analogy between writing style (abstract) and a distance runner (concrete).

The good style is the lean style. Like a good distance run- 1, 2
ner, it hasn't an ounce of excess fat anywhere on it. And like the 3
good distance runner, it moves without excess motion. Its arms 4

¶ dev
3c

don't flail out in all directions; they swing easily at the sides in a beautiful economy of effort. A good style has the same grace ⁵ and beauty in its motion as a good athlete because there's nothing wasted. Everything is there for a purpose.   ⁶

— LAURENCE PERRINE, "Fifteen Ways to
Write Five Hundred Words"

In the next paragraph Mavis Gallant draws an analogy between attitudes toward life and attitudes toward clothing.

A woman can always get some practical use from a torn-up ¹ life, Gabriel decided. She likes mending and patching it, making ² sure the edges are straight. She spreads the last shred out ³ and takes its measure: "What can I do with this remnant? How long does it need to last?" A man puts on his life ready-made. If ⁴,⁵ it doesn't fit, he will try to exchange it for another. Only a fool ⁶ of a man will try to adjust the sleeves or move the buttons; he doesn't know how.

— MAVIS GALLANT, "Baum, Gabriel, 1935–( )"

Sometimes an analogy will be offered as proof of an idea. But analogy never proves. (For a discussion of false analogy, see 4d-3.)

What are its causes or its effects? (*Cause-and-effect analysis*)

When you analyze why something happened or what is likely to happen, then you are determining causes and effects. **Cause-and-effect analysis** is especially useful in writing about social, economic, or political events or problems, as the following paragraphs illustrate. In the first, William Ouchi looks at the roots of Japanese collectivism, which he elsewhere contrasts with American individualism.

The *shinkansen* or "bullet train" speeds across the rural ¹ areas of Japan giving a quick view of cluster after cluster of farmhouses surrounded by rice paddies. This particular pattern ² did not develop purely by chance, but as a consequence of the technology peculiar to the growing of rice, the staple of the Japanese diet. The growing of rice requires the construction ³ and maintenance of an irrigation system, something that takes many hands to build. More importantly, the planting and the ⁴ harvesting of rice can only be done efficiently with the cooperation of twenty or more people. The "bottom line" is that a ⁵ single family working alone cannot produce enough rice to survive, but a dozen families working together can produce a surplus. Thus the Japanese have had to develop the capacity to ⁶ work together in harmony, no matter what the forces of disagreement or social disintegration, in order to survive.

— WILLIAM OUCHI, *Theory Z: How American Business
Can Meet the Japanese Challenge*

In the next example George Wald first presents what he thinks is a wrong link between effects and causes (sentences 1–3), then states his analysis and supporting reasons (sentences 4–5), and finally suggests new effects that might result from a change in circumstances (sentences 6–7). Thus Wald adopts the methods of both contrast and cause-and-effect analysis.

¶ *dev*
3c

We are often told that the famine already in progress in increasing parts of the Third World, and hunger among the poor in some developed countries, is somehow the fault of the hungry. This is the familiar tactic of blaming the victim. It is frequently said that the poor should not have so many children, that they are poor because they have too many children. All of us should realize by now that it's the other way around: People have too many children because they are poor. Having many children is a strategy for survival among the very poor; they need to have many children so that one or two may survive to feed them in their old age and bury them when they die. The only way to get the poor to have fewer children is to give them some assurance that the children they have will survive. Once that is achieved, they will be glad to have smaller families.
     — GEORGE WALD, "There Isn't Much Time"

1

2, 3

4

5

6

7

(For a discussion of the mistakes often made in analyzing cause-and-effect relationships, see 4d.)

How does it work? (*Process analysis*)

When you describe how something works, you describe the steps in a **process.** Paragraphs developed by analyzing a process are usually organized chronologically or spatially, as the steps in the process occur or become apparent. The following paragraph traces the process by which a rising air current known as a *thermal* is created.

The second type of rising current is heated air, known as a thermal. A field warmed by the sun heats the air above it, causing it to expand and rise. If the field is surrounded by a cooler forest, the heated pocket of air may rise in the form of a great bubble or of a column. Everyone has seen birds soaring in wide circles over land; usually they are coasting around the periphery of a rising air column. Over the ocean, when the water warms colder air above it, the air rises in a whole group of columns, packed together like the cells of a honeycomb. If the wind then freshens, it may blow the columns over until they lie horizontally on the water. The flat-lying columns of air may rotate around their axes, each in the opposite direction from its neighbor. This has been demonstrated in the laboratory by blowing smoke-filled air over a warmed surface at increasing speed, corresponding to an increase in the wind over the ocean. If

1

2

3

4

5

6

7

8

9

you put your two fists together and rotate them, the right clockwise and the left counter-clockwise, you will see that the two
inner faces of the fists rise together. Just so two adjoining air   10
cells rotating in opposite directions will push up between them
a ridge of rising air. Birds can glide in a straight line along such   11
a ridge.   — JOHN H. STORER, "Bird Aerodynamics"

Combining methods of development

Whatever method you choose as the basis for developing a
paragraph, other methods may also prove helpful. We saw one example of combined methods in Wald's paragraph on page 89.
Storer's paragraph above, developed primarily by process, also provides a definition of *thermal*. And Thurber's paragraph defining the
soap opera (p. 84) also divides the soap opera into its components.

As we will see in Section 3e, the paragraphs within an essay inevitably will be developed with a variety of methods, even when one
controlling method develops and structures the entire essay.

3
Checking length

In an essay of 500 to 750 words, the average paragraph may
contain between 100 and 150 words, or between four and eight sentences. These numbers are averages, of course; the actual length of
a paragraph will depend on its topic, its role in the development of
the thesis sentence, and its position in the essay. Nevertheless, very
short paragraphs are often inadequately developed; they may leave
readers with a sense of incompleteness. And very long paragraphs
often contain irrelevant details or develop two or more topics; readers may have difficulty sorting out or remembering ideas.

When you are revising your essay, reread the paragraphs that
seem very long or very short, checking them especially for unity and
adequate development. If the paragraph wanders, cut everything
from it that does not support your main idea. If it is underdevel-
oped, supply the specific details, examples, or reasons needed, or try
one of the methods of development we have discussed here.

EXERCISE 11

The paragraphs below are not well developed. Analyze them, looking especially for general statements that lack support or leave
questions in your mind. Then rewrite one into a well-developed
paragraph, supplying your own concrete details.

1.   Gestures are one of our most important means of commu-   1
nication. We use them instead of speech. We use them to sup-   2, 3

plement the words we speak. And we use them to communicate   4
some feelings or meanings that words cannot adequately express.

2.   The tax laws still discriminate against married people. Con-   1, 2
trary to the old saying, two people do *not* live more cheaply
than one, especially when both wife and husband are working
students. Instead, the reverse is more likely to be true. At the   3, 4
very least, single and married people should be treated equally.

3.   Children who have been disciplined too much are often   1
easy to spot. Their behavior toward adults may reflect the harsh   2
treatment they have received from adults. And their behavior   3
toward other children may be uncontrolled.

EXERCISE 12

Write a well-developed paragraph on one of the following ideas or
an idea of your own. Be sure your paragraph is unified and coherent as well as adequately developed with specific details.

1. how billboards blight (or decorate) the landscape
2. why you like (or don't like) poetry
3. a place where you feel comfortable (or uncomfortable)
4. an unusual person you know
5. an instance of unusual kindness or cruelty

EXERCISE 13

Identify the method or methods of development in each of the following paragraphs. Where does the author supply specific details
to achieve development?

1.   Computer operations occur so rapidly that we routinely   1
process data in what might be termed subliminal time — inter-
vals far too short for the human senses to detect or for human
neural response times to match. We now have computer-oper-   2
ated microprinters capable of turning out 10,000–20,000 lines
per minute — more than 200 times faster than anyone can read
them, and this is still the slowest part of computer systems. In   3
20 years, computer scientists have gone from speaking in terms
of milliseconds (thousandths of a second) to nanoseconds (bil-
lionths of a second) — a compression of time almost beyond
our powers to imagine. It is as though a person's entire working   4
life of, say, 80,000 paid hours — 2000 hours per year for 40
years — could be crunched into 4.8 minutes.
              — ALVIN TOFFLER, "The Third Wave"

2.   A dying person may pass through five separate attitude   1
stages, according to the psychiatrist Elisabeth Kübler-Ross. In   2
the first stage, denial, the patient ignores symptoms of illness
and refuses to accept diagnosis and sometimes even treatment.
Then, in a stage of anger, the patient feels outraged at the in-   3

¶ *dev*
3c

justice of dying. A stage of bargaining may follow, when the ⁴ patient tries to make an exchange with the hospital staff or his or her family or God for a little more time. Then the patient ⁵ may enter a period of depression that comes when he or she realizes that everything is soon to be finished, that life is almost over. And finally, that dying person may feel acceptance of ⁶ death, a quiet resignation to the power of death.   — A STUDENT

3.   Even allowing for the mental and physical slowdown ac- ¹ companying old age, there are many jobs and activities old people are capable of performing. I don't mean the nonsense ² make-work projects which are so eagerly dreamed up by the directors of senior citizen centers but real ways the aged could continue to contribute to society. Nothing is so depressing as ³ seeing a roomful of people engaged in performing some task for no reason other than to fill empty hours. Painting pretty pic- ⁴ tures is fine — if that is what you want to do. Playing bingo can ⁵ be fun; knitting is productive and good for arthritic fingers; square dancing is joyful besides being good exercise. But what ⁶ if those were the only alternatives offered to, say, a twenty-five-year-old Rhodes scholar? Wouldn't you say it was a disgraceful ⁷ waste? And don't you think the young person in question would ⁸ suffer from a severe loss of self-respect if he could not use the knowledge and talent he possessed? He would probably be- ⁹ come moody, withdrawn, hostile, and suicidal. Yet such is the ¹⁰ position of many of our aged. And they, too, become moody, ¹¹ withdrawn, and suicidal.
    — SHARON R. CURTIN, *Nobody Ever Died of Old Age*

4.   In American society there exist people classified by en- ¹ cyclopedia salesmen as "mooches." Mooches can be generally ² defined as people who like to buy the product; they see the encyclopedia salesman as the bearer of a rare and desirable gift. Mooches are people whose incomes and occupational levels ex- ³ ceed their educational attainments; persons whose income is in the middle-middle range but whose education doesn't exceed high school, or may not even attain that level. Without educa- ⁴ tion, mooches cannot have professional status, although they might make as much money as a professional; consequently, mooches try to assume professionalism by accruing what they think are indications of professional status. A conspicuously ⁵ displayed set of encyclopedias tells the mooch's friends that he can afford to consume conspicuously, that he values a highly normative product over creature comforts, and that he pro- vides for the long-range benefit of his protectorate. The mooch ⁶ associates all these characteristics with professional persons. For him, then, encyclopedias function as easily interpreted pro- ⁷ fessional-status indicators.
    — LYNN M. BULLER, "The Encyclopedia Game"

5.   The nightmare of the plague was compounded for the ¹ fourteenth century by the awful mystery of its cause. The idea ²

of disease carried by insect bite was undreamed of. Fleas and ₃
rats, which were in fact the carriers, are not mentioned in the
plague writings. Contagion could be observed but not ex- ₄
plained and thus seemed doubly sinister. The medical faculty ₅
of the University of Paris favored a theory of poisonous air
spread by a conjunction of the planets, but the general and fundamental belief, made official by a papal bull, was that the pes-
tilence was divine punishment for man's sins. Such horror ₆
could only be caused by the wrath of God. "In the year of our ₇
Lord, 1348," sadly wrote a professor of law at the University of
Pisa, "the hostility of God was greater than the hostility of
men."   — BARBARA W. TUCHMAN, "History as Mirror"

¶ dev

3c

EXERCISE 14

Identify the appropriate method or methods for developing a paragraph on each of the following topics. (Choose from illustration
or support, definition, division or classification, comparison and/
or contrast, analogy, cause-and-effect analysis, and process analysis.)

 1. the influences of a person's biorhythms or astrological sign on
    his or her behavior
 2. a typical situation comedy on television
 3. tuning an engine
 4. rock music and country music
 5. why rock movregrapura
 6. what loyalty is
 7. the kinds of people involved in the tax revolt
 8. the picture of aliens shown by recent science-fiction movies
 9. dancing as pure motion, like a kite in the wind
10. one consequence of the energy shortage

EXERCISE 15

Write a paragraph about a topic from Exercise 14, using the development method you chose in that exercise. Or if you prefer,
choose a topic of your own and develop it with one of the methods
discussed in the text. Be sure the paragraph is also unified and
coherent.

EXERCISE 16

Write seven unified, coherent, and well-developed paragraphs,
each one developed with a different method. Draw on the topics
provided here or in Exercise 14. Or choose your own topics.

 1. *illustration or support*
    why go to college
    why study
    having a headache
    the best sports events
    usefulness (or uselessness) of a self-help book

2. *definition*
   hunger
   humor
   an adult
   fear
   authority
3. *division and classification*
   the segments of a television news show
   factions in a campus controversy
   styles of playing poker
   parts of a barn
   kinds of sports fans
4. *comparison and/or contrast*
   driving American and foreign compact cars
   AM and FM radio announcers
   high school and college football
   movies on TV and in a theater
5. *analogy*
   running and flying
   the U.S. Constitution and a building's foundation
   graduating from high school and being released from prison
6. *cause-and-effect analysis*
   connection between tension and anger
   causes of failing a course
   one way pollution affects you
   connection between credit cards and debt
   causes of a serious accident
7. *process analysis*
   preparing for a job interview
   drying fresh herbs
   making a cabinet
   protecting your home from burglars
   making a jump shot

3d
Writing special kinds of paragraphs

Several kinds of paragraphs do not always follow our guidelines for unity, coherence, development, and length because they serve special functions. These are the essay introduction, the essay conclusion, the transitional paragraph, and the paragraph of spoken dialogue.

1
Opening an essay

Most essays open with a paragraph that draws readers from their world into the writer's world. An opening paragraph should focus readers' attention on the topic and arouse readers' curiosity about what the writer has to say. The safest kind of introduction opens with a statement of the essay's general subject, clarifies or limits the subject in one or more sentences, and then, in the thesis sentence, asserts the point of the essay (see 1d). This is the pattern in the paragraph below, which introduces an essay on the history of American bathing habits.

> We Americans are a clean people. We bathe or shower 1, 2
> regularly and spend billions of dollars each year on soaps and
> deodorants to wash away or disguise our dirt and odor. Yet 3
> cleanliness is a relatively recent habit with us. From the time of 4
> the Puritans until the turn of the twentieth century, bathing in
> the United States was rare and sometimes even illegal.
> — A STUDENT

The writer's first two sentences offer her subject and elaborate on it, leading us to focus on something within our experience. Then, by introducing a less familiar but related idea, the third sentence forms a bridge from common experience to the writer's specific purpose. The fourth sentence, the thesis, states that purpose explicitly.

Here is a more complicated example of this form of introductory paragraph.

> Whatever the institutional mechanics of it, the renovation 1
> of America must begin in Americans' minds. It must express it- 2
> self in their civic morale, their sense of individual responsibility
> for themselves, for the communities and the nation around
> them. It is not enough to say that the Government has failed, 3
> that the System has failed. That accusation subtly absolves in- 4
> dividual citizens of blame but also leaves them feeling like ab-
> jectly passive victims of immense conspiracies — bureaucra-
> cies, multinational corporations. No society can flourish, or 5
> even function, if its people do not feel responsible for it any
> more.   — LANCE MORROW, "To Revive Responsibility"

Several other types of introduction can be equally effective, though they are sometimes harder to invent and control. One kind begins with a quotation that leads into the thesis sentence.

> "It is difficult to speak adequately or justly of London," 1
> wrote Henry James in 1881. "It is not a pleasant place; it is not 2
> agreeable, or cheerful, or easy, or exempt from reproach. It is 3
> only magnificent." Were he alive today, James, a connoisseur of 4
> cities, might easily say the same thing about New York or Paris
> or Tokyo, for the great city is one of the paradoxes of history.
> In countless different ways, it has almost always been an un- 5
> pleasant, disagreeable, cheerless, uneasy and reproachful
> place; in the end, it can only be described as magnificent.
> — *Time*

Another kind of introduction opens by relating an incident that sets the stage for the thesis.

> Canada is pink. I knew that from the map I owned when I [1, 2] was six. On it, New York was green and brown, which was true [3] as far as I could see, so there was no reason to distrust the map maker's portrayal of Canada. When my parents took me across [4] the border and we entered the immigration booth, I looked excitedly for the pink earth. Slowly it dawned on me: This for- [5] eign, "different" place was not so different. I discovered that [6] the world in my head and the world at my feet were not the same.
> — ROBERT ORNSTEIN, *Human Nature*

An introduction may also start with an opinion, preferably a startling one that will grab the reader's attention.

> Caesar was right. Thin people need watching. I've been [1,2,3] watching them for most of my adult life, and I don't like what I see. When these narrow fellows spring at me, I quiver to my [4] toes. Thin people come in all personalities, most of them men- [5] acing. You've got your "together" thin person, your mechanical [6] thin person, your condescending thin person, your tsk-tsk thin person. All of them are dangerous. [7]
> — SUZANNE BRITT JORDAN, "That Lean and Hungry Look"

A historical comparison or contrast may make an effective introduction when some background to the essay topic is useful.

> Throughout the first half of this century, the American [1] Medical Association, the largest and most powerful medical organization in the world, battled relentlessly to rid the country of quack potions and cure-alls; and it is the AMA that is generally credited with being the single most powerful force behind the enactment of the early pure food and drug laws. Today, [2] however, medicine's guardian seems to have done a complete about-face and become one of the pharmaceutical industry's staunchest allies — often at the public's peril and expense.
> — MAC JEFFERY, "Does Rx Spell Rip-off?"

All these examples show basic attributes of good introductions. They are concise. They are direct because they tell us specifically what the author will discuss and what the author's viewpoint is. They seem sincere, so we believe the author will talk to us honestly. And they are interesting without misrepresenting the content of the essay that follows. To achieve these attributes, an introductory paragraph need not be long, as this opener shows.

> I've often wondered what goes into a hot dog. Now I know [1, 2] and I wish I didn't.   — WILLIAM ZINSSER, *The Lunacy Boom*

| **2**
| Closing an essay

Most essays end with a closing statement or conclusion, a signal to readers that the writer has not simply stopped writing but has actually finished. The conclusion completes the essay, bringing it to a climax while assuring readers that they have understood the writer's intention. Usually set off in its own paragraph, the conclusion may consist of a single sentence or a group of sentences. It may summarize the evidence presented in the essay, restate the thesis with a fresh emphasis, suggest a course of action, ask a question, strike a note of hope or despair, introduce a startling fact, quote an authority, or tell an anecdote.

The paragraph below concludes the essay on bathing habits whose introduction we saw on page 95. The writer summarizes her essay in sentence 1 and then, in sentence 2, echoes her introduction by proposing a link between the habits of history and the habits of today.

> Thus changed attitudes and advances in plumbing finally 1
> freed us to bathe whenever we want. Perhaps partly to make up 2
> for our ancestors' bad habits, we have transformed that free-
> dom into a national obsession.   — A STUDENT

Ada Louise Huxtable uses a different technique to conclude her highly critical essay on the Rayburn House Office Building in Washington, D.C. Instead of summarizing, she takes a final shot at the building.

> An old architectural saying has it that there's no point in 1
> crying over spilled marble. Several million pounds of it have 2
> been poured onto Capitol Hill in this latest Congressional build-
> ing venture, and there is nothing quite as invulnerable as a
> really monumental mistake. The Rayburn Building's ultimate 3
> claim to fame may well be that it is the biggest star-spangled ar-
> chitectural blunder of our time.
> — ADA LOUISE HUXTABLE, "The Rayburn Building"

Concluding an essay on environmental protection, Peter F. Drucker states his opinion on the issues he has discussed and, in his last sentence, calls for action.

> Until we get the answers, I think we had better keep on 1
> building power plants and growing food with the help of fertil-
> izers and such insect-controlling chemicals as we now have.
> The risks are well known, thanks to the environmentalists. If 2, 3
> they had not created a widespread public awareness of the eco-
> logical crisis, we wouldn't stand a chance. But such awareness 4
> by itself is not enough. Flaming manifestos and prophecies of 5

doom are no longer much help, and a search for scapegoats can
only make matters worse. The time for sensations and mani-   6
festos is about over. Now we need rigorous analysis, united ef-   7
fort and very hard work.

— PETER F. DRUCKER, "How Best to Protect the Environment"

These three paragraphs illustrate how to avoid several pitfalls
of conclusions.

1. Don't simply repeat your introduction — statement of subject,
   thesis sentence, and all. Presumably the paragraphs in the
   body of your essay have contributed something to the opening
   statements, and it's that something you want to capture in
   your conclusion.
2. Don't start off in a new direction, with a subject different from
   or broader than the one your essay has been about. For instance, Huxtable might have violated this principle (and weakened her conclusion) had she veered off to the quality of
   Washington architecture in general.
3. Don't conclude more than you reasonably can from the evidence you have presented. If your essay is about your frustrating experience trying to clear a parking ticket, you cannot reasonably conclude that *all* local police forces are too tied up in
   red tape to be of service to the people.
4. Don't use your conclusion to apologize for your essay or otherwise cast doubt on it. Don't say, "Even though I'm no expert,"
   or "This may not be convincing, but I believe it's true," or anything similar. Rather, to win your readers' confidence, display
   confidence.

3
Using transitional paragraphs

Short transitional paragraphs, often only a sentence or two,
direct a reader's attention to a turn in an essay or emphasize an idea
that will follow. Because they are separate paragraphs and longer
than words or phrases, transitional paragraphs move a discussion
from one place to another more slowly or more completely than
does a single transitional expression like *consequently* or *in contrast*
(see pp. 76–77).

> These, then, are the reasons for keeping the drinking age at
> twenty-one. Now let's look at some of the reasons for lowering it to
> eighteen.

> The conclusion would seem to be obvious. To be sure, how-
> ever, we must look at a few other facts.

> So the debates were noisy and emotion-packed. But what did
> they accomplish? Historians agree on at least three direct results.

¶
3d

Use transitional paragraphs only to shift readers' attention when your essay makes a significant turn. A paragraph like the one below betrays a writer who is stalling; it does not redirect the flow but stops it altogether.

> Now that we have examined these facts, we can look at some others that are equally important to an examination of this issue.

4
Writing dialogue

When recording a conversation between two or more people, start a new paragraph for each person's speech. The paragraphing establishes for the reader the point at which one speaker stops talking and another begins. For example:

> "Are you saying that you are going to go now and not come back?"
> "Oh, God. Yes, I'm saying that."
> Jessica began to scream.
> — Iris Murdoch, *The Nice and the Good*

Though dialogue appears most often in fictional writing (the source of the example above), it may occasionally freshen or enliven narrative or expository essays. (For guidance in using quotation marks and other punctuation in dialogue, see 24c.)

EXERCISE 17

Analyze the introductory and concluding paragraphs in the first and final drafts of the student essay in Chapter 2, pages 38–40 and 49–51. What is wrong with the first-draft paragraphs? Why are the final-draft paragraphs better? Could they be improved still further?

EXERCISE 18

Write introductory and concluding paragraphs for an essay on one of the following topics (or a topic of your own).
  1. how organized crime takes over or controls a business or neighborhood
  2. your views on aging
  3. how good and evil are depicted in a science-fiction book or movie
  4. the advantages (or disadvantages) of dogs (or cats) as pets
  5. the importance of psychology (or any field of study) in our daily lives

3e
Combining paragraphs in the essay

Paragraphs do not stand alone but contribute to a larger piece of writing. Each unified, coherent, and well-developed paragraph adds something to a unified, coherent, and well-developed essay (see Chapter 1).

In an essay of fewer than 750 words, each paragraph between the introductory and concluding ones will develop and support a part of the essay's central idea, its thesis. The devices for achieving paragraph coherence — a logical pattern of organization, repetition and restatement of words or word groups, use of transitional expressions, and the like — will also link paragraphs in a coherent whole. And the methods of developing paragraphs — definition, division, and so on — will suit the needs of each paragraph in the larger context of the essay. Thus the methods may or may not reflect the way the whole essay is developed, they may vary from one paragraph to the next, and they may even overlap in a single paragraph.

The following essay illustrates the way effective paragraphs can contribute to an effective essay.

A hyperactive committee member can contribute to efficiency. A hyperactive salesperson can contribute to profits. But when a child is hyperactive, people — even parents — may wish he had never been born. To understand hyperactivity in children, we can visualize a collage of the thoughts, feelings, and attitudes of those who must cope with the problem: doctors, parents, even the child himself.   1

The first part of our collage is the doctors. In their terminology the word *hyperactivity* is short for H-LD, a hyperkinesis–learning disability syndrome. They apply the word to children who are "abnormally or excessively busy." But doctors do not fully understand the problem and thus differ over how to treat it. For example, some recommend special diet; others, behavior-modifying drugs; and still others, who do not consider hyperactivity to be a medical problem, a psychiatrist for the entire family. The result is a merry-go-round of tests, confusion, and frustration for the parents and the child.   2

As the parent of a hyperactive child, I can say what the word *hyperactivity* means to the parents who form the second part of the collage. It means a worry that is deep and enduring. It means a despair that is a companion on dark and sleepless nights. It means a fear that is heart twisting and constant, for the hyperactive child is most destructive toward himself. It means a mixture of frustration, guilt, and anger. And finally, since there are times when that anger goes out of control and the child is in danger from the parent, it means self-loathing.   3

The weight of hyperactivity, however, rests not on the doctors or the parents but on the child. For him is reserved the fi-   4 nal and darkest part of our collage because he is most affected. From early childhood he is dragged from doctor to doctor, is attached to strange and frightening machines, and is tested or discussed by physicians, parents, neighbors, teachers, peers. His playmates dislike him because of his temper and his unwillingness to follow rules; and even his pets fear and mistrust him, for he treats them erratically, often hurting them without meaning to. As time goes on, he sees his parents more and more often in tears and anger, and he knows that he is the cause. Though he is highly intelligent, he does poorly when he enters school because of his short attention span. He is fond of sports and games but never joins the other children on the playground because he has an uncontrollable temper and poor coordination. By the time he reaches age seven or eight, he is obsessed with one thought: "Mama," my son asks me repeatedly, "why do I have to be hyperactive?"

At last the collage is completed, and it is dark and somber. 5 *Hyperactivity*, as applied to children, is a word with uncertain, unattractive, and bitter associations. But the picture does have a bright spot, for inside every hyperactive child is a loving, trustful, calm person waiting to be recognized.   — A STUDENT

The general method of development in this essay is division or analysis: The writer examines each part of the collage she creates. The essay's basic organization is general to specific or climactic, proceeding from the general notions of the seemingly distant doctors to the more specific and poignant experiences of a single child. Within this general scheme, however, each paragraph follows the course required by its topic and the writer's purpose. For instance, having shown in paragraph 2 that doctors do not agree on what hyperactivity is, the writer develops paragraph 3 by defining the word as she sees it. And she develops paragraph 4 by analyzing the effects of hyperactivity on the one most harmed by it, the child himself. This paragraph also follows a chronological organization in tracing the child's experiences.

Despite the varied patterns of organization and methods of development in her paragraphs, the writer guides us smoothly and steadily from one paragraph to the next. She recalls the promise of the thesis sentence, a three-part collage, in the topic sentence of every succeeding paragraph. She links paragraphs with transitional words to remind us where we are in the essay: *first* (paragraph 2), *second* (paragraph 3), *however* and *final* (paragraph 4), *at last* (paragraph 5). The entire first sentence of paragraph 4 is a transition from the earlier paragraphs. The writer repeats the key words of the essay, *collage* and *hyperactive* or *hyperactivity*, in the first or second sentence of every paragraph. At the end of paragraph 2 on doctors, she looks ahead to the next two paragraphs on parents and the child. In the conclusion she echoes the distinction first made in the

¶
3e

introduction between the useful hyperactivity of adults and the destructive hyperactivity of children. The combination of these techniques produces a tightly woven analysis that readers can easily understand.

EXERCISE 19

Analyze the ways in which paragraphs combine in the three student essays in Chapter 2, pages 49, 53, and 54. With what techniques, if any, does each writer link paragraphs to the thesis sentence and to each other? Where, if at all, does the writer seem to stray from the thesis or fail to show how paragraphs relate to it? How would you revise the essays to solve any problems they exhibit?

EXERCISE 20

Analyze the paragraphs below for unity, coherence, and development. Identify each paragraph's central idea (even if it is not stated explicitly), any clarification or limitation of the idea, and the shape of the whole. Identify the pattern of organization in each paragraph as well as the devices used to achieve coherence. Identify the method of development.

1. Every American sport directs itself in a general way toward certain segments of American life. Baseball is basically a leisurely, pastoral experience, offering a tableau of athletes against a lush green background, providing moments of action amid longer periods allowed for contemplation of the spectacle. In its relaxed, unhurried way, it is exactly what it claims to be — the national "pastime" rather than an intense, sustained game crammed with action. Born in a rural age, it offers still the appeal of an untroubled island where, for a few hours, a pitcher tugging at his pants leg can seem to be the most important thing in a fan's life.   — PETE AXTHELM, *The City Game*

2. My grandmother was one of millions of immigrants who arrived in this country around 1900. She was ten years old, and she could speak no English. During her first few years here, she lived in tenements and supported herself and her family with menial work in factories. Yet she survived and thrived, changing in a way that parallels the experience of many American immigrants from early in this century. When she died at the age of ninety, she was a retired schoolteacher and the widow of a carpenter. She was living in her own home, close to her four children and ten grandchildren. Over half of her descendants had graduated from college. Her existence was comfortable, secure, and happy.   — A STUDENT

3. The inner life of the White House is essentially the life of the barnyard, as set forth so graphically in the study of the

pecking order among chickens which every freshman sociology
student must read. It is a question of who has the right to peck   2
whom and who must submit to being pecked. There are only   3
two important differences. The first is that the pecking order is   4
determined by the individual strength and forcefulness of each
chicken, whereas in the White House it depends upon the relationship to the barnyard keeper. The second is that no one out-   5
side the barnyard glorifies the chickens and expects them to order the affairs of mankind. They are destined for the frying pan   6
and that is that.

       — GEORGE E. REEDY, *The Twilight of the Presidency*

4.   Shortly after World War II, decades of investigation into   1
the internal workings of the solids yielded a new piece of elec-
tronic hardware called a transistor (for its actual invention,
three scientists at Bell Laboratories won the Nobel Prize). Tran-   2
sistors, a family of devices, alter and control the flow of electricity in circuits; one standard rough analogy compares their
action to that of faucets controlling the flow of water in pipes.
Other devices then in existence could do the same work, but   3
transistors are superior. They are solid. They have no cogs and   4, 5
wheels, no separate pieces to be soldered together; it is as if
they are stones performing useful work. They are durable, take   6
almost no time to start working, and don't consume much
power. Moreover, as physicists and engineers discovered, they   7
could be made very small, indeed microscopic, and they could
be produced cheaply in large quantities.

       — TRACY KIDDER, *The Soul of a New Machine*

5.   As more products and services become available to con-   1
sumers, their quality and effectiveness seem to decline. To   2
avoid unnecessary frustration and expense, consumers should
be well informed before buying products and services. First,   3
they should shop around, hunting among dealers for the best
quality, price, and service available. Second, they should con-   4
sult guides, such as *Consumer Reports*, that are published by
nonprofit product-testing services. Finally, they should refuse   5
to accept oral promises, demand to see relevant contracts and
warranties, and decline to sign or accept any document they do
not fully understand.   — A STUDENT

6.   We may extend this conclusion for hearts to a general   1
statement about the pace of life in small versus large animals.
Small animals tick through life far more rapidly than large ani-   2
mals — their hearts work more quickly, they breathe more frequently, their pulse beats much faster. Most importantly, meta-   3
bolic rate, the so-called fire of life, increases only three-fourths
as fast as body weight in mammals. To keep themselves going,   4
large mammals do not need to generate as much heat per unit
of body weight as small animals. Tiny shrews move frenetically,   5
eating nearly all their waking lives to keep their metabolic fire

burning at the maximal rate among mammals; blue whales glide majestically, their hearts beating the slowest rhythm among active, warm-blooded creatures.

— STEPHEN JAY GOULD, *The Panda's Thumb*

7.   In the presence of grandparent and grandchild, past and future merge in the present. Looking at a loved child, one cannot say, "We must sacrifice this generation for the next. Many must die now so that later others may live." This is the argument that generations of old men, cut off from children, have used in sending young men out to die in war. Nor can one say, "I want this child to live well no matter how we despoil the earth for later generations." For seeing a child as one's grandchild, one can visualize that same child as a grandparent, and with the eyes of another generation one can see other children, just as light-footed and vivid, as eager to learn and know and embrace the world, who must be taken into account — now. My friend Ralph Blum has defined the human unit of time as the space between a grandfather's memory of his own childhood and a grandson's knowledge of those memories as he heard about them. We speak a great deal about a human scale; we need also a human unit in which to think about time.

— MARGARET MEAD, *Blackberry Winter*

4

Convincing
a Reader

In a way, all writing is meant to persuade: You try to convince readers to accept your perspective on a topic. But convincing readers is fundamental in argumentation, when you aim always for readers' agreement with your ideas.

To convince readers that your idea is sound, or even to make them take your argument seriously, you have to follow certain conventional practices of essay development. Your readers will want to know what your idea is, so you will probably state it in a thesis sentence that narrows your topic to a single, specific assertion (see 1d). Your readers will expect you to support your thesis sentence with other, more specific assertions, often the topic sentences of your paragraphs (see 3a). And your readers will expect you to support these assertions in turn with concrete and specific evidence. A well-ordered argument follows this general course. In this chapter we will examine how such an argument is put together and the hazards to be avoided along the way.

4a
Sounding moderate

In Chapter 1 we discussed the way details and tone can gain readers' interest and support. When arguing about ideas, you have a special problem with audience. Readers are naturally (and appropriately) skeptical of what they read, and they often resist being convinced of anything. If they feel a writer is shouting at them, they may see the argument as emotional rather than rational and thus close their minds to it. The best way to open readers' minds to your argument is to write moderately, reasonably, and calmly.

The writer of the following introductory paragraph is not likely to overcome the wariness or resistance of his audience.

log
4a

> Pornography is vile and putrid, the cause of all moral decay and violence in America. It unleashes ugly desires and reduces men and women to their sex organs! It separates the human bond between love and sex. Consequently, it calls for the death of humanity. Pornography must not be tolerated!

No one could doubt the writer's sincerity, but his shrill tone is repellent. He uses absolute words like *all* that allow no exceptions. He punctuates sentences with exclamation marks instead of allowing the strength of his ideas to convey his intensity. And he employs words and phrases like *putrid*, *ugly*, and *death of humanity* that have strong emotional connotations but little rational appeal. If the writer continues this approach throughout the essay, readers who do not already agree with him probably will not be persuaded.

Compare the wild and alienating tone of the preceding paragraph with the more moderate, inviting tone of the one that follows.

> Pornography is a form of free expression that causes a serious social and moral problem. Pornography may well provoke sexual crimes, and it certainly damages the moral tone of society. In addition, it degrades sexual relationships between men and women, substituting mechanical action for love. Because pornography is detrimental to society and to personal relations, it should be strictly controlled, even if free expression must be curtailed.

The writer's opinion has not changed, and we still do not doubt the sincerity of his view. But by casting his ideas in a calmer tone, the writer has invited us to see both him and his argument as reasonable.

As the revised paragraph suggests, a reasonable tone assures your audience that you have weighed the alternatives before arriving at your thesis. To this end you may want to acknowledge an opposing view and then show that it *isn't* reasonable. For example, an argument against expensive athletic programs might begin:

> Athletic directors often claim that athletic programs contribute money to academic programs; in fact, sports do not make money but *cost* money.

Another way to show your objectivity is to admit that an opposing view *is* reasonable but insist (and demonstrate) that your point is more compelling. This tactic is used in the last sentence of the revised paragraph above and in the passage below.

> A nuclear power plant will benefit the economy of this region. Granted, there are dangers associated with nuclear power. But the advantages outweigh the risks.

A moderate tone and an acknowledgment of opposing views give the *appearance* of being reasonable and fair, and to some extent you are what you show yourself to be. However, being reasonable involves not only appearances but also substance. Attending to the substance of an argument is the subject of the following sections.

log.   .
4b.

EXERCISE 1

Revise the following paragraph to make its tone moderate and appealing. Delete or add material as you think necessary to achieve moderation.

Drugs and alcohol are two really stupid ways to escape from reality. People even die from using them. That's escape, all right! The best these excuses for thinking can do is give a minute of relief from disappointment and frustration. Big deal. People are pretty sick to think they're getting anything more.

EXERCISE 2

Moderate the following sentences in one of two ways: either acknowledge a likely opposing view, or acknowledge the given view while asserting the opposite.
1. Fulfilling a science requirement is a waste of time.
2. The best way to solve the energy shortage is to perfect solar technology.
3. In a society as advanced as ours, mail service should be free.
4. The federal and local governments should do more to regulate the quality of children's television.
5. All people convicted of a crime should be jailed for a definite time.

4b
Making assertions believable

Assertions are fundamental to your argument. Thus you want your readers to suspend their natural skepticism and to believe your assertions, even before they read the supporting evidence. In part, the tone you adopt and your openness to opposing views will influence your readers' acceptance of your assertions. But to write believable assertions, you need to be mindful of other factors as well: distinctions among fact, opinion, and prejudice; clearly defined terms; and straightforward confrontation of the issue.

1
Distinguishing fact, opinion, and prejudice

Most assertions you make will be statements of fact, opinion, or prejudice. The category your assertions fall into will partly determine whether readers find them believable or convincing.

A **fact** is verifiable — that is, one can determine whether it is true. It may involve numbers or dates. (*The football field is 100 yards long. World War II ended in 1945.*) Or the numbers may be implied. (*The second book is longer than the first one. The earth is closer to the sun than Saturn is.*) Or the fact may involve no numbers at all. (*The city council adjourned without taking a vote. The forecaster predicts hail.*) If one can assume that measuring devices or records or memories are correct, then the truth of the fact is beyond argument.

An **opinion,** in contrast, is a judgment *based* on facts, an honest attempt to draw a reasonable conclusion from evidence. For example, you know that millions of people go without proper medical care because they can't afford it, and so you form the judgment that the country should institute national health insurance even though it would cost billions of dollars. This opinion expresses a viewpoint. It is contestable because the same facts might lead another person to a different opinion (for instance, that the country simply can't afford national health insurance costing billions of dollars, even if people must go without proper medical care). And an opinion is changeable. With more evidence you might conclude that other national problems such as inflation or unemployment seem as pressing as inadequate medical care. Then you would need to revise your opinion to rank national health insurance as *one of* the nation's top priorities.

Opinions form the backbone of an argument. But stated by themselves, they have little power to convince. You must always let your readers know what your evidence is and how it led you to arrive at each of your opinions (see 4c).

Opinions are not the same as expressions of personal likes and dislikes, such as *I enjoy jazz more than rock music.* Statements like this one are often called opinions because they express a viewpoint. But an opinion can be contested, whereas a statement of preference cannot (would someone say, "No, you don't enjoy jazz more"?). A statement of preference becomes an opinion only when it is reworded to allow the possibility of argument or change. For instance, *Jazz is more complex than rock music* is an opinion.

Be careful never to let a mere prejudice pass as a well-founded opinion. A **prejudice** (or prejudgment) resembles an opinion in that it expresses a viewpoint. However, a prejudice is based on little or no examination of the evidence. Very often we acquire prejudices from others — parents, friends, the communications media — without thinking. *Women belong in the home. Men should not cry. Fat people are jolly.* At best, such assertions oversimplify. *Some* women might be excellent housekeepers, but so might *some* men. At worst, assertions of prejudice reflect a narrow-minded and simplistic view of the world. And writers who are perceived as narrow-minded are not likely to impress their readers with their reasonableness.

2
Defining terms

In any argument, but especially in arguments about abstract ideas, clear and consistent definition of terms is essential. To be understood, the writer of the following paragraph needs to clarify what she means by *justice*.

> What has happened to justice in this country over the past few decades? It seems less often applied than it was when my grandparents were young. In their day both criminal and victim were treated justly. Today, however, neither receives justice.

We know that the writer regrets some change in the way criminals and their victims are dealt with, but other than that we do not know exactly what she is saying. She fails to tell us what *justice* means to her. The word is abstract; it does not refer to anything concrete and in fact has varied meanings. Compare the previous paragraph with the one following, in which the writer is careful to define the abstract word.

> If by "justice" we mean treating people fairly, punishing those who commit crimes and protecting the victims of those crimes, then justice has deteriorated in this country over the past decades. Criminals now receive more explicit protection from the laws — when they are arrested and tried and even if they are imprisoned than their victims do. Thousands of criminals go free every year because an arresting policeman forgot to say a sentence or a prosecuting attorney decided another case was more important. Meanwhile the victims are ignored.

We may need to see how this writer supports her assertions before we can accept them, but at least we have a clear sense of what her terms mean.

3
Facing the question

Almost every argument centers on an issue or question: "Is jazz more complex than rock music?" "Should the country adopt a national health insurance plan?" "Should the town allow a nuclear power plant to be built nearby?" An effective argument faces the central issue squarely. It answers the question by stating relevant opinions about it and supporting those opinions with facts. But facing the question can be difficult. It's often easier to oversimplify complex issues, or to argue superficially about them, than it is to grapple with all the evidence. Sometimes, too, a favored opinion dies hard, though the evidence fails to support it. These circumstances can cause two common faults: begging the question (also called circular reasoning) and ignoring the question by appealing to readers' emotions.

Avoid begging the question

You **beg the question** when you treat an opinion that is open to question as if it were already proved or disproved. (In essence, you are begging your readers to accept your ideas from the start.) For example, if you argue that jazz is more complex than rock music because it is harder to play, then you are begging the question. You are using complexity, as measured by playing difficulty, to establish complexity. Your statement has not proved that jazz is more complex, and you now must also prove that jazz is harder to play. In the meantime your readers may lose patience with your failure to support your view.

The following sentence begs the question in a slightly different way.

> Teenagers should be prevented from having abortions, for they would not become pregnant in the first place if they weren't allowed to terminate their "mistakes."

The writer assumes — and asks us to agree — that the option of having an abortion leads teenagers to unwanted pregnancies; therefore, removing the option of abortion will remove the problem of pregnancy. But how can we agree when we still have no proof for the fundamental assertion? The writer has merely substituted one debatable assumption for another.

Avoid ignoring the question

Writers sometimes attempt to convince readers by supporting assertions exclusively with appeals to the readers' emotions. The effect is to obscure or skip over the real question.

One way to ignore the question is with **appeals to readers' fear, pity, or sense of decency.** The following sentences do not appeal to reason.

> By electing Susan Clark to the city council, you will prevent the city's economic collapse. [Trades on people's fears. Can Clark single-handedly prevent economic collapse?]

> She should not have to pay taxes because she is an aged widow with no friends or relatives. [Touches on people's pity. Should age and loneliness, rather than income, determine a person's tax obligation?]

> Dr. Bowen is an honest man because he attends church regularly and participates in community activities. [Appeals to people's sense of decent behavior. Are churchgoers and community participants necessarily honest?]

Another way to ignore the question is to appeal to readers' sense of what other people believe or do. One approach is **snob appeal,** leading people to accept what you say because they want to be identified with others they admire.

> As any literate person knows, James Joyce is the best twentieth-century novelist. [But what qualities of Joyce's novels make them superior?]

> Paul Newman's support for the governor proves that the governor's doing a good job. [What has the governor actually accomplished?]

Writers sometimes ignore the question by trying to convince readers to agree with them because everybody else does. This is the **bandwagon approach.**

> As everyone knows, marijuana use leads to heroin addiction. [What is the evidence?]

> No one in this town would consider voting for him. [What is the basis for judging him?]

Yet another diversion involves **flattery** of readers, in a way inviting them to conspire with you on your views.

> Since you are thoughtful and perceptive, you know how corrupt the insurance commissioners are. [What is the evidence of corruption?]

> We all understand campus problems well enough to see the disadvantages of such a backward policy. [What are the disadvantages of the policy?]

All these sentences resort to appeals having nothing to do with the issues they raise. A careless reader might be momentarily swayed by snob appeal, the bandwagon approach, or flattery. But a careful reader is more likely to be put off by the writer's evasion.

One final kind of emotional appeal is to address *not* the pros and cons of the issue itself but the real or imagined negative qualities of the people who hold the opposing view. This kind of argument is called ***ad hominem,*** Latin for "to the man."

> We need not listen to her arguments against national health insurance because she is wealthy enough to afford private insurance. [Her wealth does not necessarily discredit her views on health insurance.]

> One of the scientists has been treated for emotional problems, so his pessimism about nuclear war merits no attention. [Do the scientist's previous emotional problems invalidate his current views?]

You'll recognize most of these tricks for ignoring the question from advertising and political campaigns. Are your children's teeth cavity-free? Is your kitchen floor as spotless as your neighbor's? Are you the only person who does not eat a certain brand of cereal? Is that candidate as incompetent as his opponent says? You should be wary of these pitches in what you read and hear, and you should avoid them in your own writing. A skeptical audience is unlikely to be persuaded by them.

EXERCISE 3

Identify the facts (verifiable statements), opinions (judgments based on facts), statements of personal preference, and assertions of prejudice in the following paragraphs.

1.   People probably weren't as interesting before electricity was discovered as they are today. They had many fewer contacts with others outside their immediate circle because printed matter wasn't so widely circulated, and radio and television weren't invented. They knew nothing about the arts except what they could see and hear firsthand at museums and concerts. They must have led deprived lives.

2.   I have always been a simple man. My pleasures consist of stargazing, walking in the woods, and eating homemade ice cream. The frantic pace and the constant bombardment of information experienced by most people are boring to me. I like to live as my grandparents lived.

EXERCISE 4

The following paragraph fails to define important words clearly enough for us to pin down the meaning intended. Identify the undefined terms and revise the paragraph as you see fit to eliminate the problems.

The best solution to current problems is one we don't hear of very often: self-sufficiency. If we were more self-sufficient, we would not have to rely so much on scarce resources to satisfy basic needs. Sure, some of us play at gardening, sewing, and other skills, but very few of us try to free ourselves of the grocery store's vegetables or the department store's clothes. If we were more self-sufficient, we would be more secure, because independence ultimately creates a bond between individuals.

EXERCISE 5

Identify the question raised by each of the following sentences and evaluate the writer's effectiveness in facing the question.

1. Many women are bored with their lives because their jobs are tedious.
2. Steven McRae spends too much time making himself look good to be an effective spokesman for the student body.

3. Teenagers are too young to be allowed to drink alcoholic beverages.
4. Giving nuclear capability to emerging nations is dangerous because they will probably use it to wage war.
5. Our souls are immortal because they are not made of matter and thus are indestructible.

EXERCISE 6

Leaf through a magazine or watch television for half an hour, looking for advertisements that attempt to sell a product not on the basis of its worth but by snob appeal, flattery, or appeals to emotions. Be prepared to discuss the advertisers' techniques.

4c
Supporting the assertions

As crucial as they are, moderate and believable assertions are only the beginning of a convincing argument. You must also support your assertions with evidence — the substance of any argument. Making reasonable assertions keeps your readers' minds open only long enough to get them to the evidence. If the evidence proves unsatisfactory, then your cause will be lost.

The kinds of evidence available to writers came up earlier in the context of paragraph development (see 3c-1). There you saw that to engage or convince readers, you must support your general assertions with concrete and specific details, examples, and reasons. Consider the information supplied by the author of the following paragraph to support his assertion (made earlier in his article and echoed below) that the Soviet Union would suffer considerable damage if it launched a surprise nuclear attack against the United States.

> No Soviet attack on the United States could preclude a devastating counterattack on the Soviet Union. This is because it only takes a small number of nuclear weapons to inflict awesome damage on any attacker. And the United States has *thousands* of nuclear warheads that can be delivered by a diverse array of vehicles. There is no technical possibility of an attack so successful as to deprive the United States of the number of warheads needed for a second strike of unprecedented devastation. Such a response aimed at the highly concentrated Soviet industrial base would destroy the USSR as a modern industrial state. There is no way Russian leaders could ever hope to "win" a nuclear war, and they know it. — HENRY KENDALL, "Second Strike"

The author supports his assertion about Soviet vulnerability with a complex and detailed reason: Not all of the thousands of nuclear warheads possessed by the United States would be destroyed in a surprise attack, and the remaining warheads could in turn destroy Soviet industry.

To support your assertions and convince readers, your evidence must meet four criteria: It must be *accurate, relevant, representative,* and *adequate.*

Accurate evidence is drawn from reliable sources, quoted exactly, and presented with the original meaning unchanged. In researching an essay in favor of gun control, for instance, you might consult statistics provided by the anticontrol National Rifle Association as well as those provided by procontrol groups to ensure that your evidence is sound from both perspectives. In quoting excerpts as evidence, be careful to preserve their true meaning, not just a few words that happen to support your argument. For instance, you would distort the writer's meaning if you quoted the first sentence in the following passage as evidence of the positive effects of television.

> Television can be an effective force for education and understanding, for appreciation of people and their troubles and accomplishments. But it assumes that role so rarely that we have only fleeting glimpses of the possibilities. We know better the dull-witted, narrow-minded fare that monopolizes the set from one year to the next.

(See 35e and Appendix A for more information on quoting from sources.)

Relevant evidence comes from sources with authority on your topic and relates directly to your point. Unless your uncle is a recognized expert on the Central Intelligence Agency, or unless you can establish his authority, his opinion of whether the CIA meddles illegally in other countries' affairs is not relevant to your paper on the subject. If your uncle is a member of the town council, however, his views may very well be relevant evidence in your essay on how a new shopping mall will hurt the town merchants.

Evidence is representative when it reflects the full range of the sample from which it is said to be drawn. For instance, in an essay arguing that dormitories should stay open during school holidays, you might want to cite the opinions of the school's 5000 students. But you would mislead readers if, on the basis of a poll among your roommates and dormitory neighbors, you reported as evidence that "the majority of students favor leaving the dormitories open." A few dormitory residents could not be said to represent the entire student body, particularly the nonresident students. To be representative, your poll would have to take in many more students in proportions that reflect the numbers of resident and nonresident students on campus.

Evidence is adequate when it is plentiful and specific enough to support your assertions. To convince readers of your opinion, you must tell them what information you base it on. If you are writing an essay about animal abuse, you cannot hope to win over your readers solely with statements like *Too many animals are deliberately injured or killed by humans every year.* You need to supply facts instead of the vague *too many*. How many animals are injured? How many die? You need to specify the conditions under which animals are injured or killed. And you need to demonstrate that the actions are deliberate, perhaps with examples of animal abuse. Adequate, well-selected evidence is crucial to an effective argument.

EXERCISE 7

Supply at least two specific details, examples, or reasons to support each of the following general assertions.

1. A college education should not cost as much as it does.
2. _____ is the television program (or movie, or both) that best shows life as it really is.
3. _____ is an example of a good teacher (or doctor, lawyer, politician, parent).
4. Americans are energy spendthrifts.
5. Superman is a great hero.

EXERCISE 8

Locate the details, examples, and reasons in the following paragraphs, and evaluate the quality of the evidence against the four criteria of accuracy, relevancy, representativeness, and adequacy.

1. Our rivers and streams are becoming choked by pollution. For example, swimming is now prohibited along stretches of the Mississippi River. My minister says there are portions of the river where fish can't survive. Are we a nation that does not care enough about its resources to conserve them?

2. Crime is out of control in this city. Three months ago my parents' house was burglarized. The thieves stole their food processor and their vibrating bed as well as their television and stereo. Then a month ago my roommate had her pocket picked on the subway. And last week I saw a confused old man trying to describe to the police how muggers had stolen his wallet and his groceries as he walked home from the corner market.

4d

Reasoning effectively

Our discussion so far in this chapter has mostly concerned the attributes that make an argument convincing to readers. But constructing an argument requires an understanding of the two ways in which people tend to reason, inductively and deductively. These methods figure not only in our formal writing but also in our everyday activities, as the following example illustrates.

You want to buy a reliable used car. In thinking of what kind of car to buy, you follow specific steps of reasoning. (1) You consider your friends' experiences with used cars: One has had to spend a lot of money to repair her used Volkswagen; another has complained that his used Ford handles badly; and three others have raved about their used Toyotas. (2) You recall an article in *Consumer Reports* rating Toyota highest among used cars. (3) You conclude that Toyota is the most reliable used car. So far your reasoning is **inductive.** You have made a series of observations about the reliability of different used cars. And you have induced, or inferred, from those observations the generalization that Toyota is the most reliable used car. The **generalization** is based on the assumption that what is applicable in one set of circumstances (your friends' experiences, *Consumer Reports'* tests) is or will be applicable as well in a similar set of circumstances (your own experiences). Having thus reasoned inductively, you then proceed with **deductive** reasoning, from the generalization to particular circumstances. You start with a premise (you want to buy a reliable used car), apply to it a generalization you believe to be true (Toyota is the most reliable used car), and reach a conclusion (you want to buy a used Toyota).

As this example demonstrates, induction and deduction are fundamental to our thought. They derive from our experience of the world as coherent (with one event related to another) and not fragmented. We activate these reasoning processes effortlessly and habitually in the daily business of living. We employ them more consciously in organizing essays and paragraphs from specific to general (inductively) and from general to specific (deductively). (See 1f-1 and 3b-1.) But we need to use them methodically in reasoning about complex ideas: for instance, when evaluating the thinking of others or when trying to convince others to accept our views.

1

Reasoning inductively

Induction is the dominant method of reasoning in two situations: generalizing from observations and attributing a cause to a set of observed circumstances.

We saw an example of generalizing from observations in the identification of a reliable used car. In another case you might observe that few students attend showings of the school film society, which presents only serious foreign films; that your college friends seem to prefer science-fiction, adventure, and horror movies; and that a magazine article says these three kinds of entertainment films are most popular with people under twenty-five. From these observations you infer that most college students prefer entertainment movies. The more students you talk to and the more you read about the subject, the more certain you can be that your generalization is true.

Attributing a cause to circumstances is essentially the same process as generalizing from observations. You and your friends, and presumably most students, prefer science-fiction, adventure, and horror movies. These movies entertain you and offer relief from studying. The chairman of the student film society, however, programs only weighty foreign films, and few students attend. From these observations you conclude that the chairman is unaware of students' needs and preferences. True, with a little imagination you could also conclude that the chairman knows students' preferences but is determined to ignore them because he is a snob. You could even conclude that he is ignoring them because he wants to learn foreign languages. But the conclusion you do draw is the simplest because it adheres to the available evidence: The chairman does not demonstrate awareness of students' preferences. And the simplest explanation of cause, based exclusively on what you know, is usually more reasonable than the more elaborate one for which you must invent supporting facts.

The more evidence you have, the more likely it is that your generalizations are valid, but you can't know for certain that they are correct. You can only ensure that your generalizations are reasonable — sound conclusions based on sound evidence — and that your readers perceive them as such.

2
Reasoning deductively

You reason deductively when you use some assertions to arrive at others. As when you determined that you should buy a used Toyota, in deduction you apply generalizations or conclusions that are accepted as true to slightly different but similar situations or issues. For example, if you know that all male members of your psychology class are on the football squad, and Albert is in the psychology class, then you conclude that Albert must be on the football squad. This group of three statements constitutes a **syllogism,** two

log
4d

premises stating facts or judgments that together lead to a conclusion.

1. *Premise:* English papers containing sentence fragments receive poor grades.
2. *Premise:* Your English paper contains sentence fragments.
3. *Conclusion:* Your English paper will receive a poor grade.

The first premise states a generalization arrived at by induction. The
second premise states a specific case of the generalization. The conclusion derives logically from the two premises.

Deductive reasoning underlies many arguments you read or
write. The force of such arguments depends on the reliability of the
premises and the care with which you apply them in drawing new
conclusions. Two common sources of difficulty with deduction are
unstated premises and overstated premises.

In many deductive arguments the basic premise is not explicitly stated but is understood. For instance:

Harold lived in Boston for several years, so he should know how to
get to the ball park. [Unstated premise: Anyone who lived in Boston should know the way to the ball park.]

As student-government president, Jordan will have to deal with
conflicting demands from all sides. [Unstated premise: A student-
government president must deal with conflicting demands.]

Problems arise when the unstated premise is wrong or unfounded,
as in the following sentences.

Since Jane Lightbow is a senator, she must receive money illegally
from lobbyists. [Unstated premise: All senators receive money illegally from lobbyists.]

Now that Sally Matlock's mother is in jail, Sally will become a behavior problem. [Unstated premise: All children whose mothers
are jailed become behavior problems.]

As these sentences show, when reasoning deductively you must
carefully examine your basic premises, especially when they are implied.

The second common problem in deduction, overstated premises, results from the difficulty in making a generalization that will
apply to all instances, since ordinarily we must base any generalization on only a few instances. When such generalizations are
premises in a deductive argument, they must contain or imply limiting words like *some, many,* and *often,* rather than absolute words
like *all, no one, never,* or *always.* Compare the difference in reasonableness in the following pairs of sentences.

OVERSTATED	Parents are *always* too busy to help their children solve problems.
MODIFIED	Parents are *often* too busy to help their children solve problems.
OVERSTATED	Movie theater ushers *are* a thing of the past; one *never* sees them in cinema complexes.
MODIFIED	Movie theater ushers *may be* a thing of the past; one *rarely* sees them in cinema complexes.

log
4d

Even when a premise sounds reasonable, it still must be supportable. For instance, modifying the unstated assumption about Senator Lightbow might result in this sentence:

Since Jane Lightbow is a senator, she might receive money illegally from lobbyists. [Unstated premise: *Some* senators receive money illegally from lobbyists.]

But it does not necessarily follow that Senator Lightbow is one of the "some." The sentence, though logical, is not truly reasonable unless evidence demonstrates that Senator Lightbow should be linked with illegal activities.

3
Avoiding faulty reasoning

Some kinds of faulty inductive and deductive reasoning — errors called **fallacies** — are common in all sorts of writing. Like begging the question or appealing to emotions rather than reason, these fallacies weaken an argument.

Hasty generalization

A **hasty generalization** is one based on too little evidence or on evidence that is unrepresentative (see 4c). For example:

Because it trains one for work, business is the only major worth pursuing. [Other majors train one for work, and other students may have different goals.]

When attendance is down and the team is losing, the basketball coach should be fired. [The sentence does not allow for other influences on the team's performance.]

A variation of the hasty generalization involves the use of absolute words like *all, always, never,* and *no one* when your evidence cannot support such terms and what you really mean is *some, sometimes, rarely,* and *few* (see also above).

Another common hasty generalization is the **stereotype,** a conventional and oversimplified characterization of a group of people.

log
4d

The ideas that the French are good lovers, the British reserved, and the Italians emotional are stereotypes. When you apply such a characterization to an individual Frenchman or Briton or Italian, you extend a prejudice, a judgment not based on evidence (see p. 108). Here are several other stereotypes: *People who live in cities are unfriendly. Californians are fad-crazy. Women are emotional. Men are less expressive than women.*

Oversimplification

A frequent fallacy in writing is **oversimplification** of the relation between causes and their effects. The fallacy (sometimes called the **reductive fallacy**) often involves linking two events as if one caused the other directly, whereas the causes may be more complex or the relation may not exist at all. For example:

> Poverty causes crime. [If so, then why do people who are not poor commit crimes? And why aren't all poor people criminals?]

> The better a school's athletic facilities are, the worse its academic programs are. [The sentence seems to assume a direct cause-and-effect link between athletics and scholarship.]

Post hoc *fallacy*

Related to oversimplification of cause and effect is the fallacy of assuming that because *A* preceded *B*, then *A* must have caused *B*. This fallacy is called in Latin *post hoc, ergo propter hoc*, which means "after this, therefore because of this," or the ***post hoc*** **fallacy** for short. Here are a definition and example from the humorist Max Shulman, followed by two more examples of the fallacy at work.

> "Next comes Post Hoc. Listen to this: Let's not take Bill on our picnic. Every time we take him out with us, it rains."
>
> "I know somebody just like that," she exclaimed. "A girl back home — Eula Becker, her name is. It never fails. Every single time we take her on a picnic —"
>
> "Polly," I said sharply, "it's a fallacy. Eula Becker doesn't *cause* the rain. She has no connection with the rain. You are guilty of Post Hoc if you blame Eula Becker."
>
> — MAX SHULMAN, "Love Is a Fallacy"

> In the two months since he took office, Mayor Holcomb has allowed unemployment in the city to increase 2 percent. [The increase in unemployment is no doubt attributable to conditions existing before Holcomb took office.]

> The town council erred in permitting the adult bookstore to open, for shortly afterward two women were assaulted. [It cannot be assumed without evidence that the women's assailants visited or were influenced by the bookstore.]

Either . . . or fallacy

In the **either . . . or fallacy** you assume that a complicated question has only two answers, one good and one bad, or both bad.

> City policemen are either brutal or corrupt.

> Either we institute national health insurance or thousands of people will become sick or die.

Like the illustrations of the previous fallacies, these sentences oversimplify complex issues and relationships to make the writer's perspective seem convincing. But no careful reader would be fooled. Many city policemen are neither brutal nor corrupt. And allowing people to sicken or die is not necessarily the only alternative to national health insurance.

Non sequitur

A **non sequitur** occurs when no logical relation exists between two or more connected ideas. In Latin *non sequitur* means "it does not follow." In the sentences below, the second thought does not follow from the first.

> If high school English were easier, fewer students would have trouble with the college English requirement. [Presumably, if high school English were easier, students would have more trouble.]

> Kathleen Newsome has my vote for mayor because she has the best-run campaign organization. [Shouldn't one's vote be based on the candidate's qualities, not the campaign organization's?]

False analogy

An **analogy** is a comparison between two essentially unlike things for the purpose of definition or illustration. (We saw analogy used in paragraph development; see 3c-2.) In arguing by analogy, you draw a likeness between things on the basis of a single shared feature and then extend the likeness to other features. But analogy can only illustrate a point, never prove it. It can trick you into assuming that because things are similar in one respect, they *must* be alike in other respects. Here is an example of this fallacy, which is called **false analogy.**

> The nonhuman primates like chimpanzees and gorillas care for their young, clean and groom each other, and defend themselves and sometimes the group from attack. Why, then, must the human primates go so much further — Medicare, child care, welfare, Social Security, and so on — to protect the weak? [Taken to its logical extreme, this analogy would lead us to ask why we speak to each other when gorillas do not.]

log
4d

EXERCISE 9

Study the following facts and then evaluate each of the numbered conclusions below them. Which of the generalizations are reasonable given the evidence, and which are not?

> Between the 1970 and 1980 national censuses, the population of the United States increased 11.4 percent, to 226,504,825.
> The percentage increase from 1950 to 1960 was 18.5 percent; from 1960 to 1970, 13.3 percent.
> The population of the South and West regions increased 21.4 percent between 1970 and 1980.
> The population of the Northeast and North Central regions increased just over 2 percent between 1970 and 1980.
> Over 52 percent of the nation's people now live in the South and the West.

1. The population of the United States continues to grow at the rapid pace set after World War II.
2. Americans increasingly prefer to live in the Sun Belt states of the South and West regions rather than in the states of the Northeast and North Central regions.
3. Many Americans prefer the pleasant climate of the South and West regions to the harsh climate of the Northeast and North Central regions.

EXERCISE 10

Supply the element needed to complete each of the following syllogisms.
1. a. Cigarette smokers risk lung cancer.
   b.
   c. Therefore, cigarette smokers risk death.
2. a. The challenging courses are the good ones.
   b. Biology is a challenging course.
   c.
3. a.
   b. That child receives no individual attention.
   c. Therefore, that child learns slowly.
4. a. Discus throwers develop large pectoral muscles.
   b.
   c. Therefore, Warren has large pectoral muscles.
5. a.
   b. Enrollments will certainly decline.
   c. Therefore, the school will close.

EXERCISE 11

Each of the sentences below contains one of the following: a generalization based on inadequate or invented evidence, or a deduction based on a faulty, unstated assumption or on an overstated assumption. Determine where each sentence goes wrong and revise it to make it more effective.

1. Since capital punishment prevents murder, it should be the mandatory sentence for all murderers.
2. With a mayor who was once the president of a manufacturing company, our city will experience increased air pollution because environmental controls will not be enforced.
3. The only way to be successful in the United States is to make money, because Americans measure success by income.
4. Keeping the library open until midnight has caused the increase in late-night crime on the campus.
5. Government demands so much honesty that we should not leave it to lawyers and professional politicians.

EXERCISE 12

The following sentences exemplify the fallacies discussed in the text: hasty generalization, oversimplification, *post hoc* fallacy, either . . . or fallacy, non sequitur, and false analogy. Identify the fallacy or fallacies that each sentence illustrates, and revise the sentence to make it more effective.

1. A successful marriage demands a maturity that no one under twenty-five possesses.
2. Students' persistent complaints about the grading system prove that it is unfair.
3. The United States got involved in World War II because the Japanese bombed Pearl Harbor.
4. People watch television because they are too lazy to talk or read or because they want mindless escape from their lives.
5. Working people are slaves to their corporate masters: They have no freedom to do what they want, and they can be traded to other companies.
6. The stories about welfare chiselers show that the welfare system supports only shirkers and cheats.
7. Mountain climbing is more dangerous than people think: My cousin has fainted three times since he climbed Pike's Peak.
8. Racial tension is bound to occur when people with different backgrounds are forced to live side by side.
9. If the United States does not supply military assistance to Central and South American countries, we will eventually be subjected to Communism.
10. She admits to being an atheist, so how can she be a good philosophy teacher?

EXERCISE 13

Evaluate the following brief essay for its effectiveness in convincing you (or any reader) to accept the writer's argument. Look especially for a moderate tone, believable assertions, adequate support for assertions, and sound inductive or deductive reasoning. Identify the writer's generalizations and evaluate their reasonableness. Do you see examples of any of the faults discussed in this chapter, such as begging or ignoring the question, overstating assumptions, or slipping into faulty reasoning?

Let's Hear It for Asphalt

The truly disadvantaged students on this campus are the commuters. We pay our money and work hard for our degrees, yet we can never find places to park our cars. Commuters are regularly treated as second-class citizens compared to resident students. But nowhere is the discrepancy more noticeable than in the parking situation.

The fact is, there aren't enough parking spaces for half the cars on campus. Students are lucky to make their classes at all after driving around for hours looking for a place to stop their car. If parking were easier, students would get better grades, and the school administrators would probably have the higher enrollments they're so desperate for.

The most maddening thing is that we have to pay good money for parking tickets on top of tuition and everything else. The money probably goes toward a new faculty office building or dormitory or one of the other building projects that eat up what little parking space there is. Meanwhile, we commuters are pushed farther and farther away from the center of campus. But then why should the rich folks in charge of things care what happens to a few struggling students, some with families to support, who seek to better themselves?

The commuting students are like the Jews wandering in the wilderness. We need homelands for our cars and freedom from persecution by campus cops.

II
Grammatical
Sentences

5
Understanding Sentence Grammar

Grammar describes how language works and enables us to talk about it. People who are experts in grammar don't always write well, and many people who write well no longer think consciously about grammar and would have difficulty explaining in grammatical terms how their sentences work. But when something goes wrong in a sentence, a knowledge of grammar helps in recognizing the problem and provides a language for discussing it.

Grammar can help us understand sentences even if we don't know the meaning of all the words in the sentence.

The rumfrum biggled the pooba.

We don't know what that sentence means. But we can infer that something called a *rumfrum* did something to a *pooba*. He (or she, or it) *biggled* it, whatever that means. We know this because we understand the basic grammar of simple English sentences. We understand that this sentence seems like *The boy kicked the ball* or *The student passed the test*. As in those sentences, a single word following *the* names something; words with *-ed* endings usually denote action of some sort, especially when they fall in patterns like *the rumfrum biggled;* and word groups beginning with *the* and *that,* coming after words like *biggled,* usually name something that receives the action indicated.

In the sense that we understand *The rumfrum biggled the pooba*, we can understand more complex sentences such as the following:

The stintless rumfrums biggled the jittish poobas who were kerpesting the gloots.

We don't know what *stintless* and *jittish* mean, but we do know that they describe *rumfrums* and *poobas,* respectively, and that the *poobas were kerpesting* (doing something to) *the gloots,* probably more

126

than one *gloot*. We understand these relations among the words because we recognize familiar structures that recur in everyday talking and writing. Each statement about rumfrums is a **sentence,** the
basic unit of writing.

5a
Understanding the basic sentence

The basic grammar of sentences consists of the kinds of words
that compose them, the functions of those words, the patterns on
which sentences are built, and the ways those patterns can be expanded and elaborated. Understanding basic grammar can help you
create clear sentences that effectively relate your ideas.

1
Identifying subjects and predicates

Most sentences make statements. First they name something;
then they make an assertion about or describe an action involving
that something. These two sentence parts are the **subject** and the
predicate.

SUBJECT	PREDICATE
Amanda	took the money to the bank.
Leroy	rode his bicycle down the middle of the street.
All the members of my family	were churchgoers from their earliest years.

2
Identifying the basic words: Nouns and verbs

If we study the five simple sentences below, we find that they
consist almost entirely of two quite different kinds of words.

SUBJECT	PREDICATE
The earth	trembled.
The earthquake	destroyed the city.
The result	was chaos.
The government	sent the city aid.
The citizens	declared the earthquake a disaster.

In these sentences words like *earth, earthquake, government,*
and *citizen* name things, but words like *trembled, destroyed,* and *sent*
express actions. These two groups of words work in different ways.
We can have one *earthquake* or several *earthquakes,* one *citizen* or

many *citizens;* but we cannot have one or more *declareds* or *destroyeds.* If we drop the *-ed* from *destroyed* or the *-d* from *declared,* we change the time of the action. But we cannot add *-ed* to *citizen* and have a form *citizened.* The word *citizen* just doesn't work that way.

Grammar reflects these differences by identifying **parts of speech** or **word classes.** Except for the words *the* and *a,* which simply point to and help identify the words after them, our five sentences consist of two parts of speech: **nouns,** words that name; and **verbs,** words that express an action or an occurrence or a state of being. These are the basic words in English; without them we cannot form even the simplest sentences. The nouns and verbs in our sample sentences appear below.

NOUNS	VERBS
earth	trembled
earthquake	destroyed
result	was
government	sent
citizens	declared
city	
chaos	
aid	
disaster	

We can identify nouns and verbs both by their meanings and by their forms.

Nouns

MEANING

Nouns name. They may name a person (*Paul McCartney, Johnny Carson, father*), a thing (*chair, book, spaceship*), a quality (*pain, mystery, simplicity*), a place (*city, Washington, ocean, Red Sea*), or an idea (*reality, peace, success*). Whatever exists or can be thought to exist has a name. Its name is a noun.

FORM

Almost all nouns that name countable things add an *-s* to distinguish between the singular, meaning "one," and the plural, meaning "more than one": *earthquake, earthquakes; city, cities; citizen, citizens.* A few nouns form irregular plurals: *man, men; child, children; goose, geese.* Nouns also form a possessive by adding *-'s: citizen, citizen's; city, city's; father, father's.* This possessive form shows ownership (*Sheila's books*) and source (*Auden's poems*) as well as some other relationships.

Some nouns in our sample sentences — *chaos* and *earth* — do not usually form plurals. These words belong to a subgroup called **mass nouns.** They name something that is not usually countable, like *sugar, silver,* and *gravel;* or they name qualities, like *courage, fortitude,* and *anger.* Other important groups of nouns not illustrated in our sentences are **proper nouns** such as *Betty, Detroit,* and *Amazon,* which name specific people, places, and things; and **collective nouns** such as *army, family,* and *herd,* which name groups.

NOUNS WITH *THE, A,* AND *AN*

Nouns are often preceded by *the* or *a* (*an* before a vowel sound: *an apple*). These words are usually called **articles,** but they may be described as **noun markers** since they always indicate that a noun will soon follow.

Verbs

MEANING

Verbs express an action (*bring, change, grow*), an occurrence (*become, happen*), or a state of being (*be, seem*).

FORM

Almost all verbs change form to indicate a difference between present and past time. To show past time, most verbs add *-d* or *-ed* to the form listed in the dictionary: *They play today. They played yesterday.* A few verbs indicate past time irregularly: *eat, ate; begin, began.* (See 7a.)

All verbs except *be* and *have* add *-s* or *-es* to their dictionary forms when their subjects are singular nouns or singular pronouns such as *he, she,* and *it: The bear escapes. It escapes. The woman begins. She begins.* When their subjects are plural nouns or pronouns, verbs retain their dictionary forms: *The bears escape. The women begin.* The *-s* forms of *be* and *have* are *is* and *has;* and *are* is the form of *be* with plural subjects. (See Chapter 7, pp. 169–76, for a fuller discussion of verb forms.)

VERBS WITH AUXILIARIES

The dictionary form of all verbs can combine with the words *do, does, did, can, could, may, might, will, would, shall, should,* and *must: could run, may escape, must help.* These words are called **auxiliary verbs** or **helping verbs.** They and a few others combine with special forms of verbs to make verb phrases such as *will be running, might have escaped,* and *could have been helped.* (See Chapter 7, pp. 170–71.)

gr
5a

A note on form and function

In different sentences an English word may serve different functions, take correspondingly different forms, and belong to different word classes. For example, *aid* functions as a noun in the sentence *The government sent the city aid.* But in *The government aids the city*, the word *aid* functions as a verb, taking the characteristic *-s* ending of a verb with a singular subject, *government.* In *The light burns*, the word *light* functions as a noun; but in *The lanterns light the path*, the word *light* functions as a verb. Because words can function in different ways, we must always determine how a particular word works in a sentence before we can identify what part of speech it is. The *function* of a word in a sentence always determines its part of speech in that sentence.

Pronouns

Before looking at the five basic sentence patterns in English, we need to look at a third small but important group of words, the pronouns.

> Susanne enlisted in the Air Force. *She* leaves for her training in two weeks. Susanne is one of the people *who* took advanced physics in high school.

Most **pronouns** substitute for nouns and function in sentences as nouns do. In the sentences above, the pronoun *she* substitutes for *Susanne*, and the pronoun *who* substitutes for *people.*

Pronouns fall into several subclasses depending on their form or function. **Personal pronouns** refer to a specific individual or to individuals. They are *I, you, he, she, it, we,* and *they.* **Indefinite pronouns,** such as *everybody* and *some*, do not substitute for any specific nouns, though they function as nouns (*Everybody likes Tim*). **Demonstrative pronouns,** including *this, that,* and *such*, identify or point to nouns (*This is the gun she used*). The **relative pronouns** *who, which,* and *that* relate groups of words to nouns or other pronouns (*Jim spoke to the boys who broke the window*). Intensive and reflexive pronouns have different functions but the same form: a personal pronoun plus *-self* (*himself, yourself*). **Intensive pronouns** emphasize a noun or other pronoun (*She herself asked the question*). **Reflexive pronouns** indicate that the sentence subject also receives the action of the verb (*You might hurt yourself*). Finally, **interrogative pronouns,** including *who, which,* and *what*, introduce questions (*Who will come to the concert?*).

The personal pronouns *I, he, she, we, they* and the relative pronoun *who* change form depending on their function in the sentence. (For a discussion of these form changes, see Chapter 6.)

EXERCISE 1

Identify the subject and the predicate of each sentence below. Then use each sentence as a model for creating a sentence of your own.

Example:

The Aeronautics and Space Museum displays a moon rock.

SUBJECT   PREDICATE
The Aeronautics and Space Museum | displays a moon rock.

The new car contains a tape player.

1. The radio fell.
2. Summer ends soon.
3. My brother's dog had fourteen puppies.
4. People should think carefully before joining cults.
5. Several important people will speak at commencement.

EXERCISE 2

In the sentences below, identify all words functioning as nouns with *N*, all words functioning as verbs with *V*, and all pronouns with *P*.

Example:

We took the tour through the museum

P   V   N   N
We took the *tour* through the *museum.*

1. The trees they planted are dying of blight.
2. The new speed limit has prevented many accidents.
3. Although I was absent for a month, I finished the semester with good grades.
4. When the lights went out, she looked for candles.
5. Drivers must pass a new test every ten years, or they may not drive.

EXERCISE 3

Identify each of the following words as a noun, as a verb, or as both. Then create sentences of your own, using each word in each possible function.

Example:

fly
Noun and verb.
The *fly* sat on the meat loaf. [Noun.] The planes *fly* low. [Verb.]

1. car	5. whistle	8. post
2. label	6. condition	9. attic
3. door	7. sing	10. glue
4. company		

3

Forming sentence patterns with nouns and verbs

Our five sample sentences reappear below with an *N* over each noun and a *V* over each verb.

          N   V

1. The earth trembled.

          N   V   N

2. The earthquake destroyed the city.

          N   V   N

3. The result was chaos.

          N   V   N N

4. The government sent the city aid.

          N   V   N   N

5. The citizens declared the earthquake a disaster.

These five sentences typify the five basic patterns on which we build all our sentences, even the most complex. The subjects of the sentences are similar, consisting only of a noun and an article or marker. But each predicate is different from the others because the relation between the verb and any remaining words is different. Let's examine each pattern in turn.

Pattern 1: The earth trembled.

In the simplest pattern the predicate consists only of the verb. Verbs in this pattern do not require following words to complete their meaning and thus are called **intransitive** (from Latin words meaning "not passing over").

SUBJECT	PREDICATE
	Intransitive verb
The earth	trembled.
Mosquitoes	bite.
Spring	will come.
We	have been swimming.

Pattern 2: The earthquake destroyed the city.

In sentence 2 the predicate consists of a verb followed by a noun. The noun completes the meaning of the verb by identifying who or what receives the action of the verb. This noun is a **direct object** (DO). Verbs that require direct objects to complete their meaning are called **transitive** ("passing over").

SUBJECT	PREDICATE	
	Transitive verb	*Direct object*
The earthquake	destroyed	the city.
The man	stubbed	his toe.
The people	wanted	peace.

gr
5a

Pattern 3: The result was chaos.

In sentence 3 the predicate also consists of a verb followed by a single noun. But here the verb *was* serves merely to introduce a word that renames or describes the subject. We could write the sentence *The result = chaos.* The noun following the verb in this kind of sentence is a **subject complement** (SC), or a **predicate noun.** Verbs in this pattern are called **linking verbs** because they simply link their subjects to the description that follows.

SUBJECT	PREDICATE	
	Linking verb	*Subject complement*
The result	was	chaos.
Jamison	is	an engineer.
The woman	became	an accountant.

Notice that subject complements in this sentence pattern may also be adjectives, words such as *tall, hopeful, large,* and *blind* (See 5b-1). Adjectives serving as complements are sometimes called **predicate adjectives.**

SUBJECT	PREDICATE	
	Linking verb	*Subject complement*
The result	was	chaotic.
The house	seemed	expensive.

Pattern 4: The government sent the city aid.

In sentence 4 the predicate consists of a verb followed by two nouns. The second noun is a direct object, identifying what was sent. But the first noun, *city,* is different. This noun is an **indirect object** (IO), identifying to or for whom or what the action of the verb is performed.

SUBJECT	PREDICATE		
	Transitive verb	*Indirect object*	*Direct object*
The government	sent	the city	aid.
Neighbors	gave	the dog	a bone.
The boys	asked	the man	a question.
George	tossed	me	an apple.

Pattern 5: *The citizens declared the earthquake a disaster.*

In sentence 5 the predicate again consists of a verb followed by two nouns. But in this pattern the first noun is a direct object and the second noun renames or describes it. Here the second noun is an **object complement** (OC).

SUBJECT	PREDICATE		
	Transitive verb	*Direct object*	*Object complement*
The citizens	declared	the earthquake	a disaster.
The manager	made	him	an assistant.
The class	elected	Joan	president.

Notice that the relation between a direct object and an object complement is the same as that between a subject and a subject complement in pattern 3. Just as the subject complement renames or describes a subject, so an object complement renames or describes a direct object. And just as we can use either nouns or adjectives in pattern 3, so we can use either nouns or adjectives as object complements in this last pattern.

SUBJECT	PREDICATE		
	Transitive verb	*Direct object*	*Object complement*
The citizens	declared	the earthquake	disastrous.
The people	considered	the building	beautiful.

The five sentence patterns above are the basic frameworks for most written English sentences. However long or complicated a sentence is, one or more of these basic patterns forms its foundation. A question may change the order of the subject and verb (*Is she a doctor?*), a command may omit the subject entirely (*Be quiet!*), and the order of the parts may be different in some statements (see 5e), but the same basic sentence parts will be present or clearly understood.

EXERCISE 4

In the sentences below, identify each verb as intransitive, transitive, or linking. Then identify each direct object (DO), indirect object (IO), subject complement (SC), and object complement (OC).

Example:

Parents offer their children not only love but also support.

Offer is a transitive verb.

                        IO   DO   DO

Parents offer their *children* not only *love* but also *support*.

1. Marie calls her boy friend a genius.
2. The dentist's bill was five hundred dollars.
3. Many adults find rock concerts strange.
4. I read my brother *Charlotte's Web.*
5. Then I bought him his own copy.
6. Moderate exercise is good for your heart.
7. My brothers argued.
8. The counterfeiter was a child.
9. The newspapers proclaimed the election an upset.
10. The magician showed the audience his tricks.

gr
5b

EXERCISE 5

Create a sentence by using each verb below in the pattern indicated.

> *Example:* send (S–V–IO–DO)
> Sue sent her teacher a note.

1. catch (S–V–DO)
2. bring (S–V–IO–DO)
3. cry (S–V)
4. think (S–V–DO–OC)
5. seem (S–V–SC)
6. call (S–V–DO–OC)
7. become (S–V–SC)
8. watch (S–V–DO)
9. buy (S–V–IO–DO)
10. study (S–V)

5b

Expanding the basic sentence with single words

We have been studying simple sentences and their basic structures. But most of the sentences we read, write, or speak are longer and more complex. Most sentences contain one or more of the following: (1) modifying words; (2) word groups, called phrases and clauses; or (3) combinations of two or more words or word groups of the same kind. These sentence expanders are the subjects of this and the next two sections.

1

Using adjectives and adverbs

The simplest expansion of sentences occurs when we add modifying words to describe or limit the nouns and verbs. Modifying words add details.

Recently, the earth trembled.

The earthquake *nearly* destroyed the *old* city.

The *frantic* citizens *quickly* declared the earthquake a *complete* disaster.

The added words do not all act the same way. *Old, frantic,* and *complete* modify nouns, but *recently, nearly,* and *quickly* do not. We don't speak of a *recently earthquake* or a *quickly citizen.* Nor do we say *frantic declared* or *complete destroyed.* We are encountering two different parts of speech. **Adjectives** (such as *old, frantic, complete, heartless, friendly*) describe or modify nouns and pronouns. **Adverbs** (such as *recently, nearly, quickly, never, always*) describe the action of verbs and also modify adjectives, other adverbs, and whole groups of words.

Although an *-ly* ending often signals an adverb, many adverbs — *never* and *always,* for example — have a different form. Moreover, some *adjectives* end in *-ly:* In *a gentlemanly person, a likely candidate,* and *a lovely breeze, gentlemanly, likely,* and *lovely* clearly modify nouns and are thus adjectives. Therefore, to determine whether a word is an adjective or an adverb, we must identify the word or words it modifies.

Adjectives modify only nouns and pronouns. Adverbs may modify verbs, but they may also modify adjectives and other adverbs: *extremely unhappy* (adverb-adjective); *bitterly cold* (adverb-adjective); *very quickly* (adverb-adverb). Adverbs may also modify whole sentences or groups of words within a sentence. In *Unfortunately, we have no money,* for example, *unfortunately* modifies the whole sentence that follows it. In *She ran almost to the end of the street,* the adverb *almost* modifies *to the end of the street.*

Adverbs usually indicate where, when, how, or to what extent, as in the following sentences.

Send all the mail *here.* [*Here* is *where* the mail is to be sent.]

Fred will arrive *tomorrow.* [*Tomorrow* is *when* Fred will arrive.]

Jeremy answered *angrily.* [*Angrily* is *how* Jeremy answered.]

We are *completely* satisfied. [*Completely* indicates *to what extent* we are satisfied.]

Adjectives and adverbs appear in three forms distinguished by degree. The **positive degree** is the basic form, the one listed in the dictionary: *good, green, angry; badly, quickly, angrily.* The **comparative** form indicates a greater degree of the quality named by the word: *better, greener, angrier; worse, more quickly, more angrily.* The **superlative** form indicates the greatest degree of the quality named: *best, greenest, angriest; worst, most quickly, most angrily.* (For further discussion of the forms and uses of comparatives and superlatives, see 9e.)

EXERCISE 6

Identify the adjectives and adverbs in the following sentences. Then use each sentence as a model for creating a sentence of your own.

Example:

The red barn sat uncomfortably among modern buildings.

ADJ   ADV   ADJ

The *red* barn sat *uncomfortably* among *modern* buildings.

The little girl complained loudly to her busy mother.

1. The icy rain created glassy patches on the roads.
2. Happily, children used the slippery streets as playgrounds.
3. Fortunately, no cars ventured out.
4. Wise parents stayed indoors where they could be warm and dry.
5. The dogs slept soundly near the warm radiators, seldom going outside.

gr

5b

EXERCISE 7

Change each adjective below into an adverb, and change each adverb into an adjective. Then use both the adjective and the adverb in sentences of your own.

Example:

sorrowful

sorrowfully

Her expression was *sorrowful.*

David watched *sorrowfully* as the firemen removed the charred remains of his furniture.

1. watchful	6. evenly
2. wisely	7. happy
3. new	8. painfully
4. bright	9. darkly
5. fortunately	10. sturdy

2
Using other words as modifiers

We have already observed that a particular word may function sometimes as a noun, sometimes as a verb. Similarly, nouns and special forms of verbs may sometimes serve as modifiers of other nouns. In such combinations as *morning shoppers, office buildings, Thanksgiving prayer,* and *shock hazard,* the first noun modifies the second. In combinations like *singing birds, acting president, corrected papers,* and *broken finger,* the first word is a verb form modifying the following noun. (These modifying verb forms are discussed in more detail in 5c-2.) Again, the part of speech to which we assign a word always depends on its function in a sentence.

EXERCISE 8

Use each of the following verb forms to modify a noun in a sentence of your own.

Example:

smoking
Only a *smoking cigar* remained.

1. typed
2. painted
3. written
4. burned
5. pitching
6. charging
7. ripened
8. rolling
9. known
10. driven

EXERCISE 9

To practice expanding the basic sentence patterns with single-word modifiers, combine each group of sentences below into one sentence. You will have to delete and rearrange words.

Example:

The speaker told us the facts. The speaker told us calmly. The facts were terrifying.

The speaker *calmly* told us the *terrifying* facts.

1. The shadows made the evening. The shadows were trembling. The evening was spooky.
2. The dog barked. The dog was frightened. It barked loudly.
3. A driver can avoid accidents. The driver must be careful. The accidents might be unhappy.
4. Children leave toys. The children are growing. They leave the toys behind. The toys are many. The toys are broken.
5. The wind invited kites. The wind was blustery. The kites would be flying.
6. The car is a Chevrolet. The car is wrecked. The Chevrolet is silver.
7. We bought our father a knife. We bought the knife recently. It is for carving.
8. The doors open. The doors are brass. They open inward.
9. The oceans contain fish. The oceans are deep. The fish are peculiar.
10. The boy spoke. The boy was lisping. He spoke softly.

5c
Expanding the basic sentence with word groups

We have seen that nouns and verbs are the basic words of our language. Naming and asserting, they are all we need to build the basic sentence patterns. Adjectives and adverbs are the simplest modifiers, permitting us to qualify or limit nouns and verbs. But most sentences we read or write contain whole word groups that *serve* as nouns and modifiers. Such word groups enable us to combine several bits of information into one sentence and to make the relations among them clear.

Consider the following sentence:

> When the ice cracked, the skaters, fearing an accident, sought safety at the lake's edge.

The skeleton of this sentence — the basic subject and predicate — is *The skaters sought safety.* The sentence pattern is subject (*skaters*), verb (*sought*), and direct object (*safety*). But attached to this skeleton are three other groups of words that add related information. Each word group could itself be stated as a basic sentence pattern: *The ice cracked. The skaters feared an accident. The lake's edge was safe.* In the sample sentence, however, each of these statements is reduced to something less than a sentence and then is inserted into the basic pattern *The skaters sought safety.* The reduced constructions are all phrases and clauses.

A **phrase,** such as *at the lake's edge* and *fearing an accident,* is a group of related words that lacks either a subject or a predicate or both. A **clause,** in contrast, contains both a subject and a predicate. Both *The skaters sought safety* and *When the ice cracked* are clauses, though only the first can stand alone as a sentence. We will examine the various kinds of phrases and clauses in the sections below.

1
Using prepositional phrases

Prepositions are connecting words. Unlike nouns, verbs, and modifiers, which may change form according to their meaning and use in a sentence, prepositions never change form. We use many prepositions with great frequency, but the entire list is relatively short. Here are the most common ones.

about	beside	into	through
above	between	like	throughout
across	beyond	near	till
after	by	of	to
against	concerning	off	toward
along	despite	on	under
among	down	onto	underneath
around	during	out	unlike
as	except	outside	until
at	excepting	over	up
before	for	past	upon
behind	from	regarding	with
below	in	round	within
beneath	inside	since	without

A preposition always connects a noun, a pronoun, or a word group functioning as a noun to another word in the sentence. The noun, pronoun, or word group so connected is called the **object of the preposition.** The preposition plus its object and any modifiers is called a **prepositional phrase.**

PREPOSITION	OBJECT
before	college
of	spaghetti
on	the surface
with	great satisfaction
upon	entering the room
from	where you are standing

Prepositions normally come before their objects. But sometimes the preposition comes after its object, particularly in speech.

What do you want to see him *about?*
Which *apartment* does she live *in?*

Prepositional phrases usually function as adjectives (modifying nouns) or as adverbs (modifying verbs, adjectives, or other adverbs). Occasionally, prepositional phrases also function as nouns, though rarely in writing.

PREPOSITIONAL PHRASES AS ADJECTIVES

Terry is the boy *in the pink shirt.* [Phrase describes *boy.*]

Life *on a raft in the Mississippi* gave an opportunity *for adventure.* [*On a raft* describes *life; in the Mississippi* describes *raft;* and *for adventure* describes *opportunity.*]

PREPOSITIONAL PHRASES AS ADVERBS

She had driven steadily *for four hours from Baltimore.* [Both phrases describe *driven.*]

Our Great Dane Joshua buries his bones *behind the garage.* [Phrase describes *buries.*]

PREPOSITIONAL PHRASE AS NOUN

Across the river is too far to go for ice cream. [Phrase functions as sentence subject.]

EXERCISE 10

Identify the prepositional phrases in the passage below. Indicate whether each phrase functions as an adjective or as an adverb, and name the word that the phrase modifies.

Example:
After an hour I finally arrived at the home of my professor.

ADV PHRASE   **ADV PHRASE**   **ADJ PHRASE**
After an hour I finally arrived *at the home of my professor.* [*After an hour* and *at the home* modify *arrived; of my professor* modifies *home.*]

gr
5c

The woman in blue socks ran from the policeman on horseback. She darted down Bates Street and then into the bus depot. At the depot the policeman dismounted from his horse and searched for the woman. The entrance to the depot and the interior were filled with travelers, however, and in the crowd he lost sight of the woman. She, meanwhile, had boarded a bus on the other side of the depot and was riding across town.

EXERCISE 11

To practice writing sentences with prepositional phrases, combine each pair of sentences below into one sentence that includes one or two prepositional phrases. You will have to add, delete, and rearrange words. Some items have more than one possible answer.

Example:
I will start working. The new job will pay the minimum wage.
I will start working *at a new job for the minimum wage.*

1. The band members held a party. They invited one hundred people.
2. Tiny minnows swim. The small pond is where they swim.
3. We are required to write the exam. We must use pencil and white paper.
4. The monkey chattered noisily. It had silver fur.
5. The interview continued. Two hours was the time it took.
6. Jan received a glass paperweight. An unknown admirer gave it.
7. They took a long walk. They followed the stream and crossed the bridge.
8. The wagging tail toppled the lamp. It was a dog's tail.
9. The author wants to shock readers. He introduces foul language and gruesome crimes.
10. Everyone attended the lecture. Only Vicky and Carlos did not go.

2
Using verbals and verbal phrases

Verbals are special verb forms like *smoking* or *hidden* that can function as nouns or modifiers. Verbals *cannot* stand alone as the complete verb in the predicate of a sentence. For example, *The man smoking* and *The money hidden* are not sentences. Any verbal must combine with a helping verb in order to serve as the predicate of a sentence: *The man was smoking. The money is hidden.*

Because verbals cannot serve alone as sentence predicates, they are sometimes called **nonfinite verbs** (in essence, they are "unfinished"). **Finite verbs,** in contrast, can make an assertion or express a state of being without a helping verb (they are "finished"). A simple test can distinguish finite and nonfinite verbs. Finite verbs that express present time always change form when the subject changes from singular to plural: *The prisoner escapes. The prisoners escape. The paper is written. The papers are written.* In contrast, nonfinite verbs always have the same form whether the subject is singular or plural: *the prisoner escaping, the prisoners escaping; the paper written, the papers written; the letter to mail, the letters to mail.*

There are three kinds of verbals: participles, gerunds, and infinitives.

Participles

All verbs have two participle forms, a present and a past. The **present participle** consists of the dictionary form of the verb plus the ending *-ing: beginning, completing, hiding.* The **past participle** of most verbs consists of the dictionary form plus *-d* or *-ed: believed, completed.* Some common verbs have an irregular past participle: *begun, hidden.* (See 7a.)

Both present and past participles function as adjectives to modify nouns and pronouns.

The *freezing* rain made the roads dangerous. [Modifies *rain.*]

The *exhausted* miners were rescued after four days. [Modifies *miners.*]

Oliver found his *typing* job *boring.* [Both participles modify *job.*]

Disgusted, he quit that night. [Modifies *he.*]

Gerunds

Gerund is the name given to the *-ing* form of the verb when it serves as a noun.

Unfortunately, *studying* always bored Michael. [Sentence subject.]

His sister Annie hated *swimming.* [Object of *hated.*]

Both Michael and Annie preferred *loafing* to *working.* [*Loafing* is the object of *preferred; working* is the object of the preposition *to.*]

Their principal occupation was *loafing.* [Subject complement.]

Present participles and gerunds can be distinguished *only* by their function in a sentence. If the *-ing* form functions as an adjective (*a teaching degree*), it is a present participle. If the -*ing* form functions as a noun (*Teaching is difficult*), it is a gerund.

Infinitives

The **infinitive** is the *to* form of the verb, the dictionary form preceded by the infinitive marker *to: to begin, to hide, to run*. Infinitives may function as nouns, adjectives, or adverbs.

> He is the man *to elect.* [Modifies *man.*]
> He hoped *to go.* [Object of *hoped.*]
> This physics problem is difficult *to solve.* [Modifies *difficult.*]

Verbal phrases

Like other forms of verbs, participles, gerunds, and infinitives may take subjects, objects, or complements, and they may be modified by adverbs. The verbal and all the words immediately related to it make up a **verbal phrase.**

PARTICIPIAL PHRASES

Like participles, **participial phrases** always serve as adjectives, modifying nouns or pronouns.

> *Chewing his pencil steadily,* Dick stared into the air. [Modifies *Dick.*]
> He was frustrated by the paper *lying before him.* [Modifies *paper.*]
> *Defeated by the same blank paper earlier in the day,* Dick knew he must somehow write something. [Modifies *Dick.*]

GERUND PHRASES

Gerund phrases, like gerunds, always serve as nouns.

> *Eating an entire lemon pie for lunch* was easy for Wesley. [Sentence subject.]

> His mother was annoyed at *his eating the whole pie.* [Object of preposition *at. His* is the subject of the gerund; see 6h.]

> But she had hidden a second pie because she anticipated *his doing it.* [Object of *anticipated.*]

INFINITIVE PHRASES

Infinitive phrases may serve as nouns, adjectives, or adverbs.

> *To lie repeatedly* is *to deny reality.* [The first phrase is the sentence subject; the second is a subject complement.]

> We wanted *him to go.* [Object of *wanted. Him* is the subject of the infinitive; see 6f.]

> Jimmy's is the best place *to eat pancakes.* [Modifies *place.*]

> Amy is not someone *to put off decisions.* [Modifies *someone.*]

Frank jogged *to keep himself fit*. [Modifies *jogged*.]

Jack was too young *to understand the story*. [Modifies *young*.]

NOTE: When an infinitive or infinitive phrase serves as a noun after verbs like *hear, let, help, make, see*, and *watch*, the infinitive marker *to* is omitted: *We all heard her (to) tell the story*.

EXERCISE 12

The following sentences contain participles, gerunds, and infinitives as well as participial, gerund, and infinitive phrases. Identify each verbal or verbal phrase and indicate whether it is used as an adjective, an adverb, or a noun.

Example:

Running wildly, the dog tried to rid herself of the aching cramp.

ADJ N ADJ

Running wildly, the dog tried *to rid herself* of the *aching* cramp.

1. Defeated at Waterloo, Napoleon was sent into exile.
2. We must be strong enough to face the death of loved ones.
3. Whimpering and moaning, my brother was finally dragged to be vaccinated.
4. Eating at a nice restaurant is a relaxing way to end a demanding week.
5. To fly was one of humankind's recurring dreams.
6. The dwindling water supply made the remaining vacationers decide to leave for another campground.
7. The hungry wolves were kept at bay by the periodic firing of a rifle.
8. The train moved too fast for us to enjoy the passing countryside.
9. After missing church three times in a row, I received a call from the minister.
10. Three misbehaving children ruined our attempt to stage a play in the elementary school.

EXERCISE 13

To practice writing sentences with verbals and verbal phrases, combine each pair of sentences below into one sentence. You will have to add, delete, change, and rearrange words. Each item has more than one possible answer.

Example:

My father took pleasure in mean pranks. For instance, he hid the neighbors' cat.

My father took pleasure in mean pranks such as *hiding the neighbors' cat*.

1. Lee knew she had lost the race. She was falling far behind the other runners.
2. The teenager was convicted of two burglaries. He spent six months in reform school.
3. The letter had been opened by mistake. It was lying on the table.
4. Bobby found his wallet. He could buy his books.
5. The giraffe's long neck is essential. With it the giraffe can reach leaves and bark high in trees.
6. Children shop in supermarkets with their parents. This early experience is one almost all children share.
7. I must get a job. I must support myself.
8. The retired couple used their free time well. They traveled across the country and back several times.
9. They discovered a box of old money. They were cleaning the cellar.
10. I have jogged every day for a month. I have lost five pounds.

3
Using absolute phrases

Absolute phrases consist of a noun or pronoun and a participle, plus any modifiers.

The parade passed by slowly, *the bands blaring, the crowds shouting.*

The old tree stood alone, *its trunk stripped and rotting.*

Their work nearly finished, the men rested.

These phrases are called *absolute* (from a Latin word meaning "free") because they have no specific grammatical connection to any word in the rest of the sentence.

Notice that absolute phrases, unlike participial phrases, always contain a subject. Compare the following.

The large man *standing before me* turned to speak. [Participial phrase modifying *man*, the sentence subject.]

A large man having moved in front of me, I could see nothing. [Absolute phrase having its own subject, *A large man.*]

We often omit the participle from an absolute phrase when it is some form of *be* such as *being* or *having been.*

The animal lay on its side, *its body stiff, its legs askew, its eyes wide open.*

EXERCISE 14

To practice writing sentences with absolute phrases, combine each pair of sentences below into one sentence that contains an absolute phrase. You will have to add, delete, change, and rearrange words.

> *Example:*
> The flower's petals wilted. It looked pathetic.
> *Its petals wilted,* the flower looked pathetic.

1. Her face turned pale. She stared at the woman ahead of her.
2. The steelworkers called a strike. The factory was closed down.
3. We were forced to cancel the annual picnic. The funds had run out.
4. The thief stood before the safe. His fingers twitched eagerly.
5. The swimmer's arms thrashed. He rose again to the surface.

4
Using subordinate clauses

As we noted earlier, a **clause** is any group of words that contains a subject and a predicate. There are two kinds of clauses, and the distinction between them is important. An **independent** or **main clause** can stand alone as a sentence: *The sky darkened.* A **dependent** or **subordinate clause** is just like an independent clause *except* that it begins with a subordinating word: *when the sky darkened.* *When* and other subordinating words like *because, if, who,* or *that* express particular relationships between the clauses they introduce and the independent clauses to which they are attached. Clauses that have been subordinated can *never* stand alone as sentences. The following examples show the differences between the two kinds of clauses.

TWO INDEPENDENT CLAUSES

The chair is expensive. We cannot buy it.

FIRST CLAUSE SUBORDINATED

Because the chair is expensive, we cannot buy it.

TWO INDEPENDENT CLAUSES

I met a man. He was selling boa constrictors.

SECOND CLAUSE SUBORDINATED

I met a man *who was selling boa constrictors.*

We use two kinds of subordinating words to connect subordinate clauses with independent clauses. The first kind is **subordinating conjunctions** or **subordinators.** They come always at the beginning of subordinate clauses. Like prepositions, subordinating conjunctions are few in number and never change form in any way. The following list contains some of the most common subordinating conjunctions.

after	because	in order that	than	when
although	before	once	that	whenever
as	even if	rather than	though	where
as if	even though	since	unless	wherever
as though	if	so that	until	while

The second kind of connecting word is the **relative pronoun.** It also introduces a subordinate clause and serves to link it with an independent clause. The relative pronouns are listed below.

which	what	who (whose, whom)
that	whatever	whoever (whomever)

Like subordinating conjunctions, these words link one clause with another. But unlike subordinating conjunctions, relative pronouns also usually act as subjects or objects in their own clauses, and two of them (*who* and *whoever*) change form accordingly (see 6g).

Subordinate clauses function as adjectives, adverbs, and nouns and are described as adjective, adverb, or noun clauses according to their use in a particular sentence. Only by determining its function in a sentence can we identify a particular clause.

ADJECTIVE CLAUSES

Adjective clauses modify nouns and pronouns. They usually begin with the relative pronouns *who* (*whose, whom*), *which,* and *that,* although a few adjective clauses begin with *when* or *where.* Adjective clauses ordinarily fall immediately after the noun or pronoun they modify.

My family still lives in the house *that my grandfather built.* [Modifies *house.*]

Dale is the girl *who always gets there early.* [Modifies *girl.*]

My yellow Volkswagen, *which I bought seven years ago,* has traveled 78,000 miles. [Modifies *Volkswagen.*]

There comes a time *when each of us must work.* [Modifies *time.*]

ADVERB CLAUSES

Adverb clauses, like adverbs, modify verbs, adjectives, and other adverbs. They always begin with subordinating conjunctions. And they usually tell how, why, when, under what conditions, with what result, and so on.

Calvin liked to go *where there was action.* [Modifies *go.*]

Elaine is friendlier *when she's talking on the telephone.* [Modifies *friendlier.*]

Because he did not study, Donald failed. [Modifies *failed.*]

She came as quickly *as she could.* [Modifies *quickly.*]

gr

5c

NOUN CLAUSES

Noun clauses function as subjects, objects, and complements in sentences. They begin either with relative pronouns or with the words *when, where, whether, why,* or *how*. Unlike adjective and adverb clauses, noun clauses *replace* a noun within a main clause; therefore, they can be difficult to identify.

> *The lecture* pleased the audience. [*The lecture* is the sentence subject.]
>
> *What the lecturer said* pleased the audience. [The noun clause replaces *The lecture* as sentence subject.]

Here are some typical noun clauses.

> Everyone knows *what a panther is*. [Object of *knows*.]
>
> *Whoever calls the station first* will win a case of bean soup. [Subject of sentence.]
>
> They thought about *whether they could afford the trip*. [Object of preposition *about*.]

ELLIPTICAL CLAUSES

A subordinate clause that is grammatically incomplete but clear in meaning is an **elliptical clause** (*ellipsis* means "omission"). The meaning of the clause is clear because the missing element can be supplied from the context. Most often the elements omitted are the relative pronouns *that, which,* and *whom* from adjective clauses or the predicate from the second part of a comparison.

> Thailand is among the countries (*that or which*) *he visited*.
> Ellen dances better *than Martha* (*dances*).

Here are other typical elliptical clauses.

> *When* (*she was*) *only a child*, Julia saw a great gray owl.
>
> *Though* (*they are*) *rare south of Canada*, great gray owls sometimes appear in Massachusetts.

EXERCISE 15

Identify the subordinate clauses in the following sentences and indicate whether each is used as an adjective, an adverb, or a noun. If the clause is a noun, indicate its function in the sentence.

Example:

The instructions explained how to build an underground house.

NOUN

The instructions explained *how to build an underground house*. [Object of *explained*.]

1. The auctioneer opened the bidding when everyone was seated.
2. They were unperturbed by what the strange man screamed at them.
3. Whenever the economy is uncertain, people tend to become more selfish.
4. Whoever wants to graduate must pass all the required courses.
5. I knew the ending would be unhappy when the main character started falling apart.
6. That Stefanie did not go to college was a disappointment to her parents.
7. Ever since she was a small child, they have saved money for her education.
8. Stefanie decided, though, that she wanted to work a year or two before college.
9. Until she makes up her mind, Stefanie's education money is collecting interest.
10. Her parents are the kind who let their children think for themselves.

gr
5c

EXERCISE 16

To practice writing sentences with subordinate clauses, combine each pair of independent clauses below into one sentence. Use either subordinating conjunctions or relative pronouns as appropriate, referring to the lists on page 147 if necessary. You will have to add, delete, and rearrange words. Each item has more than one possible answer.

> *Example:*
> Josh has bad grades. He may not graduate.
> *Because* Josh has bad grades, he may not graduate.

1. The hunter tried to move the stone. It was very heavy.
2. We came to the gate. We had first seen the deer tracks there.
3. Someone is fickle. This person cannot be relied on.
4. Abner won the award. This fact still amazes us.
5. The town government canceled the new playground. Then small children demonstrated in the streets.
6. We can make no exceptions. You should know this.
7. Those dogs have a master. He gives them equal discipline and praise.
8. The basketball team has had a losing season. The team shows promise.
9. He did not bother to undress for bed. He was too tired.
10. She is the teacher. She gives very few A's.

5
Using appositives

An **appositive** is a word or word group that renames the word or word group before it. (The word *appositive* derives from a Latin word that means "placed near to" or "applied to.") The most common appositives are nouns that rename other nouns.

> Bizen ware, *a dark stoneware,* has been produced in Japan since the fourteenth century. [Noun phrase as appositive.]
>
> His first love, *racing stock cars,* was his last love. [Gerund phrase as appositive.]

All appositives can replace the words they refer to: *A dark stoneware has been produced in Japan since the fourteenth century. Racing stock cars was his last love.*

Appositives are often introduced by words and phrases like *or, that is, such as, for example,* and *in other words.*

> Kangaroos, opossums, and wombats are all marsupials, *that is, mammals that carry their young in external abdominal pouches.*
>
> Jujitsu, *or judo,* is based on the principle that an opponent's strength may be used to defeat him.

Although most appositives are nouns that rename other nouns, they may also be and rename other parts of speech.

> All papers should be proofread carefully, that is, *checked for spelling, punctuation, and mechanics.* [The appositive defines the verb *proofread.*]

Appositives can always be stated as clauses with some form of the verb *be.*

> Bizen ware, (*which is*) *a dark stoneware,* has been produced in Japan since the fourteenth century.

Thus appositives are economical alternatives to adjective clauses containing a form of *be.*

EXERCISE 17

To practice writing sentences with appositives, combine each pair of sentences below into one sentence that contains an appositive. You will have to delete and rearrange words. Some items have more than one possible answer.

Example:

The largest land animal is the elephant. The elephant is also one of the most intelligent animals.

The largest land animal, *the elephant,* is also one of the most intelligent animals.

1. Jerry's aim in life is to avoid all productive labor. His aim will surely change when his parents stop supporting him.
2. Their Beatles memorabilia occupied a room in their basement. The memorabilia consisted of records, photographs, posters, and T-shirts.

3. The little boy is a nasty, spoiled brat. He cannot be left alone with other children.
4. Cactus growing attracts patient people. It is a hobby with no immediate rewards.
5. The most popular professional team sports pay their players well. They are football, baseball, basketball, and hockey.
6. Edgar Allan Poe was a writer of fantastic, scary stories. He was also a poet and a journalist.
7. The radio talk show received a call from Warren Jones. He is the escaped prisoner.
8. The house was a five-room adobe structure. It was bought by a neighborhood group.
9. The hailstorm hit at 5:30. That is the height of rush hour.
10. English adopted many words for animals from the Algonquin Indians. These are words such as *moose, opossum,* and *raccoon.*

gr
5d

5d
Compounding words, phrases, and clauses

We have seen how to modify the nouns and verbs of the basic sentence patterns and how to use word groups in place of single nouns and modifiers. Now we will examine how to combine words and word groups that are closely related and parallel in importance, as in these examples:

Bonnie spent the afternoon in the park. Her father spent the afternoon in the park.

Bonnie and her father spent the afternoon in the park.

Curt was tired. He was sick. He was depressed.

Curt was *tired, sick, and depressed.*

Brenda went to the drugstore. She bought some vitamins. She returned as soon as possible.

Brenda *went to the drugstore, bought some vitamins, and returned as soon as possible.*

In the first pair of examples we joined the two different subjects, *Bonnie* and *her father*, into a **compound subject,** thus avoiding repetition of the same predicate in two sentences. In the second pair of examples we joined the three adjective complements into a **compound complement** (*tired, sick, and depressed*) that describes the common subject *Curt* after the common linking verb *was*. And in the last pair of examples we joined the three different predicates into a **compound predicate** (*went . . . , bought . . . , and returned . . .*), using the common subject *Brenda*. In every example we used *and* to join the parts.

1
Using coordinating conjunctions and correlative conjunctions

The word *and* is a **coordinating conjunction.** Like prepositions and subordinating conjunctions, coordinating conjunctions do not change form and are few in number.

and	or	so
but	for	yet
nor		

The coordinating conjunctions *and, but, nor,* and *or* always connect words or word groups of the same kind — that is, two or more nouns, verbs, adjectives, adverbs, phrases, clauses, or whole sentences.

> Stewart *or* Linda will have to go.
> The chair was unfashionable *but* charming.
> Alison worked every day *and* partied every evening.
> He studied day and night, *but* he could not pass the course.

The conjunctions *for* and *so* cannot connect words, phrases, or subordinate clauses, but they can connect independent clauses. *For* indicates cause; *so* indicates result.

> Amy stayed home, *for* she had work to do.
> Jasper was tired, *so* he went to bed early.

The word *yet* often functions as an adverb (*She has not left yet*), but it can also function as a coordinating conjunction. Like *but*, it indicates contrast.

> He tended the goldfish carefully, *yet* it died.

Some conjunctions pair up with other words to form **correlative conjunctions.** Typical correlative conjunctions include *both . . . and, not only . . . but also, not . . . but, either . . . or,* and *neither . . . nor.*

> *Both* Bonnie *and* her father went to the park.
> The basketball is *either* on the shelf *or* in the closet.
> The class stood *neither* when he arrived *nor* when he left.
> We consume energy *not only* when we are awake *but also* when we are asleep.

2
Using conjunctive adverbs

One other kind of connecting word, called a **conjunctive adverb,** links only independent clauses, not words, phrases, or subordinate clauses. Unlike subordinating conjunctions, conjunctive adverbs indicate that the clauses they connect are equal rather than unequal. Further, conjunctive adverbs not only connect clauses but also modify the clauses they appear in. Here is a list of common conjunctive adverbs.

accordingly	furthermore	moreover	similarly
also	hence	namely	still
anyway	however	nevertheless	then
besides	incidentally	next	thereafter
certainly	indeed	nonetheless	therefore
consequently	instead	now	thus
finally	likewise	otherwise	undoubtedly
further	meanwhile		

gr
5d

Compare the use of coordinating conjunctions, conjunctive adverbs, and subordinating conjunctions in the following sentences.

The game was long and boring, *but* we stayed to the end.
The game was long and boring; *however,* we stayed to the end.
Although the game was long and boring, we stayed to the end.

The game was exciting, *and* we stayed to the end.
The game was exciting; *consequently,* we stayed to the end.
Because the game was exciting, we stayed to the end.

In the first sentence of each group, the coordinating conjunctions *but* and *and* join two main clauses and indicate the relations between them, but neither word modifies the clause that follows. In contrast, the conjunctive adverbs *however* and *consequently* join two main clauses while at the same time acting as adverbs to modify the clauses following them. In the third sentence of each group, the initial subordinating conjunction reduces the first clause from an independent clause to an adverb modifier.

Because they are adverbs, conjunctive adverbs can also be moved around within their clauses, as in the following:

However, we stayed to the end.
We stayed, *however,* to the end.
We stayed to the end, *however.*

Neither the coordinating conjunctions nor the subordinating conjunctions can be moved in this way; they must remain between the two clauses they join. These differences among coordinating conjunctions, conjunctive adverbs, and subordinating conjunctions are important because they determine very different punctuation in the clauses introduced by one or the other. (See Chapter 11 on comma splices.)

NOTE: Just as some words may serve as nouns, verbs, or modifiers depending on their function in a sentence (see pp. 130 and 137), so some connecting words may have more than one use. For example, *after, before, until,* and some other words may be either prepositions or subordinating conjunctions. Some prepositions, such as *behind, in,* and *outside,* can serve also as adverbs, as in *He trailed behind.* Most relative pronouns are used also as interrogative pronouns to ask questions: *What time is it? Who left?* And some conjunctive adverbs, particularly *however,* may also serve simply as adverbs in sentences like *However much it costs, we must have it.* Again, the part of speech of a word depends on its function in a sentence.

EXERCISE 18

To practice compounding words, phrases, and clauses, combine each pair of sentences below into one sentence that is as short as possible without altering meaning. Use the type of connecting word specified in parentheses, referring to the lists on pages 152–53 if necessary. You will have to add, delete, and rearrange words.

Example:

The encyclopedia had some information. It was not detailed enough. (*Conjunctive adverb.*)

The encyclopedia had some information; *however,* it was not detailed enough.

1. Geoffrey raked some leaves. He stopped raking before he had finished the job. (*Coordinating conjunction.*)
2. Television news will have to get better. I might give up news programs for newspapers. (*Correlative conjunction.*)
3. Physics is a difficult subject. It is an enjoyable subject. (*Coordinating conjunction.*)
4. The football team's morale was bad. The team had a losing season. (*Conjunctive adverb.*)
5. The cheerleaders missed the bus. The back-up center also missed the bus. (*Coordinating conjunction.*)
6. Politicians cannot be shy people. They must be outgoing. (*Conjunctive adverb.*)
7. The newspaper publishes interesting feature articles. It publishes feeble editorials. (*Conjunctive adverb.*)
8. The pelicans floated on the smooth water. Sometimes they dipped beneath the surface to catch fish. (*Coordinating conjunction.*)
9. My mother attended Thomas Jefferson High School. My mother-in-law also attended Thomas Jefferson High School. (*Correlative conjunction.*)
10. The news stories from Uganda were censored. They were out-of-date because the censor had held on to them for so long. (*Conjunctive adverb.*)

5e
Changing the usual order of the sentence

So far, all the examples of basic sentence grammar have been similar: The subject of the sentence comes first, naming the performer of the predicate's action, and the predicate comes second. This arrangement of subject and predicate describes most sentences that occur in writing, but we need to look briefly at four other kinds of sentences that alter this basic pattern.

1
Forming questions

We form questions in one of several ways. We may invert the normal subject-verb arrangement of statements:

The dog is barking. Is the dog barking?

We may use a question word such as *how, what, who, when, where, which,* or *why:*

What dog is barking?

Or we may use some combination of the two methods:

Why is the dog barking?

In each case a question mark signals that the sentence is a question.

2
Forming commands

We construct commands even more simply than we construct questions: We merely delete the subject of the sentence, *you.*

Open the window.
Go to the store.
Eat your spinach.

3
Writing passive sentences

In any sentence that uses a transitive verb — that is, in any sentence where the verb takes an object — we can move the object to the position of the subject and put the subject in the predicate. When we do this we create a **passive sentence,** using the **passive voice** of the verb rather than the **active voice.** (See also Chapter 7, pp. 183–84.)

Greg wrote the paper. [Active voice.]

The paper was written (by Greg). [Passive voice. *The paper,* which was the original object of *wrote,* becomes the sentence subject. The original sentence subject, *Greg,* may appear in a prepositional phrase or be omitted entirely.]

Passive sentences are so called because their subjects do not perform or initiate the action indicated by their verbs. Rather, their subjects are acted upon. In passive sentences the verb is always a phrase made up of some form of the verb *be* and the past participle of the main verb (*paper was written, exams are finished*). (See 18d for cautions against overuse of the passive voice.)

4

Writing sentences with postponed subjects

The subject follows the predicate in two sentence patterns that are neither questions, commands, nor passive voice. In one pattern the normal word order is reversed for emphasis. This pattern occurs most often when the normal order is subject–intransitive verb–adverb. Then the adverb moves to the front of the sentence while subject and predicate reverse order: *Then came the dawn. Up walked Henry.*

A second kind of sentence with a postponed subject begins with either *it* or *there,* as in the following:

         v   s
There will be eighteen people attending the meeting.

      v   ———s———
It is certain that they will be there.

The words *there* and *it* in such sentences are **expletives.** Their only function is to postpone the sentence subject. Since expletive sentences do not give emphasis, they are usually less effective than sentences stated in the usual subject-predicate order: *Eighteen people will attend the meeting. That they will be there is certain.* (See also 18e.)

EXERCISE 19

Form a question and a command from the following noun and verb pairs.

    Example:

split, wood

Did you *split* all this *wood?*
Split the *wood* for our fire.

1. water, boil
2. music, stop
3. table, set
4. blackboard, write
5. telephone, use

EXERCISE 20

Rewrite each passive sentence below as active, and rewrite each expletive construction to restore normal subject-verb order. (For additional exercises with the passive voice and with expletives, see pp. 184, 285, and 403.)

1. The football was thrown by the quarterback for more than forty yards.
2. It is uncertain whether microwave ovens are dangerous.
3. Sixty people were killed in the plane crash.
4. The lives of over one hundred others were saved by the pilot's skill.
5. There was an audience of nearly ten thousand at the concert.

5f
Classifying sentences

We describe and classify sentences in two different ways: by function (statement, question, command, exclamation, and so forth) or by their structure. Four basic sentence structures are possible: simple, compound, complex, and compound complex.

1
Writing simple sentences

Simple sentences consist of a single independent clause. The clause may contain phrases, and the subject, the verb, and its objects may be compound, but the sentence is simple as long as it contains only one complete independent clause and no subordinate clause.

Last July was unusually hot.

In fact, both July and August were vicious months.

The summer either made people leave the area for good or reduced them to bare existence. [Two predicates but only one subject.]

2
Writing compound sentences

A **compound sentence** consists of two or more simple sentences joined by a coordinating conjunction or by a semicolon.

Last July was hot, but August was even hotter.

The hot sun scorched the land to powder; the lack of rain made it totally untillable.

The government later provided assistance; consequently, those who remained gradually improved their lot.

3
Writing complex sentences

A sentence is **complex** if it contains one or more subordinate clauses as well as one independent clause.

Rain finally came, although many had left the area by then.

When the rain came, people rejoiced.

Those who remained were able to start anew because the government came to their aid.

Notice that length does not determine whether a sentence is complex or simple; both kinds can be short or long.

4
Writing compound-complex sentences

A **compound-complex sentence** has the characteristics of both the compound sentence (two or more independent clauses) and the complex sentence (at least one subordinate clause).

Even though government aid finally came, many people had already been reduced to poverty, and others had been forced to leave the area. [Subordinate clause; independent clause; independent clause.]

Some of those who had left gradually moved back to their original homes, but years passed before the land became as fertile as before. [Independent clause containing subordinate clause; independent clause; subordinate clause.]

EXERCISE 21

Identify the following sentences as simple, compound, complex, or compound-complex. Indicate which clauses are independent, which subordinate.

Example:

The police began patrolling more often when crime in the neighborhood increased.

```
                ┌─────── INDEPENDENT ───────┐
```
Complex: The police began patrolling more often
```
   ┌─────── SUBORDINATE ───────┐
```
when crime in the neighborhood increased.

1. Winters in Vermont are beautiful.
2. Summers in Vermont, by the way, are no less beautiful.
3. Although the guest of honor arrived late, no one seemed to mind.
4. The police strike lasted a week, but no robberies occurred in that time.
5. Even though some say football has supplanted baseball as the national pastime, millions of people watch baseball every year and they don't seem ready to stop.

gr

5f

EXERCISE 22

Combine each group of simple sentences below to produce the kind of sentence specified in parentheses. You will have to add, delete, change, and rearrange words.

Example:

The traffic never stopped. It passed by her house. (*Complex.*)
The traffic that passed by her house never stopped.

1. Dinner was tasty. It did not fill us up. (*Compound.*)
2. The storm was predicted to be fierce. It passed by quickly. (*Complex.*)
3. The musical notes died away. Then a strange object filled the sky. (*Complex.*)
4. The wolves were afraid. They feared the fire. (*Simple.*)
5. We wanted the rumors to stop. We hoped for that. They did not. (*Compound-complex.*)

6
Case of Nouns and Pronouns

Case is the form of a noun or pronoun that shows how it functions in a sentence — that is, whether it functions as a subject, as an object, or in some other way. The personal pronouns *I, we, he, she,* and *they* and the relative pronoun *who* have separate forms for three cases: subjective, possessive, and objective.

SUBJECTIVE

| I | we | he, she | they | who |

POSSESSIVE

| my | our | his, her | their | whose |
| mine | ours | his, hers | theirs | |

OBJECTIVE

| me | us | him, her | them | whom |

All other pronouns and all nouns have only two forms: a possessive case (for instance, *your, boy's*); and a plain case (*you, boy*), which is the form listed in the dictionary and which serves all functions except that of the possessive. Since only *I, we, he, she, they,* and *who* change form for each case, we will focus on these pronouns in this chapter.

The **subjective form** is used when a pronoun is the subject of a sentence, the subject of a clause, the complement of a subject, or an appositive identifying a subject. (See 5a and 5c.)

SUBJECT OF SENTENCE

She and *I* skied three days last week.
They tried to save the house.

SUBJECT OF SUBORDINATE CLAUSE

Give the money to the kids *who* cleaned up the house.
He is the man *who* I thought would win.

ca
6

SUBJECT OF UNDERSTOOD VERB

Sarah has more money than *he* (has).
I am not as smart as *she* (is).

SUBJECT COMPLEMENT

The editors of the paper were *he* and *I*.
They assumed it was *I*.

APPOSITIVE IDENTIFYING SUBJECT

Only two members, Susan and *I*, went to the jazz festival.

The **objective form** of a pronoun is used when the pronoun is the direct or indirect object of a verb or verbal, the object of a preposition, the subject of an infinitive, or an appositive identifying an object. (See 5a and 5c.)

OBJECT OF VERB

Lisa likes both Tom and *him*.
The woman *whom* they elected was experienced.
The exam gave *him* a headache.

OBJECT OF PREPOSITION

Most of *us* hated to get up.
I didn't know *whom* they laughed at.

OBJECT OF VERBAL

Electing *her* was easy. [Object of gerund.]
Having elected *her*, the committee adjourned. [Object of past participle.]
Mary ran to help *him*. [Object of infinitive.]

SUBJECT OF INFINITIVE

We invited *them* to eat with us.
They asked *me* to speak.

APPOSITIVE IDENTIFYING OBJECT

The judge fined both defendants, Joe and *her*.

The **possessive form** of a pronoun is used before nouns and gerunds.

BEFORE NOUNS

His sisters needed *our* bicycles.

BEFORE GERUNDS

Their flying to Nashville was my suggestion.

In addition, the possessive forms *mine, ours, yours, his, hers,* and *theirs* (and only those forms) may be used without a following noun, in the position of a noun.

IN NOUN POSITIONS

Hers is the racket on the table.
The blue Pinto is *mine (ours, yours, his, theirs).*

(For the possessive forms of nouns, see 23a.)

6a

Use the subjective case for all parts of compound subjects and for subject complements.

In compound subjects use the same pronoun form you would use if the pronoun stood alone as a subject.

SUBJECTS

Joan and *I* left, but *Bill* and *he* stayed.
After *she* and *I* left, the fight started.

If you are in doubt about the correct form, try each part of the subject in a separate sentence: *Joan left. I left.* Therefore, *Joan and I left.*

A pronoun following the forms of the verb *be (am, is, are, was, were)* is a subject complement (see 5a-3). Since it renames the subject, the pronoun is in the subjective case.

SUBJECT COMPLEMENTS

The ones who paid the bill were *you* and *I.*
It was *she* whom the governor finally appointed.

Such sentences are likely to sound stilted because expressions like *It's me* and *It was her* are common in speech. Unless we want to gain some special emphasis, we would ordinarily write our sample sentences in their more natural order: *You and I were the ones who paid the bill; The governor finally appointed her.*

6b

Use the objective case for all parts of compound objects.

In compound objects use the same pronoun form you would use if the pronoun stood alone as an object.

OBJECTS OF VERBS

We wanted to invite *Larry* and *her.* [Direct object.]
The coach gave *her* and *me* a lecture. [Indirect object.]

OBJECTS OF PREPOSITIONS

Marty gave presents to *Gloria* and *me.*
The $10 gift was divided between *him* and *me.*

If you are in doubt about the correct form, try each part of the object in a separate sentence: *We wanted to invite Larry. We wanted to invite her.* Therefore, *We wanted to invite Larry and her.*

ca

6c

EXERCISE 1

Select, from the pairs in parentheses, the appropriate subjective or objective pronoun(s) for each of the following sentences.

Example:

The correspondence between (*he, him*) and (*I, me*) continued for three years.

The correspondence between *him* and *me* continued for three years.

1. After a lot of planning, (*he, him*) and McHale launched the newsletter.
2. The reward check was made out to my friend and (*I, me*).
3. We couldn't see whether it was (*they, them*) or another group.
4. My parents had wanted all the children home for Thanksgiving but could afford to bring only Susanne and (*I, me*).
5. No one told us that (*he, him*) and George had left.
6. The woman gave money to (*he, him*) and (*I, me*).
7. The guilty ones are (*she, her*) and Allen.
8. All through the night Jimmy and (*I, me*) heard moans and strange knocks.
9. The rangers closed the mountain road after Mark and (*I, me*) reached the top.
10. My father had to leave my mother and (*I, me*) to find work in another city.

6c

Use the appropriate case when the plural pronouns *we* and *us* occur with a noun.

The case of the first-person plural pronoun used with a noun depends on the use of the noun.

Most of *us* skaters grew up together. [*Skaters* is the object of the preposition *of.*]

We skaters grew up together. [*Skaters* is the subject of the sentence.]

6d

In appositives the case of a pronoun depends on the function of the word it describes or identifies.

The class elected two representatives, Debbie and me. [*Representatives* is the object of the verb *elected,* so the words in the appositive, *Debbie and me,* take the objective case.]

Two representatives, Debbie and I, were elected. [*Representatives* is the subject of this sentence, so the words in the appositive, *Debbie and I,* take the subjective case.]

If you are in doubt about case in an appositive, try the sentence without the word the appositive identifies: *The class elected Debbie and me; Debbie and I were elected.*

EXERCISE 2

Select, from the pairs in parentheses, the appropriate subjective or objective pronoun for each of the following sentences.

> *Example:*
> The legislation provides new opportunities for (*we, us*) handicapped people.
> The legislation provides new opportunities for *us* handicapped people.

1. Implementing the new policy is up to (*we, us*) students.
2. To (*we, us*) fishermen, peace and quiet are real pleasures.
3. (*We, Us*) students appreciate clear directions on tests.
4. The best hockey players, (*she, her*) and Christine, received the awards.
5. Two of (*we, us*) children, my sister Ellen and (*I, me*), gave our parents an anniversary party.

6e

The case of a pronoun after *than* or *as* expressing a comparison depends on the meaning.

When we use *than* and *as* in comparisons, we often do not complete the clauses they introduce: *Joe likes spaghetti more than (he likes) ravioli.* This sentence is clear because it can have only one sensible meaning. But in *Annie liked Ben more than Joe,* we cannot tell whether *Annie liked Ben more than (she liked) Joe* or *Annie liked Ben more than Joe (liked him).*

When such sentences end with a pronoun, however, the case of the pronoun indicates what words have been omitted. When the pronoun is subjective, it must serve as the subject of the omitted verb.

> Annie liked Ben more than *he* (liked Ben).

When the pronoun is objective, it must serve as the object of the omitted verb.

> Annie liked Ben more than (she liked) *him*.

Be careful to choose the pronoun form that fits your meaning.

ca

6g

6f

Use the objective case for pronouns that are subjects or objects of infinitives.

SUBJECT OF INFINITIVE

We wanted Gail and *her* to win the bowling tournament. [*Gail and her* is the compound subject of the infinitive *to win*.]

OBJECT OF INFINITIVE

They expect to meet *him*. [*Him* is the object of the infinitive *to meet*.]

6g

The form of the pronoun *who* depends on its function in its clause.

1

At the beginning of questions use *who* if the question is about a subject, *whom* if it is about an object.

To determine the form of *who* at the beginning of a question, construct an answer to the question, using a personal pronoun in the answer. The case of the pronoun in the answer will indicate the required case of *who* in the question.

> *Who* left the freezer door open? *She* left it open. [Subject.]
> *Whom* do you blame? I blame *him*. [Direct object.]
> *Whom* is the pizza for? It is for *her*. [Object of preposition.]

In speech the subjective case *who* is commonly used whenever it is the first word of a question, regardless of whether it is a subject or an object. But writing requires a distinction between the forms.

SPOKEN	*Who* are you working for?
WRITTEN	*Whom* are you working for? [Object of preposition *for*.]

2

In subordinate clauses use *who* and *whoever* for all subjects, *whom* and *whomever* for all objects.

The case of a pronoun in a subordinate clause depends on its function in the clause, regardless of whether the clause itself functions as a subject, an object, or a modifier. (See 5c-4.)

Give the clothes to *whoever* needs them. [*Whoever* is the subject of the clause *whoever needs them*. The entire clause is the object of the preposition *to*.]

I don't know *whom* the mayor appointed. [*Whom* is the object of *appointed: the mayor appointed whom*. The whole clause *whom the mayor appointed* is the object of the verb *know*.]

Whom he appointed is not my concern. [Again, *whom* is the object of *appointed*. This time the clause is the subject of the sentence.]

Larry is the man *whom* most people prefer. [*Whom* is the object of *prefer: people prefer whom*. The clause *whom most people prefer* modifies the noun *man*.]

If you have trouble determining which form of *who* or *whoever* to choose, rewrite the subordinate clause as a separate sentence, substituting a personal pronoun for the *who* form. The form of the personal pronoun will be the same as the required form of *who*. For instance:

I remember (*who, whom*) was sitting on the sofa. *He* was sitting on the sofa. Therefore, I remember *who* was sitting on the sofa.

The manager hired the woman (*who, whom*) his boss recommended. His boss recommended *her*. Therefore, the manager hired the woman *whom* his boss recommended.

NOTE: Don't let expressions like *I think* and *she says* confuse you when they come between *who* as a subject and its verb.

He is the man *who* I think *was* on duty yesterday. [*Who* is the subject of *was*, not the object of *think*.]

I asked the mechanic *who* Barbara said *was* her friend. [*Who* is again the subject of *was*, not the object of *said*.]

To choose between *who* and *whom* in such constructions, delete the interrupting phrase: *I asked the mechanic who was her friend.*

EXERCISE 3

Select, from the pairs in parentheses, the appropriate form of the pronoun in each of the following sentences.

Example:

The caller asked (*who, whom*) I intended to vote for.
The caller asked *whom* I intended to vote for.

1. (*Who, Whom*) will be chosen for the All-Star team?
2. (*Whoever, Whomever*) parked this Cadillac needs to learn how to drive.
3. The teacher (*who, whom*) we most respect won the award.
4. (*Who, Whom*) is Elaine living with?
5. (*Who, Whom*) is that man at the end of the alley?
6. He is the kind of person (*who, whom*), my father says, will always be able to multiply his money.
7. There will be a five-minute break for (*whoever, whomever*) among you needs it.
8. To (*who, whom*) was the letter addressed?
9. The parents of that baby, (*whoever, whomever*) they are, shouldn't leave it alone.
10. The school administrators suspended Jurgen, (*who, whom*) they suspected of setting the fire.

EXERCISE 4

Combine each pair of sentences below into one sentence by making one of them a clause beginning *who* or *whom*. Be sure to use the appropriate case form. You will have to add, delete, and rearrange words, and you may find that more than one answer is possible in each case.

Example:

A man may have committed the robbery. The police were already seeking the man.

A man *whom* the police were already seeking may have committed the robbery. *Or:* The police were already seeking a man *who* may have committed the robbery.

1. Children may have problems seeing or hearing. These children may do poorly in school.
2. Carolyn knows the person. We invited the person to speak.
3. The woman must have been angry. The woman wrote that letter.
4. David is the candidate. We think David deserves to win.
5. Truman was a president. My father greatly admired Truman.

6h

Ordinarily, use the possessive form of a pronoun or noun immediately before a gerund.

A **gerund** is the *-ing* form of the verb (*running, sleeping*) used as a noun (see 5c-2). Like nouns, gerunds function either as subjects of verbs or as objects of verbs and prepositions. And like nouns, gerunds are commonly preceded by possessive nouns and pronouns: *her marriage* (noun), *her marrying* (gerund), *our vote* (noun), *our voting* (gerund).

ca
6h

> The doctor disapproved of *their* exercising. [Compare *their exercise.*]
>
> *Jim's* failing in mathematics surprised us all. [Compare *Jim's failure.*]

Notice the difference between the gerund and the present participle. Both have the same *-ing* form. But whereas the gerund serves as a subject or object, the participle serves as an adjective.

> We often met *John* coming home late. [*Coming home late* is a participial phrase modifying *John.*]
>
> *John's* coming home late worried us. [*Coming home late* is a gerund phrase serving as the subject of *worried.*]

Notice also that a gerund usually is not preceded by the possessive when the possessive would create an awkward construction.

> AWKWARD   We heard a rumor about everybody's on the team wanting to quit.
>
> REVISED   We heard a rumor about everybody on the team wanting to quit.
>
> BETTER   We heard a rumor that everybody on the team wants to quit.

EXERCISE 5

Correct all inappropriate case forms in the following sentences, and explain the function of each case form.

After class Tom and I drove to the warehouse to pick up Tom's trunk. Between he and I, we could just lift the trunk's lid. Us weaklings could never lift the whole trunk. We looked around for someone who could help us, someone who we could count on to supply extra muscle. The man we found proved no stronger than us, but him pulling and us pushing were enough to get the trunk on a dolly and into our car. We left him to help the next weaklings who showed up.

7

Verb Forms, Tense, Mood, and Voice

VERB FORMS

All verbs have three forms called **principal parts:** an infinitive, a past tense, and a past participle. The **infinitive** (sometimes called the **plain form**) is the dictionary form of the verb. It is the form we use when the verb's action is occurring in the present and the subject is a plural noun or the pronoun *I, we, you,* or *they.*

> We *eat* chicken three times a week.
> Our friends *leave* today.
> Examinations *frighten* me.

The **past tense** is the verb form indicating that the verb's action occurred in the past. It is usually formed by adding *-ed* to the infinitive, although for some irregular verbs it is formed in other ways (see 7a).

> The chicken *crossed* the road.
> The examination *frightened* me.
> They *went* downtown. [Irregular verb.]

The **past participle** is the verb form we use with *have, has,* or *had* (*have climbed, had opened*), and it may also be used alone to modify nouns and pronouns (*sliced bread*). Except for some irregular verbs (see 7a), the past participle is usually the same as the past-tense form.

> The chicken had *crossed* the road.
> The examination has *frightened* me.
> They have *gone* downtown. [Irregular verb.]

In addition to their three principal parts, all verbs have two other forms, a present participle and an *-s* form. We form the **present participle** by adding *-ing* to the verb's infinitive, as in *acting, eat-*

169

ing, living, studying. The present participle can modify nouns and pronouns, as in *the boiling water, the girl driving, everyone living.* In addition, the present participle may combine with the forms of the verb *be* (*am, is, are, was,* and *were*) to indicate continuing action: *is buying, was finishing, were swimming.* When two verb forms are combined in this way, they may serve together as the only verb in a sentence. Note, however, that the present participle *cannot stand alone* as the only verb in a sentence.

The **-s form** of all verbs except *be* and *have* consists simply of the infinitive plus -s or -es, as in *asks, thinks, eats, does, finishes,* and *polishes.* The -s forms of *be* and *have* are *is* and *has.* We use the -s form to indicate present time when the subject is a singular noun, a singular indefinite pronoun (*everybody, someone*), or the personal pronouns *he, she,* or *it: The roof leaks; Everybody is asleep; She works hard.*

The verb *be* has eight forms rather than the five forms of most other verbs. In addition to its infinitive *be,* its past participle *been,* and its present participle *being, be* has three distinct forms in the present tense and two in the past tense.

	I	*he, she, it*	*we, you, they*
PRESENT TENSE	am	is	are
PAST TENSE	was	was	were

Auxiliary verbs, often called **helping verbs,** combine with a verb's infinitive, present participle, or past participle to indicate time and other kinds of meaning, as in *can run, was sleeping, had been eaten.* We saw one such combination above: the forms of *be* plus the present participle to indicate continuing action (*is buying, were swimming*). These combinations are **verb phrases.** Since the infinitive, present participle, or past participle in any verb phrase always carries the principal meaning, it is sometimes called the **main verb.**

Some auxiliaries — *shall* and *will; have, has,* and *had; do, does,* and *did;* and the forms of *be* (*am, is, are, was, were, been,* and *being*) — combine with main verbs to indicate time and voice (see pp. 176 and 183).

I *will go.*   The doors *were opened.*
She *had run.*   The children *are playing.*
Sylvia *did* not *want* grapes.   They *have been playing.*

Auxiliaries such as *can, could, may, might, must, ought, shall, should, will,* and *would* combine with main verbs to indicate necessity, obligation, permission, possibility, and the like.

She *can write.*   You *must go.*
I *should study.*   I *might come.*

The two kinds of auxiliaries sometimes work together to create complex verb phrases.

> You *might have told* me.
> I *may be sleeping.*
> You *ought to have eaten.*

7a
Use the correct form of irregular verbs.

As indicated above, most verbs are **regular;** that is, they form their past tense and past participle by adding *-d* or *-ed* to the infinitive.

INFINITIVE	PAST TENSE	PAST PARTICIPLE
live	lived	lived
act	acted	acted
frighten	frightened	frightened

Some verbs, however, do not follow this pattern. About two hundred English verbs are **irregular;** that is, they form their past tense and past participle in some irregular way. We have to learn the parts of the verbs by memorizing them, just as we learn new words.

Most irregular verbs form the past tense and the past participle by changing an internal vowel.

INFINITIVE	PAST TENSE	PAST PARTICIPLE
begin	began	begun
come	came	come
ring	rang	rung

Some irregular verbs change an internal vowel and add an *-n* in the past participle.

INFINITIVE	PAST TENSE	PAST PARTICIPLE
break	broke	broken
draw	drew	drawn
grow	grew	grown

Some irregular verbs have the same form in both the past tense and the past participle or in all three forms.

INFINITIVE	PAST TENSE	PAST PARTICIPLE
let	let	let
set	set	set
sleep	slept	slept

Check a dictionary if you have any doubt about a verb's principal parts. The form listed there is the infinitive. If no other forms are listed, the verb is regular; that is, both the past tense and the past participle add *-d* or *-ed* to the infinitive: *agree, agreed; sympathize, sympathized; talk, talked.* If the verb is irregular, the dictionary will list the infinitive, the past tense, and the past participle in that order: *speak, spoke, spoken; go, went, gone.* If the dictionary gives only two forms (as in *hear, heard* or *think, thought*) then the past tense and the past participle are the same.

The following list includes the most common irregular verbs. (When a principal part has two possible forms, as in *dove* and *dived,* both are included.) Look over this list to find verbs whose parts you are unsure of. Then spend some time memorizing the parts and trying them in sentences.

vb
7a

INFINITIVE	PAST TENSE	PAST PARTICIPLE
arise	arose	arisen
become	became	become
begin	began	begun
bid	bid	bid
bite	bit	bitten, bit
blow	blew	blown
break	broke	broken
bring	brought	brought
burst	burst	burst
buy	bought	bought
catch	caught	caught
choose	chose	chosen
come	came	come
cut	cut	cut
dive	dived, dove	dived
do	did	done
draw	drew	drawn
dream	dreamed, dreamt	dreamed, dreamt
drink	drank	drunk
drive	drove	driven
eat	ate	eaten
fall	fell	fallen
find	found	found
flee	fled	fled
fly	flew	flown
forget	forgot	forgotten, forgot
freeze	froze	frozen
get	got	got, gotten
give	gave	given
go	went	gone
grow	grew	grown
hang	hung, hanged (executed)	hung, hanged

INFINITIVE	PAST TENSE	PAST PARTICIPLE
hear	heard	heard
hide	hid	hidden
hold	held	held
keep	kept	kept
know	knew	known
lay	laid	laid
lead	led	led
leave	left	left
let	let	let
lie	lay	lain
lose	lost	lost
pay	paid	paid
prove	proved	proved, proven
ride	rode	ridden
ring	rang	rung
rise	rose	risen
run	ran	run
say	said	said
see	saw	seen
set	set	set
shake	shook	shaken
sing	sang, sung	sung
sink	sank, sunk	sunk
sit	sat	sat
slide	slid	slid
speak	spoke	spoken
spring	sprang, sprung	sprung
stand	stood	stood
steal	stole	stolen
swim	swam	swum
take	took	taken
tear	tore	torn
throw	threw	thrown
wear	wore	worn
wind	wound	wound
write	wrote	written

vb
7a

EXERCISE 1

Fill in each blank below with either the past tense or the past participle of the irregular verb(s) shown in parentheses, and identify each form you used.

Example:

Though we had _____ the cash box, it was _____. (*hide; steal*)

Though we had *hidden* the cash box, it was *stolen*. [Two past participles.]

1. Every afternoon after work, we have _____ at the city pool and then _____ a party. (*swim; hold*)
2. The minister _____ to the Kiwanis Club last night. (*speak*)
3. Because the day was so dark, it seemed as though the sun had never _____. (*rise*)
4. Before we could stop him, my cousin had _____ all the chocolate milk and had _____ all the cookies. (*drink; eat*)
5. The fans were encouraged because their team had not _____ a home game all season. (*lose*)
6. She _____ hoping she would be _____ for the lacrosse team. (*keep; choose*)
7. The wind _____, and my hands almost _____. (*blow; freeze*)
8. If we had not _____ the table, we would have _____ asleep. (*leave; fall*)
9. The dry spell was _____ when the rains _____ again. (*break; begin*)
10. The halfback _____ the pass _____ by the quarterback. (*catch; throw*)

7b

Distinguish between *sit* and *set* and between *lie* and *lay*.

The principal parts of *sit* and *set* and of *lie* and *lay* are often confused, especially in speech. Here are the forms of the two verbs.

INFINITIVE	PAST TENSE	PAST PARTICIPLE
sit	sat	sat
set	set	set
lie	lay	lain
lay	laid	laid

Sit and *lie,* as in *Sit down* and *Lie down,* mean to "be seated" and to "recline," respectively. They are both **intransitive verbs:** They cannot take objects. *Set* and *lay,* as in *Set the eggs down carefully* and *Lay the floor boards there,* mean to "put" or "place" something. They are **transitive verbs** and usually take objects. (See 5a-3.)

Loretta *lies* down every afternoon. [No object.]
Clarence *laid* the plans on the table. [*Plans* is the object of *laid.*]
The dog *sits* by the back door. [No object.]
Mr. Flood *set* the jug down roughly. [*Jug* is the object of *set.*]

EXERCISE 2

Fill in each blank below with the correct past-tense or past-participle verb form. You will have to choose the correct verb from the pair given in parentheses and then supply an appropriate form of that verb.

Example:

The dishes still _____ on the counter, exactly where we had _____ them. (*lie* or *lay; sit* or *set*)

The dishes still *lay* on the counter, exactly where we had *set* them.

1. The spider _____ in its web and _____ in wait for its prey. (*sit* or *set; lie* or *lay*)
2. After she had _____ the table, she _____ a cloth over it. (*sit* or *set; lie* or *lay*)
3. Joan's wallet had _____ in the street for two days. (*lie* or *lay*)
4. The skunk _____ asleep in the trap. (*lie* or *lay*)
5. He _____ the sick child down for a nap and then _____ watching over her. (*lie* or *lay; sit* or *set*)

7C

Use the *-s* and *-ed* forms of the verb when they are required.

In speech we hear the *-s* and *-ed* endings of verbs clearly when they form a separate syllable, as in *pleases, passes, finishes, spotted,* or *demanded.* But in many verbs the final *-s* or *-ed* sound almost entirely disappears, especially if the ending does not form another syllable and if the verb's infinitive ends in certain consonant sounds, as in *asks, adds, bagged, lived,* and *used.* The *s* or *ed* sound may also fade if words immediately following the verb begin with the same or a similar sound, as in *asks Susan, used to, raced downtown,* and *supposed to.*

In your writing be sure all present-tense verbs end in *-s* when they follow singular nouns, the personal pronouns *he, she,* or *it,* and most indefinite pronouns. (See also 8a-1 and 8a-5.) Check all past-tense and past-participle forms of regular verbs to be sure they end in *-d* or *-ed.* If you are in doubt about the forms, consult a dictionary. Remember that if the dictionary lists no other forms with the plain form, the verb is regular and requires *-d* or *-ed* in the past tense and past participle.

EXERCISE 3

Supply the correct form of each verb in parentheses below. Be careful to include *-s* and *-ed* endings where they are needed.

A teacher sometimes (*ask*) too much of a student. In high school I was once (*punish*) for being sick. I had (*miss*) some school, and I (*realize*) that I would fail a test unless I had a chance to make up the class work. I (*discuss*) the problem with the teacher, but he said I was (*suppose*) to make up the work while I was sick.

At that I (*walk*) out of the class. I (*receive*) a failing grade then, but it did not change my attitudes. Today I still balk when a teacher (*make*) unreasonable demands or (*expect*) miracles.

TENSE

Tense is the attribute of a verb that shows the time of the verb's action in relation to the time at which the writer writes or the speaker speaks. The **simple tenses** indicate that an action or state of being is present, past, or future. You have met present and past already in the verb's principal parts. The future is formed with the helping verb *will* or *shall*. The **perfect tenses** indicate that an action was or will be completed before another time or action. (The term *perfect* derives from the Latin *perfectus,* meaning "completed.") The perfect tenses are formed with the helping verb *have*.

SIMPLE TENSES	REGULAR VERB	IRREGULAR VERB
Present	You *work*.	You *write*.
Past	You *worked*.	You *wrote*.
Future	You *will work*.	You *will write*.

PERFECT TENSES		
Present perfect	You *have worked*.	You *have written*.
Past perfect	You *had worked*.	You *had written*.
Future perfect	You *will have worked*.	You *will have written*.

In addition, all verbs have a set of **progressive forms,** sometimes called the **progressive tense,** that indicate continuing (therefore, progressive) action. The progressive uses the *-ing* form of the verb plus a form of *be* to show time. Regular and irregular verbs do not differ.

PROGRESSIVE FORMS	
Present	You *are working/writing*.
Past	You *were working/writing*.
Future	You *will be working/writing*.
Present perfect	You *have been working/writing*.
Past perfect	You *had been working/writing*.
Future perfect	You *will have been working/writing*.

We use the auxiliary *do* (*does*) and its past tense *did,* together with the infinitive of the verb, in asking questions, making negative statements, and showing emphasis.

Does he *write* every day? [Question.]
He *did* not *write* every day. [Negation.]
He *does write* every day. [Emphasis.]

7d

Observe the special uses of the present tense and the uses of the perfect tenses.

The present tense generally indicates action occurring at the time of speaking, as in *She understands what you mean* or *From here I see the river and the docks*. It is also used in several special situations.

TO INDICATE HABITUAL OR RECURRING ACTION

Abby *goes* to New York every Friday.
The store *opens* at ten o'clock.

TO STATE A GENERAL TRUTH

The mills of the gods *grind* slowly.
The earth *is* round.

TO DISCUSS THE CONTENT OF LITERATURE, FILM, AND SO ON

Huckleberry Finn *has* adventures we all would like to experience.
In that article the author *examines* several causes of crime.

TO INDICATE FUTURE TIME

Our friends *arrive* the day after tomorrow.
Ted *leaves* in the next half-hour.

(Notice that in sentences like the last two, time is really indicated by the phrases *the day after tomorrow* and *in the next half-hour*.)

The perfect tenses generally indicate an action completed before another specific time or action. The present perfect tense can also indicate action begun in the past and continued into the present.

PRESENT PERFECT

Hannah *has fed* the dog, so we can go. [Action is completed at the time of the statement.]

Hannah *has* always *fed* the dog. [Action began in the past but continues now.]

PAST PERFECT

Harley *had finished* his work by the time his friends arrived. [Action was completed before another past action.]

FUTURE PERFECT

He *will have finished* his work by the time his friends arrive. [The present tense *arrive* with *by the time* indicates the future. The future perfect *will have finished* indicates that his work will be completed before the future arrival.]

7e

Use the appropriate sequence of verb tenses.

vb
7e

The term **sequence of tenses** refers to the relation between the verb in a main clause and the verbs or verbals in subordinate clauses or verbal phrases (see 5c). In the sentence *He left after I arrived,* the past tense of the verb *arrived* is in normal sequence with the past tense of *left.* (For a discussion of keeping verb tenses consistent within compound sentences and from one sentence to another, see 13b.)

1

When the verb in a main clause is in any tense except the past or past perfect, the verb in the subordinate clause may be in any tense required by meaning.

The verbs in main and subordinate clauses do not have to have identical tenses, but the tense in the subordinate clause should reflect your meaning. In the following sentences all the verb forms follow a clear and natural sequence, though the tenses in main and subordinate clauses are different.

Mike *knows* that Susan *visited* New Orleans. [Mike's present knowledge is about something that happened in the past, Susan's visit.]

Mike *has known* all along that Susan *will visit* New Orleans. [Mike's knowledge began in the past and continues; Susan's going to New Orleans lies in the future.]

Susan *will explain* to Mike why she *changed* her plans. [The explanation lies in the future, but the change of plans occurred some time in the past.]

Note that any change of tense between a main and subordinate clause must be logical. The sentence *My family always keeps pets because we liked them* does not seem logical because *liked* indicates that the liking is past and thus is not a reason to keep pets in the present.

2

When the verb in a main clause is in the past or past perfect tense, the verb in the subordinate clause must also be in the past or past perfect tense.

We *talked* for a long time after we *returned* home. [Since the talking took place in the past, the return home must also have occurred in the past. The past perfect *had returned* would also indicate that the return occurred at a time before the past talking. But the present *return* or the future *will return* would make no sense in the sentence.]

My friend *had left* before I *arrived.* [The past perfect *had left* indicates that the friend's leaving occurred earlier than the past arrival.]

vb

7e

EXCEPTION: When a subordinate clause expresses a general truth such as *The earth is round,* use the present tense even though the verb of the main clause is in the past or past perfect tense.

I never *realized* that many marriages *are* genuinely happy.

3

Use a present infinitive to express action at the same time as or later than that of the verb. Use a perfect infinitive to express action earlier than that of the verb.

The **present infinitive** is the verb's plain form preceded by *to* (see 5c-2). In the following sentences the present infinitive shows action at the same time as or later than that of the verb.

I *went to see* a World Series game last year. [The going and the seeing occurred at the same time in the past.]

I *want to see* a World Series game this year. [The wanting is present; the seeing is still in the future.]

I *would have liked to see* (not *to have seen*) the other World Series games last year. [The present infinitive indicates the same past time as *would have liked.*]

The verb's **perfect infinitive** consists of *to have* followed by the past participle, as in *to have talked, to have won.* In the following sentences the perfect infinitive indicates action earlier than that of the verb.

Sarah *would like* (not *would have liked*) *to have heard* Sylvia Plath read her poetry. [The liking occurs in the present; the hearing would have occurred in the past.]

The election *was thought to have been rigged.* [The rigging of the election occurred before the thinking about it.]

4

Use a present participle to express action at the same time as that of the verb. Use a past participle or a present perfect participle to express action earlier than that of the verb.

In the sentence below, the present participle shows action occurring at the same time as that of the verb.

Driving across the United States, he *was astonished* by the vast spaces. [The driving and the astonishment occurred in the same past time.]

In the following sentences the past participle and the present perfect participle, respectively, show action occurring earlier than that of the verb.

vb

7e

Exhausted by overwork, Sheila *remained* at home for two weeks. [The exhaustion occurred before Sheila remained home.]

Having lived all his life in the country, he *is frightened* by cities. [Life in the country preceded the fear of cities.]

EXERCISE 4

Revise the following sentences so that the sequence of verb tenses is appropriate. Some items have more than one possible answer.

> *Example:*
>
> Hedy had hoped to have been elected.
> Hedy had hoped *to be elected.*

1. My grandfather died before I had arrived at the hospital.
2. The jury recommends leniency because the criminal was so young.
3. The mechanic would have liked to have owned the car.
4. The archaeologist opened the tomb when the bats inside it are killed.
5. She was on the critical list since she fell yesterday.
6. The stagehands refused to put up the set for the play because they think the design is unsafe.
7. Many shopkeepers should have done more to have protected themselves against robberies.
8. I enroll only in courses that left me time to work.
9. Having driven without my glasses on, I caused an accident.
10. The police claimed that the dog bites a child.

EXERCISE 5

The tenses in each sentence below are in correct sequence. Change the tense of the verb as instructed in parentheses. Then change the tense of infinitives, participles, and other verbs as necessary to restore correct sequence. Some items have more than one possible answer.

> *Example:*
>
> He will call when he reaches his destination. (*Change will call to called.*)
>
> He called when he *reached* (or *had reached*) his destination.

1. Everyone who auditions for the play is given a part. (*Change auditions to auditioned.*)
2. I would like to have attended that concert. (*Change would like to would have liked.*)
3. The elderly man hoped that his children would visit him over Chanukah. (*Change hoped to hopes.*)
4. Soldiers are taught to obey commands so that their nerves will be steady during combat. (*Change are taught to were taught.*)
5. Everyone believed the woman was crazy because she repeatedly claimed she had seen a ghost. (*Change believed to believes.*)

vb
7

MOOD

Mood in grammar refers to a verb form that indicates the writer's or speaker's attitude toward what he or she is saying. The **indicative mood** states a fact or opinion or asks a question. The **imperative mood** expresses a command or gives a direction. The **subjunctive mood** expresses a requirement, a desire, or a suggestion, or states a condition that is contrary to fact. The three moods are illustrated in these sentences:

INDICATIVE   They *need* our help. [Opinion.]
             Marie *works* only on Saturday. [Fact.]
             Why *does* she *work* on Saturday? [Question.]

IMPERATIVE   *Work* only on Saturdays. [Command.]
             Turn right at the light. [Direction.]

SUBJUNCTIVE   Her father urged that she *work* only on Saturdays. [Suggestion.]

             Regulations require that applications *be* in writing. [Requirement.]

             I wish that I *swam* better. [Desire.]

             If she *were* to work more, her studies would suffer. [Condition contrary to present fact.]

The imperative omits the subject of the sentence: (*You*) *Work only on Saturdays.* In the present tense the subjunctive mood uses only the infinitive of the verb no matter what the subject is (see the first subjunctive sentence above). The present subjunctive form of *be* is *be* rather than *am, is,* or *are* (second subjunctive sentence). In the past tense of the subjunctive all verbs except *be* use their past tense (third subjunctive sentence); *be* uses *were* for all subjects (fourth subjunctive sentence). (For a discussion of keeping mood consistent within and among sentences, see 13b.)

7f

Use the subjunctive verb forms appropriately.

Although in the past English used distinctive subjunctive verb forms in many contexts, such forms appear now only in two kinds of constructions and in a few idiomatic expressions.

vb

7f

1

Use the subjunctive form *were* in contrary-to-fact clauses beginning with *if* or expressing a wish.

If I *were* you, I'd see a doctor.
If the rash *were* treatable, she would have treated it.
I wish Jeannie *were* my doctor.

NOTE: The indicative form *was* (*I wish Jeannie was my doctor*) is common in speech and in some informal writing, but the subjunctive *were* is usual in formal English.

2

Use the subjunctive in *that* clauses following verbs that demand, request, or recommend.

Verbs like *ask, insist, urge, require, recommend,* and *suggest* often precede subordinate clauses beginning with *that* and containing the substance of the request or suggestion. The verb in such *that* clauses should be in the subjunctive mood.

The psychologist urged that the patient *be released.*
The law required that he *report* weekly.
Julie's mother insisted that she *stay* home.
Instructors commonly ask that papers *be finished* on time.

NOTE: These constructions have widely used alternative forms, such as *The law required him to report weekly* or *Julie's mother insisted on her staying home.*

3

Use the subjunctive in some set phrases and idioms.

Several English expressions commonly use the subjunctive. For example:

Come rain or *come* shine.
Be that as it may.
The people *be* damned.

EXERCISE 6

Revise the following sentences with appropriate subjunctive verb forms.

> *Example:*
>
> I would help the old man if there was a way I could reach him.
>
> I would help the old man if there *were* a way I could reach him.

1. If I was happier, I would not have so much trouble in school.
2. Marie asks that the motion is adopted.
3. The syllabus requires that each student writes three papers and takes two essay tests.
4. They treat me as if I was their son.
5. If a road was connecting them, the two towns could do business with each other.

VOICE

Verbs can show whether their subjects are acting or are acted upon. In the **active voice** the subject names the actor.

> *David wrote* the paper.
> *Bookies coordinate* illegal bets.

In the passive voice the subject names the object or receiver of the action.

> *The paper was written* by David.
> *Illegal bets are coordinated* by bookies.

The passive voice of a verb always consists of the appropriate form of the helping verb *be* plus the past participle of the main verb. Other helping verbs may also be present.

> Senators *are elected* for six-year terms.
> Jerry *has been given* complete freedom.

To change a sentence from active to passive voice, we convert the direct object or the indirect object of the verb into the subject of the verb. Thus, only verbs that take objects (transitive verbs) can form the passive voice.

ACTIVE	We *gave* Jerry complete freedom.
PASSIVE	Jerry *was given* complete freedom. [Indirect object becomes subject.]
PASSIVE	Complete freedom *was given* (to) Jerry. [Direct object becomes subject.]

vb

7

To change a sentence from passive to active voice, we convert the verb's subject into a direct or an indirect object and substitute a new subject for the previous one.

PASSIVE	Sally *was bitten* by Jamie's dog.
ACTIVE	Jamie's dog *bit* Sally.
PASSIVE	The statement *was read* at a press conference.
ACTIVE	The company's representative *read* the statement at a press conference.

The passive voice can be useful when the actor is either unknown or unimportant in a sentence.

Ray Appleton *was murdered* after he returned home. [The murderer is presumably unknown, and in any event Ray Appleton's death is the point of the sentence.]

In the first experiment acid *was added* to the solution. [The person who added the acid, perhaps the writer, is less important than the fact that acid was added. Passive sentences are common in scientific writing.]

Except in such situations, however, you should prefer the active voice in your writing. By omitting the actor, the passive can deprive writing of clarity and strength. The active voice is generally more concise, more forthright, and more vigorous than the passive. (See 18d and 31c-3 for additional cautions against the passive voice.)

EXERCISE 7

Convert the following sentences from active voice to passive or from passive to active. (In converting passive verbs to active, you may have to supply a subject for the new sentence.)

Example:
The building was demolished last spring.
The *city demolished* the building last spring.

1. Drugs are often prescribed to relieve depression.
2. Whales are still killed by foreign fishing fleets.
3. The plane crash killed over thirty people.
4. The survivors were discovered by a passing freighter.
5. The Church was thought very important by the people of the Middle Ages.

EXERCISE 8

Circle all the verbs in the following paragraph and correct their form, tense, or mood if necessary.

We use to know nothing about our earliest ancestors. Before Darwin's *On the Origin of Species* was published in 1859, people had thought humans are only thousands of years old. Now we know that the earliest animals to have walked upright on two legs (a sign of having been human) existed *millions* of years ago. Anthropologists in Africa discovered footprints almost like ours that were 3½ million years old. When the footprints had been excavated, they were seen to be laying beside the remains of an ancient river that has long since dried up.

vb

7

8

Agreement

Agreement refers to the correspondence in form between sub-jects and verbs and between pronouns and their **antecedents,** the nouns or other pronouns they refer to. Subjects and verbs agree in number (singular and plural) and in person (first, second, and third). Pronouns and their antecedents agree in person, number, and gender (masculine, feminine, and neuter).

The following sentences illustrate agreement between subject and verb and between pronoun and antecedent.

> *Sarah* often *speaks* up in class. [Both subject and verb are in the third-person singular form.]

> Even though *we understand, we* still *dislike* it. [Both subjects and verbs are in the first-person plural form.]

> *Claude* resented their ignoring *him.* [Both the pronoun *him* and its antecedent *Claude* are masculine, and the pronoun agrees with its antecedent's third-person singular form.]

> The *dogs* stand still while *they* are judged. [The pronoun *they* agrees with the third-person plural form of its antecedent *dogs.*]

8a
Make subjects and verbs agree in number.

What you want to say will always determine the number of the subject you select. You are unlikely to write *door* when you mean *doors.* Once you have selected a subject, it will determine the form of the verb you use: *the door opens; the doors open.*

Most subject-verb agreement problems arise when the writer omits endings from subjects or verbs, when the writer cannot easily determine whether the subject is singular or plural, or when words come between subject and verb and blur their relationship. The following conventions cover these and other problems that affect subject-verb agreement.

1

Use the verb ending *-s* or *-es* with all singular nouns and third-person singular pronouns.

Adding *-s* or *-es* to a noun usually makes the noun *plural*, whereas adding *-s* or *-es* to a present-tense verb makes the verb *singular*. Thus if the subject noun has an added *-s* or *-es*, the verb will not have it. If the subject does not have the *-s* ending, the verb will have it.

SINGULAR	PLURAL
The boy eats.	The boys eat.
The bird soars.	The birds soar.

(The only exceptions to these rules involve the nouns that form irregular plurals, such as *child, children; man, men; woman, women.*)

Writers often omit *-s* and *-es* endings because they are not pronounced clearly in speech (as in *asks* and *lists*) or because they are not used regularly in some English dialects. However, the endings are required in both spoken and written standard English.

NONSTANDARD	Julie *resist* any kind of change.
STANDARD	Julie *resists* any kind of change.

NONSTANDARD	Their *action* demand a response.
STANDARD	Their *actions* demand a response.

Remember that the verb *be* is irregular. In the present tense we use *is* with *he, she, it,* and singular nouns (*tree is*) and *are* with all plurals (*trees are*). In the past tense we use *was* with *he, she, it,* and singular nouns (*tree was*) and *were* with all plurals (*trees were*).

(See Chapter 7, pp. 170 and 175, for further discussion of these verb forms.)

2

Subject and verb should agree even when other words come between them.

When the subject and verb fall next to each other in a sentence, they usually agree naturally because they sound right. But when other words come between the subject and verb, particularly other nouns, then we may commit agreement errors because we tend to connect the verb to the nearest noun rather than to the actual subject.

> A catalog of courses and requirements often *baffles* (not *baffle*) students. [The verb must agree with the subject, *catalog*, not the nearer word *requirements*.]
>
> The profits earned by the cosmetic industry *are* (not *is*) high. [The subject is *profits*, not *industry*.]

NOTE: *As well as, together with, along with, in addition to,* and similar expressions are prepositions rather than coordinating conjunctions (see 5c-1 and 5d-1). Thus the phrases they begin do not change the number of the subject.

> The governor, as well as his advisers, *has* (not *have*) agreed to attend the protest rally.

In such a sentence if you really mean *and* (*The governor and his advisors have agreed to attend*), you can avoid confusion and awkwardness (and extra words) by using *and*. Then the subject is compound, and the verb should be plural (see 8a-3).

3
Subjects joined by *and* usually take plural verbs.

Two or more subjects joined by *and* take a plural verb whether one or all of the subjects are singular.

> Frost and Roethke *are* her favorite poets.
> The dog, the monkey, the children, and the tent *were* in the car.

EXCEPTIONS: When the two or more parts of the subject form a single idea or refer to a single person or thing, then they take a singular verb.

> Avocado and bean sprouts *is* my favorite sandwich.
> The winner and new champion *was* in the shower.

When a compound subject is preceded by the adjectives *each* or *every*, then the verb is usually singular.

> At customs, every box, bag, and parcel *is* inspected.
> Each man, woman, and child *has* a right to be heard.

But when a compound subject is *followed* by *each*, the verb is plural.

> The man and the woman each *have* different problems to contend with.

4

When parts of a subject are joined by *or* or *nor*, the verb agrees with the nearer part.

When all parts of a subject joined by *or* or *nor* are singular, the verb is singular; when all parts are plural, the verb is plural.

> Neither the teacher nor the student *knows* the answer.
> The rabbits or the woodchucks *have eaten* my lettuce.

Problems with subjects joined by *or* or *nor* occur most often when one part of the subject is singular and the other plural. In that case usage requires that the verb agree with the subject part closer to it. To avoid awkwardness in such sentences, place the plural part closer to the verb.

> **AWKWARD**   Neither the employees nor the manager *was* on time.
>
> **IMPROVED**   Neither the manager nor the employees *were* on time.

The same problem arises when the subject consists of nouns and pronouns of different person requiring different verb forms: *neither Jim nor I, either he or you.* In this case, too, the verb agrees with the part of the subject nearer to it.

> Either he or you *are* late.
> Neither Jim nor I *am* late.

Since observing this convention often results in awkwardness, avoid the problem altogether by rewording the sentence.

> **AWKWARD**   Either she or you *are* late.
>
> **IMPROVED**   Either she *is* late, or you *are*.

5

Generally, use singular verbs with indefinite pronouns.

An **indefinite pronoun** is one that does not refer to a specific person or thing. The common indefinite pronouns include *all, any, anybody, anyone, anything, each, either, everybody, everyone, everything, neither, nobody, none, no one, one, some, somebody, someone,* and *something*. Most of these are singular in meaning (they refer to a single unspecified person or thing), and they take singular verbs.

> The president said anyone *was* welcome to join.
> Something *is* wrong with that man.

But a few indefinite pronouns like *all, any, none,* and *some* may be either singular or plural in meaning. The verbs you use with these pronouns depend on the meaning of the nouns or pronouns they refer to.

> All of the money *is* reserved for emergencies. [*All* refers to *money*, so the verb is singular.]

> When the men finally arrive, all *go* straight to work. [*All* refers to *the men*, so the verb is plural.]

agr

8a

6

Collective nouns take singular or plural verbs depending on meaning.

A **collective noun** has singular form but names a group of individuals or things — for example, *army, audience, committee, crowd, family, group, team*. When used as a subject, a collective noun may take a singular or plural verb, depending on the context in which it appears. When you are considering the group as one unit, use the singular form of the verb.

> Contrary to some reports, the American family *is* still strong.
> Any band *sounds* good in that concert hall.

But when you are considering the group's members as individuals who act separately, use the plural form of the verb.

> The old group *have* gone their separate ways.
> Since their last concert, the band *have* not agreed on where to play.

NOTE: Even when the plural verb form is properly used, as in these examples, it often sounds awkward. For this reason you may prefer to rephrase such sentences with plural subjects, as in *The members of the old group have gone their separate ways*.

Number, used as a collective noun, may be singular or plural. Preceded by *a*, it is always plural; preceded by *the*, it is always singular.

> A number of my friends *have* decided to live off campus.
> The number of people in debt *is* very large.

7

The verb agrees with the subject even when the normal word order is inverted.

Most often, inverted subject-verb order occurs in so-called expletive constructions beginning with *there* or *it* and a form of *to be* (see 5e-4).

> There *are* too many students in that class. [*Students* is the subject; *are* is the verb. Compare *Too many students are in that class*.]

After many years there *is* finally peace in that country. [*Peace* is the subject; *is* is the verb. Compare *Peace is in that country.*]

In this construction, *there is* may be used before a compound subject when the first element in the subject is singular.

There *is* much work to do and little time to do it.

(Expletive constructions are often needlessly wordy. See 18e and 31c-3.)

Word order may sometimes be inverted for emphasis without use of the expletive construction. The verb still agrees with its subject.

From the mountains *comes* an eerie, shimmering light.

agr

8a

8
A linking verb agrees with its subject, not the subject complement.

When using the construction in which a subject complement follows a linking verb, you should be sure that the verb agrees with its subject, the first element, not with the noun or pronoun that serves as a subject complement.

Henry's sole support *is* his mother and father. [The subject is *support*.]

Henry's mother and father *are* his sole support. [The subject is *mother and father*.]

(See 5a-3 for review of linking verbs and subject complements.)

9
When used as subjects, *who*, *which*, and *that* take verbs that agree with their antecedents.

The relative pronouns *who*, *which*, and *that* do not have different singular and plural forms. When one of these pronouns serves as a subject, its verb should agree with the noun or other pronoun that the relative pronoun refers to (its antecedent).

Mayor Garber ought to listen to the people who *work* for her. [*Who* refers to the plural *people*, so the verb is plural.]

Jane is the person who usually *solves* our problems. [*Who* refers to the singular *Jane*, so the verb is singular.]

Agreement problems often occur with relative pronouns when the sentence includes a phrase beginning with *one of the*.

Roberts is one of the teachers who *have* a bad reputation. [*Who* refers to the plural *teachers*. Several teachers have a bad reputation; Roberts is one of them.]

Roberts is the only one of the teachers who *has* paid attention to me. [*Who* refers to *one*. Among the teachers only one, Roberts, has paid attention.]

agr
8a

10

Nouns with plural form but singular meaning take singular verbs.

Some nouns with plural form (that is, ending in -*s*) are usually regarded as singular in meaning. They include *athletics, economics, mathematics, means, measles, news, politics, physics,* and *statistics.*

After so long a wait, the news *has* to be good.
Statistics *is* required of psychology majors.

Measurements and figures ending in -*s* may also be singular when the quantity they refer to is a unit.

Three years *is* a long time to wait.
Three-fourths of her library *consists* of reference books.

These words and amounts are plural in meaning when they describe individual items rather than whole groups or whole bodies of activity or knowledge.

The statistics *prove* him wrong. [*Statistics* refers to facts.]
Two-fifths of the cars on the road *are* unsafe. [The cars are unsafe separately.]

11

Titles and words named as words take singular verbs.

When your sentence subject is the title of a work (such as a book or a movie) or a word you are defining or describing, the verb should be singular even if the title or the word is plural.

Dream Days remains one of her favorite books.
Folks is a down-home word for *people.*

EXERCISE 1

Revise the verbs in the following sentences as needed to make subjects and verbs agree in number. If the sentence is already correct as given, circle the number preceding it.

Example:
Each of the nominees deserve to win.
Each of the nominees *deserves* to win.

1. A number of students was seen among the demonstrators.
2. Neither that drawing nor those paintings appeals to my friend.
3. Margaret Gayoso is among those who is going to Washington to lobby for preservation of the wilderness.
4. The idea that the college should grant privileges to athletes are ridiculous.
5. The committee has voted unanimously to raise tuition.
6. Surely someone among all those experts know the answer.
7. Mathematics are his special problem.
8. *Seminars* have a more elegant sound than *classes*.
9. Every Tom, Dick, and Harry seems to have an opinion on how the federal dollar should be spent.
10. The police claimed that the crowd were endangering public safety.
11. He is one of those persons who breaks promises easily.
12. *Two Brothers* is the title of his newest movie.
13. Neither the chemistry instructor nor her lab assistants seems to know the assignment for today.
14. A new porch door, in addition to new windows, are needed.
15. Either the manager or his representative are responsible for handling complaints.

agr
8b

8b
Make pronouns and their antecedents agree in person and number.

The **antecedent** of a pronoun is the noun or other pronoun it refers to. The antecedent usually comes before the pronoun that refers to it, but it may follow the pronoun.

> Every *dog* in that kennel has received *its* shots. [*Dog* is the antecedent of *its*.]

> Having received *their* tax bills, the *home owners* worried about payment. [*Home owners*, the subject of the main clause, is the antecedent of *their* in the introductory phrase.]

> In *Grapes of Wrath*, *Steinbeck* shows *his* sympathy for migrant farm workers. [*Steinbeck* is the antecedent of *his*.]

As these examples show, a pronoun agrees with its antecedent in gender (masculine, feminine, neuter), person (first, second, third), and number (singular, plural). Since pronouns derive their meaning from their antecedents, pronoun-antecedent agreement is essential for the reader to understand what you are saying.

1

Antecedents joined by *and* usually take plural pronouns.

Two or more antecedents joined by *and* take a plural pronoun whether one or all of the antecedents are singular.

My adviser and I can't coordinate *our* schedules.
Their argument resolved, George and Jennifer had dinner together.

EXCEPTIONS: When the compound antecedent refers to a single idea, person, or thing, then the pronoun is singular.

The athlete and scholar forgot both *his* javelin and *his* books.

When the compound antecedent follows *each* or *every*, the pronoun is singular.

Every girl and woman took *her* seat.

2

When parts of an antecedent are joined by *or* or *nor*, the pronoun agrees with the nearer part.

When the parts of an antecedent are connected by *or* or *nor*, the pronoun's person and number should agree with the part closer to it.

Steve or John should have raised *his* hand.

Either consumers or car manufacturers will have *their* way.

Neither the student nor the elderly people will retrieve *their* deposits from that landlord.

When one subject is plural and the other singular, as in the last example, the sentence will be awkward unless you put the plural subject second.

AWKWARD	Neither my parents nor my sister filed *her* tax return last year.
IMPROVED	Neither my sister nor my parents filed *their* tax return last year.

3

Generally, use a singular pronoun when the antecedent is an indefinite pronoun.

Indefinite pronouns refer to persons or things in general rather than to a specific person or thing. The indefinite pronouns *each, either, neither,* and *no one* as well as those ending in *-body, -one,* or *-thing* (*everybody, someone, anything*) are singular in meaning. When these indefinite pronouns serve as antecedents to other pronouns, the other pronouns are singular.

> Everyone on the team had *her* own locker.
> Each of the boys likes *his* teacher.
> Something made *its* presence felt.

Sometimes using a singular pronoun to refer to an indefinite pronoun results in an awkward sentence when the indefinite pronoun clearly means "many" or "all."

> **AWKWARD**   After everyone left, I shut the door behind *him*.

In speech we commonly avoid such awkwardness with a plural pronoun: *After everyone left, I shut the door behind them*. In all but the most informal writing, however, you should rewrite the sentence.

> **REWRITTEN**   After all the guests left, I shut the door behind *them*.

The generic he

In the examples above, the gender intended by the indefinite pronoun is known and reflected in the pronouns *her, his,* and *its*. However, the meaning of indefinite pronouns more often includes both masculine and feminine genders, not one or the other. In such cases we traditionally use *he* (or *him*, or *his*) to refer to the indefinite antecedent. But many people see the so-called **generic** *he* (or generalized *he*) as unfairly excluding females. Thus many writers now avoid using *he* in these situations by rewriting their sentences.

> **ORIGINAL**   Everyone brought *his* book to class.
>
> **BROADER**   Everyone brought *his or her* book to class. [Overused, this option can be wordy or awkward.]
>
> **PLURAL**   All the students brought *their* books to class. [This option can be used frequently without creating awkwardness.]

In speech we often solve the problem of the generic *he* by combining a plural pronoun with an indefinite pronoun, as in *Everyone brought their books to class*. But this construction violates the expectations of most readers, so it should be avoided in writing.

4

Collective noun antecedents take singular or plural pronouns depending on meaning.

Collective nouns like *army, committee, family, group,* and *team* have singular form but may be referred to by singular or plural pronouns, depending on the meaning intended. When you are referring to the group as a unit — all its members acting together — then the pronoun is singular.

> The committee voted to disband *itself*.
> The team attended a banquet in *its* honor.

agr

8b

When you are referring to the individual members of the group, the pronoun is plural.

> The audience arose quietly from *their* seats.
> The old group have gone *their* separate ways.

The last example demonstrates the importance of being consistent in verb use as well as pronoun choice when assigning a singular or plural meaning to a collective noun (see also 8a-6).

| INCONSISTENT | The old group *has* gone *their* separate ways. |
| CONSISTENT | The old group *have* gone *their* separate ways. |

EXERCISE 2

Revise the following sentences so that pronouns and their antecedents agree in person and number. Some items have more than one possible answer. If the sentence is already correct as given, circle the number preceding it.

Example:

Every one of the puppies thrived in their new home.
Every one of the puppies thrived in *its* new home.

1. Each of the fifty parents visited their child's teacher.
2. Neither of the two candidates is well known for her honesty.
3. Everyone on the women's basketball team brought their own equipment.
4. No new parent feels entirely secure in their role.
5. The team had never won on their home court.
6. The town offers few opportunities for someone to let out their tensions.
7. Each of the thirty students conducted their own experiments.
8. Will either Mary or Lucy send in their application?
9. The family pulled strings to get its dog released from the pound.
10. Did any of the boys believe they would get away with cheating?

EXERCISE 3

In the following sentences subjects agree with verbs, and pronouns agree with antecedents. Make the change specified in parentheses after each sentence, and then revise the sentence as necessary to maintain agreement. Some items have more than one possible answer.

Example:

The student attends weekly conferences with her teacher. (*Change The student to Students.*)

Students *attend* weekly conferences with *their* teacher.

1. He who does poorly in school often loses respect for himself. (*Change He to People.*)
2. Teen-agers who collect baseball cards often devote much money and time to their hobby. (*Change Teen-agers to A teen-ager.*)
3. The dancer who fails to practice risks injuring herself. (*Change The dancer to Dancers.*)
4. The computers were purchased because of their simplicity. (*Change computers to computer.*)
5. Their exams over, the seniors celebrate by throwing a party. (*Change seniors to senior.*)
6. The photographs show the beauty of the landscape, but their dim light obscures details. (*Change photographs to photograph.*)
7. All workers have some complaint about their jobs. (*Change All workers to Each worker.*)
8. Even though the disarmament conferences have resulted in little change, the government continues to attend them. (*Change conferences to conference.*)
9. Judith is the one who always makes the decisions, and the rest of us resent her authority. (*Change Judith to Judith and Bill.*)
10. Since we don't know what's behind it, the locked door seems more mysterious than it probably is. (*Change door to doors.*)

EXERCISE 4

Revise the sentences in the following paragraph to correct errors in agreement between subjects and verbs or between pronouns and their antecedents.

Everyone has their favorite view of professional athletes. A common view is that the athletes are like well-paid children who have no real work to do, have no responsibilities, and simply enjoy the game and the good money. But this view of professional athletes fail to consider the grueling training the athletes have to go through to become professionals. Either training or competing lead each athlete to take risks that can result in their serious injury. The athletes have tremendous responsibility to the team they play on, which need to function as a unit at all times to win their games. Most athletes are finished as active team players by the age of forty, when he is too stiff and banged-up to go on. Rather than just listening to any of the people who criticizes professional athletes, everyone interested in sports need to defend the athletes. They take stiff physical punishment so neither the sports fanatic nor the casual observer are deprived of their pleasure.

9
Adjectives and Adverbs

Adjectives and adverbs are modifiers that describe, restrict, or otherwise qualify the words to which they relate. **Adjectives** modify nouns and pronouns. **Adverbs** modify verbs, adjectives, and other adverbs.

ADJECTIVE-NOUN	ADJ N serious student
ADJECTIVE-PRONOUN	ADJ PRON ordinary one
ADVERB-VERB	ADV V hurriedly seek
ADVERB-ADJECTIVE-NOUN	ADV ADJ N only three people
ADVERB-ADVERB	ADV ADV quite seriously

Adverbs may also modify phrases, clauses, or entire sentences.

He drove *nearly* to the edge of the cliff. [*Nearly* modifies the phrase *to the edge.*]

They arrived *just* when we were ready to leave. [*Just* modifies the clause *when we were ready to leave.*]

Fortunately, she is no longer on the critical list. [*Fortunately* modifies the entire sentence that follows.]

Many of the most common adjectives are familiar one-syllable words such as *good, bad, strange, true, false, large, right,* and *wrong.* Many others are formed by adding endings such as *-al, -able, -ful, -less, -ish, -ive,* and *-y* to nouns or verbs: *optional, fashionable, beautiful, fruitless, selfish, expressive, dreamy.*

Most adverbs are formed by adding *-ly* to adjectives: *badly, strangely, falsely, largely, beautifully, selfishly.* But note that we cannot depend on *-ly* to identify adverbs, since some adjectives also end in -*ly* (*fatherly, lonely, silly*) and since some common adverbs do not end in -*ly* (*always, forever, here, not, now, often, quite, then, there*). Thus, although certain endings sometimes help us to distinguish between adjectives and adverbs, the only sure way to distinguish them is to determine how an individual word functions in its sentence. If a word modifies a noun or pronoun, it is an adjective; if it modifies a verb, an adjective, or another adverb, it is an adverb.

9a
Don't use adjectives to modify verbs, adverbs, or other adjectives.

Adjectives modify only nouns and pronouns. Using adjectives instead of adverbs to modify verbs, adverbs, or other adjectives is nonstandard.

NONSTANDARD	They took each other *serious*.
STANDARD	They took each other *seriously*.
NONSTANDARD	Jenny read the book *easy*.
STANDARD	Jenny read the book *easily*.

The adjectives *good* and *bad* often appear where standard English requires the adverbs *well* and *badly*.

NONSTANDARD	Playing *good* is the goal of practicing baseball.
STANDARD	Playing *well* is the goal of practicing baseball.
NONSTANDARD	The band played *bad* last night.
STANDARD	The band played *badly* last night.

Although in informal speech the adjective forms *real* and *sure* are often used in place of the adverb forms *really* and *surely*, formal speech and writing require the -*ly* adverb form.

INFORMAL	After a few lessons Dan drove *real* well.
FORMAL	After a few lessons Dan drove *really* well.
INFORMAL	I *sure* was shocked by his confession.
FORMAL	I *surely* was shocked by his confession.

9b
Use an adjective after a linking verb to modify the subject. Use an adverb to modify a verb.

A **linking verb** is one that links, or connects, a subject and its complement: *They are golfers* (noun complement); *He is lucky* (adjective complement). (See also 5a-3.) The verbs most often used as linking verbs are forms of *be* and verbs associated with our five senses (*look, sound, smell, feel, taste*), as well as a few others (*appear, seem, become, grow, turn, prove, remain*). But some of these verbs may or may not be linking, depending on their meaning in the sentence. When the word after the verb modifies the subject, the verb is linking and the word should be an adjective. When the word modifies the verb, however, it should be an adverb.

> Hallie felt *bad* after she lost the race. [Adjective *bad*, meaning "ill" or "unhappy," modifies *Hallie*.]
>
> She had lost the race *badly*. [Adverb *badly* modifies *had lost*.]

> The evidence proved *conclusive*. [Adjective *conclusive* modifies *evidence*.]
>
> The evidence proved *conclusively* that the defendant was guilty. [Adverb *conclusively* modifies *proved*.]

9c
After a direct object, use an adjective to modify the object and an adverb to modify the verb.

If the direct object of a verb is followed by a word that modifies the verb, that word must be an adverb: *She repeated the words angrily*. If, in contrast, the direct object is followed by a word that modifies the object itself (an object complement), that word must be an adjective: *Campus politics made Martin angry*. (See also 5a-3.) In most sentences like these you can test whether a modifier should be an adjective or an adverb by trying to move it away from the direct object. If you can move it, it should be an adverb: *She angrily repeated the words*. If you cannot move the modifier away from the direct object, it is probably an adjective.

> The instructor considered the student's work *thorough*. [The adjective can be moved in front of *work* but not away from it.]
>
> The instructor considered the student's work *thoroughly*. [The adverb can be moved away from *work*. Compare *The instructor thoroughly considered the student's work*.]

9d
When an adverb has a short form and an *-ly* form, distinguish carefully between the forms.

Some adverbs have two forms, one with an *-ly* ending and one without. These include the following:

cheap, cheaply	loud, loudly	sharp, sharply
high, highly	near, nearly	slow, slowly
late, lately	quick, quickly	wrong, wrongly

The two forms in some pairs are interchangeable. But in other pairs the choice between the two forms is a matter of idiom. The -ly form in some adverb pairs has developed an entirely separate meaning.

ad
9d

He went *late.*
Lately he has been eating more.

Winter is drawing *near.*
Winter is *nearly* here.

When the long and short forms have the same meaning, the short forms generally occur with other short words and in informal speech and writing. The -ly forms are preferable in formal writing.

INFORMAL	Drive *slow.*
FORMAL	The funeral procession moved *slowly* through town.
INFORMAL	Jones wants to get rich *quick.*
FORMAL	Harrison became rich *quickly* when he invested in the stock market.

EXERCISE 1

Identify the adjectives and adverbs in the following sentences, and determine what part of speech each one modifies. Then compose five sentences of your own that parallel those given here.

Example:
The antique lantern sputtered noisily and went out.

    ADJ——⟍ N   V ⟋—— ADV   V ⟋ ADV
The *antique* lantern sputtered *noisily* and went *out.*

The *angry* man shouted *loudly* and moved *inside.*

1. The demonstrators quickly dispersed when the local police arrived.
2. Everyone in the class answered the hardest question wrong.
3. He was such an exciting person that everyone felt bad when he left.
4. Even in good weather, one of the surest ways to cause an accident is to follow another car too closely.
5. As the Ferris wheel slowly turned, raising him higher in the air, he became increasingly ill.

EXERCISE 2

Revise the following sentences so that adjectives are used to modify nouns and pronouns and adverbs are used to modify verbs, adjectives, and other adverbs. If any sentence is already correct as given, circle the number preceding it.

Example:

The largest bell rang loud.
The largest bell rang *loudly.*

1. I was real surprised when Martin and Emily got a divorce.
2. If you practice the piano regular, you will soon be able to play real music.
3. Thinking about the accident, Jerry felt bad.
4. After playing poor for six games, the hockey team finally had a game that was good.
5. If people learned karate, they could stop would-be robbers quick, before the robbers could steal anything.

9e

Use the comparative and superlative forms of adjectives and adverbs appropriately.

Adjectives and adverbs can show different degrees of quality or amount with the endings *-er* and *-est* or with the words *more* and *most* (to compare upward) or *less* and *least* (to compare downward). Most modifiers have three forms. The **positive form** is the dictionary form and simply describes without comparing.

a *big* book   spoke *forcefully*

The **comparative form** compares the thing modified with one other thing.

a *bigger* book   spoke *more* (or *less*) *forcefully*

The **superlative form** compares the thing modified with two or more other things.

the *biggest* book   spoke *most* (or *least*) *forcefully*

1

When word length or sound requires, use *more* and *most* instead of the endings *-er* and *-est*.

For downward comparisons, all adjectives and adverbs use *less* for the comparative (*less open*) and *least* for the superlative (*least successfully*). For upward comparisons, most one-syllable adjectives and adverbs and many two-syllable adjectives take the endings *-er* and *-est: red, redder, reddest; lucky, luckier, luckiest; fast, faster, fastest.*

Many two-syllable adjectives can either add *-er* and *-est* or use the words *more* and *most: steady, steadier* or *more steady, steadiest* or *most steady.* The use of *more* or *most* tends to draw the comparison out and so places more emphasis on it.

Using *more* and *most* is the only way to form the comparative and superlative for adjectives of three or more syllables and for most adverbs of two or more syllables (including nearly all ending in *-ly*): *beautiful, more beautiful, most beautiful; often, more often, most often; sadly, more sadly, most sadly.*

2
Use the correct form of irregular adjectives and adverbs.

The irregular modifiers change the spelling of their positive form to show comparative and superlative degrees.

POSITIVE	COMPARATIVE	SUPERLATIVE
Adjectives		
good	better	best
bad	worse	worst
little	littler, less	littlest, least
many		
some }	more	most
much		
Adverbs		
well	better	best
badly	worse	worst

3
Don't use double comparatives or double superlatives.

The comparative or the superlative is doubled when the *-er* or *-est* ending is combined with the words *more, most, less,* or *least.*

He was the *wisest* (not *most wisest*) man I ever knew.
My sister gets privileges because she's *older* (not *more older*).

4
In general, use the comparative form for comparing two things and the superlative form for comparing three or more things.

She was the *taller* of the two girls. [Comparative.]
Of all those books, *The Yearling* is the *best*. [Superlative.]

In conversation the superlative form is often used even though only two things are being compared: *When two people argue, the angriest one is usually wrong.* But the distinction between the forms should be observed in writing.

5

| In general, don't use comparative or superlative forms for modifiers that cannot logically be compared.

ad
9e

Adjectives and adverbs that cannot logically be compared include *perfect, unique, dead, impossible,* and *infinite.* These words are **absolute;** that is, they are not, strictly speaking, capable of greater or lesser degrees because their positive form describes their only state. Although they can be preceded by adverbs like *nearly* or *almost* that mean "approaching," they cannot logically be modified by *more, most, less,* or *least* (as in *most unique* or *less infinite*).

This distinction is sometimes ignored in speech, but it should always be made in writing.

| WRITING | He was a *unique* teacher. |
| SPEECH | He was the *most unique* teacher we had. |

EXERCISE 3

Write the comparative and superlative forms of each adjective or adverb below. Then use all three forms in sentences of your own.

Example:

heavy
Comparative: heavier. Superlative: heaviest.
The barbells were too *heavy* for me. The magician's trunk was *heavier* than I expected. Joe Clark was the *heaviest* person on the team.

1. interesting	5. some	8. well
2. great	6. often	9. majestic
3. lively	7. good	10. badly
4. hasty		

EXERCISE 4

Revise the following sentences so that the comparative and superlative forms of adjectives and adverbs are appropriate for formal usage.

Example:

Attending classes full-time and working at two jobs was the most impossible thing I ever did.

Attending classes full-time and working at two jobs was *impossible* (or *the hardest thing I ever did*).

1. If I study hard, I should be able to do more better on the next economics test.
2. Working last summer as an assistant to my congressman was one of the more unique experiences I have ever had.
3. My uncle is the younger of three brothers.

4. He was the most cruelest person I ever met.
5. Of the two major problems with nuclear power plants — waste disposal and radiation leakage — radiation leakage is the most terrifying.

9f

Avoid overuse of nouns as modifiers.

We often use one noun to modify another, especially in the absence of an appropriate adjective form. For example:

father figure	truth serum
flood control	child care
slave trade	security guard

Carefully conceived, such constructions can be both clear and concise: *Child care center* seems preferable to *center for the care of children*, which requires two successive prepositional phrases. But overuse of nouns to modify other nouns can lead to writing that is flat, if not senseless. To avoid awkward or confusing constructions, keep two principles in mind. First, whenever possible use a possessive or an adjective as a modifier.

NOT   Glenn took the state medical board exams to become a *dentist* technician.

BUT   Glenn took the state medical *board's* exams to become a *dental* technician.

Second, use only short nouns as modifiers and use them only in sequences of no more than two or three words.

CONFUSING   Minimex maintains a *plant employee relations improvement program.*

REVISED   Minimex maintains a *program* for *improving relations* among *plant employees.*

EXERCISE 5

Revise the following sentences so that they conform to formal usage. Make sure that adjectives modify nouns and pronouns; that adverbs modify verbs, adjectives, and other adverbs; that the comparative and superlative degrees are appropriate; and that nouns are not overused as modifiers. If a sentence is already correct as given, circle the number preceding it.

Example:

The opening lines of the long poem are the better ones.
The opening lines of the long poem are the *best* ones.

1. She and her sisters argued over which of them was smarter.
2. The university administration student absenteeism policy was controversial.
3. He rehearsed long enough to do real well in his audition for a part in the play, but he was too scared to speak loud enough.
4. Jerry was not more mature than his brother, though he was more older.
5. As we huddled over our sick guinea pig, he seemed to grow more dead by the hour.
6. The food tasted so badly that we were certain we would feel strangely or worse in the morning.
7. He remained firm, refusing to give in even though we asked him nicely.
8. One can buy a tape player cheap, but the cheap players rarely work good or last long.
9. Jessica spoke careful and calm to ensure that she would be understood.
10. Doors open easy in dry weather.

III
Clear
Sentences

10

Sentence Fragments

A **sentence fragment** is part of a sentence that is set off as if it were a whole sentence by an initial capital letter and a final period or other end punctuation. Unlike a complete sentence, a sentence fragment lacks a subject or a verb or both, or it begins with a subordinating word. In either case, a sentence fragment fails to express a complete, independent thought.

FRAGMENT	The sign leaning against the wall. [Lacks a verb.]
FRAGMENT	Feeling sick. [Lacks both a subject and a verb.]
FRAGMENT	When it is time. [Contains a subject and a verb but begins with a subordinating word.]

Fragments are serious errors in writing. They distract or confuse the reader, and they suggest that the writer has been careless or does not understand the structure of a sentence. (Before proceeding with this chapter, you may find it helpful to review 5a and 5c on sentences and clauses.)

When you are not sure whether a word group set off as a sentence is actually a complete sentence, apply the following three tests. If the word group does not pass *all three* tests, it is a fragment and needs to be revised in one of the ways suggested in this chapter.

TEST 1: Look for a verb in the group of words. If you cannot find one, the word group is a fragment.

FRAGMENT	Four years of study and then graduation. [The group contains no verb. Compare a complete sentence: *Four years of study <u>precede</u> graduation.*]

If you find a verb form, it must change at least once to show the difference in present time, past time, and future time. *Work*, for instance, is different for all three times: *Today the men work* (present); *Yesterday the men worked* (past); *Tomorrow the men will work* (future). *Hurt* remains the same for present and past but does require *will* to show future: *Today the ant bites hurt* (present); *Yesterday the ant bites hurt* (past); *Tomorrow the ant bites will hurt* (future). If the verb form does not change at least once to indicate present, past, and future time, then it is not a sentence verb, and the word group containing it is a fragment. An *-ing* form such as *working* or *hurting* does not change form and thus can never serve alone as the only verb in a sentence. It must be accompanied by a helping verb that does change form to show time.

FRAGMENT   The statue standing by the door. [The *-ing* verb form *standing* does not change in any way to show a difference in present, past, or future time. Compare a complete sentence: *The statue is* (or *was* or *will be*) *standing by the door.*]

FRAGMENT   The skies having darkened. [The helping verb *having* does not change form in any way to show a difference in time. Compare a complete sentence: *The skies have* (or *had* or *will have*) *darkened.*]

frag
10

TEST 2: If you find a sentence verb, look for its subject by asking who or what performs the action or makes the assertion of the verb. The subject will usually come before the verb. If there is no subject, the word group is a fragment unless it is a command.

FRAGMENT   And closed the door quietly. [The word group lacks a subject and is not a command. Compare complete sentences: *And he closed the door quietly. And close the door quietly.*]

TEST 3: If you find a sentence verb and its subject, look at the beginning of the word group. If the first word is a subordinating conjunction such as *after, because, before,* or *since,* the group is a fragment because it does not express a complete, independent thought. (See p. 147 for a list of subordinating conjunctions.)

FRAGMENT   As the plane lifted from the runway. [The word group contains a sentence verb, *lifted,* and a subject, *plane.* But because the group begins with the subordinating conjunction *as,* the thought is incomplete. Compare a complete sentence: *The plane lifted from the runway.*]

If the word group begins with *how, who, which, where, when, what,* or *why* — words that may introduce either subordinate clauses or questions — the group is a fragment unless it asks a question.

FRAGMENT   When she goes to her office. [The word group contains a sentence verb, *goes,* and a subject, *she.*

But it begins with *when* and does not ask a question. Compare complete sentences: *She goes to her office. When does she go to her office?*]

(For the use of commas, semicolons, and other punctuation marks in correcting sentence fragments, see also Chapters 20, 21, 22, and 25.)

10a
Don't set off a subordinate clause as a sentence.

Subordinate clauses contain both subjects and verbs, but they always begin with a subordinating conjunction (*although, because, if,* and so on) or with a relative pronoun (*who, which, that*). (See 5c-4.) Subordinate clauses cannot stand alone as complete sentences.

You can usually correct a subordinate clause set off as a sentence by combining it with the preceding or following independent clause. Or you can remove the subordinating word and thus create a new independent clause. These methods are illustrated in the following examples. (The fragments are in italics.)

FRAGMENT | Many pine trees bear large cones. *Which appear in August.* [The fragment is a subordinate clause modifying *cones.*]

REVISED | Many pine trees bear large cones, which appear in August. [The subordinate clause is attached to the independent clause.]

FRAGMENT | The decision seems perfectly correct and fair. *Although I can't say I like it.* [The fragment is a subordinate clause modifying the entire independent clause.]

REVISED | The decision seems perfectly correct and fair, although I can't say I like it. [The subordinate clause is attached to the independent clause.]

REVISED | The decision seems perfectly correct and fair. I can't say I like it. [The subordinate clause is made into a complete sentence by dropping *although.*]

EXERCISE 1

Correct any sentence fragment below either by combining it with an independent clause or by making it an independent clause. If an item contains no sentence fragment, circle the number preceding it.

Example:

Robert missed only one question on his chemistry quiz. Even though he had not studied the night before.

Robert missed only one question on his chemistry quiz, even though he had not studied the night before.

1. I enjoy New England more in the winter than in the summer. Especially now that I have learned to ski.

2. Freshman English is not as difficult as people say. Unless someone is not willing to do the work.

3. Sarah worked many hours perfecting her double somersault. Before summer ended it had become her best dive.

4. Whenever they lose touch with their children. Parents blame themselves.

5. The judgments of movie critics are often unreliable. Because they look for qualities that many people do not care about.

frag
10b

| 10b
Don't set off a verbal phrase as a sentence.

A **verbal phrase** consists of an infinitive (*to begin, to choose*), a past participle (*begun, chosen*), or a present participle (*beginning, choosing*) together with any objects and modifiers it may have (see 5c-2). Verbal phrases are always parts of sentences and can never stand alone as complete sentences.

Like fragments consisting of subordinate clauses, fragments consisting of verbal phrases are most easily corrected by combining them with the independent clauses they are related to. Verbal phrases cannot be converted into independent clauses without rewriting.

FRAGMENT	He backed closer and closer to the end of the diving board. *At last falling into the water.* [The fragment is a participial phrase modifying *he* in the independent clause.]
REVISED	He backed closer and closer to the end of the diving board, at last falling into the water. [The participial phrase is attached to the independent clause.]
REVISED	He backed closer and closer to the end of the diving board. At last *he fell* into the water. [The participial phrase is made into a complete sentence by changing the participle to the verb *fell* and by adding the subject *he.*]

EXERCISE 2

Correct any sentence fragment below either by combining it with an independent clause or by rewriting it as an independent clause. If an item contains no sentence fragment, circle the number preceding it.

Example:

Dancing has become very popular. Captivating all generations.

Dancing has become very popular. *It is* captivating all generations.

1. Drag racing is a mixed pleasure. Being both exciting and dangerous.
2. Having a hobby can be important to a fulfilling life. Engaging people in things outside their work.
3. Just to stay awake. That is the major challenge of long-distance driving.
4. Whipping back and forth in the wind. The flag made a frightening sound.
5. To be able to fly in a glider was one of my childhood dreams. I finally realized it last year.

frag

10c

10c

Don't set off a prepositional phrase as a sentence.

Prepositional phrases consist of prepositions (such as *in, on, to, over, under,* and *with*) together with their objects and modifiers (see 5c-1). Like subordinate clauses and verbal phrases, prepositional phrases always serve as parts of sentences; they cannot stand alone as complete sentences.

FRAGMENT   More than anything else, I wanted to get away from the heat. *To someplace cooler.* [The fragment is a prepositional phrase modifying *to get away* in the main clause.]

REVISED   More than anything else, I wanted to get away from the heat to someplace cooler. [The prepositional phrase is attached to the main clause.]

EXERCISE 3

Correct any sentence fragment below either by combining it with an independent clause or by rewriting it as an independent clause. If an item contains no sentence fragment, circle the number preceding it.

Example:

She was still beautiful two years later. After seven operations.

She was still beautiful two years later, after seven operations.

1. The gun was where the police expected to find it. In a garbage can behind the movie theater.
2. The science series deserved the award it received. On every show the producers helped clarify some difficult subject.
3. The house will take at least three weeks to paint. Even with two painters working full-time.
4. This weekend we discovered a new leak under the house. In a space occupied by some rodents that had decided to live with us.
5. In moving heavy things. You should be careful to lift using your legs, not your back.

10d

frag
10d

Don't set off an appositive or a part of a compound predicate as a sentence.

Appositives are nouns, or nouns and their modifiers, that rename or describe other nouns (see 5c-5). They cannot stand alone as sentences.

FRAGMENT	When I was a child, my favorite adult was an old uncle. *A retired sea captain who always told me long stories of wild adventures in faraway places.* [The fragment is an appositive identifying *uncle* in the independent clause.]
REVISED	When I was a child, my favorite adult was an old uncle, a retired sea captain who always told me long stories of wild adventures in faraway places. [The appositive is attached to the independent clause with a comma.]

Compound predicates are predicates made up of two or more verbs and their objects, if any. A verb or its object cannot stand alone as a sentence without a subject.

FRAGMENT	Pat worked all day. *And danced at night.* [The fragment is the second part of the compound predicate *worked . . . and danced.*]
REVISED	Pat worked all day and danced at night.
FRAGMENT	If his friends were in trouble, Henry always offered them much advice and many good wishes. *But no real help.* [*No real help* is the third part of the compound object of *offered* in the independent clause.]
REVISED	If his friends were in trouble, Henry always offered them much advice and many good wishes, but no real help.

Note that starting sentences with coordinating conjunctions such as *and* and *but* can lead to sentence fragments. Check every sentence you begin with a coordinating conjunction to be sure it is complete.

EXERCISE 4

Correct any sentence fragment below either by combining it with an independent clause or by rewriting it as an independent clause. If an item contains no sentence fragment, circle the number preceding it.

Example:

Harry was unable to spell. But, surprisingly, could play Scrabble well.

Harry was unable to spell but, surprisingly, could play Scrabble well.

1. During World War II Jack Armstrong was a hero for young people. The all-American boy.
2. Lynn graduated from college in 1982. And spent six months trying to find a job.
3. The college of business administration offers several degrees. And the opportunity to be an intern for one of many businesses.
4. In whatever form, tobacco is bad for one's health. Whether cigarettes, cigars, pipe tobacco, or chewing tobacco.
5. With the money her grandmother left her she bought a stereo. And she visited friends in St. Louis.

10e

Be aware of the acceptable uses of incomplete sentences.

A few word groups lacking the usual subject-predicate combination nonetheless conform to the standard expectations of most readers. Such patterns are acceptable in writing, although they occur most often in speech or in writing that records speech. They include exclamations (*Watch it! Oh no!*); questions and answers (*Where next? To Kansas. Why? To see my brother.*); and commands (*Move along. Shut the window. Finish your work.*). Commands are also used in written directions. Another kind of incomplete sentence, which occurs in special situations, is the transitional phrase (*So much for the causes, now for the results. One final point.*).

Professional writers sometimes use sentence fragments and do so effectively, particularly in narrative and descriptive writing. But such sentences are infrequent in expository writing. Unless you are experienced and thoroughly secure in your own writing, you should avoid all fragments and concentrate on writing clear, well-formed sentences.

EXERCISE 5

Break each of the following sentences at the vertical line, and then add, delete, or change words and punctuation as necessary to produce two *complete* sentences.

frag
10e

Example:

When the president came to town, | Secret Service men were everywhere.

The president came to town• Secret Service men were everywhere.

1. The drunken driver swerved across the cement median strip | and hit four parked cars in a row.
2. Classes may not resume after vacation | because the school has run out of money.
3. The child appeared at the hospital, | badly beaten and abandoned by his parents.
4. An unknown person gave the acting company an old building | and the money to convert it to a theater.
5. The old photograph shows a handsome man, | although he holds himself stiffly so as not to blur the image.

EXERCISE 6

Revise the following paragraph to eliminate sentence fragments by combining them with an independent clause or rewriting them as independent clauses.

Becoming an adult can mean moving into the best years of life. Or moving downhill from the "high" of adolescence. Depending on one's outlook. On one's experiences as a child and one's view of adulthood. Beginning at about age twenty, people enter a new world. Released from the restrictions adults place on them. They are approaching their physical and mental peak. The world is ahead. Waiting to challenge and be challenged. If their experiences as children have made them secure with themselves and others, they may welcome the challenges of adulthood. But those challenges can also seem frightening and overwhelming. If childhood and adolescence have already presented too many battles to fight. Too little security.

11

Comma Splices and Run-on Sentences

In speaking and writing we often link two or more main clauses into one sentence. In speaking we naturally pause between clauses or use a coordinating conjunction like *and* or *but* to link them. In writing we also use coordinating conjunctions, but the pauses in speech must be indicated by punctuation in writing. Two problems commonly occur in punctuating linked clauses. One is the **comma splice,** in which two or more main clauses are joined only by commas. The second is the **run-on sentence** (sometimes called the **fused sentence**), in which two or more main clauses are joined without any punctuation or conjunction between them.

COMMA SPLICE

The ship was huge, its mast stood thirty feet high. [Two main clauses are joined only by a comma.]

RUN-ON SENTENCE

The ship was huge its mast stood thirty feet high. [Two main clauses are joined with no punctuation or conjunction.]

CLAUSES AS SEPARATE SENTENCES

The ship was huge. Its mast stood thirty feet high.

CLAUSES COMBINED IN ONE SENTENCE

The ship was huge; its mast stood thirty feet high.

Like sentence fragments (see Chapter 10), comma splices and run-on sentences are serious errors because they generally force the reader to reread for sense. They also suggest that the writer has been careless or does not understand the structure of a sentence. (For the uses of commas, semicolons, and other sentence punctuation, see Chapters 20, 21, 22, and 25.)

COMMA SPLICES

11a

Don't join two main clauses with a comma unless they are also joined by a coordinating conjunction.

When a comma is the only mark of punctuation between two main clauses and there is no other connector (such as a coordinating conjunction), the relation between the two clauses is not immediately clear. Readers expect the same sentence to continue after a comma. When they find themselves reading a second sentence before they realize they have finished the first, they may have to reread in order to understand the writer's meaning.

cs
11a

> **COMMA SPLICE**   Rain had fallen steadily for sixteen hours, many basements were flooded.
>
> **COMMA SPLICE**   Cars would not start, many people were late to work.

You have four main options for correcting a comma splice: (1) make separate sentences of the main clauses; (2) insert a coordinating conjunction after the comma between the clauses; (3) insert a semicolon between the clauses; or (4) subordinate one of the clauses to the other. The option you choose depends on the relation you want to establish between the clauses. Some general principles will help you choose among the possibilities.

Making separate sentences

Revising a comma splice by making separate sentences from the main clauses will always be correct.

> Rain had fallen steadily for sixteen hours. Many basements were flooded.

The period is not only correct but preferable if the ideas expressed in the two main clauses are only loosely related.

> **COMMA SPLICE**   Chemistry has contributed much to our understanding of foods, many foods such as wheat, corn, and beans can be produced in the laboratory.
>
> **REVISED**   Chemistry has contributed much to our understanding of foods. Many foods such as wheat, corn, and beans can be produced in the laboratory.

Inserting a coordinating conjunction

When the ideas in the main clauses are closely related and parallel in importance, you may choose to correct a comma splice by inserting the appropriate coordinating conjunction between the clauses, after the comma.

Cars would not start, *and* many people were late to work.

COMMA SPLICE   He had intended to work all weekend, his friends arrived Friday and stayed until Sunday.

REVISED   He had intended to work all weekend, *but* his friends arrived Friday and stayed until Sunday.

cs

11a

Notice that the relation indicated by a coordinating conjunction can be complementary (*and*), contradictory (*but, yet*), causal (*for, so*), or alternate (*or, nor*).

Cars would not start, *so* many people were late to work.

Many people were late to work, *for* cars would not start.

People were late to work, *or* they stayed home to pump out flooded basements.

Using a semicolon

If the relation between the ideas expressed in the main clauses is very close and obvious without a conjunction, you can connect the clauses with a semicolon. (See also 11b.)

Rain had fallen steadily for sixteen hours ;many basements were flooded.

COMMA SPLICE   Rhoda and Nancy were close friends, they roomed together, ate meals together, and studied together.

REVISED   Rhoda and Nancy were close friends; they roomed together, ate meals together, and studied together.

Subordinating one clause

When the idea in one clause is more important than that in the other, you can subordinate the less important idea by expressing it in a dependent clause. Use a subordinating conjunction or a relative pronoun at the beginning of the new dependent clause.

After rain had fallen steadily for sixteen hours, many basements were flooded. [The addition of the subordinating conjunction *After* reduces the first sentence to a subordinate clause indicating time.]

In the examples below notice that subordination is more effective than forming separate sentences because it defines the relation between the clauses more precisely.

COMMA SPLICE	The examination was finally over, Becky could feel free to enjoy herself once more.
REVISED	The examination was finally over. Becky could feel free to enjoy herself once more. [Both ideas receive equal weight.]
IMPROVED	*When* the examination was finally over, Becky could feel free to enjoy herself once more. [Emphasis on the second idea.]
COMMA SPLICE	They had driven for nine hours without stopping, they were starved when they arrived home.
REVISED	They had driven for nine hours without stopping. They were starved when they arrived home.
IMPROVED	*Because* they had driven for nine hours without stopping, they were starved when they arrived home.

cs
11b

Note that other subordinating constructions, such as prepositional and participial phrases, can also express less important ideas (see 16b).

EXCEPTIONS. Commas are sometimes used between three or more brief parallel main clauses or between two brief main clauses that are balanced, particularly if they are contrasting.

Paul dislikes sports, he dislikes work, he dislikes everything. [Brief parallel main clauses.]

He's not a person, he's a monster. [Balanced and contrasting main clauses.]

| 11b
Use a period or semicolon to separate main clauses connected by conjunctive adverbs or transitional expressions.

Conjunctive adverbs are connecting words such as *also, consequently, however, nevertheless, then,* and *therefore* (see 5d-2). Typical transitional expressions include *for example, on the contrary,* and *that is* (see 3b-6). Conjunctive adverbs and transitional expressions frequently connect main clauses, and then the clauses must be separated by a period (forming two separate sentences) or by a semicolon (see 22b). The adverb or expression is also generally set off by commas.

COMMA SPLICE	Most Americans refuse to give up unhealthy habits, consequently our medical costs are higher than those of many other countries.
REVISED	Most Americans refuse to give up unhealthy habits. Consequently, our medical costs are higher than those of many other countries.
REVISED	Most Americans refuse to give up unhealthy habits; consequently, our medical costs are higher than those of many other countries.

cs
11b

Like coordinating and subordinating conjunctions, conjunctive adverbs and transitional expressions help to link the two clauses they join. But they also serve as adverbs, modifying the clause in which they appear. And unlike conjunctions, which must be placed between the word groups they join (coordinating) or at the beginning of the word group they introduce (subordinating), conjunctive adverbs and transitional expressions may be placed at the beginning, middle, or end of the clause. No matter where in the clause a conjunctive adverb or transitional expression appears, however, the clause must be separated from another main clause by a period or a semicolon.

COMMA SPLICE	The increased time devoted to watching television is not the only cause of the decline in reading ability, it is one of the important causes.
COORDINATING CONJUNCTION	The increased time devoted to watching television is not the only cause of the decline in reading ability, *but* it is one of the important causes.
SUBORDINATING CONJUNCTION	*Although* the increased time devoted to watching television is not the only cause of the decline in reading ability, it is one of the important causes.
SEMICOLON AND CONJUNCTIVE ADVERB	The increased time devoted to watching television is not the only cause of the decline in reading ability; *however,* it is one of the important causes.
SEMICOLON AND CONJUNCTIVE ADVERB	The increased time devoted to watching television is not the only cause of the decline in reading ability; it is, *however,* one of the important causes.
SEMICOLON AND CONJUNCTIVE ADVERB	The increased time devoted to watching television is not the only cause of the decline in reading ability; it is one of the important causes, *however.*
PERIOD AND CONJUNCTIVE ADVERB	The increased time devoted to watching television is not the only cause of the decline in reading ability. *However,* it is one of the important causes.

EXERCISE 1

Correct each comma splice below in *two* of the following ways: make separate sentences of the main clauses; insert a coordinating conjunction between the clauses; substitute a semicolon for the comma between clauses; or subordinate one clause to another. If an item contains no comma splice, circle the number preceding it.

> *Example:*
> Judith slept deeply at night, she had worked hard all day.
> Judith slept deeply at night *because* she had worked hard all day. [Subordination.]
> Judith slept deeply at night, *for* she had worked hard all day. [Coordinating conjunction.]

1. The election was held on a rainy day, the weather kept people away from the polls.
2. My brother enlisted in the Marines for three years, he will probably reenlist when his hitch is up.
3. We lost the game against Colliersville, though we had been favored to win.
4. Marian never seems to stop, she has so much energy.
5. Snow fell for three days in a row, consequently the superintendent had to shut down the schools.
6. Sean bought a new suit for the interview, he didn't get the job.
7. Little Orphan Annie used to be just a comic-strip character, now however she has become a character in a musical.
8. Politicians rarely deal squarely with complex issues, they are too worried about alienating potential supporters.
9. Many home owners are rebelling against property taxes, they believe they should not have to bear the expense of local government.
10. The apartment has an excellent view, it looks out over a parking lot at the expansive town dump.

cs
11c

RUN-ON SENTENCES

11c
Don't run two main clauses together without using an appropriate connector or punctuation mark between them.

When two main clauses are joined without a word to connect them or a punctuation mark to separate them, the result is a **run-on sentence,** sometimes called a **fused sentence.** Run-on sentences can rarely be understood on first reading, and they are never acceptable in standard written English.

RUN-ON	Many people would be lost without television they would not know how to amuse themselves.
RUN-ON	Our foreign policy is not well defined it confuses many countries.

Run-on sentences may be corrected in the same ways as comma splices (see 11a).

SEPARATE SENTENCES	Our foreign policy is not well defined. It confuses many countries. [The two main clauses are made into separate sentences.]
COMMA AND COORDINATING CONJUNCTION	Our foreign policy is not well defined, *and* it confuses many countries. [The two main clauses are separated by a comma and a coordinating conjunction.]
SEMICOLON	Our foreign policy is not well defined; it confuses many countries. [The two main clauses are separated by a semicolon.]
SUBORDINATING CONJUNCTION	*Because* our foreign policy is not well defined, it confuses many countries. [*Because* subordinates the first clause to the second.]

EXERCISE 2

Revise each of the run-on sentences below in *two* of the four ways shown above.

Example:

Tim was shy he usually refused invitations.
Tim was shy, *so* he usually refused invitations.
Tim was shy; he usually refused invitations.

1. The rain fell so hard that water started pouring into the kitchen from the back porch it blew in around the kitchen windows too.
2. Children sometimes misbehave just to test their elders parents should discipline them on those occasions.
3. The skills center offers job training to people who need it it can't guarantee jobs, though.
4. The parking problem in the downtown area is getting out of hand the mayor suggests a new underground parking garage.
5. Science courses teach interesting content they also teach one to think logically about the world.

EXERCISE 3

Combine each pair of sentences below into one sentence without creating comma splices or run-on sentences. Either supply a comma and a coordinating conjunction, supply a semicolon, or subordinate one clause to the other. You will have to add, delete, or change words as well as punctuation.

Example:

The sun sank lower in the sky. The colors gradually faded.

As the sun sank lower in the sky, the colors gradually faded. [The first clause is subordinated to the second.]

1. I once worked as a switchboard operator. However, after a week I was fired for hopeless incompetence.
2. The candidate's backers learned of his previous illegal activities. They withdrew their support.
3. Record prices stayed stable for a long time. In the last decade they rose sharply.
4. Teachers sometimes make unfair assignments. They don't take account of the workload in other courses.
5. I nearly froze trying to unlock the car door. I discovered I was standing next to the wrong red Rabbit.
6. Many proud people restrict their activities. They are afraid to fail at something new.
7. We thought my seven-year-old brother was a genius. He read an entire encyclopedia.
8. The driver was lucky to escape uninjured. His car was destroyed, however.
9. Some Eskimos found and nursed the sick explorer. He died two weeks later.
10. Two railroad lines cut through the town. They intersect a block from the main street.

EXERCISE 4

Identify and revise the comma splices and run-on sentences in the following paragraph.

A pleasant, inexpensive treat is a weekend in a country inn. Inns are usually located in quaint, quiet villages, there is little noise during the night except for crickets. The surrounding area is countryside, often with historical sites to visit. The innkeeper is sometimes a great cook. I have had delicious breakfasts at inns frequently they are included in the charge for the room. The rooms themselves are large and airy. The chairs are soft the beds are just right. The trip to the inn may take an hour and the weekend may cost no more than twenty dollars. It's a great break from school or work, I recommend it to everyone.

12

Pronoun Reference

A **pronoun** derives its meaning from its **antecedent,** the noun it substitutes for. Therefore, a pronoun must refer clearly and unmistakably to its antecedent in order for the sentence containing the pronoun to be clear. A sentence like *Jim spoke to Mark; he did not want to go* is not clear because the reader does not know whether *he* refers to Jim or to Mark.

Whether a pronoun and its antecedent appear in the same sentence or in adjacent sentences, you should be certain their relation is clear. One way to achieve clarity is to ensure that pronoun and antecedent agree in person and number (see 8b). The other way is to ensure that the pronoun refers unambiguously to a single, close, specific antecedent.

12a
Make a pronoun refer clearly to one antecedent.

A pronoun may, of course, refer to two or more nouns in a compound antecedent, as in the following:

Jenkins and Wilson pooled *their* resources and became partners.

But when either of two nouns can be a pronoun's antecedent, the reference will not be clear.

CONFUSING The men removed all the furniture from the room and cleaned it. [Does *it* refer to the room or to the furniture?]

CLEAR The men removed all the furniture from the room and cleaned the room (or the furniture).

CLEAR	After removing all the furniture from it, the men cleaned the room.
CLEAR	The men cleaned all the furniture after removing it from the room.

Clarifying pronoun reference may require simply replacing the pronoun with the appropriate noun, as in the first clear example above. But to avoid repetition, you may want to restructure the sentence so that the pronoun can refer to only one possible antecedent, as in the second and third clear examples.

Sentences that report what someone said, using verbs like *said* or *told*, often require direct rather than indirect quotation.

CONFUSING	Oliver told Bill that he was mistaken.
CLEAR	Oliver told Bill, "I am mistaken."
CLEAR	Oliver told Bill, "You are mistaken."

ref
12b

NOTE: Avoid the awkward device of using a pronoun followed by the appropriate noun in parentheses.

WEAK	Mary should help Joan, but *she* (*Joan*) should help herself first.
IMPROVED	Mary should help Joan, but *Joan* should help herself first.

12b

Place a pronoun close enough to its antecedent to ensure clarity.

When a relative pronoun like *who, which,* or *that* introduces a clause that modifies a noun, the pronoun generally should immediately follow its antecedent to prevent confusion. (See also Chapter 14 on misplaced modifiers.)

CONFUSING	Jody found a dress in the attic that her aunt had worn. [Her aunt had worn the attic?]
CLEAR	In the attic Jody found a dress that her aunt had worn.

Even when only one word could possibly serve as the antecedent of a pronoun, the relationship between the two may still be unclear if they are widely separated.

CONFUSING	Two brothers had built the town's oldest barn, which over the years had served as a cow barn, a blacksmith shop, a carriage house, and a garage. However, no one could remember their names.

[*Their* can sensibly refer only to *brothers*, but the pronoun is too far from its antecedent to be clear.]

CLEAR   Two brothers had built the town's oldest barn, which over the years had served as a cow barn, a blacksmith shop, a carriage house, and a garage. However, no one could remember *the brothers'* names. [The noun is repeated for clarity.]

The confusing separation of pronoun and antecedent is most likely to occur in long sentences and, as illustrated by the example above, in adjacent sentences within a paragraph. (See 3b-4.)

ref
12b

EXERCISE 1

Rewrite the following sentences to eliminate unclear pronoun reference. If you use a pronoun in your revision, be sure that it refers to only one antecedent and that it falls close enough to its antecedent to ensure clarity.

Example:

The discouraged artist looked at his canvas and at the apple he was painting and then destroyed it.

The discouraged artist looked at his canvas and at the apple he was painting and then destroyed *the apple.*

1. If your pet cheetah will not eat raw meat, cook it.
2. Dick and his cousin did not get along because he liked to have his own way.
3. Since Bill had been driving the car that rolled into the truck, he is responsible for the damage to it.
4. My father and his sister have not spoken for thirty years because she left the family when my grandfather was ill and never called or wrote. But now he is thinking of resuming communication.
5. Saul found an old gun in the rotting shed that was just as his grandfather had left it.
6. There is a difference between the heroes of today and the heroes of yesterday: They have flaws in their characters.
7. Jan held the sandwich in one hand and the telephone in the other, eating it while she talked.
8. She used a camera to take the photograph that had been in her family since the 1920s.
9. Tom told his brother that he was in trouble at home.
10. Denver was where my grandmother grew up. The city had been the scene of a mad gold rush with fortune seekers, plush opera houses, makeshift hotels, noisy saloons, and dirt streets. When I was a child, she often retold the stories she had heard of those days.

12c

Make a pronoun refer to a specific antecedent rather than to an implied one.

As a rule, the meaning of a pronoun will be clearest when it refers to a specific noun or other pronoun. When the antecedent is not specifically stated but implied by the context, the reference can only be inferred by the reader.

1

Use *this*, *that*, *which*, and *it* cautiously in referring to whole statements.

The most common kind of implied reference occurs when the pronoun *this, that, which,* or *it* refers to a whole idea or situation described in the preceding clause, sentence, or even paragraph. Such reference, often called **broad reference,** is acceptable only when the pronoun refers clearly to the entire preceding clause. In the following sentence, *which* could not possibly refer to a noun in the preceding clause and thus refers unambiguously to the whole clause.

> I can be kind and civil to people, *which* is more than you can.
> — GEORGE BERNARD SHAW

But if a pronoun might possibly confuse a reader, you should recast the sentence to avoid using the pronoun or to provide an appropriate noun.

CONFUSING	I knew nothing about economics, *which* my instructor had not learned. [*Which* could refer to *economics* or to the whole preceding clause.]
CLEAR	I knew nothing about economics, a fact my instructor had not learned.
CLEAR	I knew nothing about economics because my instructor knew nothing about it.
CONFUSING	The faculty members reached agreement on a change in the requirements, but it took time. [Does *it* refer to reaching agreement or to the change?]
CLEAR	The faculty members agreed on a change in the requirements, but arriving at agreement took time.
CLEAR	The faculty members reached agreement on a change in the requirements, but the change took time to implement.

CONFUSING	The British knew little of the American countryside and had no experience with the colonists' guerrilla tactics. This gave the colonists an advantage. [Does *This* refer to the whole preceding sentence, to the ignorance alone, or to the inexperience alone?]
CLEAR	The British knew little of the American countryside and had no experience with the colonists' guerrilla tactics. Their enemy's ignorance and inexperience gave the colonists an advantage.

ref
12c

2

Don't use a pronoun to refer to a noun implied by a modifier.

Adjectives, nouns used as modifiers, and the possessives of nouns or pronouns make unsatisfactory antecedents. Although they may imply a noun that could serve as an antecedent, they do not supply the specific antecedent needed for clarity.

WEAK	In the president's speech *he* outlined plans for tax reform.
REVISED	In his speech the president outlined plans for tax reform.
WEAK	Liz drove a red Toyota; *it* was her favorite color.
REVISED	Liz drove a red Toyota because red was her favorite color.
REVISED	Liz drove a Toyota that was red, her favorite color.

3

Don't use a pronoun to refer to a noun implied by some other noun or phrase.

WEAK	Jim talked at length about salesmanship, although he had never been *one*.
REVISED	Jim talked at length about salesmanship, although he had never been a salesman.
WEAK	Jake was bitten by a rattlesnake, but *it* was not serious.
REVISED	Jake was bitten by a rattlesnake, but the bite was not serious.

4
Don't use part of a title as an antecedent in the opening sentence of a paper.

The title of a paper is entirely separate from the paper itself, so a pronoun can't be used to refer to the title. If you open a paper with a reference to the title, repeat whatever part of the title is necessary for clarity.

TITLE	How to Row a Boat
NOT	This is not as easy as it looks.
BUT	Rowing a boat is not as easy as it looks.

12d
Avoid the indefinite use of *it* and *they*. Use *you* only to mean "you, the reader."

In conversation we commonly use expressions like *It says in the paper* or *In Texas they say.* But such indefinite use of *it* and *they* is inappropriate in all but informal writing. The constructions are not only unclear but wordy.

WEAK	In Chapter 4 of this book *it* describes the early flights of the Wright brothers.
REVISED	Chapter 4 of this book describes the early flights of the Wright brothers.
WEAK	In the average television drama *they* present a false picture of life.
REVISED	The average television drama presents a false picture of life.

Using *you* with indefinite reference to people in general is also well established in conversation: *You can take various courses in college. You can tell that my father was a military man.* The indefinite *you* frequently occurs in informal writing, too. And in all but very formal writing, *you* is acceptable when the meaning is clearly "you, the reader," as in *You can learn the standard uses of pronouns.* But the writer must consider whether the context is appropriate for such a meaning. Consider this example.

INAPPROPRIATE	In the fourteenth century *you* had to struggle simply to survive. [Clearly, the meaning cannot be "you, the reader."]
REVISED	In the fourteenth century *one* (or *a person* or *people*) had to struggle simply to survive.

12e

Avoid using the pronoun *it* more than one way in a sentence.

We use *it* idiomatically in expressions like *It is raining* or *It is growing colder daily.* We use *it* to postpone the subject in sentences like *It is true that more jobs are available to women today.* And, of course, we use *it* as a personal pronoun in sentences like *Jon wanted the book, but he couldn't find it.* All these uses are standard. But when two of these uses occur in the same sentence, the reader can be confused.

> CONFUSING When it is rainy, shelter your bicycle and wipe it often. [The first *it* is idiomatic; the second refers to *bicycle*.]
>
> REVISED In rainy weather shelter your bicycle and wipe it often.

12f

Be sure the relative pronouns *who, which,* and *that* are appropriate for their antecedents.

The relative pronouns *who, which,* and *that* commonly refer to persons, animals, or things. *Who* refers most often to persons but may also refer to animals that have names.

> Travis is the boy *who* leads the other boys into trouble.
> Their dog Wanda, *who* is growing lame, has difficulty running.

Which refers to animals and things.

> The Orinoco River, *which* is 1600 miles long, flows through Venezuela into the Atlantic Ocean.

That refers to animals and things and occasionally to persons when they are collective or anonymous.

> The jade tree *that* my grandmother gave me suddenly died.
> Infants *that* walk need constant tending.

(See also 21c-1 for the use of *which* and *that* in nonrestrictive and restrictive clauses.)

The possessive *whose* generally refers to people but may refer to animals and things in order to avoid awkward and wordy *of which* constructions.

> The book *whose* binding broke had been my father's. [Compare *The book of which the binding broke had been my father's.*]

EXERCISE 2

Revise the following sentences so that all pronouns refer clearly to specific, appropriate antecedents.

Example:

In impressionist paintings they used color to imitate reflected light.

Impressionist painters used color to imitate reflected light.

1. We receive warnings to beware of nuclear fallout, pesticides, smog, and oil shortages, but I try not to think about it.
2. In F. Scott Fitzgerald's novels he wrote about the Jazz Age.
3. By the time the firemen arrived at the scene, it was blazing out of control.
4. Carl is a master carpenter because his father, a cabinetmaker, taught him about it when he was a teen-ager.
5. Macbeth is a complicated and ambiguous hero, and that is one thing that makes it a good play.
6. After hearing Professor Eakins's lecture on marine biology, I think I want to become one.
7. In urban redevelopment projects they try to make neighborhoods safe and attractive.
8. In the nineteenth century you didn't have many options in motorized transportation.
9. My car Harriet, who has no roof, is useless when it rains.
10. We hoped we had a winning lottery ticket so that we could pay the debt, but this was not something we could count on.
11. Few people dare to wear sealskin today because their endangered status has been so well publicized.
12. It rained for a week, but it is possible that we can save the crop.
13. In most textbooks they are careful to define special terms.
14. The plant supervisor never gives you a chance to ask questions.
15. We argue constantly and he never looks straight at me, which bothers me.

ref

12

13

Shifts

A sentence should be consistent: Grammatical elements such as tense, mood, voice, person, and number should remain the same throughout the sentence, unless grammar or the meaning of the sentence requires a shift. Unnecessary shifts in these elements, either within a sentence or among related sentences, confuse the reader and distort meaning.

13a
Keep sentences consistent in person and number.

Person in grammar refers to the distinction among the person talking (first person), the person spoken to (second person), and the person, object, or concept being talked about (third person). **Number** refers to the distinction between one (singular) and more than one (plural). Both nouns and personal pronouns change form to show differences in number, but only the personal pronouns have distinctive forms for the three persons.

The most common faulty shifts in person are shifts from second to third and from third to second person. They occur because we can refer to people in general, including our readers, either in the third person (*a person, one; people, they*) or in the second person (*you*).

> *People* should not drive when *they* have been drinking.
> *One* should not drive when *he* (or *he or she*) has been drinking.
> *You* should not drive when *you* have been drinking.

Although any one of these possibilities is acceptable in an appropriate context, a mixture of more than one is inconsistent.

INCONSISTENT	If *a person* works hard, *you* can accomplish a great deal.
REVISED	If *you* work hard, *you* can accomplish a great deal.
REVISED	If a *person* works hard, *he* (or *he or she*) can accomplish a great deal.
BETTER	If *people* work hard, *they* can accomplish a great deal.

(For a discussion of avoiding the use of *he* to mean both *he* and *she*, see 8b-3.)

Inconsistency in number occurs most often between a pronoun and its antecedent (see 8b).

shift
13b

INCONSISTENT	If a *student* does not understand a problem, *they* should consult the instructor.
REVISED	If a *student* does not understand a problem, *he* (or *he or she*) should consult the instructor.
BETTER	If *students* do not understand a problem, *they* should consult the instructor.

EXERCISE 1

Revise the sentences below to make them consistent in person and number.

Example

A plumber will fix burst pipes, but they won't repair waterlogged appliances.

Plumbers will fix burst pipes, but they won't repair waterlogged appliances.

1. If a person has just moved to the city, you have trouble knowing where to go.
2. When a taxpayer does not file on time, they have to pay a penalty.
3. Writers must know what they are writing about; otherwise one cannot write.
4. If a student misses too many classes, you may fail a course.
5. One should not judge other people's actions unless they know the circumstances.

13b
Keep sentences consistent in tense and mood.

Certain shifts of tense within a sentence or from one sentence to another may be required by your meaning or by grammar (see 7e). For example:

Ramon *will graduate* from college twenty-three years after his father first *came* to the United States. [Ramon's graduation is still in the future, but his father arrived in the past.]

Readers expect such changes in tense to indicate either changes in actual time or changes in relative time. But changes that are not required by meaning distract readers. Unnecessary shifts from past to present or from present to past in sentences narrating a series of events are particularly confusing.

shift
13b

INCONSISTENT   Immediately after Booth *shot* Lincoln, Major Rathbone *threw* himself upon the assassin. But Booth *pulls* a knife and *plunges* it into the major's arm. [The writer starts narrating the events in the past and then shifts to the present.]

REVISED   Immediately after Booth *shot* Lincoln, Major Rathbone *threw* himself upon the assassin. But Booth *pulled* a knife and *plunged* it into the major's arm.

INCONSISTENT   The main character in the novel *suffers* psychologically because he *has* a clubfoot, but he eventually *triumphed* over his handicap.

REVISED   The main character in the novel *suffers* psychologically because he *has* a clubfoot, but he eventually *triumphs* over his handicap. [The present tense is ordinarily used to describe the action of a novel, a play, or a movie.]

Shifts in the mood of verbs occur most frequently in directions, because the writer moves between the imperative mood (*Unplug the appliance*) and the indicative mood (*You should unplug the appliance*). (See 7f.) Directions are usually clearer and more concise in the imperative, as long as its use is consistent.

INCONSISTENT   *Cook* the mixture slowly, and *you should stir* it until the sugar is dissolved. [Shifts from imperative to indicative.]

REVISED   *Cook* the mixture slowly, and *stir* it until the sugar is dissolved. [Consistently imperative.]

EXERCISE 2

Revise the sentences below to make them consistent in tense and mood.

Example:

Lynn ran to first, rounded the base, and keeps running until she slides into second.

Lynn ran to first, rounded the base, and *kept* running until she *slid* into second.

1. Soon after he joined the union, Lester appears at a rally and makes a speech.
2. First sand down any paint that is peeling; then you should paint the bare wood with primer.
3. Rachel is walking down the street, and suddenly she stops, as a shot rang out.
4. Rudeness occurs when people did not see themselves as others saw them.
5. To buy a tape deck, find out what features you need and you should decide what you want to pay.

13c
Keep sentences consistent in subject and voice.

When a verb is in the active voice, the subject names the actor: *Linda passed the peas.* When a verb is in the passive voice, the subject names the receiver of the action; the actor may not be mentioned or may be mentioned in a prepositional phrase: *The peas were passed (by Linda).* (See pp. 183–84.)

A shift in voice may sometimes help focus the reader's attention on a single subject.

> The candidate *campaigned* vigorously and *was nominated* on the first ballot. [*Candidate* is the subject of both the active verb *campaigned* and the passive verb *was nominated.*]

But most shifts in subject and voice not only are unnecessary but also may create confusion or error.

INCONSISTENT	In the morning the *children rode* their bicycles; in the afternoon *their skateboards were given* a good workout. [The shift in subject from *children* to *skateboards* is confusing. Without a named actor the second clause implies that someone or something other than the children gave the skateboards a workout.]
REVISED	In the morning the *children rode* their bicycles; in the afternoon *they gave* their skateboards a good workout.
INCONSISTENT	As *we looked* out over the ocean, *ships could be seen* in the distance. [Since the main clause does not name an actor, the reader cannot be sure who is looking.]
REVISED	As *we looked* out over the ocean, *we could see* ships in the distance.

EXERCISE 3

Make the sentences below consistent in subject and voice.

Example:

At the reunion they ate hot dogs and volleyball was played.
At the reunion they ate hot dogs and *played volleyball.*

1. Some arrowheads were dug up, and they found some pottery that was almost undamaged.
2. They started the game after some practice drills were run.
3. The tornado ripped off the roof, and it was deposited in a nearby lot.
4. The debate was begun by the senator when he introduced the new bill.
5. If you learn how to take good notes in class, much extra work will be avoided.

13d
Don't shift unnecessarily between indirect and direct quotation.

Direct quotation reports, in quotation marks, the exact words of a speaker. **Indirect quotation** reports what was said but not necessarily in the speaker's exact words.

DIRECT	He said, "I am going."
INDIRECT	He said that he was going.
INCONSISTENT	Sue asked whether we had repaired the car and "Is anything else likely to happen?"
REVISED	Sue asked, "Have you repaired the car? Is anything else likely to happen?"
REVISED	Sue asked whether we had repaired the car and whether anything else was likely to happen.

EXERCISE 4

Revise each of the following sentences twice, once to make the form of quotation consistently indirect and once to make it consistently direct.

Example:

Tom asked whether the guest host had arrived and "Are the cameras ready?"

Tom asked whether the guest host had arrived and *whether the cameras were ready.*

Tom asked, *"Has the guest host arrived?* Are the cameras ready?"

1. Coach Butler said that our timing was terrible and "I would rather cancel the season than watch you play."
2. The report concluded, "Drought is a serious threat" and that we must begin conserving water now.
3. Teachers who assign a lot of homework always say, "I'm doing this for your own good" and that they'd rather not hear any complaints.
4. The author claims that adults pass through emotional stages and "No stage can be avoided."
5. My grandfather says, "Gardening keeps me alive" and that, in any event, the exercise helps ease his arthritis.

EXERCISE 5

shift

13d

Identify each faulty shift in the following paragraph as inconsistent in person, number, tense, mood, subject, voice, or form of quotation. Revise the faulty sentences to eliminate the shifts.

One is always urged to conserve energy, and we try to do that. However, saving energy requires making sacrifices. My children like baths, not showers, so how can I tell them that they must keep clean and then insist, "You must not use the bath"? They won't stay clean. I don't mind a cool house, but it has to be kept warm when you have the flu. Everyone enjoys a fire in the fireplace, but they fail to realize how much heat from the furnace was released up the chimney. Nonetheless, we have to learn to live with incon-

14

Misplaced and Dangling Modifiers

In reading a sentence in English, we depend principally on the arrangement of the words to tell us how they are related. In writing, we usually follow unconsciously the arrangements readers expect. But we may create confusion if we fail to keep certain principles of arrangement in mind. The confusion is especially probable when modifiers are not connected to the words they modify.

MISPLACED MODIFIERS

We say that a modifier is **misplaced** if it appears to modify the wrong part of the sentence or if we cannot be certain what part of the sentence the writer intended it to modify.

14a
Place prepositional phrases where they will clearly modify the words intended.

A prepositional phrase serving as an adjective usually comes right after the noun it modifies (*The man in the green hat blew smoke rings*). A prepositional phrase serving as an adverb often falls right after the word it modifies (*The cat meowed in the barn*), although it may also fall elsewhere in the sentence (*In the barn the cat meowed*). Since readers tend to link prepositional phrases to the nearest possible word, writers must be careful to place them so that they clearly modify the intended word. Misplaced modifiers may be merely awkward, unintentionally amusing, or genuinely confusing.

CONFUSING   The book has a picture on the jacket *of a horse.* [The adjective phrase *of a horse* appears to modify *jacket,* the word it follows. The book's picture seems to be on a horse's jacket.]

CLEAR   The book has a picture *of a horse* on the jacket. [The phrase falls directly after *picture,* which it modifies.]

CONFUSING   She served hamburgers to the men *on paper plates.* [Surely the hamburgers, not the men, were on paper plates.]

CLEAR   She served the men hamburgers *on paper plates.* [The adjective phrase *on paper plates* directly follows the noun it modifies.]

CONFUSING   He was unhappy that he failed to break the record *by a narrow margin.* [The sentence implies that he wanted to break the record only by a narrow margin.]

CLEAR   He was unhappy that he failed *by a narrow margin* to break the record. [The adverb phrase falls directly after *failed,* the verb it modifies.]

mm
14b

14b

Place subordinate clauses where they will clearly modify the words intended.

Like adjective phrases, adjective clauses modify nouns and ordinarily fall directly after the word or words they modify. Such clauses usually begin with the relative pronouns *who, which,* or *that.* Adverb clauses usually begin with subordinating conjunctions like *after, because,* and *since.* (See 5c-4.) Like adverb phrases, they can stand at the beginning, middle, or end of a sentence.

CONFUSING   According to police records, many dogs are killed by automobiles *that roam unleashed.* [The adjective clause appears to modify *automobiles.*]

CLEAR   According to police records, many dogs *that roam unleashed* are killed by automobiles. [The clause directly follows the noun it modifies, *dogs.*]

CONFUSING   The mayor was able to cut the ribbon and then the band played *when someone found scissors.* [The adverb clause appears to modify *the band played.*]

CLEAR   *When someone found scissors,* the mayor was able to cut the ribbon and then the band played.

[Placed at the beginning of the sentence, the clause clearly modifies *the mayor was able to cut the ribbon.*]

EXERCISE 1

Revise the sentences below so that prepositional phrases and subordinate clauses clearly modify the words intended.

Example:

Sir Arthur Conan Doyle wrote a mystery about a hound on the moors in 1902.

In 1902 Sir Arthur Conan Doyle wrote a mystery about a hound on the moors.

1. The magician made a rabbit disappear with a wink.
2. The electric typewriter is running on the desk.
3. Marie opened the book given to her last Christmas by Charles Dickens.
4. We found the contact lens during lunch on the rug.
5. The little girl fed her kitten in the kitchen that she had received for Christmas.
6. The bell is an heirloom that you hear chiming.
7. The foundry delivered machines to the factory in a truck.
8. She stared at the people standing nearby with flashing eyes.
9. Buffalo gains a huge supply of hydroelectric power from Niagara Falls that will never be exhausted.
10. My father realized the mistakes he had made after the damage was done.

mm
14c

14c
Place limiting modifiers carefully.

Limiting modifiers include *almost, even, exactly, hardly, just, merely, nearly, only, scarcely,* and *simply.* They modify the expressions that immediately follow them. Compare the uses of *just* in the following sentences:

The instructor *just nodded* to me as he came in.
The instructor nodded *just to me* as he came in.
The instructor nodded to me *just as he came in.*

In speech several of these modifiers frequently occur before the verb, regardless of what they are intended to modify. In writing, however, these modifiers should fall immediately before the word or word group they modify in order to avoid any ambiguity.

UNCLEAR   They *only* saw each other during meals. [They had eyes only for each other, or they met only during meals?]

CLEAR   They saw *only* each other during meals.

CLEAR   They saw each other *only* during meals.

NOTE: *Only* is acceptable immediately before the verb when it modifies a whole statement.

He only wanted his guest to have fun.

EXERCISE 2

Use each of the following limiting modifiers in two versions of the same sentence.

> *Example:*
> only
> He is the *only* one I like.
> He is the one *only* I like.

1. almost	4. simply
2. even	5. exactly
3. hardly	

mm
14d

14d

Avoid squinting modifiers.

A **squinting modifier** is one that may refer to either the preceding or the following word, leaving the reader uncertain about which modification is intended. A modifier can modify only *one* grammatical element in a sentence. It cannot serve two elements at once.

SQUINTING   The work that he hoped would satisfy him *completely* frustrated him.

CLEAR   The work that he hoped would *completely* satisfy him frustrated him.

CLEAR   The work that he hoped would satisfy him frustrated him *completely*.

EXERCISE 3

Revise each of the following sentences twice so that the squinting modifier applies clearly first to one term and then to the other.

> *Example:*
> Those who complain often get results.
> Those who complain get results *often*.
> Those who *often* complain get results.

1. The baseball team that wins championships most of the time has excellent pitching.
2. I told my son when the game was over I would play with him.
3. A person who skis often gets cold.
4. The man who was bald totally refused to seek a remedy.
5. People who see psychologists occasionally will feel better.

14e

Avoid separating a subject from its verb or a verb from its object or complement.

When we read a sentence, we expect the subject, verb, and object or complement to be close to each other. If adjective phrases or clauses separate them, the meaning is usually clear.

The wreckers who were demolishing the old house discovered a large box of coins. [The subject, *wreckers,* and the verb, *discovered,* are separated by the adjective clause beginning *who.*]

However, if an adverb phrase or clause interrupts the movement from subject to verb to object or complement, the resulting sentence is likely to be awkward and confusing.

AWKWARD	The *wreckers,* soon after they began demolishing the old house, *discovered* a large box of coins. [The clause beginning *soon after,* which modifies the whole sentence, interrupts the movement from subject to verb.]
REVISED	Soon after they began demolishing the old house, the *wreckers discovered* a large box of coins. [The modifier is placed first, where it clearly modifies the whole sentence.]
AWKWARD	Three of the wreckers *lifted,* with great effort, *the heavy box.* [The phrase beginning *with* modifies the verb *lifted* but interrupts the movement from verb to object.]
REVISED	Three of the wreckers *lifted the heavy box* with great effort. [The modifier falls at the end of the sentence, where it still clearly modifies the verb.]

14f

Avoid separating the parts of a verb phrase or the parts of an infinitive.

A verb phrase consists of a helping verb plus a main verb, as in *will call, was going, had been writing.* Such phrases constitute close grammatical units. We regularly insert single-word adverbs in them without causing awkwardness: *Joshua* had not *entirely* completed *his assignment. He* was *seriously* considering *asking for an extension.* But when longer word groups interrupt verb phrases, the result is almost always awkward.

> **AWKWARD**   Many students *had,* by spending most of their time on the assignment, *completed* it.
>
> **REVISED**   By spending most of their time on the assignment, many students *had completed* it.
>
> **REVISED**   Many students *had completed* the assignment by spending most of their time on it.

mm

14f

Infinitives consist of the marker *to* plus the plain form of a verb, as in *to produce* or *to enjoy.* The two parts of the infinitive are widely regarded as a grammatical unit that should not be split.

> **AWKWARD**   The weather service expected temperatures *to* not *rise.*
>
> **REVISED**   The weather service expected temperatures not *to rise.*

Note, however, that a split infinitive may sometimes be natural and preferable, though it will still bother some readers.

> Several U.S. industries expect *to* more than *triple* their use of robots within the next decade.

We cannot place the modifier *more than* anywhere except between the two parts of the infinitive. We could recast the sentence entirely, as in *Several U.S. industries expect to increase their use of robots by over 200 percent within the next decade.* But the revision is less economical, so the split construction seems acceptable.

EXERCISE 4

Revise the sentences below to connect separated parts of sentences (subject-predicate, verb-object-complement, verb phrase, infinitive).

> *Example:*
> Most children have by the time they are seven lost a tooth.
> *By the time they are seven,* most children have lost a tooth.

1. The lieutenant had given, although he was later accused of dereliction of duty, the correct orders.
2. The girls loved to daily sun beside the pool.
3. Ballet will, if the present interest continues to grow, be one of the country's most popular arts.
4. The police revealed, after two days of silence, the story.
5. The beavers, when the new housing construction began, abandoned their dam.

DANGLING MODIFIERS

| 14g

Avoid dangling modifiers.

A **dangling modifier** does not sensibly modify anything in its sentence.

DANGLING   *Passing the building,* the vandalism was clearly visible. [The modifying phrase seems to describe *vandalism*. The writer has not said who was passing the building or who saw the vandalism.]

DANGLING   *Shortly after leaving home,* the accident occurred. [The modifying phrase seems to describe *accident*. The writer has not said who left home or who was in the accident.]

Dangling modifiers occur most often when certain kinds of modifying word groups precede the main clause of the sentence, as in the examples above. These word groups include participial phrases (*passing the building*); infinitive phrases (*to be seen*); prepositional phrases in which the object of the preposition is a gerund (*after leaving home*); and elliptical clauses in which the subject and perhaps the verb are understood (*while at work*). (See 5c.) Since these phrases and clauses have no expressed subject, readers take them to modify the following noun, the subject of the main clause. If they do not sensibly define or describe the following noun, they are dangling modifiers.

DANGLING   *Being very tired,* the alarm failed to disturb Morton's sleep. [Participial phrase.]

DANGLING   *To get up on time,* a great effort was needed. [Infinitive phrase.]

DANGLING   *On rising,* coffee was essential to waken Morton. [Prepositional phrase.]

DANGLING   *Until completely awake,* work was impossible. [Elliptical clause.]

These sentences are illogical because the initial modifiers do not sensibly describe the words they appear to modify: Alarm clocks don't get tired, effort doesn't get up, coffee doesn't rise, and work doesn't awaken. Note that a modifier may be dangling even when the sentence elsewhere contains a word the modifier might seem to describe, such as *Morton's* and *Morton* in the first and third examples above. In addition, a dangling modifier may fall at the end of a sentence:

DANGLING   Work came easily *when finally awake.*

We correct dangling modifiers by recasting the sentences in which they appear. We can change the subject of the main clause to the word the modifier properly defines or describes. Or we can recast the dangling modifier as a complete clause. The examples below illustrate these revisions.

DANGLING	*Being crowded in the car,* the trip was uncomfortable. [Dangling participial phrase.]
REVISED	*Being crowded in the car, we* were uncomfortable.
REVISED	*Because we were crowded in the car,* the trip was uncomfortable.
DANGLING	*After unlocking the door,* the cat refused to go out. [Dangling prepositional phrase.]
REVISED	*After I had unlocked the door,* the cat refused to go out.
DANGLING	*To take sharp action pictures,* the shutter speed should be fast. [Dangling infinitive phrase.]
REVISED	*To take sharp action pictures, a photographer* needs a fast shutter speed.
REVISED	*If a photographer wants to take sharp action pictures,* the shutter speed should be fast.
DANGLING	*Though still in the hospital,* the stitches were removed from Larry's wound. [Dangling elliptical clause.]
REVISED	*Though still in the hospital, Larry* had the stitches removed from his wound.
REVISED	*Though Larry was still in the hospital,* the stitches were removed from his wound.

dm.
14g

EXERCISE 5

Revise the sentences below to eliminate any dangling modifiers. Each item has more than one possible answer.

Example:

Having let out all the string, our kite sailed dangerously near the wires.

Having let out all the string, we watched our kite sail dangerously near the wires.

When we had let out all the string, our kite sailed dangerously near the wires.

1. Staring at the ceiling, the idea became clear.
2. Sagging and needing a new coat of paint, Mr. Preston called the house painter.
3. By repairing the transmission, our car began to run again.

4. Monday passed me by without accomplishing anything.
5. To swim well, good shoulder muscles help.
6. To obtain disability income, a doctor must certify that an employee cannot work.
7. When only a ninth grader, my grandmother tried to teach me double-entry bookkeeping.
8. Arriving by train, the stockyards dominate the landscape.
9. After weighing the alternatives, his decision became clear.
10. Although unusually hot, the rains kept the crops from being ruined.

EXERCISE 6

dm
14g

Combine each pair of sentences below into a single sentence by rewriting one as a modifier. Make sure each modifier applies clearly to the appropriate word. You will have to add, delete, and rearrange words, and you may find that more than one answer is possible in each case.

Example:

Bob demanded a hearing from the faculty. Bob wanted to appeal the decision.

Wanting to appeal the decision, Bob demanded a hearing from the faculty.

1. We were taking our seats. The announcer read the line-up.
2. I was rushing to the interview. My shoelace broke.
3. The children crowded into the buses. The children were from the fifth grade.
4. She was trying to cheer Jason up. Her Halloween mask terrified Jason instead.
5. They were holding hands. A man crept up behind them.
6. She rested her bandaged foot on the stool. She was wearing a yellow satin robe.
7. My uncle said he had never received good advice. He was fifty years old then.
8. Several people saw the ranch hand. The people had been shopping in town.
9. We reached the end of the road. A vast emptiness surrounded us.
10. Sylvie received a letter announcing she had won. The letter came the day after she returned from vacation.

15

Mixed and Incomplete Sentences

MIXED SENTENCES

A **mixed sentence** contains two or more parts that are incompatible — that is, the parts do not fit together. The misfit may be in grammar or in meaning.

MIXED GRAMMAR	After watching television for twelve hours was the reason his head hurt.
MIXED MEANING	The work involved in directing the use of resources is the definition of management.

15a

Be sure that the parts of your sentences, particularly subjects and predicates, fit together grammatically.

Many mixed sentences occur when we start a sentence with one grammatical plan or construction in mind but end it with a different one. Such sentences often result from a confusion between two ways of making a statement.

MIXED	In all his efforts to please others got him into trouble.

In this mixed sentence the writer starts with a modifying prepositional phrase and then tries to make it work as the subject of *got*. But prepositional phrases can very seldom function as sentence subjects. Here are two ways to revise the sentence.

REVISED	In all his efforts to please others, he got into trouble. [The necessary subject *he* is added to the main clause.]
REVISED	All his efforts to please others got him into trouble. [The preposition is dropped.]

247

Each group of sentences below illustrates a similar confusion between two sentence plans plus ideas for revision.

MIXED	By increasing the amount of money we spend will not solve the problem of crime. [The writer has made a prepositional phrase the subject of *will not solve.*]
REVISED	Increasing the amount of money we spend will not solve the problem of crime. [The preposition is omitted, leaving a gerund phrase as the subject.]
REVISED	We will not solve the problem of crime by increasing the amount of money we spend. [The subject *we* is supplied for the main clause, and the prepositional phrase is moved to the end of the sentence.]
MIXED	Although he was seen with a convicted thief does not make him a thief. [The writer has made an adverb clause the subject of *does.* An adverb clause cannot serve as a subject.]
REVISED	That he was seen with a convicted thief does not make him a thief. [*That* changes the clause into a noun clause, a grammatical subject.]
REVISED	Although he was seen with a convicted thief, he is not necessarily a thief. [The subject *he* is supplied for the main clause.]
MIXED	Among those who pass the entrance examinations, they do not all get admitted to the program. [The sentence subject *they* is not an appropriate subject for the modifying phrase beginning with *among.* A subject like *all* or *many* is needed.]
REVISED	Among those who pass the entrance examinations, not all get admitted to the program.
REVISED	Among those who pass the entrance examinations, many do not get admitted to the program.
REVISED	Not all those who pass the entrance examinations get admitted to the program.

mixed

15b

15b

Be sure that the subjects and predicates of your sentences fit together in meaning.

The mixed sentences we examined above were confusing because their parts did not fit together grammatically. Another kind of

mixed sentence fails because its subject and predicate do not fit together in meaning. Such a mixture is sometimes called a **faulty
predication.**

The most common form of faulty predication occurs when the
linking verb *be* connects a subject and its complement. Since such a
sentence forms a kind of equation, the subject and complement
must be items that can be sensibly equated. If they are not, the sentence goes awry.

FAULTY   A *compromise* between the city and the town
            would be the ideal *place* to live.

In this sentence the subject *compromise* is equated with the complement *place*. Thus the sentence says that *a compromise is a place*,
clearly not a sensible statement. Sometimes such mixed sentences
seem to result from the writer's effort to compress too many ideas
into a single word or phrase. The sentence above can be revised to
state the writer's meaning more exactly.

mixed
15b

REVISED   A *community* that offered the best qualities of
            both city and town would be the ideal *place* to
            live.

Faulty predications are not confined to sentences with *be*. In
the following sentences the italicized subjects and verbs highlight
the misfit between the two.

FAULTY   The *use* of emission controls *was created* to re-
            duce air pollution. [The controls, not their use,
            were created.]

REVISED   Emission *controls were created* to reduce air pol-
            lution.

FAULTY   The *area* of financial mismanagement *poses* a
            threat to small businesses. [Mismanagement, not
            the area, poses the threat.]

REVISED   Financial *mismanagement poses* a threat to small
            businesses.

A special kind of faulty predication occurs when a clause beginning *when* or *where* follows a form of *be* in a definition, as in *A
wastebasket is where you put trash.* Though the construction is common in speech, written definitions require nouns or noun clauses on
both sides of *be: A wastebasket is a container for trash.*

FAULTY   *An examination* is *when you are tested* on what
            you know.

REVISED   *An examination* is *a test* of what you know.

REVISED   *In an examination you are tested* on what you
            know.

A similar kind of faulty predication occurs when a *because* clause follows the subject-verb pattern *The reason is,* as in *The reason is because I don't want to.* This construction is also common in speech, but it is redundant since the conjunction *because* means *for the reason that.* The construction should not appear in writing.

> FAULTY   The *reason* we were late *is because* we had an accident.
>
> REVISED   The *reason* we were late *is that* we had an accident.
>
> REVISED   We were late *because* we had an accident.

mixed
15b

In some mixed sentences the combination of faults is so confusing that the writer has little choice but to start over.

> MIXED   My long-range goal is through law school and government work I hope to deal with those problems I now deal with more effectively.
>
> POSSIBLE REVISION   My long-range goal is to go to law school and then work in government so that I can deal more effectively with problems I now face.

EXERCISE 1

Revise the sentences below so that their parts fit together both in grammar and in meaning. Each item has more than one possible answer.

> *Example:*
>
> When they found out how expensive pianos are is why they were discouraged.
>
> They were discouraged *because* they found out how expensive pianos are.
>
> When they found out how expensive pianos are, *they* were discouraged.

1. Because of a broken leg is the reason Vance left the football team.
2. Schizophrenia is when a person withdraws from reality and behaves in abnormal ways.
3. Among the polished stones, they were all beyond my price range.
4. Any government that can support an expedition to Mars, they should be able to solve their country's social problems, too.
5. The different tastes of different beers is in how they are brewed.
6. Needlepoint is where you work with yarn on a mesh canvas.
7. Through the help of his staff is how the mayor got reelected.

8. After mowing the backyard was the right time for a glass of iced tea.
9. A divorce is when a judge dissolves a marriage contract.
10. The reason many people don't accept the theory of evolution is because it goes contrary to their religious beliefs.

INCOMPLETE SENTENCES

The most serious kind of incomplete sentence is the fragment (see Chapter 10). But sentences are also incomplete when the writer omits one or more words needed to make a phrase or clause clear or accurate.

inc
15c

15c
Be sure that omissions from compound constructions are consistent with grammar or idiom.

Both speech and writing commonly use **elliptical constructions,** constructions that omit words not necessary for meaning (see 5c-4). In the following sentences the words in parentheses can be omitted without confusing or distracting the reader. Notice that they all involve compound constructions.

My car has been driven 80,000 miles; his (has been driven) only 20,000 (miles).

Some people heat by oil, some (heat) by gas, others (heat) by electricity.

She had great hope for her sons and (for) their future.

Such omissions are possible only when the words omitted are common to all the parts of a compound construction. When the parts differ in grammar or idiom, all words must be included in all parts. (See also 31b-3.) In the following sentences the italicized words differ and must be included.

My car *has been driven* 80,000 miles; their cars *have been driven* only 20,000 miles.

I *am* firm; you *are* stubborn; he *is* pigheaded.

The students *were invited* and *were happy* to go. [The first *were* is an auxiliary in the passive verb phrase *were invited*. The second *were* is a linking verb with the complement *happy*.]

She had faith *in* and hopes *for* the future. [Idiom requires *in* after the noun *faith* but *for* after *hopes*. Thus both must be present.]

Notice that in the sentence *My brother and friend moved to Dallas,* the omission of *my* before *friend* indicates that *brother* and *friend* are the same person. If two different persons are meant, the modifier or article must be repeated, as in *My brother and my friend moved to Dallas.*

15d

Be sure that all comparisons are complete and logical.

Comparisons make statements about the relation between two or more things, as in *Dogs are more intelligent than cats* or *Bones was the most intelligent dog we ever had.* To be complete and logical, a comparison must state the relation between the compared items fully enough to ensure clarity; it must compare only items that can sensibly be compared; and it must include all and only the items being compared.

1
State a comparison fully enough to ensure clarity.

In a comparison such as *John likes bowling better than (he likes) tennis,* we can omit *he likes* because only one meaning is possible. But sentences such as *John likes bowling better than Jane* may mean either *better than he likes Jane* or *better than Jane likes bowling.* Therefore, we must be careful to state such sentences fully enough to prevent any misreading.

UNCLEAR	Boston is nearer to New York than Washington.
CLEAR	Boston is nearer to New York than *Washington is.*
CLEAR	Boston is nearer to New York than *it is to Washington.*

2
Be sure that the items being compared are in fact comparable.

A comparison is logical only if it compares items that can sensibly be compared. We can compare one food with another or one car with another, but we cannot sensibly compare food with cars. We are likely to make illogical comparisons unintentionally.

ILLOGICAL	The cost of a typewriter is greater than a calculator. [The writer compares the cost of something with a calculator.]
REVISED	The cost of a typewriter is greater than *the cost of* (or *that of*) a calculator.

3

In comparing members of the same class, use *other* or *any other*. In comparing members of different classes, use *any*.

When we compare a person or thing with all others in the same group, we form two units: (1) the individual person or thing and (2) all *other* persons or things in the group.

Joshua [the individual] was more stubborn than *any other* child in the family [all the others in the group].

ILLOGICAL	Los Angeles is larger than *any* city in California. [Since Los Angeles is itself a city in California, the sentence seems to say that Los Angeles is larger than itself.]
LOGICAL	Los Angeles is larger than *any other* city in California. [Adding *other* excludes Los Angeles from the group of the state's other cities.]

When a person or thing is compared with the members of a *different* group, the two units are logically separate.

Some American cars [one group] are cheaper than *any* foreign car [a different group].

ILLOGICAL	Los Angeles is larger than *any other* city in Canada. [The cities in Canada constitute a group to which Los Angeles does not belong.]
LOGICAL	Los Angeles is larger than *any* city in Canada. [Omitting the word *other* makes a separate group of the Canadian cities.]

4

Avoid comparisons that do not state what is being compared.

Brand X gets clothes *whiter*. [Whiter than what?]
Brand Y is so much *better*. [Better than what?]

15e

Be careful not to omit articles, prepositions, or other needed words.

In haste or carelessness writers sometimes omit small words such as articles and prepositions that are needed for clarity.

INCOMPLETE	Regular payroll deductions are a type painless savings. You hardly notice missing amounts, and

inc
15e

after period of years the contributions can add a
large total.

REVISED   Regular payroll deductions are a type *of* painless
savings. You hardly notice *the* missing amounts,
and after *a* period of years the contributions can
add *up to* a large total.

(See also the Glossary of Usage under *type of.*)

In both speech and writing we often omit *that* when it introduces a noun clause following a verb, as in *We knew* (*that*) *he
was coming.* But such an omission can sometimes be confusing.

inc

15e

INCOMPLETE   She observed many people who had been invited
were missing. [At first reading, *many people* appears to be the object of *observed* rather than the
subject of the entire subordinate clause.]

REVISED   She observed *that* many people who had been invited were missing.

Attentive proofreading is the only insurance against the kind
of omissions described in this section. *Proofread all your papers
carefully.*

EXERCISE 2

Revise the sentences below so that they are complete, logical, and
clear. Some items have more than one possible answer.

Example:

Our house is closer to the courthouse than the subway stop.

Our house is closer to the courthouse than *it is to* the subway
stop.

Our house is closer to the courthouse than the subway stop *is.*

1. Both of them not only believe but work for energy conserva-
tion.
2. The legal question raised by the prosecution was relevant and
considered by the judge.
3. Football interested Ralph more than his friends.
4. His tip was larger than any customer I ever waited on.
5. With an altitude of 6288 feet, New Hampshire's Mount Washington is higher than any mountain in New England.
6. The largest bookstore the United States stocks two three copies most books in print.
7. The dog is only a puppy; the cats both ten years old.
8. My chemistry text is more interesting to me than any other social science text.
9. He feared darkness and the drop in temperature would trap
the climbers on the mountain.
10. Inventors usually have an interest and talent for solving practical problems.

IV
Effective Sentences

16

Using Coordination and Subordination

To communicate effectively, you must fit thoughts together according to their relative importance. You **coordinate** the facts and ideas that you wish to emphasize equally, such as the thoughts about insurance in the sentence *Car insurance is costly, but medical insurance is almost a luxury.* You **subordinate** lesser facts and ideas to the ones you wish to emphasize. In the sentence *Because accidents and theft are frequent, car insurance is expensive,* the clause beginning *Because* is subordinate to the main clause. Subordinated information may be very important to the total meaning of the sentence, but readers will always see it as less important than the subject and predicate in the main clause of the sentence.

You coordinate the information in words, phrases, and clauses by joining them with the coordinating conjunctions *and, but, or, nor, for, so,* and *yet;* by joining them with conjunctive adverbs such as *however, moreover,* and *therefore;* and by expressing them in the same kind of grammatical construction (see Chapter 17 on parallelism). You subordinate information by expressing it in clauses introduced by subordinating conjunctions (such as *although, because, if, when, where, while*) or relative pronouns (*who, which, that*), or by expressing it in phrases and single words.

The sections that follow provide some guidelines for managing coordination and subordination effectively.

16a
Coordinating to relate equal ideas

Two or more simple sentences in a row will seem roughly equal but distinct. Thus the reader must detect whatever specific relation exists between them. Linking sentences and ideas with coordinating conjunctions enables the reader to see the relations between them more easily. Compare the following passages.

> We should not rely so heavily on coal, oil, and uranium. We have a substantial energy resource in the moving waters of our rivers. Smaller streams add to the total volume of water. The resource renews itself. Coal and oil are irreplaceable. Uranium is also irreplaceable. The cost of water does not increase much over time. The costs of coal, oil, and uranium rise dramatically.

> We should not rely so heavily on coal, oil, and uranium, for we have a substantial energy resource in the moving waters of our rivers and streams. Coal, oil, and uranium are irreplaceable and thus subject to dramatic cost increases; water, in contrast, is self-renewing and more stable in cost.

The information in both passages is essentially the same, but the second is shorter and considerably easier to read and understand. Whereas the first passage strings ideas together in short, simple sentences without relating them to each other, the second passage builds connections among coordinate ideas: the availability of water in rivers and streams (first sentence); the relation between renewal and cost (second sentence); and the contrast between water and the other resources (both sentences).

coord
16a

1
Avoiding faulty coordination

Faulty coordination occurs when no logical connection seems to exist between two coordinated statements or when the stated connection contradicts common sense. Sometimes faulty coordination occurs because the writer omits necessary information, as in this example:

FAULTY	Jacob is a foster child and has to go to the dentist often.
REVISED	Jacob is a foster child *whose biological parents neglected his teeth; consequently,* he has to go to the dentist often.
REVISED	*Because* Jacob is a foster child *whose biological parents neglected his teeth,* he has to go to the dentist often.

Often, as the last example above shows, the intended relation between clauses can be clarified by subordinating one of the ideas if it modifies or explains the other one. Here is another example.

FAULTY	John Stuart Mill was a utilitarian, and he believed that actions should be judged by their usefulness or by the happiness they cause.

| REVISED | John Stuart Mill, *a utilitarian*, believed that actions should be judged by their usefulness or by the happiness they cause. |

2
Avoiding excessive coordination

A stringy compound sentence — a sequence of main clauses linked with coordinating conjunctions — creates the same effect as a series of simple sentences: It obscures the relative importance of ideas and details.

| EXCESSIVE COORDINATION | We were near the end of the trip, and the storm kept getting worse, and the snow and ice covered the windshield, and I could hardly see the road ahead, and I knew I should stop, but I kept on driving, and once I barely missed a truck. |

coord
16a

This sentence contains two main assertions: *the storm kept getting worse* and *I kept on driving*. All the rest is detail elaborating on these simple statements. Such a loosely compounded sentence needs subordination so that main assertions and supporting detail are distinct.

| REVISED | As we neared the end of the trip, *the storm kept getting worse*, covering the windshield with snow and ice until I could barely see the road ahead. Even though I knew I should stop, *I kept on driving*, once barely missing a truck. |

Be careful not to overuse *so* as a coordinating connector.

| EXCESSIVE COORDINATION | Jim had an examination that day, so he came home late, so he missed seeing the fire, so he was not able to describe it to us. |

As with other varieties of excessive coordination, the best way to revise such sentences is to separate the main statement from dependent details.

| REVISED | *Jim was not able to describe the fire to us* because he had an examination that day and arrived home too late to see the fire. |

Excessive coordination is not always as obvious as it is in the two examples above. The passage below contains only two compound sentences, but they still connect facts so loosely that the reader is left to distinguish their importance.

EXCESSIVE
COORDINATION

A man came out of the liquor store. He wore a pair of frayed corduroy pants, and he wore a brown sweater. He started toward a blue car, and the police arrested him.

Using subordination to rewrite this passage shows clearly which ideas are important and which less important. The essential fact that the police arrested the man becomes the main clause, and all other details are incorporated into a single subordinate *when* clause.

REVISED

When a man wearing frayed corduroy pants and a brown sweater came out of the liquor store and started toward a blue car, *the police arrested him.*

EXERCISE 1

Combine sentences in the passages below to coordinate related ideas in the way that seems most effective to you. You will have to supply coordinating conjunctions.

1. Everyone read some fairy tales as a child. Everyone remembers some. Most people think they are only for children. They express the deepest fears and desires of children. They also express the deepest fears and desires of adults. Adults read them *to* children. They should read them *for* themselves.
2. Henry Hudson was an English explorer. He captained ships for the Dutch East India Company. On a voyage in 1610 he passed by Greenland. He sailed into a great bay in today's northern Canada. He thought he and his sailors could winter there. The cold was terrible. Food ran out. The sailors mutinied. The sailors cast Hudson adrift in a small boat. Eight others were also in the boat. Hudson and his companions perished.

coord
16a

EXERCISE 2

Revise the following sentences to eliminate faulty or excessive coordination. Relate ideas effectively by adding or subordinating information or by forming more than one sentence. Each item has more than one possible answer.

Example:

My dog barks, and I have to move out of my apartment.

Because my dog's barking *disturbs my neighbors*, I have to move out of my apartment.

1. The dean was furious, and she let the police know it, but they refused to listen, and they began patrolling the campus.
2. The Chinese are communists, and they believe in the common ownership of goods and the means to produce them.
3. The dogs escaped from the pen because the keeper forgot to secure the latch, and the dogs wanted freedom, and they got it by running away, and it took the rest of the day to find them.

4. The weather in March is cold and rainy, but sometimes it is warm and sunny, and the inconsistency makes it impossible to plan outdoor activities, yet everyone wants to be outdoors after the long winter.
5. The gun sounded, and I froze, but an instant later I was running with a smooth, pumping motion, and I knew I would win the race.
6. The citizens of Vermont are determined to preserve their environment, and they have some of the nation's toughest anti-pollution laws.
7. Two days last month were legal holidays, and the school held classes as usual.
8. Registering for classes the first time is confusing, and you have to find your way around, and you have to deal with strangers.
9. Robert was due to arrive at lunchtime, and he called just before dinner.
10. Air traffic in and out of major cities increases yearly, and the congestion is becoming dangerous, but the current regulations are inadequate, and they cannot control even the present traffic.

sub
16b

16b
Subordinating to distinguish the main idea

Like paragraphs, many sentences consist of a main idea amplified and supported by details. In the paragraph, the main idea appears in the topic sentence and the details in the remaining sentences (see 3a). In the sentence, the main idea appears in the main clause and the details in subordinate structures such as phrases or subordinate clauses. Subordination is crucial for distinguishing principal ideas from supporting information. In the sentence below, the writer fails to make this distinction.

> In recent years car prices have increased, and production costs have increased even more, and car makers must contend with lower profits.

The writer gives three facts: car prices have increased, production costs have increased, and profits are lower. By loosely coordinating these three facts, the writer suggests some relation among them. But *in recent years* and *even more* provide the only explicit relations. We do not know which fact the writer sees as most important or how the other facts qualify or support it. Look at the improvement in these revisions.

> *Because* production costs have increased even more than car prices in recent years, car makers must contend with lower profits.

Although car prices have increased in recent years, production costs have increased even more, *so that* car makers must contend with lower profits.

When production costs increase even more than car prices, *as* they have in recent years, car makers must contend with lower profits.

In these revisions the words *because, although, so that, when,* and *as* indicate specific cause-and-effect relations among the three facts. Each sentence makes clear that car makers' profits decline when increases in production costs outstrip increases in prices, but the emphasis varies from one version to another.

No rules can specify what information in a sentence should be primary and what subordinate, for the decision is dictated in every instance by the writer's meaning. But, in general, details of time, cause, condition, concession, purpose, and identification (size, location, and the like) usually appear in subordinate structures. Consider the following pairs of examples. (Some of the appropriate subordinating conjunctions and relative pronouns are listed in parentheses.)

sub
16b

TIME (*after, before, since, until, when, while*)

The mine explosion killed six men. The owners adopted safety measures.

After the mine explosion killed six men, the owners adopted safety measures.

CAUSE (*because, since*)

Jones has been without work for six months. He is having trouble paying his bills.

Because Jones has been without work for six months, he is having trouble paying his bills.

CONDITION (*if, provided, since, unless*)

Mike attends no lectures and studies infrequently. He has little chance of passing his biology examination.

Since Mike attends no lectures and studies infrequently, he has little chance of passing his biology examination.

CONCESSION (*although, as if, even though, though*)

The horse looked gentle. It proved high-spirited and hard to manage.

Although the horse looked gentle, it proved high-spirited and hard to manage.

PURPOSE (*in order that, so that, that*)

Congress passed new immigration laws. Many Vietnamese refugees could enter the United States.

Congress passed new immigration laws *so that* many Vietnamese refugees could enter the United States.

IDENTIFICATION (*that, when, where, which, who*)

The old factory now manufactures automobile transmissions. It stands on the south side of town and covers three acres.

The old factory, *which* stands on the south side of town and covers three acres, now manufactures automobile transmissions.

Using subordinate clauses to distinguish main ideas from supporting information is the first and most important step toward writing effective sentences. But skillful subordination depends also on other grammatical constructions that help to subordinate information. Many times, a verbal or prepositional phrase, an appositive, an absolute phrase, or even a single-word modifier will suffice to give all the weight needed to subordinate information. In general, a subordinate clause will give greatest importance to subordinate detail; verbal phrases, appositives, and absolute phrases will give somewhat less weight; prepositional phrases still less; and single words the least. We can see the differences among subordinate constructions in the examples below.

sub
16b

Old barns are common in New England. They are often painted red. [Separate sentences.]

Old barns, *which are often painted red*, are common in New England. [Subordinate clause.]

Old barns, *often painted red*, are common in New England. [Verbal phrase.]

Old *red* barns are common in New England. [Single word.]

Notice below how different grammatical constructions give different weights to the information in some of the sentence pairs we looked at above.

Jones has been without work for six months. He is having trouble paying his bills. [Separate sentences.]

Because Jones has been without work for six months, he is having trouble paying his bills. [Subordinate clause.]

Having been without work for six months, Jones is having trouble paying his bills. [Verbal phrase.]

Out of work for six months, Jones is having trouble paying his bills. [Prepositional phrase.]

The horse looked gentle. It proved high-spirited and hard to handle. [Separate sentences.]

Although the horse looked gentle, it proved high-spirited and hard to manage. [Subordinate clause.]

The horse, *a gentle-looking animal,* proved high-spirited and hard to manage. [Appositive.]

The *gentle-looking* horse proved high-spirited and hard to manage. [Single word.]

The old factory now manufactures automobile transmissions. It stands on the south side of town and covers three acres. [Separate sentences.]

The old factory, *which stands on the south side of town and covers three acres,* now manufactures automobile transmissions. [Subordinate clause.]

The *three-acre* factory *on the town's south side* now manufactures automobile transmissions. [Single word and prepositional phrase.]

1
Avoiding faulty subordination

Faulty subordination occurs when a writer uses a subordinate clause or other subordinate structure for what seems clearly to be the most important idea in the sentence. Often, faulty subordination merely reverses the dependent relation the reader expects.

> **FAULTY**   Ms. Angelo was in her first year of teaching, although she was a better instructor than others with many years of experience. [The sentence suggests that Ms. Angelo's inexperience is the main idea, whereas the writer almost certainly intended to stress her skill *despite* her inexperience.]

sub
16b.

> **REVISED**   Although Ms. Angelo was in her first year of teaching, *she was a better instructor than others with many years of experience.*

> **FAULTY**   Marty's final interview that was to determine his admission to law school began at two o'clock. [Common sense says that the important fact is the interview's purpose, not its time.]

> **REVISED**   *Marty's final interview,* which began at two o'clock, *was to determine his admission to law school.*

2
Avoiding excessive subordination

Excessive subordination sometimes occurs when a writer tries to jam too much loosely related detail into a single sentence.

> **OVERLOADED**   The boats that were moored at the dock when the hurricane, which was one of the worst in three decades, struck were ripped from their moorings, because their owners had not been adequately prepared, since the weather service had predicted the storm would blow out to sea, which they do at this time of year.

Since such sentences usually have more than one idea that deserves a main clause, they are best revised by sorting their details into more than one sentence.

> REVISED
>
> Struck by one of the worst hurricanes in three decades, *the boats at the dock were ripped from their moorings. The owners were unprepared* because the weather service had said that hurricanes at this time of year blow out to sea.

A common form of excessive subordination occurs with a string of adjective clauses beginning *which, who,* or *that,* as in the following:

> STRING OF ADJECTIVE CLAUSES
>
> Every Christmas we all try to go to my grandfather's house, which is near Louisville, which is an attractive city where my parents now live.

These sentences can often be revised by recasting some of the subordinate clauses as other kinds of modifying structures. In the revision below, for example, the clause *which is near Louisville* has been reduced to a simple modifier, and the clause *which is an attractive city* has been changed to an appositive.

> REVISED
>
> Every Christmas we all try to go to my grandfather's house *near Louisville, an attractive city* where my parents now live.

sub
16b

EXERCISE 3

Combine each of the following pairs of sentences twice, each time using one of the subordinate structures in parentheses to make a single sentence. You will have to add, delete, change, and rearrange words.

Example:

During the late eighteenth century, workers carried beverages in brightly colored bottles. The bottles had cork stoppers. (*Clause beginning* that. *Phrase beginning* with.)

During the late eighteenth century, workers carried beverages in brightly colored bottles *that had cork stoppers.*

During the late eighteenth century, workers carried beverages in brightly colored bottles *with cork stoppers.*

1. In World War I, German forces set out to capture Verdun. Verdun was a fortress in northeastern France. (*Clause beginning* which. *Appositive beginning* a fortress.)
2. One of the largest salt mines in the world lies under a city in Poland. It yields an average of 60,000 tons of salt yearly. (*Phrase beginning* lying. *Phrase beginning* yielding.)
3. Bertrand Russell was raised by his grandparents. He had been

orphaned in early childhood. (*Clause beginning because or since. Phrase beginning orphaned.*)

4. James Joyce is one of the century's most controversial writers. He has been praised as the greatest writer since Milton and condemned as a writer of "latrine literature." (*Clause beginning who. Phrase beginning praised.*)

5. The Amish live peaceful but austere lives. Most of them refuse to use modern technology. (*Absolute phrase beginning most. Phrase beginning living.*)

6. Hernando de Soto is the legendary European discoverer of the Mississippi River. He supposedly died on the river's banks. (*Clause beginning who. Appositive beginning the legendary.*)

7. Computerized newspaper operations speed up and simplify copy preparation. They are favored by editors and reporters. (*Clause beginning because. Phrase beginning favored.*)

8. Patents are the surest protection for inventions. They are difficult to obtain. (*Clause beginning although. Appositive beginning the surest.*)

9. Winston Churchill originated the phrase "the Iron Curtain." He was speaking at Westminster College in Missouri. (*Phrase beginning speaking. Phrase beginning at.*)

10. Andrew Bradford began the American magazine industry. He first published *American Magazine* in 1741. (*Clause beginning who. Clause beginning when.*)

sub

16b

EXERCISE 1

Rewrite the following paragraph in the way you think most effective to subordinate the less important ideas to the more important ones. Use subordinate clauses or other subordinating constructions as appropriate.

Many students today are no longer majoring in the liberal arts. I mean by "liberal arts" such subjects as history, English, and the social sciences. Students think a liberal arts degree will not help them get jobs. They are wrong. They may not get practical, job-related experience from the liberal arts, but they will get a broad education, and it will never again be available to them. Many employers look for more than a technical, professional education. They think such an education can make an employee's views too narrow. The employers want open-minded employees. They want employees to think about problems from many angles. The liberal arts curriculum instills such flexibility. The flexibility is vital to the health of our society.

EXERCISE 5

Revise the following sentences to eliminate faulty or excessive subordination by reversing main and subordinate ideas, by coordinating ideas, or by making separate sentences. Some items have more than one possible answer.

Example:
Scarred for life, he was severely injured in a car crash.
Severely injured in a car crash, he was scarred for life.

1. The car that my boss parked in front of the store, which rolled into my bike, was the car that he had just bought.
2. The best plays in basketball are sometimes made at the last minute because it is a game of surprises.
3. A woman who wants a career in the armed forces is better off now than she used to be because reasonable people no longer think that there's anything wrong with women who want to become career officers, which used to be a problem.
4. Children should understand that many good television shows that take some thought to enjoy are worth watching because true entertainment doesn't occur unless people have to think about what they see.
5. The speaker from the Sierra Club, whom we had invited on short notice when our planned speaker canceled, nonetheless gave an informative and moving talk about the need to preserve our wilderness areas, which he said were in danger of extinction.

sub
16c

16c
Choosing clear connectors

Most connecting words signal specific and unambiguous relationships; for instance, the coordinating conjunction *but* clearly indicates contrast, and the subordinating conjunction *because* clearly indicates cause. A few connectors, however, require careful use, either because they are ambiguous in many contexts or because they are often misused in current English.

1
Avoiding ambiguous connectors: *as* and *while*

The subordinating conjunction *as* can indicate several kinds of adverbial relations, including comparison and time.

COMPARISON   He was working *as* rapidly as he could.

TIME   The instructor finally arrived *as* the class was leaving.

As can also indicate cause, but in that sense it is often ambiguous and should be avoided.

AMBIGUOUS   *As* I was in town, I visited some old friends. [Time or cause intended?]

CLEAR	*When* I was in town, I visited some old friends. [Time.]
CLEAR	*Because* I was in town, I visited some old friends. [Cause.]

The subordinating conjunction *while* can indicate either time or concession. Unless context makes the meaning of *while* unmistakably clear, choose a more exact connector.

AMBIGUOUS	*While* we were working nearby, we did not hear the burglars enter. [Time or concession?]
CLEAR	*When* we were working nearby, we did not hear the burglars enter. [Time.]
CLEAR	*Although* we were working nearby, we did not hear the burglars enter. [Concession.]

2
Avoiding misused connectors: *as, like,* and *while*

The use of *as* as a substitute for *whether* or *that* is nonstandard.

NONSTANDARD	He was not sure *as* he could come.
ꞰꞄꞇꞋꞄꞇꞄ	Hꞇ ꞃꞇꞈ ꞇꞆꞇ ꞈꞁꞇꞆ ꞃꞃꞀꞇꞇꞃꞆꞇꞇ (ꞈꞇ ꞇꞃꞈꞇꞇ) ꞃꞇ ꞈꞆꞁꞃꞋ ꞈꞆ꞉ꞁꞇ.

Although the preposition *like* is often used as a conjunction in speech and in advertising (*Dirt-Away works like a soap should*), writing and standard speech require the conjunction *as, as if,* or *as though.*

INFORMAL SPEECH	The examination seemed *like* it would never end.
WRITING	The examination seemed *as if* (*as though*) it would never end.

The subordinating conjunction *while* is sometimes carelessly used in the sense of *and* or *but,* creating false subordination.

FAULTY	My sister wants to study medicine *while* I want to study law.
REVISED	My sister wants to study medicine, *and* I want to study law.

EXERCISE 6

Substitute a clear or correct connector in the sentences below where *as, while,* and *like* are ambiguous or misused.

Example:

He looked to me like he had slept in this clothes.
He looked to me *as if* he had slept in his clothes.

1. As I was going home for Thanksgiving, my mother cooked a squash pie for me.
2. From where I was sitting, the car looked like it would hit the baby carriage.
3. Busing schoolchildren is a controversial issue in many cities, while in others it does not seem to arouse much interest.
4. As teachers and legislators worry about the literacy of high school students, the situation may improve.
5. Many states give minimum competency tests for graduation from high school, like there weren't enough hurdles to jump over to get a high school diploma.

EXERCISE 7

sub
16c

Identify each instance of faulty, excessive, or ineffective coordination or subordination in the paragraph below. Rewrite the paragraph in the way you think most effective to emphasize main ideas.

Many people claim that chemical fertilizers and insecticides are essential for a healthy and productive vegetable garden, although they are wrong. Organic-gardening methods produce healthy gardens. Good nutritious soil will give any plant a head start on healthy growth, and the most necessary soil element is nitrogen, which can be supplied by several organic sources, which include animal manure and fishmeal. Aerated soil allows roots room to grow. It also allows water to drain easily. Pests like mites and beetles have their place in the food chain. Using insecticides to kill them can result in larger populations of other pests. These other pests can cause more trouble than mites and beetles. Mites and beetles sometimes feed on them. A strong plant in good soil will resist attack from pests. The gardener can also make exotic concoctions of strong-smelling ingredients like beer, onions, and red peppers, which will discourage many pests, which react much as we do to the strong odors. And practiced gardeners know that growing certain plants next to others also discourages pests. For example, eggplants grown near green beans will be less susceptible to beetles. Leeks keep flies away from carrots.

17
Using Parallelism

Parallelism is a similarity of grammatical form between two or more coordinated elements.

> The air is dirtied by ‖ factories ‖ belching ‖ smoke
> and ‖ cars ‖ spewing ‖ exhaust.

In a paragraph, parallel structure from one sentence to the next helps link the sentences by indicating that they are closely related in meaning and importance (see 3b-2). Parallel structure can also operate within a sentence, as the example above shows, to reinforce the close relation between compound sentence elements, whether they be words, phrases, or entire clauses. In the sentence below, the two parts of the compound predicate are both coordinate and parallel.

> Recycling old buildings both *conserves our resources* and *preserves our past.*

The principle underlying parallelism is that form should reflect meaning. Since the parts of a compound subject, predicate, object, complement, or modifier have the same function and importance, they should have the same grammatical form. Thus parallelism is both a grammatical requirement of the sentence and a device for helping readers see the connections between ideas. In the following sections we will look at parallelism in both ways.

17a
Using parallelism for coordinate elements

Parallel structure is necessary wherever coordination exists: wherever elements are connected by coordinating conjunctions or by correlative conjunctions, wherever elements are compared or contrasted, and wherever items are arranged in a list or outline. The elements should match each other in structure, though they need not match word for word, as the previous sentence of this text illustrates. In the following sentence the coordinate prepositional phrases are parallel even though the prepositions differ and the second phrase contains additional words.

> We passed *through the town* and *into the vast, unpopulated desert.*

1
Using parallelism for elements linked by coordinating conjunctions

The coordinating conjunctions *and, but, or, nor,* and *yet* always signal a need for parallelism, as the following sentences show.

> *In the kitchen* and *on the patio,* Miracle Grill will cook your food *safer, faster,* and *cheaper.*

> Political candidates *often explain what they intend to do* but *rarely explain how they are going to do it.*

> In Melanie's home, children had to account for *where they had been* and *what they had been doing.*

When elements linked by coordinating conjunctions are not parallel in structure, their coordination is weakened and the reader is distracted.

> FAULTY The disadvantages of nuclear reactors are *their great danger* and *that they are very expensive.*

> REVISED The disadvantages of nuclear reactors are *their great danger* and *their great expense.*

Do not hesitate to repeat words like *to, in, the,* and *that* when the repetition can save your readers from confusion. Such words often signal parallelism, stress relationships, and help keep meanings clear.

> CONFUSING Thoreau stood up for his principles *by not paying* his taxes and *spending* a night in jail. [Did he spend a night in jail or not?]

> REVISED Thoreau stood up for his principles *by not paying* his taxes and *by spending* a night in jail.

When the elements linked by coordinating conjunctions require different prepositions, the different words must be included. (See also 15c.)

> FAULTY The boy demonstrated an interest and a talent for writing.

//
17a

REVISED   The boy demonstrated an interest *in* and a talent for writing.

Be sure that clauses beginning with *and who* or *and which* are coordinated only with preceding *who* and *which* clauses.

FAULTY   Marie is a young woman *of great ability* and *who wants* to be a lawyer.

REVISED   Marie is a young woman *who has* great ability and *who wants* to be a lawyer.

Note that such constructions are often improved by omitting the conjunction.

Marie is a young woman *of great ability who wants* to be a lawyer.

2
Using parallelism for elements linked by correlative conjunctions

Correlative conjunctions are pairs of connectors such as *both . . . and, either . . . or, not only . . . but also*. These pairs stress the equality and balance between the two elements they connect, and those elements should be parallel to confirm their relation.

Ernest is addicted not only *to drinking* but also *to gambling*.

Off-road bikes are not only *interrupting the peacefulness of the desert* but also *destroying its vegetation*.

The common error in parallelism with correlative conjunctions is the omission of words like prepositions or the infinitive marker *to* after the second connector.

NONPARALLEL   He told the boy either *to brush* the horse or *feed* the chickens.

REVISED   He told the boy either *to brush* the horse or *to feed* the chickens.

3
Using parallelism for elements being compared or contrasted

Elements being compared or contrasted should ordinarily be cast in the same grammatical form.

It is better *to live rich* than *to die rich*.   — SAMUEL JOHNSON

WEAK   Jody wanted *a job* rather than *to apply for welfare*.

REVISED   Jody wanted *a job* rather than *welfare payments*.

REVISED   Jody wanted *to find a job* rather than *to apply for welfare.*

4
Using parallelism for items in lists or outlines

The elements of a list or outline that divides a larger subject are coordinate and should be parallel in structure. (See also 1f-1 on outlining.)

FAULTY	IMPROVED
The Renaissance in England was marked by	The Renaissance in England was marked by
1. an extension of trade routes	1. the extension of trade routes
2. merchant class became more powerful	2. the increasing power of the merchant class
3. the death of feudalism	3. the death of feudalism
4. upsurging of the arts	4. the upsurge of the arts
5. the sciences were encouraged	5. the encouragement of the sciences
6. religious quarrels began	6. the rise of religious quarrels

//
17a

EXERCISE 1

Identify the parallel elements in the following sentences. How does parallelism contribute to the effectiveness of each sentence?
1. Tonight a Santa Ana will begin to blow, a hot wind from the northeast whining down through the Cajon and San Gorgonio Passes, blowing up sandstorms out along Route 66, drying the hills and the nerves to the flash point.   — JOAN DIDION
2. The faster the plane, the narrower the seats.
                                                    — JOHN H. DURRELL
3. [The afternoon] was gray, deadened, and wintry, with a slow, moist, heavy coldness sinking in and deadening all the faculties.   — D. H. LAWRENCE
4. The mornings are the pleasantest times in the apartment, exhaustion having set in, the sated mosquitoes at rest on ceiling and walls, sleeping it off, the room a swirl of tortured bedclothes and abandoned garments, the vines in their full leafiness filtering the hard light of day, the air conditioner silent at last, like the mosquitoes.   — E. B. WHITE
5. Aging paints every action gray, lies heavy on every movement, imprisons every thought.   — SHARON CURTIN

EXERCISE 2

Revise the sentences below to make coordinate, compared, or listed elements parallel in structure. Add words or rephrase as necessary to increase the effectiveness and coherence of each sentence.

Example:

After waiting for hours, pacing the floor, and having bitten her nails to the quick, Sherry was frantic with worry.

After waiting for hours, pacing the floor, and *biting* her nails to the quick, Sherry was frantic with worry.

1. For exercise I prefer swimming and to jog.
2. After a week on a construction job, Leon felt not so much exhausted as that he was invigorated by the physical labor.
3. To lose weight, cut down on what you eat, eat fewer calories in the food you do consume, and you should exercise regularly.
4. All persons are entitled both to equal educational opportunities and employment opportunities.
5. Everyone was surprised at the election results: overwhelming approval of the bond issue; the redistricting plan was defeated; and the city's council will have all new faces.
6. My father insisted that I learn how to budget and creating and managing a bank account.
7. Her generosity, sympathetic nature, and the fact that she is able to motivate employees make her an excellent supervisor.
8. Pam hoped for either a loan or to work at a part-time job.
9. Baby-sitting children, I have learned how to keep them amused, patience, and the art of being both stern and fair.
10. The shock of having one's apartment burglarized comes less from the missing possessions than to think that a stranger has invaded one's privacy.

//

17b

17b
Using parallelism to increase coherence

Parallelism not only ensures similarity of form for coordinated structures but also enhances coherence by clearly relating paired or opposed units. Failing to use parallel form is closely related to mixing constructions within a sentence (see Chapter 15). Consider this sentence:

NONPARALLEL   During the early weeks of the semester, the course reviews fundamentals, whereas little emphasis is placed on new material or more advanced concepts.

Here "the course" is doing two things — or doing one thing and not doing the other — and these are opposites. But the construction of the sentence does not help the reader see the connection quickly. Rather, the connection is obscured by the use of the active voice in the first clause (*the course reviews*) and the passive voice in the second (*little emphasis is placed*). Revised to make these two ideas parallel, the sentence reads as follows:

> **REVISED** During the early weeks of the semester, the course *reviews fundamentals* but *places little emphasis* on new material or more advanced concepts.

Effective parallelism will enable you to combine in a single, well-ordered sentence related ideas that you might have expressed in two or three separate sentences. Compare the following three sentences with the original single sentence written by H. L. Mencken.

> Slang originates in the effort of ingenious individuals to make language more pungent and picturesque. They increase the store of terse and striking words or widen the boundaries of metaphor. Thus a vocabulary for new shades and differences in meaning is provided by slang.

> Slang originates in the effort of ingenious individuals to make the language more pungent and picturesque — to increase the store of terse and striking words, to widen the boundaries of metaphor, and to provide a vocabulary for new shades and differences in meaning. — H. L. MENCKEN

// 17b

Parallel structure works as well to emphasize the connections among related sentences in a paragraph (see 3b-2). Consider the parallelism not only within but also among sentences in this partial paragraph:

> Style is an extraordinary thing. It is one of the subtlest secrets of all art. . . . *In painting, it is* composition, colour-sense, and brushwork. *In sculpture, it is* the treatment of depths and surfaces and the choice of stones and metals. *In music, it is* surely the melodic line, the tone-colour, and the shape of the phrase. . . . *In prose and poetry, it is* the choice of words, their placing, and the rhythms and melodies of sentence and paragraph. — GILBERT HIGHET

Here, Highet clarifies and emphasizes his assertion that style is common to all forms of art by casting four successive sentences in the same structure (*In . . . , it is . . .*).

EXERCISE 3

Combine each group of sentences below into one concise sentence in which parallel elements appear in parallel structures. You will have to add, delete, change, and rearrange words. Each item has more than one possible answer.

Example:

Christin sorted the books neatly into piles. She was efficient about it, too.

Christin sorted the books neatly *and efficiently* into piles.

1. The class is held on Wednesday afternoons. Sometimes it meets on Saturday mornings.
2. Dick finally held on to a job after lasting three weeks at his previous job. He had worked at an earlier job for two weeks. And the one before that had lasted three days.
3. After making several costly mistakes, he stopped to consider the jobs available to him. He thought about his goals for a job.
4. To make a good stew, marinate the meat. There should be plenty of vegetables added. Wine should be included for flavor. Simmer the whole thing for at least two hours.
5. Carlone had three desires. First, he wanted to have money. Second, he wanted to be famous. The third desire was for happiness.
6. Driving a car with a manual transmission requires mastering the gears. It requires coordination of the clutch and gas pedals. And it requires that one attend to the sounds of the engine.
7. The sun looks small at its zenith. But it looks large when it reaches the horizon.
8. Ben walked with a limp. Moreover, his back was bent.
9. Most people who saw the movie were unimpressed with the acting. Or they frankly criticized the acting.
10. We returned from camping very tired. We were dirty. Mosquito bites covered us.

//

17

18

Emphasizing Main Ideas

Well-managed sentences clearly relate ideas and details to each other through coordination, subordination, and parallelism. They also emphasize important information by making it readily apparent within a sentence. You can control emphasis within your sentences in three ways: by placing the most important ideas in strong positions; by using repetition carefully; and, when a statement is important enough, by separating it from surrounding information.

18a
Arranging ideas effectively

Arranging ideas within sentences for emphasis involves two principles. First, the most emphatic positions within a sentence are the beginning and the ending, the ending being the more emphatic of the two. Second, parallel series of words, phrases, or clauses will be most emphatic if the elements appear in order of their increasing importance.

1
Using sentence beginnings and endings

The basic sentence in English consists of the subject and the predicate, with the predicate containing the verb and any objects or complements (see 5a). Readers automatically look to the basic sentence for the writer's principal meaning, even when words, phrases, and whole clauses modify parts or all of the basic sentence. By controlling the position of the basic sentence (the main clause) in relation to its modifiers, you can lead readers to focus on important and new information in the way that best suits your purpose.

In speech we naturally stress the beginning and the ending of a sentence, and so in reading we expect them to contain important information. Thus the most effective way to call attention to information is to place it first or last in the sentence, reserving the middle for incidentals. Look at the difference in these examples.

UNEMPHATIC | Education remains the most important single means of economic advancement, in spite of all its shortcomings.

REVISED | In spite of all its shortcomings, education remains the most important single means of economic advancement.

REVISED | Education remains, in spite of all its shortcomings, the most important single means of economic advancement.

In the first sentence our final attention rests on education's shortcomings rather than on its importance, even though the latter is clearly what the writer wished to emphasize. The first revision, by placing the qualifying phrase at the beginning of the sentence, leaves some stress on the qualification but emphasizes education's importance more. The second revision de-emphasizes the qualification even further by inserting it in the middle of the sentence, leaving both education and its importance at the emphatic points of the sentence.

emph

18a

Sentences most often begin with the subject and predicate plus their modifiers and then add modifiers at the end. Such sentences are called **cumulative** (because they accumulate information as they proceed) or **loose** (because they are not tightly structured).

CUMULATIVE | The divers searched for treasure on the smooth bottom of the bay, along the coral reef, and on the deep, rocky seabed.

CUMULATIVE | The old man bitterly hated all social planning, having been unaware of social problems during most of his life and now choosing to ignore them.

As these examples illustrate, the cumulative sentence completes its main statement first and then explains, amplifies, or illustrates it. The primary emphasis lies on the opening main clause, but the sentence continues to provide new information.

The opposite kind of sentence, called **periodic,** saves the main clause until just before the end (the period) of the sentence. Everything before the main clause points toward it by telling the reader how to interpret it.

PERIODIC | In three years, two months, and seven days, according to his view, the world will end.

<table>
<tr><td>PERIODIC</td><td>Though his lawyer defended him eloquently and he himself begged for leniency in a moving plea, the jury found him guilty.</td></tr>
</table>

A variation of the periodic sentence names the subject at the beginning, follows it with a modifier, and then fills in the predicate.

Uncle John, whom everyone calls a cheat and a liar, is actually a warm and generous man.

Whether the subject comes first or is delayed along with the predicate, the periodic sentence creates suspense for the reader by delaying the important information of the main clause until the end of the sentence.

Here, for comparison, are cumulative and periodic revisions of an unemphatic sentence.

<table>
<tr><td>UNEMPHATIC</td><td>Under half steam and spewing black smoke, the ship finally reached port with its hull battered and a hole punched in its bow.</td></tr>
<tr><td>CUMULATIVE</td><td>The ship finally reached port under half steam and spewing black smoke, with its hull battered and a hole punched in its bow.</td></tr>
<tr><td>PERIODIC</td><td>Under half steam and spewing black smoke, with its hull battered and a hole punched in its bow, the ship finally reached port.</td></tr>
</table>

emph
18a

The cumulative sentence parallels the way we naturally think (by accumulating information), and it does not tax the memory of readers. The periodic sentence is more contrived, and it requires careful planning so that the reader can remember all the information leading up to the main clause. You should save the periodic sentence for when your purpose demands climactic emphasis.

2
Arranging parallel elements effectively

Series

Parallelism requires that you express coordinate ideas in similar grammatical structures (see Chapter 17). In addition, you should arrange the coordinate ideas so that they correspond to readers' expectations of order, just as you arrange the parts of an essay or the sentences in a paragraph (see 1f-1 and 3b-1). A series of grammatically parallel elements can be weak if you arrange the elements randomly.

UNEMPHATIC   The storm ripped the roofs off several buildings, killed ten people, and knocked down many trees in town.

In this sentence the three kinds of damage are named without regard for their relative importance: Trees knocked down, the least serious damage, concludes the series, and people killed, the most serious damage, is buried in the middle of the series. The revised sentence below arranges the items in the order of their increasing importance so that the most important item comes at the end, the most emphatic point.

EMPHATIC   The storm knocked down many trees in town, ripped the roofs off several buildings, and killed ten people.

Here is another example.

UNEMPHATIC   After years of teaching, Anna decided to quit when she realized that she actually disliked children, that her fellow teachers bored her, and that she didn't have enough time for her hobbies.

EMPHATIC   After years of teaching, Anna decided to quit when she realized that she didn't have enough time for her hobbies, that her fellow teachers bored her, and that she actually disliked children

emph
18a

You may want to use an unexpected item at the end of a series for humor or for another special effect.

Early to bed and early to rise makes a man healthy, wealthy, and dead.   — JAMES THURBER

But be careful not to use such a series unintentionally. The following series seems thoughtlessly random rather than intentionally humorous.

UNEMPHATIC   The painting has subdued tone, great feeling, and a length of about three feet.

EMPHATIC   The painting, about three feet long, has subdued tone and great feeling.

Balanced sentences

When the clauses of a compound or complex sentence are parallel, the sentence is **balanced.**

The fickleness of the women I love is equalled only by the infernal constancy of the women who love me.   — GEORGE BERNARD SHAW

In a pure balanced sentence two independent clauses are exactly parallel: They match item for item.

> The love of liberty is the love of others; the love of power is the love of ourselves. — WILLIAM HAZLITT

But the term is commonly applied to sentences that are only approximately parallel or that have only some parallel parts.

> If thought corrupts language, language can also corrupt thought. — GEORGE ORWELL

> The secret of learning to act lies not in the study of methods but in the close observation of those who have already learned.

Balanced sentences are heavily emphatic but require thoughtful planning. When used carefully, they can be an especially effective way to emphasize the contrast between two ideas.

emph
18a

EXERCISE 1

Underline the main clause in each sentence below, and identify the sentence as cumulative or periodic. Then rewrite each cumulative sentence as a periodic one and each periodic sentence as a cumulative one.

1. One of the most disastrous cultural influences ever to hit America was Walt Disney's Mickey Mouse, that idiot optimist who each week marched forth in Technicolor against a battalion of cats, invariably humiliating them with one clever trick after another. — JAMES A. MICHENER
2. At length, in the beginning of May, with the help of some of my acquaintances, rather to improve so good an occasion for neighborliness than from any necessity, I set up the frame of my house. — HENRY DAVID THOREAU
3. Because they wanted a fair price for their crops and felt the government was not doing enough for them, the farmers marched on Washington.
4. Matthew's children worked two years to get him out of jail — writing letters, seeing lawyers, attending meetings — because they knew him to be honest and believed him to be innocent.
5. Its neck stretched forward, its wings beating against the water, the swan took flight.

EXERCISE 2

Combine each group of sentences below into a single cumulative sentence and then into a single periodic sentence. You will have to add, delete, change, and rearrange words, and each item has more than two possible answers. Does the cumulative or the periodic sentence seem more effective to you?

Example:

The woman refused any treatment. She felt that her life was completed. She wished to die.

Cumulative: The woman refused any treatment, feeling that her life was completed and wishing to die.

Periodic: Feeling that her life was completed and wishing to die, the woman refused any treatment.

1. The combined technology of computers and television will dramatically change our lives. The change will occur in the few years remaining before the end of the century.
2. The abandoned car was a neighborhood eyesore. Its windows were smashed. Its body was rusted and dented.
3. Two trains raced across the river. Their wheels were spinning. Their engines were parallel. Their engines were billowing smoke.
4. Carl walked with his back straight. He held his head high. He stared straight ahead. He hid his shame.
5. The leaf fell slowly. It was wafted by the wind. It was performing graceful somersaults.

emph
18b

EXERCISE 3

Revise the sentences below so that elements in a series or balanced elements are arranged to give maximum emphasis to main ideas.

Example:

The campers were stranded without matches, without food or water, and without a tent.

The campers were stranded without matches, without a tent, and without food or water.

1. The explosion at the chemical factory blew up half a city block, killed six workers, and started a fire in a building.
2. In the 1950s Americans wanted to keep up with the Joneses; keeping up with change is what America wants in the 1980s.
3. People view heaven in several ways: as the presence of God, as a myth, as just another world, or as the promise of future happiness.
4. When Claire thought of her husband, she shivered; but she smiled at the thought of her old friend Carl.
5. The football players marched triumphantly into the locker room, victorious, battered, and bruised.

18b
Repeating ideas

Although careless repetition results in weak and wordy sentences, judicious repetition of key words and phrases can be an effective means of emphasis. Such repetition often combines with parallelism. It may occur in a series of sentences within a paragraph (see 3b-3). Or it may occur in a series of words, phrases, or clauses within a sentence, as in the examples below.

> We have the tools, all the tools — we are suffocating in tools — but we cannot find the actual wood to work or even the actual hand to work it.   — ARCHIBALD MACLEISH

> Government comes from below, not above; government comes from men, not from kings or lords or military masters; government looks to the source of all power in the consent of men.
>   — HENRY STEELE COMMAGER

18c
Separating ideas

emph
18c

When you save important information for the end of a sentence, you can emphasize it even more by setting it off from the rest of the sentence. The second example below illustrates how putting an important idea in a separate sentence can highlight it.

> Boys are wild animals, rich in the treasures of sense, but the New England boy had a wider range of emotions than boys of more equable climates because he felt his nature crudely, as it was meant.

> Boys are wild animals, rich in the treasures of sense, but the New England boy had a wider range of emotions than boys of more equable climates. He felt his nature crudely, as it was meant.
>   — HENRY ADAMS

You can vary the degree of emphasis by varying the extent to which you separate one idea from the others. Separating two ideas with a semicolon provides more emphasis than separating them with a comma and a coordinating conjunction. And separating them with a period provides still greater emphasis. Compare the following sentences.

> Most of the reading which is praised for itself is neither literary nor intellectual but narcotic.

> Most of the reading which is praised for itself is neither literary nor intellectual; it is narcotic.

> Most of the reading which is praised for itself is neither literary nor intellectual. It is narcotic.   — DONALD HALL

Sometimes a dash or a pair of dashes will isolate and thus emphasize a part of a statement (see also 25b).

> His schemes were always elaborate, ingenious, and exciting — and wholly impractical.

Athletics — that is, winning athletics — have become a profitable university operation.

EXERCISE 4

Emphasize the main idea in each sentence or group of sentences below by following the instructions in parentheses: Either combine sentences so that parallelism and repetition stress the main idea, or place the main idea in a separate sentence. Each item has more than one possible answer.

> *Example:*
> I try to listen to other people's opinions. When my mind is closed, I find that other opinions open it. And they can change my mind when it is wrong. (*Parallelism and repetition.*)
>
> I try to listen to other people's opinions, for they can open my mind when it is closed and they can change my mind when it is wrong.

1. Without rain our seeds will not germinate. We will have no crops if it doesn't rain. (*Parallelism and repetition.*)
2. Roger worked harder than usual to win the chemistry prize that his father had won before him, for he could not let his father down. (*Separation.*)
3. My parents fear change. They fear change in morals. They are afraid their neighborhood will change. They are afraid of change in their own children. (*Parallelism and repetition.*)
4. By the time the rescuers reached the crash site, the wind had nearly covered the small plane with snow and no one had survived. (*Separation.*)
5. The key to staying happy is staying free. Keep free of debt. Don't become weighed down by possessions. Avoid entangling relationships. (*Parallelism and repetition.*)

emph

18d

18d
Preferring the active voice

In the active voice the subject acts (*I peeled the onions*). In the passive voice the subject is acted upon and the actor is either relegated to a phrase (*The onions were peeled by me*) or omitted entirely (*The onions were peeled*). The passive voice is thus indirect, obscuring the actor or burying him or her entirely. The active voice is more natural, direct, vigorous, and emphatic. Further, all sentences turn on their verbs, which give sentences their motion, pushing them along. And active verbs push harder than passive ones.

PASSIVE	For energy conservation it is urged that all lights be turned off when not being used. [Who is urging? Who is to turn the lights off?]

ACTIVE	To save energy, students should turn off all lights they are not using.
PASSIVE	The new outpatient clinic was opened by the hospital administration so that the costs of nonemergency medical care would be reduced.
ACTIVE	The hospital administration opened the new outpatient clinic to reduce the costs of nonemergency medical care.

Sometimes the subject of an active statement is unknown or unimportant, and then the passive voice can be useful.

The flight was canceled.
Wellington was called the "Iron Duke."
Thousands of people are killed annually in highway accidents.

Except in these situations, however, rely on the active voice. It is economical and creates movement.

**emph
18e**

18e
Being concise

Conciseness — brevity of expression — aids emphasis no matter what the sentence structure. Unnecessary words detract from necessary words. They clutter sentences and obscure ideas.

One common structure that may contribute to wordiness is the expletive construction, which inverts the normal subject-verb order by beginning a sentence with *there* or *it* and a form of the verb *be* (see 5e-4).

WEAK	*There are* likely to be thousands of people attending the rally against nuclear power plants.
EMPHATIC	*Thousands of people are* likely to attend the rally against nuclear power plants.

Some frequently used qualifying phrases such as *in my opinion, more or less,* and *for the most part* are also unnecessarily wordy. They can always be reworded more concisely and can often be omitted entirely.

WEAK	*In my opinion,* the competition for grades distracts many students from their goal of obtaining a good education.
EMPHATIC	*I think* the competition for grades distracts many students from their main goal of obtaining a good education.

MORE EMPHATIC   The competition for grades distracts many students from their goal of obtaining a good education.

(See 31c for further discussion of strengthening sentences through conciseness.)

EXERCISE 5

Revise the sentences below to make them more emphatic by converting passive voice to active voice, by eliminating expletive constructions, or by condensing or eliminating wordy phrases. (For additional exercises with the passive voice and with expletives, see pp. 157, 184, and 403.)

> *Example:*
> Under certain atmospheric conditions, the moon can be seen as purple, in a manner of speaking.
> Under certain atmospheric conditions, the moon *appears almost* purple.

1. The residents were told by the government to evacuate their homes when the government discovered dangerous amounts of contaminants in their water.
2. There must be a way that we can get out of this predicament, whether legally or illegally.
3. The problem in this particular situation is that we owe more taxes than we can afford to pay.
4. The paintings were looked over by the art dealers before the auction began.
5. After all these years there is still not a good road running between Springfield and Lyndon.

EXERCISE 6

Drawing on the advice in this chapter, rewrite the following paragraph to emphasize main ideas and to de-emphasize less important information.

The most famous fairy tale, "Cinderella," is also the most popular. The tale is about a girl who is badly treated by her stepmother and stepsisters, as we all know. They make her do all the chores. Finally, her fairy godmother rescues her, and she is married to a handsome prince. The story was first told by the Chinese in the ninth century. Its Chinese origins are shown by the episode of the glass slipper that the prince can fit only on Cinderella's tiny, delicate foot. Small feet were a mark of special beauty for Chinese women at that particular time. We are still fascinated by Cinderella's story, although we do not remain so fascinated by small feet. In Europe and the United States alone, the tale exists in over 500 versions down to this day.

emph

18e

19
Achieving Variety

In a paragraph or an essay, sentences do not stand one by one. Rather, each stands in relation to those before and after it. To make sentences work together effectively, the writer must vary their length, their emphasis, and their word order to reflect the importance and complexity of ideas. Although experienced writers generally find that variety takes care of itself as they commit ideas to paper, inexperienced writers often have difficulty achieving it without guidance and practice.

A series of similar sentences will prove monotonous and ineffective, as this passage illustrates:

> Ulysses S. Grant and Robert E. Lee met on April 9, 1865. Their meeting place was the parlor of a modest house at Appomattox Court House, Virginia. They met to work out the terms for the surrender of Lee's Army of Northern Virginia. One great chapter of American life ended with their meeting, and another began. Grant and Lee were bringing the Civil War to its virtual finish. Other armies still had to surrender, and the fugitive Confederate government would struggle desperately and vainly. It would try to find some way to go on living with its chief support gone. Grant and Lee had signed the papers, however, and it was all over in effect.

Individually, these eight sentences are perfectly clear and adequately detailed. But together they do not make pleasant reading, and their relative importance is obscure. Their lengths are roughly the same, ranging from twelve to sixteen words, and they are about equally detailed. Each sentence consists of one or two main clauses beginning with the subject. At the end of the passage we have a sense of names, dates, and events but no sure sense of how they relate.

Now compare the sentences above with the actual passage written by Bruce Catton.

> When Ulysses S. Grant and Robert E. Lee met in the parlor of a modest house at Appomattox Court House, Virginia, on April 9, 1865, to work out the terms for the surrender of Lee's Army of Northern Virginia, a great chapter in American life came to a close, and a great new chapter began.
>
> These men were bringing the Civil War to its virtual finish. To be sure, other armies had yet to surrender, and for a few days the fugitive Confederate government would struggle desperately and vainly, trying to find some way to go on living now that its chief support was gone. But in effect it was all over when Grant and Lee signed the papers.   — BRUCE CATTON, "Grant and Lee"

The information in these two passages is almost identical. The differences lie chiefly in the sentence variety of the second and the sharp focus on the end of war which that variety underscores. Catton's four sentences range from eleven to fifty-five words, and only one of the sentences begins with its subject. The first sentence brings together in one long *when* clause all the details of place, time, and cause contained in the first three sentences of the first passage. The sentence is periodic (see 18a-1), and the suspense it creates forces us to focus on the significance of the meeting described in the two main clauses at the end. The very brief second sentence, contrasting sharply with the one before it, quickly recapitulates the reason for the meeting. The third sentence, a long, cumulative one (see 18a-1), reflects the lingering obstacles to peace. And the fourth sentence, another short one, tersely indicates the futility of future struggle. Together, the four sentences clearly, even dramatically, convey that the meeting ended the war and marked a turning point in American history. The rest of this chapter suggests some ways you can vary your sentences to achieve such effectiveness.

var
19a

| 19a
Varying sentence length and emphasis

The sentences of a stylistically effective essay will differ most obviously in their length. Further, some sentences consist only of one main clause with modifiers, some consist of two main clauses, some are cumulative, and a few perhaps are periodic. (See 18a-1.) This variation in length and emphasis marks mature writing, making it both readable and clear.

Neither short sentences nor long sentences are intrinsically better. But in most contemporary writing, sentences tend to vary from between 10 and 15 words on the short side to between 35 and

40 words on the long, with an average of between 15 and 25 words depending on the writer's purpose and style. Your sentences generally should not be all at one extreme or the other, for your readers may have difficulty focusing on main ideas and seeing the relations among them. If most of your sentences contain 35 words or more, you probably need to break some up into shorter, simpler sentences. If most of your sentences contain fewer than 10 or 15 words, you probably need to add details to them or combine them through coordination and subordination. Examine your writing particularly for a common problem: strings of main clauses, subjects first, in either simple or compound sentences.

1
Avoiding strings of brief and simple sentences

var
19a

A series of brief and simple sentences is both monotonous and hard to understand because it forces the reader to sort out relations among ideas. If you find that you depend on brief, simple sentences, work to increase variety by combining some of them into longer units that emphasize and link new and important ideas while de-emphasizing old or incidental information. (See 16a, 16b, and 18a.)

Look at how a string of simple sentences can be revised into an effective piece of writing.

WEAK   The moon is now moving away from the earth. It moves away at the rate of about one inch a year. Our days on earth are getting longer. They grow a thousandth of a second longer every century. A month might become forty-seven of our present days long. We might eventually lose the moon altogether. Such great planetary movement rightly concerns astronomers. It need not worry us. The movement will take 50 million years.

REVISED   The moon is now moving away from the earth at the rate of about one inch a year. And at the rate of a thousandth of a second or so every century, our days on earth are getting longer. Someday, a month will be forty-seven of our present days long, if we don't eventually lose the moon altogether. Such great planetary movement rightly concerns astronomers, but it need not concern us. It will take 50 million years.

In the first passage the choppy movement of the nine successive simple sentences leaves the reader with nine independent facts and a lame conclusion. The revision retains all the facts of the original but compresses them into five sentences that are structured to emphasize main ideas and to show relations among them. The three most important facts of the passage — the moon's movement (sentence 1), our lengthening days (sentence 2), and the enormous span of time involved (sentence 5) — appear, respectively, in the opening main clause of a cumulative sentence, in the ending main clause of a periodic sentence, and in a terse simple sentence. The third sentence places in a subordinate clause the dramatic possibility that we may lose the moon, but the clause receives its own stress by falling at the end of the sentence. And the coordination of the fourth sentence accentuates with *but* the contrast between the astronomers' concerns and ours, thus preparing the way for the highly emphatic brief sentence at the end.

2
Avoiding excessive compounding

Because compound sentences are merely linked simple sentences, a series of them will be as weak as a series of brief simple sentences, especially if the clauses of the compound sentences are all of about the same length. Notice the seesaw effect of the passage below, and consider how it is strengthened by changing some main clauses into modifiers and by varying their positions.

var

19a

WEAK
: The hotel beach faces the south, and the main street runs along the north side of the hotel. The main street is heavily traveled and often noisy, but the beach is always quiet and sunny. It was Sunday afternoon, and we were on the hotel beach. We lay stretched out on the sand, and the sun poured down on us.

REVISED
: The main street, heavily traveled and often noisy, runs along the north side of the hotel. But on the south side the hotel beach is always quiet and sunny. On Sunday we lay there stretched out on the sand, letting the sun pour down on us.

(See 16a-2 for additional discussion of how to avoid excessive coordination within sentences.)

EXERCISE 1

Rewrite the following paragraphs to increase variety so that important ideas receive greater emphasis than supporting information. You will have to change some main clauses into modifiers and then combine and reposition the modifiers and the remaining main clauses.

1. Any supermarket shopper has seen the Red Devil. It appears on small cans of meat spreads like deviled ham. It is a trademark

of Underwood. It is the oldest registered trademark in the United States. A trademark identifies a product. It links the product clearly to a particular maker. An original trademark can become legally established with continued use. Registration of a trademark provides further protection. Trademarks are registered with the U.S. Patent Office. Infringements of trademarks are punishable by law.

2.   Nathaniel Hawthorne was one of America's first great writers, and he was descended from a judge. The judge had presided at some of the Salem witch trials, and he had condemned some men and women to death. Hawthorne could never forget this piece of family history, and he always felt guilty about it. He never wrote about his ancestor directly, but he did write about the darkness of the human heart. He wrote *The Scarlet Letter* and *The House of the Seven Gables*, and in those books he demonstrated his favorite theme of a secret sin.

var
19b

19b
Varying sentence beginnings

The basic English sentence begins with the subject, followed by the verb and its complement or object, if any. Within the basic sentence, adjectives generally precede or follow their nouns or pronouns, while adverbs generally precede or follow the verb or its complement or object. For example:

> The defendant's lawyer relentlessly cross-examined the stubborn witness for two successive days.

The majority of sentences follow this standard pattern. But, as shown by the altered passage on Grant and Lee at the start of this chapter (p. 286), an unbroken sequence of sentences beginning with the subject quickly becomes monotonous. Your final arrangement of sentence elements should always depend on two concerns: the relation of a sentence to those preceding and following it; and the emphasis required by your meaning. When you do choose to vary the subject-first pattern, you have several options.

Adverb modifiers, unlike adjective modifiers, can often be placed at a variety of spots in a sentence. Consider the different emphases created by moving the adverbs in the basic sentence above.

> *For two successive days*, the defendant's lawyer *relentlessly* cross-examined the stubborn witness.

> *Relentlessly*, the defendant's lawyer cross-examined the stubborn witness *for two successive days*.

> *Relentlessly, for two successive days*, the defendant's lawyer cross-examined the stubborn witness.

Notice that the last sentence, with both modifiers at the beginning, is periodic and thus highly emphatic (see 18a-1).

Beginning a sentence with a participial phrase also postpones the subject and sometimes creates a periodic sentence.

> The lawyer thoroughly cross-examined the witness and then called the defendant herself to testify.
>
> *Having thoroughly cross-examined the witness,* the lawyer called the defendant herself to testify.

When the relation between two successive sentences demands, you may begin the second with a coordinating conjunction or with a transitional expression such as *first, for instance, however, in addition, moreover,* or *therefore*. (See 3b-6 for a longer list of transitional expressions.)

> The witness expected to be dismissed after his first long day of cross-examination. He was not; the defendant's lawyer called him again the second day.
>
> The witness expected to be dismissed after his first long day of cross-examination. *But* he was not; the defendant's lawyer called him again the second day.

> The prices of clothes have risen astronomically in recent years. The cotton shirt that once cost $6.00 and now costs $20.00 is an example.
>
> The prices of clothes have risen astronomically in recent years. *For example,* a cotton shirt that once cost $6.00 now costs $20.00.

var
19b

Occasionally, an expletive construction — *it* or *there* plus a form of *be* — may be useful to delay and thus emphasize the subject of the sentence.

> His judgment seems questionable, not his desire.
> *It is* his judgment that seems questionable, not his desire.

However, expletive constructions are more likely to harm writing by adding extra words than they are to help it by adding variety. You should use them rarely, only when you can justify doing so. (See also 18e.)

EXERCISE 2

Revise each pair of sentences below, following the instructions in parentheses to make a single sentence that begins with an adverb modifier or a participial phrase, or to make one of the two sentences begin with an appropriate coordinating conjunction or transitional expression.

Example:

The *Seabird* left to take its place in the race. It moved quickly in the wind. (*One sentence with participial phrase beginning moving.*)

Moving quickly in the wind, the *Seabird* left to take its place in the race.

1. Voting rights for women seemed a possibility in the 1860s. Women were not actually given the vote for nearly sixty years. (*Two sentences with coordinating conjunction.*)
2. Robert had orders to stay in bed. He returned to work immediately. (*One sentence with adverb modifier beginning although.*)
3. Gasoline prices are determined by international conditions we cannot control. They may never stabilize. (*Two sentences with transitional expression.*)
4. The rescuers were careful as they handled the ropes. They lowered the frightened climber from the ledge. (*One sentence with participial phrase beginning carefully.*)
5. The building may be torn down. We will all be without homes. (*One sentence with adverb modifier beginning if.*)

EXERCISE 3

Revise the passage below to vary sentence beginnings by using each of the following at least once: an adverb modifier, a participial phrase, a coordinating conjunction, and a transitional expression.

Fred found himself cut off from the rest of the campers. He sat down to try to get his bearings. He watched the movement of the sun carefully. He thought he would find his way before nightfall. He was still lost when the stars came out. He admitted he was lost. He covered himself in leaves for warmth.

19c
Inverting the normal word order

Inverted sentences such as *Up came the dawn* and *Mutton he didn't like* are infrequent in modern prose. Because the word order of subject, verb, and object or complement is so strongly fixed in English, an inverted sentence can be emphatic.

Harry had once been a dog lover. Then his neighbors' barking dogs twice raced through his garden. Now Harry detests all dogs, especially barking dogs.

Harry had once been a dog lover. Then his neighbors' barking dogs twice raced through his garden. Now *all dogs,* especially barking dogs, *Harry detests.*

Inverting the normal order of subject, verb, and complement can be useful in two successive sentences when the second expands on the first.

> Critics have not been kind to Presidents who have tried to apply the ways of private business to public affairs. Particularly *explicit was the curt verdict* of one critic of President Hoover: Mr. Hoover was never President of the United States; he was four years chairman of the board.   — Adapted from EMMET JOHN HUGHES, "The Presidency vs. Jimmy Carter"

Inverted sentences used without need are artificial. Avoid descriptive sentences such as *Up came Larry and down went Cindy's spirits.*

| 19d
| Mixing types of sentences

Except in dialogue, most written sentences are statements. Occasionally, however, questions, commands, or, more rarely, exclamations may enhance variety. Questions may point the direction of a paragraph, as in *What does a detective do?* or *How is the percentage of unemployed workers calculated?* More often, though, the questions used in exposition or argumentation do not require answers but simply emphasize ideas that readers can be expected to agree with. These **rhetorical questions** are illustrated in the following passage.

> Another word that has ceased to have meaning due to overuse is *attractive. Attractive* has become verbal chaff. Who, by some stretch of language and imagination, cannot be described as attractive? And just what is it that attractive individuals are attracting?   — DIANE WHITE

Imperative sentences occur frequently in a description of a process, particularly in directions. In such writing they are often the principal type of sentence rather than a means to variety, as this passage on freewriting illustrates.

> The idea is simply to write for ten minutes (later on, perhaps fifteen or twenty). Don't stop for anything. Go quickly without rushing. Never stop to look back, to cross something out, to wonder how to spell something, to wonder what word or thought to use, or to think about what you are doing.   — PETER ELBOW

Notice that the authors of these examples use questions and commands not merely to vary their sentences but to achieve some special purpose. Variety occurs because a particular sentence type is effective for the context, not because the writer set out to achieve variety for its own sake.

EXERCISE 4

Imagine that you are writing an essay either on the parking problem at your school or on the problems of living in a dormitory. Practice varying sentences by composing a sentence or passage to serve each purpose listed below.

1. Write a question that could open the essay.
2. Write a command that could open the essay.
3. Write an exclamation that could open the essay.
4. For the body of the essay, write an appropriately varied paragraph of at least five sentences, including at least one short and one long sentence beginning with the subject; at least one sentence beginning with an adverb modifier; at least one sentence beginning with a coordinating conjunction or transitional expression; and one rhetorical question or command.

EXERCISE 5

var

19

Examine the following paragraphs for sentence variety. By analyzing your own response to each sentence, try to explain why the author wrote each short or long sentence, each cumulative or periodic sentence, each sentence beginning with its subject or beginning some other way, and each question.

1.   Love. We are early taught to say it. I love you. We are trained to the thought of it as if there were nothing else, or nothing else worth having without it, or nothing worth having which it could not bring with it. Love is taught, always by precept, sometimes by example. Then hate, which no one meant to teach us, comes of itself. It is true that if we say I love you, it may be received with doubt, for there are times when it is hard to believe. Say I hate you, and the one spoken to believes it instantly.
                                — KATHERINE ANNE PORTER, "The Necessary Enemy"

2.   That night in my rented room, while letting the hot water run over my can of pork and beans in the sink, I opened [H. L. Mencken's] *A Book of Prefaces* and began to read. I was jarred and shocked by the style, the clear, clean, sweeping sentences. Why did he write like that? And how did one write like that? I pictured the man as a raging demon, slashing with his pen, consumed with hate, denouncing everything American, extolling everything European or German, laughing at the weaknesses of people, mocking God, authority. What was this? I stood up, trying to realize what reality lay behind the meaning of the words. Yes, this man was fighting, fighting with words. He was using words as a weapon, using them as one would use a club. Could words be weapons? Well, yes, for here they were. Then, maybe, perhaps, I could use them as a weapon? No. It frightened me. I read on and what amazed me was not what he said, but how on earth anybody had the courage to say it.
                                — RICHARD WRIGHT, *Black Boy*

V
Punctuation

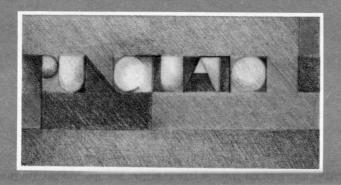

20

End Punctuation

THE PERIOD

20a

Use the period to end sentences that are statements, mild commands, or indirect questions.

STATEMENTS

These are exciting and trying times.

Some African revolutionaries hire mercenary soldiers to help them fight.

MILD COMMANDS

Please do not smoke.
Think of the possibilities.
Turn to page 146.

If you are unsure whether to use an exclamation point or a period after a command, use a period. The exclamation point should be used only rarely (see 20f).

An **indirect question** reports what someone has asked but not in the original speaker's own words.

INDIRECT QUESTIONS

The judge asked why I had been driving with my lights off.

Students sometimes wonder whether teachers read their papers.

Abused children eventually stop asking why they are being punished.

See 25e for the use of three spaced periods in an ellipsis (. . .) to indicate omissions from quotations.

20b
Use periods with most abbreviations.

Ordinarily, use periods with abbreviations.

p.	B.A.	A.D.	Mr.
D.C.	Ph.D.	A.M.	Mrs.
M.D.	e.g.	P.M.	Ms.
Dr.	B.C.		

When an abbreviation falls at the end of a sentence, use only one period: *Government, not industry, is the business of Washington, D.C.*

Periods are usually dropped from abbreviations for organizations, corporations, and government agencies when more than two words are abbreviated. For example:

IBM	NFL
EEOC	AFL-CIO

Check a dictionary for the preferred form of such abbreviations, and see Chapter 28, which concerns abbreviations.

Note that **acronyms** — pronounceable words, such as UNESCO, NATO, VISTA, and WHO, formed from the initial letters of the words in a name — never require periods (see 28b).

20c

EXERCISE 1

Revise the sentences below so that periods are used correctly.

Example:
Several times we asked whether Julie could go with us?
Several times we asked whether Julie could go with us.

1. Let the dissenters have their say
2. The police asked whose dog was barking?
3. Class begins at 3:00 PM sharp
4. The new house had 2200 sq ft of heated space
5. The Roman Empire in the West collapsed in 476 AD

THE QUESTION MARK

20c
Use the question mark after direct questions.

DIRECT QUESTIONS

Who will follow her?
What is the difference between these two people?
Will economists ever really understand the economy?

After indirect questions, use a period: *My mother asked why I came in so late.* (See 20a.)

Questions in a series are each followed by a question mark.

The officer asked how many times the suspect had been arrested. Three times? Four times? More than that?

The use of capital letters for questions in a series is optional (see 26a).

NOTE: Question marks are never combined with other question marks, exclamation points, periods, or commas.

> FAULTY   I finally asked myself, "Why are you working at a job you hate?."
>
> REVISED   I finally asked myself, "Why are you working at a job you hate?"

20d

Use a question mark within parentheses to indicate doubt about the correctness of a number or date.

The Greek philosopher Socrates was born in 470 (?) B.C. and died in 399 B.C. from drinking poison after having been condemned to death.

NOTE: Don't use a question mark within parentheses to express sarcasm or irony. Express these attitudes through sentence structure and diction. (See Chapters 18 and 31.)

> FAULTY   Her friendly (?) criticism did not escape notice.
>
> REVISED   Her criticism, *too rough to be genuinely friendly,* did not escape notice.

EXERCISE 2

Revise the sentences below so that question marks (along with other punctuation marks) are used correctly.

> *Example:*
> "When will it end?," cried the man dressed in rags.
> "When will it end?" cried the man dressed in rags.

1. Parents often wonder whether their children are getting anything out of college?
2. "What does *ontogeny* mean?," the biology instructor asked?
3. The candidate for Congress asked whether there was anything he could do to help us?
4. Will little children always ask, "Well, if God made everything, who made God?"?
5. Ulysses and his mariners took seven years to travel from Troy to Ithaca. Or was it six. Or eight?

THE EXCLAMATION POINT

20e

Use the exclamation point after emphatic statements and interjections and after strong commands.

No! We must not lose this election!
When she saw her rain-soaked term paper, she gasped, "Oh, no!"
Come here immediately!

Follow mild interjections and commands with periods or commas, as appropriate.

No, the response was not terrific.
To prolong your car's life, change its oil regularly.

NOTE: Exclamation points are never combined with other exclamation points, question marks, periods, or commas.

| FAULTY | My father was most emphatic. "I will not give you any more money!," he roared. |
| REVISED | My father was most emphatic. "I will not give you any more money!" he roared. |

20f

Avoid overusing exclamation points.

Don't express sarcasm, irony, or amazement with the exclamation point. Rely on sentence structure and diction to express these attitudes. (See Chapters 18 and 31.)

| FAULTY | After traveling 1.24 billion miles through space, *Voyager 2* missed its target by 41 miles (!). |
| REVISED | After traveling 1.24 billion miles through space, *Voyager 2* missed its target by *a mere* 41 miles. |

Relying on the exclamation point for emphasis is like crying wolf: The mark loses its power to impress the reader. Frequent exclamation points can also make the tone of your writing seem extreme. (See 4a.) In the passage below, the writer could have conveyed her ideas more effectively by punctuating sentences with periods.

Our city government is a mess! After just six months in office, the mayor has had to fire four city officials! In the same period the city councilors have done nothing but argue! And city services decline with each passing day!

EXERCISE 3

Revise the sentences below so that exclamation points (along with other punctuation marks) are used correctly. If a sentence is punctuated correctly as given, circle the number preceding it.

Example:

What a shock it was to hear her scream, "Stop"

What a shock it was to hear her scream, "Stop!"

1. The sun was so bright that it bleached all colors!
2. "Well, now!," he said loudly.
3. The child's cries could be heard next door: "Don't go. Don't go."
4. Close your books and take out a clean piece of paper.
5. As the fire fighters moved their equipment into place, police walked through the crowd shouting, "Move back!."

EXERCISE 4

Insert appropriate punctuation (periods, question marks, or exclamation points) where needed in the paragraph below.

When Maureen approached Jesse with her idea for a class gift to the school, he asked if she knew how much it would cost "Forget it if it's over $200," he said "Do you think the class can come up with even that much" Both of them knew the committee treasury contained only the $100 given by Dr Wheeler Maureen said that she thought they could raise the rest with a talent show "That's ridiculous" exclaimed Jesse "What talent Dr Wheeler's Whose" But he softened when Maureen asked him if he would perform his animal imitations Jesse loved to do animal imitations

20f !

21
The Comma

The comma is the most frequently used — and misused — mark of internal punctuation. In general, commas function within sentences to indicate pauses and to separate elements; they also have several conventional uses, as in dates. Omitting needed commas or inserting needless ones can confuse the reader, as the following sentences show.

COMMA NEEDED	Though very tall Abraham Lincoln was not an overbearing man.
REVISED	Though very tall, Abraham Lincoln was not an overbearing man.
UNNEEDED COMMAS	The hectic pace of Beirut, broke suddenly into frightening chaos when the city became, the focus of civil war.
REVISED	The hectic pace of Beirut broke suddenly into frightening chaos when the city became the focus of civil war.

21a
Use the comma before a coordinating conjunction linking main clauses.

The coordinating conjunctions are *and, but, or, nor,* and sometimes *yet, so,* and *for*. They should be preceded by a comma when they link main clauses — that is, clauses with a subject and predicate (and without a subordinating word at the beginning) that make complete statements (see 5c).

301

> She was perfectly at home in what she knew **,** *and* what she knew
> has remained what all of us want to know.
> — EUDORA WELTY on Jane Austen

> He would have turned around again without a word **,** *but* I seized
> him.   — FYODOR DOSTOYEVSKY

> Seventeen years ago this month I quit work **,** *or,* if you prefer, I re-
> tired from business.   — F. SCOTT FITZGERALD

> They made their decision with some uneasiness **,** *for* they knew
> that in such places any failure to conform could cause trouble.
> — RICHARD HARRIS

> In putting on trousers a man always inserts the same old leg first.
> ... All men do it **,** *yet* no man thought it out and adopted it of set
> purpose.   — MARK TWAIN

> Near evening I was too jittery to attend to chores **,** *so* Bailey volun-
> teered to do all before his bath.   — MAYA ANGELOU

EXCEPTIONS: Some writers prefer to use a semicolon before *so*
and *yet.*

> Many people say that the institution of marriage is in decline **;** *yet*
> recent evidence on the number and stability of marriages suggests
> that the institution is at least holding steady.

21a

When the main clauses in a sentence are very long or grammatically
complicated, or when they contain internal punctuation, a semicolon before the coordinating conjunction will clarify the division
between clauses (see 22c).

> Life would be dull without its seamier side, its violence, filth, and
> hatred **;** *for* otherwise how could we appreciate the joys?
> — ELLEN STEPIK

When main clauses are very short and closely related in meaning,
you may omit the comma between them as long as the resulting sentence is clear.

> She opened her mouth *but* no sound came out of it.
> — FLANNERY O'CONNOR
> My heart raced *and* I felt ill.

If you are in doubt about whether to use a comma in such sentences, use it. It will always be correct.

EXERCISE 1

Insert a comma before each coordinating conjunction that links
main clauses in the sentences below.

Example:

I would have dropped out of school but my physics teacher talked me into staying.

I would have dropped out of school, but my physics teacher talked me into staying.

1. Kampala is Uganda's capital and largest city and it serves as the nation's social and economic center.
2. I am looking for a job but the ones I find either pay too little or require too many skills that I do not have.
3. Housing prices continue to rise so fewer people can afford their own homes.
4. Jill wanted to go out for the tennis team but she strained a tendon in her right ankle.
5. The hikers had come a long way and they could not summon the energy for the final mile to the river and a comfortable campsite.

EXERCISE 2

Combine each pair of sentences below into one sentence that uses a comma between main clauses connected by the coordinating conjunction in parentheses.

Example:

The circus had just come to town. Everyone wanted to see it. (*and*)

The circus had just come to town, *and* everyone wanted to see it.

1. The accident must have happened at night. It could not have happened at all. (*or*)
2. The FBI used to be considered simply a crime-busting organization. Now we know it is involved in national security as well. (*but*)
3. His father sometimes hit him. The boy sometimes hit his little sister. (*so*)
4. In many bird species the female builds the nest. The male defends it. (*and*)
5. The last Super Bowl game was a bore. We all watched it from beginning to end. (*yet*)

21b

21b
Use the comma to set off introductory phrases and clauses.

Introductory phrases and clauses modify a word or words in the main clause that follows. Put a comma after introductory elements: subordinate clauses (5c-4); participles, infinitives, and participial and infinitive phrases (5c-2); prepositional phrases (5c-1); and sentence modifiers such as *unfortunately, certainly,* and *of course.*

> *If Ernest Hemingway had written comic books,* they would have been just as good as his novels. [Subordinate clause.] — STAN LEE
>
> *Exhausted,* the runner collapsed at the finish line. [Participle.]
>
> *To win the most important race of her career,* she had nearly killed herself. [Infinitive phrase.]
>
> *From Columbus and Sir Walter Raleigh onward,* America has been traveling the road west. [Prepositional phrase.] — PETER DAVISON
>
> *Unfortunately,* the diamond was fake. [Sentence modifier.]

Take care to distinguish verbals used as subjects (gerunds or gerund phrases) from verbals used as modifiers. The former never take a comma; the latter usually do.

> *Jogging through the park* has become a popular form of recreation for city dwellers. [Gerund phrase used as subject.]
>
> *Jogging through the park,* I was unexpectedly caught in a downpour. [Participial phrase used as adjective.]

The comma can be omitted following short introductory prepositional and infinitive phrases and subordinate clauses if its omission does not create confusion. (If you are in doubt, however, the comma is always correct.)

> CLEAR   *By the year 2000* the world population will be more than 6 billion. [Prepositional phrase.]
>
> CLEAR   *To write clearly* one must think clearly. [Infinitive phrase.]
>
> CLEAR   *When snow falls* the city collapses. [Subordinate clause.]
>
> CONFUSING   At eighteen people are considered young adults.
>
> REVISED   At eighteen, people are considered young adults.

21b

EXERCISE 3

Insert commas where needed after introductory elements in the sentences below. If a sentence is punctuated correctly as given, circle the number preceding it.

> *Example:*
> Not long after the rally ended a fight erupted.
> Not long after the rally ended, a fight erupted.

1. Gasping for breath the fire fighters staggered out of the burning building.

2. Because of the late morning rain the baseball game had to be canceled.
3. Collecting old Marvel comics is his favorite hobby.
4. Without so much as nodding her head Phyllis slammed the door and left.
5. Before you make any more mistakes read the directions.
6. Closing the shop was the hardest thing she had to do.
7. Even though Regina was sick last week she attended every rehearsal.
8. Tomorrow morning Mark will drive the children to the bus depot.
9. When young Robert was tall for his age.
10. In both the North and the South schools are more integrated now than they were fifteen years ago.

EXERCISE 4

Combine each pair of sentences below into one sentence that begins with an introductory phrase or clause as specified in parentheses. Follow the introductory element with a comma. You will have to add, delete, change, and rearrange words.

> *Example:*
> The girl was humming to herself. She walked upstairs. (*Phrase beginning Humming.*)
> *Humming to herself,* the girl walked up the stairs.

1. One needs information to vote wisely. One needs objective information about the candidates' backgrounds and opinions. (*Phrase beginning To.*)
2. The city may go deeper into debt. Services will have to be curtailed. (*Clause beginning If.*)
3. The flags were snapping in the wind. They made the speaker's message seem even more urgent. (*Phrase beginning Snapping.*)
4. Vatican City has only 108 acres. It is the smallest sovereign state in the world. (*Phrase beginning With.*)
5. A woman was finally appointed as a Supreme Court justice. The Court remains far from balanced. (*Clause beginning Although.*)

21c
Use the comma to set off nonrestrictive elements.

Restrictive and nonrestrictive sentence elements contribute differently to meaning and require different punctuation. A **restrictive element** limits, or restricts, the meaning of the word or words it applies to. Thus it is essential to the meaning of the sentence and cannot be omitted without significantly changing that meaning. Restrictive elements are never set off with commas.

RESTRICTIVE ELEMENT

Employees *who work hard* will receive raises.

A **nonrestrictive element** gives added information about the word or words it applies to, but it does not limit the word or words. It can be omitted from the sentence without changing the essential meaning. Nonrestrictive elements are always set off with commas.

NONRESTRICTIVE ELEMENT

Molly Berman, *who lives next door*, got a raise.

A test can help you determine if a sentence element is restrictive or nonrestrictive: Does the meaning of the word preceding the element change when the element is removed? It does in the restrictive example above, for *Employees will receive raises* does not provide the same information about employees as the original sentence did. The employees are no longer defined or limited to a specific group, the ones who work hard, but instead include all employees, whatever their work habits. Conversely, *Molly Berman got a raise* has essentially the same meaning as the original nonrestrictive example. Not knowing where Molly Berman lives does not change our understanding of the sentence; no matter where she lives, she still got the raise.

Here is another example of how the test may be applied, this time with prepositional phrases.

RESTRICTIVE OR NONRESTRICTIVE?

Travel *with three children* is tiring.
Travel *with few exceptions* is expensive.

Does the meaning of the word (*travel*) preceding each phrase change when you omit the phrase? It does in the first sentence because *Travel is tiring* no longer specifies the conditions under which travel is tiring (with three children) and thus refers to *all* travel. But the meaning of *travel* in the second sentence remains the same — *Travel is expensive* — because the phrase *with few exceptions* does not specify particular conditions or kinds of travel. Thus the phrase in the first sentence is restrictive and should *not* be set off by commas; the phrase in the second sentence is nonrestrictive and *should* be set off by commas.

RESTRICTIVE

Travel *with three children* is tiring.

NONRESTRICTIVE

Travel, *with few exceptions*, is expensive.

The presence or absence of commas around a sentence element can change the meaning of a single sentence, as the following examples illustrate.

The band *playing old music* held the audience's attention.
The band, *playing old music,* held the audience's attention.

In the first sentence the absence of commas restricts the subject to a particular band, the one playing old music, and thus implies that more than one band played more than one kind of music. In the second sentence, however, the commas setting off the phrase imply that only one band played because the phrase does not restrict the subject to a particular band. Which punctuation is correct depends on the writer's intended meaning and on the context in which the sentence appears. For example:

RESTRICTIVE

Not all the bands were equally well received, however. The band *playing old music* held the audience's attention. The other groups created much less excitement.

NONRESTRICTIVE

A new band called Fats made its debut on Saturday night. The band, *playing old music,* held the audience's attention. If this performance is typical, the group has a bright future.

(Though commas are most commonly used to set off nonrestrictive elements from other sentence parts, writers occasionally use dashes or parentheses to indicate greater separation. See 25b-2 and 25c for examples.)

1
Use the comma to set off nonrestrictive clauses and phrases.

NONRESTRICTIVE CLAUSES

Carl O'Hara, *who used to raise funds for public radio,* has joined a commercial television network. [Compare *Carl O'Hara has joined a commercial television network.* O'Hara's background does not alter the fact that he now works in commercial television.]

Science courses, *which are now required of all students,* tie up one afternoon a week for laboratory work. [Compare *Science courses tie up one afternoon a week for laboratory work.* Presumably, science courses entail laboratory work whether or not they are required, so the fact that they are now required does not restrict the meaning of the sentence.]

Three-year-old Nancy, *whose blue eyes shone with mischief,* had to be rescued more than once from her adventures. [Compare *Three-year-old Nancy had to be rescued more than once from her adventures.* The look of the child's eyes does not restrict the meaning.]

The American farming system, *which is the envy of the world,* is the despair of the American farmer. [Compare *The American farming system is the despair of the American farmer.* The meaning of the subject is unchanged.] — CHARLES KURALT

NONRESTRICTIVE PHRASES

The dog, *seeking a bone,* jumped on the boy's lap. [Compare *The dog jumped on the boy's lap.* Assuming that only one dog is present, then the dog's goal does not restrict it to a specific dog.]

The Capitol Building, *at one end of Independence Mall,* is an imposing sight. [Compare *The Capitol Building is an imposing sight.* The building's name identifies it; its location does not supply further restriction.]

The library's most valuable book, *bought at auction in 1962,* is a thirteenth-century Bible. [Compare *The library's most valuable book is a thirteenth-century Bible.* Assuming that the Bible is the most valuable book in the library's entire collection, the details of its purchase do not restrict it further.]

What families are doing, *in flamboyant and dumfounding ways,* is changing their size and their shape and their purpose. [Compare *What families are doing is changing their size and their shape and their purpose.* Since the author is emphasizing what families are doing, and not that they are doing something in a particular way, the omission of the phrase does not change the meaning.] — JANE HOWARD

21c

RESTRICTIVE CLAUSES

Books *that say something new about the world* are the only kind worth reading. [Compare *Books are the only kind worth reading.* Because it does not specify what books are worth reading, the sentence is senseless.]

The person *who vandalized the dormitory* was never caught. [Compare *The person was never caught,* which does not identify the person.]

Every question *that has a reasonable answer* is justifiable. [Compare *Every question is justifiable,* which clearly alters the writer's meaning.] — KONRAD LORENZ

He wore the look of one *who knows he is the victim of a terrible disease and understands his helplessness.* [Compare *He wore the look of one.* Without its modifying clause, *one* is meaningless.] — STEPHEN CRANE

RESTRICTIVE PHRASES

The newer houses *on the town's north side* were built *in the 1960s.* [Without either or both of its prepositional phrases, the sentence changes meaning. Compare *The newer houses were built in the 1960s; The newer houses on the town's north side were built;* and *The newer houses were built.*]

A student *seeking an easy course* should not enroll in History 101. [Compare *A student should not enroll in History 101,* which fails to limit the kind of student who should not enroll.]

The ongoing taboo *against women dating men shorter than themselves* is among the strictest of this society. [Compare *The ongoing taboo is among the strictest of this society,* which no longer specifies what taboo.] — RALPH KEYES

The sealed crates *containing the records of my past* were drawn from storage and opened. [Compare *The sealed crates were drawn from storage and opened.* The crates are no longer limited by their contents.] — JOHN GREGORY DUNNE

NOTE: Whereas both nonrestrictive and restrictive clauses may begin with *which,* only restrictive clauses begin with *that.* Some writers prefer *that* exclusively for restrictive clauses and *which* exclusively for nonrestrictive clauses. See the Glossary of Usage, page 561, for advice on the use of *that* and *which.*

2
Use the comma to set off nonrestrictive appositives.

An **appositive** is a noun or noun substitute that renames and could substitute for another noun immediately preceding it. (See 5c-5.) Many appositives are nonrestrictive; thus they are set off, usually with commas. Take care *not* to set off restrictive appositives, like restrictive phrases and clauses, they limit or define the noun or nouns they refer to.

NONRESTRICTIVE APPOSITIVES

The Chapman lighthouse, *a three-legged thing erect on a mud-flat,* shone strongly. [Compare *The Chapman lighthouse shone strongly.*] — JOSEPH CONRAD

John Kennedy Toole's only novel, *A Confederacy of Dunces,* won the Pulitzer Prize. [Compare *John Kennedy Toole's only novel won the Pulitzer Prize.*]

RESTRICTIVE APPOSITIVES

Paul Scott's novel *The Jewel in the Crown* is about India under British rule. [Compare *Paul Scott's novel is about India under British rule,* which implies wrongly that Scott wrote only one novel.]

The philosopher *Alfred North Whitehead* once wrote that the history of philosophy was a series of footnotes to Plato. [Compare *The philosopher once wrote that the history of philosophy was a series of footnotes to Plato.*]

Our language has adopted the words *garage, panache, and fanfare* from French. [Compare *Our language has adopted the words from French.*]

21c

3

Use the comma to set off parenthetical expressions.

Parenthetical expressions are explanatory, supplementary, or transitional words or phrases that interrupt the sentence structure. (Transitional expressions include *however, indeed, consequently, as a result, of course, for example,* and *in fact;* see 3b-6 for a more complete list.) Parenthetical expressions are usually set off by commas.

> The Cubist painters, *for example,* were obviously inspired by the families of crystals.   — JACOB BRONOWSKI

> The only option, *besides locking him up,* was to release him to his parents' custody.

> The film, *according to the critics,* is one of Redford's best.

> Any writer, *I suppose,* feels that the world into which he was born is nothing less than a conspiracy against the cultivation of his talent.   — JAMES BALDWIN

(Dashes and parentheses may also set off parenthetical elements; see 25b-2 and 25c.)

4

21c

Use the comma to set off *yes* and *no,* tag questions, words of direct address, and mild interjections.

YES AND NO

Yes, the editorial did have a point.
No, that can never be.

TAG QUESTIONS

Jones should be allowed to vote, *should he not?*
They don't stop to consider others, *do they?*

DIRECT ADDRESS

Cody, please bring me the newspaper.
With all due respect, *sir,* I will not do that.

MILD INTERJECTIONS

Well, you will never know who did it.
Oh, they forgot all about the baby.

(You may want to use exclamation points or dashes to set off forceful interjections. See 20e and 25b for examples.)

EXERCISE 5

Insert commas in the sentences below to set off nonrestrictive elements, and delete any commas that incorrectly set off restrictive elements. If the sentence is correct as given, circle the number preceding it.

Example:

Elizabeth Blackwell who attended medical school in the 1840s was the first American woman to receive a medical degree.

Elizabeth Blackwell**,** who attended medical school in the 1840s**,** was the first American woman to receive a medical degree.

1. *Moby Dick* a novel by Herman Melville is thought by some critics to be America's finest novel.
2. Our modern ideas about civil liberties can be traced back to the Magna Carta which was written in 1215.
3. Legionnaire's disease unknown until a few years ago has been responsible for the deaths of many people.
4. The poem is by the fiction writer, Jay Berde.
5. Please listen fellow voters while I explain my position.
6. The report concluded that Americans who pay property taxes are the most disgruntled citizens.
7. All students, working to support themselves, should be given some financial aid.
8. The port of New York which was once the busiest in the nation is not nearly as active as it was.
9. The team that conducted the research was awarded a prize.
10. Those of us, who hadn't seen the concert, felt we had missed something.

21c

EXERCISE 6

Combine each pair of sentences below into one sentence that uses the element described in parentheses. Insert commas as appropriate. You will have to add, delete, and rearrange words. Some items have more than one possible answer.

Example:

Mr. Ward's oldest sister helped keep him alive. She was a nurse in the hospital. (*Nonrestrictive clause beginning* who.)

Mr. Ward's oldest sister**,** *who was a nurse in the hospital***,** helped keep him alive.

1. The calculator has limited use. It is the size of a quarter. (*Nonrestrictive clause beginning* which.)
2. Joan Silver was leading the runners. She was the first to come in view. (*Nonrestrictive phrase beginning* leading.)
3. A house is on Langness Street. It is over two hundred years old. (*Restrictive phrase beginning* on.)
4. Men and women control our industries. They are interested primarily in profits. (*Restrictive clause beginning* who.)
5. The senator is William de Silva. He is a native of this city. (*Nonrestrictive appositive.*)
6. Winter is the best of seasons. It is a time of dazzling snows and toasty fires. (*Nonrestrictive appositive.*)

7. The island is in the middle of the river. It is a perfect hide-away. (*Nonrestrictive phrase beginning in.*)
8. The demonstrators were blocking the road. They tied up traf-fic for two hours. (*Restrictive phrase beginning blocking.*)
9. Psychologists say that children have difficulty evaluating their own performances. They need the constant support of their parents. (*Nonrestrictive clause beginning who.*)
10. Some courses sharpen communications skills. They should be required of medical and nursing students. (*Restrictive clause beginning that.*)

21d

Use the comma to set off absolute phrases.

An **absolute phrase** modifies a whole sentence rather than any word or word group in the sentence; it is not connected to the rest of the sentence by a conjunction, preposition, or relative pronoun. (See 5c-3.) Absolute phrases usually consist of at least a participle and its subject (a noun or pronoun), as in the following:

Their work finished, the men quit for the day.

Absolute constructions can occur at almost any point in the sentence. Whatever their position, they are always set off by commas.

Their homework done, the children may watch whatever they want on television.

After reaching Eagle Rock, we pointed our canoes toward shore, *the rapids ahead being rough.*

His clothes, *the fabric tattered and the seams ripped open,* looked like Salvation Army rejects.

EXERCISE 7

Insert commas in the sentences below to set off absolute construc-tions.

Example:

Prices having risen steadily the government contemplated a price freeze.

Prices having risen steadily, the government contemplated a price freeze.

1. The shooting having started the set was quiet except for the actors' voices.
2. Their exams finished the students had a party to celebrate.
3. The painters quit work early the house painted and the sup-plies put away.

4. The police drove away from the accident their investigation completed.
5. Spring coming nearer the ground felt damp and the air smelled fresh.
6. The governor had a chance the legislature being in recess to enhance his position with the voters.
7. All doors secured the guard took a nap.
8. The case was finally closed the only suspect having died.
9. Children their imaginations being vivid often suffer from terrifying nightmares.
10. The exam being difficult he was lucky to pass the course.

21e
Use the comma to set off phrases expressing contrast.

It was Saturday, *not Sunday,* when the burglary occurred.

Trout are found in fresh water, *not in salt water.*

Style is the manner of a sentence, *not its matter.* — DONALD HALL

It is not light that is needed, *but fire;* it is not the gentle shower, *but thunder.* — FREDERICK DOUGLASS

NOTE: Experienced writers do not always use commas to set off contrasting phrases containing *but*

His life was long *but sadly empty.* — HERMAN CRAISLEY

21e

EXERCISE 8

Insert commas in the sentences below to set off phrases that express contrast.

Example:

Susan not her sister was the one who succumbed to the disease.

Susan, not her sister, was the one who succumbed to the disease.

1. The president should have a single term of six years not two four-year terms.
2. The humidity not just the heat makes some summer days unbearable.
3. It was William Faulkner not F. Scott Fitzgerald who won the Nobel Prize.
4. World War II ended with the surrender of the Japanese in September 1945 not with the surrender of the Germans in May.
5. My family attends church in Cromwell not Durben because we know the minister in Cromwell.

21f

Use the comma between words, phrases, or clauses forming a series and between coordinate adjectives not linked by conjunctions.

Place commas between all elements of a **series** — that is, three or more items of equal importance.

> The names *Belial,* *Beelzebub,* *and Lucifer* sound ominous.

> He felt cut off from them *by age,* *by understanding,* *by sensibility,* *by technology,* *and by his need to measure himself against the mirror of other men's appreciation.*   — RALPH ELLISON

> The ox *was solid black,* *stood five feet high at the shoulder,* *had a five-foot span of horns,* *and must have weighed 1,200 pounds on the hoof.*   — RICHARD B. LEE

Though some writers omit the comma before the coordinating conjunction in a series (*Breakfast consisted of coffee, eggs and kippers*), the final comma is never wrong and it always helps the reader see the two items as separate. Use it consistently and your writing will be clearer, as the following example shows.

> CONFUSING   After the storm the downtown streets were littered with branches, broken glass from windows and signs advertising businesses.

> CLEAR   After the storm the downtown streets were littered with branches, broken glass from windows, and signs advertising businesses.

EXCEPTION: When items in a series are long and grammatically complicated, composed of clauses or phrases with modifiers, they may be separated by semicolons. When the items contain commas, they must, for clarity, be separated by semicolons. (See 22d.)

Coordinate adjectives are two or more adjectives that modify equally the same noun or pronoun. The individual adjectives are separated either by coordinating conjunctions or by commas.

> The *sleek* and *shiny* car was a credit to the neighborhood.

> The *dirty,* *rusty,* *dented* car was an eyesore.

> Nothing is more essential to *intelligent,* *profitable* reading than sensitivity to connotation.   — RICHARD ALTICK

Adjectives are not coordinate — and should *not* be separated by commas — when the one nearer the noun is more closely related to the noun in meaning.

> The house overflowed with *ornate electric* fixtures. [*Ornate* modifies *electric fixtures.*]

The museum's most valuable object is a *sparkling diamond neck-lace.* [*Sparkling* modifies *diamond necklace.*]

Two tests will help you determine whether adjectives are coordinate: (1) Can the adjectives be rearranged without changing the meaning? (2) Can the word *and* be inserted between the adjectives without changing the meaning? In the sentence *They are dedicated medical students,* the adjectives cannot be either rearranged (*medical dedicated students*) or separated by *and* (*dedicated and medical students*). Thus the adjectives are not coordinate, and no comma belongs between them. However, in the sentence *She was a faithful sincere friend,* the adjectives can be rearranged (*sincere faithful friend*), and they can be separated by *and* (*faithful and sincere friend*). Thus the adjectives are coordinate, and a comma belongs between them: *She was a faithful, sincere friend.*

Notice that numbers are not coordinate with other adjectives.

FAULTY   Among the junk in Grandmother's attic was *one, lovely* vase.

REVISED   Among the junk in Grandmother's attic was *one lovely* vase.

Do not use a comma between the final coordinate adjective and the noun.

FAULTY   Spring evenings in the South are *warm, sensuous, experiences.*

REVISED   Spring evenings in the South are *warm, sensuous* experiences.

21f

EXERCISE 9

Insert commas in the sentences below to separate coordinate adjectives or elements in series. Circle the number preceding each sentence whose punctuation is already correct.

Example:

The paved road became a soft sticky goo when the sun shone on it.

The paved road became a soft, sticky goo when the sun shone on it.

1. For his second birthday I'd like to buy my son a plastic hammer a punching bag and a leash.
2. Neither personal loss business setbacks nor illness defeated him.
3. The school bought a fine Victorian house to use as a faculty and alumni club.
4. That morning, fresh crisp and clear, turned out to be memorable.

---

5. Television newscasters rarely work full-time as reporters investigate only light stories if any and rarely write the copy they read on the air.
6. That was the second frightening experience of the day.
7. Several stores opened new larger branches in the shopping mall outside the city.
8. The suspect was brought in kicking hitting and cursing.
9. She was a Miamian by birth a farmer by temperament and a worker to the day she died.
10. The unset leg fracture she had as a child caused her troubling annoying pain all her life.

21g
Use the comma according to convention in dates, addresses, place names, and long numbers.

The items in a date, address, or place name are conventionally separated with commas, as illustrated below. When they appear within sentences, dates, addresses, and place names punctuated with commas are also ended with commas.

DATES

July 4, 1776, was the day the Declaration of Independence was signed.

The bombing of Pearl Harbor on December 7, 1941, prompted American entry into World War II.

Commas are not used between the parts of a date in inverted order: *Their anniversary on 15 December 1982 was their fiftieth.* Commas need not be used in dates consisting of a month or season and a year: *For the United States, the war began December 1941 and ended August 1945.*

ADDRESSES AND PLACE NAMES

Use the address 5262 Laurie Lane, Memphis, Tennessee, for all correspondence.

Send inquiries to Box 3862, Pasadena, California.

Columbus, Ohio, is the location of Ohio State University.

The population of Garden City, Long Island, New York, is 30,000.

Commas are not used between state names and zip codes in addresses: *Berkeley, California 94720, is the place of my birth.*

LONG NUMBERS

Use the comma to separate the figures in long numbers into groups of three, counting from the right. The comma with numbers of four digits is optional.

A kilometer is 3,281 feet (*or* 3281 feet).

Russia's 8,649,490 square miles make it the largest country in the world.

EXERCISE 10

Insert commas as needed in the following sentences.

> *Example:*
> The car cost $10624 when new.
> The car cost $10,624 when new.

1. The world's population exceeds 4415000000.
2. Boulder Colorado sits at the base of the Rocky Mountains.
3. The letter was postmarked October 2 1981 in Paris France.
4. Whoever writes P.O. Box 725 Asheville North Carolina 28803 will get a quick response.
5. January 1 2000 will be a big day in our lives.

21h

Use the comma with quotations according to standard practice.

The words used to explain a quotation (*he said, she replied,* and so on) may come before, after, or in the middle of the quotation. They must always be separated from the quotation by punctuation, usually a comma or commas.

1

Ordinarily, use the comma to separate introductory and concluding explanatory words from quotations.

General Sherman summed up the attitude of all thoughtful soldiers when he said, "War is hell."

"Knowledge is power," wrote Francis Bacon.

EXCEPTIONS: Do not use the comma when a quotation followed by explanatory words ends in an exclamation point or a question mark (see 20c and 20e).

"Claude!" Mrs. Harrison called.

"Why must I come home?" he asked.

Do not use commas with a quotation introduced by *that* or with a short quotation in a sentence that does more than merely introduce or explain the quotation.

The warning that "cigarette smoking is dangerous to your health" has fallen on many deaf ears.

People should always say "Excuse me" when they bump into fellow pedestrians.

Use a colon instead of a comma to separate explanatory words from a quotation when there is an emphatic break between them in meaning or in grammar or when the quotation is very formal or longer than a sentence. (See also 25a.) For instance:

The Bill of Rights is unambiguous: "Congress shall make no law respecting an establishment of religion, or prohibiting the free exercise thereof."

2

Use the comma after the first part of a quotation interrupted by explanatory words. Follow the explanatory words with the punctuation required by the quotation.

QUOTATION

"When you got nothin', you got nothin' to lose."

EXPLANATORY WORDS

"When you got nothin'," Kris Kristofferson sings, "you got nothin' to lose." [The explanatory words interrupt the quotation at a comma and thus end with a comma.]

QUOTATION

"That part of my life was over; his words had sealed it shut."

EXPLANATORY WORDS

"That part of my life was over," she wrote; "his words had sealed it shut." [The explanatory words interrupt the quotation at a semicolon and thus end with a semicolon.]

QUOTATION

"This is the faith with which I return to the South. With this new faith we will be able to hew out of the mountain of despair a stone of hope."

EXPLANATORY WORDS

"This is the faith with which I return to the South," Martin Luther King, Jr., proclaimed. "With this new faith we will be able to hew out of the mountain of despair a stone of hope." [The explanatory words interrupt the quotation at the end of a sentence and thus end with a period.]

21h

3
Place commas that follow quotations within quotation marks.

"That's my seat,**"** she said coldly.
"You gave it up,**"** I replied evenly, "so you have no right to it."

(For instructions on punctuating quotations, see 24g.)

EXERCISE 11

Insert commas in the sentences below to correct punctuation with quotations.

Example:
When asked to open her bag, the shoplifter exclaimed "I didn't steal anything."
When asked to open her bag, the shoplifter exclaimed**,** "I didn't steal anything."

1. "The mass of men lead lives of quiet desperation" Henry David Thoreau wrote in *Walden*.
2. "I'll be on the next bus for Cleveland" the woman promised.
3. In a sentence that has stirred generations of readers, Jean-Jacques Rousseau announced "Man was born free, and everywhere he is in chains."
4. "We must face reality" the president said sternly "while we have time."
5. "The team has a chance" the announcer said quietly. Then he yelled "We have a chance!"

21i
Use the comma to prevent misreading.

The comma tells the reader to pause slightly before moving on. In some sentences words may run together in unintended and confusing ways unless a comma separates them. Use a comma in such sentences even though no rule requires one.

CONFUSING	Soon after she left town for good. [A short introductory phrase does not require a comma, but clarity requires it in this sentence.]
REVISED	Soon after, she left town for good.
CONFUSING	The students who can usually give some money to the United Fund. [Without a comma the sentence seems incomplete.]
REVISED	The students who can, usually give some money to the United Fund.

EXERCISE 12

Insert commas in the sentences below to prevent misreading.

Example:

To Mary Heather promised hope.
To Mary, Heather promised hope.

1. Beginning tomorrow afternoon practice will be canceled.
2. Though old Grandfather was still spry.
3. However crude the invention is promising.
4. Of the fifty six boys can't go.
5. Those who can't regret it.

21j
Avoid misusing or overusing the comma.

Although commas are useful and often necessary to signal pauses in sentences, they can make sentences choppy and even confusing if they are used more often than needed or in violation of rules 21a through 21h. Examine every sentence you write to be sure you have used commas appropriately.

21j

1
Don't use the comma to separate a subject from its verb, or a verb or a preposition from its object, unless the words between them require punctuation.

FAULTY   The returning *soldiers, expected* a warmer welcome than they received. [Separation of subject and verb.]

REVISED   The returning *soldiers expected* a warmer welcome than they received.

FAULTY   After deciding that she could do one but not both, my sister *chose, to have children* rather than pursue a career. [Separation of verb and object.]

REVISED   After deciding that she could do one but not both, my sister *chose to have children* rather than pursue a career.

FAULTY   Amazingly, the refund from the utility company came *after, only three weeks.* [Separation of preposition and object.]

REVISED   Amazingly, the refund from the utility company came *after only three weeks.*

In the sentence below, commas are needed to set off the nonrestrictive adjective clause that interrupts subject and verb.

Americans, who are preoccupied with football, baseball, basketball, and hockey, have not developed a strong interest in professional soccer.

2
Don't use the comma with words or phrases joined by coordinating conjunctions.

FAULTY	*The defense attorney, and the presiding judge* disagreed with the verdict. [Compound subject.]
REVISED	*The defense attorney and the presiding judge* disagreed with the verdict.
FAULTY	Television advertising is *expensive, and sometimes very effective.* [Compound complement.]
REVISED	Television advertising is *expensive and sometimes very effective.*
FAULTY	The sale of *handguns, and other weapons* is increasing alarmingly. [Compound object of a preposition.]
REVISED	The sale of *handguns and other weapons* is increasing alarmingly.
FAULTY	The boys *hiked up the mountain, and camped for the night* on the summit. [Compound predicate.]
REVISED	The boys *hiked up the mountain and camped for the night* on the summit.
FAULTY	Banks *could, and should* help older people manage their money. [Compound helping verb.]
REVISED	Banks *could and should* help older people manage their money.

21j

(See 21a and 21f, respectively, for the appropriate use of commas with coordinating conjunctions between main clauses and in series.)

3
Don't use the comma to set off restrictive elements.

FAULTY	The land, *that both the Arabs and Israelis claim as theirs,* is mostly arid and unpopulated. [The clause beginning *that* restricts the meaning of the subject *land.*]
REVISED	The land *that both the Arabs and Israelis claim as theirs* is mostly arid and unpopulated.

FAULTY	Hawthorne's work, *The Scarlet Letter,* was the first major American novel. [The title of the novel is essential to distinguish the novel from the rest of Hawthorne's work.]
REVISED	Hawthorne's work *The Scarlet Letter* was the first major American novel.
FAULTY	We stayed, *at the beach,* for two days. [The phrase *at the beach* limits the verb *stayed.*]
REVISED	We stayed *at the beach* for two days.

(See 21c for further discussion of identifying and punctuating nonrestrictive and restrictive elements in sentences.)

4
Don't use the comma before the first or after the last item in a series unless a rule requires it.

FAULTY	The *forsythia, daffodils, and tulips,* turned the garden into a rush of color. [The comma after *tulips* separates subject and verb.]
REVISED	The *forsythia, daffodils, and tulips* turned the garden into a rush of color.
FAULTY	Among other things, the Europeans brought to the New World, *horses, advanced technology, and new disease.* [The comma after *World* separates verb and object.]
REVISED	Among other things, the Europeans brought to the New World *horses, advanced technology, and new disease.*

In the sentence below, the commas before and after the series are necessary because the series is an appositive.

The three major television networks, *ABC, CBS, and NBC,* face fierce competition from the cable networks.

(See 21f for further discussion of punctuating series.)

5
Don't use the comma to set off an indirect quotation or a single word unless it is a nonrestrictive appositive.

INDIRECT QUOTATION

FAULTY	The students asked, why they had to take a test the day before vacation.

21j

REVISED　　　　The students asked why they had to take a test the day before vacation.

QUOTED OR ITALICIZED WORD

FAULTY　　　　James Joyce's story, "Araby," was assigned last year, too. [The story title is a restrictive appositive. The commas imply wrongly that Joyce wrote only one story.]

REVISED　　　　James Joyce's story "Araby" was assigned last year, too.

FAULTY　　　　The word, *open,* can be both a verb and an adjective. [*Open* is a restrictive appositive.]

REVISED　　　　The word *open* can be both a verb and an adjective.

The sentence below requires a comma because the quoted title is a nonrestrictive appositive.

Her only poem about death, "Mourning," was printed in *The New Yorker.*

(See 21c-2 for more on punctuating appositives.)

EXERCISE 13

Revise the sentences below to eliminate needless or misused commas. Circle the number preceding each sentence that is already punctuated correctly.

Example:

The antique mirror, that hung above the fireplace, was destroyed by vandals.

The antique mirror that hung above the fireplace was destroyed by vandals.

1. Classes had to be held, in the hallways, because of the fire damage.
2. Charles Dickens's novel, *David Copperfield,* is still a favorite of generations of readers.
3. The split season after the baseball strike in 1981, gave more teams a chance to win the pennant.
4. The coach said, that next year the team would have a winning season.
5. The mayor apologized to the tourists whose car, trailer, and camping equipment were stolen in the city.
6. The tennis term, *love,* meaning, "zero," comes from the French word, *l'oeuf,* meaning, "the egg."
7. The complicated gears on a ten-speed bicycle, make it difficult to maintain and repair.

8. Cheese, eggs, and milk, are high in cholesterol.
9. Mary bought some of her course books at a used-book store, and borrowed the rest.
10. The runners, long since expected at the finish line, had taken a wrong turn after six miles.
11. After the New Hampshire primary, eliminates some candidates, the presidential race calms down somewhat.
12. The cat brought home a dirty, smelly, sock.
13. The point, of many of F. Scott Fitzgerald's stories, is that having money does not guarantee happiness.
14. Forest fires often benefit, the woods they burn.
15. Guidebooks single out the bird sanctuary north of town, and the marsh south of town.

EXERCISE 14

Insert commas in the paragraphs below wherever they are needed, and eliminate any misused or needless commas.

Ellis Island New York has reopened for business but now the customers are tourists not immigrants. This spot which lies in New York Harbor was the first American soil seen, or touched by many of the nation's immigrants. Though other places also served as ports of entry for foreigners none has the symbolic power of, Ellis Island. Between its opening in 1892 and its closing in 1954, over 20 million people about two-thirds of all immigrants were detained there before taking up their new lives in the United States. Ellis Island processed over 2000 newcomers a day when immigration was at its peak between 1900 and 1920.

As the end of a long voyage and the introduction to the New World Ellis Island must have left something to be desired. The "huddled masses" as the Statue of Liberty calls them indeed were huddled. New arrivals were herded about kept standing in lines for hours or days yelled at and abused. Assigned numbers they submitted their bodies to the pokings and proddings of the silent nurses and doctors, who were charged with ferreting out the slightest sign of sickness, disability or insanity. That test having been passed the immigrants faced interrogation by an official through an interpreter. Those, with names deemed inconveniently long or difficult to pronounce, often found themselves permanently labeled with abbreviations, of their names, or with the names, of their hometowns. But of course millions survived the examination humiliation and confusion, to take the last short boat ride to New York City. For many of them and especially for their descendants Ellis Island eventually became not a nightmare but the place where life began.

21j ⌃

22

The Semicolon

22a

Use the semicolon to separate main clauses not joined by a coordinating conjunction.

Main clauses contain a subject and a predicate and make complete statements (see 5c). They are often linked by a comma and a coordinating conjunction such as *and* or *but* (see 21a). When the coordinating conjunction is omitted, however, the clauses should be linked with a semicolon.

> I was not led to the university by conventional middle-class ambitions; my grip on the middle class was more tenuous than that on the school system. — ROBIN FOX

> Nobody can be promoted to a job until the person who occupies it has left. . . . If that person is about to be fired, then it is sensible to make yourself as different as you can from him; if he is about to be promoted, then it makes sense to pattern your behavior on his; if he is about to retire, you're on your own. — MICHAEL KORDA

(If instead of substituting a semicolon for an omitted conjunction, you use a comma or no punctuation at all, you will produce a comma splice or a run-on sentence. See Chapter 11.)

EXCEPTION: If one or both main clauses are very short, some writers use a comma instead of a semicolon.

The poor live, the rich just exist.

But a semicolon is safer, and it will always be correct.

EXERCISE 1

Insert semicolons or substitute them for commas to separate main clauses in the sentences below.

Example:

One man guided the group another brought up the rear.
One man guided the group; another brought up the rear.

1. Karate is not just a technique for self-defense, like a religion, it teaches inner calm.
2. He is still playing baseball at the age of sixty-three he is still no good.
3. The Himalayas are the loftiest mountain range in the world, they culminate in the highest mountain in the world, Mount Everest.
4. Subways in New York City are noisy, dirty, and dangerous they are also a superbly efficient means of transportation.
5. The pony express was slow but competent the Postal Service is just slow.

EXERCISE 2

Combine each set of three sentences below into one sentence containing only two main clauses, and insert a semicolon between the clauses. You will have to add, delete, change, and rearrange words. Each item has more than one possible answer.

Example:

The city's older neighborhoods offer a lesson in building design. They contain many elegant houses. These houses are sometimes open to visitors.

The city's older neighborhoods offer a lesson in building design; they contain many elegant houses that are sometimes open to visitors.

1. They said they were willing to work. They would work for little pay. The summer had been boring so far.
2. She drove a good car. She wore expensive clothes. She relied on these external symbols to gain her popularity.
3. Indian rugs are deceptively decorative. Their designs have religious meanings for the weavers. The colors also have religious meanings.
4. The storm blew down trees. It blew down all the trees but the poplars. They stood in a row, undamaged.
5. The legend is that Betsy Ross designed the first American flag. The legend is probably untrue. Historians have never found any evidence to support it.

;
22b

22b

Use the semicolon to separate main clauses joined by a conjunctive adverb.

Conjunctive adverbs include *accordingly, besides, consequently, furthermore, hence, however, indeed, instead, moreover, nonetheless, otherwise, still, then, therefore,* and *thus*. (See 5d-2.) When a conjunctive adverb links two main clauses, the clauses should be connected by a semicolon.

> The Labor Department lawyers will be here in a month; *therefore,* the grievance committee should meet as soon as possible.

> For the first time in twenty years, the accident rate in St. Louis did not rise; *indeed,* it actually declined.

The position of the semicolon between main clauses never changes, but the conjunctive adverb may appear in several positions within a clause. When the adverb immediately follows the semicolon, follow the adverb with a comma. When the adverb does not immediately follow the semicolon, surround the adverb with commas or, if the adverb falls at the end of a sentence, precede it with a comma.

> Blue jeans have become fashionable all over the world; *however,* the American originators still wear more jeans than anyone else.

> Blue jeans have become fashionable all over the world; the American originators, *however,* still wear more jeans than anyone else.

> Blue jeans have become fashionable all over the world; the American originators still wear more jeans than anyone else, *however.*

(If you use a comma or no punctuation at all between main clauses connected by a conjunctive adverb, you will produce a comma splice or run-on sentence. See Chapter 11.)

; 22b

EXERCISE 3

Insert semicolons and commas in the following sentences to separate main clauses linked by conjunctive adverbs and to set off the conjunctive adverbs from the rest of the clause they appear in.

> *Example:*
> She had heard that the auditions were going to be mobbed she went early to the gym therefore and was one of the first to try out.

> She had heard that the auditions were going to be mobbed; she went early to the gym, therefore, and was one of the first to try out.

1. Thanksgiving was fewer than three weeks away still they had made no plans for the big turkey dinner.
2. Environmentalists are trying to preserve the meadow outside town moreover they sued some land developers who were planning to build in the city park.
3. The elevator shakes when it goes down the inspector says it is safe however.

4. We must cut down on our fuel consumption otherwise we'll find ourselves with *no* fuel, not just less.
5. The air was suddenly calm consequently we had to paddle our sailboat to shore.

EXERCISE 4

Combine each set of three sentences below into one sentence containing only two main clauses, and link the clauses with a semicolon and the conjunctive adverb in parentheses. (Be sure conjunctive adverbs are punctuated appropriately.) You will have to add, delete, and rearrange words. Each item has more than one possible answer.

Example:

The Russians censor their news. We get little news from them. And what we get is unreliable. (*therefore*)

The Russians censor their news; *therefore,* the little news we get from them is unreliable.

1. They didn't enjoy their first swim in the ocean. They were afraid of the waves. Also, the salty water was unpleasant. (*besides*)
2. He was alarmed by the shadow. It stood suddenly in his path. But he kept walking. (*nonetheless*)
3. My grandfather grew up in Italy. But he never spoke Italian in the United States. He always spoke English. (*instead*)
4. Peanuts thrive in light, sandy soil. They are an ideal crop for the South. In the South such soil is common. (*thus*)
5. The speaker's nervousness showed in his damp brow. His trembling voice also indicated nervousness. His hands shook so badly that he could barely hold his notes. (*moreover*)

22c

Use the semicolon to separate main clauses if they are very long and complex or if they contain commas, even when they are joined by a coordinating conjunction.

You would normally use a comma with *and, but, or, nor,* and *for* between main clauses. But placing semicolons between clauses punctuated with commas or between long and grammatically complicated clauses makes a sentence easier to read.

Lewis and Clark led the men of their party with consummate skill, inspiring and encouraging them, doctoring and caring for them; *and* they kept voluminous notes and journals.   — PAGE SMITH

By a conscious effort of the mind, we can stand aloof from actions and their consequences; *and* all things, good and bad, go by us like a torrent.   — HENRY DAVID THOREAU

Many writers prefer to use a semicolon instead of a comma between main clauses joined by the conjunctions *so* and *yet*, even when the clauses are not internally punctuated or complicated.

The day was rainy and blustery; *so* the food vendors kept their fruits and vegetables indoors.

Three truckloads of supplies arrived at the construction site; *yet* we still did not have enough cement.

EXERCISE 5

Substitute semicolons for commas in the following sentences to separate main clauses that are long or grammatically complicated or that are internally punctuated.

Example:

She enjoyed dancing to popular music, often joined a group for square dancing, and even danced the fox trot with her father and brothers, but she preferred ballet.

She enjoyed dancing to rock music, often joined a group for square dancing, and even danced the fox trot with her father and brothers; but she preferred ballet.

1. By evening, having looked at every house on the realtor's list, the Morianis were exhausted and crabby, but they still hadn't found anything they could afford to buy.

2. James did whatever he wanted, without regard for the feelings or welfare of those around him or for the harm he was doing to himself, and eventually he got in trouble.

3. Seeking lower taxes, businesses moved to the suburbs, and merchants closed their downtown stores in favor of new ones in the shopping mall, and the city's center died.

4. She had a challenging job, a decent income, and good prospects for the future, but she remained miserable.

5. The inside of the dorm has to be cleaned, painted, and furnished by September, or two hundred students will have no place to live.

22c

EXERCISE 6

Combine each set of sentences below into one sentence containing only two main clauses. Link the clauses with a semicolon and the coordinating conjunction in parentheses. You will have to add, delete, and rearrange words. Each item has more than one possible answer.

Example:

The election will be very close. Perhaps it will even be a tie. The nominees have hardly campaigned. They do not seem concerned. (*but*)

The election will be very close, perhaps even a tie; *but* the nominees have hardly campaigned and do not seem concerned.

1. Scientists cannot count the stars, planets, and moons in the universe. They do not have the means. They must rely on estimates. (*so*)
2. Transportation is scarce and expensive in Alaska. One reason is the extremely cold climate. Another is the sparse population. The difficulties of transportation discourage businesses from locating there. (*and*)
3. Legends of the towns of the Old West create a lively picture. The picture consists of constant saloon brawls, bank robberies, and gunfights. The picture is inaccurate. (*but*)
4. Most Americans believe that the Internal Revenue Service reads their tax returns carefully. They believe that the IRS checks and double-checks all the information they provide. The IRS counts on this belief to keep taxpayers honest. (*and*)
5. In the office Mrs. Brown was a tyrant. She expected her subordinates to do exactly as she said. At home she was a pushover. She let her children do whatever they pleased. (*yet*)

22d

Use the semicolon to separate items in a series if they are long or contain commas.

;
22d

You normally use commas to separate items in a series (see 21f). But use semicolons instead when the items are long or internally punctuated. The semicolons help the reader identify the items.

The custody case involved Mark and Amy Dalton, the children; Ellen and George Dalton, the parents; and Ruth and Harold Blum, the grandparents.

One may even reasonably advance the claim that the sort of communication that really counts, and is therefore embodied into permanent records, is primarily written; that "words fly away, but written messages endure," as the Latin saying put it two thousand years ago; and that there is no basic significance to at least fifty per cent of the oral interchange that goes on among all sorts of persons, high and low. — MARIO PEI

EXERCISE 7

Substitute semicolons for commas in the following sentences to separate long or internally punctuated items in a series.

Example:

No public transportation alternative is ideal: Buses are cheap, but they take time, planes are fast, but they cost too much, and trains both take time and cost too much.

No public transportation alternative is ideal: Buses are cheap, but they take time; planes are fast, but they cost too much; and trains both take time and cost too much.

1. The picnic was a disaster from the start because Brian forgot the beach blankets and chairs, Julie forgot the beer, potato salad, and hot dogs, and Sam forgot his bathing suit.
2. The convocation droned on and on, with the college president intoning the challenges of education, the dean, first thanking the president, detailing the joys of education, and the student government president, thanking both the president and the dean, listing students' responsibilities to the college.
3. We have a cat who is the size of a cocker spaniel, with a bark to match, a dog who is so big we can't trust him in the house, and neighbors who, for some reason, won't speak to us.
4. The car, with its headlights out, swerved into oncoming traffic, narrowly missed a large, loaded oil truck, and headed, nose first, into a deep, muddy ditch.
5. The farm we visited has a clear, fast-moving brook, a shallow but clear pond, and trees, hundreds of trees that keep the waters and the house delightfully cool.

EXERCISE 8

Combine each set of sentences below into one sentence that includes a series punctuated with semicolons. You will have to add, delete, and rearrange words. Each item has more than one possible answer.

Example:

He lived in a dream world. It was populated by servants who fulfilled his every wish. Chauffeurs drove him about in expensive, fast cars. Politicians and corporate executives sought his favors.

He lived in a dream world populated by servants who fulfilled his every wish; chauffeurs who drove him about in expensive, fast cars; and politicians and corporate executives who sought his favors.

1. Driving west from Pennsylvania, we saw vast expanses of tall corn and shorter soybean plants. We saw many cows, some horses, and a few sheep grazing in rolling pastures. And sturdy, well-kept houses appeared with matching barns.
2. The campaign took an unexpected turn when three events occurred. The Republican had to undergo an operation that kept her in the hospital for two weeks. The Democrat's wife gave birth to twins, a boy and a girl. And an independent candidate accused the other two of graft.
3. California's Fresno County, the nation's leading county in farm production, produces vegetables such as potatoes and tomatoes. It produces fruits such as figs, peaches, and nectarines. It produces seed crops such as alfalfa, barley, and cotton.

22d

4. When the new building opened, visitors reacted to it. Some visitors reacted with praise for the architect's choice of materials, sense of style, and imagination. Some visitors reacted with criticism of the building's excessive use of glass and too-sharp corners. Some visitors reacted with boredom at the sight of yet another high-rise office tower.

5. With attention and practice we Americans should have no trouble learning the essential metric weights and measures. These include the meter, about 39 inches. They also include the kilogram, about 2.2 pounds, and the liter, about 1.06 quarts.

22e
Avoid misusing or overusing the semicolon.

The semicolon links sentence elements with a longer pause than that signaled by the comma. Misused or overused, the semicolon will halt the flow of a sentence and often confuse the reader.

1
Don't use the semicolon to link subordinate clauses or phrases to main clauses.

FAULTY	According to African authorities; only about 35,000 Pygmies exist today, and their number is dwindling.
REVISED	According to African authorities, only about 35,000 Pygmies exist today, and their number is dwindling.
FAULTY	The world would be less interesting; if clothes were standardized.
REVISED	The world would be less interesting if clothes were standardized.

2
Don't use the semicolon to introduce a list.

Colons and dashes, not semicolons, introduce explanations, lists, and so forth. (See 25a and 25b.)

FAULTY	The teacher had heard all the students' reasons for doing poorly in her course; psychological problems, family illness, too much work, too little time.

REVISED	The teacher had heard all the students' reasons for doing poorly in her course: psychological problems, family illness, too much work, too little time.
REVISED	The teacher had heard all the students' reasons for doing poorly in her course — psychological problems, family illness, too much work, too little time.

3
Don't overuse the semicolon.

Use the semicolon only occasionally and only when required by a rule. Too many semicolons, even when they are required by rule, often indicate repetitive sentence structure. Compare these two versions of the same paragraph. The first overuses the semicolon. The second, with fewer semicolons, is clearer and contains more varied sentences.

We live in an industrialized and urbanized society; men and women no longer share in tasks of production in accordance with strength and ability. The man disappears to the factory or office; the woman concentrates exclusively on managing consumption. This is a conventional arrangement; it is not an efficiently necessary division of labor; at a simple level of consumption it is perfectly possible for one person to do both. The family retains other purposes, including those of love, sex, and child rearing; however, it is no longer an economic necessity.

With industrialization and urbanization, men and women no longer share in tasks of production in accordance with strength and ability. The man disappears to the factory or office; the woman concentrates exclusively on managing consumption. This is a conventional arrangement, not an efficiently necessary division of labor; at a simple level of consumption it is perfectly possible for one person to do both. Without denying that the family retains other purposes, including those of love, sex, and child rearing, it is no longer an economic necessity.
— JOHN KENNETH GALBRAITH

EXERCISE 9

Revise the sentences or groups of sentences below to eliminate misused or overused semicolons, substituting other punctuation as appropriate.

Example:

The table was ready to be stained; all the old finish had been removed, the raw wood had been sanded smooth, and the dust had been wiped off with a clean rag.

The table was ready to be stained; All the old finish had been removed, the raw wood had been sanded smooth, and the dust had been wiped off with a clean rag.

1. Thinking of her future; Marie decided to major in economics.
2. The bus line finally went out of business; because more and more students drove themselves to school.
3. Even though the National League usually wins the All-Star Game; I think the American League is superior.
4. Despite all our grasping for material goods, only three things are necessary for survival; sound shelter, warm clothes, and simple food.
5. Walking is great fun; we don't do enough of it. You see things when you're walking that you don't see when you're driving; you can smell and feel different things, too. Walking makes you a part of life; driving just races you through it.

EXERCISE 10

Insert semicolons in the paragraph below wherever they are needed. Eliminate any misused or needless semicolons, substituting other punctuation as appropriate.

The movie's set, sounds, and actors captured the essence of horror films. The set was ideal; dark, deserted streets, trees dipping their branches over the sidewalks, mist hugging the ground and creeping up to meet the trees, looming shadows of unlighted, turreted houses. The sounds, too, were appropriate, especially terrifying was the hard, hollow sound of footsteps echoing throughout the film. But the movie's best feature was its actors; all of them tall, pale, and thin to the point of emaciation. With one exception, they were dressed uniformly in gray and had gray hair. The exception was an actress who dressed only in black; as if to set off her pale yellow, nearly white, long hair; the only color in the film. The glinting black eyes of another actor stole almost every scene, indeed, they were the source of all the film's mischief.

;
22e

23

The Apostrophe

23a
Use the apostrophe to indicate the possessive case for nouns and indefinite pronouns.

The **possessive case** shows ownership or possession of one person or thing by another (see Chapter 6). Possession may be shown with an *of* phrase (*the hair of the dog*); or it may be shown with the addition of an apostrophe and, usually, an *-s* (*the dog's hair*)

1
Add -'s to form the possessive case of singular or plural nouns or indefinite pronouns *not* ending in -s.

The *cat's* paw was mangled.
He was fired after a *week's* work.
The *children's* parents performed *Snow White.*
Laura felt she was *no one's* friend.

2
Add -'s to form the possessive case of singular words ending in -s.

Henry *James's* novels reward the patient reader.
Doris's term paper was read aloud in our English class.
The *business's* customers filed suit.

EXCEPTION: We typically do not pronounce the possessive *-s* of a few singular nouns ending in an *s* or *z* sound, especially when these nouns are followed by a word beginning in *s*. In these cases, add only the apostrophe to indicate possession.

> For *conscience'* sake she confessed her lie.
>
> *Jesus'* moral principles guide the behavior of people even today.
>
> Two thousand years after it was written, *Aristophanes'* humor can still hit the mark.

3

Add only an apostrophe to form the possessive case of plural words ending in *-s*.

> The *teachers'* association called a strike.
>
> *Workers'* incomes have risen over the past decade but not fast enough.
>
> She took two *years'* leave from school.
>
> The *Murphys'* car was stolen.

4

Add *-'s* only to the last word to form the possessive case of compound words or word groups.

> My *father-in-law's* birthday was yesterday.
> The *council president's* address was a bore.
> Go bang on *somebody else's* door.

5

When two or more words show individual possession, add *-'s* to them all. If they show joint possession, add *-'s* only to the last word.

INDIVIDUAL POSSESSION

Harry's and *Gerry's* dentists both use hypnotism. [Harry and Gerry have different dentists.]

JOINT POSSESSION

That living room is an example of *John and Martha's* bad taste. [John and Martha are jointly responsible for the living room.]

EXERCISE 1

Form the possessive case of each word or word group in parentheses below.

Example:
The (*men*) team lost to the (*women*).
The *men's* team lost to the *women's*.

1. The (*mayor*) announcement was expected.
2. Higher pay and three (*weeks*) vacation were the focus of the (*garbage collectors*) strike.
3. John (*Adams*) letters to his wife illuminate his character.
4. Her (*sister-in-law*) family was wealthy.
5. (*Everyone*) books were stolen from the gym.
6. The (*Reagans*) life-style was often criticized.
7. (*Children*) clothes are ridiculously expensive.
8. (*Marvin and Colleen*) child has a learning disability.
9. (*Susan and Sarah*) husbands are both out of work.
10. The (*utility companies*) recent price increases are unlawful.
11. We studied (*Keats*) poetry.
12. An (*hour*) reading was the only assignment.
13. (*Charles*) new car was a lemon.
14. The (*Hickses*) decision to move upset their children.
15. For (*goodness*) sake, don't holler.

23b

Don't use the apostrophe in forming noun plurals or the possessive case of personal pronouns.

The plurals of nouns are generally formed by adding -*s* or -*es* (*boys, Smiths, families, Joneses*). Don't mistakenly add an apostrophe to form the plural.

FAULTY   The unleashed *dog's* began traveling in a pack.

REVISED   The unleashed *dogs* began traveling in a pack.

His, hers, its, ours, yours, theirs, and *whose* are possessive forms of the personal pronouns. They do not need apostrophes.

FAULTY   Credit for discovering the house is really *her's.*

REVISED   Credit for discovering the house is really *hers.*

The personal pronouns are often confused with contractions. See 23c below.

EXERCISE 2

Revise the sentences below to correct mistakes in the formation of plurals or of the possessive case of personal pronouns. Circle the number preceding any sentence that is already correct.

Example:
Was the responsibility their's?
Was the responsibility *theirs?*

1. The neatest room was her's.
2. Its color was shocking.
3. The White's yard made our's look good.
4. Theirs was far messier.
5. Book's can be good friend's.
6. The schools in the district offer no music courses.
7. Some of the world's people live in nearly uninhabitable climates.
8. Street crime was a particular focus of their's.
9. Open crate's, each with it's contents intact, cluttered my grandmother's attic.
10. Its rough wood floor was barely visible.

23c

Use the apostrophe to indicate the omission of one or more letters, numbers, or words in standard contractions.

it is	it's	does not	doesn't
they are	they're	were not	weren't
you are	you're	class of 1987	class of '87
who is	who's	of the clock	o'clock
cannot	can't	madam	ma'am

Contractions of verb phrases (*don't won't, isn't*) and of pronoun-verb pairs (*I'll, we're, she's*) are common in speech and in informal writing. They may also be used to relax style in more formal kinds of writing, as they are in this handbook. But be aware that many people disapprove of contractions in any kind of formal writing.

NOTE: Don't confuse the personal pronouns *its, their, your,* and *whose* with the contractions *it's, they're, you're,* and *who's.*

FAULTY   *It's* place of origin is not *you're* problem or *they're* problem. But *who's* is it?

REVISED   *Its* place of origin is not *your* problem or *their* problem. But *whose* is it?

EXERCISE 3

Form contractions from each set of words below. Use each contraction in a complete sentence.

Example:
we are
we're
We're open to ideas.

1. they are
2. he is
3. she will
4. is not

5. cannot
6. should not
7. hurricane of
   1962

8. we would
9. will not
10. are not

EXERCISE 4

Revise the sentences below to correct mistakes in the use of contractions and personal pronouns. Circle the number preceding any sentence that is already correct.

Example:
The cat darted suddenly from it's resting place.
The cat darted suddenly from *its* resting place.

1. They're hope for financial aid was dashed.
2. The investigators wondered whose gun it was.
3. Its a wonder that any rivers remain unspoiled.
4. The college will grant you admission whenever your ready.
5. Business is a good major because it's certain that corporations will always need competent managers.
6. The Soltis, who's daughter was married last year, retired to Florida.
7. Now, months after the flood, their finally moving back home.
8. When it's star halfback was injured, the team fell apart.
9. The only way of avoiding a fine is to pay you're taxes on time.
10. The children know its time for bed when the clock strikes eight times.

23d

Use the apostrophe plus -*s* to form the plurals of letters, numbers, and words named as words.

That sentence has too many *but*'s.

At the end of each chapter the author had written two *3*'s.

Remember to dot your *i*'s and to cross your *t*'s, or your readers may not be able to distinguish them from *e*'s and *l*'s.

Notice that the letters, numbers, and words are italicized (underlined in typed or handwritten copy) but that the apostrophe and added -*s* are not. (See 27d on this use of italics or underlining.)

EXCEPTION: References to the years in a decade are not italicized and often omit the apostrophe. Thus either *1960's* or *1960s* is acceptable as long as usage is consistent.

EXERCISE 5

Form the plural of each letter, number, or word by using an apostrophe and -*s* and by underlining (italicizing) appropriately. Use the new plural in a complete sentence.

> *Example:*   x
> Erase or white out typing mistakes. Do not use *x*'s.

1. and
2. q
3. if
4. 4
5. stop

EXERCISE 6

Correct any mistakes in the use of the apostrophe or any confusion between personal pronouns and contractions in the paragraph below.

Landlocked Chad is among the worlds most troubled countries. The people's of Chad are poor: They're average per capita income equals $73 a year. No more than 15 percent of Chads population is literate, and every thousand people must share only two teacher's. The natural resources of the nation have never been plentiful, and now, as its slowly being absorbed into the growing Sahara Desert, even water is scarce. Chads political conflicts go back beyond the turn of the century, when the French colonized the land by brutally subduing it's people. The rule of the French — who's inept government of the colony did nothing to ease tensions among racial, tribal, and religious group's — ended with independence in 1960. But since then the Chadians experience has been one of civil war and oppression, and now their threatened with invasions from they're neighbors.

23d

24
Quotation Marks

The principal function of quotation marks — either double (" ") or single (' ') — is to enclose direct quotations from speech and from writing. Always use quotation marks in pairs, one at the beginning of a quotation and one at the end.

(Several quotation practices are discussed in the appropriate sections of this book. See 25d for the use of brackets within quotations to separate your own comments from the words of the author you quote. See 25e for the use of the ellipsis mark [. . .] to indicate an omission from a quotation. And see 35g-? for information on integrating quotations into your own writing.)

24a

Use double quotation marks to enclose direct quotations.

Direct quotations report what someone has said or written in the exact words of the original. Always enclose direct quotations in quotation marks.

> "If a sentence does not illuminate your subject in some new and useful way," says Kurt Vonnegut, "scratch it out."

Indirect quotations report what has been said or written, but not in the exact words. Indirect quotations are *not* enclosed in quotation marks.

> Kurt Vonnegut advises inexperienced writers to scratch out any sentence that does not illuminate their subject in some new and useful way.

341

24b

Use single quotation marks to enclose a quotation within a quotation.

When you quote a writer or speaker, use double quotation marks (see 24a). When the material you quote contains yet another quotation, enclose the second quotation in single quotation marks.

> "In formulating any philosophy," Woody Allen writes, "the first consideration must always be: What can we know? . . . Descartes hinted at the problem when he wrote, 'My mind can never know my body, although it has become quite friendly with my legs.' "

Notice that two quotation marks appear at the end of the sentence — one single (to finish the interior quotation) and one double (to finish the main quotation).

EXERCISE 1

Insert single and double quotation marks as needed in the following sentences. Circle the number preceding each sentence that is already correct.

Example:

Shakespeare's phrase salad days to describe youth means more to me as I grow older, Mr. Bowman said.

"Shakespeare's phrase 'salad days' to describe youth means more to me as I grow older," Mr. Bowman said.

1. She tells us, Dance is poetry, Marsha said, but I don't understand what she means.
2. Mark Twain quipped, Reports of my death are greatly exaggerated.
3. We shall overcome, sang the civil rights workers of the 1960s. I think we should still be singing those words.
4. After a long pause he said that the man in the red shirt had stolen the car.
5. Now that spring is here, Ms. Radley said, we can hold classes on the lawn.

" "
24c

24c

Set off quotations of dialogue, poetry, and long prose passages according to standard practice.

Dialogue

When quoting conversations, begin a new paragraph for each speaker.

"Say something, son," the detective said.
"I didn't hold this guy up," said the suspect in a dead voice.
— BERNARD MALAMUD

NOTE: When you quote a single speaker for more than one paragraph, put quotation marks at the beginning of each paragraph but at the end of only the last paragraph. The absence of quotation marks at the end of each paragraph but the last tells readers that the speech is continuing.

Poetry

When you quote a single line from a poem, song, or verse play, place the line in the running text and enclose it in quotation marks.

Dylan Thomas remembered childhood as an idyllic time, "About the lilting house and happy as the grass was green."

Poetry quotations of two or three lines may be placed in the text or displayed separately. If you place such a quotation in the text, enclose it in quotation marks, and indicate the end of the first line with a slash (see 25f).

Robert Frost's incisiveness shows in two lines from "Death of the Hired Man": "Home is the place where, when you have to go there, / They have to take you in."

To separate the quotation from the text, insert space above and below it and indent it from the left margin.

24c

Robert Frost's incisiveness shows in two lines from "Death of the Hired Man":

> Home is the place where, when you have to go there,
> They have to take you in.

The *MLA Handbook*, the standard guide to manuscript format in English and some other disciplines, recommends the following spacings for displayed quotations in research papers: Triple-space above and below the quotation, indent it ten spaces from the left margin, and double-space the quoted lines. Unless your instructor specifies otherwise, follow these guidelines as well in shorter essays, both typewritten and handwritten. (See Chapter 35, p. 498, for an example of a displayed quotation in a typed paper.)

Always set off and indent quotations of more than three lines of poetry, using the format given above.

Emily Dickinson rarely needed more than a few lines to express her complex thoughts:

> To wait an Hour – is long –
> If Love be just beyond –
> To wait Eternity – is short –
> If Love reward the end –

NOTE: Be careful when quoting poetry to reproduce faithfully all line indentions, space between lines, spelling, capitalization, and punctuation, such as the capitals and dashes in the Dickinson poem above.

Long prose passages

Separate a prose quotation of more than four typed or handwritten lines from the body of your paper. Following the guidelines of the *MLA Handbook* (see above), triple-space above and below the quotation, indent it ten spaces from the left margin, and double-space the quoted lines. Don't add quotation marks.

While deploring the effects of the social sciences on English prose style, Malcolm Cowley can still use his sense of humor:

> Considering this degradation of the verb, I have wondered how one of Julius Caesar's boasts could be translated into Socspeak. What Caesar wrote was *"Veni, vidi, vici"* — only three words, all of them verbs. The English translation is in six words: "I came, I saw, I conquered," and three of the words are first-personal pronouns, which the sociologist is taught to avoid. I suspect that he would have to write: "Upon the advent of the investigator, his hegemony became minimally coextensive with the areal unit rendered visible by his successive displacements in space."

" "
24d

EXERCISE 2

Practice using quotation marks in quoted dialogue, poetry, and long prose passages by completing each of the exercises below.
1. Write a short sketch of dialogue between two people.
2. Write a sentence that quotes a single line of poetry.
3. Write two sentences, each quoting the same two lines of poetry. In one, place the poetry lines in the text. In the other, separate the two lines from the text.
4. Write a sentence introducing a prose passage of over four lines, and then set up the quotation appropriately.

24d

Put quotation marks around the titles of songs, short poems, articles in periodicals, short stories, essays, episodes of television and radio programs, and the subdivisions of books.

SONGS

"Lucy in the Sky with Diamonds"
"Mr. Bojangles"

SHORT POEMS

" Stopping by Woods on a Snowy Evening"
" Sunday Morning"

ARTICLES IN PERIODICALS

" Comedy and Tragedy Transposed" (in *The Yale Review*)
" Does 'Scaring' Work?" (in *Newsweek*)

SHORT STORIES

" The Battler"
" The Gift of the Magi"

ESSAYS

" Politics and the English Language"
" Joey: A 'Mechanical Boy' "

EPISODES OF TELEVISION AND RADIO PROGRAMS

" The Mexican Connection" (on *60 Minutes*)
" Cooking with Clams" (on *Eating In*)

SUBDIVISIONS OF BOOKS

" Voyage to the Houyhnhnms" (Part IV of *Gulliver's Travels*)
" The Mast Head" (Chapter 35 of *Moby Dick*)

See 27a on the use of italics (or underlining) for all other titles. And see 26b for guidelines on the use of capital letters in titles.

" "

24e

24e

Occasionally, quotation marks may be used to enclose defined words and words used in a special sense.

By " charity," I mean the love of one's neighbor as oneself.
An architect refers to one view of a building as its " aspect."
Pardon my pun, but I find that lawyer " appealing."

NOTE: In definitions, italics (or underlining) are more common than quotation marks (see 27d).

By *charity*, I mean the love of one's neighbor as oneself.
An architect refers to one view of a building as its *aspect*.

EXERCISE 3

Insert quotation marks as needed for titles and words in the sentences below. If quotation marks should be used instead of italics, insert them.

Example:
How can you call him sir when he doesn't show any respect for you?

How can you call him "sir" when he doesn't show any respect for you?

1. Doom means simply judgment as well as unhappy destiny.
2. The article that appeared in *Mental Health* was titled *Children of Divorce Ask, "Why?"*
3. The encyclopedia's discussion under Modern Art filled less than a column.
4. In Chapter 2, titled *The Waiter,* the novelist introduces the villain.
5. The Rolling Stones perform Satisfaction at almost all their concerts.

24f
Avoid using quotation marks where they are not required.

Don't use quotation marks in the titles of your papers unless they contain or are themselves direct quotations.

Not	"The Death Wish in One Poem by Robert Frost"
But	The Death Wish in One Poem by Robert Frost
Or	The Death Wish in "Stopping by Woods on a Snowy Evening"

66 99

24f

Don't use quotation marks to enclose common nicknames or technical terms that are not being defined.

Not	Even as president, "Jimmy" Carter preferred to use his nickname.
But	Even as president, Jimmy Carter preferred to use his nickname.
Not	"Mitosis" in a cell is fascinating to watch.
But	Mitosis in a cell is fascinating to watch.

Don't use quotation marks in an attempt to justify or apologize for the use of slang and trite expressions that are inappropriate to your writing. If slang is appropriate, use it without quotation marks.

Not	It "rained cats and dogs" for the whole week, so we did not make any "bread" in our temporary construction jobs.
But	It rained hard for the whole week, so we did not make any money in our temporary construction jobs.

(See 31a-1 and 31b-5 for a discussion of slang and trite expressions.)

24g

Place other marks of punctuation inside or outside quotation marks according to standard practice.

1

Place commas and periods inside quotation marks.

"Your first check will come next month," the social worker said.
Without pausing he pointed and said, "That's the man."

(See 21h for the use of commas to separate quotations from words used to introduce or explain them.)

2

Place colons and semicolons outside quotation marks.

A few years ago the slogan in elementary education was "learning by playing"; now educators are concerned with teaching basic skills.
We all know what is meant by "inflation": More money buys less.

3

Place dashes, question marks, and exclamation points inside quotation marks only if they belong to the quotation.

When a dash, question mark, or exclamation point is part of the quotation, put it *inside* quotation marks.

"But must you —" Marcia hesitated, afraid of the answer.
"Who is she really?" he mused.
"Go away!" I yelled.

When a dash, question mark, or exclamation point applies only to the larger sentence, not to the quotation, place it *outside* quotation marks.

One of the most evocative lines in English poetry — "After many a summer dies the swan"— was written by Alfred, Lord Tennyson.
Who said, "Now cracks a noble heart"?
Believe it or not, she even said, "I'll have you fired"!

EXERCISE 4

Revise the sentences below for the proper use of quotation marks. Insert quotation marks where they are needed, remove them when they are not needed, and be sure that other marks of punctuation are correctly placed inside or outside the quotation marks. Circle the number preceding any sentence that is already punctuated correctly.

Example:

In America the signs say, Keep off the grass; in England they say, Please refrain from stepping on the lawn.

In America the signs say, "Keep off the grass"; in England they say, "Please refrain from stepping on the lawn."

1. In *King Richard II* Shakespeare calls England This precious stone set in the silver sea.
2. The doctors gave my father an "electrocardiogram" but found nothing wrong.
3. The commercial says, Aspirin will relieve the pain of neuritis and neuralgia; but what are they?
4. In his three-piece suit he looked like a real "man about town."
5. Poe's story The Tell-Tale Heart has terrorized more than a few readers.
6. Years ago an advertising campaign said, The family that prays together stays together; today born-again Christians are saying the same thing.
7. You — come here! David commanded.
8. Our forests — in Longfellow's words, "The murmuring pines and the hemlocks" — are slowly succumbing to land development.
9. Must we regard the future with what Kierkegaard called fear and trembling?
10. My son asked, What sort of person would hurt an animal?

" "

24g

EXERCISE 5

Insert quotation marks where they are needed in the paragraph below.

In one class we talked about two lines from Shakespeare's Sonnet 55:

Not marble, nor the gilded monuments
Of princes, shall outlive this powerful rime.

Why is this true? the teacher asked. Why does Shakespeare's powerful rime indeed live longer than the gilded monuments / Of princes? She then asked if the lines were protected only by Shakespeare's status as our greatest writer. No, said one student. It has more to do with the power of the language. Then another student added, Even though paper is less durable than stone, ideas are more durable than monuments to dead princes. The whole discussion was an eye opener for some of us (including me) who had never given much credit to rhymes or the words that made them.

25

Other Punctuation Marks

THE COLON

25a

Use the colon to introduce and to separate.

1

Use the colon to introduce summaries, explanations, series, appositives ending sentences, long or formal quotations, and statements introduced by *the following* or *as follows*.

SUMMARY

The facts can lead us to only one conclusion: We're putting more cancer-causing chemicals into our bodies and they're doing their work superbly.

EXPLANATION

The conditioning starts very early: with the girl child who wants the skin that Ivory soap has reputedly given her mother, with the nine-year-old who brings back a cake of Camay instead of the male deodorant her father wanted.　　　— MARYA MANNES

SERIES

It is impossible to dissociate language from science or science from language, because every natural science always involves three things: the sequence of phenomena on which the science is based; the abstract concepts which call these phenomena to mind; and the words in which the concepts are expressed.

— ANTOINE LAVOISIER

FINAL APPOSITIVE

Two chief elements make work interesting: first, the exercise of skill, and second, construction.　　　— BERTRAND RUSSELL

LONG OR FORMAL QUOTATIONS

Scarcely had the moon flight been achieved before one U.S. senator boldly announced: "We are the masters of the universe. We can go anywhere we choose." — LOREN EISELEY

STATEMENT INTRODUCED BY *THE FOLLOWING* OR *AS FOLLOWS*

The relation between leisure and income is as follows: The quality of play depends on the quantity of pay.

NOTE: Usage varies on whether to begin a complete sentence following a colon with a capital letter or a small letter. Either is acceptable.

2
Use the colon to separate subtitles and titles, the subdivisions of time, and the parts of biblical citations.

TITLES AND SUBTITLES

Charles Dickens: An Introduction to His Novels
Eros and Civilization: A Philosophical Inquiry into Freud

TIME	BIBLICAL CITATIONS
1:30	Isaiah 28:1–6
12:26	1 Corinthians 3:6–7

25a.

3
Avoid misusing the colon.

Use the colon only at the end of an independent clause. Avoid using it between a verb and its object or between a preposition and its object.

NOT	Three entertaining movies, all directed by Stephen Spielberg, are: *E.T., Close Encounters of the Third Kind,* and *Raiders of the Lost Ark.*
BUT	Three entertaining movies, all directed by Stephen Spielberg, are *E.T., Close Encounters of the Third Kind,* and *Raiders of the Lost Ark.*
NOT	Shakespeare showed the qualities of a Renaissance man, such as: humanism and a deep interest in classical Greek and Roman literature.
BUT	Shakespeare showed the qualities of a Renaissance man, such as humanism and a deep interest in classical Greek and Roman literature.

EXERCISE 1

Insert colons as needed in the sentences below.

Example:

You can find the state park as follows get on the expressway going south, take Exit 27, and drive 20 miles due east.

You can find the state park as follows: Get on the expressway going south, take Exit 27, and drive 20 miles due east.

1. He concluded with an ultimatum "Either improve the mass transit system, or anticipate further decay in your downtown area."
2. He based his prediction of the Second Coming on John 21 17–30.
3. She left her cottage at 800 in the morning with only one goal in mind to murder the man who was blackmailing her.
4. After providing a general view of the harbor, the author then describes: the deck of the ship, its rigging, and the men on board.
5. The Pilgrims had one major reason for coming to the New World they sought religious freedom.

THE DASH

25b

Use the dash or dashes to indicate sudden changes in tone or thought and to set off some sentence elements.

1

Use the dash or dashes to indicate sudden shifts in tone, new or unfinished thoughts, and hesitation in dialogue.

SHIFT IN TONE

He tells us— does he really mean it?— that he will speak the truth from now on.

UNFINISHED THOUGHT

If she found out— he did not want to think about what she would do.

HESITATION IN DIALOGUE

"I was worried you might think I had stayed away because I was influenced by— " he stopped and lowered his eyes.

Astonished, Howe said, "Influenced by what?"

"Well, by— " Blackburn hesitated and for answer pointed to the table.   — LIONEL TRILLING

2

Use the dash or dashes to emphasize appositives and parenthetical expressions.

APPOSITIVES

The year of her birth — 1945 — also marked the end of World War II.

The qualities Monet painted — sunlight, rich shadows, deep colors — were abundant around the rivers and gardens he used as subjects.

PARENTHETICAL EXPRESSIONS

Though they are close together — separated by only a few blocks — the two neighborhoods might as well exist in different countries.

At any given time there exists an inventory of undiscovered embezzlement in — or more precisely not in — the country's businesses and banks. This inventory — it should perhaps be called the bezzle — amounts at any moment to millions of dollars.

— JOHN KENNETH GALBRAITH

(See also 21c on commas and 25c on parentheses.)

3

Use the dash to set off introductory series and summaries.

INTRODUCTORY SERIES

Shortness of breath, skin discoloration or the sudden appearance of moles, persistent indigestion, the presence of small lumps — can signify cancer.

SUMMARY

It was love on the run, love on the lam, love in a pressure cooker, love on the barricades, love all mixed up with political passion and suicidal despair, love born of broken hearts and cracking brains — for all of them the most intense emotional experience of their short lives.

— SHANA ALEXANDER

4

Avoid misusing or overusing the dash.

Don't use the dash when commas, semicolons, and periods are more appropriate. And don't use too many dashes. They can create a jumpy or breathy quality in writing.

NOT   In all his life — eighty-seven years — my great-grandfather never allowed his picture to be taken — not even once. He claimed the "black box" — the camera — would steal his soul.

But   In all his eighty-seven years my great-grandfather did not allow his picture to be taken even once. He claimed the "black box" — the camera — would steal his soul.

EXERCISE 2

Insert dashes as needed in the sentences below.

Example:

What would we do if someone like Adolf Hitler that monster appeared among us?

What would we do if someone like Adolf Hitler — that monster — appeared among us?

1. The religious I should say fanatic quality of their belief was almost frightening.
2. The three cats on the ledge one Persian, one Siamese, and one Manx make a pleasant late-afternoon picture.
3. Carnivals, circuses, rodeos, amusement parks all the wonders of childhood Joey had seen.
4. "The dream just" she paused, then continued slowly. "Actually, it terrifies me."
5. To feed, clothe, and find shelter for the needy these are real achievements.

PARENTHESES

25c

Use parentheses to enclose nonessential elements within sentences.

1

Use parentheses to enclose parenthetical expressions.

Parenthetical expressions include explanations, facts, minor digressions, and examples that may aid understanding but are not essential to meaning.

EXPLANATION

He drove trucks (tractor-trailers, actually) to earn money for college tuition.

FACT

The population of Philadelphia (now about 1.7 million) has been declining steadily since 1950.

MINOR DIGRESSION

Queen Victoria's death in 1901 (a traumatic event for the British people) more or less officially ended the historical period since named for her.

EXAMPLE

Unlike the creatures (some insects, for instance) that have been unchanged for five, ten, even fifty million years, man has changed over this time-scale out of all recognition.   — JACOB BRONOWSKI

Be careful not to misuse or overuse parenthetical expressions. Their content may not be essential to your meaning, but it should be relevant. Too many parenthetical expressions, even relevant ones, can weigh down your sentences or make them choppy.

NOTE: Don't put a comma before a parenthetical expression enclosed in parentheses.

> **NOT**   The dungeon, (really the basement) haunted us.
>
> **BUT**   The dungeon (really the basement) haunted us.

A comma or period falling after a parenthetical expression should be placed outside the closing parenthesis.

> We received numerous complaints (125 to be exact), but most harped on the same old theme (namely, high prices).

( )
25c

When it falls between other complete sentences, a complete sentence enclosed in parentheses has a capital letter and end punctuation.

> In general, coaches will tell you that scouts are just guys who can't coach. (But then, so are brain surgeons.)   — ROY BLOUNT, JR.

(See also 21c-3 and 25b-2 for the uses of commas and dashes, respectively, to set off parenthetical expressions. Both give the content of the expression more emphasis than parentheses do, and dashes are more emphatic than commas.)

2

Use parentheses to enclose letters and figures labeling items in lists within sentences.

My father could not, for his own special reasons, even *like* me. He spent the first twenty-five years of my life acting out that painful fact. Then he arrived at two points in his own life: (1) his last years, and (2) the realization that he had made a tragic mistake.
— RAY WEATHERLY

When lists are set off from the text, the numbers or letters labeling them are usually not enclosed in parentheses.

EXERCISE 3

Insert parentheses as needed in the sentences below.

Example:

Students can find good-quality, inexpensive furniture for example, desks, tables, chairs, sofas, even beds in junk stores.

Students can find good-quality, inexpensive furniture (for example, desks, tables, chairs, sofas, even beds) in junk stores.

1. Our present careless use of coal and oil will lead to a series of unpleasant events: 1 all of us will have to cut back drastically on our use of resources; 2 only the rich will have access to these resources; and 3 no one will have access to them for they will be exhausted.
2. Some exotic pets monkeys and fragile breeds of dog require too much care to be enjoyable.
3. Charles Darwin's *On the Origin of Species* 1859 remains a controversial book to this day.
4. The Rocky Mountains and they are rocky look ominous as well as beautiful.
5. The Hundred Years' War 1337–1453 between England and France was not a continuous war but a series of widely spaced battles.

[ ]
25d

BRACKETS

25d

Use brackets only within quotations to separate your own comments from the words of the writer you quote.

If you need to explain, clarify, or correct the words of the writer you quote, place your additions in brackets.

"That Texaco station [just outside Chicago] is one of the busiest in the nation," said a company spokesman.

You may also use a bracketed word or words to substitute for parts of the original quotation that would otherwise be unclear. In the sentence below, the bracketed word substitutes for *they* in the original.

"Despite considerable achievements in other areas, [humans] still cannot control the weather."

The word *sic* (Latin for "in this manner") in brackets indicates that an error in the quotation appeared in the original and was not made by you.

> According to the newspaper report, "The car slammed thru [*sic*] the railing and into oncoming traffic."

But don't use *sic* to make fun of a writer or to note errors in a passage that is clearly nonstandard or illiterate.

THE ELLIPSIS MARK

25e

Use the ellipsis mark to indicate omissions within quotations.

The **ellipsis mark** consists of three spaced periods (. . .). It is used most often to show that something has been left out of a quotation.

ORIGINAL QUOTATION

"It took four years for Bernice Gera to walk onto that ball field, four years of legal battles for the right to stand in the shadow of an 'Enjoy Silver Floss Sauerkraut' sign while the crowd cheered and young girls waved sheets reading 'Right On, Bernice!' and the manager of the Geneva Phillies welcomed her to the game. 'On behalf of professional baseball,' he said, 'we say good luck and God bless you in your chosen profession.' And the band played and the spotlights shone and all three networks recorded the event. Bernice Gera had become the first woman in the 133-year history of the sport to umpire a professional baseball game."

— NORA EPHRON

OMISSION OF PART OF A SENTENCE

"Bernice Gera had become the first woman . . . to umpire a professional baseball game."

OMISSION OF TWO SENTENCES

"It took four years for Bernice Gera to walk onto that ball field, four years of legal battles for the right to stand in the shadow of an 'Enjoy Silver Floss Sauerkraut' sign while the crowd cheered and young girls waved sheets reading 'Right On, Bernice!' and the manager of the Geneva Phillies welcomed her to the game. . . . Bernice Gera had become the first woman in the 133-year history of the sport to umpire a professional baseball game."

Notice that when the ellipsis mark follows a sentence, as in the example immediately above, four equally spaced periods result: the sentence period (closed up to the last word of the sentence) and the three periods of the ellipsis mark. Notice also that although Ephron's essay goes on after the quoted paragraph, an ellipsis mark is not used at the end of the quotation.

If you omit one or more lines of poetry or paragraphs of prose from a quotation, use a separate line of ellipsis marks across the full width of the quotation to show the omission.

NOTE: Pauses and unfinished statements in quoted speech may be indicated with the ellipsis mark. (See 25b-1 for the use of the dash for this purpose.)

"I wish . . ." His voice trailed off.

EXERCISE 4

To practice using ellipsis marks to show omissions from quotations, follow each instruction below, using the following paragraph by Stewart Udall.

> The most common trait of all primitive peoples is a reverence for the life-giving earth, and the native American shared this elemental ethic: the land was alive to his loving touch, and he, its son, was brother to all creatures. His feelings were made visible in medicine bundles and dance rhythms for rain, and all of his religious rites and land attitudes savored the inseparable world of nature and God, the master of life. During the long Indian tenure the land remained undefiled save for scars no deeper than the scratches of cornfield clearings or the farming canals of the Hohokams on the Arizona desert.   — STEWART UDALL

1. Quote the first sentence from the paragraph, but omit the words *its son* (and punctuation as necessary). Show the omission with an ellipsis mark.
2. Quote the paragraph, but omit the second sentence. Show the omission with an ellipsis mark.

THE SLASH

25f

Use the slash between options and to separate lines of poetry that are run in to the text.

OPTION

I don't know why some teachers oppose pass /fail courses.

NOTE: The options *and/or* and *he/she* should be avoided. (See the Glossary of Usage, pp. 548 and 554.)

POETRY

More than fifty years after its introduction, people are still baffled by E. E. Cummings's unique form of expression, as in lines like "next to of course god america i **/** love you land of the pilgrims' and so forth oh."

(See 24c for more on quoting poetry.)

EXERCISE 5

Insert colons, dashes, parentheses, brackets, ellipsis marks, or slashes as needed in the sentences below, or remove them where they are not needed. When two or more different marks would be appropriate in the same place, be able to defend the choice you make. Circle the number preceding any sentence that is already correct as written.

> *Example:*
>
> The sidewalks of Venice some as old as the city are regularly immersed in water from flooded canals.
>
> The sidewalks of Venice — some as old as the city — are regularly immersed in water from flooded canals. [Dashes set off and emphasize the parenthetical expression.]

1. The old Sorensen mansion has all the qualities of a building destined for demolition it is vacant, it is decrepit, the taxes on it are high, and the land under it is immensely valuable.
2. "Barbra Streisand's sole talent . . . . is singing."
3. "Buy the new Universal Dictionery *sic*," the ad said. But how could anybody buy a dictionary that can't spell *dictionary?*
4. James Joyce's *Ulysses* first published in 1922 is a beautiful, shocking novel.
5. The sudden warmth, the palest green, the splashy, cleansing rain these signs of an eastern spring were what she missed most in California.
6. In the letter he quoted two lines of poetry that John Donne once wrote in a letter of his own "Sir, more than kisses, letters mingle souls; For thus friends absent speak."
7. As everyone knows (well, almost everyone), playing professional sports pays very well.
8. Paying taxes one of life's certainties is only a little less painful than the other certainty.
9. The book is filled with behind-the-scenes anecdotes about some of the all-time most popular television shows, including *I Love Lucy, Gunsmoke, All in the Family,* and *Dallas.*
10. The caged gorillas gigantic and glaring at their surroundings seem more vicious than they really are.

/

25f

VI
Mechanics

26
Capitals

Experienced writers generally agree on when to use capitals, but the conventions are constantly changing. Consult a recent dictionary if you have any doubt about whether a particular word should be capitalized.

26a
Capitalize the first word of every sentence.

Every writer should own a good dictionary.
Will this rain ever stop?
Watch out!

NOTE: Capitalization of the questions in a series is optional. Both of the following examples are correct.

Is the ideal population for a city a hundred thousand? Half a million? Over a million?

Is the ideal population for a city a hundred thousand? half a million? over a million?

Also optional is capitalization of the first word in a complete sentence after a colon (see 25a).

26b
Follow standard practice in capitalizing the titles of your own papers and of books and their parts, periodicals, articles, films, television and radio programs, poems, plays, and other works.

Capitalize all words in a title *except* articles (*a, an, the*) and prepositions and conjunctions of fewer than five letters. Capitalize

even these short words when they are the first or last word in a title
or when they fall after a colon or semicolon.

"The Love Song of J. Alfred
  Prufrock"
The Sound and the Fury
"Courtship Through the Ages"
*Merry England; Or, the History
  of a People*

What Do I Live For?
"Once More to the Lake"
Gone with the Wind
"The World Is Too Much
  with Us"
Management: A New Approach

NOTE: Always capitalize the prefix or first word in a hyphenated word within a title. Capitalize the second word only if it is a
noun or an adjective or is as important as the first word.

"How to Apply Stage Make-up"   *Through the Looking-Glass*
The Pre-Raphaelite Imagination

26c

**Always capitalize the pronoun *I* and the interjection *O*.
Don't capitalize *oh* unless it begins a sentence.**

I love to stay up at night, but, oh, I hate to get up in the morning.
He who thinks himself wise, O heavens, is a great fool. — VOLTAIRE

26d

**Capitalize proper nouns, proper adjectives, and words
used as essential parts of proper nouns.**

1

cap
26d

Capitalize proper nouns and proper adjectives.

Common nouns name general classes of persons, places, and
things. **Proper nouns** name specific persons, places, and things.
Proper adjectives are formed from some proper nouns. Capitalize
all proper nouns and proper adjectives but not the articles (*a, an,
the*) that precede them.

COMMON NOUNS	PROPER NOUNS	PROPER ADJECTIVES
state	California	Californian
man	Shakespeare	Shakespearean
building	Radio City Music Hall	—

SPECIFIC PERSONS AND THINGS

Stephen King
Napoleon Bonaparte
Jane Fonda

the Leaning Tower of Pisa
Boulder Dam
the Empire State Building

SPECIFIC PLACES AND GEOGRAPHICAL REGIONS

New York City
China
Europe
North America

the Mediterranean Sea
Lake Victoria
the Northeast
the Rocky Mountains

DAYS OF THE WEEK, MONTHS, HOLIDAYS

Monday
May
Thanksgiving

Yom Kippur
Christmas
Columbus Day

HISTORICAL EVENTS, DOCUMENTS, PERIODS, MOVEMENTS

World War II
the Vietnam War
the Boston Tea Party
the Treaty of Ghent
the Constitution

the Middle Ages
the Age of Reason
the Renaissance
the Great Depression
the Romantic Movement

GOVERNMENT OFFICES OR DEPARTMENTS AND INSTITUTIONS

House of Representatives
Department of Defense
Social Security Admin-
    istration
Postal Service
York Municipal Court

Warren County General
    Hospital
Northeast Regional High
    School
Springfield Board of
    Education

**POLITICAL, SOCIAL, ATHLETIC, AND OTHER ORGANIZATIONS
AND ASSOCIATIONS AND THEIR MEMBERS**

Democratic Party, Democrats
Communist Party, Communist
Daughters of the American
    Revolution
Girl Scouts of America, Scout
Young Men's Christian
    Association

B'nai B'rith
Rotary Club, Rotarians
Elks
Eastern Star
League of Women Voters
Boston Celtics
Chicago Symphony Orchestra

RACES, NATIONALITIES, AND THEIR LANGUAGES

Native American
Afro-American, Negro
Caucasian
But: blacks, whites

Germans
Swahili
Italian

RELIGIONS AND THEIR FOLLOWERS

Christianity, Christians
Protestantism, Protestants
Catholicism, Catholics
Hinduism, Hindu

Judaism, Jews
Orthodox Judaism, Reform
    Jew
Islam, Moslems or Muslims

cap
26d

RELIGIOUS TERMS FOR SACRED PERSONS AND THINGS

God	Buddha
Allah	the Bible (*but* biblical)
Christ	the Koran

NOTE: Capitalization of pronouns referring to God is optional in most contexts, but it is often used in religious texts and should be used where necessary to avoid confusion.

AMBIGUOUS	Our minister spoke of God as though *he* loved every member of our congregation.
REVISED	Our minister spoke of God as though *He* loved every member of our congregation.

2
Capitalize common nouns used as essential parts of proper nouns.

The common nouns *street, avenue, park, river, ocean, lake, company, college, county,* and *memorial* are capitalized when they are part of proper nouns naming specific places or institutions.

Main Street	Lake Superior
Park Avenue	Ford Motor Company
Central Park	Madison College
Mississippi River	Kings County
Pacific Ocean	George Washington Memorial Park

3
Capitalize trade names.

Trade names identify individual brands of certain products. When a trade name loses its association with a brand and comes to refer to a product in general, it is not capitalized. Refer to a dictionary for current usage when you are in doubt about a name.

Scotch tape	Xerox
Chevrolet	Bunsen burner

But: nylon, thermos

cap
26e

26e
Capitalize titles when they precede proper names but generally not when they follow proper names or are used alone.

Professor Otto Osborne	Otto Osborne, a professor of English
Doctor Jane Covington	Jane Covington, a medical doctor

| Senator Robert Dole | Robert Dole, senator from Kansas |
| General Omar Bradley | Omar Bradley, the general |

EXCEPTION: Many writers capitalize a title denoting very high rank even when it follows a proper name or is used without one.

Ronald Reagan, the President of the United States
the Chief Justice of the United States

26f
Avoid unnecessary capitalization.

In general, modern writers capitalize fewer words than earlier writers did. Don't capitalize a word unless a rule says you must.

1
Don't capitalize common nouns used in place of proper nouns.

UNNECESSARY	I am determined to take an Economics course before I graduate from College.
REVISED	I am determined to take an economics course before I graduate from college.
REVISED	I am determined to take Economics 101 before I graduate from Madison College.

2
Don't capitalize compass directions unless they refer to specific geographical areas.

The storm blew in from the northeast and then veered to the south along the coast. [Here *northeast* and *south* refer to general directions.]

Students from the South have trouble adjusting to the Northeast's bitter winters. [Here *South* and *Northeast* refer to specific regions of the country.]

3
Don't capitalize the names of seasons or the names of academic years or terms.

spring	winter quarter
fall	freshman year
autumn	summer term

4

Don't capitalize the names of relationships unless they form part of or substitute for proper names.

my mother
John's brother
the father of my friend

BUT

I remember how Father scolded us.

Aunt Annie, Uncle Jake, and Uncle Irvin died within two months of each other.

EXERCISE

Capitalize words as necessary in the sentences below, or substitute small letters for unnecessary capitals. Consult a dictionary if you are in doubt. If the capitalization in a sentence is already correct, circle the number preceding the sentence.

Example:

The last book i read, *The american way of death,* is about American burial customs.

The last book I read, *The American Way of Death,* is about American burial customs.

1. The building is too tall. it dominates its neighbors.
2. The grand canyon is in arizona, not too far from phoenix.
3. Colson, the doctor, knew his medicine, but his manner made his patients nervous.
4. My grandmother never approved of uncle William's choice of career.
5. The bible, koran, and bhagavad-gita are the holy books of jews and christians, moslems, and hindus, respectively.
6. The text for my psychology course, *A study of psycho-social development,* opened my eyes about how children learn.
7. Our scavenger-hunt map directed us two blocks Southeast and two blocks Northeast to find an old sink.
8. The Suwannee river rises in the Okefenokee swamp and moves through Georgia and Florida to the gulf of Mexico.
9. The new Saunders theater is an acoustical triumph, but, Oh, it was expensive to build.
10. Never one to take sides, father says that both general Douglas MacArthur and president Harry Truman were fine men and it's just too bad they had to argue.

cap
26f

27
Italics

Type that slants upward to the right is known as *italic type*. We use italics to distinguish or emphasize certain words and phrases. In your handwritten or typed papers, underline to indicate material that would be italicized if set into type.

27a
Underline the titles of books, long poems, plays, periodicals, pamphlets, published speeches, long musical works, movies, television and radio programs, and works of visual art.

Titles that do not fall under any of the categories below — for instance, essays, short stories, short poems — are enclosed in quotation marks rather than underlined. See 24d.

BOOKS

Catch-22
War and Peace
The Promise

LONG POEMS

Beowulf
The Song of Roland
Paradise Lost

PLAYS

Equus
Hamlet
Summer and Smoke

PERIODICALS

Time
Philadelphia *Inquirer*
Yale Law Review

PAMPHLETS

The Truth About Alcoholism
*On the Vindication of the
    Rights of Women*

PUBLISHED SPEECHES

Lincoln's *Gettysburg Address*
Pericles' *Funeral Oration*

LONG MUSICAL WORKS	MOVIES
Tchaikovsky's *Swan Lake*	*Gone with the Wind*
Bach's *St. Matthew Passion*	*Star Wars*
The Beatles' *Revolver*	*Invasion of the Body Snatchers*

TELEVISION AND RADIO PROGRAMS	WORKS OF VISUAL ART
60 Minutes	Michelangelo's *David*
The Shadow	the *Mona Lisa*

NOTE: Be careful to underline articles and marks of punctuation only if they are part of the title (the *Reader's Digest,* not *The Reader's Digest*). In titles of newspapers the initial *the* and the name of the city in which the paper is published may or may not be part of the title.

the Manchester *Guardian*
The New York Times

EXCEPTIONS: Legal documents, the Bible, and their parts are generally not italicized.

NOT	They registered their *deed.*
BUT	They registered their deed.

NOT	We just studied the *Book of Revelation* in the *Bible.*
BUT	We just studied the Book of Revelation in the Bible.

27b
Underline the names of ships, aircraft, spacecraft, and trains.

Queen Elizabeth II	*Apollo XI*
Spirit of St. Louis	*Orient Express*

27c
Underline foreign words and phrases that are not part of the English language.

English tends to absorb foreign words and phrases that speakers and writers find useful. The French expression "bon voyage," for example, is now part of our language and need not be underlined. If a foreign word or phrase has not been absorbed into our language, it should be underlined. A dictionary will tell you whether or not the words you wish to use should be underlined.

The scientific name for the brown trout is *Salmo trutta*. [The scientific names for plants and animals are always underlined.]

What a life he led! He was a true *bon vivant*.

The Latin *De gustibus non est disputandum* translates roughly as "There's no accounting for taste."

27d
Underline words, letters, numbers, and phrases named as words.

Some people pronounce *th*, as in *thought*, with a faint *s* or *f* sound.

Carved into the middle of the column, twenty feet up, was a mysterious 7.

Try pronouncing *unique New York* ten times fast.

Italics may also be used instead of quotation marks in definitions (see 24e).

The word *syzygy* refers to a straight line formed by three celestial bodies, as in the alignment of earth, sun, and moon that produces an eclipse.

27e
Occasionally, underlining may be used for emphasis.

Compare these sentences:

ital
27e

I thought you had the key.   I *thought* you had the key.
I thought you had the key.   I thought *you* had the key.

In the absence of clues from context, the first sentence doesn't tell us where the emphasis should lie. The three following sentences, however, tell us exactly what word to emphasize, and the different emphases create different meanings. In this way italics (or underlining) can stress an important word or phrase, especially in reporting how someone said something. But such emphasis should be used sparingly. Excessive underlining will make your writing sound immature or hysterical, as the following example illustrates.

The hunters had *no* food and *no* firewood. But they were *too* tired to do anything more than crawl into their *sopping* sleeping bags. Had it been ten degrees colder, *they might have frozen to death*.

If you find that you rely too much on underlining to achieve emphasis, consult Chapter 18 for other techniques to help you accent your writing.

EXERCISE

Underline (italicize) words and phrases as needed in the following sentences, or circle any words or phrases that are italicized unnecessarily.

Example:

Of Hitchcock's movies, Psycho is the scariest.
Of Hitchcock's movies, <u>Psycho</u> is the scariest.

1. The clock has long since been stolen, but the sign below its old spot still reads tempus fugit.
2. Both the *Old Testament* and the *New Testament* of the *Bible* offer profound lessons in human nature.
3. Esquire was the forerunner of magazines like Playboy, Penthouse, and GQ.
4. No matter how many times I say it, the word euphemism comes out wrong.
5. The Chronicle and the Examiner are San Francisco's major newspapers.
6. Homo sapiens has evolved further than any other species.
7. When Elizabeth Taylor and Richard Burton fell in love while filming Cleopatra, their romance was described as une grande passion.
8. According to the Chronicle of Higher Education, enrollments in business courses are climbing rapidly, whereas enrollments in the social sciences and humanities are plummeting.
9. The mountains were *so* beautiful that I had to *force* myself to leave them.
10. Whether he's watching Masterpiece Theatre, Wide World of Sports, or the silliest situation comedy, Larry is happy in front of the television.

ital
27

28

Abbreviations

Everyone uses certain standard abbreviations because they are convenient and readily understood. Nevertheless, only a few abbreviations are acceptable in general writing. For a list of abbreviations used in footnotes and bibliographies, see 35h.

28a

Use standard abbreviations for titles immediately before and after proper names.

BEFORE THE NAME	AFTER THE NAME
Dr. James Hsu	James Hsu, M.D.
Mr., Mrs., Ms., Hon.,	D.D.S., D.V.M., Ph.D.,
St., Rev., Msgr., Gen.	Ed.D., O.S.B., S.J., Sr., Jr.

(Note that the title *Ms.*, used before a name instead of *Mrs.* or *Miss* when a woman's marital status is unknown or irrelevant, is not actually an abbreviation, though it is followed by a period: *Ms. Judith Boyer.*)

Use abbreviations such as *Rev., Hon., Prof., Rep., Sen., Dr.,* and *St.* (for *Saint*) only if they appear with a proper name. Spell them out in the absence of a proper name.

FAULTY	By then my head hurt so badly that I was forced to call the *Dr.*
REVISED	By then my head hurt so badly that I was forced to call the *doctor.*
REVISED	By then my head hurt so badly that I was forced to call *Dr. Kaplan.*

The abbreviations for academic degrees — *Ph.D., M.A., B.A.,* and the like — may be used without a proper name.

My brother took seven years to get his *Ph.D.* It will probably take me just as long to earn my *B.A.*

28b

Familiar abbreviations and acronyms for the names of organizations, corporations, people, and some countries are acceptable in most writing.

An **acronym** is an abbreviation that spells a pronounceable word. *Radar,* which we no longer capitalize, is an acronym for "*ra*dio *de*tecting *a*nd *r*anging." Other acronyms include WHO, UNESCO, and NATO. These abbreviations, written without periods, are acceptable in most writing as long as they are familiar. So are several familiar abbreviations of the names of organizations, corporations, people, and countries. When these abbreviate three or more words, they are usually written without periods.

ORGANIZATIONS	CIA, FBI, YMCA, AFL-CIO
CORPORATIONS	IBM, CBS, ITT
PEOPLE	JFK, LBJ, FDR
COUNTRIES	U.S.A. (or USA), U.S.S.R. (or USSR)

(See 20b for more information on when to use periods in abbreviations.)

NOTE: If a name or term (such as *operating room*) appears often in a piece of writing, then its abbreviation (*O.R.*) can cut down on extra words. Spell out the full term at its first appearance, indicate its abbreviation in parentheses, and use the abbreviation from then on. However, if the term occurs only a few times in a paper, the abbreviation will serve no useful purpose and may even confuse readers. In that case spell out the term each time it occurs.

ab
28c

28c

Use the abbreviations B.C., A.D., A.M., P.M., *no.*, and the symbol $ with specific dates and numbers only.

The abbreviation B.C. ("before Christ") always follows a date, whereas A.D. (*anno Domini,* Latin for "year of our Lord") precedes a date.

44 B.C.	8:05 P.M.	no. 36
A.D. 1492	11:26 A.M.	$7.41

FAULTY   Hospital routine is easier to follow in the A.M. than in the P.M.

REVISED   Hospital routine is easier to follow in the *morning* than in the *afternoon or evening.*

NOTE: As shown here, B.C., A.D., A.M., and P.M. are set in small capital letters, which is a printer's convention. In handwriting and typewriting, use capitals for B.C. and A.D. (B.C., A.D.) and either capitals or small letters for A.M. and P.M. (A.M., a.m., P.M., p.m.). The abbreviation for *number* may be either capitalized or not (No., no.).

28d

Generally, reserve common Latin abbreviations such as *i.e., e.g.,* **and** *etc.* **for use in footnotes, bibliographies, and comments in parentheses.**

i.e.   that is (*id est*)
c.f.   compare (*confer*)
e.g.   for example (*exempli gratia*)
et al.   and others (*et alii*)
etc.   and so forth (*et cetera*)
N.B.   note well (*nota bene*)

He said he would be gone a fortnight (i.e., two weeks).
Bloom et al., editors, *Anthology of Light Verse*
Trees, too, are susceptible to disease (e.g., Dutch elm disease).

(Note that these abbreviations are generally not italicized or underlined.) In formal writing use the appropriate English phrases instead of these Latin abbreviations.

FAULTY   The cabs of some modern farm machines — e.g., combines — look like airplane cockpits.

INFORMAL   The cabs of some modern farm machines (e.g., combines) look like airplane cockpits.

FORMAL   The cabs of some modern farm machines (for example, combines) look like airplane cockpits.

FORMAL   The cabs of some modern farm machines — for example, combines — look like airplane cockpits.

ab
28e

28e

Don't use *Inc., Bros., Co.,* **or the ampersand (& for** *and***) except when they are part of the official name of a business firm.**

FAULTY   *The Santini bros.* operate a large moving firm in New York City.

REVISED	*The Santini brothers* operate a large moving firm in New York City.
REVISED	*Santini Bros.* is a large moving firm in New York City.
FAULTY	As a child I read every story about the Hardy Boys & Nancy Drew.
REVISED	As a child I read every story about the Hardy Boys *and* Nancy Drew.

28f

In most writing don't abbreviate units of measurement; geographical names; names of days, months, and holidays; names of people; courses of instruction; and labels for divisions of written works.

UNITS OF MEASUREMENT

The dog is thirty *inches* (not *in.*) high.
Dig a hole six *feet* (not *ft.*) deep.

EXCEPTIONS: Long phrases such as *miles per hour* (m p h) or *cycles per second* (c.p.s.) are conventionally abbreviated and may or may not be punctuated with periods: *The speed limit on that road was once 75 m.p.h.* (or *mph*).

GEOGRAPHICAL NAMES

The publisher is in *Massachusetts* (not *Mass.* or *MA*).
He came from Aukland, *New Zealand* (not *N.Z.*).
She lived on Morrissey *Boulevard* (not *Blvd.*).

EXCEPTIONS: The United States is often referred to as the U.S.A. (USA) or the U.S., and the Soviet Union as the U.S.S.R. (USSR).

NAMES OF DAYS, MONTHS, AND HOLIDAYS

The truce was signed on *Tuesday* (not *Tues.*), *January* (not *Jan.*) 16.

NAMES OF PEOPLE

James (not *Jas.*) Bennett ran for that seat.
Robert (not *Robt.*) Frost writes accessible poems.

COURSES OF INSTRUCTION

I'm majoring in *political science* (not *poli. sci.*).
Economics (not *Econ.*) is a tough course.

LABELS FOR DIVISIONS OF WRITTEN WORKS

The story begins on *page* (not *p.*) 15.
Read *Chapter* (not *Ch.*) 6.
We finally finished *Volume* (not *Vol.*) I of our history text.

ab
28f

EXERCISE 1

Revise the following sentences as needed to correct faulty use of abbreviations. Circle the number preceding any sentence in which the abbreviations are already correct as written.

Example:

One prof. spent five class hrs. reading from the textbook.

One *professor* spent five class *hours* reading from the textbook.

1. They bought a house with 100 ft. of lake frontage.
2. Mount Vesuvius erupted in *anno Domini* 79 and buried Pompeii.
3. Mr. and Mrs. Harold Marsh, Jr., donated a new wing for the library.
4. The city built a new office building at the corner of Juniper and Cowen Sts.
5. A dictionary — e.g., *The American Heritage Dictionary* — will tell you whether to punctuate an abbreviation with periods.
6. FDR died on Thurs., Apr. 12, 1945, in Warm Springs, Ga.
7. The Lynch bros., Wm. & Robt., went bankrupt in the same year.
8. The Cold War between the U.S.A. and the U.S.S.R. dominated international affairs in the 1950s.
9. They asked the rev. to marry them on horseback.
10. There, in the middle of Ch. 6, between pp. 128 & 129, was a leaf my mother had pressed as a child.

EXERCISE 2

ab
28

Spell out all inappropriate abbreviations in the following paragraph. If an abbreviation is appropriate in its context, leave it as is.

The advantages of a grad. degree are not lost on me. With a Ph.D. I might become a college prof., a job that would allow me to work only in the P.M., so I wouldn't have to get up before 11:00 A.M., and only on Tues., Wed., and Thurs., my favorite days. Or I could get an M.D. and become a dr. Though I might have to work long hrs., I could earn plenty of $ and, by serving on a professional association like the AMA, could have a lot of influence. I know about these advantages because my two older bros. are Prof. Giordano and Dr. Giordano. I also know how hard they had to work for their degrees, so I think I'll stick with poli. sci. courses and look for a nice, safe govt. job after I get my B.A.

29

Numbers

Experienced writers vary in their choice between writing numbers out and using figures. In scientific and technical writing, numbers are usually written as figures. In general writing, numbers are more often spelled out. The rules below give conventions for general writing.

29a
Use figures for numbers that require more than two words to spell out.

The leap year has *366* days.
The population of Minot, North Dakota, is about *32,500*.

Spell out numbers of one or two words. (See also 29b.)

That hotel can accommodate no more than *seventy-five* people.

The first writing we know of was done over *six thousand* years ago.

The museum's collection included almost *twelve hundred* drawings and paintings.

A hyphenated number can be considered one word.

The ball game drew *forty-two thousand* people.

EXCEPTION: When you use several numbers together, they should be consistently spelled out or consistently expressed in figures.

INCONSISTENT	Only *ninety-nine* students attended the first lecture, but the audience increased to *126* for the second lecture and *two hundred* for the third.

REVISED   Only *99* students attended the first lecture, but the audience increased to *126* for the second lecture and *200* for the third.

29b

Use figures for days and years; numbers of pages, chapters, volumes, acts, scenes, and lines; numbers containing decimals, percentages, and fractions; addresses; scores and statistics; exact amounts of money; and the time of day.

DAYS AND YEARS

June 18, 1981   A.D. 12   456 B.C.

EXCEPTION: The day of a month may be expressed in words (*June fifth; October first*) when it is not followed by a year.

NUMBERS OF PAGES, CHAPTERS, VOLUMES, ACTS, SCENES, LINES	NUMBERS CONTAINING DECIMALS, PERCENTAGES, AND FRACTIONS
Chapter 9, page 123	22.5
Encyclopaedia Britannica, Volume 14	48% (or 48 percent)
Hamlet, Act V, Scene 3, lines 35–40	3½

ADDRESSES	SCORES AND STATISTICS
355 Clinton Avenue	21 to 7
419 Stonewall Street	a mean of 26
Washington, D.C. 20036	a ratio of 8 to 1

EXACT AMOUNTS OF MONEY	THE TIME OF DAY
$4.50	9:00
$3.5 million (or $3,500,000)	3:45
$2,763.00 (or $2763.00)	2:30

EXCEPTIONS: Round dollar or cent amounts of only a few words may be expressed in words: *seventeen dollars; fifteen hundred dollars; sixty cents.* When the word *o'clock* is used for the time of day, also express the number in words: *two o'clock* (not *2 o'clock*).

29c

Always spell out numbers that begin sentences.

We are so accustomed to seeing a capital letter at the beginning of a sentence that a number there can make reading difficult. Therefore, always spell out any number that begins a sentence. If

the number requires more than two words, avoid further awkwardness by rewording the sentence so the number falls later and can be
expressed as a figure.

AWKWARD	*103* of the opening-night audience asked for a re-fund.
AWKWARD	*One hundred and three* of the opening-night au-dience asked for a refund.
REVISED	Of the opening-night audience, *103* asked for a re-fund.

EXERCISE

Revise the following sentences to correct the use of numbers.
Circle the number preceding any sentence in which numbers are
already used appropriately.

Example:

The texts for my courses cost me one hundred and twelve dollars.

The texts for my courses cost me *$112.00*.

1. A liter is equal to almost one and six-hundredths quarts.
2. Not until page ninety-nine, in the middle of Chapter five, does
   the author introduce the main character.
3. I was born on May fifteenth, six days after my dog.
4. Peter Minuit bought Manhattan Island from the Indians for
   twenty-four dollars.
5. Dominating the town's skyline was a sign that stood thirty feet
   off the ground and measured 112 feet by thirty-seven feet.
6. 166 people in the county installed some form of solar-heating
   system in their homes this year.
7. Outside twenty-seven Ogden Street, the mayor's house, over a
   hundred and fifty people were demonstrating.
8. A disappointing 52 percent of the voters showed up at the
   polls.
9. The new school cost a million and three-quarters dollars.
10. Because of the snow, only two hundred and ten students at-
    tended the dance.

num

29c

30

Word Division

As much as possible, avoid dividing words. If you must divide a word between the end of one line and the beginning of the next, do so only between syllables. Put a hyphen at the end of the first line, never at the beginning of the second. Never divide the last word on a page, because in the act of turning the page the reader may forget the beginning of the word. If you are in doubt about how to break any word into syllables, consult a dictionary. Note, however, that not all syllable breaks are appropriate for word division. Use the following rules to decide when and how to divide words.

30a
Don't make a division that leaves a single letter at the end of a line or fewer than three letters at the beginning of a line.

FAULTY	A newspaper or television editorial for or *a-against* a candidate can sway an election.
REVISED	A newspaper or television editorial for or *against* a candidate can sway an election.
FAULTY	Counseling is required for every child *abus-er.*
REVISED	Counseling is required for every child *abuser.*

30b
Don't divide one-syllable words.

Since one-syllable words have no break in pronunciation, they should not be divided.

FAULTY	The shiny, spinning space capsule *dropped* suddenly from the clouds.
REVISED	The shiny, spinning space capsule *dropped* suddenly from the clouds.

30c
Divide compound words only between the words that form them or at fixed hyphens.

Compound words are made up of two or more words (*drawback, homecoming*). Their component words may be separated by a hyphen (*well-paying, cross-reference*), in which case the hyphen is called **fixed.**

FAULTY	If you want to have friends, be *good-natured.*
REVISED	If you want to have friends, be *good-natured.*
FAULTY	Sherlock Holmes exemplifies the *mastermind.*
REVISED	Sherlock Holmes exemplifies the *mastermind.*

(See 34d for guidelines on when to use hyphens in spelling compound words.)

30d
Avoid confusing word divisions.

Some word divisions may momentarily confuse the reader because the first or second part by itself forms a pronounceable (or unpronounceable) unit that does not fit with the whole. For example: *poi-gnant, read-dress, in-dict.* Avoid word divisions like these.

CONFUSING	Her walking out of class was an act of *heroism.*
CLEAR	Her walking out of class was an act of *heroism.*
CONFUSING	He claims that stealing never bothered his *conscience.*
CLEAR	He claims that stealing never bothered his *conscience.*

EXERCISE

Revise the sentences below so that words are divided properly.

Example:

I thought Harry's joke was sidesplit-
ting, but no one else even smiled.

I thought Harry's joke was *side-
splitting*, but no one else even smiled.

1. Instead of going to college, she joined the army.
2. Each of the twenty-three apartments he looked at was rented before he could make a deposit on it.
3. Americans find any number of ways to keep from feeling mid-
dle-aged.
4. While the photographers snapped pictures, Dan blush-
ed with embarrassment.
5. After the lecture Dotty felt she knew e-
nough about the subject to pass the test.

div
30

VII
Effective Words

31

Controlling Diction

Diction is the choice and use of words. To control your diction, you should select the words that fit your purpose and express your meaning most accurately and clearly, and you should prune all words that do not make your meaning more exact. Because the substance and the effectiveness of what you say depend finally on the words you choose, you will waste much of your effort in writing unless you develop a respect for words and a sensitivity to their shades of meaning. The following sections present criteria for choosing the appropriate and exact word, but they cannot cover all instances. You must rely on your own judgment to select words that suit your subject, your purpose, and your audience. The first rule, perhaps, is to be suspicious of the first word that comes to mind. You can probably discover another one with a shade of meaning closer to your intention.

31a
Choosing the appropriate word

Words are appropriate when they suit your subject and the purpose of your writing, the image of yourself that you want to project, and the readers you are writing for. We all use various kinds of language — various sets of words — depending on the context in which we are speaking or writing. Talking to friends, for example, you might say, *My sister decided to bag therapy because her shrink seemed even more strung out than she was.* Writing for general audience, however, you would convey the same information quite differently, perhaps writing, *My sister decided to abandon therapy because her psychiatrist seemed even more disturbed than she was.* In each case the diction fits the occasion: When you talk to people you know well and share experiences with, you can relax into informal or slang expressions like *bag, shrink,* and *strung out;* when you write for a general audience, you must be more formal, using more widely understood words like *abandon, psychiatrist,* and *disturbed.*

Most of your writing in college and after will be analyzing, discussing, explaining, and sometimes defending your understanding and interpretation of facts, events, and ideas. The words appropriate to such writing, like the conventions of grammar and usage described earlier in this handbook, are those which educated readers and writers normally expect. The huge vocabulary in what is called standard or educated English excludes words that only limited groups of people use and understand: slang, colloquial language, regional words and expressions, nonstandard language, obsolete words, technical terms, euphemisms, and pretentious words. These more limited vocabularies, discussed below, should be avoided altogether or else used cautiously and only in special contexts. Whenever you doubt the status of a word, always consult a dictionary (see 32b-2).

1
Avoiding slang

All groups of people — from musicians and computer scientists to vegetarians and gangsters — create **slang,** novel and colorful expressions that reflect the group's special experiences and set it off from others. Slang displays endless inventiveness. Some of it gives new meanings to old words. During the 1950s, for example, the word *cool* gained a meaning of "self-controlled" (*Stay cool*) or "pleasing, excellent" (*The movie was cool*). During the 1960s *freak* came to describe a person on drugs (*a speed freak*) and, later, anyone with long hair, patched jeans, and a fondness for drugs (*He's a freak, so I think you'll like him*). More recently, *into* has described personal commitment (*I'm really into plants*), and *get off* has meant "to become excited" (*I really get off on old Rolling Stones records*). Some slang comes from other languages: Our word *chow* ("food" or "a meal") comes from the Chinese *chao,* meaning "to stir or fry"; *hoosegow* ("jail") comes from the Spanish *juzgado,* "courtroom"; and *schlep* ("to lug" or "a clumsy person") comes from the Yiddish *schleppen,* "to drag." Sometimes the slang of a particular ethnic group is widely adopted by the rest of the population. *Out to lunch, put on ice,* and *pad,* for example, are contributions of black slang.

Among those who understand it, slang may be vivid, lively, and forceful. And much slang, such as *dropout* (*She was a high school dropout*), has proven so useful that it has passed into the general vocabulary. But most slang is flippant, short-lived, and mean-

appr

31a

ingful only to a narrow audience. In addition, it is generally too vague and imprecise for effective communication. The writer who says that *many students start out pretty straight but then get weird* not only has deprived her writing of seriousness but also has not said what specifically happens to the students. The same is true of this sentence: *The mayor has put out some new hype for the city.* In each case, avoiding imprecise slang and including specific, informative language would strengthen the sentence.

2
Avoiding colloquial language

Colloquial language designates the words and expressions appropriate to spoken language. Regardless of our backgrounds and how we live, we all try to *get along with* each other. We sometimes *get together with* our neighbors. We play with *kids, go crazy* about one thing, *crab* about something else, and in our worst moments try to *get back at* someone who has made us do the *dirty work.* These italicized words and expressions are not "wrong"; quite the contrary, more formal language might sound stilted and pompous in casual conversation.

Some informal writing that tries to create the casual, relaxed effect of conversation draws intentionally on spoken language. And some formerly colloquial words (*rambunctious, trigger* as a verb) have gained acceptance in more formal, written English. But the colloquial language so natural to conversation does not provide the exactness needed in more formal college, business, and professional writing. In such writing you should generally avoid any words and expressions labeled "informal" or "colloquial" in your dictionary. Take special care to avoid **mixed diction,** a combination of standard and colloquial words.

MIXED DICTION	According to a Native American myth, the Great Creator *had a dog hanging around with him* when he created the earth.
CONSISTENT	According to a Native American myth, the Great Creator *was accompanied by a dog* when he created the earth.
MIXED DICTION	The events of Watergate were too complex to interest us grade-schoolers, but we thought Nixon's resignation was *really wild.*
CONSISTENT	The events of Watergate were too complex to interest us grade-schoolers, but we thought Nixon's resignation was *extraordinary* (or *exciting*).

3
Avoiding regional words and expressions

Most national languages vary slightly from one geographical area to another. In American English, regional differences are most marked in pronunciation. A Texan overhearing a conversation between a New Yorker and a Georgian will not mistake either of the speakers for a fellow Texan. But some regional differences also occur in vocabulary. Southerners may say they *reckon*, meaning they "think" or "suppose." People in Maine invite their Boston friends to come *down* rather than *up* (north) to visit. In the Northeast, people *catch a cold* and *get sick*, but in some other parts of the country they *take a cold* and *take sick*. Regional expressions are perfectly appropriate in writing that addresses local readers and may give color and realism to regional description, but they should be avoided in writing intended for a general audience.

REGIONAL   The house where I spent my childhood was *down the road a piece* from a federal prison.

GENERAL   The house where I spent my childhood was *a short distance* from a federal prison.

4
Avoiding nonstandard language

Words and grammatical forms called **nonstandard,** though spoken by many intelligent people, are never acceptable in standard written English. Examples include *nowheres;* such pronoun forms as *hisn, hern, hisself,* and *theirselves; them* as an adjective, as in *them dishes, them courses;* the expressions *this here* and *that there*, as in *that there elevator;* verb forms such as *knowed, throwed, hadn't ought*, and *could of;* and double negatives such as *didn't never* and *haven't no*. Dictionaries label such expressions "nonstandard," "illiterate," or "substandard." Avoid all nonstandard expressions in speech and especially in writing.

appr
31a

5
Avoiding obsolete or archaic words and neologisms

Since our surroundings and our lives are constantly changing, some words gradually pass out of use and others are created to fill new needs. **Obsolete** and **archaic** are dictionary labels for words or meanings of words that we never or rarely use but that appear in older documents and literature still read today. The label *obsolete* indicates that the word or a particular meaning is no longer used at all. Thus *enwheel*, meaning "to encircle," and *cote*, meaning "to pass," are now obsolete. The label *archaic* indicates that the word or meaning occurs now only in special contexts, such as in poetry. The sense of *fast* meaning "near" (*fast by the schoolhouse*) and the word *belike*, meaning "perhaps," are archaic.

Whereas obsolete and archaic words have passed out of common use, **neologisms** are words created (or coined) so recently that they have not come into established use. Some neologisms do become accepted as part of our general vocabulary. *Motel*, coined from *motor* and *hotel*, and *brunch*, meaning a combination of breakfast and lunch, are examples. But most neologisms pass quickly from the language. In the late 1970s newsmagazines coined the words *equalimony* and *palimony* to refer to changing attitudes and court interpretations of alimony rights, but these words have not gained much wider use. Unless such words serve a special purpose in your writing and are sure to be understood and appreciated by your readers, you should avoid them.

6
Using technical words with care

All disciplines and professions from accounting to zoology rely on special words or give common words special meanings. Chemists speak of *esters* and *phosphatides*, geographers and mapmakers refer to *isobars* and *isotherms*, and literary critics write about *motifs* and *personae*. Golfers talk about *mashies* and *niblicks*. Printers use common words like *cut*, *foul*, and *slug* in special senses. Such technical language allows specialists to communicate precisely and economically with other specialists who share their vocabulary. But without explanation these words are meaningless to the nonspecialist. When you are writing for a general reader, avoid unnecessary technical terms. If your subject requires words the reader may not understand, be careful to define them. (See 31c-4 for a discussion of jargon and overly technical and inflated language.)

appr
31a

7
Avoiding euphemisms and pretentious writing

A **euphemism** is a presumably inoffensive word that a writer or speaker substitutes for a word deemed potentially offensive or too blunt. We speak euphemistically when we say that someone *passed on* rather than *died*. Government officials employ euphemism when they describe an effort to cut waste in military spending as an *acquisitions-improvement program* or when they describe nuclear war as *nuclear engagement*. Because euphemisms conceal meaning instead of clarifying it, you should use them only when you know that blunt, truthful words would needlessly offend members of your audience.

People who write euphemistically also tend to decorate their prose with ornate phrases. Any writing that is more elaborate than its subject requires will sound pretentious or excessively showy. Good writers choose their words for their exactness and economy. Pretentious writers choose them in the belief that fancy words will impress readers. They rarely will.

PRETENTIOUS	Many institutions of higher education recognize the need for youth at the threshold of maturity to confront the choice of life's endeavor and thus require students to select a field of concentration.
REVISED	Many colleges and universities force students to make decisions about their careers by requiring them to select a major.

When either of two words will say what you mean, prefer the small word to the big one, the common word to the uncommon one. If you want to say *It has begun to rain,* say so. Don't say *I perceive that moisture has commenced to precipitate earthward.*

EXERCISE 1

Insert words appropriate for standard written English in the sentences below to replace slang, colloquialisms, regionalisms, nonstandard expressions, obsolete or archaic words, neologisms, technical words, euphemisms, or pretentious expressions. Consult a dictionary as needed to determine a word's appropriateness and to find suitable substitutes.

Example:
We did not tell our father we had crashed on the beach because we were afraid he'd get bent out of shape.
We did not tell our father we had *spent the night* on the beach because we were afraid he'd *become angry.*

1. The food shortages in some parts of North Africa are so severe that thousands of people have met their demise.
2. A few stockholders have been down on the company ever since it refused to stop conducting business in South Africa.
3. The most stubborn members of the administration still will not hearken to our pleas for a voice in college doings.
4. Though it never became popular, quadraphonic stereo, playing music out of four speakers, was quadriffic.
5. I almost failed Western Civ, because the jerk who borrowed my notes lost them.
6. We realized after we asked him to cut class with us that he might foul up the afternoon by ratting on us.

appr
31a

7. Her arm often aches, but she says it doesn't bother her none.
8. Because he understands the finest intricacies of democratic management and can thus covertly persuade the most recalcitrant legislator to do his every bidding, we should return the governor to his position as chief executive of our fair state.
9. Whenever I hear someone boast about the famous people he or she knows, I suspect a put-on.
10. The lecture on Charlemagne was fantastic, but I missed some of it because the mike kept going on the blink.

31b
Choosing the exact word

Good writers labor to find the words within the large vocabulary of standard English that fit their meaning, that say precisely what they want to say with exactly the overtones they intend. Inexact, fuzzy, or inappropriate words weaken writing and often confuse readers.

1
Understanding denotation and connotation

A word's **denotation** is the thing or idea it refers to, the meaning listed in the dictionary without reference to any of the emotional associations it may arouse in a reader. Using words according to their established denotations is the first rule of clear diction. The person who writes *My dog is inflicted with fleas* or *Older people must often endure infirmaries* has mistaken *inflicted* for *afflicted* and *infirmaries* for *infirmities*. In using the wrong word, the writer has said something different from what was intended, and the result will either amuse or confuse the reader. The writer who says *The divergence between the estimate and the stadium's actual cost is surprising* has also missed the mark, though not as widely. The word needed is *discrepancy*, not *divergence*. The two words are second or third cousins, but they are not interchangeable. Some mistakes in diction occur because of confusion of **homonyms,** words such as *principle/principal* or *rain/reign/rein* that sound alike but have different spellings and meanings. (See 34a-1 for an extensive list of commonly confused homonyms and their meanings.) Consult your dictionary whenever you are unsure of a word's exact meaning.

Writers miss the exact word they want more often by misjudging its connotation than by mistaking its denotation. **Connotation** refers to the association a word carries with it. Personal connotations derive from one's particular experiences. A person whose only experience with dogs was being bitten three times will have a different reaction to the word *dog* than will someone who lives with the warm memories of a childhood pet. People whose family lives are punctuated by quarrels and bitterness will react to the word *home* very differently from those who find their homes secure and comfortable. But in spite of such personal associations, most people agree about the favorable or unfavorable connotations of a word. To most readers, the connotations of *love, home,* and *peace* are favorable, whereas those of *lust, shack,* and *war* are unfavorable. Most of us would prefer to be described as *slim* rather than *skinny* or as *portly* rather than *fat.* And we would prefer to hear our tastes described as *inexpensive* rather than *cheap.*

Understanding connotation is especially important in choosing among **synonyms,** words with approximately, but often not exactly, the same meanings. *Cry* and *weep* are similar words, both denoting the shedding of tears; but *cry* more than *weep* connotes a sobbing sound accompanying the tears. *Sob* itself connotes broken, gasping crying, with tears, whereas *wail* connotes sustained sound, rising and falling in pitch, perhaps without tears. Filling in the blank in the sentence *We were disturbed by his _____ing,* each of these words would evoke different sounds and images. Tracking down the word whose connotation is exactly what you want can take time and effort. The most convenient resource is a dictionary, particularly the discussions of synonyms and their shades of meaning at the end of many entries (see 32b-2 and 33c-2 for samples). Other useful resources are a thesaurus, which lists groups of synonyms, and a dictionary of synonyms, which both lists and defines them. (See 32a-3 for specific titles.)

EXERCISE 2

Revise the sentences below to replace any italicized word that is not used according to its established denotation. If the italicized word in a sentence is used correctly, circle the number preceding the sentence. Consult a dictionary if you are uncertain of a word's precise meaning.

Example:

Sam and Dave are going to Bermuda and Mattapan, *respectfully,* for spring vacation.

Sam and Dave are going to Bermuda and Mattapan, *respectively,* for spring vacation.

1. The *enormity* of the beached whale — and its horrible stench — both amazed and repelled us.
2. My parents have the *allusion* that I will enter the family business when I graduate.
3. The jury did not find the defendant's testimony *credible* and so convicted her.

4. The pond's water was always *defiled*, so we had to keep from swallowing it when we swam.
5. When students boycotted the school cafeteria, I was *disinterested* in their childish protest.
6. We've been without furniture for days, but now the movers are due to arrive *momentously*.
7. The *sight* for the new bank had formerly held apartments for seventy-five elderly people.
8. After trying *continually* to see my teacher for two weeks, I finally complained to the dean.
9. The *affect* of the town's hasty decision to close the library this summer has been to deprive poor people of reading material.
10. Having been *deferred* from acting on impulse, she felt paralyzed by indecision.

EXERCISE 3

Describe how the connotation of each italicized word in the sentences below contributes to the writer's meaning. Give at least one synonym or related word that the writer could have used instead of the italicized word, and describe how the new word would alter meaning. Consult a dictionary or thesaurus as necessary.

1. [The river] *slumbers* between broad prairies, *kissing* the long meadow grass, and *bathes* the overhanging boughs of elder bushes and willows or the roots of elms and ash trees and clumps of maples.   — NATHANIEL HAWTHORNE
2. The new earth, freshly *torn* from its parent sun, was a ball of *whirling* gases, *intensely* hot, *rushing* through the black spaces of the universe on a path and a speed controlled by *immense* forces.   — RACHEL CARSON
3. When the country loved it with a passion, baseball was boyhood eternal, all *bluster*, innocence, and *bravado flashing* across green *meadows* in the sunlight.   — RUSSELL BAKER
4. I think all theories are suspect, that the finest principles may have to be *modified*, or may even be *pulverized* by the demands of life, and that one must find, therefore, one's own moral *center* and move through the world hoping that this center will guide one aright.   — JAMES BALDWIN
5. After a long straight *swoop* across the pancakeflat prairies, hour after hour of harvested land *streaked* with yellow *wheatstubble* to the horizon, it's exciting to see hills ahead, *dark* hills under clouds against the west.   — JOHN DOS PASSOS

exact
31b

2
Balancing the abstract and concrete, the general and specific

To understand a subject as you understand it, to experience it as you experience it, your readers need ample guidance from your words. When you describe a building as beautiful and nothing more, you force readers to fill in both the kind of building and the features that make it beautiful. If readers trouble to do the work you have assigned them — and they may not — they will summon up diverse images of the many beautiful buildings they have seen, not a coherent image of the one you have seen. In evading your responsibility to be exact, you will have failed to communicate your meaning. Effective writing demands that abstract and general words like *beautiful* and *building*, which convey the broad outlines of objects and ideas, be balanced by concrete and specific words that make the objects and ideas sharp and firm. For instance, you might describe a *Victorian brick courthouse faced with stately arched windows and trimmed with ornate sandstone carvings.*

Abstract words name qualities and ideas: *beauty, inflation, depression, labor, management, truth, culture, integration, liberal, conservative.* **Concrete words** name things we can know by our senses: *brick, sandstone, arched, bacon, apple, sticky, crisp, hard.*

General words name classes or groups of things, such as *buildings, weather, birds,* or *professional people,* and include all the varieties of the class. **Specific words** limit a general class like *buildings* by naming one of its varieties, such as *Victorian courthouse, office tower,* or *hut. Professional people* include *doctors, scientists, teachers,* or *public accountants. Weather* includes *sunshine, drought, rain, windstorm,* and *cyclone. Birds* include *sparrows, eagles, geese, parrots, bobolinks,* and *vultures.* But *general* and *specific* are relative terms. *Doctor* becomes a general word in relation to *radiologist* and *surgeon,* and *surgeon* is general in relation to *neurosurgeon* and *orthopedic surgeon. Rain* is the general class for *drizzle, sprinkle,* and *downpour,* and *downpours* can be *continuous* or *sudden.* You become more and more specific as you move from a general class to a unique item, from *bird* to *pet bird* to *parrot* to *my parrot Moyshe.*

Abstract and general words are useful in the broad statements that set the course for your writing and tell readers what to expect.

The wild horse in America has a *romantic* history.

We must be *free* from *government interference* in our *affairs.*

Relations between the sexes today are only a *little* more *relaxed* than they were in the past.

exact

31b

But statements like these, which rely heavily on abstract and general words, must be developed and supported by concrete and specific detail. Writing seldom fails because it lacks abstraction and generality. It often fails because it lacks the concrete and specific words that nail down meaning and make writing vivid, real, and clear. In your own writing choose the concrete and specific word over the general and abstract. When your meaning does call for an

abstract or general word, make sure you define it, explain it, and
narrow it with the concrete and specific words that most precisely
reflect your knowledge and experience. Look at how concrete and
specific information turns vague sentences into exact ones in the examples below.

VAGUE   The size of his hands made his smallness real.
[How big were his hands? How small was he?]

EXACT   Not until I saw his white, doll-like hands did I realize that he stood at least a full head shorter
than most other men.

VAGUE   The long flood caused a lot of awful destruction
in the town. [How long did the flood last? What
destruction did it cause, and why was the destruction awful?]

EXACT   The flood waters, which rose swiftly and then
stayed stubbornly high for days, killed at least six
townspeople and made life a misery for the hundreds who had to evacuate their ruined homes
and stores.

EXERCISE 4

Make the following paragraph vivid for the reader by expanding
the sentences with appropriate details of your own. Concentrate
especially on substituting concrete and specific words for the abstract and general ones in italics.

   I have learned how *bad* noise pollution can be since I moved
into a *place near* a *highway*. The cars and trucks *going* by make *different sounds*, but together they produce a *steady noise*. Even when
all the windows are *closed* and *covered*, the *noise comes in* through
the *walls* of the *old* apartment building. To be heard over the *noise*,
conversation must be *loud*, and the television and stereo must be
at *high volume*. Even the *early morning* is not *quiet*, and the *noise*
forms a constant background to an *unrestful* sleep.

exact
31b

EXERCISE 5

For each abstract or general word below, give at least two other
words or phrases that illustrate increasing specificity or concrete-
ness. Consult a dictionary as needed. Use the most specific or concrete word from each group in a sentence of your own.

   Example:

   tired, *sleepy, droopy-eyed*

   We stopped for the night when I became so *droopy-eyed* that
   the road blurred.

1. fabric
2. delicious
3. car
4. narrow-minded
5. reach (*verb*)
6. green
7. walk (*verb*)
8. flower
9. serious
10. pretty
11. teacher
12. nice
13. virtue
14. angry
15. crime
16. smile (*verb*)
17. sick
18. desire (*verb*)
19. candy
20. misfortune

3
Using idioms

Idioms are expressions whose meanings cannot be determined simply from the words in them or whose component words cannot be predicted by any rule of grammar; often, they violate conventional grammar. Examples include *put up with, plug away at,* and *make off with.* People learn the common idioms of their language naturally, just as they learn other common words, and generally they pose no problem for writers. But even experienced writers of English have difficulty with some idiomatic combinations of an adjective or verb and a preposition. For instance, *conform to the rules* is idiomatic, whereas *conform with the rules* is not. Some typical idioms are listed below for reference. Check a dictionary if you are unsure of what preposition to use with an idiom (see 32b-2).

in accordance *with*
according *to*

accuse *of* a crime

agree *with* a person
agree *to* a proposal
agree *on* a plan

angry *with*

capable *of*

charge *for* a purchase
charge *with* a crime

compare *to* something in a different class
compare *with* something in the same class

concur *with* a person
concur *in* an opinion

contend *with* a person
contend *for* a principle

differ *with* a person
differ *from* in appearance
differ *about* or *over* a question

independent *of*

impatient *at* her conduct
impatient *of* restraint
impatient *for* a raise
impatient *with* a person

inferior *to*

occupied *by* a person
occupied *in* study
occupied *with* a thing

part *from* a person
part *with* a possession

prior *to*

rewarded *by* the judge
rewarded *for* something done
rewarded *with* a gift

superior *to*

wait *at* a place
wait *for* a train, a person
wait *on* a customer

exact
31b

EXERCISE 6

Insert the preposition that correctly completes each idiom in the sentences below. Consult the preceding list or a dictionary as needed.

Example:

I disagree _____ many feminists who say women should not be homemakers.

I disagree *with* many feminists who say women should not be homemakers.

1. He had waited for years, growing impatient _____ her demands and _____ the money that she would leave to him.
2. The writer compared gorilla society _____ human society.
3. They agreed _____ most things, but they differed consistently _____ how to raise their child.
4. I was rewarded _____ my persistence _____ an opportunity to meet the senator.
5. He would sooner part _____ his friends than part _____ his Corvette.

4
Using figurative language

Figurative language expresses or implies comparisons between different ideas or objects. The sentence *As I try to write, I can think of nothing to say* is literal. The sentence *As I try to write, my mind is a blank slab of black asphalt* is figurative. The abstract concept of having nothing to say has become concrete, something the reader can visualize. The blank slab of black asphalt is bare, hard, and unyielding, just as the frustrated writer's mind seems bare, resisting all attempts at writing.

Figurative language is commonplace. We sprinkle our conversation with figures: Having *slept like a log,* we get up to find it *raining cats and dogs* but have to *pluck up our courage* and *battle the storm.* The sports pages abound in figurative language: The Yankees *shell* the Royals, the Cowboys *embark* on another season, and basketball players make *barrels* of money. Slang, too, is largely figurative: You may be *hung up* on chemistry, but you *get off* on physics.

The rapid exchange of speech leaves little time for inventiveness, and most figures of daily conversation, like hastily written news stories, are worn and hackneyed. But writing gives you time to reject the tired figure and to search out the fresh words and phrases that will carry meaning concretely and vividly.

The two most common figures of speech are the **simile** and the **metaphor.** Both compare two things of different classes, often one

exact

31b

abstract and the other concrete. A simile makes the comparison explicit, usually beginning with *like* or *as.*

> We force their [children's] growth as if they were chicks in a poultry factory.   — ARNOLD TOYNBEE

> When he tried to think of the future he was like some blundering insect that tries, again and again, to climb up the smooth wall of a dish into which it has fallen.   — ROBERT PENN WARREN

> To hold America in one's thoughts is like holding a love letter in one's hand — it has so special a meaning.   — E. B. WHITE

Instead of stating a comparison, the metaphor implies it, omitting such words as *like* or *as.*

> I refuse to accept the notion that nation after nation must spiral down a militaristic stairway into the hell of nuclear war.
>   — MARTIN LUTHER KING, JR.

> A school is a hopper into which children are heaved while they are young and tender; therein they are pressed into certain standard shapes and covered from head to heels with official rubber stamps.
>   — H. L. MENCKEN

> Cape Cod is the bared and bended arm of Massachusetts; the shoulder is at Buzzard's Bay; the elbow or crazy bone at Cape Mallebarre, the wrist at Truro; the sandy fist at Provincetown.
>   — HENRY DAVID THOREAU

Two other figures of speech, **personification** and **hyperbole,** are less common than metaphor and simile. Personification treats ideas and objects as if they were human.

> The economy consumes my money and gives me little in return.

> I could hear the whisper of snowflakes, nudging each other as they fell.

Hyperbole deliberately exaggerates.

> She appeared in a mile of billowing chiffon, flashing a rhinestone as big as an ostrich egg.

> I'm going to cut him up in small cubes and fry him in deep fat.

exact
31b

To be successful, figurative language must be fresh and unstrained, calling attention not to itself but to the writer's meaning. If readers reject your language as trite or overblown, they may reject your message. One kind of figurative language gone wrong is the **mixed metaphor,** in which the writer combines two or more incompatible figures.

MIXED   He often hatched new ideas, using them to unlock the doors of opportunity.

Since metaphors often generate visual images in the mind of the reader, a mixed metaphor can create a ludicrous scene.

> MIXED   Various thorny problems that one would prefer to sweep under the rug continue to bob up all the same.

To revise a mixed metaphor, follow through consistently with just one metaphor.

> IMPROVED   Various thorny problems that one would prefer to weed out continue to sprout up all the same.

EXERCISE 7

Identify each figure of speech in the sentences below as a simile or a metaphor and analyze how it contributes to the writer's meaning.

1. All artists quiver under the lash of adverse criticism.
   — CATHERINE DRINKER BOWEN
2. Louisa spends the entire day in blue, limpid boredom. The caressing sting of it appears to be, for her, like the pleasure of lemon, or the coldness of salt water.   — ELIZABETH HARDWICK
3. Every writer, in a roomful of writers, wants to be the best, and the judge, or umpire, or referee is soon overwhelmed and shouted down like a chickadee trying to take charge of a caucus of crows.   — JAMES THURBER
4. See enough and write it down, I tell myself, and then some morning when the world seems drained of wonder, some day when I am only going through the motions of doing what I am supposed to do, which is write — on that bankrupt morning I will simply open my notebook and there it all will be, a forgotten account with accumulated interest, paid passage back to the world out there. . . .   — JOAN DIDION
5. At best today it [the railroad in America] resembles a fabled ruin, a vast fallen empire. More commonly it suggests a stodgy and even dirtier-looking subway; a sprawling anachronism that conveys not ruin but mess, not age but senility, not something speeding across continents but stalled between stations.
   — LOUIS KRONENBERGER

exact

31b

EXERCISE 8

Invent appropriate figurative language of your own (simile, metaphor, hyperbole, or personification) to describe each scene or quality below, and use the figure effectively in a sentence.

Example:

the attraction of a lake on a hot day
The small waves *like fingers beckoned* us irresistibly.

1. the sound of a kindergarten classroom
2. people waiting in line to buy tickets to a rock concert
3. the politeness of strangers meeting for the first time
4. a streetlight seen through dense fog
5. the effect of watching television for ten hours straight

5
Avoiding trite expressions

Trite expressions, or **clichés,** are phrases so old and so often repeated that they become stale. They include worn figures of speech, such as *heavy as lead, thin as a rail, wise as an owl;* stale scraps from literature, such as *to be or not to be, trip the light fantastic, gone with the wind;* adjectives and nouns that have become inseparable, such as *acid test, crushing blow, ripe old age;* and simply overused phrases, such as *point with pride, easier said than done, better late than never.* Many of these expressions were probably once fresh and forceful, but constant use has dulled them. They can slide almost automatically into your writing unless you are alert to them. If you let a few slip through, they will weaken your writing by suggesting that you have not thought about what you are saying and have used the easiest expression.

The following list contains some of the trite expressions you should work to avoid.

add insult to injury	ladder of success
beyond the shadow of a doubt	moving experience
brought back to reality	needle in a haystack
cool, calm, and collected	on a silver platter
diabolical skill	sadder but wiser
dyed in the wool	sneaking suspicion
face the music	sober as a judge
gentle as a lamb	stand in awe
hard as a rock	strong as an ox
hit the nail on the head	tired but happy
hour of need	tried and true

exact
31b

EXERCISE 9

Revise the sentences below to eliminate trite expressions.

Example:

The basketball team had almost seized victory, but it faced the test of truth in the last quarter of the game.

The basketball team *seemed about to win,* but the last quarter of the game *tested it further.*

1. These disastrous consequences of the war have shaken the small nation to its roots.

2. The handwriting is on the wall: Either cut the federal government down to size or face the music of having more bureaucrats than citizens.
3. When my father retired from the gas company after thirty long years, he was honored to receive a large clock in recognition of his valued service.
4. Sam shouldered his way through the crowd, hoping to catch a glimpse of the actress who had become the woman of his dreams.
5. After years of unprecedented prosperity and nearly uninterrupted peace and quiet, Americans have been brought back to reality by internal discord and economic confusion.

31c
Being concise

The word *concise* comes from a Latin word meaning "to cut," and being concise in writing requires cutting whatever adds nothing to your meaning. In revising your sentences, search for forceful and exact words and details that are essential to your meaning. Cross out all the empty words; cut out repetition that neither clarifies nor emphasizes your meaning; and be sure you have used the most direct grammatical form to express your ideas. Don't mistake brevity for conciseness; they are not the same thing. Concise writing states without wasting words but does not exclude the concrete and specific details that make meaning clear and exact.

1
Cutting empty words and phrases

Writers sometimes resort to empty words and phrases, either thinking that they sound authoritative or leaning on them when solid words will not come. But empty expressions simply fill space, and they should be eliminated in revision.

Filler phrases say in several words what a single word can say as well.

For	Substitute
at all times	always
at the present time	now
at this point in time	now
in the nature of	like
for the purpose of	for
in order to	to
until such time as	until
for the reason that	because

con
31c

FOR	SUBSTITUTE
due to the fact that	because
because of the fact that	because
by virtue of the fact that	because
in the event that	if
by means of	by
in the final analysis	finally

Some filler phrases — such as *all things considered, as far as I'm concerned,* and *for all intents and purposes* — can be cut entirely with no loss in meaning.

WORDY   For all intents and purposes, few women have yet achieved equal pay for equal work.

CONCISE   Few women have yet achieved equal pay for equal work.

All-purpose words, as their name implies, could mean almost anything. They include *angle, area, aspect, case, character, factor, field, kind, situation,* and *type.* Because all-purpose words convey so little information, they almost always clutter and complicate the sentences they appear in.

WORDY   Because I chose the field of chemistry as my major, the whole character of my attitude toward the area of learning has changed.

CONCISE   My choice of chemistry as a major has changed my attitude toward learning.

WORDY   The type of large expenditures on advertising that manufacturers must make is a very important aspect of the cost of detergent cleansers.

CONCISE   Manufacturers' large advertising expenditures increase the cost of detergents.

EXERCISE 10

Revise the following sentences as necessary to achieve conciseness. Concentrate on cutting filler phrases and all-purpose words.

Example:

I came to college because of many factors, but most of all because of the fact that I want a career in medicine.

I came to college *primarily because* I want a career in medicine.

1. When making plans of any sort, one cannot discount the element of chance.
2. The fact is that most people are too absorbed in their own lives to care much about the situations of others.

con
31c

3. The baseball situation I like best is when the game seems to be over, for all intents and purposes, and the home team's slugger hits the winning run out of the park.
4. The nature of cooking — the attention to detail it demands and the creativity it allows — is what drew me into cooking school.
5. One aspect of majoring in Asian studies is a distinct drawback: Except for a few rare teaching and curatorial positions, jobs are not available now and probably will not be available for some time to come.

2
Avoiding unnecessary repetition

Deliberately repeating words for parallelism or emphasis may clarify meaning and enhance coherence (see 17b and 18b). But unnecessary repetition weakens sentences. Avoid flabby repetition like that illustrated in the following examples.

WORDY	When he died, Fitzgerald was writing a book that promised to be his best book.
CONCISE	When he died, Fitzgerald was writing what promised to be his best book.
WORDY	The plane was flying directly in the direction of Dallas when it crashed.
CONCISE	The plane was flying toward Dallas when it crashed.
WORDY	The machine crushes the ore into fine bits and dumps the crushed ore into a bin.
CONCISE	The machine pulverizes the ore and then dumps it into a bin.

Notice that using one word two different ways within a sentence is especially confusing.

con
31c

CONFUSING	In grade school and high school I always had good grades.
CLEAR	In both grammar and high school I always had good grades.

The simplest kind of useless repetition is the **redundant phrase,** a phrase that says the same thing twice, such as *few in number* and *large in size.* Some of the most common redundant phrases are listed below. (The unneeded words are italicized.)

biography *of his life*	*final* completion
consensus *of opinion*	*habitual* custom
cooperate *together*	*important* (*basic*) essentials

large (small) *in size*	return *again*
puzzling *in nature*	square (round, oblong) *in shape*
repeat *again*	*surrounding* circumstances

A related form of redundancy is repetition of the same idea in slightly different words. In the sentences below, the unneeded phrases are italicized.

WORDY   We planned to meet just before sunrise *very early in the morning.*

WORDY   Many unskilled workers *without training in a particular job* are unemployed *and don't have any work.*

EXERCISE 11

Revise the following sentences to achieve conciseness. Concentrate on eliminating unnecessary or confusing repetition and redundancy.

Example:

Because the circumstances surrounding the cancellation of classes were murky and unclear, the editor of the student newspaper assigned a staff reporter to investigate and file a report on the circumstances.

Because the circumstances leading to the cancellation of classes were unclear, the editor of the student newspaper assigned a staffer to investigate and report the story.

1. In today's world in the last quarter of the twentieth century, security has become a more compelling goal than social reform.
2. Deadly nightshade is aptly named. It has small white flowers and deep black fruit. The fruit looks like night, and it also looks like death. The fruit does happen to be poisonous, too.
3. The fire that destroyed my apartment also destroyed my books and research notes. Now, with the research for my term paper destroyed, I'll have to start it all over again from the beginning.
4. The disastrous drought was devastating to crops, but the farmers cooperated together to help each other out.
5. In his autobiography of his life, and particularly in his version of the Watergate scandal, Richard Nixon rehashed old claims and did not reveal anything new.

con
31c

3
Simplifying word groups and sentences

Choose the simplest and most direct grammatical construction that fits your meaning. Don't use a clause if a phrase will do; don't use a phrase if a word will do. *The strength that the panther has, the strength of the panther,* and *the panther's strength* mean the same thing. But the first takes six words, the last only three.

WORDY	The figurine, which was carved from a piece of ivory, measured three inches.
REVISED	The figurine, carved of ivory, measured three inches.
CONCISE	The carved ivory figurine measured three inches.
WORDY	On a corner of Main Street a man was selling mice that were mechanical.
CONCISE	On a Main Street corner a man was selling mechanical mice.

(See 16b for advice on the ways to subordinate information.)

You can streamline and strengthen sentences by choosing strong verbs that advance the action rather than weak verbs that merely mark time. Weak verbs, along with their usual baggage of inflated nouns and unnecessary adjectives and prepositional phrases, flatten sentences just where they should be liveliest and pad them with unnecessary words.

WORDY	The painting *is a glorification of* Queen Victoria.
CONCISE	The painting *glorifies* Queen Victoria.

The first sentence takes three more words than the second to convey the same information. In the second sentence the direct, evocative verb *glorifies* substitutes for both the long noun *glorification* (which requires a prepositional phrase) and the colorless linking verb *is*. Wordy constructions of a weak verb like *is, has,* or *make* plus an adjective or noun commonly clutter writing.

WORDY	I *am desirous* of teaching music to children.
CONCISE	I *want* to teach music to children.
WORDY	He *had the sense* that she would die.
CONCISE	He *sensed* that she would die.
WORDY	Though they *made some advancement* in the next hours, they still failed to reach camp.
CONCISE	Though they *advanced* in the next hours, they still failed to reach camp.

con
31c

Passive constructions usually contain more words (and much more indirectness) than active constructions. Revise passive constructions by shifting their verbs to the active voice and positioning the actor as the subject.

WORDY   *The building had been designed by architects* six years earlier, and *the plans had been reviewed by no one* before *construction was begun.*

CONCISE   *Architects had designed the building* six years earlier, and *no one had reviewed the plans* before *construction began.*

Whenever possible, avoid sentences beginning with the expletive constructions *there is* and *there are.* Revise expletive constructions by removing *there*, moving the subject to the beginning of the sentence, and substituting a strong verb for *is* or *are.*

WORDY   *There are several plots that are repeated* in television drama.

CONCISE   *Several plots occur repeatedly* in television drama.

(See also 18d and 18e on passives and expletives.)

EXERCISE 12

Make the following sentences as concise as possible. Simplify grammatical structures, replace weak verbs with strong ones, and eliminate passive and expletive constructions.

> *Example:*
>
> He was taking some exercise in the park when several thugs were suddenly ahead in his path.
>
> He was *exercising* (or *jogging* or *strolling* or *doing calisthenics*) in the park when several thugs suddenly *loomed* in his path.

1. The new goal posts were torn down by vandals before the first game, and the science building windows were broken.
2. The house on Hedron Street that is brightly lighted belongs to a woman who was once a madam.
3. I am aware that most people of about my age are bored by politics, but I myself am becoming more and more interested in the subject.
4. When a social reform is taking root, such as affirmative action in education and business, it is followed by backlash from those for whom the reform is not directly beneficial.
5. The attendance at the conference was lower than we expected, but there is evidence that the results of the meeting have been spread by word of mouth.

4
Avoiding jargon

Jargon is the special vocabulary of any discipline or profession; medical and economic terms are examples. (See 31a-6.) But *jargon* also commonly describes any vague, inflated language that states relatively simple ideas in unnecessarily complicated ways.

con

31c

The directions for using a shower head tell us that *the nozzle with which this spray system is equipped will allow the user to reduce the mean diameter of the spray spectrum* instead of simply saying that *the nozzle will concentrate the spray.* Jargon often sounds as if the writer had studied all the guidelines for being exact and concise and then had set out to violate every one.

JARGON   The necessity for the individual to become a separate entity in his own right may impel a child to engage in open rebelliousness against parental authority or against sibling influence, with resultant confusion of those being rebelled against.

TRANSLATION   A child's natural desire to become himself may make him rebel against bewildered parents or siblings.

JARGON   Please interface with employees by spending time on the floor for information getting and listening to employees' inputs and feedbacks as they offer same.

TRANSLATION   Spend time with employees and listen to their complaints and suggestions.

EXERCISE 13

Make the following passage as concise as possible. Eliminate jargon by cutting unneeded or repeated words and by simplifying both words and grammatical structures. Consult a dictionary as needed. Be merciless.

Example:

The nursery school teacher education training sessions involve active interfacing with preschool children of the appropriate age as well as intensive peer interaction in the form of role plays.

Training for nursery school teachers involves *interaction* with *preschoolers* and *role playing with peers.*

con

31c

At the end of a lengthy line of reasoning, he came to the conclusion that the situation with carcinogens [cancer-causing substances] should be regarded as analogous to the situation with the automobile. Rather than giving in to an irrational fear of cancer, we should consider all aspects of the problem in a balanced and dispassionate frame of mind, making a total of the benefits received from potential carcinogens (plastics, pesticides, and other similar products) and measuring said total against the damage done by such products. This is the nature of most discussions about the automobile. Rather than responding irrationally to the visual, aural, and oral pollution caused by automobiles, we have decided to live with them (while simultaneously working to improve on them) for the benefits brought to society as a whole.

32

Using the Dictionary

Consulting a dictionary can strengthen your choice of words. It can show you what words fit your needs (see Chapter 31); it can help you build your vocabulary (see Chapter 33); and it can show you how to spell words (see Chapter 34). It can answer most of the questions about words you may ask. This chapter will show you how to choose a dictionary that suits your purpose, how to read a dictionary without difficulty, and how to work with a dictionary as a flexible, compact, and thorough word reference.

An ordinary dictionary records in an alphabetical list the current usage and meaning of the words of a language. To do this, it includes a word's spelling, syllables, pronunciation, origin, meanings, grammatical functions, and grammatical forms. For some words the dictionary may provide a label indicating the status of the word according to geography, time, style, or subject matter. It may also list other words closely related in meaning and explain the distinctions among them. Some dictionaries include quotations illustrating a word's history or special uses. Many dictionaries include additional reference information, such as an essay on the history of English, rules for punctuation and spelling, a vocabulary of rhymes, names and locations of colleges, and tables of weights and measures.

32a

Choosing a dictionary

1

Abridged dictionaries

Abridged dictionaries are the most practical for everyday use. Often called desk dictionaries because of their convenient size, they usually list 100,000 to 150,000 words and concentrate on fairly common words and meanings. Though you may sometimes need to consult an unabridged or a more specialized dictionary, a good abridged dictionary will serve most reference needs for writing and reading. Any of the following abridged dictionaries, listed alphabetically, is dependable.

The American Heritage Dictionary of the English Language. 2nd coll. ed. Boston: Houghton Mifflin, 1982. This dictionary's most obvious feature is its wealth of illustrations: more than 4000 photographs, drawings, and maps. The dictionary includes foreign words, abbreviations, and geographical and biographical names among the main entries. The definitions are arranged so that the most common meaning comes first. Usage labels (*slang, informal,* and so on) are applied liberally. Many words are followed by usage notes, which reflect the consensus of a panel of one hundred writers, editors, and teachers. The dictionary uses as few abbreviations and symbols as practicable. It includes guides to usage, grammar, spelling, and punctuation, and an appendix on Indo-European roots.

Oxford American Dictionary. New York: Oxford Univ. Press, 1980. A descendant of the unabridged *Oxford English Dictionary* (see below), this abridged dictionary is somewhat briefer than any of the others listed here. Its pronunciation symbols are particularly straightforward and easy to use. Its word meanings, arranged according to the frequency of their use, are short and simple. The dictionary emphasizes correct American usage, applies usage labels frequently, and includes over 600 usage notes. Unlike most other abridged dictionaries, this one contains no special appendixes and no etymologies, or word histories.

The Random House Dictionary of the English Language. Coll. ed. New York: Random House, 1982. Based on the unabridged *Random House Dictionary* (see below), this dictionary includes abbreviations and biographical and geographical names in the main alphabetical listing. Its list of words is particularly up to date. Appendixes include a manual of style.

Webster's New Collegiate Dictionary. 8th ed. Springfield, Mass.: Merriam, 1981. This dictionary, based on the unabridged *Webster's Third New International Dictionary* (see below), concentrates on standard English and applies usage labels (such as *slang*) less frequently than do other dictionaries. Word definitions are listed in chronological order of their appearance in the language rather than in order of preferred meaning. The main alphabetical listing includes abbreviations, but geographical and biographical names and foreign words and phrases appear in appendixes, as does a manual of style.

Webster's New World Dictionary of the American Language. 2nd coll. ed. New York: Simon & Schuster, 1978. This dictionary in-

32a

cludes foreign words, abbreviations, and geographical and biographical names in the main alphabetical listing. The definitions of
words are arranged in chronological order. Usage labels (*colloquial,
slang,* and so on) are applied liberally, and words and phrases of
American origin are starred. Appendixes on punctuation and mechanics and on manuscript form are included.

2
Unabridged dictionaries

Unabridged dictionaries are the most scholarly and comprehensive of all dictionaries, sometimes consisting of several volumes.
They emphasize the history of words and the variety of their uses.
An unabridged dictionary is useful when you are studying a word in
depth, reading or writing about the literature of another century, or
looking for a quotation containing a particular word. The following
unabridged dictionaries are available at most libraries.

The Oxford English Dictionary. 13 volumes plus 4 supplements
(in progress). New York: Oxford Univ. Press, 1933, 1972, 1976. Also
available in a compact, photographically reduced, two-volume edition, 1971. This is the greatest dictionary of our language. Its purpose is to show the histories and current meanings of all words. Its
entries illustrate the changes in a word's spelling, pronunciation,
and meaning with quotations from writers of every century. Some
entries span pages. The main dictionary focuses on British words
and meanings, but the supplements include American words and
meanings.

The Random House Dictionary of the English Language. New
York: Random House, 1980. This dictionary is smaller (and less expensive) than many unabridged dictionaries (it has 260,000 entries
compared to 450,000 in *Webster's Third New International*). Its entries and definitions are especially up to date. Its appendixes include
short dictionaries of French, Spanish, Italian, and German; a list of
reference books; a manual of style; a brief atlas with color maps;
and a list of major dates in history.

*Webster's Third New International Dictionary of the English
Language.* Springfield, Mass.: Merriam, 1981. This dictionary attempts to record our language more as it *is* used than as it *should* be
used. Therefore, usage labels (such as *slang*) are minimal. Definitions are given in chronological order of their appearance in the language. Most acceptable spellings and pronunciations are provided.
Plentiful illustrative quotations show variations in the uses of words.
The dictionary is unusually strong in new scientific and technical
terms.

32a

3

Special dictionaries

Special dictionaries limit their attention to a single class of word (for example, slang, engineering terms, abbreviations), to a single kind of information (synonyms, usage, word origins), or to a specific subject (black culture, biography, history). Thus special dictionaries provide more extensive and complete information about their topics than general dictionaries do.

Special dictionaries on slang or word origins not only can help you locate uncommon information but also can give you a sense of the great richness and variety of language.

FOR INFORMATION ON SLANG

Partridge, Eric. *Dictionary of Slang and Unconventional English.* 7th ed. New York: Macmillan, 1970.

Wentworth, Harold, and Stuart Berg Flexner. *Dictionary of American Slang.* 2nd supp. ed. New York: Crowell, 1975.

FOR THE ORIGINS OF WORDS

Morris, William, and Mary Morris. *Dictionary of Word and Phrase Origins.* 3 vols. New York: Harper & Row, 1971.

Partridge, Eric. *Origins: A Short Etymological Dictionary of Modern English.* 4th ed. New York: Macmillan, 1966.

Two kinds of special dictionaries — a usage dictionary and a dictionary of synonyms — are such useful references for everyday writing that you may want one of each on your own reference shelf. A dictionary of usage contains extensive entries for the words, phrases, and constructions that most frequently cause problems and controversy.

FOR GUIDANCE ON ENGLISH USAGE

Follett, Wilson. *Modern American Usage.* Ed. Jacques Barzun. New York: Hill and Wang, 1966.

Fowler, H. W. *A Dictionary of Modern English Usage.* 2nd ed. Rev. and ed. Sir Ernest Gowers. New York: Oxford Univ. Press, 1965.

Morris, William, and Mary Morris. *Harper Dictionary of Contemporary Usage.* New York: Harper & Row, 1975.

32a

A dictionary of synonyms provides lists of words with closely related meanings. The lists are much more extensive than the usage notes in a general dictionary. Some dictionaries of synonyms contain extended discussions and illustrations of various shades of meaning.

FOR INFORMATION ABOUT SYNONYMS

Lewis, Norman. *The New Roget's Thesaurus of the English Language in Dictionary Form.* New York: Putnam's, 1964.

Webster's New Dictionary of Synonyms. Springfield, Mass.: Merriam, 1973.

See 35b for an extensive list of special dictionaries in fields such as literature, business, history, psychology, and science.

32b
Working with a dictionary's contents

1
Finding general information

The dictionary is a convenient reference for information of every sort. Most abridged dictionaries will tell you the atomic weight of oxygen, Napoleon's birth and death dates, the location of Fort Knox, the population of Gambia, what the Conestoga wagon of the Old West looked like, the origin and nature of surrealism, or the number of cups in a quart. Finding such information may require a little work — for instance, checking the entry *periodic table* or *element* as well as *oxygen,* or consulting an appendix of biographical names for Napoleon. But a dictionary is often the quickest and most accessible reference for general information when an encyclopedia, textbook, or other reference book is unavailable or inconvenient to refer to.

2
Answering specific questions

Dictionaries use abbreviations and symbols to squeeze a lot of information into a relatively small book. This system of condensed information may at first seem difficult to read. But all dictionaries include in their opening pages detailed information on the arrangement of entries, pronunciation symbols, and abbreviations. And the format is quite similar from one dictionary to another, so becoming familiar with the abbreviations and symbols in one dictionary makes reading any dictionary an easy routine. The labeled parts of the two entries below — *conjecture* from the *American Heritage Dictionary* (referred to from now on as *AHD*) and *reckon* from *Webster's New Collegiate Dictionary* — are discussed in the following sections.

32b

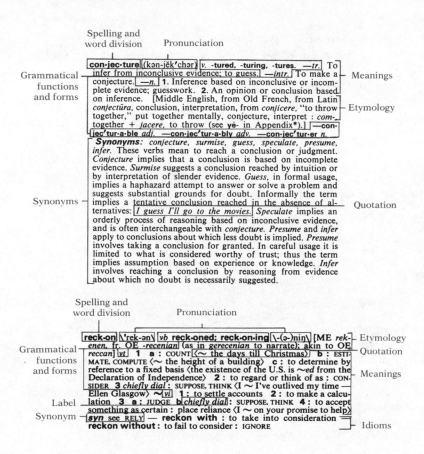

Spelling and word division

Grammatical functions and forms

Pronunciation

Meanings

Etymology

Synonyms

Quotation

Spelling and word division

Pronunciation

Grammatical functions and forms

Etymology

Quotation

Meanings

Label

Synonym

Idioms

Spelling and word division

The small initial letters for both *conjecture* and *reckon* indicate that these words are not normally capitalized. (In contrast, *Franklin stove* is capitalized in both the *AHD* and *Webster's Collegiate* because *Franklin* is a proper noun.)

The centered periods in **con·jec·ture** and **reck·on** show the divisions of these words into syllables. If you are writing or typing a word of more than one syllable and need to break it at the end of a line, follow the dictionary's division of the word into syllables. (See also Chapter 30 for general rules about word division.)

If a word is a hyphenated compound word, such as *cross-reference*, a dictionary shows the hyphen as part of the spelling: **cross-ref·er·ence.** The treatment of foreign words such as *joie de vivre* or *ex post facto*, which are normally italicized (or underlined) in writing, is more varied. *Webster's New World Dictionary* places a special symbol (‡) before each one. The *AHD* simply designates

32b

them as *French* and *Latin*, respectively, thereby indicating they
should be italicized.

Dictionaries provide any variant spellings of a word at the beginning of an entry. Thus, for the word *dexterous, Webster's Collegiate* has **"dex·ter·ous** *or* **dex·trous,"** indicating that the more common spelling is *dexterous*, although *dextrous* is acceptable.

EXERCISE 1

Check the spelling of the following words in a dictionary. Correct
any incorrect spellings, and divide all the words into syllables.

1. England	5. inheritence	9. grievance
2. innoculate	6. over-estimate	10. secretery
3. reccommend	7. depreciation	11. trans-Atlantic
4. methodical	8. excruciating	12. crossreference

Pronunciation

Dictionaries use symbols to indicate how to pronounce a word
because the alphabet itself does not record all the sounds in the language. (Listen, for example, to the different sounds of *a* in only three
words: *far, make,* and *answer.*) Most dictionaries provide a key to
the pronunciation symbols at the foot of each page or every two facing pages.

The entries for *conjecture* and *reckon* show two slightly different pronunciation systems. In the *AHD*'s *conjecture* the pronunciation appears in parentheses; in *Webster's Collegiate* it appears in reversed slashes (\ \ ). In both entries the stressed syllable is
indicated by an accent mark (' and ꞌ); but in the *AHD* the mark follows the stressed syllable (kən-jĕk′chər), whereas in *Webster's Collegiate* it precedes the stressed syllable (ꞌrek-ən).

Most unabridged and some abridged dictionaries provide variant pronunciations, including regional differences. The *AHD*, for example, provides two pronunciations for the last syllable of *licorice*,
indicating that the word may be pronounced either of two ways:
"lĭk′ər-ĭs, -ĭsh."

32b

EXERCISE 2

Consult a dictionary for the correct pronunciation of the following
words. Write out the pronunciation as given, using the dictionary's
symbols. (If more than one pronunciation is given, write them all
out.)

1. crucifixion	5. bathos	9. polemic
2. mnemonics	6. epitome	10. yacht
3. timorous	7. miserable	11. promenade
4. utilitarian	8. obelisk	12. insouciance

Grammatical functions and forms

Dictionaries give helpful information about a word's function and forms. The *Webster's Collegiate* entry for *reckon* shows the word to be a verb (*vb*), with the past tense and past participle *reckoned* and the present participle *reckoning*, and with both transitive (*vt*) and intransitive (*vi*) meanings. The *AHD* entry for *conjecture* shows it to be an even more versatile word. It is a verb (*v.*): past tense and past participle *conjectured*, present participle *conjecturing*, and third-person singular present tense *conjectures*. The verb has both transitive (*tr.*) and intransitive (*intr.*) meanings. And *conjecture* is also a noun (*n.*), with separate meanings in that function.

Most dictionaries provide not only the principal forms of regular and irregular verbs but also the plural forms of irregular nouns and the comparative and superlative forms of adjectives and adverbs that commonly show degree with *-er* and *-est*. An adjective or adverb without *-er* and *-est* forms in the dictionary requires the addition of *more* and *most* to show the comparative and superlative.

When other parts of speech are formed from the word being defined and have related meanings, those words are grouped at the end of the entry, where they are spelled, divided, accented, and identified by part of speech but not defined. Several of these so-called derivative forms are provided at the end of the *AHD* entry for *conjecture: conjecturable* (*adj.*), *conjecturably* (*adv.*), and *conjecturer* (*n.*).

The *Webster's Collegiate* entry for *reckon* ends with two uses of the word in idiomatic expressions (*reckon with* and *reckon without*). These phrases are defined (unlike the related parts of speech of *conjecture*) because, as with all idioms, their meanings cannot be inferred simply from the words they consist of (see 31b-3).

32b

EXERCISE 3

Consult a dictionary to determine the part of speech of each of the following words. If the word functions as more than one part of speech, list them all. If the word is a verb, list its principal parts; if a noun, its plural form; if an adjective or adverb, its comparative and superlative.

1. little	5. machine	9. upset
2. that	6. orient	10. steal
3. study	7. roof	11. manifest
4. happen	8. ring	12. firm

Etymology

Dictionaries provide the **etymology** of a word (its history) to indicate its origin and the evolution of its meanings and forms. The dictionary can compress much information about a word into a small space through symbols, abbreviations, and different type-faces. An explanation of these systems appears in the dictionary's opening pages. The *AHD* traces *conjecture* first to Middle English (twelfth to fifteenth centuries), back through Old French (ninth to sixteenth centuries), and then to Latin. The final parenthetical reference to the Appendix directs us to a list of roots in Indo-European, the unwritten parent language of most modern languages of India and Europe. (See 33a for a brief history of the English language.) As the entry in *Webster's Collegiate* shows, *reckon* came to English by a different route, arriving from Old English (OE) by way of Middle English (ME).

Sometimes dictionaries will not give the etymology for a word. Their practices differ (and are explained in their opening pages), but in general they omit etymology when it is obvious, unknown, or available elsewhere in the dictionary.

EXERCISE 4

Consult a dictionary for the etymologies of the following words Use the dictionary's own explanations of abbreviations and symbols to get the fullest history of the word, and write out that history in your own words.

1. grammar	5. penetrate	9. calico
2. engage	6. promote	10. chauvinism
3. leaf	7. retrieve	11. assassin
4. moon	8. toxic	12. water

Meanings

Dictionaries divide the general meaning of a word into particular meanings on the basis of how the word is or has been actually used. They arrange a word's meanings differently, however, explaining the basis of their arrangement in their opening pages. *Webster's Collegiate* and *Webster's New World* list meanings in order of their appearance in the language, earliest first. The *AHD*, *Oxford American*, and abridged *Random House*, in contrast, place the word's most basic or most common meaning first and follow it with the other meanings. These different policies will result in roughly the same arrangement of meanings only when the oldest meaning of a word is also the most common. Thus you should be sure you know the system of arrangement used by any dictionary you are consulting. Then read through the entire entry before settling on the meaning that most closely fits the context of what you're reading or writing.

Most dictionaries provide any special technical and scientific

32b

meanings of a word in separately numbered entries that are usually labeled. These labels are discussed in more detail below.

EXERCISE 5

Consult a dictionary for the meanings of the following words. How many distinct meanings does each word have? How does the dictionary list meanings, chronologically or in order of importance? If chronologically, is the oldest meaning also the most common? What changes have occurred in each word's use over time?

1. weight	5. order	9. prefer
2. recipe	6. apt	10. quit
3. color	7. astrology	11. spring
4. condition	8. offered	12. sue

Synonyms and antonyms

Synonyms are words whose meanings are approximately the same, such as *small* and *little*. **Antonyms** are words whose meanings are approximately opposite, such as *small* and *big*. When a word has many closely related synonyms that are hard to distinguish, an abridged dictionary may devote a separate paragraph to them. The *AHD* does so in distinguishing the verb *conjecture* from the verbs *surmise, guess, speculate, presume,* and *infer,* each of which can also be looked up in its alphabetical place. *Webster's Collegiate* defines *reckon* with some words in small capital letters (COUNT, ESTIMATE, COMPUTE, and so on). These are both synonyms and cross-references, in that each word may be looked up in its alphabetical place. At the boldface **syn** at the end of the entry, the phrase "see RELY" directs us to a brief treatment of synonyms at the entry for *rely*. Dictionaries specify antonyms less often than synonyms, usually with a boldface **ant** at the end of the entry.

Reading through the lists and discussions of synonyms and antonyms for a word can help you locate its meaning in a given context more exactly. (See 33c-2 for a discussion of how to use the synonyms provided by a dictionary to increase your vocabulary.)

32b

EXERCISE 6

Consult a dictionary for the synonyms and antonyms of the following words. Use the word itself and each synonym or antonym appropriately in a sentence of your own.

1. suggest	4. discover	7. kind (*adj.*)
2. plain (*adj.*)	5. change (*v.*)	8. memory
3. high (*adj.*)	6. beautiful	9. serious

Labels

Dictionaries apply labels to a word or one of its meanings that has a certain status or a special use. The labels are usually of four kinds: subject, style, region, and time.

Subject labels tell us that a word or one of its meanings has a special use in a field of knowledge or a profession. In its entry for *relaxation*, for instance, the *AHD* presents specialized meanings with the subject labels *physiology, physics*, and *mathematics*.

Style labels restrict a word or one of its meanings to a particular level of usage, such as *slang, colloquial* or *informal, nonstandard* or *substandard, vulgar*, and *poetic* or *literary*. The label *slang* indicates that a word should be used in writing only for a special effect. For example, all the abridged dictionaries label *crumb* as slang when it means "a worthless or despicable person." The label *informal* or *colloquial* is applied to words that are appropriate for conversation and informal writing but not for formal writing. For instance, the *AHD* labels as informal the use of *sure* in the sentence *We sure need that money* (the more formal word is *surely*). The label *nonstandard* or *substandard* is applied to words or their meanings that are considered inappropriate for standard speech and writing. The *AHD* labels all uses of *ain't* as nonstandard, whereas *Webster's Collegiate* remarks that *ain't* is "disapproved by many" but labels expressions like *I ain't got no* substandard. The label *vulgar*, or sometimes *vulgar slang*, is applied to words or their meanings that are normally considered offensive in speech and writing. The label *poetic* or *literary* designates words or their meanings (such as *eve* for *evening* and *o'er* for *over*) used only in poetry or the most formal writing.

Region labels indicate that a particular spelling, pronunciation, or meaning of a word is not national but limited to some area. A regional difference may be indicated by the label *dialect*. *Webster's Collegiate* labels as dialect (*dial*) the uses of *reckon* to mean "suppose" or "think" (as in *I reckon I'll do that*). More specific region labels may designate areas of the United States or other countries. The word *bloke* (meaning "fellow") is labeled as British by most dictionaries. And the *AHD* labels *arroyo*, "a deep gully" or "a dry gulch," as Southwestern U.S.

Time labels indicate words or their meanings that the language, in evolving, has discarded. These words and meanings are included in the dictionary primarily to help readers of some older texts that contain them. The label *obsolete* designates words or specific meanings that are no longer used, whereas the label *archaic* designates words or specific meanings that are out-of-date though still in occasional use.

See 31a for further discussion of levels of usage and their appropriateness in your writing.

32b

EXERCISE 7

Consult at least two dictionaries to determine the status of each of the following words or any one of their meanings according to subject, style, region, or time.

1. impulse	5. goof	9. mad
2. OK	6. goober	10. sing
3. irregardless	7. lift	11. brief (*n.*)
4. neath	8. potlatch	12. joint

Illustrative quotations

Dictionaries are made by collecting quotations showing actual uses of words in all kinds of speech and writing. Some of these quotations, or others that the dictionary makers invent, may appear in the dictionary's entries as illustrations of how a word may be used. Unabridged dictionaries usually provide many such examples, not only to illustrate a word's current uses but also to show the changes in its meanings over time. Abridged dictionaries use quotations more selectively: to illustrate an unusual meaning of the word, to help distinguish between two closely related meanings of the same word, or to show the differences between synonyms. The *AHD* entry for *conjecture* and the *Webster's Collegiate* entry for *reckon* (p. 410) both employ quotation.

EXERCISE 8

Consult a dictionary to find a quotation illustrating at least one meaning of each word below. Then write an illustrative sentence of your own for each word.

1. jolt	4. ceremonial	7. legitimate
2. inarticulate	5. sensuous	8. inquire
3. discreet	6. tremble	9. nether

32b

33

Improving Your Vocabulary

A precise and versatile vocabulary is essential to effective communication. As you gain experience writing, you will want to improve the precision with which you use familiar words (see Chapter 31) and increase the number of words you can use appropriately.

This chapter briefly describes the development of English and explains how words are formed. Then it offers some advice for learning to use new words. The chapter has a twofold purpose: to provide a sense of the potential of English by acquainting you with its history and range of words; and to help you increase the range, versatility, and precision of your own vocabulary.

33a
Understanding the sources of English

People change their language as they and their surroundings change. They revise spellings, pronunciation, and syntax, alter meanings, and even add or drop words to keep the language fresh and useful. English changes continuously, but its subtle and complex character stays the same.

English has over 500,000 words, probably more than any other language. This exceptional vocabulary and the power and range of expression that accompany it derive from its special mix of word sources. For English, unlike many other languages, has borrowed a large number of words.

How English drew on its several sources and acquired its large vocabulary is the story of historical changes. The ancestor of English, Indo-European, was spoken (but not written) perhaps as far back as 500 B.C., and it eventually spread to cover the area from India west to the British Isles. In what is now England, an Indo-European offshoot called Celtic was spoken extensively until the fifth century A.D. But over the next few centuries invaders from the European continent, speaking a dialect of another Indo-European language, Germanic, overran the native Britons. The Germanic dialect became the original source of English.

Old English, spoken from the eighth to the twelfth centuries, was a rugged, guttural language, as the passage at the end of this paragraph illustrates. Old English used a slightly different alphabet from ours (including the characters ð and þ for *th*), which has been transcribed in the sample below. The sample shows the opening lines of the Lord's Prayer, which we know today as "Our father, who art in heaven, hallowed be thy name. Thy kingdom come. Thy will be done on earth as it is in heaven."

> Fæder ure thu the eart on heofonum, si thin nama gehalgod. Tobecume thin rice. Gewurthe thin willa on eorthan swa swa on heofonum.

Many of our nouns, such as *stone, word, gift,* and *foot*, come from Old English. So do most of our pronouns, prepositions, and conjunctions, some — such as *he, under,* and *to* — without any change in spelling. Other Germanic tribes, using a similar dialect but settling on the European continent instead of in England, fostered two other languages, Dutch and German. As a result, Dutch, German, and English are related languages with some similar traits.

In 1066 the Normans, under William the Conqueror, invaded England. The Normans were originally Vikings who had settled in northern France and had forsaken Old Norse for their own dialect of Old French. They made Norman French the language of law, literature, and the ruling class in England. As a result, English acquired many French words, including many military and governmental words like *authority, mayor, crime, army,* and *guard*. The common English people kept English alive during the Norman occupation, but they adopted many French words intact (*air, point, place, age*), and eventually the French influence caused the language to shift from Old to Middle English, which lasted from the twelfth through the fifteenth centuries. During this time a great many Latin words also entered English, for Latin formed the background of Norman French, and it was the language of the Church and of scholars. English words that entered Middle English directly from Latin or from Latin through French include *language, luminous, memory, liberal,* and *sober.*

Middle English, as the following passage from Geoffrey Chaucer's *Canterbury Tales* shows, was much closer to our own language than to Old English.

33a

A clerk there was of Oxenford also,
That unto logyk hadde longe ygo.
As leene was his hors as is a rake,
And he nas nat right fat, I undertake,
But looked holwe, and therto sobrely.

Modern English evolved in the fourteenth and fifteenth centuries as the language's sound and spellings changed. This was the time of the Renaissance in Europe. Ancient Latin and Greek art, learning, and literature were revived, first in Italy and then throughout the continent. English vocabulary expanded rapidly, not only with more Latin and many Greek words (such as *democracy* and *physics*) but also with words from Italian and French. Advances in printing, beginning in the fifteenth century, made publications widely available to an increasingly literate audience. The Modern English of twentieth-century America is four centuries and an ocean removed from the Modern English of sixteenth-century England, but the two are fundamentally the same. The differences and the similarities are evident in this passage from the King James Bible, published in 1611:

And the Lord God commanded the man, saying, Of euery tree of the garden thou mayest freely eate. But of the tree of the knowl edge of good and euill, thou shalt not eate of it: for In the day that thou eatest thereof, thou shalt surely die.

33b
Learning the composition of words

Words can often be divided into meaningful parts. A *handbook*, for instance, is a book you keep at hand (for reference). A *shepherd* herds sheep (or other animals). Knowing what the parts of a word mean by themselves, as you do here, can often help you infer approximately what they mean when combined.

The following explanations of roots, prefixes, and suffixes provide information that can open up the meanings of words whose parts may not be familiar or easy to see. For more information, refer to a dictionary's etymologies, which provide the histories of words (see 32b).

33b

1
Learning roots

A **root** is the unchanging component of words related in origin and usually in meaning. Both *illiterate* ("unable to read and write") and *literal* ("sticking to the facts or to the first and most obvious meaning of an idea") share the root *liter*, derived from *littera*, a Latin word meaning "letter." A person who cannot understand the letters that make up writing is *illiterate*. A person who wants to understand the primary meaning of the letters (the words) in a contract is seeking the *literal* meaning of that contract.

At least half our words come from Latin and Greek. The list below includes some common Latin and Greek roots, their meanings, and examples of English words containing them.

ROOT (SOURCE)	MEANING	ENGLISH WORDS
aster, astr (G)	star	astronomy, astrology
audi (L)	to hear	audible, audience
bene (L)	good, well	benefactor, benevolent
bio (G)	life	biology, autobiography
dic, dict (L)	to speak	dictator, dictionary
fer (L)	to carry	transfer, referral
fix (L)	to fasten	fix, suffix, prefix
geo (G)	earth	geography, geology
graph (G)	to write	geography, photography
jur, jus (L)	law	jury, justice
log, logue (G)	word, thought, speech	astrology, biology, neologism
luc (L)	light	lucid, translucent
manu (L)	hand	manual, manuscript
meter, metr (G)	measure	metric, thermometer
op, oper (L)	work	operation, operator
path (G)	feeling	pathetic, sympathy
ped (G)	child	pediatrics
phil (G)	love	philosophy, Anglophile
phys (G)	body, nature	physical, physics
psych (G)	soul	psychic, psychology
scrib, script (L)	to write	scribble, manuscript
tele (G)	far off	telephone, television
ter, terr (L)	earth	territory, extraterrestrial
vac (L)	empty	vacant, vacuum, evacuate
verb (L)	word	verbal, verbose
vid, vis (L)	to see	video, vision, television

33b

EXERCISE 1

Define the following italicized words, using the list of roots above and any clues given by the rest of the sentence. Check the accuracy of your meanings in a dictionary.

1. After guiding me through college, my *benefactor* will help me start a career.
2. Always afraid of leading a *vacuous* life, the heiress immersed herself in volunteer work.
3. The posters *affixed* to the construction wall advertised a pornographic movie.

4. After his *auditory* nerve was damaged, he had trouble catching people's words.
5. The child *empathized* so completely with his mother that he felt pain when she broke her arm.

2
Learning prefixes

Prefixes are standard syllables fastened to the front of a word to modify its meaning. For example, the word *prehistory* is a combination of the word *history*, meaning "based on a written record explaining past events," and the prefix *pre-*, meaning "before." Together, prefix and word mean "before a written record explaining past events," or before events were recorded. Learning standard prefixes can help you improve vocabulary and spelling just as learning word roots can. The following lists group prefixes according to sense so that they are easier to remember. When two or more prefixes have very different spellings but the same meaning, they usually derive from different languages, most often Latin and Greek.

Prefixes showing quantity

MEANING	PREFIXES IN ENGLISH WORDS
half	*semi*annual; *hemi*sphere
one	*uni*cycle; *mon*arch, *mono*rail
two	*bi*nary, *bi*monthly; *di*lemma, *dicho*tomy
three	*tri*angle, *tri*logy
four	*quad*rangle, *quar*tet
five	*quint*et; *penta*gon
six	*sex*tuplets; *hexa*meter
seven	*sept*uagenarian; *hept*archy
eight	*oct*ave, *octo*pus
nine	*nona*genarian
ten	*deca*de, *deca*thlon
hundred	*cent*ury, *percent*age; *hecto*liter
thousand	*milli*meter; *kilo*cycle

33b

Prefixes showing negation

MEANING	PREFIXES IN ENGLISH WORDS
without, no, not	*a*sexual; *il*legal, *im*moral, *in*valid, *ir*reverent; *un*skilled
not, absence of, opposing, against	*non*breakable; *ant*acid, *anti*pathy, *contra*dict
opposite to, complement to	*counter*clockwise, *counter*weight

422 *Improving Your Vocabulary*

MEANING	PREFIXES IN ENGLISH WORDS
do the opposite of, remove, reduce	*de*horn, *de*vitalize, *de*value
do the opposite of, deprive of	*dis*establish, *dis*arm
wrongly, bad	*mis*judge, *mis*deed

Prefixes showing time

MEANING	PREFIXES IN ENGLISH WORDS
before	*ante*cedent; *fore*cast; *pre*cede; *pro*logue
after	*post*war
again	*re*write

Prefixes showing direction or position

MEANING	PREFIXES IN ENGLISH WORDS
above, over	*super*vise
across, over	*trans*port
below, under	*infra*sonic; *sub*terranean; *hypo*dermic
in front of	*pro*ceed; *pre*fix
behind	*re*cede
out of	*e*rupt, *ex*plicit; *ec*stasy
into	*in*jection, *im*merse; *en*courage, *em*power
around	*circum*ference; *peri*meter
with	*co*exist, *col*loquial, *com*municate, *conse*quence, *cor*respond; *sym*pathy, *syn*chronize

EXERCISE 2

Provide meanings for the following italicized words, using the lists of prefixes and any clues given by the rest of the sentence. Check the accuracy of your meanings in a dictionary.

1. In the twenty-first century some of our oldest cities will celebrate their *quadricentennials*.
2. Most poems called sonnets consist of fourteen lines divided into an *octave* and a *sestet*.
3. When the Congress seemed ready to cut Social Security benefits again, some representatives proposed the *countermeasure* of increasing Medicare payments.
4. By increasing Medicare payments, the representatives hoped to *forestall* the inevitable financial squeeze on the elderly.
5. Ferdinand Magellan, a Portuguese sailor, commanded the first expedition to *circumnavigate* the globe.

33b

3
Learning suffixes

Suffixes are standard syllables fastened to the end of a word to modify its meaning and usually its part of speech. The word *popular* is an adjective. With different suffixes, it becomes a different adjective, an adverb, a noun, and two different verbs.

ADJECTIVE	popul*ar*	**NOUN**	popul*ation*
	popul*ous*	**VERB**	popul*ate*
ADVERB	popul*arly*		popul*arize*

Many words change suffixes in the same way. In fact, suffixes help us recognize what parts of speech many words are, as the following examples show.

Noun suffixes

mis*ery*	min*er*	intern*ship*	random*ness*
refer*ence*	base*ment*	presid*ency*	brother*hood*
relev*ance*	national*ist*	discus*sion*	king*dom*
operat*or*	national*ism*	agit*ation*	

Verb suffixes

harden	pur*ify*
national*ize*	agit*ate*

Adjective suffixes

miser*able*	president*ial*	wonder*ful*	use*less*
ed*ible*	gigant*ic*	fibr*ous*	self*ish*
nation*al*	friend*ly*	adopt*ive*	flatul*ent*

The only suffix regularly applied to adverbs is *-ly:* openly, selfishly.

NOTE: Inflectional endings, such as the plural *-s*, the possessive *-'s*, the past tense *-ed*, and the comparative *-er* or *-est*, appear at the ends of words but do not change a word's grammatical function.

33b

EXERCISE 3

Identify the part of speech of each word below, and then change it to the part or parts of speech in parentheses by deleting, adding, or changing a suffix. Use the given word and each created word in a sentence. Check a dictionary if necessary to be sure suffixes and spellings are correct.

1. magic (*adjective*)
2. durable (*noun; adverb*)
3. refrigerator (*verb*)
4. self-critical (*noun*)
5. differ (*noun; adjective*)

6. equal (*noun; adverb*)
7. conversion (*verb; adjective*)
8. strictly (*adjective; noun*)
9. assist (*noun*)
10. qualification (*verb; adjective*)

33c
Learning to use new words

You can learn a new word not only by understanding its composition but also by examining the context in which it appears and by looking it up in a dictionary — both ways to increase your vocabulary by multiplying and varying your experience with language.

1
Examining context

Most people guess the meaning of an unfamiliar word by looking at familiar words around it. Imagine, for example, that you overheard someone saying the following:

> I was so tired I didn't bother with a real bed. I just lay down on the liclac in the living room. As soon as my feet rested at one end and my head at the other, I fell asleep. In the morning I was cramped from pushing against the back of the liclac.

To guess what *liclac* means, you could examine all the familiar words and learn that (1) a liclac isn't a bed, but you can lie on it; (2) it's part of a living room; (3) it's the length of a person; (4) it's narrow and has a back. From these clues you might guess that the nonsense word *liclac* represents a piece of living room furniture similar to a couch or sofa.

Parallelism shows you which ideas line up or go together and can often suggest the meaning of a new word. Watch for parallel ideas in the following sentence.

> The kittens see their mother hunt and kill, and they in turn take up *predatory* behavior.

If you did not know the word *predatory*, you could put together clues from the context: parallel construction (*kittens see . . . and they . . . take up*); the tip-off phrase *in turn;* and the suggested idea of imitation (kittens watching their mother and taking up her behavior). These clues produce the correct assumption that predatory behavior consists of hunting and killing.

The phrase *is called* or the word *is* often signals a definition.

The point where the light rays come together is called the *focus* of the lens.

Sometimes definitions are enclosed in parentheses or set off by commas or dashes.

In early childhood these tendencies lead to the development of *schemes* (organized patterns of behavior).

Many Chinese practice *Tai Chi*, an ancient method of self-defense performed as exercise in slow, graceful motions.

At *burnout* — the instant a rocket stops firing — the satellite's path is fixed.

Noticing examples can also help you infer the meaning of a word. The expressions *such as, for example, for instance, to illustrate,* and *including* often precede examples.

Society often has difficulty understanding *nonconformists* such as criminals, inventors, artists, saints, and political protesters.

The parallel examples help explain *nonconformist* because they all seem to be exceptions, people who go beyond the average or beyond the rules. This is close to an understanding of *nonconformists* as people who do not adapt themselves to the usual standards and customs of society.

Sometimes an example that reveals the meaning of an unfamiliar word is spread throughout the sentence or paragraph and is not announced by a phrase.

During the first weeks of *rehabilitation*, Brian exercised as best he could, took his medicine daily, and thought constantly about the physical condition he once possessed.

Guessing the meaning of *rehabilitation* requires considering what occurred during it: (1) exercising "as best he could" — as if Brian had some kind of handicap; (2) taking medicine — as if he were ill; and (3) thinking about his past physical condition — as if he were wishing for the good shape he used to be in. Putting these examples together suggests that *rehabilitation* is returning to a healthy condition, which is one of its meanings. (The more precise definition is "restoring a former capacity"; and that idea includes reviving a skill as well as recuperating from a sickness.)

33c

EXERCISE 4

Use context to determine the meanings of the words italicized below (not including titles). Check the accuracy of your guess by consulting a dictionary.

1. Like America, Michael [Corleone, in *The Godfather*] began as a clean, brilliant young man *endowed* with incredible resources and believing in a humanistic idealism. Like America, Michael was an innocent who had tried to correct the ills and injustices of his *progenitors.* — FRANCIS FORD COPPOLA
2. Everything about man is a *paradox.* The *magnanimous* man grown rich becomes mean. The creative artist for whom everything is made easy nods. Every doctrine swears that it will breed men, but none can tell us in advance what sort of men it will breed. — ANTOINE DE SAINT-EXUPÉRY
3. "And this, too, shall pass away." How much [this sentence] expresses! How *chastening* in the hour of pride! How *consoling* in the depths of *affliction!* — ABRAHAM LINCOLN
4. As long as there is one upright man, as long as there is one compassionate woman, the *contagion* may spread and the scene is not *desolate.* Hope is the thing that is left to us in a bad time. — E. B. WHITE
5. In a community where public services have failed to keep *abreast* of private consumption, . . . in an atmosphere of private *opulence* and public *squalor,* the private goods have full sway. — JOHN KENNETH GALBRAITH

2
Using the dictionary

The dictionary is a quick reference for the meaning of words (see 32b). It can give the precise meaning of a word whose general meaning you have guessed by examining the word's context. It can also help you fix the word in your memory by showing its spelling, pronunciation, grammatical functions and forms, etymology, and synonyms and antonyms.

For example, suppose you did not understand the word *homogeneous* in the following sentence:

Its homogeneous population makes the town stable but dull.

33c

The dictionary gives the meanings of the word: "of the same kind," "of similar composition throughout." Thus the town's population is made up of similar kinds of people. *Homogeneous* comes from the Greek words *hom*, meaning "same," and *genos*, meaning "kind, type." Obviously, the composition of the word reinforces its definitions. Looking down the dictionary's column under *homogeneous*, you would find a related word, *homogenize*, which might be more familiar because of the common phrase *homogenized milk*. To *homogenize* means "to blend into a smooth mixture" and "to break up the fat globules of milk by forcing them through minute openings." The relation between this familiar word and the other, less familiar one gives added meaning to both words. A similar expansion of meaning could come from examining an antonym of *homogeneous*, such as *heterogeneous*, meaning "consisting of dissimilar ingredients." Thinking of the two opposite words together might fix them both in your memory.

A dictionary of synonyms is the best source for the precise meanings of similar words (see 32a-3). But even an abridged dictionary will supply much information about synonyms (see 32a-1). Most abridged dictionaries list a word's common synonyms and either direct you to the entries for the synonyms or distinguish among them in one place. An example of the latter format is the paragraph below, which follows the main entry for the word *real* in *The American Heritage Dictionary of the English Language*. By drawing on this information as you write, you can avoid overreliance on the word *real* when a more precise word is appropriate.

re·al[1] (rē′əl, rēl) *adj.* **1.** Being or occurring in fact or actuality; having verifiable existence: *The child shows real intelligence.* **2.** True and actual; not illusory or fictitious: *real people.* **3.** Genuine and authentic; not artificial or spurious: *real mink; real humility.* **4.** *Philosophy.* Existing actually and objectively. **5.** *Optics.* Of, pertaining to, or designating an image formed by light rays that converge in space. **6.** *Mathematics.* Of, pertaining to, or designating the nonimaginary part of a complex quantity. **7.** *Law.* Of or pertaining to stationary or fixed property, as buildings or land. Compare **personal.** —*adv. Informal.* Very: *real sorry.* [Middle English, of real property or things, from Norman French, from Late Latin *reālis*, actual, real, from Latin *rēs* thing. See *rei-* in Appendix.*] —**real′ness** *n.*

Synonyms: *real, actual, true, authentic, concrete, existent, genuine, tangible, veritable.* *Real,* although frequently used interchangeably with the terms that follow, pertains basically to that which is not imaginary but is existent and identifiable as a thing, state, or quality. *Actual* connotes that which is demonstrable. *True* implies belief in that which conforms to fact. *Authentic* implies acceptance of historical or attributable reliability rather than visible proof. *Concrete* implies the reality of actual things. *Existent* applies to concepts or objects existing either in time or space: *existent tensions. Genuine* presupposes evidence or belief that a thing or object is what it is claimed to be. *Tangible* stresses the mind's acceptance of that which can be touched or seen. *Veritable,* which should be used sparingly, applies to persons and things having all the qualities claimed for them.

EXERCISE 5

The dictionary entry above lists the following words as synonyms for *real: actual, true, authentic, concrete, existent, genuine, tangible,* and *veritable.* Using the dictionary entry and consulting a dictionary of synonyms if necessary, write nine sentences that make precise use of *real* and each of its eight synonyms.

33c

34
Spelling

Because of the history and complexity of English, spelling English words according to standard usage requires consistent attention. However, learning to spell well is worth the effort because misspelling can make writing seem incompetent or lazy. This chapter will show you how to recognize typical spelling problems, how to follow a handful of rules as a guide to spelling, and how to develop spelling skills through conscious effort.

34a
Avoiding typical spelling problems

Spelling well involves recognizing situations that commonly lead to misspelling. Pronunciation can mislead you in several ways; different forms of the same word may have different spellings; and some words have more than one acceptable spelling. Watching for the errors these situations encourage will prevent many spelling mistakes.

1
Avoiding excessive reliance on pronunciation

In English, unlike some languages, pronunciation of words is an unreliable guide to their spelling. The same letter or combination of letters may have different sounds in the pronunciation of different words. For an example, say aloud these different ways of pronouncing the letters *ough: tough, dough, cough, through, bough*. And say aloud these ways of pronouncing *ea: beat, tread, pear, search, fear*. Another problem is that some words contain letters that are not pronounced clearly or at all, such as the *ed* in *asked*, the silent *e* in *swipe*, or the unpronounced *gh* in *tight*.

Pronunciation is a particularly unreliable guide to the spelling of **homonyms,** words pronounced the same though they have different spellings and meanings: for example, *great/grate, to/too/two, threw/through, horse/hoarse, board/bored, break/brake.* Homonyms and words with very similar pronunciations, such as *gorilla/ guerrilla* and *accept/except,* are common sources of spelling errors. Studying the following list of homonyms and similar-sounding words will help you avoid spelling errors caused by word sounds. (See 34c-3 for some tips on how to use spelling lists.)

accept (to receive)
except (other than)

affect (to have an influence on)
effect (result)

all ready (prepared)
already (by this time)

allude (to refer to indirectly)
elude (to avoid)

allusion (indirect reference)
illusion (erroneous belief or perception)

ascent (a rise)
assent (agreement)

bare (unclothed)
bear (to carry, or an animal)

board (a plank of wood)
bored (uninterested)

born (brought into life)
borne (carried)

brake (stop)
break (smash)

buy (purchase)
by (next to)

capital (the seat of a government)
capitol (the building where a legislature meets)

cite (to quote an authority)
sight (the ability to see)
site (a place)

descent (a movement down)
dissent (disagreement)

desert (to abandon)
dessert (after-dinner course)

discreet (reserved, respectful)
discrete (individual or distinct)

elicit (to bring out)
illicit (illegal)

fair (average, or lovely)
fare (a charge for transportation)

formally (conventionally)
formerly (in the past)

forth (forward)
fourth (after *third*)

gorilla (a large primate)
guerrilla (a kind of soldier)

hear (to perceive by ear)
here (in this place)

heard (past tense of *hear*)
herd (a group of animals)

hole (an opening)
whole (complete)

its (possessive of *it*)
it's (contraction of *it is*)

lead (heavy metal)
led (past tense of *lead*)

lessen (to make less)
lesson (something learned)

meat (flesh)
meet (encounter)

no (the opposite of *yes*)
know (to be certain)

sp
34a

passed (past tense of *pass*)
past (after, or a time gone by)

patience (forbearance)
patients (persons under medical care)

peace (the absence of war)
piece (a portion of something)

plain (clear)
plane (a carpenter's tool, or an airborne vehicle)

presence (the state of being at hand)
presents (gifts)

principal (most important, or the head of a school)
principle (a basic truth or law)

rain (precipitation)
reign (to rule)
rein (a strap for controlling an animal)

raise (to build up)
raze (to tear down)

right (correct)
rite (a religious ceremony)
write (to make letters)

road (a surface for driving)
rode (past tense of *ride*)

scene (where an action occurs)
seen (past participle of *see*)

stationary (unmoving)
stationery (writing paper)

straight (unbending)
strait (a water passageway)

their (possessive of *they*)
there (opposite of *here*)
they're (contraction of *they are*)

to (toward)
too (also)
two (following *one*)

waist (the middle of the body)
waste (discarded material)

weak (not strong)
week (Sunday through Saturday)

which (one of a group)
witch (a sorcerer)

who's (contraction of *who is*)
whose (possessive of *who*)

your (possessive of *you*)
you're (contraction of *you are*)

2
Distinguishing between different forms of the same word

Other spelling problems occur when the noun form and the verb form of the same word are spelled differently. For example:

VERB	NOUN	VERB	NOUN
advise	advice	enter	entrance
argue	argument	marry	marriage
describe	description	omit	omission

Sometimes the noun and the adjective forms of the same word differ.

NOUN	ADJECTIVE	NOUN	ADJECTIVE
comedy	comic	height	high
courtesy	courteous	Britain	British
generosity	generous		

The principal parts of irregular verbs are usually spelled differently.

begin, began, begun	know, knew, known
break, broke, broken	ride, rode, ridden
do, did, done	ring, rang, run

Irregular nouns change spelling from singular to plural.

child, children	shelf, shelves
goose, geese	tooth, teeth
mouse, mice	woman, women

Notice, too, that the stem of a word may change its spelling in different forms.

four, forty	thief, theft

3
Using preferred spellings

Many words have variant spellings as well as preferred spellings (see 32b-2). Since the variant spellings listed in an American dictionary are often British spellings, you should know the main differences between American and British spellings.

AMERICAN	BRITISH
encyclop*e*dia	encyclop*ae*dia
col*or*, hum*or*	col*our*, hum*our*
theat*er*, cent*er*	theat*re*, cent*re*
cance*l*ed, trave*l*ed	cance*ll*ed, trave*ll*ed
judgment	judg*e*ment
reali*z*e	reali*s*e

34b
Following spelling rules

sp
34b

Misspelling is often a matter of misspelling a syllable rather than the whole word. The following general rules focus on troublesome syllables, with notes for the occasional exceptions.

1
Distinguishing between *ie* and *ei*

Words like *believe* and *receive* sound alike in the second syllable, but the syllable is spelled differently. How do you know which word should have *ie* and which one *ei*? The answer is in the familiar jingle:

I before *e*, except after *c*, or when pronounced "ay" as in *neighbor* and *weigh*.

i BEFORE *e*	believe	bier	hygiene
	grief	thief	friend
	chief	fiend	
ei AFTER *c*	ceiling	conceive	perceive
	receive	deceit	conceit
ei SOUNDED AS "AY"	neighbor	freight	beige
	sleigh	eight	heinous
	weight	vein	

EXCEPTIONS: Some words are spelled with an *ei* combination even though it doesn't follow *c* and isn't pronounced "ay." These words include *either, neither, foreign, forfeit, height, leisure, weird, seize,* and *seizure.* This sentence might help you remember some of them:

The weird foreigner neither seizes leisure nor forfeits height.

EXERCISE 1

Insert *ie* or *ei* in the words below. Check doubtful spellings in a dictionary.

1. br__f
2. dec__ve
3. rec__pt
4. s__ze
5. for__gn
6. pr__st
7. gr__vance
8. f__nd
9. l__surely
10. ach__ve
11. pat__nce
12. p__rce
13. h__ght
14. fr__ght
15. f__nt

2
Keeping or dropping a final *e*

Many words end with an unpronounced or silent *e:* for instance, *move, brave, late, rinse.* When adding endings like *-ing* or *-ly* to these words, do you keep the final *e* or drop it? You drop it if the ending begins with a vowel.

advise + able = advisable
force + ible = forcible
surprise + ing = surprising

You keep the final, silent *e* if the ending begins with a consonant.

advance + ment = advancement
accurate + ly = accurately
care + ful = careful

EXCEPTIONS: The silent *e* is sometimes retained before an ending beginning with a vowel. It is kept when *dye* becomes *dyeing,* to avoid confusion with *dying.* It is kept to prevent mispronunciation of words like *shoeing* (not *shoing*) and *mileage* (not *milage*). And the final *e* is often retained after a soft *c* or *g*, to keep the sound of the consonant soft rather than hard.

courageous	changeable	noticeable
outrageous	manageable	embraceable

The silent *e* is also sometimes *dropped* before an ending beginning with a consonant, when the *e* is preceded by another vowel.

argue + ment = argument
true + ly = truly
due + ly = duly

EXERCISE 2

Combine the following words and endings, keeping or dropping final *e*'s as necessary to make correctly spelled words. Check doubtful spellings in a dictionary.

1. malice + ious	5. sue + ing	9. suspense + ion
2. love + able	6. virtue + ous	10. astute + ness
3. service + able	7. note + able	
4. retire + ment	8. battle + ing	

3
Keeping or dropping a final *y*

Words ending in *y* often change their spelling when an ending is added to them. The basic rule is to change the *y* to *i* when it follows a consonant.

beauty, beauties	worry, worried	supply, supplier
folly, follies	merry, merrier	deputy, deputize

But keep the *y* when it follows a vowel; when the ending is *-ing;* or when it ends a proper name.

day, days	cry, crying	O'Malley, O'Malleys
obey, obeyed	study, studying	Minsky, Minskys
key, keyed	beautify, beautifying	

sp
34b

EXERCISE 3

Combine the following words and endings, changing or keeping final *y*'s as necessary to make correctly spelled words. Check doubtful spellings in a dictionary.

1. imply + s
2. messy + er
3. apply + ing
4. delay + ing
5. defy + ance
6. say + s
7. solidify + s
8. Murphy + s
9. misty + er
10. supply + ed

4
Doubling consonants

Words ending in a consonant sometimes double the consonant when adding an ending. Whether to double the final consonant depends on the word's number of syllables, on the letters preceding the final consonant, and on which syllable is stressed in pronunciation.

In one-syllable words, double the final consonant when a single vowel precedes the final consonant.

slap, slapping   flat, flatter
tip, tipped   pit, pitted

However, *don't* double the final consonant when two vowels or a vowel and another consonant precede the final consonant.

pair, paired   park, parking
real, realize   rent, rented

In words of more than one syllable, double the final consonant when a single vowel precedes the final consonant and the stress falls on the last syllable of the stem once the ending is added.

submit, submitted   refer, referring
occur, occurred   begin, beginning

But *don't* double the final consonant when it is preceded by two vowels or by a vowel and another consonant, or when the stress falls on other than the stem's last syllable once the ending is added.

refer, reference   despair, despairing
relent, relented   beckon, beckoned

sp
34b

EXERCISE 4

Combine the following words and endings, doubling final consonants as necessary to make correctly spelled words. Check doubtful spellings in a dictionary.

1. repair + ing
2. admit + ance
3. benefit + ed
4. shop + ed
5. fear + ing
6. conceal + ed
7. allot + ed
8. drip + ing
9. declaim + ed
10. parallel + ing

5
Attaching prefixes

Adding prefixes such as *dis-*, *mis-*, and *un-* does not change the spelling of the word. When adding a prefix, do not drop a letter from or add a letter to the original word.

uneasy	disappoint	misinform
unnecessary	dissatisfied	misstate
antifreeze	defuse	misspell
anti-intellectual	de-emphasize	

(See also 34d-4 on when to use hyphens with prefixes.)

6
Forming plurals

Nouns

Most nouns form plurals by adding *-s* to the singular form.

boy, boys   table, tables   carnival, carnivals

Some nouns ending in *f* or *fe* form the plural by changing the ending to *ve* before adding *-s*.

leaf, leaves   life, lives   yourself, yourselves

Singular nouns ending in *-s*, *-sh*, *-ch*, or *-x* form the plural by adding *-es*.

kiss, kisses	church, churches
wish, wishes	fox, foxes

(Notice that verbs ending in *-s*, *-sh*, *-ch*, or *-x* form the third-person singular in the same way. *Taxes* and *lurches* are examples.)

Nouns ending in *o* preceded by a vowel usually form the plural by adding *-s*.

ratio, ratios   zoo, zoos

Nouns ending in *o* preceded by a consonant usually form the plural by adding *-es*.

hero, heroes   tomato, tomatoes

Some English nouns that were originally Italian, Greek, Latin, or French form the plural according to their original language: *piano, pianos; medium, media; datum, data; alumnus, alumni; alumna, alumnae.*

sp
34b

Compound nouns

Compound nouns form plurals in two ways. An -*s* is added to the last word when two or more main words (usually nouns and verbs) make up the compound word, whether or not they are hyphenated.

city-states	bucket seats	breakthroughs
painter-sculptors	booby traps	

When the parts of the compound word are not equal — when a noun is combined with other parts of speech — then *s* is added to the noun.

fathers-in-law   passersby

Note, however, that most modern dictionaries give the plural of *spoonful* as *spoonfuls.*

EXERCISE 5

Make correct plurals of the following words. Check doubtful spellings in a dictionary.

1. pile	6. box	11. libretto
2. donkey	7. switch	12. sister-in-law
3. beach	8. rodeo	13. mile-per-hour
4. summary	9. criterion	14. cargo
5. thief	10. cupful	15. hiss

34c
Developing spelling skills

You should habitually consult a dictionary for spellings you are unsure of (see Chapter 32). Start by looking up the word as you think it is spelled. Then try different variations based on the pronunciation of the word. Once you think you have found the correct spelling, check the definition to make sure you have the word you want. In addition to consulting the dictionary regularly, you can improve spelling in several other ways: by pronouncing words carefully; by inventing tricks to help you remember troublesome words; and by memorizing the spellings of words that cause problems for many people.

sp
34c

1
Pronouncing carefully

Pronunciation will not always work to tell you how to spell because, as we observed in 34a, accurate pronunciation may not give you all the information you need. In addition, speakers of some English dialects pronounce words differently from the way they are spelled. Nevertheless, careful pronunciation can help you spell many words in which sounds are frequently added, omitted, or reversed in pronunciation.

athletics (not atheletics)	library (not libary)
disastrous (not disasterous)	recognize (not reconize)
mischievous (not mischievious)	strictly (not stricly)
lightning (not lightening)	government (not goverment)
height (not heighth)	history (not histry)
irrelevant (not irrevelant)	temperament (not temperment)
perform (not preform)	representative (not representive)
nuclear (not nucular)	

2
Using mnemonics

Mnemonics (pronounced with an initial *"n"* sound) are techniques for assisting your memory. The *er* in *letter* and *paper* can remind you that *stationery* (meaning "writing paper") has an *er* near the end; *stationary* with an *a* means "standing in place." Or the word *dome* with its long *o* sound can remind you that the building in which the legislature meets is spelled *capitol*, with an *o*. The *capital* city is spelled with *al* like *Albany*, the capital of New York. If you identify the words you have trouble spelling, you can take a few minutes to think of your own mnemonics, which may work better for you than someone else's.

3
Studying spelling lists

Learning to spell commonly misspelled words will reduce your spelling errors. As you work with the following list, study only a small group of words at a time. (Learning tests have demonstrated that seven items is a good number to work with.) Be sure you understand the meaning of the word before you try to memorize its spelling. Look it up in a dictionary if you are uncertain, and try using it in a sentence. Pronounce the word out loud, syllable by syllable, and write the word out. (Additional words that are commonly misspelled appear in the list of similar-sounding words on pp. 429–30. That list should be considered an extension of the one below.)

sp
34c

absence	accidentally	acknowledge	address
absorption	accommodate	acquaintance	admission
abundance	accuracy	acquire	adolescent
acceptable	accustomed	across	advice
accessible	achieve	actually	advising

against
aggravate
aggressive
all right
all together
almost
although
altogether
amateur
analysis
analyze
angel
annihilate
annual
answer
apology
apparent
appearance
appetite
appreciate
appropriate
approximately
argument
arrest
ascend
assassinate
assistance
associate
atheist
athlete
attendance
audience
auxiliary
average

bargain
basically
beginning
belief
believe
beneficial
benefited
boundary
breath
breathe
Britain
bureaucracy
burial
business

calculator
calendar
carrying
category
cede
cemetery
certain
changeable
changing
characteristic
chief
chocolate
choose
chose
climbed
coarse
column
coming
commercial
commitment
committed
committee
competent
competition
complement
compliment
conceit
conceive
concentrate
concert
condemn
conquer
conscience
conscientious
conscious
consistency
consistent
continuous
controlled
controversial
convenience
convenient
coolly
council
counsel
course
courteous
criticism
criticize

crowd
cruelty
curiosity
curious

deceive
deception
decide
decision
definitely
degree
dependent
descend
descendant
describe
description
desirable
despair
desperate
destroy
determine
develop
device
devise
dictionary
difference
dining
disagree
disappear
disappoint
disapprove
disastrous
discipline
discriminate
discussion
disease
dispel
dissatisfied
distinction
divide
divine
division
doctor
drawer
drunkenness

easily
ecstasy
efficiency

efficient
eighth
either
eligible
embarrass
emphasize
empty
enemy
entirely
environment
equipped
especially
essential
every
exaggerate
exceed
excellent
exercise
exhaust
existence
expense
experience
experiment
explanation
extremely

familiar
fascinate
favorite
February
finally
financially
forcibly
foreign
foresee
forty
forward
friend
frightening
fulfill

gauge
generally
government
grammar
grief
guarantee
guard
guidance

happily
harass
height
heroes
hideous
humorous
hungry
hurriedly
hurrying
hypocrisy
hypocrite

ideally
illogical
imaginary
imagine
imitation
immediately
immigrant
incidentally
incredible
independence
independent
indispensable
individually
inevitably
influential
initiate
innocuous
inoculate
insistent
integrate
intelligence
interest
interference
interpret
irrelevant
irresistible
irritable
island

jealousy
judgment

knowledge

laboratory
leisure
length

lenient
library
license
lightning
likelihood
literally
livelihood
loneliness
loose
lose
luxury
lying

magazine
maintenance
manageable
maneuver
marriage
mathematics
meant
medicine
miniature
minor
minute
mirror
mischievous
missile
misspelled
morale
morals
mournful
muscle
mysterious

naturally
necessary
neighbor
neither
nickel
niece
ninety
ninth
noticeable
nuclear
nuisance
numerous

obstacle
occasion

occasionally
occur
occurrence
official
omission
omit
omitted
opponent
opportunity
opposite
ordinarily
originally

paid
panicky
paralleled
particularly
pastime
peaceable
peculiar
pedal
perceive
perception
performance
permanent
permissible
persevere
persistence
personnel
perspiration
persuade
persuasion
petal
physical
pitiful
planning
pleasant
poison
politician
pollute
possession
possibly
practically
practice
prairie
precede
preference
preferred
prejudice

preparation
prevalent
primitive
privilege
probably
procedure
proceed
process
professor
prominent
pronunciation
prophecy
prophesy
psychology
purpose
pursue
pursuit

quandary
quantity
quiet
quizzes

realistically
realize
really
rebel
rebelled
recede
receipt
receive
recognize
recommend
reference
referred
relief
relieve
religious
remembrance
reminisce
renown
repetition
representative
resemblance
resistance
restaurant
rhythm
ridiculous
roommate

sp
34c

sacrifice	speak	technical	unnecessary
sacrilegious	speech	technique	until
safety	sponsor	temperature	usually
satellite	stopping	tendency	
scarcity	strategy	than	vacuum
schedule	strength	then	vegetable
science	strenuous	thorough	vengeance
secretary	stretch	though	vicious
seize	strict	throughout	villain
separate	studying	together	visible
sergeant	succeed	tomorrow	
several	successful	tragedy	weather
sheriff	sufficient	transferred	Wednesday
shining	summary	truly	weird
shoulder	superintendent	twelfth	wherever
significance	supersede	tyranny	whether
similar	suppress		wholly
sincerely	surely	unanimous	woman
sophomore	surprise	unconscious	women
source	suspicious	undoubtedly	writing

34d
Using the hyphen to form compound words

The hyphen (-) is a mark of punctuation used either to divide a word or to form a compound word. Always use a hyphen to divide a word at the end of a line and continue it on the next line as explained in Chapter 30 on word division. Using a hyphen to form compound words is somewhat more complicated.

Compound words express a combination of ideas. They may be written as a single word, like the noun *breakthrough;* as two words, like the noun *decision making;* or as a hyphenated word, like the noun *cave-in.* Sometimes compound words using the same element are spelled differently — for example, *cross-reference, cross section,* and *crosswalk.* Because of the variations in spelling compound words, you should check a recent edition of a dictionary for their current standard spelling. However, several reliable generalizations can be made about using the hyphen for compound adjectives, for fractions and compound numbers, for coined compounds, for certain prefixes and suffixes, and for clarity.

1
Forming compound adjectives

When two or more words serve together as a single modifier before a noun, the hyphen or hyphens form the modifying words clearly into a unit.

well-known actor
out-of-date statistics
English-speaking people

When the same compound adjectives follow the noun, hyphens are unnecessary and are usually left out.

The actor is *well known.*
The statistics were *out of date.*
Those people are *English speaking.*

Hyphens are also unnecessary in compound modifiers containing an *-ly* adverb, even when these fall before the noun. In a phrase like *clearly defined terms,* the *-ly* in *clearly* serves as a sufficient link between the two parts of the modifier.

When the main part of a compound adjective appears only once in a pair or a series of parallel compound adjectives, hyphens indicate which words the reader should mentally join with the main part.

School-age children should have eight- or nine-o'clock bedtimes.

2
Writing fractions and compound numbers

Hyphens join the numerator and denominator of fractions.

three-fourths
one-half

The whole numbers twenty-one to ninety-nine are always hyphenated regardless of their function or of their position in relation to the noun or verb.

Eighteen girls and twenty-four boys took the bus.
The total is eighty-seven.

3
Forming coined compounds

sp
34d

Writers sometimes create (coin) temporary compounds and join the words with hyphens.

Muhammad Ali gave his opponent a classic come-on-over-here-and-get-me look.

4
Attaching some prefixes and suffixes

Prefixes are usually attached to word stems without hyphens: *predetermine, unnatural, disengage.* However, when the prefix precedes a capitalized word, or when a capital letter is combined with a word, a hyphen usually separates the two: *un-American, pre-Eisenhower, non-European, A-frame.* And some prefixes, such as *self-, all-,* and *ex-* (meaning "formerly"), usually require hyphens whether or not they precede capitalized words: *self-control, all-inclusive, ex-student.*

The only suffix that regularly requires a hyphen is *-elect,* as in *president-elect.*

5
Avoiding confusion

If you wrote the sentence *Doonesbury is a comic strip character,* the reader might stumble briefly over your meaning. Is Doonesbury a character in a comic strip or a comic (funny) character who strips? Presumably you would mean the former, but a hyphen would prevent any possible confusion: *Doonesbury is a comic-strip character.*

Adding prefixes to words can sometimes create ambiguity. *Recreation* (*creation* with the prefix *re-*) could mean either "a new creation" or "diverting, pleasurable activity." Using a hyphen, *re-creation,* limits the word to the first meaning. Without a hyphen the word suggests the second meaning.

Combinations of prefixes and stems that place two vowels or the same three consonants together are often more readable when a hyphen separates them.

preeminent, pre-eminent
trilllike, trill-like
reevaluate, re-evaluate

Check a dictionary for the standard form, particularly for words that join two *e*'s.

sp 34d

EXERCISE 6

Insert hyphens as needed in the following compounds. Circle all compounds that are correct as given. Consult a dictionary as needed.

1. reimburse
2. deemphasize
3. forty odd soldiers
4. little known bar
5. seven eighths
6. seventy eight
7. happy go lucky
8. preexisting
9. senator elect
10. postman
11. two and six person cars
12. ex songwriter
13. V shaped
14. reeducate

VIII

Special Writing Assignments

35
Writing a Research Paper

A **research paper** is a composition based on investigation and interpretation of other people's work rather than solely on your own experience or observation. Many of the steps in planning and writing a research paper — such as limiting a subject, developing a thesis, and organizing material — are the same as those you follow in writing other kinds of essays (see Chapter 1). But the research paper takes you further, leading you to study a topic in depth by finding and presenting what others have written about it.

Your role in writing a research paper will depend on your assignment. You may be expected to function primarily as a reporter or surveyor who locates, organizes, and presents the available knowledge and beliefs about a topic (for instance, the causes of a historical event or the reasons for some human behavior). Or you may be expected to serve more as an interpreter or analyst who evaluates published facts and opinions on a topic and presents independent conclusions (for instance, the meaning of a literary work or the solution to a social problem). The two roles and kinds of papers overlap, however, because the report or survey requires that you determine which information is most worthwhile, and the interpretation or analysis requires that you survey others' conclusions as a basis for your own. Thus, although the advice in this chapter leans toward the interpretive paper, the general research and writing process described applies equally to the survey paper.

Preparing either a survey or an interpretive research paper not only leads to an in-depth examination of a topic but also teaches several important and practical skills. You will learn how to locate and evaluate a library's resources to increase your knowledge. You will learn how to draw on the information in sources to support your thesis and how to acknowledge the use you make of others' facts and opinions. In college these skills are essential in the many

444

courses that require research papers. In most kinds of work research skills will give you an edge in the daily activities of investigating and solving problems. And in life outside work research skills will help you resolve anything from a consumer complaint to a tax question to a community issue.

The primary activities of preparing a research paper — reading, evaluating, and organizing — underlie the following steps in the process:

1. Find and limit a researchable topic (p. 445).
2. Find information on the topic and read to refine the topic further (p. 448).
3. Record where the information is located (p. 459).
4. Read to strengthen your overview of the topic and work up a tentative thesis and outline (p. 467).
5. Take detailed notes (p. 469).
6. Revise the thesis and write a formal outline (p. 474).
7. Write and revise the paper (p. 477).
8. Prepare the footnotes (p. 480).
9. Prepare the bibliography (p. 490).

As this list implies, a research paper, like any other essay, evolves gradually. While you do research, your reading leads you to organize ideas. And while you organize ideas, you discover where you need to do more research. You begin to limit your topic as soon as you have chosen it, and you continue to limit it as you progress. The working thesis and outline you develop must later be refined. If you anticipate changes like these and allow time for them within the span of your assignment of perhaps four to six weeks, writing a research paper will be straightforward and rewarding.

35a
Finding and limiting a researchable topic

Before reading this section, you may want to review the suggestions for finding and limiting an essay topic described in Chapter 1. Generally, the same procedure applies to writing a research paper: Take a subject assigned to you, or think of one that interests you, and narrow it to manageable dimensions by making it specific.

One student, Paul Fuller, uses this method to find a topic for a research paper whose development we will follow in this chapter. Fuller is interested in marketing, and he first divides that subject into several others that also seem interesting to him: product development, advertising, wholesaling, and retail sales. He asks himself questions about each of these — such as who performs each func-

35a

tion and what its goals and methods are — to arrive at the one function that he most wants to learn about. Choosing advertising, he then lists several topics suggested by his questions, such as advertising's use of the mass media, the role of advertising agencies, the effect of advertising on consumers, and the case history of a single advertising campaign. Again, Fuller asks himself questions about each of these to narrow his focus and thus choose a specific path for investigation. Some of the questions he poses about advertising and consumers seem promising: "Do commercials give a product a recognizable personality?" "How do advertisers persuade consumers?" "What do consumers think of commercials?" He finally settles on the second — "How do advertisers persuade consumers?" — as the topic with which to begin his research. Diagrammed, Fuller's narrowing of his subject looks like this:

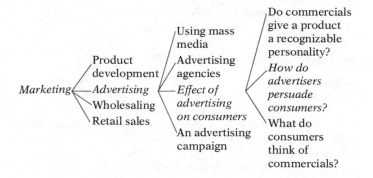

Though it will have to be narrowed more later, Fuller's topic does seem to satisfy four main requirements of a subject for a research paper. First, Fuller is likely to find many published sources of information. The topic is not too recent, as the newest fad or yesterday's news item would be, so people will have had a chance to produce evidence, weigh it, and write about it. Nor is the topic so removed geographically that the sources on it would be inaccessible, as they might be for someone in Ohio writing about a minor event in California history. Second, the topic needs to be researched in a variety of sources so that Fuller can present a range of opinion and facts. A topic that requires only personal opinion and experience, such as "How I see housewives being depicted in detergent commercials," might be suitable for a personal essay but not for a research paper. Nor would a topic be suitable if it required research in only one source. For this reason straight factual biographies of well-known people and how-to topics like "Operating a television camera" or "Making lenses for eyeglasses" generally make poor research subjects.

35a

The third requirement satisfied by Fuller's topic is that it promises to foster the objective evaluation of sources that will lead to defensible conclusions. Even when a research paper is intended to be argumentative, the success of the argument will depend on the balanced presentation of all points of view. Controversial topics that rest on belief, dogma, or prejudice — such as "When human life begins" or "Why women (or men) are superior" — are certainly arguable, but they are risky because the writer's preconceptions can easily slant either the research itself or the conclusions.

Fourth, and finally, Fuller's topic suits the length of paper he's been assigned (1500 to 2000 words, or about seven to ten pages) and the amount of time he's been given to prepare the paper (four weeks). In seven to ten pages Fuller could not cover one of his broader topics like "The effect of advertising on consumers" because he would need to deal with so many aspects of the relation (as suggested by the three questions he came up with) that no one aspect could be explored fully. Such a broad topic would also require research in so many sources (including the writings not only of advertising specialists and psychologists but also of consumers and consumer representatives) that Fuller might need months, not weeks, to complete his research. The same would be true of a topic like "Infant perception," which requires delving into complex biology, chemistry, and psychology. However, "What a three-month-old infant can see" might be appropriate for a ten-page paper that takes four weeks to prepare.

EXERCISE 1

Choose three of the following subjects and narrow each one to at least one topic suitable for beginning library work on a research paper. Or list and then limit three subjects of your own that you would enjoy investigating. (This exercise can be the first step in a research paper project that continues through Exercises 2, 5, 6, 9, 11, 12, 14, and 15.)

1. the United States in world affairs
2. the Opium War
3. dance in America
4. the history of women's suffrage
5. food additives
6. illegal aliens in the United States
7. exploration of the moon (or Mars)
8. energy sources other than oil and coal
9. the effect of television on professional sports
10. religious cults in America
11. the modern automobile engine
12. recent developments in cancer research
13. the European exploration of North America before Columbus
14. the Sacco and Vanzetti trial
15. Social Security
16. microwaves

35a

17. Native American tribal rights today
18. science fiction
19. irrigation rights
20. water pollution
21. women writers
22. the history of child labor practices
23. the novels of Kurt Vonnegut
24. comic film actors
25. genetic engineering
26. computers in the home
27. computers and the privacy of the individual
28. gothic or romance novels in the nineteenth and twentieth centuries
29. the social responsibility of business
30. trends in popular music

35b

Finding information on the topic and reading to refine the topic further

When you go to the library with a topic to investigate, you should start by surveying at least three kinds of sources: reference books, periodicals, and general books. Reference books are a good place to begin because they provide either a summary of a topic or information on where to find out about the topic. Periodicals (magazines, journals, and newspapers) usually contain detailed and current information on the topic. General books, which constitute the bulk of a library's collection and contain almost every kind of information, are those generally available for circulation. If you are unsure of how to locate or use your library's resources, ask the reference librarian, whose job is to help people with research.

Much information for a brief research paper will appear in **secondary sources,** works that report and analyze information drawn from other sources. Whenever possible, however, you should also seek **primary sources,** which include works of literature as well as historical documents (letters, diaries, speeches, and the like) that provide eyewitness accounts of an issue, event, or period. Primary sources may also include your own interviews, experiments, observations, or correspondence. (Paul Fuller uses a primary source — his own survey of magazine advertisements — in his research paper. See p. 604.)

35b

1
Using reference books

Reference books available in the library include encyclopedias, dictionaries, digests, bibliographies, indexes, atlases, almanacs, and handbooks. Although your research must go beyond these sources, they can help you decide whether your topic really interests you and whether it meets the requirements for a research paper (pp. 446–47). Preliminary research in reference books will also direct you to more detailed information on your topic.

The following list gives the types of reference works and suggests when each may be profitable. Once you have a topic, you can scan this list for a reference book with which to start. If you want a more comprehensive catalog and explanation of reference works than this list provides, consult Eugene P. Sheehy, *Guide to Reference Books*, 9th ed. (Chicago: American Library Association, 1976; supplement 1980).

General encyclopedias

General encyclopedias give brief overviews and brief bibliographies. Because they try to cover all fields, they are a convenient, but very limited, starting point. Look for the most recent edition.

> *Collier's Encyclopedia.* 24 vols. New York: Macmillan Educational
>   Corporation, 1977.
> *Encyclopedia Americana.* 30 vols. New York: Americana Corpo-
>   ration, 1977.
> *Encyclopedia International.* 20 vols. New York: Grolier, 1963–64.
> *The New Columbia Encyclopedia.* 1 vol. New York: Columbia Univ.
>   Press, 1975.
> *The New Encyclopaedia Britannica.* 30 vols. Chicago: Encyclo-
>   paedia Britannica, 1980.
> *Random House Encyclopedia.* 1 vol. New York: Random House,
>   1977.

Special encyclopedias, dictionaries, bibliographies

These reference works specialize, trying to cover one field completely. They can give you more detailed and more technical information than a general reference book can.

THE ARTS

> Apel, Willi. *The Harvard Dictionary of Music.* 2nd rev. ed. Cam-
>   bridge, Mass.: Harvard Univ. Press, 1969.
> Chujoy, Anatole, and P. W. Manchester. *The Dance Encyclopedia.*
>   New York: Simon & Schuster, 1978.
> *Encyclopedia of World Art.* 15 vols. New York: McGraw-Hill,
>   1959–68.
> Maillard, Robert, ed. *New Dictionary of Modern Sculpture.* Trans.
>   Bettina Wadia. New York: Tudor, 1971.
> Moore, Frank L. *Crowell's Handbook of World Opera.* Westport,
>   Conn.: Greenwood, 1974.
> Sadie, Stanley, ed. *The New Grove Dictionary of Music and Musi-
>   cians.* 20 vols. London: Macmillan, 1980.
> Stambler, Irwin. *Encyclopedia of Pop, Rock, and Soul.* New York:
>   St. Martin's, 1977.

35b

Stierlin, Henri. *Encyclopedia of World Architecture.* 2nd ed. 2 vols. New York: Facts on File, 1979.

Thompson, Oscar. *International Cyclopedia of Music and Musicians.* 10th ed. Ed. Bruce Bohle. New York: Dodd, Mead, 1975.

BUSINESS AND ECONOMICS

Buell, Victor P., ed. *Handbook of Modern Marketing.* New York: McGraw-Hill, 1970.

Graham, Irwin. *Encyclopedia of Advertising.* 2nd ed. New York: Fairchild, 1969.

Heyel, Carl. *The Encyclopedia of Management.* 2nd ed. New York: Van Nostrand Reinhold, 1973.

Munn, Glenn G. *Encyclopedia of Banking and Finance.* 7th ed. Ed. Ferdinand L. Garcia. Boston: Bankers, 1973.

Seidler, Lee J., and Douglas R. Carmichael. *Accountant's Handbook.* 6th ed. 2 vols. New York: Wiley, 1981.

Sloan, Harold S., and Arnold Zurcher. *A Dictionary of Economics.* 5th ed. New York: Barnes & Noble, 1970.

HISTORY

American Historical Association. *Guide to Historical Literature.* New York: Macmillan, 1961.

Binder, Leonard, ed. *The Study of the Middle East: Research and Scholarship in the Humanities and Social Sciences.* New York: Wiley, 1976.

Cambridge Ancient History. 12 vols. London: Cambridge Univ. Press, 1923–39. Revision in progress.

Cambridge Mediaeval History. 9 vols. London: Cambridge Univ. Press, 1911–36. Revision in progress.

Fairbank, John K., and Denis Twitchett. *Cambridge History of China.* 14 vols. London: Cambridge Univ. Press, 1978–. In progress.

Freidel, Frank, and Richard K. Showman eds. *Harvard Guide to American History.* Rev. ed. 2 vols. Cambridge, Mass.: Belknap Press of Harvard Univ. Press, 1974.

Hammond, N. G. L., and H. H. Scullard. *Oxford Classical Dictionary.* 2nd ed. New York: Oxford Univ. Press, 1970.

Martin, Michael R., et al. *An Encyclopedia of Latin-American History.* Rev. ed. Westport, Conn.: Greenwood, 1981.

Miller, Elizabeth W., and Mary Fisher, eds. *The Negro in America: A Bibliography.* Cambridge, Mass.: Harvard Univ. Press, 1970.

New Cambridge Modern History. 14 vols. London: Cambridge Univ. Press, 1957–80.

Prucha, Francis P. *A Bibliographical Guide to the History of Indian-White Relations in the United States.* Chicago: Univ. of Chicago Press, 1977.

35b

LITERATURE, THEATER, FILM, AND TELEVISION

Aaronson, C. S., ed. *International Television Almanac.* New York: Quigley Publications, published annually since 1956.

Adelman, Irving, and R. Dworkin. *Modern Drama: A Checklist of Critical Literature on Twentieth Century Plays.* Metuchen, N.J.: Scarecrow, 1967.

Benét, William Rose. *The Reader's Encyclopedia.* 2nd ed. New York: Crowell, 1965.

Bukalski, Peter J. *Film Research: A Critical Bibliography with Annotations and Essays.* Boston: G. K. Hall, 1972.

Hart, James D., ed. *The Oxford Companion to American Literature.* 4th ed. New York: Oxford Univ. Press, 1965.

Hartnoll, Phyllis, ed. *The Oxford Companion to the Theatre.* 3rd ed. New York: Oxford Univ. Press, 1967.

Harvey, Paul, and Dorothy Eagle, eds. *The Oxford Companion to English Literature.* 4th ed. New York: Oxford Univ. Press, 1967.

Holman, C. Hugh. *A Handbook to Literature.* 4th ed. Indianapolis: Bobbs-Merrill, 1980.

MLA International Bibliography of Books and Articles on the Modern Languages and Literatures. New York: Modern Language Association, published annually since 1922.

Schweik, Robert C., and Dieter Riesner. *Reference Sources in English and American Literature: An Annotated Bibliography.* New York: Norton, 1977.

Spiller, Robert E. *Literary History of the United States: Bibliography.* New York: Macmillan, 1974.

Trent, W. P., et al. *Cambridge History of American Literature.* New York: Macmillan, 1943.

Ward, A. W., and A. R. Waller, eds. *The Cambridge History of English Literature.* 15 vols. New York: Putnam's, 1907–33.

Watson, G., ed. *New Cambridge Bibliography of English Literature.* 4 vols. New York: Cambridge Univ. Press, 1972–76.

PHILOSOPHY AND RELIGION

Broderick, Robert, ed. *The Catholic Encyclopedia.* New York: Thomas Nelson, 1981.

Buttrick, George Arthur, and Keith R. Crim. *The Interpreter's Dictionary of the Bible.* 5 vols. Nashville: Abingdon, 1976.

Cross, F. L., and Elizabeth A. Livingston. *The Oxford Dictionary of the Christian Church.* New York: Oxford Univ. Press, 1974.

Edwards, Paul, ed. *The Encyclopedia of Philosophy.* 4 vols. New York: Free Press, 1973.

Ferm, Vergilius, ed. *An Encyclopedia of Religion.* Westport, Conn.: Greenwood, 1976.

Rice, Edward. *Eastern Definitions: A Short Encyclopedia of Religions of the Orient.* Garden City, N.Y.: Doubleday, 1978.

Roth, Cecil, ed. *The New Standard Jewish Encyclopedia.* 5th ed. New rev. ed. edited by Geoffrey Wigoder. Garden City, N.Y.: Doubleday, 1977.

35b

SOCIAL SCIENCES

Brock, Clifton. *The Literature of Political Science.* New York: Bowker, 1969.

Ebel, R. L. *Encyclopedia of Educational Research.* 4th ed. New York: Macmillan, 1969.
Eysenck, Hans Jurgen, ed. *Encyclopedia of Psychology.* 2nd ed. New York: Continuum, 1979.
Foreign Affairs Bibliography. 5 vols. New York: Bowker, 1960–76.
Leach, Maria, ed. *Funk and Wagnalls Standard Dictionary of Folklore, Mythology and Legend.* 2 vols. New York: Crowell, 1972.
Mitchell, G. Duncan, ed. *A Dictionary of Sociology.* Chicago: Aldine, 1967.
Sills, David L., ed. *International Encyclopedia of the Social Sciences.* 8 vols. plus supplement. New York: Free Press, 1977.
UNESCO International Committee for Social Science Documentation, ed. *International Bibliography of the Social Sciences.* New York: Methuen, 1960–78.
White, Carl M., et al. *Sources of Information in the Social Sciences: A Guide to the Literature.* 2nd ed. Chicago: American Library Association, 1973.
Winnick, Charles. *Dictionary of Anthropology.* Totowa, N.J.: Littlefield, 1977.

SCIENCES

Belzer, Jack, et al., eds. *Encyclopedia of Computer Science and Technology.* 14 vols. New York: Dekker, 1975–80.
Fairbridge, Rhodes W., ed. *The Encyclopedia of Oceanography.* New York: Academic, 1966.
Gray, Peter. *The Encyclopedia of Biological Sciences.* 2nd ed. New York: Van Nostrand Reinhold, 1970.
Hampel, Clifford A., and Gessner G. Hawley, eds. *The Encyclopedia of Chemistry.* 3rd ed. New York: Van Nostrand Reinhold, 1973.
Jobes, Gertrude, and James Jobes. *Outer Space: Myths, Names, Meanings, Calendars.* Metuchen, N.J.: Scarecrow, 1965.
The Larousse Encyclopedia of Animal Life. London: Hamlyn, 1967.
The McGraw-Hill Encyclopedia of Science and Technology. 4th ed. New York: McGraw-Hill, 1977.
Sarton, George. *An Introduction to the History of Science.* 5 vols. Melbourne, Fla.: Krieger, 1927–75.
Thewlis, J., ed. *Encyclopaedic Dictionary of Physics.* 9 vols. plus supplements. Elmsford, N.Y.: Pergamon, 1961–75.

Unabridged dictionaries and special dictionaries on language

Unabridged dictionaries are more comprehensive than abridged or college dictionaries. Special dictionaries give authoritative information on individual aspects of language. (See Chapter 32 for more on the kinds of dictionaries and how to use them.)

35b

UNABRIDGED DICTIONARIES

Craigie, Sir William, and James R. Hulbert. *A Dictionary of American English on Historical Principles.* 4 vols. Chicago: Univ. of Chicago Press, 1938–44.

The Oxford English Dictionary. 13 vols. plus supplements. New York: Oxford Univ. Press, 1933–76. *The Compact Edition,* 2 vols., was issued in 1971.
The Random House Dictionary of the English Language. New York: Random House, 1981.
Webster's Third New International Dictionary of the English Language. Springfield, Mass.: Merriam, 1976.

SPECIAL DICTIONARIES

Follett, Wilson. *Modern American Usage.* Ed. Jacques Barzun. New York: Hill and Wang, 1966.
Fowler, H. W. *Dictionary of Modern English Usage.* 2nd ed. Rev. and ed. Sir Ernest Gowers. New York: Oxford Univ. Press, 1965.
Lewis, Norman. *The New Roget's Thesaurus of the English Language in Dictionary Form.* New York: Putnam's, 1964.
Onions, Charles T., et al., eds. *The Oxford Dictionary of English Etymology.* New York: Oxford Univ. Press, 1966.
Partridge, Eric. *Dictionary of Slang and Unconventional English.* 7th ed. New York: Macmillan, 1970.
Partridge, Eric. *Origins: A Short Etymological Dictionary of Modern English.* New York: Macmillan, 1977.
Webster's New Dictionary of Synonyms. Springfield, Mass.: Merriam, 1978.
Wentworth, Harold, and Stuart Berg Flexner. *Dictionary of American Slang.* 2nd supp. ed. New York: Crowell, 1975.

Biographical reference works

If you want to learn about someone's life, achievements, credentials, or position, or if you want to learn the significance of a name you've come across, consult one of these reference works.

American Men and Women of Science. 12th ed. 8 vols. New York: Bowker, 1971.
Contemporary Authors. 96 vols. Detroit: Gale, 1967–80.
Current Biography. New York: Wilson, published annually since 1940.
Dictionary of American Biography. 16 vols. plus supplements. New York: Scribner's, 1927–81.
Dictionary of Literary Biography. 8 vols. Detroit: Gale, 1978–81.
Dictionary of National Biography (British). 22 vols. plus supplements. New York: Oxford Univ. Press, 1882–1972.
James, Edward T., and Janet W. James, eds. *Notable American Women.* 4 vols. Cambridge, Mass.: Belknap Press of Harvard Univ. Press, 1971–80.
Webster's Biographical Dictionary. Springfield, Mass.: Merriam, 1972.
Who's Who in America. 2 vols. Chicago: Marquis Who's Who, published biennially since 1899.

35b

Atlases and gazetteers

Atlases are bound collections of maps; gazetteers are geographical dictionaries.

Columbia Lippincott Gazetteer of the World. New York: Columbia Univ. Press, 1962.
Cosmopolitan World Atlas. Chicago: Rand McNally, 1981.
Encyclopaedia Britannica World Atlas International. Chicago: Encyclopaedia Britannica, 1969.
National Geographic Atlas of the World. 5th ed. Washington, D.C.: National Geographic Society, 1981.
The Times Atlas of the World. Boston: Houghton Mifflin, 1975.

Almanacs and yearbooks

Both almanacs and yearbooks are annual compilations of facts. Yearbooks record information about the previous year. Almanacs give facts and statistics about a variety of fields.

Americana Annual. New York: Americana Corporation, published annually since 1923.
Britannica Book of the Year. Chicago: Encyclopaedia Britannica, published annually since 1938.
Facts on File Yearbook. New York: Facts on File, published annually since 1940.
U.S. Bureau of the Census. *Statistical Abstract of the United States.* Washington, D.C.: GPO, published annually since 1878.
World Almanac and Book of Facts. New York: World-Telegram, published annually since 1868.

As a starting point for his topic of how advertising persuades consumers, Paul Fuller goes first to a general encyclopedia and skims the article on advertising. He learns that most advertisements are meant not so much to persuade consumers to buy as to make them aware that the product exists. The article also mentions that consumers often buy for irrational reasons and that advertisers' research into motivation has taught them to include in their ads scientific-sounding claims and symbols of comfort, sex, love of family, and so on. Fuller decides he can narrow his topic to the use of such nonrational, emotional appeals in advertising. He then consults the *Encyclopedia of Advertising,* where he finds references to several books, including *The Hidden Persuaders* and *Motivation in Advertising,* whose titles make them seem promising sources for his topic.

35b

2
Using indexes to periodicals

Periodicals — journals, magazines, and newspapers — are invaluable sources of information in research. The difference between journals and magazines lies primarily in their content, readership, frequency of issue, and page numbering. Magazines, such as *Psychology Today, Newsweek,* and *Esquire,* are nonspecialist publications intended for diverse readers. Most magazines appear weekly or monthly. Journals, in contrast, often appear quarterly and contain specialized information intended for readers in a particular field. Examples include *American Anthropologist, Journal of Black Studies,* and *Journal of Chemical Education.* In most magazines the page numbering begins anew with each issue. Many journals also page each issue separately, but others do not. Instead, the issues for an entire year make up an annual volume, and the pages are numbered continuously throughout the volume; thus issue number 3 (the third issue of the year) may open on page 327. (The method of pagination determines how you cite a journal article in your bibliography and notes; see pp. 463 and 483.)

Several guides provide information on the articles in journals, magazines, and newspapers. The contents, formats, and systems of abbreviation in these guides vary widely, but each one includes in its opening pages an introduction and explanation to aid the inexperienced user.

A typical and general periodical guide is the *Readers' Guide to Periodical Literature,* published since 1900 and updated semimonthly. It lists, by author, title, and subject, articles published each year in more than a hundred popular magazines. For a paper on a current topic you should consult at least several years' *Readers' Guide* volumes. Paul Fuller, checking the volumes as far back as the one for March 1977–February 1978, finds two pertinent articles under the main heading "Advertising" and the subheading "Psychological aspects." (Only a quarter of the "Advertising" entries in that volume of the *Readers' Guide* are reproduced here.)

ADVERTISING

Art director who has a way with words also has a book coming from Abrams; publication of The art of advertising; interview, ed by R. Dahlin. G. Lois. Pub W 211:55+ Ja 17 '77

Giving impact to ideas; address, October 11, 1977. L. T. Hagopian. Vital Speeches 44:154-7 D 15 '77

News behind the ads. See alternate issues of Changing times

Preaching in the marketplace. America 136:457 My 21 '77

Selling it. Consumer Rep 42:385, 458, 635 Jl-Ag, N '77
    See also
Photography in advertising
Religious advertising
Television advertising
Women in advertising
    also subhead Advertising under various subjects, e.g. Books—Advertising

Awards, prizes, etc.
Saturday review's 23rd annual Advertising Awards. C. Tucker. il Sat R 4:34-5 Jl 23 '77

35b

Laws and regulations
Crackdown ahead on advertising: what the government plans next; interview. M. Pertschuk. pors U.S. News 83:70-2 O 17 '77
FTC broadens its attack on ads. Bus **W** p27-8 Je 20 '77

Moral aspects
See Advertising ethics

Psychological aspects
Art of implying more than you say; work of Richard Harris. S. Bush. Psychol Today 10: 36+ My '77
Genderisms; reinforcement of sex role stereotypes. E. Goffman. il Psychol Today 11:60-3 Ag '77

Rates
Challenge to ad discounts; effect on small retailers of rate structure used in newspaper and magazine advertising. il Bus **W** p 146 S 19 '77
Drop in TV viewing, but not in ad pricing. il Bus **W** p33-4 Ja 16 '78

Other general indexes to periodicals include the following:

The New York Times Index. New York: The New York Times Company/Bowker, published annually since 1913. This index to the most complete United States newspaper can serve as a guide to national and international events and can indicate what issues of unindexed newspapers to consult for local reactions to such events.

Poole's Index to Periodical Literature. Boston: Houghton Mifflin, 1802–1907. An index by subject to British and American periodicals of the nineteenth century.

Popular Periodicals Index. Camden, N.J.: Popular Periodicals, published annually since 1973. An index to about twenty-five contemporary, popular periodicals not listed in major indexes.

Many special indexes and indexes to scholarly articles are available in most libraries. The following is a partial list.

America: History and Life. Santa Barbara: ABC-Clio Press, published three times a year since 1964.

Applied Science and Technology Index. New York: Wilson, published monthly since 1958. From 1913 to 1957 this work was combined with the *Business Periodicals Index* in the *Industrial Arts Index.*

Art Index. New York: Wilson, published quarterly since 1929.

Biological Abstracts. Philadelphia: Biological Abstracts, published semimonthly since 1926.

Biological and Agricultural Index. New York: Wilson, published monthly since 1964. From 1916 to 1963 this work was called the *Agricultural Index.*

Business Periodicals Index. New York: Wilson, published annually since 1958. From 1913 to 1957 this work was combined with the *Applied Science and Technology Index* in the *Industrial Arts Index.*

35b

The Education Index. New York: Wilson, published monthly since 1929.

Humanities Index. New York: Wilson, published quarterly since 1974. From 1965 to 1974 this author and subject index was combined with the *Social Sciences Index* in the *Social Sciences and Humanities Index.* From 1907 to 1965 the combined volume was called the *International Index.*

Index Medicus. Washington, D.C.: National Library of Medicine, published monthly since 1960. From 1927 to 1959 this work was called *Quarterly Cumulative Index Medicus.* From 1899 to 1926 it was *Index Medicus.*

MLA International Bibliography of Books and Articles in the Modern Languages and Literatures. New York: Modern Language Association, published annually since 1922.

Psychological Abstracts. Washington, D.C.: American Psychological Association, published monthly since 1927.

Science Citation Index. Philadelphia: Institute for Scientific Information, published quarterly since 1961.

Social Sciences Index. New York: Wilson, published quarterly since 1974. From 1965 to 1974 this author and subject index was combined with the *Humanities Index* in the *Social Sciences and Humanities Index.* From 1907 to 1965 the combined volume was called the *International Index.*

The recent issues of a periodical are generally held in the library's periodical room. To find out where and how the back issues are stored, locate the name of the periodical either in the main catalog (see the following section) or in a separate catalog of the library's periodical holdings. The catalog will tell you whether the issue you want is bound in an annual volume or stored in a much-reduced form on **microfilm,** a filmstrip showing pages side by side, or on **microfiche,** a sheet of film with pages arranged in rows and columns. Consulting periodicals stored on microfilm or microfiche requires using a special machine, or "reader," that locates and enlarges the page and projects it on a screen. Any member of the library's staff will show you how to operate the reader.

3
Using guides to books

The library's catalog lists books alphabetically by authors' names, titles of books, and subjects. (In some catalogs authors and titles are alphabetized separately from subjects.) If you are starting research on a subject you don't know very well, begin by looking under subject headings. If you know of an expert in the field and you want to find his or her books, look under the author's name. If you know the title of a relevant book but not the author's name, look for the title.

35b

The library's card catalog may be the familiar card file, cabinets of drawers containing 3″ × 5″ cards. But to save space and time, many libraries have converted their catalogs to other forms. A printed catalog in bound volumes contains small reproductions of the cards traditionally found in drawers. A catalog on microfilm or microfiche (see above) shows the library's collection on film viewed with a special reader. Increasingly, libraries are computerizing their holdings and storing their catalog in a computer as well. The user gains access to the computer's memory by typing a code onto a keyboard. A screen displays the requested information, and a printer may provide a paper copy. If you are uncertain about the location, form, or use of your library's catalog, seek help from a member of the library's staff.

Though the storage systems vary, catalogs in cabinets, in books, on film, or in computers contain similar information and follow a similar organization. By far the most widely used catalog format is that of the Library of Congress card. Here are samples of author, title, and subject cards.

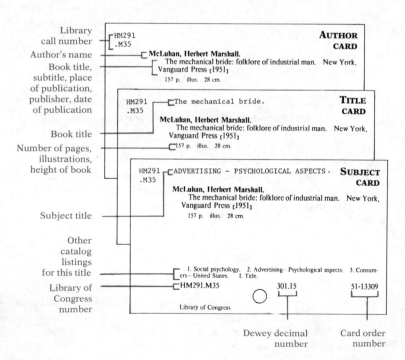

35b

Two types of reference books can help you to identify general books that have information about your topic: publishing bibliographies and digests. Publishing bibliographies tell whether a book is still in print, whether a paperback edition is available, what books were published on a certain topic in a certain year, and so on. These bibliographies include the following:

> *Books in Print.* New York: Bowker, published and supplemented annually since 1873. Books indexed by author, title, and subject.
>
> *Cumulative Book Index.* New York: Wilson, published monthly since 1898.
>
> *Paperbound Books in Print.* New York: Bowker, published semiannually since 1955.

You might, for example, want to know if the author of an encyclopedia article has published any relevant books since the date of the encyclopedia. You could look up the author's name in the latest *Books in Print* to find out.

If you want to evaluate a book's relevance to your topic before you search for it, you can consult the *Book Review Digest* (New York: Wilson, published annually since 1905). This digest tells you where to find reviews of current books and summarizes reviews. Another general digest is *Book Review Index* (Detroit: Gale, published annually since 1965). There are also digests for separate subjects such as *Recent Publications in the Social and Behavioral Sciences* (New York. American Behavioral Scientists, published annually).

EXERCISE 2

List at least five sources you can consult for further leads on each of the three topics you produced in Exercise 1 (p. 447), or for three other topics. Use the information provided in the preceding section and additional information at your library.

35c
Making a working bibliography

Trying to pursue every source lead as you came across it would prove inefficient and probably ineffective. Instead, you'll want to find out what is available before deciding which leads to follow, and that requires systematically keeping track of where information is and what it is. You can keep track of sources by making a working bibliography, a card file of the books, articles, and other sources you believe will help you. When you have a substantial card file of material, you can decide which sources seem most promising and look them up first.

A working bibliography records all the information you need to find the source. Putting each source on an individual 3″ × 5″ card will allow you to arrange your sources alphabetically by author, to discard irrelevant sources without disrupting your list, and later to transfer the information easily to your final bibliography.

Make a bibliography card for each source you think may be useful, whether you find it in the card catalog, in a reference book, or in an index to periodicals. Include, in standard bibliographical form (see the models below), all the information you will need for your final bibliography; getting all the information the first time will save you from having to retrace your steps later. For sources you find in the card catalog, list the call number on the bibliography card to save time later. (However, you will not transfer the call number to the final bibliography.) Here are two examples of bibliography cards, the first for a book and the second for a periodical.

HF
5813
V6655

Glatzer, Robert. *The New Advertising: The Great Campaigns.* New York: Citadel Press, 1970.

Gregg, Mary. "To Sell Your Product, Admit It's Not Perfect." *Psychology Today*, Oct. 1974, pp. 35-36.

35c

Listed below are some of the standard guides to the format of bibliographic entries and source citations. Except for the first two general works, each guide is published for a particular academic discipline. All the guides recommend formats that encourage the writer to include all the information needed for someone else to check the source. But the formats differ in the amount, arrangement, and punctuation of information. Your instructor will tell you which guide you should follow.

> *The Chicago Manual of Style.* 13th ed. Chicago: Univ. of Chicago Press, 1982.
>
> Turabian, Kate L. *A Manual for Writers of Term Papers, Theses, and Dissertations.* 4th ed. Chicago: Univ. of Chicago Press, 1973.
>
> *CBE Style Manual.* 4th ed. Bethesda, Md.: Council of Biology Editors, 1978.
>
> *Handbook for Authors.* Washington, D.C.: American Chemical Society, 1978.
>
> *MLA Handbook for Writers of Research Papers, Theses, and Dissertations.* New York: Modern Language Association, 1977.
>
> *Publication Manual of the American Psychological Association.* 2nd ed. Washington, D.C.: American Psychological Association, 1974.
>
> *Style Manual for Guidance in the Preparation of Papers.* 3rd ed. New York: American Institute of Physics, 1978.

The bibliographic models below are based on the *MLA Handbook,* the standard guide in the study of English and widely accepted in other disciplines as well. (The format of the American Psychological Association follows on pp. 465–66.) Note that models may have to be combined; for example, in citing the second edition of a multivolume work by two authors, you will need to draw on the models below labeled "Book with two or three authors," "A later edition," and "A work in more than one volume."

Books

BOOK WITH ONE AUTHOR

Kael, Pauline. <u>Going Steady</u>. Boston: Atlantic-Little, Brown, 1970.

TWO BOOKS WITH SAME AUTHOR

Gardner, Howard. <u>The Arts and Human Development</u>. New York:

Wiley, 1973.

----------. <u>The Quest for Mind: Piaget, Lévi-Strauss, and the</u>

<u>Structuralist Movement</u>. New York: Knopf, 1973.

BOOK WITH TWO OR THREE AUTHORS

Wimsatt, William K., and Cleanth Brooks. <u>Literary Criticism:</u>

<u>A Short History</u>. Chicago: Univ. of Chicago Press, 1978.

BOOK WITH MORE THAN THREE AUTHORS

Lopez, Robert S., et al. <u>Civilizations: Western and World</u>.

Boston: Little, Brown, 1975.

35c

Book with corporate authorship

Editors of The Progressive. The Crisis of Survival. Glenview,

Ill.: Scott, Foresman, 1970.

A later edition

Bollinger, Dwight L. Aspects of Language. 2nd ed. New York:

Harcourt Brace Jovanovich, 1975.

A modern reprint of an older edition

James, Henry. The Golden Bowl. New York: 1904; rpt. London:

Penguin, 1966.

A work in more than one volume

Blotner, Joseph. Faulkner: A Biography. 2 vols. New York:

Random House, 1974.

Blotner, Joseph. Faulkner: A Biography. New York: Random House,

1974. Vol. II.

A translation

Alighieri, Dante. The Inferno. Trans. John Ciardi. New York:

New American Library, 1971.

A work in a series

Bergman, Ingmar. The Seventh Seal. Modern Film Scripts Series.

New York: Simon & Schuster, 1968.

A book with an editor

Spradley, James P., and David W. McCurdy, eds. Conformity and

Conflict. 4th ed. Boston: Little, Brown, 1980.

A book with an author and an editor

Melville, Herman. The Confidence Man: His Masquerade. Ed. Hershel

Parker. New York: Norton, 1971.

A selection from a collection of original pieces or pieces by one author

Twain, Mark. "The War Prayer." In The Complete Essays of Mark

Twain. Ed. Charles Neider. Garden City, N.Y.: Doubleday,

1963.

A selection from a collection of reprinted pieces by different authors

Flynn, John T. "The Muckrakers." In God's Gold. New York:

Harcourt, Brace, 1932. Rpt. in John D. Rockefeller: Robber

35c

Baron or Industrial Statesman? Ed. Earl Latham. Boston:

Heath, 1942, pp. 1-6.

Periodicals: Journals, magazines, and newspapers

**A SIGNED ARTICLE IN A JOURNAL WITH CONTINUOUS
PAGINATION THROUGHOUT THE ANNUAL VOLUME (SEE P. 455)**

Gubar, Susan, and Anne Hedin. "A Jury of Our Peers: Teaching and

Learning in the Indiana Women's Prison." College English,

43 (1981), 779-89.

**A SIGNED ARTICLE IN A JOURNAL THAT PAGES ISSUES SEPARATELY
OR THAT NUMBERS ONLY ISSUES, NOT VOLUMES (SEE P. 455)**

Boyd, Sarah. "Nuclear Terror." Adaptation to Change, No. 7

(1981), pp. 20-23.

A SIGNED ARTICLE IN A MONTHLY MAGAZINE

Stein, Harry. "Living with Lies." Esquire, Dec. 1981, p. 23.

A SIGNED ARTICLE IN A WEEKLY MAGAZINE OR NEWSPAPER

Katz, Donald R. "Drawing Fire: Cartoonist Bill Mauldin and His

35-Year Fight for Truth, Justice, and the American Way."

Rolling Stone, 4 Nov. 1976, pp. 52-54, 56, 58, 60, 89.

A SIGNED ARTICLE IN A DAILY NEWSPAPER

Bowman, David. "Wrath: My Cow O'Leary's Plan for a Greater

Memphis." Center City, 11 Nov. 1976, pp. 1-2, col. 1.

AN UNSIGNED ARTICLE

"Notes on Personal Computers." Microcomputer, 2 (1980), 242.

"500 March Against Death Penalty." Boston Sunday Globe, 13 May

1979, Sec. 1, p. 21, col. 4.

"The Right to Die." Time, 11 Oct. 1976, p. 101.

Encyclopedias and almanacs

AN UNSIGNED ARTICLE IN AN ENCYCLOPEDIA

"Mammoth." The New Columbia Encyclopedia. 1975 ed.

A SIGNED ARTICLE IN AN ENCYCLOPEDIA

Hutton, J. E. "Moravian Brethren." Encyclopaedia Britannica.

1911 ed.

35c

Bulletins, pamphlets, and government documents

Zasloff, J. J. "Origins of the Insurgency in South Vietnam, 1954-
        1960." RAND Corporation Collection RM-4703/2-ISA/ARPA. Santa
        Monica, Cal.: RAND Corporation, May 1968.

Resource Notebook. Washington, D.C.: Project on Institutional
        Renewal Through the Improvement of Teaching, 1976.

National Endowment for the Humanities. "National Endowment for the
        Humanities Education Program Guidelines, 1978-1979." Washing-
        ton, D.C.: GPO, 1978.

U.S. Dept. of Labor. Employment and Earnings, 27, No. 9 (1981),
        18-20.

Unpublished dissertations and theses

Wilson, Stuart M. "John Stuart Mill as a Literary Critic." Diss.
        Univ. of Michigan 1970.

Films and television programs

Allen, Woody, dir. Manhattan. With Woody Allen, Diane Keaton,
        Michael Murphy, Meryl Streep, and Anne Byrne. United Artists,
        1979.

King of America. Writ. B. J. Merholz. Music Elizabeth Swados.
        With Larry Atlas, Andreas Katsulas, Barry Miller, and Michael
        Walden. PBS American Playhouse, 19 Jan. 1982.

Plays and concerts

Wheeler, David, dir. Richard III. By William Shakespeare. With
        Al Pacino. Cort Theatre, New York. 28 June 1979.

Ozawa, Seiji, cond. Boston Symphony Orchestra Concert. Symphony
        Hall, Boston. 25 April 1982.

35c

Records

Mitchell, Joni. For the Roses. Asylum, SD 5057, 1972.

Interviews

Smithson, Councilman John. Personal interview. 6 Sept. 1980.

Other bibliographic formats

Most of the social sciences and physical sciences employ a bibliographic style that differs from that recommended by the *MLA Handbook.* (The difference is even more marked in the style of source citations; see pp. 480–89.) These other styles differ among themselves, too — for instance, bibliographic entries are sometimes numbered — so you should ask your instructor which one to follow. But the format recommended by the widely used *Publication Manual of the American Psychological Association* is representative. Compare the models below with those from the *MLA Handbook* on the preceding pages. Note especially differences in the treatment of names, the capitalization and quotation of titles, and the listing of two or more books by the same author.

BOOK WITH ONE AUTHOR

Kael, P. Going steady. Boston: Atlantic-Little, Brown, 1970.

TWO WORKS WITH SAME AUTHOR, PUBLISHED IN SAME YEAR

Gardner, H. The arts and human development. New York: Wiley,

    1973. (a)

Gardner, H. The quest for mind: Piaget, Lévi-Strauss, and the

    structuralist movement. New York: Knopf, 1973. (b)

BOOK WITH TWO OR MORE AUTHORS

Lopez, R. S., Barnes, T., Blum, J., & Cameron, R. Civilizations:

    Western and world. Boston: Little, Brown, 1975.

BOOK IN A LATER EDITION

Bollinger, D. L. Aspects of language (2nd ed.). New York: Harcourt

    Brace Jovanovich, 1975.

35c

BOOK WITH AN EDITOR

Spradley, J. P., & McCurdy, D. W. (Eds.). Conformity and conflict

    (4th ed.). Boston: Little, Brown, 1980.

A SELECTION FROM AN EDITED ANTHOLOGY

Twain, M.   The war prayer.   In C. Neider (Ed.), <u>The complete essays</u>

   <u>of Mark Twain</u>.   Garden City, N.Y.: Doubleday, 1963.

AN ARTICLE IN A JOURNAL

Gubar, S., & Hedin, A.   A jury of our peers: Teaching and learning

   in the Indiana Women's Prison.   <u>College English</u>, 1981, <u>43</u>,

   779–789.

AN ARTICLE IN A MAGAZINE

Stein, H.   Living with lies.   <u>Esquire</u>, December 1981, p. 23.

EXERCISE 3

Prepare bibliography entries from the following information. Follow the models of the *MLA Handbook* given on pages 461–65, or use the format suggested by your instructor.

1. A book called *Black Voices: An Anthology of Afro-American Literature*, published in 1968 by The New American Library in New York, edited by Abraham Clapham.
2. An article in *Southern Folklore Quarterly*, volume 24, published in 1960. The article is "The New Orleans Voodoo Ritual Dance and Its Twentieth-Century Survivals," written by John Q. Anderson, on pages 135–43. The journal is paged continuously throughout the annual volume.
3. The fifth volume of *The History of Technology*, published in 1958 in London by Oxford University Press, written by Charles Singer, E. J. Holmroyd, A. R. Hall, and Trevor I. Williams.
4. A pamphlet entitled *George Segal*, published in 1979 by the Whitney Museum of American Art in New York.
5. A book by John Bartlett called *Familiar Quotations*, in its fifteenth edition, which was edited by Emily Morison Beck, published in 1980 by Little, Brown and Company in Boston, Massachusetts.

EXERCISE 4

35c

Prepare a working bibliography of at least ten sources for a research paper on one of the following people or on someone of your own choosing. Begin by limiting the subject to a manageable size. Then consult reference books, periodical indexes, and the library card catalog. Record bibliographic information on note cards, using the models of the *MLA Handbook* or a format suggested by your instructor.

1. John Lennon, or another performer
2. Ronald Reagan, or another politician
3. Emily Dickinson, or another writer
4. Muhammad Ali, or another sports figure
5. Andrew Wyeth, or another artist

EXERCISE 5

Using one of the topics and the possible references for it from Exercise 2 (p. 459), or starting with a different topic and references, prepare a working bibliography of at least ten sources for a research paper. List on 3″ × 5″ cards the complete bibliographic information for each source. Use the format of the *MLA Handbook* or the format chosen by your instructor.

35d
Reading to strengthen your overview and working up a tentative thesis and outline

When to stop looking for sources and start reading depends, of course, on the assigned length of the paper and on the complexity of your subject. You are probably ready to begin reading when your working bibliography suggests that you have explored most aspects of your topic and at least some sources that deal directly with your central concern. For a paper of fifteen hundred to two thousand words, ten to fifteen promising titles should give you a good base.

Once you have a satisfactory working bibliography, scan the cards for the titles that are most likely to help you work up a tentative outline and thesis. For his topic, the use of emotional appeals in advertising, Paul Fuller begins by looking at sources on research into motivation as well as more general sources on advertising.

As you glance quickly through your sources, your purpose is to evaluate their usefulness and to shape your thinking, not to collect information. A source is potentially useful to you if it is relevant to your topic and if it is reliable. Scanning the introductions to books and articles and the tables of contents and indexes of books can help you determine whether a source is relevant. Reliability is more difficult to judge. Look for information about the author's background. Once you are satisfied that the author has sufficient expertise in your subject, try to determine whether he or she might be biased. For instance, a book on parapsychology by someone identified as the president of the National Organization of Psychics may contain an authoritative explanation of psychic powers, but the author's view is likely to be biased. It should be balanced by research in other sources whose authors are more skeptical of psychic powers. Determine also whether the source is current and whether it treats the subject responsibly. Look for documentation of the author's sources, ample specific (and convincing) evidence to support general assertions, and a fair presentation of opposing views. If a source lacks any of these features, be sure you have another to balance it or back it up.

Read your sources quickly and selectively to obtain an overview of your topic so that your thesis encompasses the range of available information and represents your informed interpretation. Don't allow yourself to get bogged down in taking very detailed notes at this stage. Without a sense of what information is pertinent, you may not leave time to cover all the potentially relevant sources.

While reading and learning about your topic, do write down general ideas that seem fundamental to your topic. Be especially careful to record ideas of your own, such as a connection between statements by two different writers, because these may not occur to you later. When you have consulted the sources in your working bibliography, think of how you can arrange your list of ideas into groups of related thoughts. These rough groups — similar to the groups of ideas you use in writing an essay (see 1c) — will give you a view of your topic that should help you write a thesis for your paper.

Your thesis should state, in one or two sentences, your general idea and the perspective you take (see 1d). Drafting a thesis at this early stage helps keep you on track while you do further research. For his paper on advertising Fuller writes the following tentative thesis:

> Advertisers appeal to consumers' emotions, rather than to their reason, because they want to manipulate consumers.

This thesis states Fuller's central idea (that advertisers appeal to consumers' emotions) and also his view that advertisers use emotional appeals because they want to manipulate consumers. Fuller may have to revise his thesis to reflect his further research and to ensure that it adequately communicates his topic and perspective to readers. But for now his thesis gives Fuller a focus and a way to organize his work.

Having written a tentative thesis for your paper, you will be ready to prepare an **informal outline** that will guide your subsequent research. Like the informal outline for an essay (see 1f), the outline should show the main divisions of your paper, in the order you think you will cover them, and it should include the important supporting ideas for each division. Fuller's informal outline, below, is probably sufficient. Notice that the organization corresponds to the arrangement of ideas in the thesis sentence: Fuller's central idea comes first, followed by his perspective on it. Notice also that Fuller questions some ideas he has not found evidence for and must research further.

35d

Advertisers appeal to consumers' emotions
    Shows in the ads
      — full of adventure, humor, sex, status, and other emotional subjects
      — little information on quality and performance of product or sound reasons to buy
    Advertisers admit they emphasize emotional appeals
      — they say advertising is communication and therefore emotional
      — they say consumers choose irrationally
      — they say sales increase when ads stress emotion
Advertisers appeal to emotions because they want to manipulate consumers
    So say critics: McLuhan, Packard
    Research proves that advertisers use emotional appeals to manipulate (?)
      — consumers are manipulated by emotional appeals (?)
      — consumers would respond to rational appeals if they were provided (?)

If at this point you feel you don't have enough information to complete an informal outline, or that one of your ideas lacks support (as Fuller's last idea about research seems to), consult sources in your working bibliography that you skipped before, or reexamine the ones you skimmed. But don't try to construct a detailed, final outline now. Both your organization and your thesis will undoubtedly change as you do more research.

EXERCISE 6

Read through the sources in the working bibliography you made in Exercise 5 (p. 467). Jot down the main ideas related to your topic. Draft a thesis based on those ideas that both states the topic and implies your perspective on it. Finally, construct an informal outline that contains your main divisions and several supporting ideas for each, returning to your sources as needed.

35e
Taking detailed notes

After you have written a thesis statement and prepared an informal outline, you are ready to gather, interpret, and analyze information. To begin this stage, take detailed notes from your sources to help verify and expand your ideas and to record supporting evidence.

    Keep a copy of your informal outline with you in the library as a guide to give order to your search. Try to research the headings and subheadings of your outline one at a time. But don't let the out-

35e

line constrain your thinking. As you learn more about your topic, you will probably revise your outline by changing a heading, by dropping or adding one, or by rearranging headings. Revising is an inevitable, necessary, and beneficial part of research writing.

The most efficient method of reading during research is skimming, reading quickly to look for pertinent information. When skimming, you do not read randomly in hopes of hitting what you want. Rather, you read with a specific question in mind. Consult the table of contents or index to find what you want, and concentrate on headings and main ideas, skipping material unrelated to the specific question you are researching. When you find something relevant, read slowly and thoroughly to evaluate and interpret the material and to decide what information to write down.

Taking notes is not a mechanical process of copying from books and periodicals. If it is effective, your final paper will show that you have digested and interpreted the information in your sources — work that can be performed most efficiently in note taking. As you read and take notes, you decide what information supports your thesis, and you interpret and organize that information according to your thesis and outline. Thus your notes both prompt and preserve your thoughts.

Using a system for taking notes helps simplify the process and later makes writing the paper easier. The most common method involves note cards (4″ × 6″ cards allow more room than 3″ × 5″). Write only one fact or idea on a card so that you can easily rearrange information when you want to. (Such rearrangement is extremely difficult when notes are combined on sheets of paper.) If the same source gives you more than one idea or fact, make more than one card. At the top of every card, write the author, title, and page numbers of the source so that you will always know where the note

35e

Advertising as communication

Martineau, *Motivation in Advertising,*
p. 139.

Advertising is a form of human communication, so emotional and rational meanings are communicated at the same time.

came from. In addition, write the outline heading that this note belongs under so that you can remember what you intended to do with it. This format is illustrated on the preceding page by one of Paul Fuller's note cards.

You can use four different kinds of notes: (1) summary, (2) paraphrase, (3) direct quotation, and (4) a combination of summary or paraphrase and direct quotation. When you **summarize,** you condense an extended idea or argument into a sentence or two in your own words. When you **paraphrase,** you follow much more closely the author's original presentation, but you still restate it in your own words. Paraphrase is most useful when you want to reconstruct an author's line of reasoning but don't feel the original words merit direct quotation. As you summarize and paraphrase, be careful not to distort the author's meaning, but don't feel you have to put down in new words the whole passage or all the details. Select what is pertinent and restate only that. In this way you will be developing your thoughts about the topic as you read and take notes.

The sample note on the previous page is a paraphrase. Compare this note to the original statement by Pierre Martineau from *Motivation in Advertising* (New York: McGraw-Hill, 1957), p. 139:

> Advertising combines forces of both logical thought and emotive, aesthetic thought. Because it is communication from one set of humans to another set of humans, part of the meaning will be rational; but also there will be much meaning conveyed by nonrational symbols.

Notice how Fuller has used his own sentence structure and words to express Martineau's statement: "form of human communication" instead of "communication from one set of humans to another set of humans"; "emotional and rational meanings" instead of "logical thought and emotive, aesthetic thought . . . part of the meaning will be rational; but also there will be much meaning conveyed by nonrational symbols." (For more on paraphrasing, see Appendix A.)

Summary and paraphrase are the methods of making notes you will use most often. Use **direct quotation** sparingly — only when you feel the source's words give a special effect you want to include, when you are discussing an author's writing, when you want to give impact to an authority's opinion, or when you plan to use a graph, table, or diagram from the source. (See also 35g-2 on introducing quotations in the paper.) When you quote directly, keep in mind that you can use brackets to show any additional words needed for understanding (see 25d) and ellipses to show omissions of irrelevant words or sentences (see 25e). The note card on the next page shows how Fuller might have quoted rather than paraphrased Martineau, using both ellipses and brackets to make the quotation more concise without changing its meaning.

35e

Advertising as communication

Martineau, Motivation in Advertising,
p. 139.

"Advertising combines ... logical thought
and emotive, aesthetic thought. Because
it is [human] communication..., part
of the meaning will be rational; but
also there will be much meaning
conveyed by non-rational symbols."

Be sure to proofread any direct quotation *at least twice* to ensure complete accuracy in wording, spelling, capitalization, punctuation, and the like. And be sure you have supplied the quotation marks so that later you won't confuse the direct quotation card with a paraphrase or summary card. Researchers sometimes photocopy long quotations to save time and to ensure accuracy. If you choose to photocopy, write the author's name, source title, and page number on the page as you would on a note card. But resort to this method only occasionally. Photocopying is expensive, and copied pages can be inconvenient when you need to sift through your notes. More important, running pages through a copying machine hardly generates the creative, interpretive thinking about sources that is so crucial in taking notes.

Using quotation in combination with paraphrase helps you shape the material to suit your purposes (although you must be careful not to distort the author's meaning). The card on the next page shows how Fuller might have used a combination of quotation and paraphrase to record the statement by Martineau. Notice that the quotation marks are clearly visible and that the quotations are absolutely exact.

If the material you are quoting, summarizing, or paraphrasing runs from one page to the next in the source, make a mark (such as a check mark or a slash) at the exact spot where one page ends and the next begins. When writing your paper, you may want to use only a part of the material (say, the first or second half). The mark will save you from having to go back to your source to find which page the material actually occurred on.

When you have enough note cards to support or explain all the divisions of your informal outline, you can move to the next step of revising your thesis and writing a formal outline.

35e

Advertising as communication
Martineau, *Motivation in Advertising*,
p. 139.

One advertiser says, "Advertising combines forces of both logical thought and emotive, aesthetic thought" because of its nature as "communication from one set of humans to another."

A note on plagiarism

Plagiarism — presenting someone else's ideas as your own, whether deliberately or accidentally — is a serious offense, and a separate section of this book is devoted entirely to it (see Appendix A). If you use another writer's words or ideas in your final draft without citing a source for them, you will be committing plagiarism. The problem can start in careless note taking. For instance, if you copy even a phrase from a source without using quotation marks, you may, in writing the paper from your notes, assume that the phrase is your own paraphrase or summary and use it without quotation marks. Or if you paraphrase an author's idea and neglect to note the source, you might later forget that the idea was not yours originally but another's. Even though you did not intend to do so, you would be plagiarizing in both these cases. Thus be sure your note cards show sources and the exact use you are making of them. And read Appendix A (p. 530).

EXERCISE 7

Prepare two note cards, one containing a summary of the entire paragraph below and the other containing a paraphrase of the first four sentences (ending with the word "autonomy"). Use the format for a note card provided in the preceding section, omitting only the outline heading.

35e

Federal organization [of the United States] has made it possible for the different states to deal with the same problems in many different ways. One consequence of federalism, then, has been that people are treated differently, by law, from state to state.

The great strength of this system is that differences from state to state in cultural preferences, moral standards, and levels of wealth can be accommodated. In contrast to a unitary system in which the central government makes all important decisions (as in France), federalism is a powerful arrangement for maximizing regional freedom and autonomy. The great weakness of our federal system, however, is that people in some states receive less than the best or the most advanced or the least expensive services and policies that government can offer. The federal dilemma does not invite easy solutions, for the costs and benefits of the arrangement have tended to balance out.

— PETER K. EISINGER ET AL., *American Politics*, p. 44

EXERCISE 8

Prepare a note card containing a combination of paraphrase or summary and direct quotation that states the major idea of the passage below. Use the format for a note card provided in the preceding section, omitting only the outline heading.

Most speakers unconsciously duel even during seemingly casual conversations, as can often be observed at social gatherings where they show less concern for exchanging information with other guests than for asserting their own dominance. Their verbal dueling often employs very subtle weapons like mumbling, a hostile act which defeats the listener's desire to understand what the speaker claims he is trying to say (but is really not saying because he is mumbling!). Or the verbal dueler may keep talking after someone has passed out of hearing range — which is often an aggressive challenge to the listener to return and acknowledge the dominance of the speaker. — PETER FARB, *Word Play*, p. 107

EXERCISE 9

Continuing from Exercise 5 (p. 467), as the next step in preparing a research paper, make notes of specific information from your sources. As much as practicable, adhere to your thesis and follow your informal outline. Use paraphrase, direct quotation, and a combination of the two. Mark each card with the author's name, title, and page number as well as your outline heading.

35f

35f

Revising the thesis and writing a formal outline

As you took notes, you began to revise your thesis and outline in your mind and perhaps in your writing. These revisions occupy most of the next step in writing a research paper. After investigating your topic thoroughly through reading and note taking, you will want to evaluate your thesis sentence in light of what you now know. At this point the thesis should be close to final in its wording and in its description of your topic and what you have to say about it. In his research, for example, Paul Fuller could not find evidence to support his belief that consumers would make rational choices if they were given advertisements that appealed to reason. (See his informal outline on p. 469.) Instead, he found the opposite: Consumers choose products emotionally and do not use reason even when they are given the chance. Consequently, he revises his informal outline and his thesis so that his paper will reflect the evidence as it exists, not as he imagined it.

TENTATIVE THESIS

Advertisers appeal to consumers' emotions, rather than to their reason, because they want to manipulate consumers.

REVISED THESIS

Advertisers appeal to consumers' emotions, rather than to their reason, because consumers choose products irrationally.

After revising your thesis sentence, you will probably want to prepare a detailed outline from which to write your paper. This **formal outline,** like the formal outline for an essay (see 1f), is more complete than an informal outline and arranges ideas in a logical way. Inadequate coverage of the thesis, overlapping ideas, ideas that are not parallel yet are in parallel positions, and imprecise phrasing — all of these are corrected in the process of writing a formal outline. The goal is to produce an outline that presents your ideas in a sensible and persuasive sequence and that supports ideas at each level with enough explanation and evidence.

Before actually beginning work on your formal outline, you should group your note cards according to their headings, which are also the headings of your informal outline. You can begin revising your outline by rearranging and retitling cards to reflect your changed ideas and the sense of your revised thesis sentence. Gradually, a complete outline of your thinking will evolve.

A formal outline is usually written either in phrases — a **topic outline** — or in sentences — a **sentence outline.** A complete topic outline is illustrated in Chapter 1, pages 30–31. A complete sentence outline accompanies Paul Fuller's research paper on pages 494–95. Either is suitable for a research paper, though a sentence outline, because it requires complete statements, conveys more information. The example below shows the formal outline's format and schematic content.

35f

I. First main idea
   A. First subordinate idea
      1. First evidence for subordinate idea
         a. First detail of evidence
         b. Second detail of evidence
      2. Second evidence for subordinate idea
   B. Second subordinate idea
II. Second main idea

In this model main ideas are labeled with Roman numerals, the first sublevel with capital letters, the second with Arabic numerals, and the third with small letters. (A fourth sublevel, if needed, is labeled with Arabic numerals enclosed in parentheses.) Each level of the outline is indented farther than the one it supports.

To be an effective organizer for your thoughts, a formal outline should be detailed and should adhere to several principles of logical arrangement, clarity, balance, and completeness. These are discussed in detail and illustrated in Chapter 1, pages 31–32. Briefly: (1) The outline should divide material into groups that indicate which ideas are primary and, under them, which subordinate. A long, undivided list of parallel items probably needs to be subdivided. (2) Parallel headings should represent ideas of parallel importance and should not overlap one another. (3) Single sublevels should be avoided because they illogically imply that something is divided into only one part.

If you compare Paul Fuller's sentence outline on pages 494–95 with his informal outline on page 469, you can see that the formal outline has more information and a tighter, more logical arrangement of ideas and details.

EXERCISE 10

Identify the flaws in the following partial outline for a research paper. Check especially for departures from formal outline form, including illogical subdivision of topics, inconsistent wording of items, and nonparallel placement of ideas of parallel importance.

THESIS SENTENCE

Food additives, which aid in processing foods and in preserving them or improving their appearance, are more useful to us than they are dangerous.

FORMAL OUTLINE

I. Processing, preservation, appearance
   A. Processing
      1. Leavening agents
      2. Antifoaming agents
      3. Emulsifiers
         a. Bind ingredients together

35f

B. Preservation
  1. Protect from internal destruction
     a. Natural enzymes can cause discoloration or over-ripening
     b. Must remove or disable enzymes
  2. External destruction
     a. Bacteria
     b. Fungus
  3. Environment
     a. Heat, moisture, humidity
     b. Humectants protect foods from excess moisture
C. Appearance
  1. Glazing agents
  2. Foaming agents cause bubbles to appear in hot chocolate
  3. Firming agents
     a. Keep fruits and vegetables firm in cans
     b. Thickeners
        1. Prevent ice crystal formation, as in ice cream
        2. Improve texture
  4. Sequestrants prevent discoloration

EXERCISE 11

Using the note cards you prepared in Exercise 9 (p. 474), revise the thesis statement from Exercise 6 (p. 469) and construct a formal sentence or topic outline from which to write a paper.

35g
Writing and revising the paper

After you have taken notes from your sources, revised your thesis as necessary, and written a formal outline for your paper, you are ready to begin writing the first draft. Take time to organize your notes carefully according to your formal outline. Once you have arranged your notes, go through them slowly, considering which of your ideas each note supports, how you will link the evidence in one note with that in others, and how you will move from one idea and block of evidence to the next.

1
Writing the paper

Remember that a primary reason for doing a research paper is learning how to evaluate and interpret the evidence in sources, draw your own conclusions from the evidence, and weave the two together in a convincing whole. The weaving will be easier if you think and write in units, each one corresponding to a principal idea from your outline. Depending on the importance of the idea to your scheme, on its complexity, and on the amount of evidence needed to support it, a unit may be a single paragraph or a block of two or three paragraphs. Begin each unit by stating the idea, which should be a conclusion you have drawn from reading and taking notes. Follow the statement with the specific support from your notes: facts, quotations or paraphrases of experts, quotations of passages from literature, and so on. If your research has uncovered a disagreement among experts, present the disagreement fairly and, if your evidence allows, side with one expert or the other. As much as possible, work in transitions from one bit of evidence to the next and then from one unit to the next; and try to remain open to new interpretations or new arrangements of ideas that occur to you. But save the work of smoothing and clarifying until the second draft if you find it interfering with your ability to get everything down on paper.

As you write, always think of your audience (see 1e). Unless you know otherwise, consider your potential readers to be general college-level readers — serious and thoughtful, but perhaps uninformed about your topic. They will need and appreciate clear, specific, and comprehensive explanations. They will expect all your assertions to be supported with evidence (see 4c). Adopt a rational, straightforward tone by remaining moderate in your expression (see 4a), by using standard diction (see 31a), and by employing a variety of sentence structures (see Chapter 19).

2
Introducing summaries, paraphrases, and quotations

One of your challenges in writing a research paper will be deciding when, where, and how to introduce summaries, paraphrases, and quotations from your sources into your text. Whether you summarize, paraphrase, or quote, make others' facts and opinions serve your ideas; don't allow them to overwhelm your own point of view. Except when you are discussing passages of literature, favor paraphrases over quotations. Quote a source only when the original wording is essential to understanding the exact meaning or is particularly succinct, forceful, or otherwise interesting (for instance, a bold statement from an acknowledged authority, or an inventive comparison). Keep quotations short by eliminating sentences and phrases that are not essential to the intended meaning and that do not contribute to your purpose. Most papers of seven to ten pages should not need more than two or three quotations that are longer than a few lines. More than that may bury rather than enhance your argument.

Smooth the way for summaries, paraphrases, and quotations

35g

by integrating them into your own sentences with expressions like "according to" and "one writer observes that." For example:

QUOTATION   Yet not all authorities agree with this view. Harold Lyman, a newspaper editor for over forty years, grants that "news reporters, like everyone else, form impressions of what they see and hear." But, he insists, "a good reporter does not fail to separate his opinions from his facts."[8]

PARAPHRASE   Yet not all authorities agree with this view. Harold Lyman, a newspaper editor for over forty years, argues instead that news reporters are responsible for identifying the opinions they inevitably develop and for distinguishing them from facts.[8]

Notice that both examples accomplish two other purposes. First, the opening sentence and words like "grants," "insists," and "argues" tell us something of what to expect in the paraphrase or quotation. Second, both examples provide the source's credentials: "a newspaper editor for over forty years." Thus readers will understand clearly why the writer paraphrases or quotes any source at all and this source in particular. (See Paul Fuller's paper, pp. 496–517, for more examples of integrating quotations into the text.)

| 3
| **Revising the first draft**

When you have written a first draft, take a break for at least a day so that you can gain some objectivity about your work and read the draft critically when you begin to revise. Then evaluate your first draft according to the advice and revision checklist in 2b (p. 42). Proofread, of course, to catch simple mistakes. More important, however, rethink the content and effectiveness of every sentence and of the whole. Start with your thesis sentence (Does it accurately describe your topic and your perspective? Is the paper unified around it?), and proceed through each paragraph. Be alert for major structural problems that may not have been apparent in your outline: for instance, illogical arrangements of ideas; inadequate emphasis of important points and overemphasis of minor ones; or imbalance between the views of others (support) and your own views (interpretation). Check for clear and smooth transitions between main ideas, between ideas and their supporting evidence, and between pieces of evidence. Hunt out irrelevant ideas and facts that crept in just because you had note cards on them. Look for places where supporting evidence is weak, for points that once seemed strong but are now unclear. Try to read the paper from the point of

35g

view of someone who has not spent hours planning and researching but instead has come fresh to the paper — skeptical, perhaps, but capable of being informed and convinced. Take the time to solve the problems you find; if you spot them, your readers probably will, too.

EXERCISE 12

Write the research paper you have been preparing in Exercises 1, 2, 5, 6, 9, and 11. Before beginning the first draft, study your notes. While writing, follow your note cards (Exercise 9) and formal outline (Exercise 11) as closely as you need to, but stay open to new ideas, associations, and arrangements. Then revise thoroughly, working to improve not only your presentation of ideas but also the ideas themselves, if necessary.

35h
Preparing the footnotes

The primary purpose of footnotes is to acknowledge all sources of information and quotation used in the text of the paper. (You may also use footnotes to provide additional explanation or comment, as Paul Fuller does twice in his final draft; see pp. 506 and 512. But such notes should contain information that is clearly relevant, not a departure from the paper's topic.) You *must* acknowledge sources of direct quotation as well as of tables and diagrams. You *must also* acknowledge sources of ideas, facts, or associations between them that you paraphrase or summarize from books, magazines, newspapers, movies, television programs, interviews, letters, and the like. Acknowledge all quotations, summaries, and paraphrases no matter what their length or how often you have already cited the source. You do not need to acknowledge your own ideas or ideas that are considered common knowledge, such as well-known historical and scientific facts, when you express these in your own words. (For a detailed discussion of what to acknowledge and when, see Appendix A on avoiding plagiarism.)

As you read through your paper, check your note cards. Identify each summary, paraphrase, and quotation in the text, proofread every quotation a final time, then locate the corresponding bibliography card. The page numbers on your note cards and the information on your bibliography cards give you everything you need to write your footnotes.

From discipline to discipline, the format of source acknowledgments differs even more than the format of bibliographic entries (see 35c). Your instructor will tell you which format to follow. Whatever the form, *be consistent*. In the system recommended by the

MLA Handbook, you place a raised numeral ([1]) in the text at the end of the material you are acknowledging, and you number the citations consecutively throughout the paper. The source acknowledgments themselves then fall in the same order. The *MLA Handbook* suggests that you collect all acknowledgments on separate pages at the end of your paper, but your instructor may ask that you place them at the bottom of appropriate text pages. (Footnotes collected at the end of a paper are often called *endnotes* or simply *notes.*) For a graph, table, or diagram, place the word "Source" under the illustration, follow it with a colon, and then give the note. Start each note on a new line, indenting the first line five spaces from the left margin. Begin the note with a raised numeral corresponding to the one in the text, leave one space, and then cite the source. Double-space all lines of endnotes; single-space footnotes (at the bottoms of pages), but double-space between them. (See Paul Fuller's research paper starting on p. 496 for examples of note references in the text; see his endnotes and the comments opposite them, pp. 512–15 for the form to use in typing that section.)

The following models for footnotes and notes are based on the *MLA Handbook.* (Two other styles of source citation, used in many social and physical sciences, are described on pp. 487–89.) Notice how the note models differ from the bibliography models (pp. 461–65), though the information given is essentially the same.

BIBLIOGRAPHY

Wimsatt, William K., and Cleanth Brooks. <u>Literary Criticism:</u>

    <u>A Short History</u>. Chicago: Univ. of Chicago Press, 1978.

NOTE

    [2] William K. Wimsatt and Cleanth Brooks, <u>Literary Criticism:</u>

<u>A Short History</u> (Chicago: Univ. of Chicago Press, 1978), p. 312.

In the bibliography entry you start the first line at the left margin and indent the second and subsequent lines five spaces; but in the note you indent the first line and not the others. The note is intended to be read as a sentence, so a period appears only at the end while the body of the note is punctuated with commas and colons. In the note, unlike the bibliography entry, you enclose the publication information (place of publication, publisher, date of publication) in parentheses. Whereas you start the bibliography entry with the first author's last name, to make it easier to find the name in an alphabetical listing, in the note you give the author's name in normal order. And in the note you include the specific page number in the source from which the summary, paraphrase, or quotation is taken.

35h

Be sure to use note models for your notes and bibliography models for your bibliography.

Like the bibliography models, the note models may be combined if necessary; for example, the model for a book with an editor may be combined with that for a multivolume book if your source is a multivolume, edited work. The following note models are those for first reference to a source. When you acknowledge the same source more than once in the same paper, you should use a shortened form of reference. Two different ones are described on pages 485–86 and 487.

Books

BOOK WITH ONE AUTHOR

[1] Pauline Kael, <u>Going Steady</u> (Boston: Atlantic–Little, Brown, 1970), p. 87.

BOOK WITH TWO OR THREE AUTHORS

[2] William K. Wimsatt and Cleanth Brooks, <u>Literary Criticism:</u> <u>A Short History</u> (Chicago: Univ. of Chicago Press, 1978), p. 312.

BOOK WITH MORE THAN THREE AUTHORS

[3] Robert S. Lopez et al., <u>Civilizations: Western and World</u> (Boston: Little, Brown, 1975), pp. 281–82.

BOOK WITH CORPORATE AUTHORSHIP

[4] Editors of <u>The Progressive</u>, <u>The Crisis of Survival</u> (Glenview, Ill.: Scott, Foresman, 1970), p. 61.

A LATER EDITION

[5] Dwight L. Bollinger, <u>Aspects of Language</u>, 2nd ed. (New York: Harcourt Brace Jovanovich, 1975), p. 20.

A MODERN REPRINT OF AN OLDER EDITION

[6] Henry James, <u>The Golden Bowl</u> (New York: 1904; rpt. London: Penguin, 1966), p. 163.

A WORK IN MORE THAN ONE VOLUME

[7] Joseph Blotner, <u>Faulkner: A Biography</u> (New York: Random House, 1974), II, 82.

35h

A TRANSLATION

[8] Dante Alighieri, The Inferno, trans. John Ciardi (New York: New American Library, 1971), pp. 73-74.

A WORK IN A SERIES

[9] Ingmar Bergman, The Seventh Seal, Modern Film Scripts Series (New York: Simon & Schuster, 1968), p. 6.

A BOOK WITH AN EDITOR

[10] James P. Spradley and David W. McCurdy, eds., Conformity and Conflict, 4th ed. (Boston: Little, Brown, 1980), p. 4.

A BOOK WITH AN AUTHOR AND AN EDITOR

[11] Herman Melville, The Confidence Man: His Masquerade, ed. Hershel Parker (New York: Norton, 1971), p. 49.

A SELECTION FROM A COLLECTION OF ORIGINAL PIECES OR PIECES BY ONE AUTHOR

[12] Mark Twain, "The War Prayer," in The Complete Essays of Mark Twain, ed. Charles Neider (Garden City, N.Y.: Doubleday, 1963), p. 681.

A SELECTION FROM A COLLECTION OF REPRINTED PIECES BY DIFFERENT AUTHORS

[13] John T. Flynn, "The Muckrakers," in God's Gold (New York: Harcourt, Brace, 1932); rpt. in John D. Rockefeller: Robber Baron or Industrial Statesman? ed. Earl Latham (Boston: Heath, 1942), p. 4.

Periodicals: Journals, magazines, and newspapers

A SIGNED ARTICLE IN A JOURNAL WITH CONTINUOUS PAGINATION THROUGHOUT THE ANNUAL VOLUME (SEE P. 455)

[14] Susan Gubar and Anne Hedin, "A Jury of Our Peers: Teaching and Learning in the Indiana Women's Prison," College English, 43 (1981), 781.

A SIGNED ARTICLE IN A JOURNAL THAT PAGES ISSUES SEPARATELY OR THAT NUMBERS ONLY ISSUES, NOT VOLUMES (SEE P. 455)

[15] Sarah Boyd, "Nuclear Terror," Adaptation to Change, No. 7 (1981), pp. 20-21.

35h

A SIGNED ARTICLE IN A MONTHLY MAGAZINE

[16] Harry Stein, "Living with Lies," Esquire, Dec. 1981, p. 23.

A SIGNED ARTICLE IN A WEEKLY MAGAZINE OR NEWSPAPER

[17] Donald R. Katz, "Drawing Fire: Cartoonist Bill Mauldin and His 35-Year Fight for Truth, Justice, and the American Way," Rolling Stone, 4 Nov. 1976, p. 56.

A SIGNED ARTICLE IN A DAILY NEWSPAPER

[18] David Bowman, "Wrath: My Cow O'Leary's Plan for a Greater Memphis," Center City, 11 Nov. 1976, p. 2, col. 1.

AN UNSIGNED ARTICLE

[19] "Notes on Personal Computers," Microcomputer, 2 (1980), 242.

[20] "500 March Against Death Penalty," Boston Sunday Globe, 13 May 1979, Sec. 1, p. 21, col. 4.

[21] "The Right to Die," Time, 11 Oct. 1976, p. 101.

Encyclopedias and almanacs

AN UNSIGNED ARTICLE IN AN ENCYCLOPEDIA

[22] "Mammoth," The New Columbia Encyclopedia, 1975 ed.

A SIGNED ARTICLE IN AN ENCYCLOPEDIA

[23] J. E. Hutton, "Moravian Brethren," Encyclopaedia Britannica, 1911 ed.

Bulletins, pamphlets, and government documents

[24] J. J. Zasloff, "Origins of the Insurgency in South Vietnam, 1954-1960," RAND Corporation Collection RM-4703/2-ISA/ARPA (Santa Monica, Cal.: RAND Corporation, May 1968), p. ii.

[25] Resource Notebook (Washington, D.C.: Project on Institutional Renewal Through the Improvement of Teaching, 1976), p. 17.

[26] National Endowment for the Humanities, "National Endowment for the Humanities Education Program Guidelines, 1978-1979" (Washington, D.C.: GPO, 1978), p. 8.

35h

²⁷ U.S. Dept. of Labor, <u>Employment and Earnings</u>, 27, No. 9 (1981), 19.

Unpublished dissertations and theses

²⁸ Stuart M. Wilson, "John Stuart Mill as a Literary Critic," Diss. Univ. of Michigan 1970, p. 7.

Films and television programs

²⁹ Woody Allen, dir., <u>Manhattan</u>, with Woody Allen, Diane Keaton, Michael Murphy, Meryl Streep, and Anne Byrne, United Artists, 1979.

³⁰ <u>King of America</u>, writ. B. H. Merholz, music Elizabeth Swados, with Larry Atlas, Andreas Katsulas, Barry Miller, and Michael Walden, PBS American Playhouse, 19 Jan. 1982.

Plays and concerts

³¹ David Wheeler, dir., <u>Richard III</u>, by William Shakespeare, with Al Pacino, Cort Theatre, New York, 28 June 1979.

³² Seiji Ozawa, cond., Boston Symphony Orchestra Concert, Symphony Hall, Boston, 25 April 1982.

Records

³³ Joni Mitchell, <u>For the Roses</u>, Asylum, SD 5057, 1972.

Interviews

³⁴ Personal interview with Councilman John Smithson, 6 Sept. 1980.

Subsequent references to the same source

To minimize clutter in your footnotes or notes, and to give readers a quick sense of how often you acknowledge a source, you should use a shortened form for subsequent references to a source you have already cited fully. When you refer to only one source by the author cited (or only one source bearing the title cited if there is no author), the *MLA Handbook* recommends that subsequent references carry only the author's name (or the title) and the page refer-

35h

ence appropriate for the later citation. Here are two examples, both preceded by the full citations.

[11] Herman Melville, The Confidence Man: His Masquerade, ed.
Hershel Parker (New York: Norton, 1971), p. 49.

[35] Melville, p. 62.

[21] "The Right to Die," Time, 11 Oct. 1976, p. 101.
[36] "The Right to Die," p. 101.

However, if two of your sources are by the same author or bear the same title, give the title or the name of the source so there can be no confusion about the work you are citing. You may shorten the title or name of the source. For example:

[1] Pauline Kael, Going Steady (Boston: Atlantic–Little, Brown, 1970), p. 87.

[37] Pauline Kael, Kiss Kiss Bang Bang (Boston: Little, Brown, 1968), p. 263.

[38] Kael, Kiss Kiss, p. 266.

[22] "Mammoth," The New Columbia Encyclopedia, 1975 ed.

[39] "Mammoth," Encyclopaedia Britannica, 1911 ed.

[40] "Mammoth," Columbia Encyclopedia.

If you have previously cited one volume of a multivolume work, be sure to note the volume number in the new, shortened citation, even if it is the same.

[7] Joseph Blotner, Faulkner: A Biography (New York: Random House, 1974), II, 82.

[41] Blotner, II, 83.

35h

NOTE: Although the *MLA Handbook* does not recommend it, the Latin abbreviation "ibid.," for *ibidem* ("in the same place"), is still a common means of indicating that a citation refers to the source in the preceding note, though perhaps to a different page of the source:

[3] Robert S. Lopez et al., Civilizations: Western and World (Boston: Little, Brown), pp. 181–82.

[4] Ibid., p. 284.

Internal documentation

If your paper is devoted to the analysis of a single author's work (for instance, several novels by Faulkner or a play by Shakespeare), you can reduce the number of notes by using citations in the text itself. The first time you cite each work, provide an appropriate, full note and end it with the following sentence: "All further references to this work appear in parentheses in the text." In each subsequent citation provide the needed reference information immediately after the quotation or paraphrase in the text. For instance:

Later in <u>King Lear</u> the disguised Edgar says, "The prince of darkness

is a gentleman" (III.iv.147).

(When the parenthetical reference follows a long quotation set off from the text, end the last sentence with a period and omit any punctuation after the reference.) The reference to Shakespeare's *King Lear* shows the play's act number in a capitalized Roman numeral, the scene number in a small Roman numeral, and the line number in an Arabic numeral. Other sources may require different information, such as page or part numbers, the important thing is that the information be adequate for a reader to look up the quotation or paraphrase.

Other styles of documentation

Most of the social and physical sciences eliminate footnotes or endnotes by keying text references directly to the bibliography (often titled "Reference List" or "Literature Cited"). The text reference may consist of the author's last name and the year of the source's publication, together in parentheses, or simply of a number in parentheses or brackets. Again, you should ask your instructor about the preferred style.

The *Publication Manual of the American Psychological Association* and the style guides in some other disciplines recommend the **name-year style:**

One researcher (Herskowitz, 1974) found that mice fight each other

more frequently when they are hungry.

The reader locates the source by referring to the author's name (Herskowitz) in the list of references at the end of the text. If the list contains more than one source by that author, the reader then refers to the year of publication (1974) as well. When the author's name already appears in the discussion, then you need provide only the date in parentheses, immediately after the name.

35h

```
Herskowitz (1974) found that mice fight each other more frequently

when they are hungry.
```

If a source has two authors, give both last names. If it has three or more authors, give all their last names the first time you cite the source, but in subsequent references give only the first author's name followed by "et al." (Note the use of the ampersand [&] instead of *and* in the examples below.)

```
Factory accidents can be dramatically reduced when employees receive

periodic instruction in safety (Jones & Oman, 1979).

A large-scale study of child-rearing patterns (Sears, Maccoby,

& Levin, 1957) discovered that highly permissive parents tend to

have highly aggressive children.

This conclusion appears to contradict that of Sears et al. (1957).
```

When you need to identify the page number in a source you are paraphrasing or quoting, place it inside the parentheses as well.

```
Jacob Bronowski (1973, p. 353) maintains that an important

achievement of twentieth-century physics has been to prove that

we will never attain a complete understanding of the material

world.
```

When your bibliography includes two or more works by the same author published in the same year, arrange them in the list of references alphabetically by title, and follow each entry with (a), (b), and so on (see the bibliographic models on p. 465). In the text reference give the letter as well as the date so that the reader knows which source you are citing.

```
At least two researchers (Dolman, 1980a; Howard, 1979b) are highly

critical of the experimental work being performed on prisoners.
```

In the **number style** of source citation, used in many physical sciences, you number the entries in a list of references arranged either alphabetically or in the order of their citation in the text. The text reference then consists of the appropriate number (with or without the author's name, depending on the style) enclosed in parentheses or brackets.

35h

```
In an earlier study Herskowitz (15) found that mice also fight when

they have been deprived of sleep.
```

```
Some researchers (e.g., Philby, 19) doubt that the human brain will

ever fully understand itself.

Four studies [9-12] have isolated the virus responsible for the

disease.
```

Abbreviations

The styles of documentation illustrated above eliminate many abbreviations. However, they still use some, and you may encounter many more in your reading. The most common abbreviations appear below.

anon.	anonymous
bk., bks.	book(s)
c., ca.	*circa* ("about"), used with approximate dates
cf.	*confer* ("compare")
ch., chs	chapter(s)
col., cols.	column(s)
comp., comps.	compiled by, compiler(s)
diss.	dissertation
ed., eds.	edition(s), editor(s)
et al.	*et alii* ("and others")
ff.	and the following pages, as in pp. 17 ff.
ibid.	*ibidem* ("in the same place")
illus.	illustrated by, illustrator, illustration(s)
l., ll.	line(s)
loc. cit.	*loco citato* ("in the place cited")
ms, mss	manuscript(s)
n., nn.	note(s), as in p. 24, n. 2
n.d.	no date (of publication)
no., nos.	number(s)
n.p.	no place (of publication), no publisher
n. pag.	no pagination
op. cit.	*opere citato* ("in the work cited")
p., pp.	page(s)
passim	throughout
q.v.	*quod vide* ("which see")
rev.	revision, revised by
rpt.	reprint, reprinted
sec.	section
supp., supps.	supplement(s)
trans.	translator, translated by
univ.	university
vol., vols.	volume(s)

35h

EXERCISE 13

Prepare footnotes from the following information. Follow the models of the *MLA Handbook* given on pages 482–86, or use the style suggested by your instructor.

1. In the first note, cite page 95 in a book called *The Old Stone Age*, which was written by François Bordes and translated by J. E. Anderson. The translation was published in 1973 by McGraw-Hill in New York.
2. In the second note, cite page 121 in the book above.
3. In the third note, cite Abraham Maslow's article entitled "Self-Actualizing People," which appeared in 1950 on page 26 of volume 1 of *Personality Symposia.*
4. In the fourth note, cite page 34 in a book by Abraham Maslow called *Motivation and Personality*, published in 1954 by Harper & Row in New York.
5. In the fifth note, cite page 164 in Maslow's book above.

EXERCISE 14

Prepare the footnotes or notes, as specified by your instructor, for the research paper you wrote and revised in Exercise 12 (p. 480). Use the format of the *MLA Handbook*, or follow the style suggested by your instructor.

35i
Preparing the final bibliography

When you have completed your paper, prepare a final bibliography from the working bibliography you used throughout your research and writing. Include in the final bibliography all sources from which you quoted, paraphrased, or summarized. Unless your instructor requests it, don't include sources you examined but did not acknowledge in notes. Use the bibliography models of the *MLA Handbook*, given on pages 461–65, or the style recommended by your instructor.

Place the bibliography at the end of your paper after the footnotes. List your sources in alphabetical order. Double-space all the entries, indenting the second and subsequent lines of each one five spaces. (See Paul Fuller's bibliography and the comments opposite it, pp. 516–17, for the form to follow in typing this section.)

35i

EXERCISE 15

Prepare the final bibliography for the research paper you wrote and revised in Exercise 12 (p. 480). Follow the *MLA Handbook* models on pages 461–65, or the style suggested by your instructor.

35j
Examining a sample research paper

Paul Fuller's research paper, presented on the following pages, illustrates the advice explained in this chapter. Fuller follows the style for endnotes and bibliography described in the *MLA Handbook*. He types the paper following the advice on manuscript preparation in Appendix B. The comments on the pages facing the research paper, keyed by number, explain the details of format. The comments also describe some of the decisions Fuller makes in moving from research to writing, other options he could follow, and some ways he could improve the paper.

35j

How Advertisers Make Us Buy   1

By

Paul Fuller

English 101, Section A

Mr. R. Macek

March 12, 1982

1. **Title page format.** On his title page Fuller includes the title of his paper about a third of the way down the page, his own name (preceded by *By*) about an inch below the title, and, starting about an inch below his name, some identifying information requested by his instructor (course number, section label, and instructor's name) and the date. He centers all lines in the width of the page and separates them from each other with at least one line of space.

Next two pages

2. **Outline format.** If your instructor asks you to include your final outline, place it between the title page and the text, as Fuller does on the following pages. You may leave its pages unnumbered, or you may number them with small Roman numerals, as Fuller does. If you number the outline pages, omit the number on the first page and begin numbering with *ii* on the second page. Place the heading "Outline" at the top of the first page.

3. **Outline content.** Fuller includes his final thesis sentence as part of his outline so that his instructor can see how the parts relate to the whole.

4. Fuller casts his final outline in full sentences. Some instructors request topic outlines, in which ideas appear in phrases instead of in sentences and do not end with periods.

5. Notice that each main division (numbered with Roman numerals) refers directly to a portion of the thesis sentence and that all the subdivisions relate directly to their main division. Notice, too, the use of parallel phrasing for parallel levels. You need not repeat words such as *advertisers say*, but in this case they help Fuller relate his ideas to each other logically and clearly.

35j

Outline   2

<u>Thesis</u>: Advertisers appeal to consumers' emotions, rather   3
          than to their reason, because consumers choose
          products irrationally.

  I. Critics of advertising say advertisers deliberately   4
      use strong emotional and irrational appeals.

      A. Marshall McLuhan says the appeals of advertising
          are directed to the unconscious.

      B. Vance Packard says the methods of advertisers
          represent regression for the rational nature of
          human beings.

      C. David Ogilvy says that most advertising treats
          consumers as if they were idiots, unable to
          reason.

 II. Advertisers say they appeal to emotion because   5
      consumers choose products irrationally.

      A. Advertisers say that advertising by its nature as
          human communication expresses both emotional and
          rational messages.

      B. Advertisers say human beings choose irrationally.

      C. Advertisers say that appealing to emotion
          increases sales.

          1. Adding color to products or their ads
              increases sales.

35j

ii

      2.   Adding cartoon characters to products or their packages increases sales.

      3.   Adding emotional symbols to ads increases sales.

III. Studies of advertising indicate that advertisers do appeal to emotions, as both critics and advertisers claim, and that consumers seem to choose products emotionally, as advertisers claim.

    A. An informal survey of ads indicates that the average ad uses much more emotional appeal than rational appeal.

    B. Experiments by independent researchers suggest that consumers respond to emotional appeals in advertising and that they do not examine ads rationally.

      1.   One study showed that consumers make an emotional choice in favor of ads that merely sound truthful.

      2.   Another study showed that consumers do not examine ads rationally, but do respond emotionally to a claim that merely sounds rational.

35j

How Advertisers Make Us Buy   6

    Against a background of rolling music and a deep voice   7
speaking of "winning the world," a woman descends from a
swirl of sailcloth and clouds. This view widens to take in
the whole scene--ship, ocean, sky--in a panorama that seems
cosmic. The purpose of this drama is to make a television
audience buy some coffee. The advertisement's outsized play
for emotional attention and response is typical of contemporary advertising. Critics of such advertising accuse
it of ignoring the human capacity for reason, the ability
to make purchasing decisions on the basis of a product's
performance and quality, while appealing instead to consumers' emotions about humor, sex, status, and adventure
and to their unquestioning faith in science. In fact,
advertisers do appeal to consumers' emotions, rather than
to their reason, because consumers choose products
irrationally.

    The critics of advertising stress its manipulativeness   8
and mindlessness. Marshall McLuhan, the philosopher of   9
mass-media culture, says that advertising directs its
appeals to the unconscious:

            Ours is the first age in which many thousands of   10
            the best-trained individual minds have made it a
            full-time business to get inside the collective
            public mind . . . to manipulate, exploit, con-   11

35j

6. **Title.** Although a title such as "Appeals to Emotion in Advertising" would reflect Fuller's thesis more accurately, it would also be less forceful. **Paper format.** The title is typed two inches from the top of the page and is separated from the text by four lines of space. The text is double-spaced. The first page of the paper is not numbered, so the first numbered page is page 2.

7. **Introduction.** Fuller opens by summarizing a television commercial to demonstrate how illogical advertising can be and to introduce readers to the issues of the thesis. The example is concrete and effective. However, Fuller could have begun his paper without it by rephrasing the first sentence after the word *coffee:* "Outsized plays for emotional attention and response are typical of contemporary advertising." The following sentence elaborates on this idea while also introducing advertising's critics and clarifying two central terms of the thesis sentence and the entire paper: *appeal to reason* and *appeal to emotion.*

8. **Relation to outline.** This paragraph corresponds to Part I of Fuller's outline. Part II of the outline begins with the next paragraph and continues until page 4 of the paper.

9. **Introducing quotations.** Fuller effectively introduces his quotations here and on the next two pages: He establishes the credentials of each author in an identifying phrase, he summarizes each author's point of view; and, with the shorter quotation from Packard, he integrates the author's sentence structure into his own. (But see also comment 33, p. 513, on the Ogilvy quotation.)

10. **Format of long quotations.** The McLuhan and Ogilvy quotations on this page and the next exceed four typed lines, so Fuller sets these off from the text. These block quotations are set off by triple spacing above and below, are themselves double-spaced, and are indented ten spaces from the left margin.

11. **Editing quotations.** Fuller uses ellipses in the two long quotations to show that he has eliminated irrelevant material (see 25e). All the ellipses consist of three spaced periods; but the second one in the McLuhan quotation is preceded by a sentence period closed up to the last word, and the ellipsis in the Ogilvy quotation is followed by a space and a comma from the original. Fuller's editing of the McLuhan quotation is not entirely successful. The sentence after the ellipsis strays from the idea Fuller wants to capture (that advertising appeals are directed to the unconscious), so he should have omitted it as well.

35j

2

trol. . . . Why not assist the public to observe
consciously the drama intended to operate unconsciously?[1]

12

Vance Packard, who brought national attention to the manipu-
lations of advertisers in his best-selling The Hidden Persuaders, asserts that the methods of advertisers "represent
regress rather than progress for man in his long struggle to
become a rational and self-guiding being."[2] David Ogilvy,
one of advertising's most famous successes, concedes that
most advertising treats consumers as if they were unable to
reason:

13

> When I first began making advertisements . . . ,
> I looked at the so-called mass magazines and I was
> impressed by the extraordinary gap between edi-
> torial content and advertising content. I saw
> that the editors were writing with taste to an
> intelligent audience, and the advertising writers
> were writing to idiots.[3]

Advertisers themselves say that ads combine rational
and emotional appeals.[4] This mixture, they claim, comes
from advertising's nature as another form of human communication. Regular conversation illustrates how all human
communication, including advertising, works. In regular
conversation how something is said is often as important
as what is said. The speaker's voice, gestures, and facial
expression carry emotional messages just as important as
the rational content of what the speaker says. In printed

14

35j

12. **Footnote numbers.** Fuller raises footnote numbers above the line of type and makes sure that the number always follows punctuation after the idea or quotation being acknowledged. The numbers will run consecutively through the text, a new number for each citation, even when the source was acknowledged earlier. (For a system of internal documentation to be used when the paper concerns a single work or several works by one author, see p. 487.)

13. **Paragraphing.** Fuller does not begin a new paragraph after the McLuhan quotation because the following material (the Packard and Ogilvy quotations) is directly related. After the Ogilvy quotation, Fuller does begin a new paragraph because he's embarking on a new thought.

14. **Footnoting and introducing paraphrases.** Here Fuller is summarizing a source, so he cites the source as he would the source of a quotation. The rest of this paragraph is a paraphrase from another source cited at the end (note 5). Fuller has put the note reference in the right place, but he has failed to introduce the lengthy paraphrase adequately. As a result, the second sentence ("This mixture, they claim, . . .") appears to be undocumented, and the note reference seems to document only the last sentence in the paragraph. Fuller should have introduced the paraphrase in the second sentence and then made it clear that other sentences in the paragraph derive from the same source: *"Advertiser Pierre Martineau claims that the mixture comes from advertising's nature as another form of human communication. He notes that regular conversation. . . ."*

35j

3

advertising, art, layout, and typeface carry the emotional messages. In television advertising, the personalities of announcers and actors, the music, and the visual imagery become symbols of emotional meaning.[5]

Advertisers maintain that their emotional appeals are appropriate because human beings are essentially irrational. Car salespeople have noticed that customers on the verge of buying an expensive car for an emotional motive, such as a desire for status, like to talk at the last minute about superior performance in order to justify their emotional decision with a rational motive.[6] Pierre Martineau explains this behavior more generally:

> The entire personality of every individual is built around basic emotional needs, and the whole system of his thinking is determined by these needs, even though superficially the individual defends his point of view on purely rational grounds. Experiments repeatedly show that his rationality is highly selective rationality (or in other words, not rational at all). [Emphasis added.][7]

Other recent studies confirm the same view of consumers by advertisers.[8]

Advertisers claim many sales successes through appeals to emotion. One technique for increasing the emotional appeal of products is "color engineering." Adding color to an ad or to a product in which color has no practical

15

16

17

18

19

35j

15. **Summary statement.** This sentence is not footnoted because it is Fuller's summary of evidence from the sources cited in notes 6, 7, and 8, following.

16. **Paraphrasing.** Fuller paraphrases the example about car salespeople even though his note card contains the exact quotation from the source. He decides not to quote directly because he can reduce several sentences in the original to one of his own, and he does not want two long quotations in a row. Here is the original note card:

Consumers' irrational choices

Smith, *Motivation Research,* p. 6.

"Car salesmen joke that their product knowledge — performance statistics, repair record, etc. — doesn't make them a dime. What sells an expensive car is the customer's feeling about luxury, good looks, status. So he does not appear impulsive, the customer may ask about performance — just as he is about to sign the papers, but at that moment the salesman could say almost anything without jeopardizing what is essentially an irrational purchase."

---

17. **Adding emphasis to quotations.** Fuller underlines certain words in the quotation that reinforce his thesis especially clearly. He acknowledges this change in brackets at the end of the quotation, before the footnote number. The brackets indicate clearly that the emphasis was not part of the original citation.

18. **Footnoting supplementary information.** Instead of continuing to quote and paraphrase the same view of consumers, Fuller lets readers know that further support is available, and his note tells where to find it. This kind of summary sentence, with added documentation, can help prevent a long-winded discussion.

19. **Selecting supporting evidence.** In these paragraphs listing sales successes that resulted from appeals to emotion, Fuller has selected from his sources the most dramatic and vivid success stories he found. He provides concrete facts that support his case. And he carefully cites his sources.

35j

4

function increases sales. For example, until the 1920s
fountain pens were made of hard black rubber. When colored
plastic pens were introduced, sales improved "astro-
nomically."[9] Using aluminum paint instead of black on bed-
springs improved sales by 25 percent for one manufacturer.[10]
A Gloucester fish packer increased his sales 33 percent
simply by adding color to his advertising circular.[11] Currently, the emotional appeal of cartoon characters increases
sales 10 to 20 percent when the characters are printed on
products or their packages.[12] Experts disagree on just why
color and cartoons have such appeal--for instance, do the
cartoons trigger hero worship or nostalgia?[13]--but clearly
the appeal _is_ emotional and sales improve because of it.

    Two classic advertising campaigns that relied on emo-
tional appeals are Hathaway's and Marlboro's. After ads for
Hathaway shirts began to include a well-built, mysterious
man with a patch over one eye, sales of the shirts tripled.[14]
The manufacturers of Marlboro cigarettes experienced an even
more dramatic increase in sales because of a change in advertising. In 1954 Philip Morris decided to enter one of its
worst-selling cigarettes, Marlboro, in the new filter-tip
market.[15] To change the product's image as a woman's
cigarette, the advertisers eliminated all women from the
ads and substituted virile men. Each new ad emphasized a
tattoo on the hand of the man smoking a Marlboro. The
tattoos were a symbol that seemed to give the whole ad
campaign an emotional unity.[16] This shift in emotional
appeal improved Marlboro's sales drastically: from near

20

21

35j

20. **Going back to sources.** In his first draft Fuller described his examples of sales successes with phrases like "sales increased" and "sales improved" rather than with actual figures, and his assertions lacked force. When he realized he needed to be more specific, he referred to his bibliography cards (showing the call numbers) and to his note cards (showing page numbers) and was able to collect the figures he wanted in a quick trip to the library. In the note card below Fuller has added to the information originally gathered from the source cited in notes 12 and 13.

Johnson, "The Cartoon Creature," <u>N Y Times</u>, 2/11/79, sec. 3, p. 3.

Printing cartoon characters — Mickey Mouse, Snoopy, Superman — on products or packages can significantly increase sales.

average increase 10-20% can be 50-100%

21. **Using sources effectively.** In this paragraph Fuller blends material from two sources to make one point about the success of emotional appeals. Instead of merely stringing together other people's ideas, he arranges the material in order of increasing drama and thus shapes his research to express and support his own views. Notice that notes 14 and 16 refer to one source and notes 15 and 17 refer to the other (see p. 514). All four notes are necessary because Fuller is moving back and forth between sources.

35j

5

zero in 1954 to 6.4 billion in 1955, 14.3 billion in 1956, and 19.5 billion in 1957.[17]

But advertisers' success stories are not the last word. An informal survey and more formal studies of advertising show that appeals to emotion predominate and that consumers seem to go out of their way to make choices for emotional reasons.

My own informal survey of ads in an issue of <u>Newsweek</u> revealed that most of the ads (thirty of forty-two) used a predominantly emotional appeal (see Table 1, next page). Only one-fifth of the ads (nine of forty-two) depended on rational appeal as much as 50 percent. Some ads of products for which rational appeal would be easy or likely--products such as a newsletter, an economy car, and insurance--barely used appeals to reason (under 20 percent rational appeal). This limited (one-reader, one-magazine) study leads to several conclusions: (1) that most ads appeal primarily to consumers' emotions; (2) that only a tiny fraction of ads (one of forty-two) appeal primarily to reason; and (3) that no ads use rational appeal 100 percent, although many (twelve of forty-two) use emotional appeal 100 percent.

In an experimental study of advertising, Robert Settle and Linda Golden found that admitting a product's inferiority on one or two minor points of comparison was more effective in advertising than claiming the product's superiority on all counts. The researchers asked 120 business students to evaluate a series of ads. (The products advertised were fictitious.) Half the ads claimed that the fictitious

22

23

24

25

35j

22. **Transitional paragraph and relation to outline.** Here Fuller devotes a paragraph to the transition between Part II and Part III of the outline, between sales evidence supporting advertisers' claims about consumers and equally supportive studies by nonadvertisers.
23. **Original research.** Because he is a consumer, Fuller feels that his subjective reactions to ads are legitimate responses to evaluate and use. Nevertheless, he wisely admits the limitations of his survey. **Primary and secondary sources.** Fuller's study of magazine ads is a primary source because it is direct, firsthand information. His other sources are secondary because they contain other people's reports and interpretations of primary or secondary sources. In several instances he relies on secondhand sources when he should have used original sources; see comments 33, 38, and 39 on pages 513 and 515.
24. **Reference to illustration.** Here Fuller refers specifically to the table that shows the complete results of his survey.
25. **Reporting studies.** Fuller's descriptions of experiments here are detailed enough to let readers know how the experiments were conducted, yet not so detailed that readers will get bogged down in the experiments and lose track of his ideas. Again, as in presenting the examples of successful advertising campaigns earlier, Fuller arranges material in order of increasing detail and drama. He might have enlivened his description by including more quotations from the studies as well as even more specific information (such as some of the products evaluated in the first study). He had the specific details on his note card but failed to use them.

> Research on consumer responses
> Gregg, "To Sell Your Product," *Psych. Today,* 10/74, p. 35.
>
> Repts. study by Robert Settle and Linda Golden in *Jrnl. of Marketing Research,* 11 (May 1974).
>
> 120 bus. students evaluated fictitious ads for a pen, a watch, a blender, a camera, and a clock radio. Half the ads claimed the product was five ways superior to a well-known competitor; the other half claimed superiority on only three points and _inferiority_ on two points. 80% of students found ads admitting some inferiority to be more persuasive.

35j

See also comment 38, page 515.

6

TABLE 1

SURVEY OF ADVERTISEMENTS IN <u>NEWSWEEK</u>, 19 FEBRUARY 1979[a]

Advertisement	Percentages Emotional/ Rational	Advertisement	Percentages Emotional/ Rational
Tobacco Institute	100/0	Jameson Irish	
American Forest		Whiskey	100/0
Institute	50/50	Jack Daniels	90/10
Jeep	80/20	Ronrico Rum	90/10
Datsun	60/40	Canadian Club	100/0
Horizon TC3	90/10	Royal copier	60/40
MGB	80/20	Sharp copier	50/50
Ford Pinto	60/40	Mutual Life	
VW	100/0	Insurance	100/0
Winnebago	80/20	Sun Life Insurance	100/0
Exxon	50/50	GE TV	10/90
Lonestar Building		Vivitar lens	50/50
Supplier	80/20	Book ad	95/5
Alcoa aluminum	50/50	Famolare shoes	50/50
Tareyton	100/0	Trinity missions	100/0
L&M Lights	50/50	St. Elizabeth	
Marlboro	100/0	Hotel	90/10
Doral II	90/10	Newsletter on	
Merit	80/20	new products	80/20
Winston Lights	100/0	Anderson	
Salem	100/0	Windowwalls	50/50
Beechcraft Aviation	80/20	Anacin	50/50
Pan Am	50/50	Preparation H	50/50
Pakistan Airlines	80/20	United Cerebral	
Chivas Regal	90/10	Palsy	100/0

[a]My method for determining what percentage of an ad
appealed to emotion and what percentage to reason involved
(1) recording the overall impact of the ad as emotional or
rational; (2) evaluating the proportions of space given to
different purposes and the effects of layout, color, type,
and artwork; (3) thinking of the possible ways to advertise
the product without appealing to emotions and evaluating the
ad against these; and (4) weighing my observations and
assigning percentages to emotional and rational appeals.
As an example, the Ronrico Rum ad contains an illustration
occupying 80 percent of the space. It shows an upright
bottle of rum (label facing out) and the shape of a bottle,
tilted at 60°, containing a photograph of a couple kissing,
palm trees, beautiful water--a scene whose greenness stands
out against the mostly white ad and the pale bottle of rum. .
The angle of the bottle outline suggests it is about to fall
and makes the viewer want to reach out and grab it. The ad's
brief copy discusses the rum's "authentic" relation with
Puerto Rico. Only the words "smooth, light taste" describe
a rationally desirable quality of rum. I rated the ad (perhaps generously) 90 percent emotional, 10 percent rational.

27

26. **Table format.** Fuller places the table after the table reference (p. 5 of the paper) and on a separate sheet of paper. He numbers the table with an Arabic numeral (1) and capitalizes both the label and the title. The title tells readers what magazine the advertisements appeared in. His column headings clearly label the information beneath them. Generally, tables like this one should be double-spaced throughout, but Fuller single-spaces his so it fits on one page.

27. **Source acknowledgment.** Since the table contains Fuller's original material, no acknowledgment (source note) is needed. If one were, the table itself would not contain a note reference, but the source would be given immediately after the table and preceded by the word "source" and a colon. **Explanatory note.** Fuller's table does need an explanation of his method so that readers can judge the value of his survey. The note is keyed as a footnote, but a raised letter ([a]) is used instead of a raised number to prevent possible confusion of text notes with the table note.

7

product was superior to the best-selling and well-known actual product on five points of comparison. The other half claimed the fictitious product was superior on only three counts and inferior on two minor points. The students found the latter ads, which admitted some inferiority, to be more successful in persuading them to buy the new (fictitious) product instead of the best seller.[18] They made an emotional choice in favor of ads that simply sounded truthful without having evidence that the claims of truth were in fact valid.

28

In another study with experimental ads, Seymour Lieberman had an advertising agency create two television ads for each of six fictitious products. Each product had one deceitful ad containing a false or made-up scientific claim and one truthful ad that did not contain the scientific claim. For instance, the deceitful ad for a fictitious plant fertilizer stressed that the fertilizer contained protein (though in fact protein does not help plants grow), whereas the truthful ad did not mention protein. The deceitful ad for a fictitious bunion remedy stated that the remedy contained "four times as much methylglyoxal" (although methylglyoxal does not help treat bunions), whereas the truthful ad did not mention methylglyoxal. Both pairs of ads used the same actors and the same language; the only difference was the presence or absence of the scientific claim. After being asked to say which products interested them, one hundred middle-income consumers watched the deceitful ads and another hundred middle-income consumers watched the truthful ads. More consumers showed interest in the deceitful fertilizer ad than

29

28. **Drawing conclusions.** Fuller places note numbers 18 and 19 (on the next page) after his descriptions of the experiments but before the conclusions he draws to support the second part of his thesis (that consumers choose products irrationally). In fact, the experimenters did not use their results for quite the same purposes as Fuller does. For example, a note card from the source cited in note 18 quotes the researchers' conclusion:

By separating the studies' results from his own conclusions about the results, Fuller demonstrates the amount of thought he has given his sources, and he hopes to avoid misrepresenting them (always a danger in reporting and interpreting the work of others). However, since Fuller's conclusions are not those of the researchers, he might have mentioned briefly the researchers' goals and conclusions so that his readers could evaluate his use of their results. (See also comments 38 and 39, p. 515.)

29. **Use of quotation.** Fuller's quotation of a key phrase from the study makes his description more concrete and also illustrates how successfully the researchers imitated real ads in their fictitious ones. As noted in comment 25 (p. 505), Fuller might have made greater use of such quotations and details from the studies he cites.

35j

8

showed interest in the truthful ad. And four times as many consumers showed interest in the deceitful four-times-as-much methylglyoxal ad for a bunion remedy as showed interest in the truthful ad. Similar results occurred with two of the other four pairs of ads tested.[19] The consumers did not examine the ads' claims rationally. Instead, they gravitated to what sounded like fact, responding emotionally to claims of scientific improvements without rationally evaluating the claims.

The critics of advertising accuse advertisers of using emotional appeals deliberately and irresponsibly. They imply that consumers would make rational decisions about products if the ads for those products gave them facts about performance and quality on which to base a rational choice. Advertisers freely admit their emphasis on emotional appeals but maintain that consumers make choices irrationally. As proof, they offer the sales successes brought about by purely emotional appeals. One informal survey verifies advertisers' reliance on emotional appeals. And formal experiments suggest that consumers do not require hard information on which to base decisions but will accept the appearance of truth or fact as a substitute for the real thing. We may say we object to the overblown advertisement with no informative content. That is certainly the kind of ad we see most often. But it also seems to be the kind of ad we deserve.

30

35j

30. **Conclusion.** Fuller's conclusion might be faulted for lack of imagination, but it suits his purpose. He shows that his thesis is valid by summarizing the evidence he has presented in the paper. In his last few sentences he switches to *we* in a way that emphasizes the relevance of his conclusion for himself and his readers. His last sentence provides a final edge.

35j

Notes 31

[1] Herbert Marshall McLuhan, <u>The Mechanical Bride: Folk-</u> 32
<u>lore of Industrial Man</u> (Boston: Beacon, 1951), p. v.

[2] Vance Packard, <u>The Hidden Persuaders</u> (New York: Pocket
Books, 1958), p. 4.

[3] Quoted in Robert Glatzer, <u>The New Advertising: The</u> 33
<u>Great Campaigns</u> (New York: Citadel, 1970), p. 85.

[4] David Bernstein, <u>Creative Advertising</u> (London: Longman,
1974), p. 295.

[5] Pierre Martineau, <u>Motivation in Advertising: Motives</u>
<u>That Make People Buy</u> (New York: McGraw-Hill, 1957), pp. 139-
40.

[6] George H. Smith, <u>Motivation Research in Advertising</u> 34
<u>and Marketing</u> (1954; rpt. Westport, Conn.: Greenwood Press,
1971), p. 6.

[7] Martineau, p. 120. 35

[8] See, for example, James F. Engel, David T. Kollats, 36
and Roger D. Blackwell, <u>Consumer Behavior</u>, 2nd ed. (New York:
Holt, Rinehart and Winston, 1973), p. 58. There the same
idea is stated in a complex diagram, the "Complete Model of
Consumer Behavior Showing Purchasing Processes and Outcomes."
Out of twenty-three boxes of factors only one box, "Evaluative
Criteria," seems to represent rationality.

[9] Howard Ketcham, <u>Color Planning: For Business and</u>
<u>Industry</u> (New York: Harper & Bros., 1958), p. 7.

[10] Ketcham, p. 8.

35j

31. **Format of notes.** The word "Notes" is centered two inches from the top of the page and is followed by four lines of space. The notes are double-spaced. The first line of each entry is indented five spaces and preceded by a raised number corresponding to the number used in the text. A space separates the number and the note. The first page of notes is not numbered. The notes are numbered as part of the paper, however, so the second page of notes is page 10 of the paper.

32. Notes 1, 2, 4, 5, and 6 each show a **first reference to a book with a single author.** The page number, *v*, in note 1 refers to material (probably the preface or introduction) that occurs near the front of the book and is numbered with lower-case Roman numerals. Here is the bibliography card from which Fuller drew this note:

HM 291
.M35

McLuhan, Herbert Marshall. *The*
Mechanical Bride: Folklore of
Industrial Man. Boston:
Beacon Press, 1951.

33. Note 3 shows how to indicate a **direct quotation from secondary material.** Since Ogilvy, the original speaker, is mentioned clearly in the text, Fuller does not need to identify him here. Fuller should have consulted Ogilvy directly instead of relying on another author's report of his words. Since Fuller identifies Ogilvy as "one of advertising's most famous successes," he might have found significant information in Ogilvy's autobiography, a primary source.

34. Note 6 shows how to acknowledge a **reprint of an earlier edition.**

35. Note 7 shows a **second reference** to a source already cited (in note 5). (See also comment 37, p. 515.)

36. Note 8 demonstrates the use of a note to provide **additional relevant information or examples.** Fuller could include this material in the text (in fact, he did so in the first draft), but it is more evidence than he needs at that point and could weigh down his discussion. This note also shows how to acknowledge a **book with three authors** and an **edition other than the first.**

35j

10

[11] George Burton Hotchkiss, <u>An Outline of Advertising</u>:
<u>Its Philosophy, Science, Art, and Strategy</u>, 3rd ed. (New
York: Macmillan, 1950), p. 164.

[12] Sharon Johnson, "The Cartoon Creature as Salesman,"
<u>The New York Times</u>, 11 Feb. 1979, Sec. 3, p. 3.

37

[13] Johnson, p. 3.

[14] Martineau, p. 148.

[15] Glatzer, pp. 122–23.

[16] Martineau, p. 147.

[17] Glatzer, p. 134.

[18] Gary Gregg, "To Sell Your Product, Admit It's Not
Perfect," <u>Psychology Today</u>, Oct. 1974, pp. 35–36. This
article concerned an experiment published in <u>The Journal of
Marketing Research</u>, 11 (May 1974).

38

[19] "Truth Doesn't Sell," <u>Time</u>, 14 May 1973, pp. 96–97.

39

37. Note 12 shows how to acknowledge a **signed article in a daily newspaper.** Here is the bibliography card from which Fuller drew this note:

> Johnson, Sharon. "The Cartoon Creature
> as Salesman." The New York
> Times, 11 Feb. 1979, Sec. 3,
> p. 3.

The style shown in note 13 for **second reference** to a source already cited is that recommended by the *MLA Handbook.* If his instructor required it, Fuller might have used "ibid." instead: "[13] Ibid., p. 3."

38. Note 18 shows how to acknowledge a **signed article in a monthly magazine** and also how to indicate a **journal's volume number.** Fuller explains that his description of the experiment derives from another writer's description, not from the original report of the experiment. However, he should have consulted the original report, not only to be sure his description is accurate but also to check for additional information.

39. Note 19 shows how to acknowledge an **unsigned article in a weekly magazine.** Again, Fuller is describing an experiment as reported by a secondary source. He should have consulted the original report of the experiment.

Bibliography   40

Bernstein, David. Creative Advertising. London: Longman,   41
    1974.

Engel, James F., David T. Kollats, and Roger D. Blackwell.   42
    Consumer Behavior. 2nd ed. New York: Holt, Rinehart
    and Winston, 1973.

Glatzer, Robert. The New Advertising: The Great Campaigns.
    New York: Citadel, 1970.

Gregg, Gary. "To Sell Your Product, Admit It's Not Perfect."   43
    Psychology Today, Oct. 1974, pp. 35-36.

Hotchkiss, George Burton. An Outline of Advertising: Its
    Philosophy, Science, Art, and Strategy. 3rd ed. New
    York: Macmillan, 1950.

Johnson, Sharon. "The Cartoon Creature as Salesman." The   44
    New York Times, 11 Feb. 1979, Sec. 3, p. 3.

Ketcham, Howard. Color Planning: For Business and Industry.
    New York: Harper & Bros., 1958.

McLuhan, Herbert Marshall. The Mechanical Bride: Folklore
    of Industrial Man. Boston: Beacon, 1951.

Martineau, Pierre. Motivation in Advertising: Motives That
    Make People Buy. New York: McGraw-Hill, 1957.

Packard, Vance. The Hidden Persuaders. New York: Pocket
    Books, 1958.

Smith, George H. Motivation Research in Advertising and   45
    Marketing. 1954; rpt. Westport, Conn.: Greenwood,
    1971.

"Truth Doesn't Sell." Time, 14 May 1973, pp. 96-97.   46

35j

40. **Format of bibliography.** The word "Bibliography" is centered two inches from the top of the page and followed by four lines of space. The entries are double-spaced. The first line of each entry begins at the left margin; subsequent lines of the same entry are indented five spaces. The entries are alphabetized. The page is not numbered but is counted in the numbering of the entire paper; thus if Fuller's bibliography continued on a second page, the page would be numbered 12.

41. Typical entry for a **book with one author.**

42. Entry for a **book with three authors** in an **edition other than the first.** Here is Fuller's bibliography card for this source:

HF 541
.7
.E5

> Engel, James F., David T. Kollats, and Roger D. Blackwell. <u>Consumer Behavior</u>: 2nd ed. New York: Holt, Rinehart and Winston, 1973.

---

43. Entry for a **signed article in a monthly magazine.**
44. Entry for a **signed article in a daily newspaper.**
45. Entry for a **reprint of an older edition.**
46. Entry for an **unsigned article in a weekly magazine.** Here is Fuller's bibliography card for this source:

> "Truth Doesn't Sell." <u>Time</u>, 14 May 1973, pp. 96-97.

35j

36
Practical Writing

Writing an essay examination or a business letter or memorandum requires the same attention to unity, coherence, and development that writing an essay or research paper does (Chapters 1 and 35). The special problems of writing essay examinations, business letters, and memos are the subject of this chapter.

36a
Answering essay questions

In writing an essay for an examination, you summarize or analyze a topic, usually in several paragraphs or more and usually within a time limit. An essay question not only tests your knowledge of a subject (as short-answer and objective questions also do), but also tests your control and synthesis of that knowledge and helps you see it in a new way (as other kinds of questions usually cannot do).

1
Preparing for an essay examination

Taking lecture notes, thoughtfully reading the assigned texts or articles, and reviewing regularly will help you prepare for any kind of examination. (See Appendix C on study skills.) In addition, for an essay examination you can practice synthesizing what you know by creating summaries or outlines that reorganize the course material. For instance, in a business course you could evaluate the advantages and disadvantages of several approaches to management. In a short-story course you could look for a theme running through all the stories you have read by a certain author or from a certain period. In a psychology course you could contrast various theorists' views of what causes a disorder like schizophrenia. Any one of these is a likely topic for an essay question. Thinking of such categories not only can help you anticipate the kinds of questions you may be asked but also can increase your mastery of the material.

2
Planning your time and your answer

When you first look at your examination, always read it all the way through at least once before you start answering any questions. As you scan the examination, determine which questions seem most important, which ones are going to be most difficult for you, and approximately how much time you'll need for each question. (Your instructor may help by assigning a point value to each question as a guide to its importance or by suggesting an amount of time for you to spend on each question.) You will want to provide your best answer for every question, so this initial planning is important.

To avoid straying from an essay question or answering only part of it, read it at least twice. Examine the words and consider their implications. Look especially for words like *describe, define, explain, summarize, analyze, evaluate,* and *interpret,* each of which requires a different kind of response. For instance, the instruction *Define dyslexia and compare and contrast it with two other learning disabilities* contains important clues for how an essay should be written. *Define dyslexia* tells you to specify the meaning of the term. A description of how children with dyslexia feel about their disability, however well done, would be irrelevant. Instead, you should say what dyslexia is — a perceptual impairment causing a reader to reverse or scramble letters — and extend the definition by providing distinctive characteristics, ways the impairment seems to work, examples of its effects, and so on. The words *compare and contrast it with two other learning disabilities* tell you to analyze not only its similarities with but also its differences from the other disabilities. Answering this part of the question thus involves thinking of categories for comparison, such as causes, treatments, frequency of occurrence, and severity of effect. An essay that described only similarities, or only differences, would not answer the question completely.

After you're sure you understand the question, make a brief outline of the main ideas you want to include in your essay. Use the back of the test sheet or exam booklet for scratch paper. Jot down a brief thesis for your essay that represents your view of the topic. (If you have any doubts about how to write a thesis, see 1d and 35d.)

36a

Include key phrases that you can expand with supporting evidence for your view. This stage is much like the planning of an essay or a research paper. Though you don't have as much time to refine and rearrange your ideas, planning will help make your essay unified, coherent, well supported, and concise.

3
Starting the essay

A well-constructed thesis will contribute much to an examination essay. Drawing on the brief thesis you devised during planning, you can begin an essay effectively by stating your thesis immediately and including in it an overview of the rest of your essay. Such a capsule version of your answer tells your reader (and grader) generally how much command you have and also how you plan to develop your answer.

The opening statement should address the question directly and exactly. The following thesis, in response to the question below, does *not* meet these criteria.

QUESTION

Given humans' natural and historical curiosity about themselves, why did a scientific discipline of anthropology not arise until the twentieth century? Explain, citing specific details.

TENTATIVE THESIS

The discipline of anthropology, the study of humans, actually began in the early nineteenth century and was strengthened by the Darwinian revolution, but the discipline did not begin to take shape until people like Franz Boas and Alfred Kroeber began doing scientific research among nonindustrialized cultures.

This tentative thesis says nothing about *why* anthropology did not arise as a scientific discipline until the twentieth century. Instead, it supplies an unspecific (and unrequested) definition of anthropology, vaguely reasserts the truth implied by the question, and adds irrelevant details about the history of anthropology. The following thesis — revised to address the question directly, to state the writer's view, and to preview the essay — begins the answer more effectively.

REVISED THESIS

36a

Anthropology did not emerge as a scientific discipline until the twentieth century because nineteenth-century Westerners' limited contact with remote peoples and the corresponding failure to see those other people as human combined to overcome natural curiosity and to prevent objective study of different cultures.

This thesis specifies the writer's view of the two main causes of the slow emergence of anthropology — limited contact with remote peoples and, related to that, a narrow definition of humanity — that she will analyze in her essay.

4
Developing the essay

You develop your essay by supporting your thesis with sound generalizations, which you support in turn with *specific* evidence. (See Chapter 4.) Avoid filling out your essay by repetition. Avoid substituting purely subjective feelings about the topic for real analysis of it. (It may help to abolish the word *I* from your essay.)

The student answering the anthropology question must show that contact between Western and non-Western cultures was limited and must specify how the limitations dulled curiosity, prevented objective study, and hampered the development of anthropology. She also needs to demonstrate how a consequently narrow definition of humanity had the same results. And she *must* support her assertions with concrete examples. For instance, she might cite nineteenth-century writings that illustrate disinterest or feelings of superiority toward distant peoples.

The student would not be providing effective evidence if she introduced unsupported generalizations or substituted her subjective feelings for an objective analysis of the problem. For instance, a blanket statement that all nineteenth-century Westerners were narrow-minded or a paragraph condemning their narrow-mindedness would only pad the essay.

5
Rereading the essay

The time limit on an essay examination does not allow for the careful rethinking and revision you would give an essay or research paper. You need to write clearly and concisely the first time. If you do have a few minutes after you have finished the entire exam, re-read the essay (or essays) to correct illegible passages, misspellings, grammatical mistakes, and accidental omissions. Verify that your thesis is accurate — that it does, in fact, introduce what you ended up writing about. Check to ensure that you have supported all your generalizations thoroughly. Cross out irrelevant ideas and details, and add any information that now seems important. (Write on another page if necessary, keying the addition to the page on which it belongs.)

36a

36b
Writing business letters, job applications, and memos

When you write a letter to request information, to complain about a product or bill, or to apply for a job, or when you write a memo or report to someone you work with, you are addressing busy people who want to see quickly why you are writing and how they should respond to you. A wordy, incoherent letter or memo full of errors in grammar and spelling may prevent you from getting what you want, either because the reader·cannot understand your wish or because you present yourself so poorly. In business writing, state your purpose at the very start. Be straightforward, clear, objective, and courteous, and don't hesitate to be insistent if the situation warrants it. Observe conventions of grammar and usage, for these not only make your writing clear but also impress a reader with your care.

1
Writing business letters and job applications

Using a standard form

Business correspondence customarily adheres to one of several acceptable forms. Use either unlined white paper measuring at least 5½″ × 8½″ or what is called letterhead stationery with your address printed at the top of the sheet. Type the letter if possible, single-spaced, on only one side of a sheet. Follow a standard form for each of the letter's parts. (The form described below and illustrated in the sample letters on pp. 523 and 526 is one common model.)

The return address heading of the letter gives your address (but not your name) and the date. (If you're using letterhead stationery, you need add only the date.) Align the lines of the heading on the left, and place the whole heading on the right of the page, allowing enough space above it to center the entire letter vertically on the page.

The inside address shows the name, title, and complete address of the person you are writing to, just as this information will appear on the envelope. Begin the address a few lines below the heading at the left side of the page.

The salutation greets the addressee. Place it two lines below the address and two lines above the body of the letter. Always follow it with a colon, not a comma or dash. If you are not addressing a particular person, use a general salutation such as *Dear Sir or Madam* or *Dear Smythe Shoes* (the company name). Use *Ms.* as the

17A Revere St.
Boston, MA 02106
January 1, 1983

Return
address
heading

Ms. Ann Herzog
Circulation Supervisor
Sporting Life
25 W. 43rd St.
New York, NY 10036

Inside
address

Dear Ms. Herzog:

Salutation

Thank you for your letter of December 20, which notifies me
that Sporting Life will resume my subscription after stopping
it in error after I had received the July issue. Since I
missed at least five months' issues because of the magazine's
error, I expected my subscription to be extended for five
months after it would have lapsed--that is, through June 1983.
Instead, you tell me that the magazine will send me the back
issues that it failed to send and that the January issue
(which I haven't received) will complete my current subscription.

Body

I have no interest in receiving the back issues of Sporting
Life because the magazine is not useful or interesting
unless it is current. Since Sporting Life erred in stopping
my subscription prematurely, I still expect it to make up
the difference on the other end of my subscription.

Unless I hear otherwise from you, I will count on your
extending my subscription at least through June 1983. If
Sporting Life cannot compensate for its error in this way,
I will cancel my subscription and request a refund.

Close —— Sincerely,

Signature —— *Janet M. Marley*

Janet M. Marley

Janet M. Marley
17A Revere St.
Boston, MA 02106

Envelope

Ms. Ann Herzog
Circulation Supervisor
Sporting Life
25 W. 43rd St.
New York, NY 10036

36b

title for a woman when she has no other title, when you don't know how she prefers to be addressed, or when you know that she prefers to be addressed as *Ms.* If you know a woman prefers to be addressed as *Mrs.* or *Miss,* use the appropriate title.

The body of the letter, containing its contents, begins at the left margin. Instead of indenting paragraphs, you may place an extra line of space between them so that they are readily visible.

The letter's close begins two lines below the last line of the body and aligns at the left with the heading at the top of the page. Typical closes include *Yours truly* and *Sincerely.* Only the first word is capitalized, and the close is followed by a comma.

The signature of a business letter has two parts: a typed one, four lines below the close, and a handwritten one filling in the space. The signature should consist only of your name, as you sign checks and school documents.

Below the signature, at the left margin, you may want to include additional information such as *Enc.* (something is enclosed with the letter), *cc: Margaret Newton* (a carbon copy is being sent to the person named), or *CHC/enp* (the initials of the author/the initials of the typist).

The envelope for the letter (see p. 523) should show your name and address in the upper left corner and the addressee's name, title, and address to the right of the center. Use an envelope that is the same width as your stationery and about a third the height. Fold the letter horizontally, in thirds.

Writing requests and complaints

Letters requesting something — for instance, a pamphlet, information about a product, a T-shirt advertised in a magazine — must be specific and accurate about the item you are requesting. The letter should describe the item completely and, if applicable, include a copy or description of the advertisement or other source that prompted your request.

Letters complaining about a product or a service (such as a wrong billing from the telephone company) should be written in a reasonable but firm tone. (See the sample letter on p. 523.) Assume that the addressee is willing to resolve the problem when he or she has the relevant information. In the first sentence of the letter, say what you are writing about. Then provide as much background as needed, including any relevant details from past correspondence (as in the sample letter). Describe exactly what you see as the problem, sticking to facts and avoiding discourses on the company's social responsibility or your low opinion of its management. In the clearest

36b

possible words and sentences, proceed directly from one point to
the next without repeating yourself. Always include your opinion of
how the problem can be solved. Many companies are required by
law to establish a specific procedure for complaints about products
and services. If you know of such a procedure, be sure to follow it.

Writing a job application and résumé

   In writing to apply for a job or to request a job interview, you
should announce at the outset what job you desire and how you
heard about it. (See the sample letter below.) Then summarize your

```
                                  3712 Swiss Ave.
                                  Dallas, TX  75204
                                  March 2, 1983

Personnel Manager
Dallas News
Communications Center
Dallas, TX  75222

Dear Sir or Madam:

In response to your announcement posted in the English
department of Southern Methodist University, I am applying
for the summer job of part-time editorial assistant for the
Dallas News.

I am now enrolled at Southern Methodist University as a
sophomore, with a dual major in English literature and
journalism.  As the enclosed résumé shows, I have worked on
the university newspaper for nearly two years, I have
published articles in my hometown newspaper, and I worked
a summer there as a copy boy.  My goal is a career in
journalism.  I believe my educational background and my
work experience qualify me for the opening you have.

I am available for an interview at any time and would be
happy to send you samples of my newspaper work.  My tele-
phone number is 744-3816.

                                  Sincerely,

                                  Ian M. Irvine

Enc.
```

36b

RÉSUMÉ

Ian M. Irvine
3712 Swiss Ave.
Dallas, TX 75204

Position desired   Part-time editorial assistant.

Education

1981 to present   Southern Methodist University.
                   Current standing: sophomore.
                   Major: English literature and journalism.

1977–1981   Abilene (TX) Senior High School.
                   Graduated with academic degree.

Experience

1981 to present   Reporter on the Daily Campus, student
                   newspaper of Southern Methodist University.
                   Responsibilities include writing feature
                   stories and sports coverage; proofreading;
                   some editing.

Summer 1982   House painter and free-lance writer.
                   Published two articles in the Abilene (TX)
                   Reporter-News: "A Hundredth Birthday
                   Party" (7/1/82) and "A New Way to Develop
                   Photographs" (8/6/82).

Summer 1981   Copy boy at Abilene Reporter-News. Respon-
                   sible for transmitting copy among writers,
                   editors, and typesetters. Watched over
                   teleprinter, ran errands, occasionally
                   accompanied reporters and photographers
                   on assignments.

Special interests Fiction writing, photography, reading,
                   squash.

References   Academic references available from the
                   placement office at Southern Methodist
                   University, Dallas, TX 75275.

                   Employment   Ms. Millie Stevens
                   reference   Abilene Reporter-News
                                   Abilene, TX 79604

                   Personal   Ms. Sheryl Gipstein
                   reference   26 Overland Dr.
                                   Abilene, TX 79604

36b

qualifications for the job, including facts about your education and employment history. Include only the relevant facts, mentioning that additional information appears in an accompanying résumé. Include any special reason you have for applying, such as a specific career goal. At the end of the letter, mention that you are available for an interview at the convenience of the addressee, or else specify when you will be available (for instance, when your current job or classes leave you free).

The résumé that you enclose with your letter of application should contain, in table form, your education, your employment history, your other interests, and information about how to obtain your references. (See the sample résumé on the opposite page.)

2
Writing business memos

Unlike business letters, which address people in other organizations, business memorandums (memos, for short) address people within the same organization. A memo can be quite long, but more often it reports briefly and directly on a very specific topic: an answer to a question, a progress report, an evaluation. Both the form and the structure of a memo are designed to get to the point and dispose of it quickly.

The memo has no return address, inside address, salutation, or close. Instead, as shown in the sample memo on page 528, the heading typically consists of the date, the addressee's name, the writer's name, and a subject description or title. (If you are sending copies of the memo to someone besides the addressee, give his or her name after *cc*, meaning "carbon copy." See the sample.) Type the body of the memo as you would the body of a business letter: single-spaced, double-spaced between paragraphs, and no paragraph indentions. Never sign a business memo, though you may initial your name in the heading.

Immerse your reader in your subject at the very beginning of the memo. State your reason for writing in the first sentence, but do not waste words with expressions like "The purpose of this memo is. . . ." Devote the first paragraph to a succinct presentation of your answer, conclusion, or evaluation. In the rest of the memo explain how you arrived at your answer, the facts on which you base your conclusion, and your method of evaluation. The paragraphs may be numbered so that the main divisions of your message are easy to see.

A business memo can be more informal in tone than a business letter, particularly if you know the addressee; but it should not

36b

be wordy. Use technical terms if your reader will understand them, but otherwise keep language simple and use short sentences. Provide only the information that your reader needs to know.

The sample memo below, from a sales representative to her district manager, illustrates these guidelines. Notice especially the form of the memo, the writer's immediate statement of her purpose, the clear structure provided by the three numbered paragraphs, and the direct tone of the whole.

December 20, 1982

To: Chuck Tufts

cc: Jim Burch

From: Becky Gough

Subject: 1982 sales of Quick Wax in territory 12

Since it was introduced in January of this year, Quick Wax has been unsuccessful in my territory and has not affected sales of our Easy Shine. Discussions with customers and my own analysis of Quick Wax suggest three reasons for its failure to compete with our product.

1. Quick Wax has not received the promotion necessary for a new product. Advertising--primarily on radio--has been sporadic and has not developed a clear, consistent image for the product. In addition, the Quick Wax sales rep in this territory is new and inexperienced; he is not known to customers, and his sales pitch (which I once overheard) is weak. As far as I can tell, his efforts are not supported by phone calls or mailings from his home office.

2. When Quick Wax does make it to the store shelves, buyers do not choose it over our product. Though priced competitively with our product, Quick Wax is poorly packaged. The container seems smaller than ours, though in fact it holds the same eight ounces. The lettering on the Quick Wax package (red on blue) is difficult to read, in contrast to the white-on-green lettering on our package.

3. Our special purchase offers and my increased efforts to serve existing customers have had the intended effect of keeping customers satisfied with our product and reducing their inclination to stock something new.

36b

Appendixes

Appendix A
Avoiding Plagiarism

Plagiarism (from a Latin word for "kidnapper") is the presentation of someone else's ideas or words as your own. If you copy a sentence from a book and pass it off as your writing, if you summarize or paraphrase someone else's ideas without acknowledging your debt, or if you buy a term paper to hand in as your own, you plagiarize deliberately. If you carelessly forget quotation marks or a footnote to show that words or ideas originated with someone else, you plagiarize accidentally. Whether deliberate or accidental, plagiarism is a serious and often punishable offense.

You do not plagiarize, however, when you draw on other writers' material and acknowledge your sources. That procedure is a crucial part of honest research writing (see Chapter 35). Nevertheless, because a research paper requires by definition that you integrate other people's ideas with your own, you may not always be sure what constitutes plagiarism. This appendix shows you how to avoid plagiarism by acknowledging sources when necessary and by using them accurately and fairly.

A1
Knowing what to acknowledge

When you write a research paper, you coordinate information from three kinds of sources: (1) your independent thoughts and experiences; (2) common knowledge, the basic knowledge people share; and (3) other people's independent thoughts and experiences. Of the three, you *must* acknowledge the third, the work of others.

Your independent material

You need not acknowledge your own independent material — your thoughts, compilations of facts, or experimental results, expressed in your words or format — to avoid plagiarism. Such material includes observations from your experience (for example, a conclusion you draw about crowd behavior by watching crowds at concerts or shopping centers) as well as diagrams you construct from information you gather yourself. Though you generally should describe the basis for your independent conclusions, so that readers can evaluate your thinking, you need not cite sources for them. However, someone else's ideas and facts are not yours; even when you express them entirely in your words and format, they require acknowledgment.

Common knowledge

Common knowledge consists of the standard information of a field of study as well as folk literature and commonsense observations. Standard information includes, for instance, the major facts of history. The dates of Charlemagne's rule as emperor of Rome (800–814) and the fact that his reign was accompanied by a revival of learning — both facts available in many reference books — do not need to be acknowledged, even if you have to look up the information. However, an interpretation of facts (for instance, a theory of how writing began) or a specialist's observation (for instance, an Asian historian's opinion of the effects of Chinese wall posters) is considered independent, not common, knowledge and must be documented.

Folk literature, which is popularly known and cannot be traced to particular writers, is considered common knowledge. Mother Goose nursery rhymes and fairy tales like "Snow White" are examples. However, all literature traceable to a particular writer should be acknowledged. Even a familiar phrase like "miles to go before I sleep" (from Robert Frost's poem "Stopping by Woods on a Snowy Evening") is literature, not folk literature, and requires acknowledgment.

Commonsense observations, such as the idea that weather affects people's spirits or that inflation is most troublesome for people with low and fixed incomes, are considered common knowledge and do not require acknowledgment, even when they also appear in someone else's writing. But a scientist's findings about the effects of high humidity on people with high blood pressure, or an economist's argument about the effects of inflation on immigrants from China, will require acknowledgment.

You may treat common knowledge as your own, even if you have to look it up in a reference book. You may not know, for example, the dates of the French Revolution or the standard definition of *photosynthesis*, although these are considered common knowledge. If you do not know a subject well enough to determine whether a piece of information is common knowledge, make a record of the source as you would for any other quotation or paraphrase. As you read more about the subject, the information may come up repeatedly without acknowledgment, in which case it is probably common knowledge. But if you are still in doubt when you finish your research, always acknowledge the source.

Someone else's independent material

A2

You must always acknowledge other people's independent material — that is, any facts or ideas that are not common knowledge or your own. The source may be a book, letter, magazine, newspaper, movie, speech, interview, television program, or microfilmed document. You must acknowledge not only ideas or facts themselves but also the language and format in which the ideas or facts appear, if you use them. That is, the wording, sentence structures, arrangement of thoughts, and special graphic format (such as a table or diagram) created by another writer belong to that writer just as his or her ideas do. The following example baldly plagiarizes the original quotation from Jessica Mitford's *Kind and Usual Punishment* (New York: Random House, 1973), p. 9.

ORIGINAL	The character and mentality of the keepers may be of more importance in understanding prisons than the character and mentality of the kept.
PLAGIARISM	But the character and mentality of prison officials (the keepers) is of more importance in understanding prisons than the character and mentality of prisoners (the kept).

Though the writer has made some changes in Mitford's original and even altered the meaning slightly (by changing *may be* to *is*), she has plagiarized on several counts. She has copied key words (*character, mentality, keepers, kept*), duplicated the entire sentence structure, and lifted the idea — all without acknowledging the source. As illustrated in the following section, the writer must either enclose the exact quotation in quotation marks or state the idea in her own words and in her own sentence. Whichever she does, she must acknowledge Mitford as the source.

You need to acknowledge another's material no matter how you use it, how much of it you use, or how often you use it. Whether you are quoting a single important word, paraphrasing a single sentence, or summarizing three paragraphs, and whether you are using the source only once or a dozen times, you must acknowledge the original author every time.

If you read someone else's material during your research but do not include any of that material in your final draft, you need not acknowledge the source with a note because you have not actually used the material. However, your instructor may ask you to include such sources in your bibliography.

(See 35h for information on how to acknowledge sources with footnotes or endnotes.)

A2
Quoting, summarizing, and paraphrasing

When writing a research paper, you can present the ideas of others through direct quotation, through summary, or through paraphrase, depending on your purpose. (See 35e, p. 471, and 35g, p. 478, for information on deciding when and how to employ these methods.) For **direct quotation,** copy the material from the source *carefully,* place it in quotation marks within your running text (see 24c for the style to use with poetry and long quotations), and acknowledge the source. Put quotation marks around even a single word if the original author used it in a special or central way. Do not change any wording, spelling, capitalization, or punctuation. Be careful not to leave out or add any words or punctuation marks accidentally. Use an ellipsis mark (three spaced periods) to indicate the exact point at which you have deliberately left out part of a direct quotation (see 25e). Use brackets to surround any word, comment, or punctuation mark you add within the quotation (see 25d). Place the word *sic* (meaning "in this manner") in brackets immediately after any mistake in spelling, grammar, or common knowledge that your reader might otherwise believe to be a misquotation. To correct the plagiarism of Mitford's sentence above, the writer would place Mitford's exact words in quotation marks and cite the source properly.

> **QUOTATION**   "The character and mentality of the keepers," maintains Jessica Mitford, "may be of more importance in understanding prisons than the character and mentality of the kept."[7]

When you summarize or paraphrase, you state in your own words and sentence structures the meaning of someone else's writing. In a **summary** you extract the central idea from several sentences, paragraphs, or even pages, condensing it into one or more sentences of your own. In a **paraphrase** you follow the original more closely, often sentence by sentence, recording in your own words the author's line of reasoning. (See also 35e.) Since the words and the sentence structures are yours, you do not enclose either a summary or a paraphrase in quotation marks, although, of course, you must acknowledge the author of the idea. Here is a paraphrase of the Mitford quotation above.

> **PARAPHRASE**   Jessica Mitford maintains that we may be able to learn more about prisons from the psychology of the prison officials than from that of the prisoners.[7]

If you adopt the source's sentence pattern and simply substitute synonyms for key words, or if you use the original words and merely change the sentence pattern, you are not paraphrasing but plagiarizing, even if you acknowledge the source, because both methods use someone else's expression without quotation marks. The inadequate paraphrase below plagiarizes the original source, Frederick C. Crews's *The Tragedy of Manners: Moral Drama in the Later Novels of Henry James* (1957; rpt. Hamden, Conn.: Shoe String Press, 1971), p. 8.

> **ORIGINAL**   In each case I have tried to show that all the action in a "Jamesian novel" may be taken as a result of philosophical differences of opinion among the principal characters, and that these

differences in turn are explainable by reference to the characters' differing social backgrounds.

PLAGIARISM   According to Crews, the action in a "Jamesian novel" comes from philosophical differences of opinion between characters. These differences can be explained by examining the characters' differing social backgrounds.[5]

The plagiarized passage lifts several expressions verbatim from the source, without change and without quotation marks: "action in a 'Jamesian novel' "; "philosophical differences of opinion"; "the characters' differing social backgrounds." Thus even though the writer acknowledges the author's work (indicated by the use of Crews's name and the note number 5), he plagiarizes because he does not also acknowledge the author's words with quotation marks. The paraphrase below both conveys and acknowledges the author's meaning without stealing his manner of expression.

PARAPHRASE   According to Crews, the characters in Henry James's novels live out philosophies acquired from their upbringing and their place in society.[5]

In this paraphrase, although the writer retains Crews's essential meaning, he restates that meaning in a sentence that he himself has clearly constructed and designed to fit his larger purpose.

In paraphrasing or summarizing you must not only devise your own form of expression (or place quotation marks around the author's expressions) but also represent the author's meaning exactly without distorting it. In the following inaccurate paraphrase the writer has avoided plagiarism but has stated a meaning exactly opposite to that of the original. The original quotation, from the artist Henri Matisse, appears in Jack D. Flam, *Matisse on Art* (London: Phaidon, 1973), p. 148.

ORIGINAL   For the artist creation begins with vision. To see is itself a creative operation, requiring an effort. Everything that we see in our daily life is more or less distorted by acquired habits, and this is perhaps more evident in an age like ours when cinema posters and magazines present us every day with a flood of ready-made images which are to the eye what prejudices are to the mind.

INACCURATE   Matisse said that seeing is the first step of the ar-
PARAPHRASE   tistic act and that we learn how to see by looking at posters and magazines.[7]

The revision below combines paraphrase and quotation to represent the author's meaning exactly.

IMPROVED   Matisse said that seeing is the first step of the ar-
PARAPHRASE   tistic act because we must overcome our visual "habits" and "prejudices," particularly those we

develop in response to the popular images of our culture.[7]

(For additional discussion of quoting and paraphrasing, see 35e.)

A2

To be sure you acknowledge sources fairly and do not plagiarize, review this checklist both before beginning to write your paper and again after you have completed your first draft.

1. What type of source are you using: your own independent material, common knowledge, or someone else's independent material?
2. If you are quoting someone else's material, is the quotation exact? Have you inserted quotation marks around quotations run into the text? Have you shown omissions with ellipses and additions with brackets?
3. If you are paraphrasing someone else's material, have you rewritten it in your own words and sentence structures? Does your paraphrase employ quotation marks when you resort to the author's exact language? Have you represented the author's meaning without distortion?
4. Is each use of someone else's material acknowledged with a note?
5. Do all notes contain complete and accurate information on the sources you have cited?
6. Does your bibliography include all the sources you have drawn from in writing your paper?

Appendix B
Preparing a Manuscript

A legible, consistent, and attractive manuscript is a service to readers because it makes reading easier. This appendix discusses the materials necessary for manuscript preparation and some conventions of format. (Most of these guidelines are standard, but your instructor may request that you follow different conventions in some matters.)

B1
Choosing the appropriate materials

Typewritten papers

For typewritten papers, use 8½″ × 11″ white bond paper of sixteen- or twenty-pound weight. Some instructors also accept the same size surface-coated bond paper (called "erasable" or "corrasable"), but ink smears easily on such paper. Onionskin sheets, paper torn from notebooks, colored paper, and paper smaller or larger than 8½″ × 11″ are unacceptable. Use the same type of paper throughout a project. Type on only one side of a sheet and double-space.

Use a black typewriter ribbon that is fresh enough to make a dark impression, and make sure the keys of the typewriter are clean. To avoid smudging the page when correcting mistakes, use a liquid correction fluid or a correction tape. Don't use hyphens or x's to cross out mistakes, and don't type corrections (strikeovers) on top of mistakes.

Handwritten papers

For handwritten papers, you can use regular white paper, 8½″ × 11″, with horizontal lines spaced about a half inch apart. Don't use paper torn from a notebook, unlined paper, paper with narrow lines, colored paper, or paper other than 8½″ × 11″ (such as legal or stenographer's pads). Use the same type of paper throughout a project. Write on only

536

one side of a sheet, and write either on every line or on every other line as specified by your instructor.

Use black or blue ink, not pencil. If possible, use an ink eraser or eradicator to correct mistakes instead of drawing a single line through them. Don't scribble over or black out a mistake, and don't write corrections on top of mistakes.

B2

B2
Following a standard format

A consistent physical format makes the script, margins, paging, title, and identification visually effective and avoids the illegibility and the confusion of inconsistencies. See the sample research paper in Chapter 35, pages 492–517, for examples of the items below. (For the special formats of a bibliography and of footnotes or endnotes, neither of which is discussed below, see pp. 461–66, 480–89, 513, and 517.)

Script

Handwritten script should be reasonably uniform and clear. Be sure letters are easily distinguishable. Cross all *t*'s; dot all *i*'s with dots, not circles; form the loops of letters carefully. Make capital letters and small letters clearly different. Space consistently between words and between sentences. If your handwriting is difficult to read, submit a typed paper if possible. If you don't have access to a typewriter and your handwriting is illegible or unusual in size, decoration, or slant, make it more legible or conventional when writing the final manuscript. Indent the first line of every paragraph about an inch.

In typewritten script, leave one space between words and after commas, semicolons, and colons. Leave two spaces after sentence periods, question marks, and exclamation points. Use one space before and after as well as between the three periods of an ellipsis mark. To make a dash, use two consecutive hyphens with no space before or after. To make symbols that are not on your typewriter, leave three or four spaces and insert the symbol by hand in ink. Indent the first line of every paragraph five spaces.

For both typewritten and handwritten script, try to avoid breaking words at the ends of lines. If you must break a word, follow the guidelines provided in Chapter 30. Don't start a line with any mark of punctuation other than a dash, an opening parenthesis, an opening quotation mark, or an ellipsis mark when one of these is called for.

Set off quotations of more than four typed lines of prose or of two or more lines of poetry. (If you are quoting many passages of poetry, you may want to set off only quotations of more than two lines.) In handwritten copy, indent all lines of the quotation an inch from the left margin. In typewritten copy, indent all lines ten spaces. Triple-space above and below each quotation. Double-space the quotation itself. (See 24c.)

B3

Margins

Leave about one and a half inches for the margins at the left and top of each page. Leave one-inch margins at the right and bottom of each page. (The right margin will be uneven but should not be narrower than an inch.)

Paging

Don't number or count in your numbering the title page of your paper. The outline pages at the front of a research paper may be numbered with small Roman numerals (i, ii). The first text page in a paper is considered number 1 but goes unnumbered. Number with Arabic numerals (2, 3, 4) all pages after the first text page. Don't place a period after the numeral or insert parentheses or hyphens around it. Place the numeral two lines above the top line of text (approximately half an inch from the top of the page), and align it with the right margin.

Title and identification

If you don't use a separate title page for an essay, center your title about two inches from the top of a typed page and on the top line of a handwritten page. Leave four lines of space or two ruled lines before starting the first paragraph. Capitalize the first and last words of the title, any word after a colon or semicolon, and all other words *except* articles (*a, an, the*) and conjunctions and prepositions of less than five letters. Don't underline the title or place quotation marks around it. Place your name, the date, the course number, and any other information your instructor requests at the top right corner of the first page or wherever your instructor specifies.

For research papers, use a separate title page. Center the title about a third of the way down the page. If the title is long, break it into two lines so that the longer line is on top, and leave a line of space between lines of the title. Center the word *By* about an inch below the title. Two lines below that, center your name. Starting about an inch below your name, and double-spacing, provide the date, the course number, and any other information your instructor requests.

B3
Proofreading, correcting, and submitting the final manuscript

Proofread each page of your paper carefully. Concentrate on spelling, punctuation, mechanics, grammar, and manuscript format. If a page has several errors, retype or rewrite the page. If it has one or two errors and you can't eradicate them, correct them in ink. Draw a single line through a word you want to delete. Don't try to correct a misspelled word without crossing out and rewriting the whole word. To replace a word or mark of punctuation, draw a line through the item, place a caret (^) underneath it, and write the new word or mark in the space above the old one. To add words or marks of punctuation, place a caret underneath the line at the point where you wish to insert the word or mark; then center the word or mark over the caret in the space above the line.

```
                                        organisms
        An ecosystem is a community of ^organisms interacting
                              the
        with each other and with^environment.
```

If you have to add more words than will fit between the lines of text, rewrite or retype the page.

When you submit your final paper, be sure the pages will stay together when the paper is shuffled in with others. Depending on the wishes of your instructor, you may fold the paper in half lengthwise, paperclip or staple the pages in the upper left corner, or place the paper in a special binder.

Appendix C
Improving Study Skills

Three basic qualities underlie effective study skills: organization, repetition, and motivation. This appendix will show briefly how to employ these qualities in reading, taking notes, and preparing for tests.

It is possible to study anywhere and at any time, but you will benefit from a place that is moderately comfortable, well lighted, and undistracting. Have handy the materials you'll need while studying, such as paper, pencils, pens, and a highlighter. Keep your expectations realistic. Don't plan to accomplish more in an hour or a day than you ever have before. Concentrate on specific goals, such as answering a question about a textbook chapter or even passing a test, rather than on more general, longer-term goals, such as getting a certain grade-point average or graduating from college. And plan to take a break after every hour or so of studying to refresh yourself.

C1
Remembering

In memorizing, you use short-term storage, where information may stay a few seconds or a few minutes, and long-term storage, where information may stay indefinitely — or at least through the final examination. Most academic learning requires a conscious effort to move material from short-term storage into long-term storage.

The more organized your learning is, the more it will penetrate your long-term memory. Read a book's introduction before you read the book; skim a whole chapter before you read the chapter. Organize information into small groups of ideas or facts that make sense to you. For instance, memorize French vocabulary words in related groups such as words for parts of the body or parts of a house. Keep the groups small: Psychological research has shown that we can easily memorize about seven items at a time but have trouble with more.

As you accumulate new information, make associations between it and what you already know. For instance, to remember a sequence of four dates in twentieth-century English history, link the occurrences in England with simultaneous, and more familiar, events in the United States. Or use **mnemonic devices,** tricks for improving your memory. Say the history dates you want to remember are separated by five then four then nine years. By memorizing the first date and then 5 + 4 = 9, you'll have command of all four dates.

Reviewing the material you want to learn will improve not only how long but also how completely and accurately you remember it. Since you forget a great deal right after you read a chapter or listen to a lecture, try to spend five minutes going over the material immediately after you first encounter it. You will probably remember more from that brief review than you will from a much longer review several days later. In addition, try to spread subsequent study over half-hour sessions three or four days a week, instead of concentrating all study time in a single, long session.

C2
Scheduling

To organize your time effectively for studying, examine how you spend your days. For a week, keep track of your activities and the time they absorb. How many of the 168 hours in a week do you spend eating, sleeping, watching television, attending classes, studying, working at a job, commuting, doing laundry, socializing, and so forth? If you think it will help you organize your time, make a chart like a calendar that divides the week into seven vertical columns (one for each day) and one horizontal row for each hour you are awake. Block out on the chart your activities that occur regularly and at specific times, such as commuting, attending classes, and working. Then fill in your other regular activities (such as exercise, eating, and studying) that do not necessarily occur at fixed times.

Set aside regular time for study each week. During any given week you will want to adjust how you spend the studying time to allow for different assignments in different courses. For courses requiring extensive reading or creative work such as writing, try to include several large blocks of time per week. If you have been given a long-term assignment (such as a research paper), include time for it in your planning.

When devising a weekly schedule, don't overorganize so that you have no time left for relaxing. An unrealistic schedule that assigns all available time to studying will quickly become so difficult to live by that you'll be forced to abandon it and start over.

C3
Reading

The assigned reading you do for college courses — in textbooks, journal articles, and works of literature — requires a greater focus on

C3

comprehension, analysis, and retention than does reading for entertainment or for practical information. For most course reading, especially textbook reading, you will benefit from at least three separate examinations of the material: once skimming, once reading carefully, word by word, and once reviewing. Though these processes may seem redundant and time-consuming, with practice you will be able to perform some steps simultaneously and follow all the steps almost habitually.

The purpose of **skimming** is to give you an overview of the material that will aid your understanding of any part of it. Your goal is not to comprehend all the details or even the structure of the author's argument. Rather, you want to achieve a general sense of how a piece of writing is organized and what its principal ideas are. The steps outlined below constitute a typical procedure for skimming a textbook chapter.

1. Examine the chapter title. What does it mean? What do you already know about this subject?
2. Read the first couple of paragraphs carefully to introduce yourself to the topic and to the author's writing style. The author often gives an overview of his or her ideas at the start.
3. Move through the chapter from heading to heading, reading each one as if it were a headline. Viewing the headings as the levels of an outline will give you a feeling for which ideas the author sees as central or as subordinate.
4. As you move from one heading to the next, scan the text and note any key words that are in color, **boldface,** or *italic* type.
5. Slow down for all pictures, diagrams, tables, graphs, and maps. These often contain concentrated information.
6. Read the last paragraph of the chapter or its summary carefully. These often give an overview of the main ideas of the chapter.
7. Take a moment to think over what you've skimmed. Try to recall the sequence of ideas. Ask yourself what the main idea or thesis is.

As soon as possible after you have skimmed a chapter, read it carefully for a thorough understanding of each idea or group of ideas. Here is a procedure you might follow for such word-by-word reading.

1. Distinguish the main ideas from the supporting ideas. Look for the chapter's thesis or central argument, for the central idea in each section or paragraph, and for terms the author takes pains to define and perhaps highlights with special type.
2. Read the chapter's structure as if it were a map of the author's ideas. Look for the introduction to the chapter, which outlines the ideas that follow; for the step-by-step explanations of main ideas found in the body of the chapter; for transitions between ideas that signal shifts in thought and highlight relationships; and for summaries or conclusions at the ends of sections or the end of the chapter that condense the text to its main concepts.
3. After reading a section or a group of ideas, test your comprehension by summarizing the material in your own words and then skimming it to check your understanding. Reread parts you have forgotten or misunderstood until you're sure of your comprehension.

4. Once you feel you understand the entire chapter, go back to underline important phrases or passages and to add marginal notes (or to make separate notes if you don't want to mark your book). Underline or take notes on only main ideas, key terms, and specific supporting evidence you've chosen to remember. In marginal notes, add your own ideas or summarize the author's.

When you review a chapter, reread headings, summaries, and key terms as well as the passages you have underlined or taken notes on. Concentrate on how the parts fit together. Stop to read carefully any passages that don't seem familiar or clear. Before a test, skim the material a section at a time, and then recite or write out the main ideas before going on to the next section. If you have trouble remembering, reread the section instead of skimming it.

C4
Taking notes in class

Your aim in taking notes from a class lecture or discussion is to record it as completely as possible while sorting out the main ideas from the secondary and supporting ones. By doing so, you not only provide yourself with complete material for study later but also learn about the instructor's integration of the course material.

As you take notes, use your own words as much as possible to help you comprehend and retain the material, but resort to the speaker's words if necessary to catch everything. If you miss some material while making notes, leave a space to be filled in later. Don't count on going back to copy over and expand your notes. You may not be able to recall the missing information, and copying is little more than a time-wasting, mechanical activity. If you have already read the textbook chapter related to the lecture, you may be tempted to omit from your notes any lecture material you could find in the text. But you would be missing an important opportunity to integrate all the components of the course — the text material, your instructor's views, and your own thoughts. And you would risk forgetting exactly how your instructor made use of the text.

If, when you review your notes, you discover holes in them or confusing shifts in thought, consult a fellow student for his or her version of that part of the lecture. When you feel you understand the material, underline key words and important ideas in the notes and add comments (or cross-references to the text) in the margins.

C5
Preparing for examinations

No matter how much time you have, what material you are studying, or what kind of test you will be taking, studying for an examination

C5

involves three main steps, each requiring about a third of the total preparation time: (1) reviewing the material; (2) organizing summaries of the material; and (3) testing yourself. Your main goals are to strengthen your understanding of the subject, making both its ideas and its details more memorable, and to increase the flexibility of your new knowledge so that you can recognize it and apply it in new contexts.

As you begin studying for a test, organize your class notes and reading assignments into manageable units. Reread the material, recite or write out the main ideas and selected supporting ideas and examples, and then skim for an overview. Proceed in this way through all the units, returning to earlier ones as necessary to refresh your memory or to relate ideas.

Allow time to reorganize the material in your own way, to create categories that will help you apply the information in various contexts. For instance, in studying for a biology examination, work to understand a process, such as how a plant develops or how photosynthesis occurs. Or in studying for an American government test, explain the structures of the local, state, and federal levels of government, or outline the differences among the levels. Other useful categories include advantages or disadvantages, causes or effects, and repeated ideas. Develop categories that bring together as much of the material as possible, and think through each one as completely as you can. Such analytical thinking will enhance your mastery of the course material and may even prepare you directly for specific essay questions (see 36a).

Spend the last portion of your preparation time testing yourself. Convert to a question each heading in your lecture notes or textbook and each general category you have devised. Recite to yourself or write out the answers to the questions, going back to the course material to fill in missing information. Be sure you can define and explain all key terms. For subjects that require solving problems (such as mathematics, statistics, chemistry, and physics), work out a difficult problem for every type on which you will be tested. For history, test yourself on events and their causes or consequences. For a subject like psychology, be certain you understand the principal theories of behavior and their implications. For a literature course, test your knowledge of each work by thinking of the author's style and meaning, the main characters, and the plot developments; and trace the development of movements, genres, or periods to be sure you comprehend the relations among works.

ABOUT CRAMMING: Everything psychologists report about learning under stress suggests that cramming for an examination is about the least effective way of preparing for one. It takes longer to learn under stress, and the learning is shallower, more difficult to apply, and more rapidly forgotten. Information learned under stress is even harder to apply under conditions of stress, such as the stress of taking an examination. And the lack of sleep that usually accompanies cramming makes a good performance even more unlikely. If you must cram for a test, determine what is most important. Skim chapters and notes to select central ideas. Face the fact that you can't learn everything that will be on the test, and spend what time you have reviewing main concepts and facts.

Glossaries

Glossary of Usage
Glossary of Grammatical Terms

Glossary
of Usage

This glossary provides notes on words or phrases that often cause problems for writers. The recommendations for standard, written English are based on current dictionaries and usage guides like the ones listed on pages 408–9. Items labeled *nonstandard* should be avoided in speech and especially in writing. Those labeled *colloquial* occur commonly in speech and informal writing but are best avoided in the more formal writing usually expected in college and business. (Words and phrases labeled here as *colloquial* also include those labeled by many dictionaries with the equivalent term *informal*.) See Chapter 31 for further discussion of word choice and for exercises in usage. See 32b-2 for a description of dictionary labels. Also see 34a-1 for a list of commonly confused words that are pronounced the same or similarly. The words and definitions provided there supplement this glossary.

The glossary is necessarily brief. Keep a dictionary handy for all your writing, and make a habit of referring to it whenever you doubt the appropriateness of a word or phrase.

a, an Use *a* before words beginning with consonant sounds, including those spelled with an initial, pronounced *h* and those spelled with vowels that are sounded as consonants: *a historian, a one-o'clock class, a university.* Use *an* before words that begin with vowel sounds, including those spelled with an initial, silent *h: an orgy, an L, an honor.*

When you use an abbreviation or acronym in writing (see 28b), the article that precedes it depends on how the abbreviation is to be read: *She was once an HEW undersecretary.* (*HEW* is to be read as three letters, not as a word or as *Health, Education and Welfare.*) *Many Americans opposed a SALT treaty.* (*SALT* is to be read as one word, *salt,* not as four separate letters.)

accept, except *Accept* is a verb meaning "receive." *Except* is usually a preposition or conjunction meaning "but for" or "other than"; when it is used as a verb, it means "leave out." *I can accept all your suggestions except the last one. I'm sorry you excepted my last suggestion from your list.*

546

adverse, averse *Adverse* and *averse* are both adjectives, and both mean "opposed" or "hostile." But *adverse* describes someone or something opposed to the subject, whereas *averse* describes the subject's opposition: *The president was averse to adverse criticism.*

advice, advise *Advice* is a noun, and *advise* is a verb: *Take my advice; do as I advise you.*

affect, effect Usually *affect* is a verb, meaning "to influence," and *effect* is a noun, meaning "result": *The drug did not affect his driving; in fact, it seemed to have no effect at all.* But *effect* occasionally is used as a verb meaning "to bring about": *Her efforts effected a change.* And *affect* is used in psychology as a noun meaning "feeling or emotion": *One can infer much about affect from behavior.*

aggravate *Aggravate* should not be used in its colloquial meaning of "irritate" or "exasperate" (for example, *We were aggravated by her constant arguing*). *Aggravate* means "make worse": *The president was irritated by the Senate's stubbornness, because he feared any delay might aggravate the unrest in the Middle East.*

agree to, agree with *Agree to* means "consent to," and *agree with* means "be in accord with": *How can they agree to a treaty when they don't agree with each other about the terms?*

ain't Nonstandard for *am not, isn't,* or *aren't.*

all, all of Usually *all* is sufficient to modify a noun: *all my loving, all the things you are.* Before a pronoun or proper noun, *all of* is usually appropriate: *all of me, in all of France.*

all ready, already *All ready* means "completely prepared," and *already* means "by now" or "before now": *We were all ready to go to the movie, but it had already started.*

all right *All right* is always two words. *Alright* is a common misspelling.

all together, altogether *All together* means "in unison," or "gathered in one place." *Altogether* means "entirely." *It's not altogether true that our family never spends vacations all together.*

allusion, illusion An *allusion* is a reference to something, and an *illusion* is a deceptive appearance: *Paul's constant allusions to Shakespeare created the illusion that he was an intellectual.*

almost, most *Almost* is an adverb meaning "nearly"; *most* is an adjective meaning "the greater number (or part) of." In formal writing, *most* should not be used as a substitute for *almost: We see each other almost* (not *most*) *every day.*

a lot *A lot* is always two words. *Alot* is a common misspelling.

among, between In general, *among* is used for relationships involving more than two people or things. *Between* is used for relationships involving only two or for comparing one thing to a group to which it belongs. *The four of them agreed among themselves that the choice was be-*

tween New York and Los Angeles. Increasingly, though, *between* is used for relationships involving three or more comparable people or things: *Let's keep this just between the three of us, shall we?*

amount, number *Amount* refers to a quantity of something (a singular noun) that cannot be counted. *Number* refers to countable items (a plural noun). *The amount of leftover ice we can save depends on the number of containers we have to put it in.*

an, and *An* is an article (see *a, an*). *And* is a coordinating conjunction. Do not carelessly omit the *d* from *and*.

and etc. *Et cetera* (*etc.*) means "and the rest"; *and etc.* therefore is redundant. See also *et al., etc.*

and/or *And/or* is awkward, and it can be confusing. A sentence like *The decision will be made by the mayor and/or the council* implies that either one or the other or both will make the decision. If both will, use *and;* if either will, use *or.* Use *and/or* only when you mean three options.

and which, and who When *which* or *who* is used to introduce a relative clause, *and* is superfluous: *WCAS is my favorite AM radio station, which* (not *and which*) *I listen to every morning. And which* or *and who* is correct only when used to introduce a second clause beginning with the same relative pronoun: *Jill is my cousin who goes to school here and who always calls me at seven in the morning.*

ante-, anti- The prefix *ante-* means "before" (*antedate, antebellum*); *anti-* means "against" (*antiwar, antinuclear*). Before a capital letter or *i, anti-* takes a hyphen: *anti-Freudian, anti-isolationist.*

anxious, eager *Anxious* means "nervous" or "worried" and is usually followed by *about. Eager* means "looking forward" and is usually followed by *to. I've been anxious about getting blisters. I'm eager* (not *anxious) to get new running shoes.*

anybody, any body; anyone, any one *Anybody* and *anyone* are indefinite pronouns; *any body* is a noun modified by an adjective; *any one* is a pronoun or adjective modifed by *any. How can anybody communicate with any body of government? Can anyone help Amy? She has more work than any one person can handle.*

any more, anymore *Any more* is used in negative constructions to mean "no more." *Anymore,* an adverb meaning "now," is also used in negative constructions. *He doesn't want any more. She doesn't live here anymore.*

anyplace Colloquial for *anywhere.*

anyways, anywheres Nonstandard for *anyway* and *anywhere.*

apt, liable, likely *Apt* and *likely* are interchangeable. Strictly speaking, though, *apt* means "having a tendency to": *Horace is apt to forget his lunch in the morning if Trudy doesn't remind him. Likely* means "probably going to": *Horace is leaving so early today that he's likely to catch the first bus.*

Liable is normally used to mean "in danger of" and should be confined to situations with undesirable consequences: *If Horace doesn't watch out, he is liable to trip over that lawn sprinkler.* In the strictest sense, *liable* means "responsible" or "exposed to": *If Horace trips over that lawn sprinkler, the owner will be liable for damages.*

as   *As* is often used to mean *because, since, while, whether,* or *who.* It may be vague or ambiguous in these senses: *As we were stopping to rest, we decided to eat lunch.* (Does *as* mean "while" or "because"?) Usually a more precise word is preferable. See also 16c.

As never should be used as a substitute for *whether* or *who: I'm not sure whether (not as) we can make it. That's the man who (not as) gave me directions.*

as, like   In formal speech and writing, *as* may be either a preposition or a conjunction; *like* functions as a preposition only. Thus, if the construction being introduced is a full clause rather than a phrase, the preferred choice is *as* or *as if* (see 16c): *This cigarette tastes good, as (not like) a cigarette should. This cigarette tastes as if (not like) it were made of oregano. This cigarette tastes like oregano.*

When *as* serves as a preposition, the distinction between *as* and *like* depends on meaning. *As* suggests that the subject is equivalent or identical to the description; *She was hired as an engineer. Like* suggests resemblance but not identity: *People like her do well in such jobs. See also like, such as*

assure, ensure, insure   *Assure* means "to promise": *He assured us that if we left early, we would miss the traffic. Ensure* and *insure* often are used synonymously, meaning "make certain," but some reserve *insure* for matters of legal and financial protection and use *ensure* for more general meanings: *We left early to ensure that we would miss the traffic. It's expensive to insure yourself against floods.*

as, than   In comparisons, *as* and *than* may be followed by either subjective- or objective-case pronouns: *You are as tall as he* (subjective). *They treated you better than him* (objective). The case depends on whether the things compared are subjects or objects of verbs. To determine which case to use, supply the omitted verb: *I love you more than he* (*loves you*) (*he* is the subject of the missing verb *does*). *I love you more than* (*I love*) *him* (*him* is the object of the missing verb *love*). See also 6e.

as to   A stuffy substitute for *about: The suspect was questioned about* (not *as to*) *her actions.*

at   The use of *at* after *where* is wordy and should be avoided: *Where are you meeting him?* is preferable to *Where are you meeting him at?*

at this point in time   Wordy for *now, at this point,* or *at this time.*

averse, adverse   See *adverse, averse.*

awful, awfully   Strictly speaking, *awful* means "awe-inspiring." As intensifiers meaning "very" or "extremely" (*He tried awfully hard*), *awful* and *awfully* are colloquial and should not be used in formal speech or writing.

a while, awhile *Awhile* is an adverb; *a while* is an article and a noun. Thus *awhile* can modify a verb but cannot serve as the object of a preposition, and *a while* is just the opposite: *I will be gone awhile* (not *a while*). *I will be gone for a while* (not *awhile*).

bad, badly In formal speech and writing, *bad* should be used only as an adjective; the adverb is *badly*. *He felt bad because his tooth ached badly*. In *He felt bad*, the verb *felt* is a linking verb and the adjective *bad* is a subject complement. See also 9b.

being as, being that Colloquial for *because*, the preferable word in formal speech or writing: *Because* (not *Being as*) *the world is round, Columbus never did fall off the edge*.

beside, besides *Beside* is a preposition meaning "next to." *Besides* is a preposition meaning "except" or "in addition to" as well as an adverb meaning "in addition." *Besides, several other people besides you want to sit beside Dr. Christensen*.

between, among See *among, between*.

bring, take Use *bring* only for movement from a farther place to a nearer one and *take* for any other movement. *First, take these books to the library for renewal, then take them to old Mr. Daniels. Bring them back to me when he's finished*.

bunch In formal speech and writing, *bunch* (as a noun) should be used only to refer to clusters of things growing or fastened together, such as bananas and grapes. Its use to mean a group of items or people is colloquial; *crowd* or *group* is preferable.

burst, bursted; bust, busted *Burst* is a standard verb form meaning "to fly apart suddenly" (principal parts *burst, burst, burst*). The past-tense form *bursted* is nonstandard. The verb *bust* (*busted*) is slang.

but, hardly, scarcely These words are negative in their own right; using *not* with any of them to indicate negation is redundant. *We have but an hour* (not *We haven't got but an hour*) *before our plane leaves. I could hardly* (not *I couldn't hardly*) *make out her face in the dark*.

but however, but yet These and similar expressions, in which *but* is combined with another conjunction, are redundant and should be avoided: *He said he had finished, yet* (not *but yet*) *he continued*.

but that, but what These wordy substitutes for *that* and *what* should be avoided: *I don't doubt that* (not *but that*) *you are right*.

calculate, figure, reckon As substitutes for *expect* or *imagine* (*I figure I'll go*), these words are colloquial.

can, may Strictly, *can* indicates capacity or ability, and *may* indicates permission: *If I may talk with you a moment, I believe I can solve your problem*.

can't help but This idiom is common but redundant. Either *I can't help wishing* or the more formal *I cannot but wish* is preferable to *I can't help but wish*.

case, instance, line   Expressions such as *in the case of, in the instance of,* and *along the lines of* are usually unnecessary padding in a sentence and should be avoided.

censor, censure   To *censor* is to edit or remove from public view on moral or some other grounds; to *censure* is to give a formal scolding. *The lieutenant was <u>censured</u> by Major Taylor for <u>censoring</u> the letters his men wrote home from boot camp.*

center around   *Center on* is generally considered more logical than, and preferable to, *center around.*

climatic, climactic   *Climatic* comes from climate and refers to weather: *Last winter's low temperatures may indicate a <u>climatic</u> change. Climactic* comes from *climax* and refers to a dramatic high point: *During the <u>climactic</u> duel between Hamlet and Laertes, Gertrude drinks poisoned wine.*

complement, compliment   To *complement* something is to add to, complete, or reinforce it: *Her yellow blouse <u>complemented</u> her sun tan.* To *compliment* something is to make a flattering remark about it: *He <u>complimented</u> her sun tan. Complimentary* also can mean "free": *a <u>complimentary</u> sample of our new product; <u>complimentary</u> tickets.*

conscience, conscious   *Conscience* is a noun meaning "a sense of right and wrong"; *conscious* is an adjective meaning "aware" or "awake." *Though I was barely <u>conscious</u>, my <u>conscience</u> told me to confess.*

contact   Often used imprecisely as a verb when a more exact word such as *consult, talk with, telephone,* or *write to* would be appropriate.

continual, continuous   *Continual* means "constantly recurring": *Most movies on television are <u>continually</u> interrupted by commercials. Continuous* means "unceasing": *Cable television often presents movies <u>continuously</u> without commercials.*

convince, persuade   In the strictest sense, to *convince* someone means to change his or her opinion; to *persuade* someone means to move him or her to action. *Convince* thus is properly followed by *of* or *that,* whereas *persuade* is followed by *to: Once he <u>convinced</u> Othello <u>of</u> Desdemona's infidelity, Iago easily <u>persuaded</u> him <u>to</u> kill her.*

could of   See *have, of.*

couple of   Used colloquially to mean "a few" or "several."

credible, creditable, credulous   *Credible* means "believable": *It's a strange story, but it seems <u>credible</u> to me. Creditable* means "deserving of credit" or "worthy": *Asked to play "Red River Valley," Steve gave a <u>creditable</u> performance. Credulous* means "gullible": *The <u>credulous</u> Claire believed Tim's statement that he was quitting school.* See also *incredible, incredulous.*

criteria   The plural of *criterion* (meaning "standard for judgment"): *Of all our <u>criteria</u> for picking a roommate, the most important <u>criterion</u> is a sense of humor.*

data   The plural of *datum* (meaning "fact"): *Out of all the <u>data</u> generated* *by these experiments, not one* <u>*datum*</u> *supports our hypothesis.* Usually, a more common term like *fact, result,* or *figure* is preferred to *datum.* Though *data* is very often used as a singular noun, it is still treated as plural in much formal speech and writing: *The data* <u>*fail*</u> (not <u>*fails*</u>) *to support the hypothesis.*

device, devise   *Device* is the noun, and *devise* is the verb: *Can you* <u>*devise*</u> *some* <u>*device*</u> *for getting his attention?*

differ from, differ with   To *differ from* is to be unlike: *The twins* <u>*differ*</u> <u>*from*</u> *each other only in their hairstyles.* To *differ with* is to disagree with: *I have to* <u>*differ with*</u> *you on that point.*

different from, different than   *Different from* is preferred: *His purpose is* <u>*different from*</u> *mine.* But *different than* is widely accepted when a clause follows, particularly when a construction using *from* would be wordy: *I'm a different person now* <u>*than*</u> *I used to be* is preferable to *I'm a different person now* <u>*from the person*</u> *I used to be.*

discreet, discrete   *Discreet* (noun form *discretion*) means "tactful": *What's a* <u>*discreet*</u> *way of telling Maud to be quiet? Discrete* (noun form *discreteness*) means "separate and distinct": *Within a computer's memory are millions of* <u>*discrete*</u> *bits of information.*

disinterested, uninterested   *Disinterested* means "impartial": *We chose Pete, as a* <u>*disinterested*</u> *third party, to decide who was right. Uninterested* means "bored" or "lacking interest": *Unfortunately, Pete was completely* <u>*uninterested*</u> *in the question.*

don't   *Don't* is the contraction for *do not,* not for *does not: I* <u>*don't*</u> *care, you* <u>*don't*</u> *care,* but *he* <u>*doesn't*</u> (not <u>*don't*</u>) *care.*

due to   *Due to* is always acceptable as a subject complement: *His gray hairs were* <u>*due to*</u> *age.* Many object to *due to* as a preposition meaning "because of" (<u>*Due to*</u> *the holiday, there will be no class tomorrow*). A rule of thumb is that *due to* is always correct after a form of the verb *be* but questionable otherwise.

due to the fact that   Wordy for *because.*

each and every   Wordy for *each* or *every.* Write *each one of us* or *every one of us,* not *each and every one of us.*

eager, anxious   See *anxious, eager.*

effect   See *affect, effect.*

ensure   See *assure, ensure, insure.*

enthused   Used colloquially as an adjective meaning "showing enthusiasm." The preferred adjective is *enthusiastic: The coach was* <u>*enthusiastic*</u> (not <u>*enthused*</u>) *about the team's victory.*

especially, specially   *Especially* means "particularly" or "more than other things"; *specially* means "for a specific reason." *I* <u>*especially*</u> *treasure my boots. They were made* <u>*specially*</u> *for me.*

et al., etc. *Et al.,* the Latin abbreviation for "and other people," is often used in source references for works with more than one author: *Jones et al.* (see 35c, 35h). *Etc.,* the Latin abbreviation for "and other things," should not be used to refer to people. See also *and etc.*

everybody, every body; everyone, every one *Everybody* and *everyone* are indefinite pronouns: *Everybody* (*everyone*) *knows Tom steals. Every one* is a pronoun modified by *every, every body* a noun modified by *every.* Both refer to each thing or person of a specific group and are typically followed by *of: The game commissioner has stocked every body of fresh water in the state with fish, and now every one of our rivers is a potential trout stream.*

everyday, every day *Every day* is a noun modified by *every; everyday* is an adjective meaning "used daily" or "common": *Every day she had to cope with everyday problems.*

everywheres Nonstandard for *everywhere.*

except See *accept, except.*

except for the fact that Wordy for *except that.*

explicit, implicit *Explicit* means "stated outright": *I left explicit instructions. The movie contains explicit sex. Implicit means "implied, unstated": We had an implicit understanding. I trust Marcia implicitly.*

farther, further *Farther* refers to additional distance (*How much farther is it to the beach?*), and *further* refers to additional time, amount, or other abstract matters (*I don't want to discuss this any further*). The distinction often is blurred in current usage.

fewer, less *Fewer* refers to individual countable items (a plural noun), *less* to general amounts (a singular noun): *Skim milk has fewer calories than whole milk. We have less milk left than I thought.*

field The phrase *the field of* is wordy and generally unnecessary: *Margaret plans to specialize in* (not *in the field of*) *family medicine.*

figure See *calculate, figure, reckon.*

flaunt, flout *Flaunt* means "show off": *If you have style, flaunt it. Flout* means "scorn" or "defy": *Hester Prynne flouted convention and paid the price.*

flunk A colloquial substitute for *fail.*

former, latter *Former* refers to the first-named of two things, *latter* to the second-named: *I like both skiing and swimming, the former in the winter and the latter all year round.* To refer to the first- or last-named of three or more things, say *first* or *last: I like jogging, swimming, and hang gliding, but the last is inconvenient in the city.*

further See *farther, further.*

get This common verb is used in many slang and colloquial expressions: *get lost, get with it, get your act together, that really gets me, getting* *on. Get* is easy to overuse; watch out for it in expressions like *it's getting better* (substitute *it's improving*) and *we got done* (substitute *we finished*).

good, well *Good* is an adjective, and *well* is nearly always an adverb: *Larry's a good dancer. He and Linda dance well together. Well* is properly used as an adjective only to refer to health: *You don't look well. Aren't you feeling well? (You look good,* in contrast, means "Your appearance is pleasing.")

good and Colloquial for "very": *I was very* (not *good and*) *tired.*

had better A legitimate way of saying *ought to. Had better* is a verb modified by an adverb; the verb is necessary and should not be omitted: *you had better* or *you'd better,* not *you better.*

had ought The *had* is unnecessary and should be omitted: *He ought* (not *had ought*) *to listen to his mother.*

half Either *half a* or *a half* is appropriate usage, but *a half a* is redundant: *Half a loaf* (not *A half a loaf*) *is better than none. We'd like a half bottle* (not *a half a bottle*) *of the house wine, please.*

hanged, hung Though both are past-tense forms of *hang, hanged* is used to refer to executions and *hung* is used for all other meanings: *Tom Dooley was hanged* (not *hung*) *from a white oak tree. I hung* (not *hanged*) *the picture you gave me.*

hardly See *but, hardly, scarcely.*

have, of After verbs such as *could, should, may,* and *might,* use *have,* not *of: You should have* (not *should of*) *told me when you were coming.*

he, she; he/she Many people today object to the use of *he* to mean *he or she* because nearly all readers think of *he* as male, whether or not that is the writer's intention. *He/she,* one substitute for *he,* is awkward and objectionable to most readers. The better choice is to make *he* plural, to use *he or she,* or to rephrase. For instance, *After the infant learns to crawl, he progresses to creeping* might be rewritten as follows: *After infants learn to crawl, they progress to creeping. After the infant learns to crawl, he or she progresses to creeping. After learning to crawl, the infant progresses to creeping.*

herself, himself See *myself, herself, himself, yourself.*

hisself Nonstandard for *himself.*

hopefully *Hopefully* means "with hope": *Freddy waited hopefully for a glimpse of Eliza.* The use of *hopefully* to mean "it is to be hoped," "I hope," or "let's hope" is now very common; but since many readers continue to object strongly to the usage, you should avoid it. *I hope* (not *Hopefully*) *Eliza will be here soon.*

if, whether For clarity, begin a subordinate clause with *whether* rather than *if* when the clause expresses an alternative: *If I laugh hard, people can't tell whether I'm crying.*

illusion See *allusion, illusion.*

impact Careful writers use both the noun and the verb *impact* to connote forceful or even violent collision. Avoid the increasingly common diluted meanings of *impact:* "an effect" (noun) or "to have an effect on" (verb). The diluted verb (*The budget cuts impacted social science research*) is bureaucratic jargon.

implicit See *explicit, implicit.*

imply, infer Writers or speakers *imply*, meaning "suggest": *Jim's letter implies he's having too good a time to miss us.* Readers or listeners *infer*, meaning "conclude": *From Jim's letter I infer he's having too good a time to miss us.*

in, into *In* indicates location or condition: *He was in the garage. She was in a coma. Into* indicates movement or a change in condition: *He went into the garage. She fell into a coma.* Colloquially, *into* has also come to mean "interested in" or "involved in": *I am into Zen.*

in . . . A number of phrases beginning with *in* are unnecessarily wordy and should be avoided: *in the event that* (for *if*); *in the neighborhood of* (for *approximately* or *about*); *in this day and age* (for *now* or *nowadays*); *in spite of the fact that* (for *although* or *even though*); and *in view of the fact that* (for *because* or *considering that*). Certain other *in* phrases are nothing but padding and can be omitted entirely: *in the case of, in nature, in number, in reality, in terms of,* and *in a very real sense.* See also 31c.

incredible, incredulous *Incredible* means "unbelievable"; *incredulous* means "unbelieving": *When Nancy heard Dennis's incredible story, she was frankly incredulous.* See also *credible, creditable, credulous.*

individual, person, party *Individual* should refer to a single human being in contrast to a group or should stress uniqueness: *The U.S. Constitution places strong emphasis on the rights of the individual.* For other meanings *person* is preferable: *What person* (not *individual*) *wouldn't want the security promised in that advertisement? Party* means "group" (*Can you seat a party of four for dinner?*) and should not be used to refer to an individual except in legal documents.

infer See *imply.*

in regards to Nonstandard for *in regard to* (or *as regards* or *regarding*). See also *regarding.*

inside of, outside of The *of* is unnecessary when *inside* and *outside* are used as prepositions: *Stay inside* (not *inside of*) *the house. The decision is outside* (not *outside of*) *my authority. Inside of* may refer colloquially to time, though in formal English *within* is preferred: *I'll meet you within* (not *inside of*) *an hour.*

instance See *case, instance, line.*

insure See *assure, ensure, insure.*

irregardless Nonstandard for *regardless.*

is because See *reason is because.*

is when, is where Mixed constructions (faulty predication; see 15b) in sentences that define: *Adolescence is a stage* (not *is when a person is*) *between childhood and adulthood. Socialism is a system in which* (not *is where*) *government owns the means of production.*

its, it's *Its* is a possessive pronoun: *That plant is losing its leaves. It's* is a contraction for *it is: It's likely to die if you don't water it.* Many people confuse *it's* and *its* because possessives are most often formed with -*'s;* but *its* in the possessive sense, like *his* and *hers,* never takes an apostrophe.

-ize, -wise The suffix -*ize* is frequently used to change a noun or adjective into a verb: *revolutionize, immunize.* The suffix -*wise* commonly changes a noun or adjective into an adverb: *clockwise, otherwise, likewise.* But the two suffixes are used excessively and often unnecessarily, especially in bureaucratic writing. Avoid their use except in established words: *The two nations are ready to settle on* (not *finalize*) *an agreement. I'm highly sensitive* (not *sensitized*) *to that kind of criticism. From a financial standpoint* (not *Moneywise*), *it's a good time to buy real estate.*

kind of, sort of, type of In formal speech and writing, avoid using *kind of* or *sort of* to mean "somewhat": *He was rather* (not *kind of*) *tall.*

Kind, sort, and *type* are singular and take singular modifiers and verbs: *This kind of dog is easily trained.* Agreement errors often occur when these singular nouns are combined with the plural demonstrative adjectives *these* and *those: These kinds* (not *kind*) *of dogs are easily trained. Kind, sort,* and *type* should be followed by *of* but not by *a: I don't know what type of* (not *type* or *type of a*) *dog that is.*

Use *kind of, sort of,* or *type of* only when the word *kind, sort,* or *type* is important: *That was a strange* (not *strange sort of*) *statement. He's a funny* (not *funny kind of*) *guy.*

later, latter *Later* refers to time; *latter* refers to the second-named of two items. See *former, latter.*

lay, lie *Lay* is a transitive verb (principal parts *lay, laid, laid*) that means "put" or "place"; it is nearly always followed by a direct object. *If we lay this tablecloth in the sun next to the shirt Sandy laid out there this morning, it should dry quickly. Lie* is an intransitive verb (principal parts *lie, lay, lain*) that means "recline" or "be situated": *I lay awake all night last night, just as I had lain the night before. The town lies east of the river.* See also 7b.

leave, let *Leave* and *let* are interchangeable only when followed by *alone; leave me alone* is the same as *let me alone.* Otherwise, *leave* means "depart" and *let* means "allow": *Julia would not let Susan leave.*

less See *fewer, less.*

let See *leave, let.*

liable See *apt, liable, likely.*

lie, lay See *lay, lie.*

like, as See *as, like.*

like, such as   When you are giving an example of something, use *such as* to indicate that the example is a representative of the thing mentioned, and use *like* to compare the example to the thing mentioned: *Steve has recordings of many great saxophonists* <u>*such as*</u> *Ben Webster, Coleman Hawkins, and Lee Konitz. Steve wants to be a great jazz saxophonist* <u>*like*</u> *Ben Webster, Coleman Hawkins, and Lee Konitz.*

Most writers prefer to keep *such* and *as* together: *Steve admires saxophonists* <u>*such as*</u> *. . .* , rather than *Steve admires* <u>*such*</u> *saxophonists* <u>*as*</u>*. . . .*

likely   See *apt, liable, likely.*

line   See *case, instance, line.*

lose, loose   *Lose* is a verb meaning "mislay": *Did you* <u>*lose*</u> *a brown glove? Loose* is an adjective meaning "unrestrained" or "not tight": *Don't open the door; Ann's canary got* <u>*loose*</u>*. Loose* also can function as a verb meaning "let loose": *They* <u>*loose*</u> *the dogs as soon as they spot the bear.*

lots, lots of   Colloquial substitutes for *very many, a great many,* or *much.*

may, can   See *can, may.*

may be, maybe   *May be* is a verb, and *maybe* is an adverb meaning "perhaps": *Tuesday* <u>*may be*</u> *a legal holiday.* <u>*Maybe*</u> *we won't have classes.*

may of   See *have, of.*

media   *Media* is the plural of *medium: Of all the news* <u>*media*</u>*, television is the only* <u>*medium*</u> *with more visual than verbal content.*

might of   See *have, of.*

moral, morale   As a noun, *moral* means "ethical conclusion" or "lesson": *The* <u>*moral*</u> *of the story escapes me. Morale* means "spirit" or "state of mind": *Victory improved the team's* <u>*morale*</u>*.*

most, almost   See *almost, most.*

must of   See *have, of.*

myself, herself, himself, yourself   The *-self* pronouns are reflexive or intensive, which means they refer to or intensify an antecedent (see 5a-3): *Paul and I did it* <u>*ourselves*</u>*; Jill* <u>*herself*</u> *said so.* Though the *-self* pronouns often are used colloquially in place of personal pronouns, especially as objects of prepositions, they should be avoided in formal speech and writing unless the noun or pronoun they refer to is also present: *No one except* <u>*me*</u> *(not* <u>*myself*</u>*) saw the accident. Our delegates will be Susan and* <u>*you*</u> *(not* <u>*yourself*</u>*).*

nohow   Nonstandard for *in no way* or *in any way.*

nothing like, nowhere near   As colloquial substitutes for *not nearly,* these idioms are best avoided in formal speech and writing: *The human bones found in Europe are* <u>*not nearly*</u> *(not* <u>*nowhere near*</u>*) as old as those found in Africa.*

nowheres   Nonstandard for *nowhere.*

number   See *amount, number.*

of, have See *have, of.*

off of *Of* is unnecessary. Use *off* or *from* rather than *off of: He jumped off* (or *from*, not *off of*) *the roof.*

OK, O.K., okay All three spellings are acceptable, but avoid this colloquial term in formal speech and writing.

on, upon In modern English, *upon* is usually just a stuffy way of saying *on.* Unless you need a formal effect, use *on: We decided on* (not *upon*) *a location for our next meeting.*

on account of Wordy for *because of.*

on the other hand This transitional expression of contrast should be preceded by its mate, *on the one hand: On the one hand, we hoped for snow. On the other hand, we feared that it would harm the animals.* However, the two combined can be unwieldy, and a simple *but, however, yet,* or *in contrast* often suffices: *We hoped for snow. Yet we feared that it would harm the animals.*

outside of See *inside of, outside of.*

owing to the fact that Wordy for *because.*

party See *individual, person, party.*

people, persons In formal speech and writing, *people* refers to a general group: *We the people of the United States.* . . . *Persons* refers to a collection of individuals: *Will the person or persons who saw the accident please notify.* . . . Except when emphasis on individuals is desired, *people* is preferable to *persons.*

per Except in technical writing, an English equivalent is usually preferable to the Latin *per: $10 an* (not *per*) *hour; sent by* (not *per*) *parcel post; requested in* (not *per* or *as per*) *your letter.*

percent (per cent), percentage Both these terms refer to fractions of one hundred and should be avoided except when specifying actual statistics. Use an expression such as *part of, a number of,* or *a high* (or *small*) *proportion of* when you mean simply "part."
   Percent always follows a numeral (*40 percent of the voters*), and the word should be used instead of the symbol (%) in formal writing. *Percentage* usually follows an adjective (*a high percentage*).

person See *individual, person, party.*

persons See *people, persons.*

persuade See *convince, persuade.*

phenomena The plural of *phenomenon* (meaning "perceivable fact" or "unusual occurrence"): *We phoned the Center for Short-Lived Phenomena to find out whether the phenomenon we had witnessed might be a flying saucer.*

plenty A colloquial substitute for *very: He was going very* (not *plenty*) *fast when he hit that tree.*

plus   *Plus* is standard as a preposition meaning *in addition to: His income plus mine is sufficient.* But *plus* is colloquial as a conjunctive adverb: *Our organization is larger than theirs; moreover* (not *plus*), *we have more money.*

practicable, practical   *Practicable* means "capable of being put into practice"; *practical* means "useful" or "sensible": *We figured out a practical new design for our kitchen, but it was too expensive to be practicable.*

gl/us

precede, proceed   The verb *precede* means "to come before": *My name precedes yours in the alphabet.* The verb *proceed* means "to move on": *We were told to proceed to the waiting room.*

pretty   Overworked as an adverb meaning "rather" or "somewhat": *He was somewhat* (not *pretty*) *irked at the suggestion.*

previous to, prior to   Wordy for *before.*

principal, principle   *Principal* is a noun meaning "chief official" or, in finance, "capital sum." As an adjective, *principal* means "foremost" or "major." *Principle* is a noun only, meaning "rule" or "axiom." *Her principal reasons for confessing were her principles of right and wrong.*

proceed, precede   See *precede, proceed.*

question of whether, question as to whether   Wordy for *whether.*

raise, rise   *Raise* is a transitive verb and takes a direct object, and *rise* is intransitive: *The Bennetts have to rise at dawn because they raise cows.*

real, really   In formal speech and writing, *real* should not be used as an adverb; *really* is the adverb and *real* an adjective. *Popular reaction to the announcement was really* (not *real*) *enthusiastic.*

reason is because   Mixed construction (faulty predication; see 15b). Although the expression is colloquially common, formal speech and writing require a *that* clause after *reason is: The reason he is absent is that* (not *is because*) *he is sick.* Or: *He is absent because he is sick.*

reckon   See *calculate, figure, reckon.*

regarding, in regard to, with regard to, relating to, relative to, with respect to, respecting   Stuffy substitutes for *on, about,* or *concerning: Mr. McGee spoke about* (not *with regard to*) *the plans for the merger.*

respectful, respective   *Respectful* means "full of (or showing) respect": *If you want respect, be respectful of other people. Respective* means "separate": *After a joint Christmas celebration, the French and the Germans returned to their respective trenches.*

rise, raise   See *raise, rise.*

scarcely   See *but, hardly, scarcely.*

sensual, sensuous   *Sensual* suggests sexuality; *sensuous* means "pleasing to the senses." *Stirred by the sensuous scent of meadow grass and flowers, Cheryl and Paul found their thoughts growing increasingly sensual.*

set, sit   *Set* is a transitive verb (principal parts *set, set, set*) that describes something a person does to an object: *He set the pitcher down. Sit* is an intransitive verb (principal parts *sit, sat, sat*) that describes something done by a person who is tired of standing: *She sits on the sofa.* See also 7b.

shall, will *Will,* originally reserved for the second and third persons, is now generally accepted as the future-tense auxiliary for all three persons: *I will go, you will go, they will go.* The main use of *shall* is for first-person questions requesting an opinion or consent: *Shall I order a pizza? Shall we dance?* (Questions that merely inquire about the future use *will: When will I see you again?*) *Shall* can also be used for the first person when a formal effect is desired: *I shall expect you around three.*

should, would *Should* expresses obligation for first, second, and third persons: *I should fix dinner. You should set the table. Jack should wash the dishes. Would* expresses a wish or hypothetical condition for all three persons: *I would do it. Wouldn't you? Wouldn't anybody?* When the context is formal, however, *should* is sometimes used instead of *would* in the first person: *We should be delighted to accept your kind invitation.*

should of See *have, of.*

since *Since* is often used to mean "because": *Since you ask, I'll tell you.* Its primary meaning, however, relates to time: *I've been waiting since noon.* To avoid confusion, some writers prefer to use *since* only in contexts involving time. If you do use *since* in both senses, watch out for ambiguous constructions, such as *Since you left, my life is empty,* where *since* could mean either "because" or "ever since."

sit, set See *set, sit.*

situation Often unnecessary, as in *The situation is that we have to get some help* (revise to *We have to get some help*) or *The team was faced with a punting situation* (revise to *The team was faced with punting* or *The team had to punt*).

some *Some* is colloquial as an adverb meaning "somewhat" or "to some extent" and as an adjective meaning "remarkable": *We'll have to hurry somewhat* (not *some*) *to get there in time. Those are remarkable* (not *some*) *photographs.*

somebody, some body; someone, some one *Somebody* and *someone* are indefinite pronouns; *some body* is a noun modified by an adjective; and *some one* is a pronoun or an adjective modified by *some. Somebody ought to invent a shampoo that will give hair some body. Someone told Janine she should choose some one plan and stick with it.*

someplace Informal for *somewhere.*

sometime, sometimes, some time *Sometime* means "at an indefinite time in the future": *Why don't you come up and see me sometime? Sometimes* means "now and then": *I still see my old friend Joe sometimes. Some time* means "span of time": *I need some time to make the payments.*

somewheres Nonstandard for *somewhere.*

sort of, sort of a See *kind of, sort of, type of.*

specially   See *especially, specially*.

such   Avoid using *such* as a vague intensifier: *It was such a cold winter.* *Such* should be followed by *that* and a clause that states a result: *It was such a cold winter that Napoleon's troops had to turn back.*

such as   See *like, such as*.

supposed to, used to   In both these expressions, the *-d* is essential: *I used to* (not *use to*) *think so. He's supposed to* (not *suppose to*) *meet us.*

sure   Colloquial when used as an adverb meaning *surely: James Madison sure was right about the need for the Bill of Rights.* If you merely want to be emphatic, use *certainly: Madison certainly was right.* If your goal is to convince a possibly reluctant reader, use *surely: Madison surely was right. Surely Madison was right.*

sure and, sure to; try and, try to   *Sure to* and *try to* are the preferred forms: *Be sure to* (not *sure and*) *buy milk. Try to* (not *Try and*) *find some decent tomatoes.*

take, bring   See *bring, take*.

than, as   See *as, than*.

than, then   *Than* is a conjunction used in comparisons, *then* an adverb indicating time: *Holmes knew then that Moriarty was wilier than he had thought.*

that, which   *That* always introduces restrictive clauses: *We should see the lettuce that Susan bought* (*that Susan bought* identifies the specific lettuce being referred to). *Which* can introduce both restrictive and nonrestrictive clauses, but many writers reserve *which* only for nonrestrictive clauses: *The leftover lettuce, which is in the refrigerator, would make a good salad* (*which is in the refrigerator* simply provides more information about the lettuce). See also 21c.

their, there, they're   *Their* is the possessive form of *they: Give them their money. There* indicates place (*I saw her standing there*) or functions as an expletive (*There is a hole behind you*). *They're* is a contraction for *they are: Get them now — they're going fast.*

theirselves   Nonstandard for *themselves*.

then, than   See *than, then*.

these kind, these sort, these type, those kind   See *kind of, sort of, type of*.

this here, these here, that there, them there   Nonstandard for *this, these, that,* or *those*.

thusly   A mistaken form of *thus*.

till, until, 'til   *Till* and *until* have the same meaning; both are acceptable. *'Til*, a contraction of *until*, is an old form that has been replaced by *till*.

to, too   *To* is a preposition, *too* an adverb meaning "also" or "excessively": *I too have been to Europe.*

gl/us

toward, towards   Both are acceptable, though *toward* is preferred. Use one or the other consistently.

try and, try to   See *sure and, sure to; try and, try to.*

type of   See *kind of, sort of, type of.* Don't use *type* without *of: It was a family type of* (not *type*) *restaurant.* Or, better: *It was a family restaurant.*

uninterested   See *disinterested, uninterested.*

unique   As an absolute adjective (see 9e-5), *unique* cannot sensibly be modified with words such as *very* or *most: That was a unique* (not *a very* or *the most unique*) *movie.*

until   See *till, until, 'til.*

upon, on   See *on, upon.*

usage, use   *Usage* refers to conventions, most often those of a language: *Is "hadn't ought" proper usage? Usage* is often misused to mean *use: Wise use* (not *usage*) *of insulation can save fuel.*

use, utilize   *Utilize* means "make use of": *We should utilize John's talent for mimicry in our play.* In most contexts, *use* is equally or more acceptable and much less stuffy.

used to   See *supposed to, used to.*

wait for, wait on   In formal speech and writing, *wait for* means "await" (*I'm waiting for Paul*), and *wait on* means "serve" (*The owner of the store herself waited on us*).

ways   Colloquial as a substitute for *way: We have only a little way* (not *ways*) *to go.*

well   See *good, well.*

whether, if   See *if, whether.*

which   See *that, which.*

which, who   *Which* never refers to people. Use *who* or sometimes *that* for a person or persons and *which* or *that* for a thing or things: *The baby, who was left behind, opened the door, which we had closed.* See also 12f.

who's, whose   *Who's* is the contraction of *who is: Who's at the door? Whose* is the possessive form of *who: Whose book is that?*

will, shall   See *shall, will.*

-wise   See *-ize, -wise.*

with regard to, with respect to   See *regarding.*

would   See *should, would.*

your, you're   *Your* is the possessive form of *you: Your dinner is ready. You're* is the contraction of *you are: You're bound to be late.*

yourself   See *myself, herself, himself, yourself.*

Glossary of Grammatical Terms

absolute phrase A phrase that consists of a noun or pronoun and a participle, modifies a whole clause or sentence (rather than a single word), and is not joined to the rest of the sentence by a connector: *Our accommodations arranged, we set out on our trip. They will hire a local person, other things being equal.* When the participle in an absolute phrase is a form of the verb *be* (*being, been*), the participle is often omitted: *They will hire a local person, other things equal.* See also 5c-3 and 21d.

abstract noun See *noun.*

acronym A pronounceable word formed from the initial letter or letters of each word in an organization's title: NATO (North Atlantic Treaty Organization). See also 20b and 28b.

active voice See *verb.*

adjectival A term sometimes used to describe any word or word group, other than an adjective, that is used to modify a noun. Common adjectivals include nouns (*wagon train, railroad ties*), phrases (*fool on the hill*), and clauses (*the man that I used to be*). See *clause* and *phrase.* See also 5c.

adjective A word used to modify a noun or a word or word group used as a noun.

> **Descriptive adjectives** name some quality of the noun: *beautiful morning; dark horse.*

> **Limiting adjectives** narrow the scope of a noun. They include **possessives** (*my, their*); words that show number (*eight, several*); **demonstrative adjectives** (*this train, these days*); and **interrogative adjectives** (*what time? whose body?*)

> **Proper adjectives** are derived from proper nouns: *French fries, Machiavellian scheme.*

Adjectives also can be classified according to position.

> **Attributive adjectives** appear next to the nouns they modify: *full moon.*

Predicate adjectives are connected to their nouns by linking verbs: *The moon is full.* See also *complement.*

See also *comparison,* 5b-1, and Chapter 9.

adjective clause   See *clause.*

adjective phrase   See *phrase.*

adverb   A word used to modify a verb, an adjective, another adverb, or a whole sentence. Any one-word modifier that is not an adjective, a word used as an adjective, or an article is an adverb: *If you go south you'll hit a more heavily traveled road. South* modifies the verb *go; heavily* modifies the adjective *traveled;* and *more* modifies the adverb *heavily.*) See also *comparison,* 5b-1, and Chapter 9.

adverb clause   See *clause.*

adverbial   A term sometimes used to describe any word or word group, other than an adverb, that is used to modify a verb, adjective, other adverb, or whole sentence. Common adverbials include nouns (*This little piggy stayed home*), phrases (*This little piggy went to market*), and clauses (*This little piggy went wherever he wanted*). See *clause* and *phrase.* See also 5c.

adverbial conjunction   See *conjunctive adverb.*

adverb phrase   See *phrase.*

agreement   The correspondence of one word to another in person, number, or gender. A verb must agree with its subject; a pronoun must agree with its antecedent; and a demonstrative adjective must agree with its noun: *Every week the commander orders these kinds of sandwiches for his troops.* (The verb *orders* and the pronoun *his* both agree with the noun *commander.* The demonstrative adjective *these* agrees with the noun *kinds.*) See Chapter 8.

antecedent   The noun, or word or word group acting as a noun, to which a pronoun refers: *Jonah, who is not yet ten, has already chosen the college he will attend.* (*Jonah* is the antecedent of the pronouns *who* and *he.*) See also 8b.

appositive   A word or phrase appearing next to a noun or pronoun, or to a word or word group acting as a noun, which explains or identifies it and is equivalent to it: *My brother Michael, the best horn player in town, won the state competition.* (*Michael* is a restrictive appositive that identifies which brother is being referred to. *The best horn player in town* is a nonrestrictive appositive that adds information about *My brother Michael.*) See also 5c-5 and 21c-2.

article   The words *a* and *an* (**indefinite articles**) and the word *the* (**definite article**). Articles are usually classed as adjectives; they are sometimes called **determiners** because they always signal that a noun will follow.

auxiliary verb   A verb (also called a **helping verb**) used with a main verb in a verb phrase: *will give, has been seeing, could depend.* Auxiliaries indicate tense and sometimes also indicate voice, person, number, or mood. **Modal auxiliaries** include *can, could, may, might, must, ought, shall, should, will,* and *would.* They indicate a necessity, possibility, capability, willingness, or the like: *He can lift 250 pounds. You should write to your grandmother.* See also 5a-2 and Chapter 7.

cardinal number   The type of number that shows amount: *two, sixty, ninety-seven.* Contrast *ordinal number* (such as *second, ninety-seventh*).

case   The form of a noun or pronoun that indicates its function in the sentence. Nouns have two cases: the **plain case** (*John, ambassador*), for all uses except to show possession; and the **possessive** (or **genitive**) **case** (*John's, ambassador's*). Pronouns have three cases: the **subjective** (or **nominative**) **case** (*I, she*), denoting the subject of a verb or a subject complement; the **possessive case,** for use as either an adjective (*my, her*) or a noun (*mine, hers*); and the **objective case** (*me, her*), denoting the object of a verb, verbal, or preposition. See *declension* for a complete list of the forms of personal and relative pronouns. See also Chapter 6.

clause   A group of related words containing a subject and predicate. Clauses are either **main** (**independent**) or **subordinate** (**dependent**). A main clause can stand by itself as a sentence; a subordinate clause cannot.

MAIN CLAUSE	*We can go to the movies*
SUBORDINATE CLAUSE	We can go *if Julie gets back on time.*

Subordinate clauses may function as adjectives, adverbs, or nouns.

Adjective clauses modify nouns or pronouns: *The car that hit Fred was running a red light* (clause modifies *car*).

Adverb clauses modify verbs, adjectives, other adverbs, or whole clauses or sentences: *The car hit Fred when it ran a red light* (clause modifies *hit*).

Noun clauses, like nouns, function as subjects, objects, or complements: *Whoever was driving should be arrested* (clause is sentence subject).

See also 5c-4.

collective noun   See *noun.*

comma splice   A sentence error in which two main clauses are linked by a comma with no coordinating conjunction.

COMMA SPLICE	The book was long, it contained useful information.
REVISED	The book was long; it contained useful information.
REVISED	The book was long, *but* it contained useful information.

See 11a and 11b.

common noun   See *noun.*

comparative See *comparison.*

comparison The inflection of an adverb or adjective that shows its relative intensity. The **positive degree** is the simple, uncompared form: *gross, clumsily.* The **comparative degree** compares the thing modified to at least one other thing: *grosser, more clumsily.* The **superlative degree** indicates that the thing modified exceeds all other things to which it is being compared: *grossest, most clumsily.* The comparative and superlative degrees are formed either by adding the endings *-er* and *-est* or by preceding the modifier with the words *more* and *most, less* and *least.* See also 5b-1 and 9e.

gl/gr

complement A word or word group that completes the sense of a subject, an object, or a verb.

> **Subject complements** follow a linking verb and modify or refer to the subject. They may be adjectives, nouns or pronouns, or words or word groups acting as adjectives or nouns: *I am a lion tamer, but I am not yet experienced.* (The noun *lion tamer* and the adjective *experienced* complement the subject *I.*) Adjective complements are also called **predicate adjectives.** Noun complements are also called **predicate nouns** or **predicate nominatives.**
>
> **Object complements** follow and modify or refer to direct objects. The complement can be an adjective, a noun, or a word or word group acting as an adjective or noun: *If you elect me president, I'll keep the unions satisfied.* (The noun *president* complements the direct object *me,* and the adjective *satisfied* complements that direct object *unions.*)
>
> **Verb complements** are direct and indirect objects of verbs. They may be nouns, pronouns, or words or word groups acting as nouns: *Don't give the chimp that peanut.* (*Chimp* is the indirect object and *peanut* is the direct object of the verb *give.* Both objects are verb complements.)

See also *object* and 5a-3.

complete predicate See *predicate.*

complete subject See *subject.*

complex sentence See *sentence.*

compound Consisting of two or more words that function as a unit. **Compound words** include **compound nouns** (*milestone, featherbrain*); **compound adjectives** (*two-year-old, downtrodden*); and **compound prepositions** (*in addition to, on account of*). **Compound constructions** include **compound subjects** (*Harriet and Peter poled their barge down the river*) and **compound predicates** (*The scout watched and waited*), or parts of predicates (*He grew tired and hungry*). See also 5d.

compound-complex sentence See *sentence.*

compound predicate See *compound.*

compound sentence See *sentence.*

compound subject See *compound.*

concrete noun See *noun.*

conjugation A list of the forms of a verb showing tense, voice, mood, person, and number. The conjugation of the verb *know* in present tense, active voice, indicative mood is *I know, you know, he/she/it knows, we know, you know, they know.* See also Chapter 7.

conjunction A word that links and relates two parts of a sentence. **Coordinating conjunctions** (*and, but, or, nor, for, so, yet*) connect words or word groups of equal grammatical rank: *The lights went out, but the doctors and nurses cared for their patients as if nothing were wrong.* See also 5d-1. **Correlative conjunctions** or **correlatives** (such as *either . . . or, not only . . . but also*) are pairs of coordinating conjunctions that work together: *He was certain that either his parents or his brother would help him.* See also 5d-1. **Subordinating conjunctions** (*after, although, as if, because, if, when, while,* and so on) begin a dependent clause and link it to an independent clause. *The seven dwarfs whistle while they work.* See also 5c-4.

conjunctive adverb (adverbial conjunction) An adverb (such as *also, besides, consequently, indeed,* and *therefore*) that links two main clauses in a sentence: *We had hoped to own a house by now; however, housing costs have risen too fast.* See also 5d-2.

connector (connective) Any word or phrase that links words, phrases, clauses, or sentences. Common connectors include coordinating, correlative, and subordinating conjunctions; conjunctive adverbs; and prepositions.

connotation An association called up by a word, beyond its dictionary definition. See 31b-1. Contrast *denotation.*

construction Any group of grammatically related words, such as a phrase, a clause, or a sentence.

contraction A condensation of an expression, with an apostrophe replacing the missing letters: for example, *doesn't* (for *does not*), *we'll* (for *we will*). See also 23c.

coordinating conjunction See *conjunction.*

coordination The use of grammatically parallel constructions to indicate that parts of a sentence, compound units within a sentence, or successive sentences within a paragraph are of equal importance: *He laughed, and I winced.* See also 16a. Contrast *subordination.*

correlative conjunction (correlative) See *conjunction.*

dangling modifier A word or phrase modifying a term that has been omitted or to which it cannot easily be linked.

DANGLING	*Having arrived late,* the concert had already begun.
REVISED	Having arrived late, *we* found that the concert had already begun.

gl/gr

    REVISED   *Because we arrived late,* we missed the beginning of the concert.

See also 14g.

declension   A list of the forms of a noun or pronoun, showing inflections for person (for pronouns), number, and case. See Chapter 6. The following chart shows a complete declension of the personal and relative pronouns.

Personal pronouns	*Subjective*	*Objective*	*Possessive*
Singular			
First person	I	me	my, mine
Second person	you	you	your, yours
Third person			
Masculine	he	him	his
Feminine	she	her	her, hers
Neuter	it	it	its
Plural			
First person	we	us	our, ours
Second person	you	you	your, yours
Third person	they	them	their, theirs
Relative pronouns	who	whom	whose
	which	which	whose, of which
	that	that	—

degree   See *comparison.*

demonstrative adjective   See *adjective.*

demonstrative pronoun   See *pronoun.*

denotation   The main or dictionary definition of a word. See 31b-1. Contrast *connotation.*

dependent clause   See *clause.*

derivational suffix   See *suffix.*

descriptive adjective   See *adjective.*

determiner   A word such as *a, an, the, my,* and *your* which indicates that a noun follows. See also *article.*

diagramming   A visual method of identifying and showing the relations among various parts of a sentence.

direct address   A construction in which a word or phrase indicates the person, group, or thing spoken to: *Have you finished, John? Farmers, unite.*

direct object   See *object.*

direct quotation (direct discourse)   See *quotation.*

double negative   A nonstandard form consisting of two negative words used in the same construction so that they effectively cancel each other: *I don't have no money.* Rephrase as *I have no money* or *I don't have any money.*

double possessive   A possessive using both the ending *-'s* and the preposition *of: That is a favorite expression of Mark's.*

ellipsis   The omission of a word or words from a quotation, indicated by the three spaced periods of an **ellipsis mark:** *"that all . . . are created equal."* See also 25e.

elliptical clause   A clause omitting a word or words whose meaning is understood from the rest of the clause: *David likes Minneapolis better than (he likes) Chicago.* See also 5c-4.

expletive   A sentence construction that postpones the subject by beginning with *there* or *it* followed by a form of the verb *be: It is impossible to get a ticket; I don't know why there aren't more seats available.* (*To get a ticket* is the subject of *is; seats* is the subject of *aren't.*) See also 5e-4.

finite verb   A term used to describe any verb that makes an assertion or expresses a state of being and can stand as the main verb of a sentence or clause: *The moose eats the leaves.* See also 5c-2. Contrast *gerund, participle,* and *infinitive* — all formed from finite verbs but unable to stand alone as the main verb of a sentence: *I saw the moose eating the leaves* (participle). Contrast also *verbal (nonfinite verb).*

fragment   See *sentence fragment.*

function word   A word, such as an article, conjunction, or preposition, that serves primarily to clarify the roles of and relations between other words in a sentence: *We chased the goat for an hour but finally caught it.* Contrast *lexical word.*

fused sentence   See *run-on sentence.*

future perfect tense   See *tense.*

future tense   See *tense.*

gender   The classification of nouns or pronouns as masculine (*he, boy, handyman*), feminine (*she, woman, actress*), or neuter (*it, typewriter, dog*).

genitive case   Another term for possessive case. See *case.*

gerund   A verbal that ends in *-ing* and functions as a noun. The form of the gerund is the same as that of the present participle. Gerunds may have subjects, objects, complements, and modifiers: *Working is all right for killing time.* (*Working* is the subject of the verb *is; killing* is the object of the preposition *for* and takes the object *time.*) See also 5c-2, *verbal,* and *participle.*

helping verb   See *auxiliary verb.*

idiom   An expression that is peculiar to a language and that may not make sense if taken literally: for example, *dark horse, bide your time,* and *by and large.* See 31b-3 for a list of idioms involving prepositions, such as *agree with them* and *agree to the contract.*

imperative   See *mood.*

indefinite pronoun   See *pronoun.*

independent clause   See *clause*.

indicative   See *mood*.

indirect object   See *object*.

indirect quotation (indirect discourse)   See *quotation*.

infinitive   The plain form of a verb, the form listed in the dictionary: *buy, sharpen, rinse.* Usually in combination with the **infinitive marker** *to,* infinitives form verbals and verbal phrases that function as nouns, adjectives, or adverbs. They may have objects, complements, or modifiers: *Alex's goals are to make money and to live well.* (*To make* and *to live,* following a linking verb, are complements of the subject *goals. To make* takes the object *money* and *to live* is modified by the adverb *well.*) See also 5c-2.

infinitive marker   See *infinitive*.

infinitive phrase   See *phrase*.

inflection   The variation in the form of a word that indicates its function in a particular context. See *declension,* the inflection of nouns and pronouns; *conjugation,* the inflection of verbs; and *comparison,* the inflection of adjectives and adverbs.

inflectional suffix   See *suffix*.

intensifier   A modifier that adds emphasis to the word(s) it modifies: for example, *very slow, so angry.*

intensive pronoun   See *pronoun*.

interjection   A word standing by itself or inserted in a construction to exclaim or command attention: *Hey! Ouch! What the heck did you do that for?*

interrogative   Functioning as or involving a question.

interrogative adjective   See *adjective*.

interrogative pronoun   See *pronoun*.

intransitive verb   See *verb*.

inversion   A reversal of usual word order in a sentence, as when a verb precedes its subject or an object precedes its verb: *Down swooped the hawk. Our aims we stated clearly.*

irregular verb   A verb that forms its past tense and past participle in some other way than by the addition of *-d* or *-ed* to the plain form: for example, *go, went, gone; give, gave, given.* See also 5a; and see 7a for a list of irregular verbs. Contrast *regular verb.*

lexical word   A word, such as a noun, verb, or modifier, that carries part of the meaning of language. Contrast *function word.*

linking verb   A verb that relates a subject to its complement: *Julie is a Democrat. He looks harmless. Those flowers smell heavenly.* Common linking verbs are the forms of *be;* the verbs relating to the senses, such as *feel* and *smell;* and the verbs *become, appear,* and *seem.* See also 5a-3 and *verb.*

main clause See *clause.*

misplaced modifier A modifier so far from the term it modifies or so close to another term it could modify that its relation to the rest of the sentence is unclear.

MISPLACED	The boys played with firecrackers that they bought illegally *in the field.*
REVISED	The boys played *in the field* with firecrackers that they bought illegally.

A misplaced modifier that falls between two nouns and could modify either is called a **squinting modifier.**

SQUINTING	The plan we considered *seriously* worries me.
REVISED	The plan we *seriously* considered worries me.
REVISED	The plan we considered worries me *seriously.*

See also 14a to 14f.

mixed construction A sentence containing two or more parts that do not fit together in grammar or in meaning.

MIXED	Of those who show up, they will not all be able to get in.
REVISED	Not all of those who show up will be able to get in.

See also 15a and 15b.

modal auxiliary See *auxiliary verb.*

modifier Any word or word group that limits or qualifies the meaning of another word or word group. Modifiers include adjectives and adverbs as well as words, phrases, and clauses that act as adjectives and adverbs.

mood The form of a verb that shows how the speaker views the action. The **indicative mood,** the most common, is used to make statements or ask questions: *The play will be performed Saturday. Did you get us tickets?* The **imperative mood** gives a command: *Please get good seats. Don't let them put us in the top balcony.* The **subjunctive mood** expresses a wish, a condition contrary to fact, a recommendation, or a request: *I wish George were coming with us. Did you suggest that he join us?* See also 7f.

nominal A noun, a pronoun, or a word or group of words used as a noun: *Joan and I talked. The rich owe a debt to the poor* (adjectives acting as subject and object). *Baby-sitting can be exhausting* (gerund acting as subject). *I like to play with children* (infinitive phrase acting as object).

nominative See *case.*

nonfinite verb See *verbal.*

nonrestrictive modifier A modifying word, phrase, or clause that does not limit the term or construction it modifies and that is not essential to the meaning of the sentence's main clause. Nonrestrictive modifiers are usually set off by commas: *This electric mixer, on sale for one week only, can be plugged directly into your kitchen counter* (nonrestrictive adjective phrase). *Sleep, which we all need, occupies a third of our lives* (nonrestrictive adjective clause). See also 21c. Contrast *restrictive modifier.*

noun A word that names a person, place, thing, quality, or idea: *Maggie, Alabama, clarinet, satisfaction, socialism.* Nouns normally form the possessive case by adding *-'s* (*Maggie's*) and the plural by adding *-s* or *-es* (*clarinets, messes*), although there are exceptions (*men, women, children*).

> **Common nouns** refer to general classes: *book, government, music.*
>
> **Proper nouns** name specific people or places: *Susan, Athens, Candlestick Park.*
>
> **Collective nouns** name groups: *team, class, jury, family.*
>
> **Count nouns** name things that can be counted: *ounce, camera, pencil.*
>
> **Mass nouns** name things that are not normally counted: *jewelry, milk.*
>
> **Concrete nouns** name tangible things: *ink, porch, bird.*
>
> **Abstract nouns** name ideas or qualities: *equality, greed, capitalism.*

See also 5a-2.

noun clause See *clause.*

number The form of a noun, pronoun, demonstrative adjective, or verb that indicates whether it is singular or plural: *woman, women; I, we; this, these; runs, run.* See also Chapter 8.

object A noun, a pronoun, or a word or word group acting as a noun that receives the action of or is influenced by a transitive verb, a verbal, or a preposition.

> **Direct objects** receive the action of verbs and verbals and frequently follow them in a sentence: *We sat watching the stars. Emily caught whatever it was you had.*
>
> **Indirect objects** tell for or to whom or what something is done: *I lent Stan my car. Reiner bought us all champagne.*
>
> **Objects of prepositions** usually follow prepositions and are linked by them to the rest of the sentence: *They are going to New Orleans for the jazz festival.*

See also 5a-3 and 5c-1.

object complement See *complement.*

objective See *case.*

ordinal number The type of number that shows order: *first, eleventh, twenty-fifth.* Contrast *cardinal number* (such as *one, twenty-five*).

parenthetical element A word or construction that interrupts a sentence and is not part of its main structure, called *parenthetical* because it could (or does) appear in parentheses: *We will continue (barring further interruptions) with the next paragraph. This book, incidentally, is terrible.*

participial phrase See *phrase.*

participle A verbal showing continuing or completed action, used as an adjective, adverb, or part of a verb phrase but never as the main verb of a sentence or clause.

> **Present participles** end in *-ing*: *My heart is breaking* (participle as part of verb with auxiliary). *I like to watch the rolling waves* (participle as adjective). *He came running* (participle as adverb).

> **Past participles** most commonly end in *-d, -ed, -n,* or *-en* (*wished, shown, given*) but often change the spelling of the verb (*sung, done, slept*): *Jeff has broken his own record* (participle as part of verb with auxiliary). *The meeting occurred behind a closed door* (participle as adjective).

See also *gerund,* 5b-2, and 5c-2.

parts of speech The classes into which words are commonly grouped according to their form, function, and meaning: nouns, pronouns, verbs, adjectives, adverbs, conjunctions, prepositions, and interjections. See separate entries for each part of speech. See also 5a to 5d.

passive voice See *verb.*

past participle See *participle.*

past perfect tense See *tense.*

past tense See *tense.*

perfect tenses See *tense.*

person The form of a verb or pronoun that indicates whether the subject is speaking, spoken to, or spoken about. In English only personal pronouns and verbs change form to indicate difference in person. In the **first person,** the subject is speaking: *I am* (or *We are*) *planning to go to the party tonight.* In the **second person,** the subject is being spoken to: *Are you coming?* In the **third person,** the subject is being spoken about: *She was* (or *They were*) *going.*

personal pronoun See *pronoun.*

phrase A group of related words that lacks a subject or a predicate or both and that acts as a single part of speech. There are several common types of phrases:

> **Verb phrases** are verb forms of more than one word that serve as predicates of sentences or clauses: *He says the movie has started.*

> **Prepositional phrases** consist of a preposition and its object, plus any modifiers. They function as adjectives, as adverbs, and occasionally as nouns: *We could come back for the second show* (adverb).

gl/gr

Infinitive phrases consist of an infinitive and its object, plus any modifiers, and they sometimes also include a subject. They function as nouns, adjectives, and adverbs: *I'd hate to go all the way home* (noun).

Participial phrases consist of a participle and its object, plus any modifiers. They function as adjectives and adverbs: *The man collecting tickets says we may not be too late* (adjective).

Gerund phrases consist of a gerund (the *-ing* form of a verb used as a noun) and its object, plus any modifiers, and they sometimes also include a subject. They function as nouns: *Missing the beginning is no good, though.*

Absolute phrases consist of a noun or pronoun and usually a participle. They modify whole clauses or sentences: *Our seats being reserved, we probably should stay.* See also *absolute phrase.*

See also 5c-3.

plain case See *case.*

plain form The infinitive or dictionary form of a verb. See *infinitive.*

positive degree See *comparison.*

possessive See *case.*

predicate The part of a sentence other than the subject and its modifiers. A predicate must contain a finite verb and may contain modifiers and objects of the verb as well as object and subject complements. The **simple predicate** consists of the verb and its auxiliaries: *A wiser person would have made a different decision.* The **complete predicate** includes the simple predicate and any modifiers, objects, and complements: *A wiser person would have made a different decision.* See also 5a and 5b.

predicate adjective See *complement.*

predicate noun (predicate nominative) See *complement.*

prefix A letter or group of letters (such as *sub-, in-, dis-, pre-*) that can be added at the beginning of a root or word to create a new word: *sub-* + *marine* = *submarine; dis-* + *grace* = *disgrace.* See also 33b-2. Contrast *suffix.*

preposition A word that links a noun, a pronoun, or a word or word group acting as a noun (the object of the preposition) to the rest of a sentence: *If Tim doesn't hear from that plumber by four, he'll call someone else before dinner.* Common prepositions include those in the preceding example as well as *about, after, beside, between, for, in,* and *to.* See 5c-1 for a more complete list. See also *object* and *phrase.*

prepositional phrase See *phrase.*

present participle See *participle.*

present perfect tense See *tense.*

present tense See *tense.*

principal clause   An independent or main clause. See *clause*.

principal parts   The three forms of a verb from which its various tenses are formed: the **plain form** or **infinitive** (*stop, go*); the **past tense** (*stopped, went*); and the **past participle** (*stopped, gone*). See *infinitive*, *participle*, and *tense*. See also 5a-2 and Chapter 7.

progressive tense   See *tense*.

pronoun   A word used in place of a noun or noun phrase (its antecedent). There are eight types of pronouns, many of which differ only in function, not in form:

> **Personal pronouns** (*I, you, he, she, it, we, they*): *They want you to come with us.*
>
> **Reflexive pronouns** (*myself, themselves*): *Can't you help yourselves?*
>
> **Intensive pronouns** (*myself, themselves*): *I myself saw it. She herself said so.*
>
> **Interrogative pronouns** (*who, which, what*): *What was that? Which is mine?*
>
> **Relative pronouns** (*who, which, that*): *The noise that scared you was made by the boy who lives next door.*
>
> **Demonstrative pronouns** (*this, that, these, those*): *These are fresher than those.*
>
> **Indefinite pronouns** (*each, one, anybody, all*): *One would think somebody must have seen it.*
>
> **Reciprocal pronouns** (*each other, one another*): *I hope we'll see each other again.*

See also 5a-3, Chapter 6, 8b, Chapter 12.

proper adjective   See *adjective*.

proper noun   See *noun*.

quotation   Repetition of what someone has written or spoken. In **direct quotation** (**direct discourse**), the person's words are duplicated exactly and enclosed in quotation marks: *Polonius told his son Laertes, "Neither a borrower nor a lender be."* An **indirect quotation** (**indirect discourse**) reports what someone said or wrote but not in the exact words and not in quotation marks: *Polonius advised his son Laertes not to borrow or lend.* See also 13d and Chapter 24.

reciprocal pronoun   See *pronoun*.

reflexive pronoun   See *pronoun*.

regular verb   A verb that forms its past tense and past participle by adding *-d* or *-ed* to the plain form: *dip, dipped, dipped; open, opened, opened.* See also 5a and Chapter 7. Contrast *irregular verb*.

relative pronoun   See *pronoun*.

restrictive modifier   A word, phrase, or clause that is essential to the meaning of a sentence because it limits the thing modified. Restrictive modifiers are not set off by commas: *The keys to the car are on the table. That man who called about the apartment said he'd try to call you tonight.* See also 21c. Contrast *nonrestrictive modifier.*

rhetoric The principles for finding and arranging ideas and for using language in speech or writing so as to achieve the writer's purpose in addressing his or her audience.

rhetorical question A question asked for effect, with no answer expected. The person asking the question either intends to provide the answer or assumes it is obvious: *If we let one factory pollute the river, what does that say to other factories that want to dump wastes there?*

run-on sentence (fused sentence) A sentence error in which two main clauses are joined with no punctuation or connecting word between them.

> RUN-ON   I heard his lecture it was dull.
>
> REVISED   I heard his lecture; it was dull.

See 11c.

sentence A complete unit of thought, consisting of at least a subject and a predicate that are not introduced by a subordinating word. Sentences can be classed on the basis of their structure in one of four ways: *simple, compound, complex,* or *compound-complex.*

> **Simple sentences** contain one main clause: *I'm leaving.*
>
> **Compound sentences** contain at least two main clauses: *I'd like to stay, but I'm leaving.*
>
> **Complex sentences** contain one main clause and at least one subordinate clause: *If you let me go now, you'll be sorry.*
>
> **Compound-complex sentences** contain at least two main clauses and at least one subordinate clause: *I'm leaving because you want me to, but I'd rather stay.*

See also *clause* and Chapter 5.

sentence fragment A sentence error in which a group of words is set off as a sentence even though it begins with a subordinating word or lacks either a subject or a predicate or both. See also Chapter 10.

> FRAGMENT   She wasn't in shape for the race. *Which she had hoped to win.* [*Which,* a relative pronoun, makes the italicized clause subordinate.]
>
> REVISED   She wasn't in shape for the race, which she had hoped to win.
>
> FRAGMENT   He could not light a fire. *And thus could not warm the room.* [The italicized word group lacks a subject.]
>
> REVISED   He could not light a fire. Thus he could not warm the room.

gl/gr

sentence modifier   An adverb or a word or word group acting as an adverb that modifies the idea of the whole sentence in which it appears rather than any specific word: *In fact, people will always complain.*

simple predicate   See *predicate.*

simple sentence   See *sentence.*

simple subject   See *subject.*

simple tenses   See *tense.*

split infinitive   The often awkward interruption of an infinitive and its marker *to* by an adverb: *The mission is to boldly go where no one has gone before.* See also *infinitive,* and see 14f.

squinting modifier   See *misplaced modifier.*

subject   The noun, or word or word group acting as a noun, that is the agent or topic of the action or state expressed in the predicate of a sentence or clause. The **simple subject** consists of the noun alone: *The quick brown fox jumps over the lazy dog.* The **complete subject** includes the simple subject and its modifiers: *The quick brown fox jumps over the lazy dog.* See also 5a and 5b.

subject complement   See *complement.*

subjective   See *case.*

subjunctive   See *mood.*

subordinate clause   See *clause.*

subordinating conjunction (subordinator)   See *conjunction.*

subordination   The use of grammatical constructions to make one element in a sentence dependent on rather than equal to another and thus to convey the writer's sense that the dependent element is less important to the whole: *Although I left six messages for him, the doctor failed to call me back.* See also 16b. Contrast *coordination.*

substantive   A word or word group used as a noun.

suffix   A **derivational suffix** is a letter or group of letters that can be added to the end of a root word to make a new word, often a different part of speech: *child, childish; shrewd, shrewdly; visual, visualize.* See also 33b-3. **Inflectional suffixes** adapt words to different grammatical relations: *boy, boys; fast, faster; tack, tacked.* See also 5a and 5b.

superlative   See *comparison.*

syntax   The division of grammar that is concerned with the relations among words and means by which those relations are indicated.

tag question   A question attached to the end of a statement and consisting of a pronoun, a helping verb, and sometimes the word *not: It isn't raining, is it? It is sunny, isn't it?*

tense   The form of a verb that expresses the time of its action, usually indicated by the verb's inflection and by its auxiliaries.

The **simple tenses** include the **present** (*I race, you go*); the **past** (*I raced, you went*); and the **future,** formed with the auxiliary *will* (*I will race, you will go*).

The **perfect tenses,** formed with the auxiliaries *have* and *had,* indicate completed action. They include the present perfect (*I have raced, you have gone*); the **past perfect** (*I had raced, you had gone*); and the **future perfect** (*I will have raced, you will have gone*).

The **progressive tense,** formed with the auxiliary *be* plus the present participle, indicates continuing action (*I am racing, you are going*).

See also Chapter 7.

transitive verb   See *verb.*

verb   A word or group of words indicating the action or state of being of a subject. A **transitive verb** conveys action that has an object: *He <u>shot</u> the sheriff.* An **intransitive verb** does not have an object: *The sheriff <u>died</u>.* A **linking verb** connects the subject and a complement that describes or renames the subject: *The sheriff <u>was</u> brave.* Often the same verb may be transitive, intransitive, or linking, depending on its use in the sentence: *The dog <u>smelled</u> the bone* (transitive). *The dog <u>smelled</u>* (intransitive). *The dog <u>smelled</u> bad* (linking).

Transitive verbs also may be either in the **active voice,** when the subject is the agent of the action, or in the **passive voice,** when the subject is the recipient of the action. Active: *We all <u>made</u> the decision together.* Passive: *The decision <u>was made</u> by all of us.*

The inflection of a verb and the use of auxiliaries with it indicate its tense, mood, number, and sometimes person: *shall go, were going, have gone.*

See 5a, 5e-3, and Chapter 7. See also *tense* and *mood.*

verbal (nonfinite verb)   A verb form used as a noun (*<u>Swimming</u> is good exercise*), an adjective (*<u>Blocked</u> passes don't make touchdowns*), or an adverb (*We were prepared <u>to run</u>*). A verbal can never function as the main verb in a sentence. Verbals may have subjects, objects, complements, and modifiers. See *participle, gerund, infinitive,* and *phrase.* Contrast *finite verb.* See also 5c-2.

verbal phrase   A phrase consisting of a participle, gerund, or infinitive and its related words, used as an adjective, adverb, or noun. See *phrase.* See also 5c-2.

verb phrase   See *phrase.*

voice   The active or passive aspect of a transitive verb. See *verb.* See also 5e-3.

word order   The arrangement of the words in a sentence, which plays a large part in determining the grammatical relation among words in English.

(continued from page iv)

Index

Index

Plan of the book and guide to correction code and symbols